Lecture Notes in Artificial Intelligen

Edited by R. Goebel, J. Siekmann, and W. Wahlstei

Subseries of Lecture Notes in Computer Science

Hector Geffner   Rui Prada
Isabel Machado Alexandre   Nuno David (Eds.)

Advances in Artificial Intelligence – IBERAMIA 2008

11th Ibero-American Conference on AI
Lisbon, Portugal, October 14-17, 2008
Proceedings

 Springer

Series Editors

Randy Goebel, University of Alberta, Edmonton, Canada
Jörg Siekmann, University of Saarland, Saarbrücken, Germany
Wolfgang Wahlster, DFKI and University of Saarland, Saarbrücken, Germany

Volume Editors

Hector Geffner
ICREA & Universitat Pompeu Fabra
Paseo de Circumvalacion 8, 08003 Barcelona, Spain
E-mail: hector.geffner@upf.edu

Rui Prada
IST-UTL and INESC-ID
Av. Prof. Cavaco Silva - Taguspark, 2744-016 Porto Salvo, Portugal
E-mail: rui.prada@gaips.inesc-id.pt

Isabel Machado Alexandre
Nuno David
ADETTI/ISCTE and ISCTE, Lisbon University Institute
Av. das Forças Armadas, 1649-026 Lisbon, Portugal
E-mail: {isabel.alexandre,nuno.david}@iscte.pt

Library of Congress Control Number: 2008936470

CR Subject Classification (1998): I.2.6, I.2.9, F.4.1, I.2.3, I.2.11

LNCS Sublibrary: SL 7 – Artificial Intelligence

ISSN   0302-9743
ISBN 978-3-540-88308-1 Springer Berlin Heidelberg New York

Springer is a part of Springer Science+Business Media

springer.com

© Springer-Verlag Berlin Heidelberg 2008

Typesetting: Camera-ready by author, data conversion by Scientific Publishing Services, Chennai, India
Printed on acid-free paper   SPIN: 12538447   06/3180   5 4 3 2 1 0

Preface

IBERAMIA is the international conference series of the Ibero-American Artificial Intelligence community that has been meeting every two years since the 1988 meeting in Barcelona. The conference is supported by the main Ibero-American societies of AI and provides researchers from Portugal, Spain, and Latin America the opportunity to meet with AI researchers from all over the world. Since 1998, IBERAMIA has been a widely recognized international conference, with its papers written and presented in English, and its proceedings published by Springer in the LNAI series.

This volume contains the papers accepted for presentation at Iberamia 2008, held in Lisbon, Portugal in October 2008. For this conference, 147 papers were submitted for the main track, and 46 papers were accepted. Each submitted paper was reviewed by three members of the Program Committee (PC), coordinated by an Area Chair. In certain cases, extra reviewers were recruited to write additional reviews. The list of Area Chairs, PC members, and reviewers can be found on the pages that follow.

The authors of the submitted papers represent 14 countries with topics covering the whole spectrum of themes in AI: robotics and multiagent systems, knowledge representation and constraints, machine learning and planning, natural language processing and AI applications.

The program for Iberamia 2008 also included three invited speakers: Christian Lemaitre (LANIA, México), R. Michael Young (NCSU, USA) and Miguel Dias (Microsoft LDMC, Lisbon) as well as five workshops.

The IBERAMIA Conference series is coordinated by the Executive Committee of IBERAMIA. This committee is in charge of planning and supervising the conferences, and its members are elected by the IBERAMIA board which is made up of representatives from the following national AI associations: AEPIA (Spain), APPIA (Portugal), SBC (Brazil), and SMIA (Mexico).

We would like to thank all the people who helped bring about Iberamia 2008. First of all, the contributing authors, for ensuring the high scientific standard of the conference and their cooperation in the preparation of this volume. Second, the Area Chairs, PC members, and reviewers whose participation was crucial for assessing the papers, providing the authors with feedback, and recommending the papers to be accepted for the main program and in this volume. Some of the Area Chairs and PC members went well beyond their duties and provided their help up to the last minute with papers requiring additional reviews or opinions. While the list is longer, in this regard, we would like to make special mention of Lluis Marquez. Last but not last, we are grateful to the IBERAMIA Executive Committee, and in particular to its current Secretary, Francisco Garijo, for the advice and for keeping the conference series alive and healthy.

We also would like to thank the IBERAMIA 2008 sponsoring organizations: ISCTE - Lisbon University Institute, Fundação para a Ciência e Tecnologia (FCT), Associação Portuguesa para a Inteligência Artificial (APPIA), Asociación Española de la Inteligencia Artificial (AEPIA), and Microsoft.

October 2008

Hector Geffner
Rui Prada
Isabel Machado Alexandre
Nuno David

Organization

The 11th Ibero-American Conference on Artificial Intelligence (IBERAMIA) was held in Lisbon, Portugal, October 14–17, 2008, and was organized by ADETTI/ISCTE (Associação para o Desenvolvimento das Telecomunicações e Técnicas de Informática) and ISCTE (Lisbon University Institute).

Organizing Committee

General and
  Publication Chairs: Isabel Machado Alexandre (ADETTI/ISCTE, Portugal)

Nuno David (ADETTI/ISCTE, Portugal)

Program Chair: Hector Geffner (ICREA and Univ. Pompeu Fabra, Spain)

Workshop Chair: Rui Prada (IST-UTL and INESC-ID, Portugal)

Local Executive Organization: Fátima Estevens (ADETTI, Portugal)

Sónia Ferro (ADETTI, Portugal)

Area Chairs

Alexander Gelbukh	Instituto Politécnico Nacional, Mexico
Ana Bazzan	Universidade Federal do Rio Grande do Sul, Brazil
Anna Helena Reali Costa	Universidade de São Paulo, Brazil
Blai Bonet	Universidad Simón Bolívar, Venezuela
Carlos A. Coello Coello	CINVESTAV-IPN, Mexico
Carlos Linares	Univ. Carlos III, Madrid, Spain
Carme Torras	IRI, CSIC-UPC, Barcelona, Spain
Eugénio de Oliveira	Universidade do Porto, Portugal
Eva Onaindia	Universidad Politecnica Valencia, Spain
Fábio Gagliardi Cozman	Universidade de São Paulo, Brazil
Gabriela Henning	INTEC, Argentina
Guilherme Bittencourt	Universidade Federal de Santa Catarina, Brazil
Guillermo R. Simari	Universidad Nacional del Sur, Argentina
João Gama	LIAAD, Univ. Porto, Portugal
Jordi Vitria	Centre de Visió per Computador, UB, Spain
Jorge Louçã	ISCTE - DCTI, Portugal
José C. Riquelme	Universidad de Sevilla, Spain
Juan Pavon	Univ. Complutense, Spain
Lawrence Mandow	Universidad de Málaga, Spain

Leliane Nunes de Barros   Universidade de São Paulo, Brazil
Lluís Marquez   Technical University of Catalonia - UPC, Spain
Luis Enrique Succar   Instituto Nacional de Astrofísica, Óptica y
                            Electrónica, Mexico
Pedro Larranaga   Universidad Politécnica de Madrid, Spain
Pedro Meseguer   IIIA - CSIC, Bellaterra, Spain
Ricardo Conejo   Universidad de Málaga, Spain
Rosa Viccari   Universidade Federal do Rio Grande do Sul,
                            Brazil

Program Committee

Adi Botea
Alejandro Garcia
Alex Coddington
Alfredo Vellido
Alfredo Weitzenfeld
Alma Kharrat
Ana Arruarte
Analía Amandi
Anders Jonsson
Andre Carvalho
Andreia Malucelli
Andrew Kusiak
Antonio Bahamonde
Antonio Berlanga
Antonio Garrido
Antonio Peregrin
Arturo Hernández-Aguirre
Augusto Loureiro da Costa
Beatriz Barros Blanco
Bertrand Braunschweig
Brahim Hnich
Camino Rodríguez Vela
Candelaria Sansores
Carles Sierra
Carlos Bento
Carlos Chesnevar
Carlos Ribeiro
Carolina Ivette Martinez
Cassio Polpo de Campos
Christophe Garcia
Concha Bielza
Cristina Urdiales
Dan Cristea

David Bueno
Dídac Busquets
Dimitris Vrakas
Duncan Gillies
Enric Celaya
Enrique Alba
Enrique Amigó
Fabio Ramos
Fabiola Lopez
Felip Manya
Felipe Trevizan
Filiberto Pla
Flavien Balbo
Flavio Tonidandel
Francisco Fernández de Vega
Fred Freitas
Francisco Javier Diez
Gladys Castillo Jordan
Guillermo Leguizamon
Hector Palacios
Horacio Leone
Horacio Rodríguez
Iñaki Alegria
Iñaki Inza
Ines Lynce
Ivon Arroyo
Jaime Sichman
Javier Larrosa
Jerusa Marchi
Jesse Hoey
Jesus Aguilar-Ruiz
João Balsa
Jomi Hübner

Jorge Baier
Jorge Casillas
Jorge Marques
Jose Campo Avila
José Hernández-Orallo
José Juárez Herrero

Jose A. Lozano
José A. Gámez
José Carlos Ferreira da Rocha
José Luis Pérez de la Cruz Molina
Juan Botía

Sponsoring Institutions

IBERAMIA 2008 received financial support from the following institutions:

ISCTE - Lisbon University Institute
FCT - Fundação para a Ciência e Tecnologia
AEPIA - Asociación Española de Inteligencia Artificial
APPIA - Associação Portuguesa para a Inteligência Artificial

Additional Referees

Elder Santos
Katya Rodríguez-Vazquez
Alípio Jorge
Ana Paula Rocha
Arlindo Oliveira
Cesar Alberto Collazos Ordoñez
Debrup Chakraborty
Demetrio Arturo Ovalle Carranza
Eva Armengol
Hernan Aguirre
Jaume Bacardit
Jianjun Hu
Jordi Turmo
Juan Rodriguez-Aguilar
Jovani Alberto Jiménez Builes

Lluís Belanche
Luis Alberto Guerrero Blanco
Marcelo Errecalde
Marco Schorlemmer
Maria Esther Vidal
Mario Martín
Montse Cuadros
Muntsa Padró
S. Fidanova
Yulia Ledeneva
Norhashimah Morad
Petia Radeva
Stefka Fidanova
Vincent Chevrier

Table of Contents

Machine Learning

Multiagent Systems

Natural Language Processing

Intelligent Information Systems and NLP

Robotics

Applications

Topology and Knowledge of Multiple Agents

Bernhard Heinemann

Fakultät für Mathematik und Informatik, FernUniversität in Hagen
58084 Hagen, Germany
Bernhard.Heinemann@FernUni-Hagen.de

Abstract. A multi-agent version of Moss and Parikh's logic of knowledge and effort is developed in this paper. This is done with the aid of particular modalities identifying the agents involved in the system in question. Throughout the paper, special emphasis is placed on foundational issues.

Keywords: knowledge of agents, epistemic logic, topological reasoning, spatial logics.

1 Introduction

The development of spatial calculi in AI (like, eg, RCC [1]) has directed the interest of researchers back to one of the earliest interpretations of modal logic, the *topological* one [2].[1] In modern terminology, a formula $\Box\alpha$ holds at some point x of a topological space iff there exists an open neighbourhood of x in which α is everywhere valid; cf [4]. Thus the modal box stands for a kind of nested quantification in this spatial context, viz an existential one concerning (open) sets followed by a universal one concerning points.

Moss and Parikh [5] discovered that breaking up this interlocking of quantifiers brings to light a certain relationship of topology and *knowledge*. In fact, regarding points as *system states* and sets as *knowledge states of some agent*, the above quantification over sets induces an S4-like modality of *shrinking* while the point quantifier, being S5-like, directly describes knowledge. But shrinking a knowledge state means gaining knowledge so that the first modality corresponds to some knowledge acquisition procedure and was called the *effort operator* thus. The semantic domains of the language underlying the Moss-Parikh system are obtained by releasing the class of all admissible structures. Now, every *subset space* can be taken for that, i.e., every triple $(X, \mathcal{O}, V)$ consisting of a non-empty set X of states, a set $\mathcal{O}$ of subsets of X representing the knowledge states of the agent,[2] and a valuation V determining the states where the atomic propositions are true. The *knowledge operator, K*, then quantifies over some knowledge state $U \in \mathcal{O}$, whereas the effort operator, denoted $\Box$ as well, quantifies 'downward' over $\mathcal{O}$.

---

[1] See [3] for bringing the precise connection with RCC about.
[2] Since these sets are of topological origin they are still called *the opens* sometimes.

H. Geffner et al. (Eds.): IBERAMIA 2008, LNAI 5290, pp. 1–10, 2008.

Following that initial work, a rich theory on the connection between knowledge and topology has emerged; see Ch. 6 of the recent handbook [6] for an overview of the state of the art. The original class of all topological spaces could be characterized within the broader framework, in particular; see [7]. In addition, several extensions including temporal or dynamic aspects of knowledge have been proposed. An essential shortcoming of the system remains up to now though: Regarding its applicability to real-life scenarios in computer science or AI, a corresponding multi-agent version is still missing. (This is at least true regarding the usual semantics as the paper [8] is based on a different one.)

This deficiency is rectified in the present paper. At first glance, we have two options in doing so. On the one hand, we could assume that there is one subset space $(X, \mathcal{O}, V)$ comprising the knowledge states of all the agents. If $\mathcal{O}$ is unstructured, then the agents are semantically indistinguishable. This means that they share all of their knowledge states. Thus the resulting theory reduces to that of a single agent, which is rather uninteresting for our problem. On the other hand, if a separate subset space is associated with every agent, then we get, among other things, into trouble when trying to capture the interplay of the knowledge of the agents. The latter leads us to a possible solution nevertheless: Adressing a particular agent will here be arranged by an appropriate modality distinguishing the agent. This entails that, unlike the usual logic of knowledge (see [9]) we do no longer have a knowledge operator K_A in the formal language, for every agent A. Instead, K_A is 'decomposed' into two modalities, K and the new one belonging to A. Thus the agents are 'super-imposed' on the original system, which, therefore, can essentially be preserved. This idea is carried out in the technical part of this paper.

On looking more carefully, representing an agent by a modal operator seems to be quite natural since it is thereby indicated that agents are acting entities rather than indices to knowledge operators. But most notably, the new approach enables us to present a multi-agent version of Moss and Parikh's system in a smooth and satisfactory way.

The body of the paper is organized as follows. In the next section, we precisely define the spatio-epistemic multi-agent language indicated above. Moreover, we reason about its expressiveness there. Section 3 contains a list of basic subset space validities and a discussion referring to this. Section 4 deals with the question of completeness. We also discuss effectivity issues, in Section 5. Concluding the paper, we sum up and point to variants, extensions, and future research assignments.

2   Multi-agent Subset Spaces

In this section, we define the extended language, $\mathcal{L}$. The syntax of $\mathcal{L}$ is based on a denumerable set Prop $= \{p, q, \ldots\}$ of symbols called *proposition letters*. Let $m \in \mathbb{N}$. Then, the set Form$_m$ of all *formulas* over Prop is given by the rule $\alpha ::= p \mid \neg \alpha \mid \alpha \wedge \alpha \mid K\alpha \mid \Box \alpha \mid [A_i] \alpha$, where $i \in \{1, \ldots, m\}$. The letters A_i should represent the agents involved in the scenario under discussion. While K

and $\square$ denote the modalities of knowledge and effort as above, the new operators $[A_i]$ identify the respective agent in a way to be made precise in a minute. The duals of K, $\square$ and $[A_i]$ (i.e., the operators $\neg K\neg$, $\neg\square\neg$ and $\neg[A_i]\neg$) are denoted L, $\Diamond$ and $\langle A_i \rangle$, respectively. The missing boolean connectives are treated as abbreviations, as needed. – We now fix the relevant semantic domains. It turns out that every agent induces a substructure of the set of all opens in a natural way. Let $\mathcal{P}(X)$ designate the powerset of a given set X.

Definition 1 (Multi-agent structures)

1. *Let X be a non-empty set, $\mathcal{O} \subseteq \mathcal{P}(X)$ be a set of subsets of X such that $X \in \mathcal{O}$, and $\mathcal{A} : \{1, \dots, m\} \to \mathcal{P}(\mathcal{P}(X))$ be a mapping such that the union $\bigcup \mathrm{Im}(\mathcal{A})$ of all the image sets $\mathcal{A}(i)$, where $i = 1, \dots, m$, is contained in $\mathcal{O}$. Then $\mathcal{S} := (X, \mathcal{O}, \mathcal{A})$ is called a multi-agent subset frame.*
2. *Let $\mathcal{S} = (X, \mathcal{O}, \mathcal{A})$ be a multi-agent subset frame. Then the elements of the set $\mathcal{N}_\mathcal{S} := \{(x, U) \mid x \in U \text{ and } U \in \mathcal{O}\}$ are called the neighbourhood situations of the frame $\mathcal{S}$.*
3. *Let $\mathcal{S} = (X, \mathcal{O}, \mathcal{A})$ be a multi-agent subset frame and $V : \mathrm{Prop} \to \mathcal{P}(X)$ be a mapping. Then V is called an $\mathcal{S}$-valuation.*
4. *Let $\mathcal{S} = (X, \mathcal{O}, \mathcal{A})$ be a multi-agent subset frame and V be an $\mathcal{S}$-valuation. Then $\mathcal{M} := (X, \mathcal{O}, \mathcal{A}, V)$ is called a multi-agent subset space, or, in short, a MASS (based on $\mathcal{S}$).*

Some points are worth mentioning here. First, the function $\mathcal{A}$ is added to subset spaces in such a way that the set of all opens is not necessarily exhausted by the knowledge states of the agents. Having in mind certain spatial settings, this more general approach is quite reasonable. Second, neighbourhood situations are the atomic semantic objects of our language. They will be used for evaluating formulas. In a sense, the set component of a neighbourhood situation measures the uncertainty about the associated state component at any one time. And third, we are mainly interested in *interpreted systems,* which are here formalized by MASSs. The assignment of sets of states to proposition letters by means of valuations is in accordance with the usual logic of knowledge; cf [9] again.

Our next task is defining the relation of satisfaction. This is done with respect to a MASS $\mathcal{M}$. Thus satisfaction, which should hold between neighbourhood situations of the underlying frame and formulas from Form$_m$, is designated $\models_\mathcal{M}$. In the following, neighbourhood situations are written without brackets.

Definition 2 (Satisfaction and validity). *Let $\mathcal{M} = (X, \mathcal{O}, \mathcal{A}, V)$ be a MASS based on $\mathcal{S} = (X, \mathcal{O}, \mathcal{A})$, and let $x, U \in \mathcal{N}_\mathcal{S}$ be a neighbourhood situation. Then*

$$x, U \models_\mathcal{M} p \quad :\Longleftrightarrow \quad x \in V(p)$$
$$x, U \models_\mathcal{M} \neg\alpha \quad :\Longleftrightarrow \quad x, U \not\models_\mathcal{M} \alpha$$
$$x, U \models_\mathcal{M} \alpha \wedge \beta : \Longleftrightarrow \quad x, U \models_\mathcal{M} \alpha \text{ and } x, U \models_\mathcal{M} \beta$$
$$x, U \models_\mathcal{M} K\alpha \quad :\Longleftrightarrow \quad \text{for all } y \in U : y, U \models_\mathcal{M} \alpha$$
$$x, U \models_\mathcal{M} \square\alpha \quad :\Longleftrightarrow \quad \forall U' \in \mathcal{O} : \text{if } x \in U' \subseteq U, \text{ then } x, U' \models_\mathcal{M} \alpha$$
$$x, U \models_\mathcal{M} [A_i]\alpha : \Longleftrightarrow \quad U \in \mathcal{A}(i) \text{ implies } x, U \models_\mathcal{M} \alpha,$$

for all $p \in \text{Prop}$, $i \in \{1, \ldots, m\}$ and $\alpha, \beta \in \text{Form}_m$. In case $x, U \models_{\mathcal{M}} \alpha$ is true we say that α is valid in $\mathcal{M}$ at the neighbourhood situation x, U. Furthermore, a formula α is called valid in $\mathcal{M}$ iff it is valid in $\mathcal{M}$ at every neighbourhood situation. (Manner of writing: $\mathcal{M} \models \alpha$.)

Note that the meaning of proposition letters is independent of the opens by definition, hence 'stable' with respect to $\square$. This fact will find expression in the logical system considered later on. Additionally, note that the operator $[A_i]$ conditions the validity of formulas at the actual neighbourhood situation on agent A_i.

The rest of this section is concerned with some aspects of the expressiveness of $\mathcal{L}$. First of all, we show that the usual knowledge operator associated with an agent A is definable in the new language. In fact, the formula $\langle A_i \rangle K\alpha$ exactly says that A_i knows α at the actual neighbourhood situation (where $i \in \{1, \ldots, m\}$). This means that, with regard to subset spaces, $\mathcal{L}$ is at least as expressive as the usual language for knowledge of agents.

Actually, we have a little more expressive power. To see this, note first that the modalities $[A_i]$ remind one of the binding procedures which are known from *hybrid logic;* cf [10], Sec. 6, or [11], Ch. 14. Though there is a rather weak connection only, a kind of naming system is constituted by these modalities for one component of the semantics (the opens) nevertheless. For instance, the formula $\langle A_i \rangle \top$ means that the actual open represents a knowledge state of agent A_i.

It can easily be inferred from Definition 2 that the knowledge operator and the agent operators commutate in the following sense.

Proposition 1. *Let $\mathcal{M}$ be any MASS. Then, for all $i \in \{1, \ldots, m\}$ and $\alpha \in \text{Form}_m$, we have $\mathcal{M} \models [A_i] K\alpha \leftrightarrow K[A_i]\alpha$.*

Thus it is known that the validity of α is conditioned on agent A_i if and only if it is conditioned on A_i that α is known. This is an example of a basic MASS-validity which will be part of the axiomatization of MASSs we propose in the next section. Concluding this section, we give a concrete example.

Example 1. Let be given a two-agent scenario with three states, x_1, x_2, x_3. Let $X = \{x_1, x_2, x_3\}$. Assume that a knowledge acquisition procedure P_1, which, for $k = 1, 2, 3$, step-by-step eliminates x_k from the set of all possible alternatives, is available to agent A_1. Thus $\mathcal{A}(1) = \{\{x_1, x_2, x_3\}, \{x_2, x_3\}, \{x_3\}\}$. On the other hand, assume that a corresponding procedure P_2, which successively eliminates x_{3-k}, is available to A_2 so that $\mathcal{A}(2) = \{\{x_1, x_2, x_3\}, \{x_1, x_2\}, \{x_1\}\}$. Then, each agent can obviously reach an 'exclusive state of complete knowledge'. In other words, for every $i, j \in \{1, 2\}$ such that $i \neq j$, there is a knowledge state $\in \mathcal{A}(i) \setminus \mathcal{A}(j)$ in which every valid formula α is known by A_i. A specification of this fact reads

$$\bigwedge_{i,j \in \{1,2\}, \, i \neq j} L\Diamond \left(\langle A_i \rangle (\alpha \to K\alpha) \wedge [A_j] \bot \right),$$

which is valid at the neighbourhood situation x_k, X, for every $k \in \{1, 2, 3\}$.

3 Axiomatizing Multi-agent Subset Spaces

Our starting point to this section is the system of axioms for the usual logic of subset spaces from [12]. We later add several schemata involving the agent modalities. After that we define the arising multi-agent logic, MAL. – The axioms from [12] read as follows:

1. All instances of propositional tautologies.
2. $K(\alpha \to \beta) \to (K\alpha \to K\beta)$
3. $K\alpha \to (\alpha \wedge KK\alpha)$
4. $L\alpha \to KL\alpha$
5. $\Box(\alpha \to \beta) \to (\Box\alpha \to \Box\beta)$
6. $(p \to \Box p) \wedge (\Diamond p \to p)$
7. $\Box\alpha \to (\alpha \wedge \Box\Box\alpha)$
8. $K\Box\alpha \to \Box K\alpha$,

where $p \in$ Prop and $\alpha, \beta \in$ Form$_m$. In this way, it is expressed that, for every Kripke model M validating these axioms,

- the accessibility relation $\xrightarrow{K}$ of M belonging to the knowledge operator is an equivalence,
- the accessibility relation $\xrightarrow{\Box}$ of M belonging to the effort operator is reflexive and transitive,
- the composite relation $\xrightarrow{\Box} \circ \xrightarrow{K}$ is contained in $\xrightarrow{K} \circ \xrightarrow{\Box}$ (this is usually called the *cross property*[3]), and
- the valuation of M is constant along every $\xrightarrow{\Box}$ -path, for all proposition letters (see the remark right after Definition 2).

We now present the axioms containing the operators $[A_i]$:

9. $[A_i](\alpha \to \beta) \to ([A_i]\alpha \to [A_i]\beta)$
10. $\alpha \to [A_i]\alpha$
11. $K[A_i]\alpha \to [A_i]K\alpha$,

where $i \in \{1, \ldots, m\}$ and $\alpha, \beta \in$ Form$_m$. – Some comments are appropriate here. Item 9 contains the usual distribution schema being valid for every normal modality. The next schema, 10, says that the accessibility relation $\xrightarrow{A_i}$ belonging to the operator $[A_i]$ has *height 1;* that is, $\forall s, t :$ if $s \xrightarrow{A_i} t$, then $s = t$ (where s and t are any points of the frame under discussion). This fact can be proved in the standard way. Finally, item 11 is one half of the commutation relation between the knowledge operator and the agent operators stated in Proposition 1. Note the formal similarity between the schemata 8 and 11. – It is somewhat surprising at first glance that no other interaction axioms between the modalities are needed.

---

[3] The cross property is caused by Axiom 8, which is, therefore, called the *Cross Axiom;* see [12].

By adding two of the standard rule schemata of modal logic, viz *modus ponens* and *necessitation with respect to each modality* (cf [13], Sec. 1.6), we obtain a logical system denoted MAL. The following proposition about MAL is quite obvious.

Proposition 2 (Soundness). *If $\alpha \in$ Form$_m$ is MAL-derivable, then α is valid in all MASSs.*

The proof of the opposite assertion, i.e., the completeness of MAL with respect to the class of all MASSs, is highly non-trivial. We turn to it in the next section.

4   Completeness

A completeness proof for MAL must clearly use the associated canonical model in some way. We fix several notations concerning that model first. Let $\mathcal{C}$ be the set of all maximal MAL-consistent sets of formulas. Furthermore, let $\xrightarrow{K}$, $\xrightarrow{\square}$ and $\xrightarrow{A_i}$ be the accessibility relations induced on $\mathcal{C}$ by the modalities K, $\square$ and $[A_i]$, respectively. Let $\alpha \in$ Form$_m$ be non-MAL-derivable. We attain to a multi-agent subset space falsifying α by an infinite 'multi-dimensional' step-by-step construction. In every step, an approximation to the claimed model, which will be the 'limit' of the intermediate ones, is defined. In order to ensure that the final structure behaves as desired, several requirements on the approximations have to be kept under control during the process.

Suppose that $\Gamma_0 \in \mathcal{C}$ is to be realized (i.e., $\neg\alpha \in \Gamma_0$). We choose a denumerably infinite set of points, Y, fix an element $x_0 \in Y$, and construct inductively a sequence of quintuples $(X_n, P_n, i_n, a_n, t_n)$ such that, for every $n \in \mathbb{N}$,

1. $X_n \subseteq Y$ is a finite set containing x_0,
2. P_n is a finite set partially ordered by $\leq$ and containing $\perp$ as a least element,
3. $i_n : P_n \to \mathcal{P}(X_n)$ is a function such that $p \leq q \iff i_n(p) \supseteq i_n(q)$, for all $p, q \in P_n$,
4. $a_n : \{1, \ldots, m\} \to \mathcal{P}(\mathcal{P}(X_n))$ is a function satisfying $\bigcup_{1 \leq i \leq m} a_n(i) \subseteq \mathrm{Im}(i_n)$,
5. $t_n : X_n \times P_n \to \mathcal{C}$ is a partial function such that, for all $x, y \in X_n$ and $p, q \in P_n$,
   (a) $t_n(x, p)$ is defined iff $x \in i_n(p)$; in this case it holds that
      i. if $y \in i_n(p)$, then $t_n(x, p) \xrightarrow{K} t_n(y, p)$,
      ii. if $q \geq p$, then $t_n(x, p) \xrightarrow{\square} t_n(x, q)$,
      iii. for all $i \in \{1, \ldots, m\}$: if $i_n(p) \in a_n(i)$, then $t_n(x, p) \xrightarrow{A_i} t_n(x, p)$,
   (b) $t_n(x_0, \perp) = \Gamma_0$.

The next five conditions say to what extent the structures $(X_n, P_n, i_n, a_n, t_n)$ approximate the final model. Actually, it will be guaranteed that, for all $n \in \mathbb{N}$,

6. $X_n \subseteq X_{n+1}$,

7. P_{n+1} is an *end extension* of P_n (i.e., a superstructure of P_n such that no element of $P_{n+1} \setminus P_n$ is strictly smaller than any element of P_n),

8. $i_{n+1}(p) \cap X_n = i_n(p)$ for all $p \in P_n$,

9. for all $i \in \{1, \ldots, m\}$ and $U \in a_{n+1}(i) : U \notin a_n(i)$ or $U \cap X_n \in a_n(i)$,

10. $t_{n+1} \mid_{X_n \times P_n} = t_n$.

Finally, the construction complies with the following requirements on existential formulas: For all $n \in \mathbb{N}$,

11. if $L\beta \in t_n(x, p)$, then there are $n < k \in \mathbb{N}$ and $y \in i_k(p)$ such that $\beta \in t_k(y, p)$,

12. if $\Diamond\beta \in t_n(x, p)$, then there are $n < k \in \mathbb{N}$ and $p \leq q \in P_k$ such that $\beta \in t_k(x, q)$,

13. for all $i \in \{1, \ldots, m\} :$ if $\langle A_i \rangle \beta \in t_n(x, p)$, then there is some $n < k \in \mathbb{N}$ such that $i_k(p) \in a_k(i)$ and $\beta \in t_k(x, p)$.

With that, the desired model can easily be defined. Furthermore, a relevant *Truth Lemma* (cf [13], 4.21) can be proved for it, from which the completeness of MAL follows immediately. Thus it remains to construct $(X_n, P_n, i_n, a_n, t_n)$, for all $n \in \mathbb{N}$, in a way meeting all the above requirements. This makes up the core of the proof. The case $n = 0$ is still easy. In the induction step, some existential formula contained in some maximal MAL-consistent set $t_n(x, p)$, where $x \in X_n$ and $p \in P_n$, must be realized. We confine ourselves to the case of the operator $\langle A_i \rangle$ here, where $i \in \{1, \ldots, m\}$.[4]

So let $\langle A_i \rangle \beta \in t_n(x, p)$. The first three components of the approximating structure are unaltered in this case, i.e., $X_{n+1} := X_n$, $P_{n+1} := P_n$, and $i_{n+1} = i_n$. From the *Existence Lemma* of modal logic (cf [13], 4.20) we know that there is some point s of $\mathcal{C}$ such that $t_n(x, p) \xrightarrow{A_i} s$ and $\beta \in s$. Axiom 10 now implies that $t_n(x, p) = s$. We therefore define $a_{n+1}(i) := a_n(i) \cup \{i_n(p)\}$. This already determines a_{n+1} since the agents with index $j \neq i$ are not affected in this case. Finally, we define $t_{n+1} := t_n$.

We must now check that the properties 1 – 10, and 13, remain valid (11 and 12 are irrelevant to the present case). Apart from 5 and 13, all items are more or less obvious from the construction. Concerning item 13, see the remark at the end of this proof outline.

Thus the verification of the property 5 is left. Since 5 (b) too is evident we concentrate on 5 (a). First, the condition on the domain of t_{n+1} is obviously satisfied. Second, (i) and (ii) are clear from the validity of this condition for n. Hence only for (iii) some arguments are needed. If $j \neq i$, where i is from above, then the property is valid because of the induction hypothesis, for $a_{n+1}(j)$ equals $a_n(j)$ then. So let $j = i$ and assume that $i_{n+1}(q) \in a_{n+1}(i)$, where $q \in P_{n+1}$. We distinguish two cases. First, let $i_{n+1}(q) \notin a_n(i)$. Then both $q = p$ and $i_{n+1}(p) = i_n(p)$ must hold due to the construction. It follows from Axiom 11 (and Axiom 10 as well) that $t_{n+1}(y, p) \xrightarrow{A_i} t_{n+1}(y, p)$, where $y \in X_{n+1}$. Second,

---

[4] Note that the axioms not mentioned below are used for the other cases.

let $i_{n+1}(q) \cap X_n \in a_n(i)$. Then the above construction step forces that $i_{n+1}(q) = i_n(q)$, and the assertion again follows from the induction hypothesis.

In order to ensure that *all* possible cases are eventually exhausted, processing has to be suitably scheduled with regard to each of the modalities involved. This can be done by means of appropriate enumerations. Regarding this and the construction in case of a modality of the usual subset space logic, the reader is referred to the paper [12] for further details. – Summarizing this section, we can state the first of the main results of this paper:

Theorem 1 (Completeness). *If $\alpha \in$ Form$_m$ is valid in all MASSs, then α is MAL-derivable.*

5   Decidability

In this final technical section of the paper, we prove that the set of all MAL-derivable formulas is decidable. Since the finite model property does not apply to the usual subset space logic with respect to the class of all subset spaces (see [12], Sec. 1.3), the same is true for MAL with respect to the class of all MASSs. Thus we have to make a little detour in order to obtain the desired decidability result. We shall single a certain subclass out of the class of all Kripke models and prove that MAL satisfies the finite model property with respect to *that* class of structures. This gives us the decidability of MAL in a standard fashion. – In the following definition, R and K, S and $\Box$, and T_i and $[A_i]$, respectively, correspond to each other ($i \in \{1, \ldots, m\}$).

Definition 3 (MACA-model). *Let $M := (W, R, S, T_1, \ldots, T_m, V)$ be a multimodal model, where $R, S, T_1, \ldots, T_m \subseteq W \times W$ are binary relations and V is a valuation. Then M is called a* multi-agent cross axiom model *(or, in short, a MACA-model) iff the following conditions are satisfied:*[5]

1. *R is an equivalence relation, and S is reflexive and transitive,*
2. *for all $i \in \{1, \ldots, m\}$, the relations T_i have height 1,*
3. *$S \circ R \subseteq R \circ S$ and, for all $i \in \{1, \ldots, m\} : T_i \circ R \subseteq R \circ T_i$ (where $\circ$ denotes composition of relations),*
4. *for all $w, v \in W$ and $p \in$ Prop : if $w\,T\,w'$, then $w \in V(p) \iff v \in V(p)$.*

Note that, by taking neighbourhood situations as points, every subset space induces a semantically equivalent MACA-model.

It is easy to see that all the axioms from Section 3 are sound with respect to the class of all MACA-models. Moreover, the canonical model of MAL belongs to this class of structures. These facts imply the following theorem.

Theorem 2 (Kripke completeness). *The logical system MAL is sound and complete with respect to the class of all MACA-models.*

---

[5] The term 'cross axiom model' was introduced in [12], Sec. 2.3.

In the following, we use the method of *filtration* in order to prove the finite model property of MAL with respect to the class of all MACA-models; cf [14], Sec. 4. For a given MAL-consistent formula $\alpha \in \text{Form}_m$, we define a filter set $\Sigma \subseteq \text{Form}_m$ as follows. We first let $\Sigma_0 := \text{sf}(\alpha) \cup \{\neg\beta \mid \beta \in \text{sf}(\alpha)\}$, where $\text{sf}(\alpha)$ designates the set of all subformulas of α. Second, we form the closure of Σ_0 under finite conjunctions of pairwise distinct elements of Σ_0. Third, we close under single applications of the operator L. And finally, we form the set of all subformulas of elements of the set obtained last. Let Σ then denote the resulting set of formulas.

Now, the *smallest* filtrations of the accessibility relations $\xrightarrow{K}$, $\xrightarrow{\square}$ and $\xrightarrow{A_i}$ of the canonical model are taken, where $i = 1, \ldots, m$; cf [14], Sec. 4. Let $M := (W, R, S, T_1, \ldots, T_m, V)$ be the corresponding filtration of a suitably generated submodel of the canonical model, for which the valuation V assigns the empty set to all proposition letters not occurring in Σ. Then we have the following lemma.

Lemma 1. *The structure M is a finite MACA-model of which the size computably depends on the length of α.*

Proof. Most of the assertion is clear from the definitions and the proof of [12], Theorem 2.11. Only item 2 and the second part of item 3 from Definition 3 have to be checked. – For item 2, let Γ, Θ be two points of the canonical model such that $[\Gamma] \, T_i \, [\Theta]$, where the brackets $[\ldots]$ indicate the respective classes ($i \in \{1, \ldots, m\}$). Since we are working with smallest filtrations, there are $\Gamma' \in [\Gamma]$ and $\Theta' \in [\Theta]$ such that $\Gamma' \xrightarrow{A_i} \Theta'$. From this we conclude that $\Gamma' = \Theta'$ since $\xrightarrow{A_i}$ has height 1. It follows that $[\Gamma] = [\Theta]$. Thus T_i too has height 1. – For item 4, we remember the formal similarity of the axiom schemata 8 and 11 (see Sec. 3). Thus the cross property for K and T_i can be established on the filtrated model in the same way as it was established for K and $\square$ there; see [12], Lemma 2.10. Note that the special form of Σ is used for exactly that purpose.

Since the model M realizes α according to the *Filtration Theorem* (cf [13], 2.39), the decidability result we strived for follows readily from Theorem 2 and Lemma 1.

Theorem 3 (Decidability). *The set of all MAL-derivable formulas is decidable.*

6   Concluding Remarks

We developed a multi-agent version of Moss and Parikh's topological logic of knowledge. To this end, we introduced appropriate modalities addressing the knowledge states of the agents in question. The main issues of the paper are corresponding soundness, completeness and decidability results.

The generalization put forward here is quite natural in many respects. First, the original approach is preserved to a large extent. Second, the new system is open to variations and extensions depending on the applications one has in mind. For example, it is easy to characterize axiomatically those MASSs for which the union of all sets of knowledge states of the agents coincides with the set of all opens. Moreover, further-reaching concepts from the usual logic of knowledge can be incorporated.

We are particularly interested in topological spaces. A corresponding extension of the system presented above as well as the treatment of complexity problems are postponed to future research.

References

1. Randell, D.A., Cui, Z., Cohn, A.G.: A spatial logic based on regions and connection. In: Nebel, B., Rich, C., Swartout, W. (eds.) Principles of Knowledge Representation and Reasoning (KR 1992), San Mateo, CA, pp. 165–176. Morgan Kaufmann, San Francisco (1992)
2. McKinsey, J.C.C.: A solution to the decision problem for the Lewis systems S2 and S4, with an application to topology. Journal of Symbolic Logic 6, 117–141 (1941)
3. Nutt, W.: On the translation of qualitative spatial reasoning problems into modal logics. In: Burgard, W., Christaller, T., Cremers, A.B. (eds.) KI 1999. LNCS (LNAI), vol. 1701, pp. 113–125. Springer, Heidelberg (1999)
4. Aiello, M., van Benthem, J., Bezhanishvili, G.: Reasoning about space: The modal way. Journal of Logic and Computation 13, 889–920 (2003)
5. Moss, L.S., Parikh, R.: Topological reasoning and the logic of knowledge. In: Moses, Y. (ed.) Theoretical Aspects of Reasoning about Knowledge (TARK 1992), Los Altos, CA, pp. 95–105. Morgan Kaufmann, San Francisco (1992)
6. Aiello, M., Pratt-Hartmann, I.E., van Benthem, J.F.A.K.: Handbook of Spatial Logics. Springer, Heidelberg (2007)
7. Georgatos, K.: Knowledge theoretic properties of topological spaces. In: Masuch, M., Polos, L. (eds.) Logic at Work 1992. LNCS (LNAI), vol. 808, pp. 147–159. Springer, Heidelberg (1994)
8. Pacuit, E., Parikh, R.: The logic of communication graphs. In: Leite, J.A., Omicini, A., Torroni, P., Yolum, p. (eds.) DALT 2004. LNCS (LNAI), vol. 3476, pp. 256–269. Springer, Heidelberg (2005)
9. Meyer, J.J.C., van der Hoek, W.: Epistemic Logic for AI and Computer Science. Cambridge Tracts in Theoretical Computer Science, vol. 41. Cambridge University Press, Cambridge (1995)
10. Blackburn, P.: Representation, reasoning, and relational structures: a hybrid logic manifesto. Logic Journal of the IGPL 8, 339–365 (2000)
11. Blackburn, P., van Benthem, J., Wolter, F.: Handbook of Modal Logic. Studies in Logic and Practical Reasoning, vol. 3. Elsevier, Amsterdam (2007)
12. Dabrowski, A., Moss, L.S., Parikh, R.: Topological reasoning and the logic of knowledge. Annals of Pure and Applied Logic 78, 73–110 (1996)
13. Blackburn, P., de Rijke, M., Venema, Y.: Modal Logic. Cambridge Tracts in Theoretical Computer Science, vol. 53. Cambridge University Press, Cambridge (2001)
14. Goldblatt, R.: Logics of Time and Computation, 2nd edn. CSLI Lecture Notes, vol. 7. Center for the Study of Language and Information, Stanford (1992)

A Propositional Dynamic Logic Approach for Order of Magnitude Reasoning*

A. Burrieza[1], E. Muñoz-Velasco[2], and M. Ojeda-Aciego[2]

[1] Dept. Filosofía. Universidad de Málaga. Spain
burrieza@uma.es
[2] Dept. Matemática Aplicada. Universidad de Málaga. Spain
{emilio,aciego}@ctima.uma.es

Abstract. We introduce a Propositional Dynamic Logic for order of magnitude reasoning in order to formalize qualitative operations of sum and product. This new logic has enough expressive power to consider, for example, the concept of closeness, and to study some interesting properties for the qualitative operations, together with the logical definability of these properties. Finally, we show the applicability of our approach on the basis of some examples.

1 Introduction

Qualitative reasoning (QR) is the area of AI which tries to develop representation and reasoning techniques for dealing with situations in which the information is not sufficiently precise (e.g., exact numerical values are not available) or when numerical models are too complex. QR is somewhere in between heuristic models, based on symbolic manipulations and numerical models, based on numerical calculations.

A form of qualitative reasoning is illustrated by the management of numerical data in terms of orders of magnitude (see, for example, [19, 20, 16]). Order of magnitude reasoning stratifies values according to some notion of scale, for instance, by including hyperreal numbers, numerical thresholds, or logarithmic scales. Three issues faced by all these formalisms are the conditions under which many small effects can combine to produce a significant effect, the soundness of the reasoning supported by the formalism, and the efficiency of using them.

The introduction of a logical approach to QR tries to face the problem about the soundness of the reasoning supported by the formalism, and to give some answers about the efficiency of its use. Several logics have been defined to use QR in different contexts, [2,24,11], e.g., spatial and temporal reasoning. In particular, logics dealing with order of magnitude reasoning have been developed in [8, 7] defining different qualitative relations (*order of magnitude*, *negligibility*, *non-closeness*, etc.) on the basis of qualitative classes obtained from the real line divided in intervals [23].

---

* Partially supported by projects TIN2006-15455-C03-01 and P6-FQM-02049.

H. Geffner et al. (Eds.): IBERAMIA 2008, LNAI 5290, pp. 11–20, 2008.

In this paper, we introduce a logic approach in order to formalize qualitative operations of sum and product between our intervals (like "add a small positive number" or "multiply by a negative large number"). We consider that the introduction of this logic represents an important step stone, because, as said in [18], it contributes to model aspects of human knowledge which, together with the intrinsic qualities of the operators, are used in performing qualitative computations. To this end, we present a Propositional Dynamic Logic (henceforth PDL) with constants. The main purpose of extending modal logics to PDL [13,15,4], is to allow not only many fixed accessibility relations (as in multi-modal logic) but also the construction of complex relations from simple ones by using operators as union, composition, transitive closure, etc.

Recent applications of PDL in communication scenarios, message-passing systems, multiagent real-time systems and knowledge acquisition, can be seen in [3, 14,6,5], respectively. In our case, we introduce some nominals in order to represent the milestones which divide the different qualitative classes, for this reason we could say that our logic is a *hybrid* PDL, as a part of the Combinatory PDL [1,17]. This *hybrid dynamism* will give us enough expressive power to represent different situations, for example the important concept of closeness [19], and to consider some interesting properties for the qualitative operations, together with the logical definability of these properties. The introduction of closeness is one of the main differences of this approach with respect to the previous works in logic for order of magnitude reasoning. In these works, negligibility, order of magnitude, non-closeness and distance relations where introduced; however, a specific closeness relation was not provided. In our case, PDL will give us theoretical support in order to have, not only complete axiomatic systems to deal with this new relation, but also to study its decidability and complexity.

The paper is organized as follows. In Section 2, the syntax and semantics of the proposed logic is introduced. In Section 3, we study some properties of the qualitative sum and product and its definability, together with an example of application of our logic. Finally, some conclusions and prospects of future work are presented in Section 4.

2   Syntax and Semantics

We consider the real line $\mathbb{R}$ divided into seven equivalence classes using five landmarks $c_i \in \mathbb{R}$, chosen depending on the context [22], being $i \in \{1, 2, 3, 4, 5\}$ such that $c_i < c_{i+1}$, for all $i \in \{1, 2, 3, 4\}$:

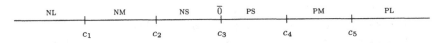

The labels correspond, respectively, to the qualitative classes representing "negative large", "negative medium", "negative small", "zero", "positive small", "positive medium", and "positive large", being:

$$\text{NL} = (-\infty, c_1), \quad \text{NM} = [c_1, c_2) \quad \text{NS} = [c_2, c_3), \quad \overline{0} = \{c_3\}$$

$$\text{PS} = (c_3, c_4], \quad \text{PM} = (c_4, c_5], \quad \text{PL} = (c_5, +\infty)$$

In order to introduce the language of our logic, we consider a set of formulas Φ and a set of programs Π, which are defined recursively on disjoint sets Φ_0 and Π_0, respectively. Φ_0 is called the set of *atomic formulas* which can be thought as abstractions of properties of states. Similarly, Π_0 is called the set of *atomic programs* which are intended to represent basic instructions.

Formulas

- Φ_0 is a denumerable set of propositional variables which contains the finite set $\mathbb{C} = \{c_i \mid i \in \{1, 2, 3, 4, 5\}\}$ of constants together with $\top$ (true) and $\bot$ (false).
- If φ and ψ are formulas and a is a program, then $\varphi \vee \psi$, $\neg\varphi$, $\langle a \rangle \varphi$ are formulas.

As usual in propositional modal logic, $\varphi \rightarrow \psi$ represents $\neg\varphi \vee \psi$, and $[a]$ represents $\neg\langle a \rangle \neg$.

Programs

- $\Pi_0 = \{<, >, +_{\text{Eq}}, \cdot_{\text{Eq}}, \theta\}$, where $\text{Eq} \in \{\text{nl}, \text{nm}, \text{ns}, 0, \text{ps}, \text{pm}, \text{pl}\}$ represents the equivalence classes defined above and θ is the null program.
- If a and b are programs and φ is a formula, then $(a; b)$ ("do a followed by b"), $a \cup b$ ("do a or b, nondeterministically"), a^* ("repeat a a finite, but nondeterministically determined, number of times") and φ? ("proceed if φ is true, else fail") are also programs.

As an example of formulas, we can consider $\langle +_{\text{ps}} \cup +_{\text{ns}} \rangle$, $\langle \cdot_{\text{pl}}; \cdot_{\text{pl}} \rangle$ and $\langle \text{ns}?; +_{\text{pl}} \rangle$ in order to represent, respectively, the intuitive meanings of adding a (positive or negative) small number, multiplying twice by a positive large number and adding a positive large number to a negative small number.

We now define the *semantics* of our logic. A *model* $\mathcal{M}$ is a pair (W, m), where W is a non-empty subset[1] of $\mathbb{R}$ and m is a meaning function such that $m(\varphi) \subseteq W$, for all formula φ, and $m(a) \subseteq W \times W$, for all programs a. Moreover, for every formula φ and ψ and for all programs a, b, we have:

- $m(\top) = W$ and $m(\bot) = \varnothing$
- $m(c_i) \in W$, for all $i \in \{1, 2, 3, 4, 5\}$
- $m(\varphi \vee \psi) = m(\varphi) \cup m(\psi)$
- $m(\neg\varphi) = W - m(\varphi)$
- $m(\langle a \rangle \varphi) = \{w \in W : \exists v \in W \text{ such that } (w, v) \in m(a) \text{ and } v \in m(\varphi)\}$
- $m(<)$ is the restriction to W of the usual strict linear ordering of $\mathbb{R}$, such that $(m(c_i), m(c_{i+1})) \in m(<)$, for all $i \in \{1, 2, 3, 4\}$.
- $m(\theta) = \varnothing$
- $m(a \cup b) = m(a) \cup m(b)$

---

[1] We could use any strict linearly ordered set with two internal operations $+$ and $\cdot$.

- $m(a; b) = m(a); m(b)$ (composition of relations $m(a)$ and $m(b)$)
- $m(a^*) = m(a)^*$ (reflexive and transitive closure of relation $m(a)$).
- $m(\varphi?) = \{(w, w) : w \in m(\varphi)\}$

Given a model $\mathcal{M} = (W, m)$, a formula φ is *true* in $w \in W$ whenever $w \in m(\varphi)$. We say that φ is *valid in a model* $\mathcal{M} = (W, m)$ if φ is true in all $w \in W$, that is, if $m(\varphi) = W$. Finally, φ is *valid* iff φ is valid in all models.

The informal meaning of some of our connectives is given as follows:

- $\langle < \rangle \varphi$ is true in w iff there exists w', greater than w, such that φ is true in w'.
- $\langle +_{\text{pm}} \rangle \varphi$ is true in w iff there exists w', obtained by adding a positive medium number to w, such that φ is true in w'.
- $[\cdot_{\text{pl}}] \varphi$ is true in w iff for every w', obtained by multiplying w by a positive large number, φ is true in w'.
- $\langle \text{nl?} \rangle \varphi$ is true in w iff w is a negative large number and φ is true in w.
- $\langle +_{\text{ns}}^* \rangle \varphi$ is true in w iff there exists w', obtained by adding a finite number of small negative numbers to w, such that φ is true in w'.

Notation: In the rest of the paper, we will use the intuitive notation ps as a formula which is true exactly in the set PS, that is, $\text{ps} \equiv (\langle > \rangle c_3 \wedge \langle < \rangle c_4) \vee c_4$, and similarly for the rest of intervals. Moreover, we use the abbreviation $\Diamond \varphi \equiv (\langle > \rangle \varphi \vee \varphi \vee \langle < \rangle \varphi)$, for any formula φ, and similarly for $\Box$.

As said before, one of the main advantages of using PDL is the possibility of constructing complex programs from basic ones. As a consequence, following the ideas presented in [7], we can use our connectives in order to represent some relations as *negligibility* and *distance*. Moreover, we introduce a notion of *closeness* which was not included in the previous approaches of logics for order of magnitude reasoning. Thus, for any formula φ, we have:

$$\langle \text{c} \rangle \varphi = \langle +_{\text{ns}} \cup +_0 \cup +_{\text{ps}} \rangle \varphi \qquad \langle \text{d} \rangle \varphi = \langle +_{\text{nl}} \cup +_{\text{pl}} \rangle \varphi$$

$$\langle \text{n} \rangle \varphi = \langle c_3? \rangle \Diamond \varphi \vee \langle (\text{ns} \vee \text{ps})? \rangle \Diamond (\langle c_2?; +_{\text{nl}} \rangle \varphi \vee \langle c_4?; +_{\text{pl}} \rangle \varphi)$$

The intuitive interpretation of the closeness relation is that x is close to y if, and only if, y is obtained from x by adding a small number. On the other hand, x is distant from y if and only if y is obtained from x by adding a large number. Moreover, we assume that zero is negligible with respect to any real number and a small number is negligible with respect to any number *sufficiently large*, that is, distant either from c_2 or c_4.

Example 1. In this example, inspired in that given in [10], we show the expressiveness of our logic in order to make different comparisons. Let us consider three computational tasks with different ranges of difficulty. For instance:

(a) Add up a column of 100 numbers.
(b) Sort a list of 10,000 elements.
(c) Invert a 100×100 matrix.
(d) Add up a column of 120 numbers.

We can say that the time required by (a) and (d) are much shorter than the others, and task (b) is much shorter than (c). For example, we may assume that the time required by (b) is obtained from the time required by (a) by adding a positive medium number, that the time required by (a) is negligible with respect to the time required by (c) and that the time required by (a) is close to the time required by (d).

If formulas $time\_a, time\_b, time\_c$ and $time\_d$ represent the time required by (a), (b), (c) and (d) respectively, then the following formulas hold:

$$time\_a \rightarrow \langle +_{\mathsf{pm}} \rangle\, time\_b, \quad time\_a \rightarrow \langle \mathsf{n} \rangle\, time\_c, \quad time\_a \rightarrow \langle \mathsf{c} \rangle\, time\_d$$

If we assume also that the time required by (c) is obtained by multiplying by a positive large number the time required by (b), then we have:

$$time\_b \rightarrow \langle \cdot_{\mathsf{pl}} \rangle\, time\_c, \quad time\_a \rightarrow \langle +_{\mathsf{pm}}; \cdot_{\mathsf{pl}} \rangle\, time\_c$$

3   Some Properties of Qualitative Sum and Product

This section is devoted to study different properties of some classes of our models with respect to the qualitative operations sum and product defined previously. For simplicity, in the rest of the paper, we will consider the class $\mathbb{L}$ of models $\mathcal{M} = (U, m)$ such that:

1. $U \subseteq \mathbb{R}$, such that $0, \alpha, \beta \in U$
2. $m(c_3) = 0,\ -m(c_2) = m(c_4) = \alpha,\ -m(c_1) = m(c_5) = \beta$

To begin with, some elementary results of qualitative arithmetic are recalled; then, some relevant properties regarding sum and product are stated. Finally, we study the definability of these properties and give some examples.

Following [19], we consider the sum and product between non-empty sets and between elements and non-empty sets defined as follows:

Definition 1. *Let $X, Y \subseteq \mathbb{R}$ and $x \in \mathbb{R}$ such that $X, Y \neq \varnothing$, we define the sets $x + Y$ and $x \cdot Y$, $X + Y$ and $X \cdot Y$ as follows:*

$$x + Y = \{x + y \mid y \in Y\} \qquad\qquad X + Y = \{x + y \mid x \in X \text{ and } y \in Y\}$$
$$x \cdot Y = \{xy \mid y \in Y\} \qquad\qquad X \cdot Y = \{xy \mid x \in X \text{ and } y \in Y\}$$

In the following proposition, we particularize the definition above to the seven qualitative classes of our order of magnitude model and obtain a number of intuitive properties.

The properties stated in the proposition below can be verified by straightforward inspection:

Proposition 1

1. $0 + \mathrm{EQ} = \mathrm{EQ}$, *for all* $\mathrm{EQ} \in \{\mathrm{NL}, \mathrm{NM}, \mathrm{NS}, 0, \mathrm{PS}, \mathrm{PM}, \mathrm{PL}\}$
2. $\mathrm{PL} + (\mathrm{PS} \cup \mathrm{PM} \cup \mathrm{PL}) \subseteq \mathrm{PL}$

3. $\text{PL} + \text{NM} \subseteq (\text{PS} \cup \text{PM} \cup \text{PL})$
4. $\text{PM} + (\text{PS} \cup \text{PM}) \subseteq (\text{PM} \cup \text{PL})$
5. $\text{PM} + \text{NS} \subseteq (\text{PS} \cup \text{PM})$
6. $\text{PS} + \text{NS} \subseteq (\text{NS} \cup 0 \cup \text{PS})$
7. If $\beta \geq 2\alpha$, we have $\text{PL} + \text{NS} \subseteq (\text{PM} \cup \text{PL})$ and $\text{PS} + \text{PS} \subseteq (\text{PS} \cup \text{PM})$
8. If $\beta \geq 1$, $(\text{PL} \cdot \text{PL}) \cup (\text{NL} \cdot \text{NL}) \subseteq \text{PL};\quad \text{PL} \cdot \text{NL} \subseteq \text{NL}$
9. If $\alpha \geq 1$, we have:
    (a) $(\text{PM} \cdot \text{PL}) \cup (\text{NM} \cdot \text{NL}) \subseteq \text{PL}$
    (b) $(\text{PM} \cdot \text{NL}) \cup (\text{NM} \cdot \text{PL}) \subseteq \text{NL}$.
    (c) $(\text{NM} \cdot \text{NM}) \cup (\text{PM} \cdot \text{PM}) \subseteq (\text{PM} \cup \text{PL})$

Note that additional properties are obtained when interchanging negative and positive numbers in the items from 2 to 7.

The following concept of definability based on models gives us a relationship between properties of our models and formulas of our logic.

Definition 2. *Let $\mathbb{K}$ be a class of models and $\mathbb{J} \subseteq \mathbb{K}$ the class of all models in $\mathbb{K}$ having a certain property P. We say that P is definable by a formula φ in the class $\mathbb{K}$ if for every model $\mathcal{M} \in \mathbb{K}$, we have that $\mathcal{M} \in \mathbb{J}$ iff φ is valid in $\mathcal{M}$.*

In our case, we will say that P is definable in the class $\mathbb{K}$ if there exists a formula φ such that P is definable by φ in $\mathbb{K}$.

Proposition 2. *All the properties in Table 1 are definable in the class $\mathbb{L}$ defined above, but the exceptions stated below:*

- *Property 7 is definable in the class $\mathbb{L}_1$ of models in $\mathbb{L}$ such that $\beta \geq 2\alpha$.*
- *Property 8 is definable in the class $\mathbb{L}_2$ of models in $\mathbb{L}$ such that $\beta \geq 1$.*
- *Property 9 is definable in the class $\mathbb{L}_3$ of models in $\mathbb{L}$ such that $\alpha \geq 1$.*

Proof. We only show the definability of the first property in 7, that is, $\text{PL} + \text{NS} \subseteq (\text{PM} \cup \text{PL})$. The proof in the rest of the cases is similar.

To obtain the validity of the formula $\varphi = \langle \text{pl?} \rangle\, [+_{\text{ns}}]\, (\text{pm} \vee \text{pl})$, let (W, m) be a model in $\mathbb{L}_1$ and suppose $(\text{PL} + \text{NS}) \subseteq (\text{PM} \cup \text{PL})$. If $w \in W$ such that $w \in m(\text{pl})$, this means that $w \in \text{PL}$. By hypothesis, this implies that, for every $w' \in W$ such that $(w, w') \in m(+_{\text{ns}})$, we have that $w' \in m(\text{pm} \cup \text{pl})$, hence $w \in m(\langle \text{pl?} \rangle\, [+_{\text{ns}}]\, (\text{pm} \cup \text{pl}))$. This means that φ is valid.

Conversely, consider a model (W, m) in which $(\text{PL} + \text{NS}) \not\subseteq (\text{PM} \cup \text{PL})$ holds. Then, there exists $w' \in \text{PL} + \text{NS}$, such that $w' \notin \text{PM} \cup \text{PL}$. Thus, $w' = w + w''$, being $w \in \text{PL}$ and $w'' \in \text{NS}$, hence $w \notin m(\langle \text{pl?} \rangle\, [+_{\text{ns}}]\, (\text{pm} \vee \text{pl}))$. This means that formula φ is not true in w, that is, φ is not valid in (W, m).

We now present some examples which show up the expressiveness of our logic and the applicability of the previous properties.

Example 2. We continue with the Example 1, by assuming now that the time required by tasks (a), (b) and (c) are positive small, medium and large numbers, respectively. This means that:

Table 1. Definability of Properties

	PROPERTY	DEFINED BY
1	$0 + \mathrm{EQ} = \mathrm{EQ}$	$\bar{0} \to [+_{Eq}]\mathsf{Eq}$
2	$\mathrm{PL} + (\mathrm{PS} \cup \mathrm{PM} \cup \mathrm{PL}) \subseteq \mathrm{PL}$	$\langle \mathsf{pl?}\rangle\,[+_{\mathsf{ps}} \cup +_{\mathsf{pm}} \cup +_{\mathsf{pm}}]\mathsf{pl}$
3	$(\mathrm{PL} + \mathrm{NM}) \subseteq (\mathrm{PS} \cup \mathrm{PM} \cup \mathrm{PL})$	$\langle \mathsf{pl?}\rangle\,[+_{\mathsf{nm}}]\,(\mathsf{ps} \vee \mathsf{pm} \vee \mathsf{pl})$
4	$\mathrm{PM} + (\mathrm{PS} \cup \mathrm{PM}) \subseteq (\mathrm{PM} \cup \mathrm{PL})$	$\langle \mathsf{pm?}\rangle\,[+_{\mathsf{ps}} \cup +_{\mathsf{pm}}]\,(\mathsf{pm} \vee \mathsf{pl})$
5	$(\mathrm{PM} + \mathrm{NS}) \subseteq (\mathrm{PS} \cup \mathrm{PM})$	$\langle \mathsf{pm?}\rangle\,[+_{\mathsf{ns}}]\,(\mathsf{ps} \vee \mathsf{pm})$
6	$(\mathrm{PS} + \mathrm{NS}) \subseteq (\mathrm{NS} \cup 0 \cup \mathrm{PS})$	$\langle \mathsf{ps?}\rangle\,[+_{\mathsf{ns}}]\,(\mathsf{ns} \vee \bar{0} \vee \mathsf{ps})$
7	$\mathrm{PL} + \mathrm{NS} \subseteq (\mathrm{PM} \cup \mathrm{PL})$ $\mathrm{PS} + \mathrm{PS} \subseteq (\mathrm{PS} \cup \mathrm{PM})$	$\langle \mathsf{pl?}\rangle\,[+_{\mathsf{ns}}]\,(\mathsf{pm} \vee \mathsf{pl})$ $\langle \mathsf{ps?}\rangle\,[+_{\mathsf{ps}}]\,(\mathsf{ps} \vee \mathsf{pm})$
8	$(\mathrm{PL} \cdot \mathrm{PL}) \cup (\mathrm{NL} \cdot \mathrm{NL}) \subseteq \mathrm{PL}$	$(\langle \mathsf{pl?}\rangle\,[\cdot_{\mathsf{pl}}]\,\mathsf{pl}) \wedge (\langle \mathsf{nl?}\rangle\,[\cdot_{\mathsf{nl}}]\,\mathsf{pl})$
9	$(\mathrm{PM} \cdot \mathrm{PL}) \cup (\mathrm{NM} \cdot \mathrm{NL}) \subseteq \mathrm{PL}$	$(\langle \mathsf{pl?}\rangle\,[\cdot_{\mathsf{pm}}]\,\mathsf{pl}) \wedge (\langle \mathsf{nl?}\rangle\,[\cdot_{\mathsf{nm}}]\,\mathsf{pl})$
	$(\mathrm{PM} \cdot \mathrm{NL}) \cup (\mathrm{NM} \cdot \mathrm{PL}) \subseteq \mathrm{NL}$	$(\langle \mathsf{nl?}\rangle\,[\cdot_{\mathsf{pm}}]\,\mathsf{nl}) \wedge (\langle \mathsf{pl?}\rangle\,[\cdot_{\mathsf{nm}}]\,\mathsf{nl})$
	$(\mathrm{NM} \cdot \mathrm{NM}) \cup (\mathrm{PM} \cdot \mathrm{PM}) \subseteq (\mathrm{PM} \cup \mathrm{PL})$	$(\langle \mathsf{nm?}\rangle\,[\cdot_{\mathsf{nm}}]\,(\mathsf{pm} \vee \mathsf{pl})) \wedge (\langle \mathsf{pm?}\rangle\,[\cdot_{\mathsf{pm}}]\,(\mathsf{pm} \vee \mathsf{pl}))$

$$time\_a \to \mathsf{ps} \quad time\_b \to \mathsf{pm}, \quad time\_c \to \mathsf{pl}$$

If we assume that $\beta \geq 2\alpha$, properties 4 and 7 of Proposition 1 can be applied to obtain, respectively:

$$time\_b \to [+_{\mathsf{ps}}]\,(\mathsf{pm} \vee \mathsf{pl}), \quad time\_a \to [+_{\mathsf{ps}}]\,(\mathsf{ps} \vee \mathsf{pm})$$

The intuitive reading of the formula $time\_b \to [+_{\mathsf{ps}}]\,(\mathsf{pm} \vee \mathsf{pl})$, is "if we add the time required by task (b) to the required one by any task with the same order of magnitude to task (a) (in this case ps), the time obtained has the same order of magnitude than the one required by task (b) or by task (c), i.e., pm or pl." In the same way, formula $time\_a \to [+_{\mathsf{ps}}]\,(\mathsf{ps} \vee \mathsf{pm})$ can be interpreted as "if we add the time required by task (a) to the time required by any task with the same order of magnitude than (a), the time obtained has the same order of magnitude than the one required by any task (a) or (b)".

Example 3. We consider now the heat exchanger studied, for example, in [20]. Let DTH be the temperature drop of the hot stream, DTC is the temperature rise of the cold stream, and DT1, DT2 are the driving force in the left and right ends of the device, respectively. Moreover, FH and KH are, respectively, the molar-flowrate and molar-heat of the hot stream and FC, KC the molar-flowrate and molar-heat of the cold stream. Notice that DTH, DTC, DT1, DT2, FH, KH, FC and KC are all positive real numbers.

The following equations are consequence of the previous definition and energy conservation:

$$\mathrm{DTH} - \mathrm{DT1} - \mathrm{DTC} + \mathrm{DT2} = 0 \tag{1}$$

$$\mathrm{DTH} \cdot \mathrm{KH} \cdot \mathrm{FH} = \mathrm{DTC} \cdot \mathrm{KC} \cdot \mathrm{FC} \tag{2}$$

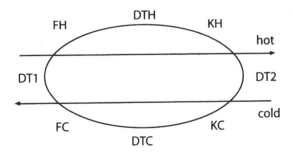

Fig. 1. The heat exchanger

In this example, we use models such that every value of DTH, DTC, ... is represented as a current state in the real line, being the milestones α and β such that $\beta \geq 2\alpha$ and $\alpha \geq 1$.

We define dth as the formula which is true iff the current value is DTH, and similarly for the rest of values dtc, dt1, etc. Assume that DTH is a positive large number and DT1, DT2 are positive small numbers, that is, the following formulas hold:

$$\text{dth} \rightarrow \text{pl} \qquad (\text{dt1} \vee \text{dt2}) \rightarrow \text{ps}$$

From (1) and our previous assumptions, we have that $\text{DTC} \in (\text{DTH} + \text{PS}) + \text{NS}$, which implies that the following formula is true:

$$\text{dth} \rightarrow \langle +_{\text{ps}}; +_{\text{ns}} \rangle \text{dtc}$$

Thus[2], we have $\text{DTC} \in (\text{PL} + \text{PS}) + \text{NS}$. Now, from Proposition 1(2), we have that $\text{PL} + \text{PS} \subseteq \text{PL}$, and from Proposition 1(7), we obtain $\text{PL} + \text{NS} \subseteq (\text{PM} \cup \text{PL})$. As a consequence, $(\text{PL} + \text{PS}) + \text{NS} \subseteq (\text{PM} \cup \text{PL})$. This means that $\text{DTC} \in (\text{PM} \cup \text{PL})$. Hence, the following formula is true:

$$\text{dtc} \rightarrow (\text{pm} \vee \text{pl})$$

This means that if DTH is *large*, then DTC is *medium* or *large*, that is, if we want that the device decreases very much the temperature of the hot stream, we have to accept that the temperature of the cold stream increases much.

On the other hand, from (1) again and our previous assumptions, we have that $\text{DTC} - \text{DTH} \in \text{PS} + \text{NS}$. Now, Proposition 1(6), we have that $\text{PS} + \text{NS} \subseteq (\text{NS} \cup 0 \cup \text{PS})$.

As a consequence, the difference between DTC and DTH is a small number while DTH is a large number.

Finally, if we assume also that KH and KC are positive medium numbers, by Proposition 1(9a,c), we have: $(\text{PM} \cdot \text{PL}) \subseteq \text{PL}$ and $(\text{PM} \cdot \text{PM}) \subseteq (\text{PM} \cup \text{PL})$, from (2), we have:

$$\langle \text{fh?} \rangle \langle \cdot_{\text{pl}} \rangle \text{pl} \rightarrow \Box \langle \text{fc?} \rangle \langle \cdot_{\text{pm}} \cup \cdot_{\text{pl}} \rangle \text{pl}$$

---

[2] Notice that although qualitative sum is not necessarily associative, in this case we could eliminate the brackets.

The meaning of this formula is: if we make the product of FH by a large number (as the product DTH · KH) and we obtain, for example, a positive large number, then we have the same order of magnitude if we make the product of FC by a medium or large number (as the product DTC · KC).

4 Conclusions and Future Work

A PDL for order of magnitude reasoning has been introduced, which gives us enough expressive power to introduce different qualitative operations of sum and product. As a consequence, we are able to define notions as negligibility, closeness and distance. Moreover, we have studied the definability of interesting properties of sum and product of real numbers and its applicability has been shown on the basis of an example.

As a future work, the introduction of PDL will give us the theoretical support in order to give a complete axiomatization of this logic and to study its decidability and complexity [13, 17]. Last, but not least, we want to give a relational proof system based on dual tableaux for this extension in the line of [9, 12].

Acknowledgements

We thank Prof. Andrzej Salwicki for suggesting the subject of this work.

References

1. Areces, C., ten Cate, B.: Hybrid Logics. In: Blackburn, P., Van Benthem, J., Wolter, F. (eds.) Handbook of Modal Logic. Studies in Logic and Practical Reasoning, vol. 3, pp. 821–868. Elsevier, Amsterdam (2007)
2. Bennett, B., Cohn, A.G., Wolter, F., Zakharyaschev, M.: Multi-Dimensional Modal Logic as a Framework for Spatio-Temporal Reasoning. Applied Intelligence 17(3), 239–251 (2002)
3. Benthem, J., Eijck, J., Kooi, B.: Logics of communication and change. Information and Computation 204(11), 1620–1662 (2006)
4. Blackburn, P., Van Benthem, J.: Modal Logic: A semantic perspective. In: Blackburn, P., Van Benthem, J., Wolter, F. (eds.) Handbook of Modal Logic. Studies in Logic and Practical Reasoning, vol. 3, pp. 58–61. Elsevier, Amsterdam (2007)
5. Bollig, B., Kuske, D., Meinecke, I.: Propositional dynamic logic for message-passing systems. In: Arvind, V., Prasad, S. (eds.) FSTTCS 2007. LNCS, vol. 4855, pp. 303–315. Springer, Heidelberg (2007)
6. Bugaychenko, D., Soloviev, I.: MASL: A logic for the specification of multiagent real-time systems. In: Burkhard, H.-D., Lindemann, G., Verbrugge, R., Varga, L.Z. (eds.) CEEMAS 2007. LNCS (LNAI), vol. 4696, pp. 183–192. Springer, Heidelberg (2007)
7. Burrieza, A., Muñoz-Velasco, E., Ojeda-Aciego, M.: A Logic for Order of Magnitude Reasoning with Negligibility, Non-closeness and Distance. In: Borrajo, D., Castillo, L., Corchado, J.M. (eds.) CAEPIA 2007. LNCS (LNAI), vol. 4788, pp. 210–219. Springer, Heidelberg (2007)

8. Burrieza, A., Ojeda-Aciego, M.: A multimodal logic approach to order of magnitude qualitative reasoning with comparability and negligibility relations. Fundamenta Informaticae 68, 21–46 (2005)
9. Burrieza, A., Ojeda-Aciego, M., Orłowska, E.: Relational approach to order of magnitude reasoning. In: de Swart, H., Orłowska, E., Schmidt, G., Roubens, M. (eds.) TARSKI 2006. LNCS (LNAI), vol. 4342, pp. 105–124. Springer, Heidelberg (2006)
10. Davis, E.: Order of Magnitude Comparisons of Distance. Journal of Artificial Intelligence Research 10, 1–38 (1999)
11. Duckham, M., Lingham, J., Mason, K., Worboys, M.: Qualitative reasoning about consistency in geographic information. Information Sciences 176(6,22), 601–627 (2006)
12. Golińska-Pilarek, J., Muñoz-Velasco, E.: Relational approach for a logic for order of magnitude qualitative reasoning with negligibility, non-closeness and distance. Technical Report (2008)
13. Harel, D., Kozen, D., Tiury: Dynamic logic. In: Gabbay, D., Guenthner, F. (eds.) Handbook of Philosophical Logic, 2nd edn., vol. 4, pp. 99–218 (2002)
14. Heinemann, B.: A PDL-like logic of knowledge acquisition. In: Diekert, V., Volkov, M.V., Voronkov, A. (eds.) CSR 2007. LNCS, vol. 4649, pp. 146–157. Springer, Heidelberg (2007)
15. Mirkowska, C., Salwicki, A.: Algorithmic Logic. Kluwer Academic Publishers, Norwell (1987)
16. Nayak, P.: Causal Approximations. Artificial Intelligence 70, 277–334 (1994)
17. Passy, S., Tinchev, T.: An essay in combinatory dynamic logic. Information and Computation 93(2), 263–332 (1991)
18. Piera, N., Agell, N.: Binary Relations for Qualitative Reasoning. In: IEEE International Conference on Systems, Man and Cybernetics, vol. 1, pp. 267–271 (1992)
19. Raiman, O.: Order of magnitude reasoning. Artificial Intelligence 51, 11–38 (1991)
20. Sanchez, M., Prats, F., Piera, N.: Una formalización de relaciones de comparabilidad en modelos cualitativos. Boletín de la AEPIA (Bulletin of the Spanish Association for AI) 6, 15–22 (1996)
21. Shults, B., Kuipers, B.J.: Proving properties of continuous systems: qualitative simulation and temporal logic. Artificial Intelligence 92, 91–129 (1997)
22. Travé-Massuyès, L., Ironi, L., Dague, P.: Mathematical Foundations of Qualitative Reasoning. AI Magazine, American Asociation for Artificial Intelligence, 91–106 (2003)
23. Travé-Massuyès, L., Prats, F., Sánchez, M., Agell, N.: Relative and absolute order-of-magnitude models unified. Annals of Mathematics and Artificial Intelligence 45, 323–341 (2005)
24. Wolter, F., Zakharyaschev, M.: Qualitative spatio-temporal representation and reasoning: a computational perspective. In: Lakemeyer, G., Nebel, B. (eds.) Exploring Artificial Intelligence in the New Millenium. Morgan Kaufmann, San Francisco (2002)

Quantum-Based Belief Merging

Laurent Perrussel[1], Jerusa Marchi[2], and Guilherme Bittencourt[2]

[1] IRIT - Université Toulouse I
F-31042 - Toulouse - France
laurent.perrussel@univ-tlse1.fr

[2] Departamento de Automação e Sistemas - Universidade Federal de Santa Catarina
88040-900 - Florianópolis - SC - Brazil
{jerusa,gb}@das.ufsc.br

Abstract. Belief merging aims at building a common belief set issued from multiple belief sets. The quality of the resulting set is usually considered in terms of a closeness criterion between the initial belief sets and an integrity constraint with respect to the aim of the merging procedure. The notion of distance between belief sets is thus a crucial issue when we face the merging problem. The aim of this paper is to revisit belief merging operators, notably the majority and the arbitration operators, with the help of a new distance that considers, in a syntactical way, the importance of each symbol in the belief set.

Keywords: belief merging, prime implicants, prime implicates, knowledge compilation.

1 Introduction

The goal of *belief merging* is to aggregate in a consistent way multiple beliefs usually represented as sets of logical statements so as to obtain a new set of statements [9,7].

This paper considers distance-based belief merging which is based on three main components [6]: a notion of distance between propositional models, a function to aggregate the distances, and a procedure to select the closest eligible resulting sets w.r.t. the aggregation stage. Typical distances are usually based on Dalal distance [3] which evaluates the closeness in terms of truth value of the propositional symbols. In [2] it was shown that belief change based on Dalal's notion of minimal change entails some drawbacks. Indeed, minimal change in Dalal's work means changing a minimal number of truth values, but without consider how many statements are supported by each literal. This means that literals are considered with no connection to agents' beliefs. In this paper, we define a distance that takes into account the structure of the statements, i.e., the relations that occur between symbols and what they represent. For this, we propose to express beliefs in terms of prime implicants and prime implicates. Indeed, these two representations enable to represent how symbols are related: in terms of models (implicants) but also in terms of structure (implicates). Our assumption is that each clause in the prime implicates set is more relevant than an isolated symbol, once it represents better the notion of knowledge unit. In order to support this notion, we introduce the *quantum notation* that correlates prime implicants and implicates in a syntactical way.

H. Geffner et al. (Eds.): IBERAMIA 2008, LNAI 5290, pp. 21–30, 2008.

Using this enriched representation, we can at first define a new distance; second we show the consequences on the behavior of belief merging procedures by focusing on two classical belief merging operators: arbitration [12] and majority operators [10].

The paper is structured as follows: in section 2, we introduce the quantum notation by presenting the formal definitions of prime implicants and prime implicates, and how we can use the quantum notation to characterize these forms. In section 3, we briefly recall the belief merging postulates, and the main characteristics of arbitration and majority operators. Section 4 revisits the arbitration and majority operators by showing how quantum-based merging operator behaves. Finally, we conclude the paper by considering some open issues.

2   Quantum Notation

Let $\mathcal{L}(P)$ be a propositional logic language defined using a set of propositional symbols $P = \{p_1, \ldots, p_n\}$. There are algorithms, e.g., [13], to convert a formula $\phi \in \mathcal{L}(P)$ into *conjunctive normal form* (CNF) or into *disjunctive normal form* (DNF), such that $\phi \equiv CNF_\phi \equiv DNF_\phi$. A conjunctive normal form of formula ϕ is a conjunction of clauses, $CNF_\phi = C_1 \wedge \cdots \wedge C_m$, where each clause C_i is a disjunction of literals, $C_i = L_1 \vee \cdots \vee L_{k_{C_i}}$, with $L_i = p_j$ or $L_i = \neg p_j$. Similarly a disjunctive normal form of ϕ is a disjunction of dual clauses or terms, $DNF_\phi = D_1 \vee \cdots \vee D_w$, where each term, D_j is a conjunction of literals, $D_j = L_1 \wedge \cdots \wedge L_{k_{D_j}}$. We note $\overline{D}$ a term D where the sign of all literals have been flipped, e.g., if $D = p_1 \wedge \neg p_2$ then $\overline{D} = \neg p_1 \wedge p_2$. Given a formula ϕ, represented by a conjunctive normal form CNF_ϕ and by a disjunctive normal form DNF_ϕ, we introduce the concepts of a *conjunctive* and *disjunctive quantum*:

Definition 1 (Conjunctive and Disjunctive quantum). *Let ϕ be a propositional formula. A* conjunctive quantum *is a pair (L, F_c), where L is a literal that occurs in ϕ and $F_c \subseteq CNF_\phi$ is its set of conjunctive coordinates that contains the subset of clauses in CNF_ϕ to which literal L belongs. Dually, a* disjunctive quantum *is a pair (L, F_d), where L is a literal that occurs in ϕ and $F_d \subseteq DNF_\phi$ is its set of disjunctive coordinates that contains the subset of terms in DNF_ϕ to which literal L belongs.*

In the following, a quantum (L, F) is noted L^F. The rationale behind the choice of the name *quantum* is to emphasize that our *minimal* unit of interest is the literal and its situation with respect to the theory in which it occurs.

Example 1. Consider theory ϕ_1 given by the following CNF:

$$0 : \neg p_1 \vee p_2 \vee p_3 \qquad 2 : p_4 \vee \neg p_2 \vee p_3 \qquad 4 : \neg p_1 \vee \neg p_3$$
$$1 : p_4 \vee \neg p_2 \vee \neg p_3 \qquad 3 : \neg p_1 \vee \neg p_2 \qquad 5 : \neg p_3 \vee \neg p_2$$

The literals that occur in ϕ_1 can be represented by the following set of conjunctive quanta: $\{\neg p_1^{\{0,3,4\}}, p_2^{\{0\}}, \neg p_2^{\{1,2,3,5\}}, p_3^{\{0,2\}}, \neg p_3^{\{1,4,5\}}, p_4^{\{1,2\}}\}$, where for conciseness, the sets of conjunctive coordinates contain the clause numbers instead of the clauses themselves.

The quantum notation can be used to characterize implicates and implicants as well as prime implicates and prime implicants of a formula ϕ given a CNF_ϕ and a DNF_ϕ.

Proposition 1 (Implicant and Implicate in quantum notation). *Let* $D = L_1 \wedge \cdots \wedge L_k$ *be a term represented by a set of conjunctive quanta* $L_1^{F_c^1} \wedge \cdots \wedge L_k^{F_c^k}$. *D is an implicant of* ϕ *if* $\cup_{i=1}^k F_c^i = CNF_\phi$ *with no pair of contradictory literals allowed. Dually, let* $C = L_1 \vee \cdots \vee L_k$ *be a clause represented by a set of disjunctive quanta* $L_1^{F_d^1} \vee \cdots \vee L_k^{F_d^k}$. *C is an implicate of* ϕ *if* $\cup_{i=1}^k F_d^i = DNF_\phi$ *with no pair of contradictory literals allowed.*

To characterize prime implicates and prime implicants, clauses C and terms D have to satisfy the *non redundancy condition*, i.e., each of their literals should represent *alone* at least one term in DNF_ϕ and respectively, one clause in CNF_ϕ. To define the non redundancy condition, we introduce the notion of *exclusive conjunctive* and *exclusive disjunctive coordinates*.

Definition 2 (Exclusive Conjunctive and Exclusive Disjunctive Coordinates). *Let* D *be a term and* $L_i \in D$ *a literal s.t.* $1 \le i \le k$, *where k is the number of clauses in a given conjunctive normal form of* ϕ, CNF_ϕ. $\widehat{F}_c^i$ *represents the exclusive conjunctive coordinates of* $L_i \in D$, *defined by* $\widehat{F}_c^i = F_c^i - \cup_{j=1, j \ne i}^k F_c^j$. $\widehat{F}_c^i$ *are the clauses in set F_c^i to which no other literal of D belongs. Similarly, let C be a clause and $L_i \in C$ a literal s.t. $1 \le i \le k$, where k is the number of terms in a given DNF_ϕ.* $\widehat{F}_d^i$ *represents the exclusive disjunctive coordinates of* $L_i \in C$, *defined by* $\widehat{F}_d^i = F_d^i - \cup_{j=1, j \ne i}^k F_d^j$. $\widehat{F}_d^i$ *are the terms in set F_d^i, to which no other literal of C belongs.*

Definition 3 (Non redundancy condition). *Let C be a clause represented as* $L_1^{F_d^1} \vee \cdots \vee L_k^{F_d^k}$. *C satisfies the non redundancy condition iff* $\forall i \in \{1, \ldots, k\}$, $\widehat{F}_d^i \ne \emptyset$. *Similarly, let D be a term represented as* $L_1^{F_c^1} \wedge \cdots \wedge L_k^{F_c^k}$. *D satisfies the non redundancy condition iff* $\forall i \in \{1, \ldots, k\}$, $\widehat{F}_c^i \ne \emptyset$.

Proposition 2 (Prime Implicate and Prime Implicant in quantum notation). *Let C be a clause. C is a prime implicate iff C is an implicate and satisfies the non redundancy condition as presented in definition 3. Dually, let D be a term. D is a prime implicant iff D is an implicant and satisfies the non redundancy condition.*

Example 2. Consider theory ϕ_1 introduced in example 1. The set $D = \{\neg p_1^{\{0,3,4\}}, \neg p_2^{\{1,2,3,5\}}, \neg p_3^{\{1,4,5\}}\}$ is an implicant of ϕ_1 because the union of the conjunctive coordinates associated with its quanta is equal to the set of clauses in CNF_ϕ:

$$\{0, 3, 4\} \cup \{1, 2, 3, 5\} \cup \{1, 4, 5\} = \{0, 1, 2, 3, 4, 5\}$$

The exclusive conjunctive coordinates of the quanta in D are: $\neg p_1^{\{0\}}, \neg p_2^{\{2\}}, \neg p_3^{\{\}}$. Because $\neg p_3$ has empty exclusive coordinates, D is not a prime implicant.

Given a theory ϕ, it is possible to determine the sets of conjunctive and disjunctive quanta that define, respectively, IP_ϕ with respect to PI_ϕ and PI_ϕ with respect to IP_ϕ. This is a minimal and enriched representation for prime implicates and implicants sets, in the sense that it explicitly contains the "holographic" relation between literals in one form and clauses (or terms) in which they occur in the other form.

Example 3. Consider theory ϕ_1 introduced in example 1. Using a dual transformation algorithm (as presented in [1]), it is possible to determine the following sets of prime implicates/implicants, represented as sets of quanta:

PI_{ϕ_1}	IP_{ϕ_1}
$0 : \neg p_2^{\{1\}} \vee \neg p_3^{\{0\}}$	$0 : \neg p_1^{\{2\}} \wedge \neg p_3^{\{0\}} \wedge p_4^{\{1\}}$
$1 : \neg p_2^{\{1\}} \vee p_4^{\{0\}}$	$1 : \neg p_1^{\{2\}} \wedge \neg p_2^{\{0,1\}}$
$2 : \neg p_1^{\{0,1\}}$	

Let us observe that, according to the quantum notation, each literal in a clause $C \in PI_{\phi_1}$ represents a subset of terms in IP_{ϕ_1}, similarly each literal in a term $D \in IP_{\phi_1}$ represents a subset of clauses in PI_{ϕ_1}. Both clauses and terms are unique and not subsumed by any other. We propose to consider a clause in the PI_ϕ set as *minimal knowledge unit*, once a clause represents a *fact* in the belief set. In order to know how many clauses in the PI_ϕ set are affected by a literal we use the exclusive coordinates, i.e., the literal that represents alone more clauses in the PI_ϕ set than others literals in the same term is considered *critical* by that term. We formalize this notion as follows:

Definition 4 (Critical literal). *Let ϕ be a theory represented in quantum notation by the sets PI_ϕ and IP_ϕ, and $D \in IP_\phi$ a term. A literal $L_i \in D$ is critical iff $| \widehat{F}_c^i | \geq | \widehat{F}_c^j |$ for all $L_j \in D$.*

Example 4. Consider the sets PI_{ϕ_1} and IP_{ϕ_1} of theory ϕ_1 presented in example 3. Exclusive conjunctive coordinates mentioned in prime implicant $\neg p_1^{\{2\}} \wedge \neg p_2^{\{0,1\}}$ show that p_2 is more critical than p_1 since two prime implicates are related to p_2.

3   Belief Merging

Belief merging [7] consists in aggregating different belief sets $\phi_i, i = 1, \ldots, n$ into one belief set. The initial belief sets may be inconsistent, i.e., $\phi_1 \wedge \cdots \wedge \phi_n \vdash \bot$, and thus the aggregation method should merge belief sets ϕ_i in a consistent way. Among the different merging operators, let us mention the well known majority operators [10] and arbitration operators [12,9]. In order to evaluate merging operators general properties have to be asserted. Such properties are described by the belief merging postulates [7,8]. These postulates describe how merging should behave based on the following main principles: syntax independence and fairness (i.e., no preferences between beliefs ϕ_i).

In order to introduce the merging postulates and operators we first give some technical notations. Let sets $\phi_1, \ldots, \phi_n$ be propositional formulas and $IP_{\phi_1}, \ldots, IP_{\phi_n}$ be their associated sets of prime implicants. Following [7], Ψ represents the set $\{\phi_1, \ldots, \phi_n\}$ and $IP_\Psi = \{IP_{\phi_1}, \ldots, IP_{\phi_n}\}$. Indeed, IP_Ψ is a multi-set consisting of sets of prime implicants. Let $\bigwedge IP_\Psi$ be the conjunction of all prime implicant sets: $IP_{\phi_1} \wedge \ldots \wedge IP_{\phi_n}$. Equivalence of sets $IP_\Psi = \{IP_{\phi_1}, \ldots, IP_{\phi_n}\}$ and $IP_{\Psi'} = \{IP_{\phi'_1}, \ldots, IP_{\phi'_n}\}$ is defined as the equivalence of each set of prime implicants $IP_\Psi \leftrightarrow IP_{\Psi'} \iff \bigwedge_{i=1}^{n} IP_{\phi_i} \leftrightarrow IP_{\phi'_i}$. $IP_{\Psi \sqcup \Psi'}$ denotes the union of IP_Ψ and $IP_{\Psi'}$. If $IP_\Psi = \{IP_{\phi_1}, \ldots, IP_{\phi_n}\}$ and $IP_{\Psi'} = \{IP_{\phi'_1}, \ldots, IP_{\phi'_n}\}$ then $IP_{\Psi \sqcup \Psi'} = \{IP_{\phi_1}, \ldots, IP_{\phi_n}, IP_{\phi'_1}, \ldots, IP_{\phi'_n}\}$. If IP_Ψ denotes a set of sets of prime implicants, $\Delta(IP_\Psi)$ is a set of terms representing the aggregation of the elements of IP_Ψ.

3.1   Behavior of the Operators

We rephrase belief merging postulates [7] as follows. Let μ be an integrity constraint and $\Delta_\mu(IP_\Psi)$ be the resulting belief merging base s.t. integrity constraint μ holds:

(P0) $\exists D \in \Delta_\mu(IP_\Psi), D_\mu \in IP_\mu$ such that $D_\mu \subseteq D$.

(P1) if $IP_\mu \neq \emptyset$ then $\Delta_\mu(IP_\Psi) \neq \emptyset$.

(P2) If $IP_{\bigwedge IP_\Psi \wedge \mu} \neq \emptyset$ then $IP_{\Delta_\mu(IP_\Psi)} = IP_{\bigwedge IP_\Psi \wedge \mu}$.

(P3) If $IP_\Psi \leftrightarrow IP_{\Psi'}$ and $\mu \leftrightarrow \mu'$ then $\Delta_\mu(IP_\Psi) \leftrightarrow \Delta_{\mu'}(IP_{\Psi'})$.

(P4) If $\exists D \in IP_\phi, D_\mu \in IP_\mu$ s.t. $D_\mu \subseteq D$ and $\exists D' \in IP_{\phi'}, D'_\mu \in IP_{\mu'}$ s.t. $D'_\mu \subseteq D'$
   then if $IP_{\Delta_\mu(IP_{\{\phi\} \sqcup \{\phi'\}}) \wedge \phi} \neq \emptyset$ then $IP_{\Delta_{\mu'}(IP_{\{\phi\} \sqcup \{\phi'\}}) \wedge \phi'} \neq \emptyset$

(P5) $\Delta_\mu(IP_\Psi) \wedge \Delta_\mu(IP_{\Psi'}) \vdash \Delta_\mu(IP_{\Psi \sqcup \Psi'})$

(P6) If $IP_{\Delta_\mu(IP_\Psi) \wedge \Delta_\mu(IP_{\Psi'})} \neq \emptyset$ then $\exists D \in IP_{\Delta_\mu(IP_{\Psi \sqcup \Psi'})}, D' \in \Delta_\mu(IP_\Psi) \wedge$
   $\Delta_\mu(IP_{\Psi'})$ s.t. $D' \subseteq D$.

(P7) $\Delta_\mu(IP_\Psi) \wedge \mu' \vdash \Delta_{\mu \wedge \mu'}(IP_\Psi)$

(P8) If $IP_{\Delta_\mu(IP_\Psi) \wedge \mu'} \neq \emptyset$ then $\exists D \in \Delta_{\mu \wedge \mu'}(IP_\Psi), D' \in \Delta_\mu(IP_\Psi)$ s.t. $D' \in D$.

This paper focus on two classical distance-based merging operators [6], *majority* and *arbitration*. Arbitration characterizes the principle of the median alternative choice [9], as suggested by the following postulate:

$$\left.\begin{array}{l} \Delta_\mu(IP_\phi) \leftrightarrow \Delta_{\mu'}(IP_{\phi'}) \\ \Delta_{\mu \leftrightarrow \neg\mu'}(IP_{\phi \sqcup \phi'}) \leftrightarrow (\mu \leftrightarrow \neg\mu') \\ \mu \nvdash \mu' \\ \mu' \nvdash \mu \end{array}\right\} \quad \Rightarrow \quad \Delta_{\mu \vee \mu'}(IP_{\phi \sqcup \phi'}) \quad \leftrightarrow \quad \Delta_\mu(IP_\phi) \quad \text{(Arb)}$$

A majority operator characterizes the principle that if an alternative occurs at least n times in Ψ then this alternative should be present in the resulting base. Formally, majority merging is characterized by the following postulate:

$$\exists D \quad \in \quad IP_{\Delta_\mu(\Psi \sqcup \Psi')} \exists n \exists D' \quad \in \quad IP_{\Delta_\mu(\Psi \sqcup (\Psi')^n)} \text{ such that } D \quad \subseteq \quad D' \quad \text{(Maj)}$$

4   Quantum-Based Merging

The proposed distance is based on the notion of distance between terms, which is analogous to the notion of distance between models. The distance between two models is based on Dalal's one [3] and it has been widely used in belief change [5,4] and belief merging [6,8]. This distance represents the number of contradicting propositional symbols among two models. In this paper, we use the quantum notation, representing a belief base ϕ by PI_ϕ and IP_ϕ, and assume the new minimal knowledge unit as presented in section 2. The distance between two implicants is defined as follows: suppose a term $D_\phi \in IP_\phi$ and a second term D, let $L_i \in D_\phi \cap \overline{D}$ be the set of contradicting literals. Now, let us focus on the set of exclusive conjunctive coordinates $\widehat{F}_c^i$ associated to each of these contradicting literals and issued from D_ϕ. This set represents the set of prime implicates that could no longer hold in PI_ϕ if L_i does not hold. Let κ be this distance:

Definition 5 (κ). *Let IP_ϕ be the set of prime implicants of ϕ. Let $D_\phi \in IP_\phi$ and D be two terms and $\kappa(D, D_\phi)$ be the set of prime implicates in PI_ϕ associated, through the conjunctive coordinates, with the set of literals of D_ϕ that conflict with literals in D:*

$$\kappa(D, D_\phi) = \bigcup_{L_i \in D_\phi \cap \overline{D}} \widehat{F}_c^i$$

In the following, we focus on the cardinality of the set given by κ. The distance between a conjunctive term D and a set of prime implicants IP_ϕ is defined as the minimal value given by κ:

$$\widehat{d}(D, IP_\phi) = \min(\{|\kappa(D, D_\phi)| \mid D_\phi \in IP_\phi\})$$

Example 5. Suppose the following belief sets $\Psi = \{\phi_1, \phi_2, \phi_3\}$ such that:

$IP_{\phi_1} = \{0 : (p_0^{\{3\}} \wedge p_1^{\{1,2\}} \wedge \neg p_3^{\{0,2\}}), 1 : (p_0^{\{3\}} \wedge p_2^{\{0,1\}} \wedge \neg p_3^{\{0,2\}}),$
$\quad 2 : (p_0^{\{3\}} \wedge p_1^{\{1,2\}} \wedge p_2^{\{0,1\}})\}$

$PI_{\phi_1} = \{0 : (p_2^{\{2,1\}} \vee \neg p_3^{\{1,0\}}), 1 : (p_1^{\{2,0\}} \vee p_2^{\{2,1\}}), 2 : (p_1^{\{2,0\}} \vee \neg p_3^{\{1,0\}})$
$\quad 3 : (p_0^{\{2,1,0\}})\}$

$IP_{\phi_2} = \{0 : (\neg p_0^{\{2,3,4\}} \wedge p_2^{\{0\}} \wedge \neg p_3^{\{1,4\}}), 1 : (\neg p_0^{\{2,3,4\}} \wedge \neg p_1^{\{0,1,2\}}),$
$\quad 2 : (\neg p_1^{\{0,1,2\}} \wedge \neg p_3^{\{3\}} \wedge \neg p_3^{\{1,4\}})\}$

$PI_{\phi_2} = \{0 : (\neg p_1^{\{2,1\}} \vee p_2^{\{0\}}), 1 : (\neg p_1^{\{2,1\}} \vee \neg p_3^{\{2,0\}}), 2 : (\neg p_0^{\{1,0\}} \vee \neg p_1^{\{2,1\}}),$
$\quad 3 : (\neg p_0^{\{1,0\}} \vee \neg p_2^{\{2\}}), 4 : (\neg p_0^{\{1,0\}} \vee \neg p_3^{\{2,0\}})\}$

$IP_{\phi_3} = \{0 : (p_0^{\{2,3\}} \wedge \neg p_1^{\{0\}} \wedge p_2^{\{1,3\}}), 1 : (\neg p_0^{\{0\}} \wedge p_1^{\{1,2\}} \wedge p_2^{\{1,3\}}),$
$\quad 2 : (p_0^{\{2,3\}} \wedge p_1^{\{1,2\}} \wedge \neg p_2^{\{0\}})\}$

$PI_{\phi_3} = \{0 : (\neg p_0^{\{1\}} \vee \neg p_1^{\{0\}} \vee \neg p_2^{\{2\}}), 1 : (p_1^{\{2,1\}} \vee p_2^{\{1,0\}}), 2 : (p_0^{\{2,0\}} \vee p_1^{\{2,1\}}),$
$\quad 3 : (p_0^{\{2,0\}} \vee p_2^{\{1,0\}})\}$

The following table details the distance between each term and profile $\Psi = \{\phi_1, \phi_2, \phi_3\}$; we also mention between parenthesis the number of contradicting literals given by Dalal distance, calculated as $d(D, IP_\phi) = \min(\{|D \cap \overline{D_\phi}| \mid D_\phi \in IP_\phi\})$, in order to stress the difference between the two distances:

D	$\widehat{d}(D, IP_{\phi_1})$	$\widehat{d}(D, IP_{\phi_2})$	$\widehat{d}(D, IP_{\phi_3})$
$p_0 \wedge p_1 \wedge \neg p_3$	0(0)	2(1)	0(0)
$p_0 \wedge p_2 \wedge \neg p_3$	0(0)	1(1)	0(0)
$p_0 \wedge p_1 \wedge p_2$	0(0)	2(1)	1(1)
$\neg p_0 \wedge p_2 \wedge \neg p_3$	1(1)	0(0)	0(0)
$\neg p_0 \wedge \neg p_1$	1(1)	0(0)	1(1)
$\neg p_1 \wedge \neg p_2 \wedge \neg p_3$	1(1)	0(0)	1(1)
$p_0 \wedge \neg p_1 \wedge p_2$	0(0)	1(1)	0(0)
$\neg p_0 \wedge p_1 \wedge p_2$	1(1)	0(0)	0(0)
$p_0 \wedge p_1 \wedge \neg p_2$	0(0)	2(1)	0(0)

According to distance $\widehat{d}$, we now revisit the arbitration and majority operators. The arbitration operator is defined as follows. First, we define the distance between a term D and set Ψ as the max distance between D and each $\phi \in \Psi$:

$$\widehat{d_a}(D, \Psi) = \max(\bigcup_{IP_\phi \in IP_\Psi} \widehat{d}(D, IP_\phi))$$

Next, we characterize the arbitration merging operator based on the quantum notation:

Definition 6 (Quantum-arbitration)

$$\widehat{\Delta}^a_\mu(IP_\Psi) = \{D_\mu \cup \overline{D} \mid D_\mu \in IP_\mu, D \in \bigcup_{IP_\phi \in IP_\Psi} IP_\phi \text{ and } \widehat{d_a}(D_\mu \cup \overline{D}, \Psi) =$$

$$\min(\{\widehat{d_a}(D_\mu \cup \overline{D}, \Psi) \mid D_\mu \in IP_\mu, D \in \bigcup_{IP_\phi \in IP_\Psi} IP_\phi\})\}$$

The key difference between the proposed operator and the classical definitions of arbitration [12,9,7] is related to the notion of quantum. In the existing definitions of arbitration, the underlying principle is to determine the models that represent a median solution: the solution "is not so far" from each ϕ_i in terms of truth values. The quantum-arbitration operator aims at calculating a median result which "is not so far" from each ϕ_i in terms of relations between literals, i.e., what are the "average" implicates? There is a second key difference between the proposed definition of merging operator and the classical ones which are based on a selection of models. Those merging operators select the models which are the closest from the profile and for this, all the possible models are considered. In our context, only a subset of models is considered; the subset given by the prime implicants of each ϕ_i. In our view, it is more realistic to focus on models that are directly issued from Ψ. It entails that if $\mu = \top$ then the result is a subset of the union of all prime implicants:

Proposition 3. $\widehat{\Delta}^a_\top(IP_\Psi) \vdash \bigvee_{IP_\phi \in IP_\Psi} IP_\phi$

Now, let us focus on the behavior of the quantum-arbitration operator:

Theorem 1. $\widehat{\Delta}^a$ does not satisfy P0 and P1 and P4. P2, P3, P5 through P8 hold.

Sketch of the proof: Postulates P0 and P1 do not hold in the limited case where all belief bases of Ψ are inconsistent. In that case, set IP_Ψ is empty and thus the set of eligible implicants $D_\mu \cup D_\Psi$ is also empty. Since the conjunction of every belief bases and μ is consistent then there always exists an implicant D s.t. $\widehat{d_a}(D, \Psi) = 0$ and $D = D_\mu \cup D_{\Psi_1} \cup \cdots \cup D_{\Psi_n}$. P3 holds because the usage of the prime forms representation entails the syntax independence. Proposition 1 entails that P4 does not hold, P5 and P6 hold because of the definition of prime implicants and $\widehat{\Delta}^a$: let us focus on P5, consider two terms D and D' s.t. $D \wedge D'$ is satisfiable and which respectively belong to $\widehat{\Delta}^a_\mu(IP_\Psi)$ and $\widehat{\Delta}^a_\mu(IP_{\Psi'})$, by definition of prime implicants and $\widehat{\Delta}^a$ there exists $D'' \in \widehat{\Delta}^a_\mu(IP_{\Psi \sqcup \Psi'})$ s.t. $D \cup D' \subseteq D''$. Definition of $\widehat{\Delta}^a$ entails P7 and P8.

The remaining question is to know whether the quantum-arbitration operator is actually an arbitration operator:

Theorem 2. *Operator $\widehat{\Delta}^a$ satisfies postulate (Arb).*

The proof is straightforward. We conclude the characterization of quantum-arbitration operator with a result on the complexity aspect.

Proposition 4. *The computation of $\widehat{\Delta}^a(IP_\Psi)$ is polynomial w.r.t. to the number of prime implicants that appear in IP_μ and IP_Ψ.*

Despite of the knowledge compilation in prime forms can lead to an exponential number of clauses in the number of atoms, the experimental results obtained in belief change area [2,11] allow us to stress that the number of prime implicants is usually significantly lower than the number of models and it means an increase in the computational efficiency.

The quantum notation and distance $\widehat{d}_a$ emphasize the preservation of the implicates. It entails that the majority operator seems more accurate than the arbitration operator: keeping the most representative prime implicates. In order to define a quantum-majority operator, we first define distance $\widehat{d}_\Sigma$ which gives the overall number of prime implicates that are violated by a term D:

$$\widehat{d}_\Sigma(D,\Psi) = \sum_{IP_\phi \in IP_\Psi} \widehat{d}(D,IP_\phi)$$

Based on this new distance, we introduce the majority merging operator based on the quantum notation:

Definition 7 (Quantum-majority)

$$\widehat{\Delta}_\mu^\Sigma(IP_\Psi) = \{D_\mu \cup \overline{D} | D_\mu \in IP_\mu, D \in \bigcup_{IP_\phi \in IP_\Psi} IP_\phi \text{ and } \widehat{d}_\Sigma(D_\mu \cup \overline{D},\Psi) =$$

$$\min(\{\widehat{d}_\Sigma(D_\mu \cup \overline{D},\Psi) | D_\mu \in IP_\mu, D \in \bigcup_{IP_\phi \in IP_\Psi} IP_\phi\})\}$$

The quantum-majority operator runs as follows: first, it considers all the implicants based on constraint μ and prime implicant D_ϕ from Ψ. Since μ has to hold, for every D_μ, the inconsistent part of D_ϕ w.r.t. to D_μ is removed so that it can be added to D_μ. Second, the distance evaluates the quantity of prime implicates that will no longer hold; it follows that if the inconsistent part between D_μ and D_ϕ is related to many implicates that appear in each ϕ_i, the distance will be quite high. Thus, as we want, the majority principle focuses on the prime implicates, i.e., the usage of the literals. Finally, the min function selects the resulting implicants that maximize the number of implicates that could still hold in the resulting base.

As for the quantum arbitration operator, the resulting base is defined w.r.t. the prime implicants that belong to IP_μ and IP_Ψ. Hence, if μ is skipped ($\mu = \top$), we get that:

Proposition 5. $\widehat{\Delta}_\top^\Sigma(IP_\Psi) \vdash \bigvee_{IP_\phi \in IP_\Psi} IP_\phi$

Again, as for arbitration operator, we focus on a subset of models, the subset characterized by the prime implicants of Ψ. Now, let us focus on the behavior of the quantum-majority operator:

Theorem 3. $\widehat{\Delta}^\Sigma$ *does not satisfy P0 and P1 and P4. P2, P3, P5 through P8 hold.*

The proof is similar to the proof given for the quantum-arbitration operator. The remaining question is to know whether operator $\widehat{\Delta}^\Sigma$ is a majority operator:

Theorem 4. *Operator* $\widehat{\Delta}^a$ *satisfies postulate (Maj).*

The proof is straightforward. We conclude the characterization of quantum-majority operator with a result on the complexity aspect.

Proposition 6. *The computation of* $\widehat{\Delta}^\Sigma(IP_\Psi)$ *is polynomial w.r.t. to the number of prime implicants that appear in* IP_μ *and* IP_Ψ.

To split the different stages (computing IP_Ψ and Δ) allow us to give more importance to the merging stage. That is, since this stage is polynomial it is easier to evaluate and compare the resulting bases and thus to possibly reconsider the principle that have guided the process (arbitration or majority).

Example 6. Let us pursue example 5. For the sake of conciseness, we suppose that we do not consider any integrity constraint, i.e., $\mu = \top$. Hereunder is the table that gives a summary of the results obtained using the quantum arbitration and majority operators. Minimal distances are emphasized (bold) in the table.

D	$\widehat{d}_a(D,\Psi)$	$\widehat{d}_\Sigma(D,\Psi)$	D	$\widehat{d}_a(D,\Psi)$	$\widehat{d}_\Sigma(D,\Psi)$
$p_0 \wedge p_1 \wedge \neg p_3$	$2(1)$	$2(1)$	$\neg p_1 \wedge \neg p_2 \wedge \neg p_3$	$1(1)$	$2(2)$
$p_0 \wedge p_2 \wedge \neg p_3$	$1(1)$	$1(1)$	$p_0 \wedge \neg p_1 \wedge p_2$	$1(1)$	$1(1)$
$p_0 \wedge p_1 \wedge p_2$	$2(1)$	$3(2)$	$\neg p_0 \wedge p_1 \wedge p_2$	$1(1)$	$1(1)$
$\neg p_0 \wedge p_2 \wedge \neg p_3$	$1(1)$	$1(1)$	$p_0 \wedge p_1 \wedge \neg p_2$	$2(1)$	$2(1)$
$\neg p_0 \wedge \neg p_1$	$1(1)$	$2(2)$			

It follows that:

$$\widehat{\Delta}_a(\Psi) \equiv IP_{\phi_2} \vee (p_0 \wedge p_2 \wedge \neg p_3) \vee (p_0 \wedge \neg p_1 \wedge p_2) \vee (\neg p_0 \wedge p_1 \wedge \neg p_2)$$

$$\widehat{\Delta}_\Sigma(\Psi) \equiv (p_0 \wedge p_2 \wedge \neg p_3) \vee (\neg p_0 \wedge p_2 \wedge \neg p_3) \vee (p_0 \wedge \neg p_1 \wedge p_2) \vee (\neg p_0 \wedge p_1 \wedge p_2)$$

Notice that, we get results that really differ from the results given by the classical definitions of belief merging operators (showed in italic). For classical arbitration all terms would be chosen and for classical majority, besides of the terms chosen by our operator, the terms $p_0 \wedge p_1 \wedge \neg p_3$ and $p_0 \wedge p_1 \wedge \neg p_2$ would be chosen.

5 Conclusion

In this paper, we have proposed two new merging operators. These two operators take advantage of the representation of beliefs in a specific syntax: prime implicants and implicates and the quantum notation. We have shown that this specific syntax enables to revisit the notion of minimal unit of knowledge. By stressing the fact that the way the literals are used in each belief base should not be forgotten, we have defined a new distance and proposed two merging operators based on this distance. We have shown the properties of these new operators. The main characteristics are that (i) the Fairness postulate ($P4$) no longer hold and (ii) the complexity results which emphasize the evaluation. Concerning postulate $P4$, since we advocate that the result should be obtained by only considering the implicants of the initial belief base, we also advocate that this result is not so disadvantageous. Our work is clearly related to [7,8] which have proposed many merging operators. The key characteristic of every proposed operators is to focus on models. None of the proposed distances (drastic distance, weighted Dalal) or operators (max, $Gmax$, Σ^n) enable to represent the proposed quantum-based operators. The closest definition of distance is the weighted Dalal which associates a numerical value to each propositional symbol. The key difference is at first the definition of the distance: the value of p may differ from the value of $\bar{p}$; second the underlying rationale: taking into account the structure of the beliefs and third limiting the calculation of merging base by only using the initial implicants. This lead to get operators that behave differently. Our aim is to extend the results so that quantum-based merging operators can be expressed with the help of preferences as shown in [8]; it will enable to characterize prime implicants/implicates belief merging in terms of representation theorems.

References

1. Bittencourt, G., Marchi, J., Padilha, R.S.: A syntactic approach to satisfaction. In: Konev, B., Schmidt, R. (eds.) Proc. of the 4th Inter. Workshop on the Implementation of Logics, pp. 18–32. University of Liverpool and University of Manchester (2003)
2. Bittencourt, G., Perrussel, L., Marchi, J.: A syntactical approach to revision. In: de Mántaras, R.L., Saitta, L. (eds.) Proc. of the 16th Eureopean Conf. on Artificial Intelligence, ECAI 2004, Valencia, Spain, August 22–27, pp. 788–792. IOS Press, Amsterdam (2004)
3. Dalal, M.: Investigations into a theory of knowledge base revision: Preliminary report. In: Rosenbloom, P., Szolovits, P. (eds.) Proc. of the 7th National Conf. on Artificial Intelligence, vol. 2, pp. 475–479. AAAI Press, Menlo Park (1988)
4. Forbus, K.: Introducing actions into qualitative simulation. In: Proc. of IJCAI 1989, Detroit, MI, pp. 1273–1278 (1989)
5. Gärdenfors, P.: Knowledge in Flux: Modelling the Dynamics of Epistemic States. Bradford Books/MIT Press (1988)
6. Konieczny, S., Lang, J., Marquis, P.: Distance-based merging: a general framework and some complexity results. In: Proc. of KR 2002, pp. 97–108 (2002)
7. Konieczny, S., Pérez, R.P.: Merging information under constraints: a logical framework. Journal of Logic and Computation 12(5), 773–808 (2002)
8. Konieczny, S., Pérez, R.P.: Propositional belief base merging or how to merge beliefs/goals coming from several sources and some links with social choice theory. European Journal of Operational Research 160(3), 785–802 (2005)
9. Liberatore, P., Schaerf, M.: Arbitration (or how to merge knowledge bases). IEEE Transactions on Knowledge and Data Engineering 10(1), 76–90 (1998)
10. Lin, J., Mendelzon, A.: Knowledge base merging by majority. Kluwer, Dordrecht (1999)
11. Marchi, J., Bittencourt, G., Perrussel, L.: A syntactical approach to belief update. In: Gelbukh, A., de Albornoz, Á., Terashima-Marín, H. (eds.) MICAI 2005. LNCS (LNAI), vol. 3789, pp. 142–151. Springer, Heidelberg (2005)
12. Revesz, P.Z.: On the Semantics of Arbitration. Journal of Algebra and Computation 7(2), 133–160 (1997)
13. Socher, R.: Optimizing the clausal normal form transformation. Journal of Automated Reasoning 7(3), 325–336 (1991)

A Study of Schedule Robustness for Job Shop with Uncertainty

Inés González-Rodríguez[1], Jorge Puente[2],
Ramiro Varela[2], and Camino R. Vela[2]

[1] Department of Mathematics, Statistics and Computing,
University of Cantabria, Spain
ines.gonzalez@unican.es
[2] A.I. Centre and Department of Computer Science,
University of Oviedo, Spain
{puente,ramiro,crvela}@uniovi.es
http://www.aic.uniovi.es/Tc

Abstract. We consider a job shop problem with uncertain processing times modelled as triangular fuzzy numbers and propose a methodology to study solution robustness with respect to different perturbations in the durations. This methodology is applied to obtain experimental results for several problem instances, using a hybrid genetic algorithm that minimises the expected makespan. We conclude that taking into account the uncertainty information provided by fuzzy numbers produces proactive solutions, coping well with posterior changes in processing times.

1 Introduction

Scheduling problems form an important body of research since the late fifties, with multiple applications in industry, finance and science [1]. Traditionally, scheduling has been treated as a deterministic problem that assumes precise knowledge of all data. However, modelling real-world problems usually involves processing uncertainty and flexibility. In the literature we find different proposals for dealing with uncertainty in scheduling [2], either finding solutions which adapt dynamically to changes or incorporating available knowledge about possible changes to the solution. Fuzzy scheduling comprises diverse approaches to dealing with both uncertainty and flexibility, ranging from representing incomplete or vague states of information to using fuzzy priority rules with linguistic qualifiers or preference modelling [3],[4].

The complexity of scheduling problems such as job shop means that practical approaches to solving them usually involve heuristic strategies [1]. Extending these strategies to problems with uncertain durations represented as fuzzy numbers usually requires a significant reformulation of both the problem and solving methods. Proposals from the literature include genetic algorithms [5],[6],[7], simulated annealing [8] and genetic algorithms hybridised with local search [9].

In the sequel, we concentrate on a job shop problem where uncertain task durations are given as fuzzy numbers. Based on a semantics of fuzzy schedules

H. Geffner et al. (Eds.): IBERAMIA 2008, LNAI 5290, pp. 31–41, 2008.

from the literature, we propose a new methodology to test the robustness of the obtained schedule with respect to posterior changes in task durations. Following this methodology, experimental results are obtained for modified benchmark problems using a hybrid algorithm, illustrating how the use of fuzzy numbers allows for robust proactive solutions.

2   Job Shop Scheduling with Uncertain Durations

The *job shop scheduling problem*, also denoted *JSP*, consists in scheduling a set of jobs $\{J_1, \ldots, J_n\}$ on a set of physical resources or machines $\{M_1, \ldots, M_m\}$, subject to a set of constraints. There are *precedence constraints*, so each job J_i, $i = 1, \ldots, n$, consists of m tasks $\{\theta_{i1}, \ldots, \theta_{im}\}$ to be sequentially scheduled. Also, there are *capacity constraints*, whereby each task θ_{ij} requires the uninterrupted and exclusive use of one of the machines for its whole processing time. A solution to this problem is a schedule (an allocation of starting times for all tasks) which, besides being *feasible*, in the sense that precedence and capacity constraints hold, is optimal according to some criteria, for instance, that the makespan is minimal.

2.1   Uncertain Durations

In real-life applications, it is often the case that the exact duration of a task, i.e. the time it takes to be processed, is not known in advance, and only some uncertain knowledge is available. Such knowledge can be modelled using a *triangular fuzzy number* or TFN, given by an interval $[n^1, n^3]$ of possible values and a modal value n^2 in it. For a TFN N, denoted $N = (n^1, n^2, n^3)$, the membership function takes the following triangular shape:

$$\mu_N(x) = \begin{cases} \frac{x - n^1}{n^2 - n^1} & : n^1 \leq x \leq n^2 \\ \frac{x - n^3}{n^2 - n^3} & : n^2 < x \leq n^3 \\ 0 & : x < n^1 \text{ or } n^3 < x \end{cases} \tag{1}$$

In the job shop, we essentially need two operations on fuzzy numbers, the sum and the maximum. These are obtained by extending the corresponding operations on real numbers using the *Extension Principle*. However, computing the resulting expression is cumbersome, if not intractable. For the sake of simplicity and tractability of numerical calculations, we follow [8] and approximate the results of these operations, evaluating the operation only on the three defining points of each TFN. It turns out that for any pair of TFNs M and N, the approximated sum $M + N \approx (m^1 + n^1, m^2 + n^2, m^3 + n^3)$ coincides with the actual sum of TFNs; this may not be the case for the maximum $M \vee N \approx (m^1 \vee n^1, m^2 \vee n^2, m^3 \vee n^3)$, although they have identical support and modal value.

The membership function of a fuzzy number can be interpreted as a possibility distribution on the real numbers. This allows to define its expected value [10], given for a TFN N by $E[N] = \frac{1}{4}(n^1 + 2n^2 + n^3)$. It coincides with the neutral scalar substitute of a fuzzy interval and the centre of gravity of its mean value [3]. It induces a total ordering $\leq_E$ in the set of fuzzy numbers [8], where for any two fuzzy numbers M, N $M \leq_E N$ if and only if $E[M] \leq E[N]$.

2.2 Fuzzy Job Shop Scheduling

For a job shop problem instance of size $n \times m$ (n jobs and m machines), let p be a duration matrix and let ν be a machine matrix such that p_{ij} is the processing time of task θ_{ij} and ν_{ij} is the machine required by θ_{ij}, $i = 1, \ldots, n$, $j = 1, \ldots, m$. Let σ be a feasible task processing order, i.e., a lineal ordering of tasks which is compatible with a processing order of tasks that may be carried out so that all constraints hold. A feasible schedule may be derived from σ using a *semi-active schedule builder*: if $S_{ij}(\sigma, p, \nu)$ and $C_{ij}(\sigma, p, \nu)$ denote respectively the starting and completion times of task θ_{ij}, these times are given by:

$$S_{ij}(\sigma, p, \nu) = C_{i(j-1)}(\sigma, p, \nu) \vee C_{rs}(\sigma, p, \nu) \tag{2}$$
$$C_{ij}(\sigma, p, \nu) = S_{ij}(\sigma, p, \nu) + p_{ij} \tag{3}$$

where θ_{rs} is the task preceding θ_{ij} in the machine according to the processing order σ, $C_{i0}(\sigma, p, \nu)$ is assumed to be zero and, analogously, $C_{rs}(\sigma, p, \nu)$ is taken to be zero if θ_{ij} is the first task to be processed in the corresponding machine. The completion time of job J_i will then be $C_i(\sigma, p, \nu) = C_{im}(\sigma, p, \nu)$ and the *makespan* $C_{max}(\sigma, p, \nu)$ is the maximum completion time of all jobs:

$$C_{max}(\sigma, p, \nu) = \vee_{1 \leq i \leq n} (C_i(\sigma, p, \nu)) \tag{4}$$

For the sake of a simpler notation, we may write $C_{max}(\sigma)$ when the problem (hence p and ν) is fixed or even C_{max} when no confusion is possible.

If task processing times are TFNs, the resulting schedule is fuzzy in the sense that starting and completion times and the makespan are TFNs. Each TFN can be seen as a possibility distributions on the values that the time may take. Notice however that there is no uncertainty regarding the task processing ordering σ that determines the schedule. To illustrate these ideas, consider a problem of 3 jobs and 2 machines with the following matrices for fuzzy processing times and machine allocation:

$$p = \begin{pmatrix} (3,4,7) & (1,2,3) \\ (4,5,6) & (2,3,4) \\ (1,2,6) & (1,2,4) \end{pmatrix} \nu = \begin{pmatrix} 1 & 2 \\ 2 & 1 \\ 2 & 1 \end{pmatrix}$$

Figure 1 shows the Gantt chart (adapted to TFNs following [8]) of the schedule given by the task order $\theta_{11}, \theta_{21}, \theta_{31}, \theta_{22}, \theta_{12}, \theta_{32}$. For instance, for task θ_{22} we have $S_{22} = C_{21} \vee C_{11} = (4,5,7)$ and $C_{22} = S_{22} + p_{22} = (6,8,11)$, meaning that θ_{22} completion time will be between 6 and 11, with 8 as most pausible value.

Since we may build a feasible schedule from a feasible task processing order, we restate the goal of the job shop problem as that of finding an optimal task processing order, in the sense that the makespan for the derived schedule is optimal. It is not trivial to optimise a fuzzy makespan, since neither the maximum

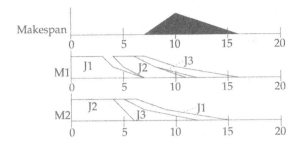

Fig. 1. Gantt chart of the schedule represented by $\theta_{11}, \theta_{21}, \theta_{31}, \theta_{22}, \theta_{12}, \theta_{32}$

nor its approximation define a total ordering in the set of TFNs. Following [9], we use the total ordering provided by the expected value and consider that the objective is to minimise the expected makespan $E[C_{max}(\sigma, \boldsymbol{p}, \boldsymbol{\nu})]$.

2.3 A Hybrid Algorithm

Evolutionary strategies have been shown to perform well in presence of uncertainty [11]. In particular, hybrid methods combining a genetic algorithm (GA) with local search (LS) have proved successful for the fuzzy flow shop problem [12] and the fuzzy job shop problem [9]. For the latter, experimental results show a clear synergy between the GA and the LS, with the hybrid method also comparing favourably with other heuristic methods from the literature [8], [5].

The *genetic algorithm* proposed in [9] uses permutations with repetition as chromosomes. These are decoded using an extension of G&T algorithm to fuzzy durations, with the fitness function being the expected makespan of the obtained schedule. Pairs of chromosomes are selected using tournament and mated using job order crossover (JOX) to obtain two offsprings; acceptance consists in selecting the best individuals from both parents and their offsprings. JOX operator has an implicit mutation effect and therefore, no explicit mutation operator is actually introduced, with the consequent simplification of parameter setting, as crossover and mutation probabilities being 1 and 0 respectively.

The *local search procedure* is applied to every chromosome immediately after its generation. Starting from this given processing order, its neighbourhood is calculated and neighbours are evaluated using the aforementioned semiactive schedule builder in the search of an improving solution. The selection criterion is *steepest descent hill-climbing*, i.e. all neighbours are evaluated, selecting the best one, which replaces the original solution if it is an improving neighbour (with a smaller $E[C_{max}]$). Local search starts again from that improving neighbour, so the procedure finishes when no neighbour satisfies the acceptance criterion. In [9] it is proposed that the neighbourhood structure be an extension of that defined for the crisp job shop in [13]. Here, a *move* for a feasible task processing order σ is defined as the change in the order of a pair of consecutive tasks (x, y) in a critical block. The *neighbourhood* of σ, denoted $H(\sigma)$, is defined as the set of processing orders obtained from σ after applying all possible moves.

A key aspect then for the neighbourhood is the definition of critical block in the fuzzy case. In general, a job shop problem instance may be represented by a directed graph $G = (V, A \cup D)$, where each node in the set V represents a task of the problem, except for the dummy nodes *start* and *end*, representing tasks with null processing times. Arcs in A, or *conjunctive arcs*, represent precedence constraints (including arcs from node *start* to the first task of each job and arcs form the last task of each job to node *end*). Arcs in D, called *disjunctive arcs*, represent capacity constraints: set D is partitioned into subsets D_i, where D_i corresponds to machine M_i and includes an arc for each pair of tasks requiring that machine. Each arc is weighted with the processing time of the task at the source node (a TFN in our case).

A feasible task processing order σ is represented by a *solution graph*, an acyclic subgraph of G, $G(\sigma) = (V, A \cup R(\sigma))$, where $R(\sigma) = \cup_{i=1...m} R_i(\sigma)$, $R_i(\sigma)$ being a hamiltonian selection of D_i. In the fuzzy case, from $G(\sigma)$ we obtain the *parallel solution graphs* $G^i(\sigma)$, $i = 1, 2, 3$, which are identical to $G(\sigma)$ except for the cost of arc $(x, y) \in A \cup R(\sigma)$, which for graph $G^i(\sigma)$ will be the i-th defining point of p_x, that is, p_x^i. Each parallel solution graph $G^i(\sigma)$ is a disjunctive graph with crisp arc weights, so in each of them a critical path is the longest path from node *start* to node *end*. For the fuzzy solution graph $G(\sigma)$, a path will be considered to be *critical* if and only if it is critical in some $G^i(\sigma)$. Nodes and arcs in a critical path are termed critical and a critical path is naturally decomposed into critical blocks $B_1, \ldots, B_r$, where a *critical block* is a maximal subsequence of operations of a critical path requiring the same machine.

3   Robustness of Processing Orders

According to a classification of the most representative situations of uncertainty in optimisation problems given in [11], the uncertainty addressed in the fuzzy job shop problem lies in the robustness category, where design variables are subject to perturbations or changes after the optimal solution has been determined. A common requirement in this case is that a solution should still work satisfactorily when the design variables change slightly, for instance, due to manufacturing tolerances. Solutions fulfilling this requirement are termed *robust solutions*. Several methods have been proposed to deal with duration uncertainty in the framework of scheduling problems ([4], [8], [5]) but less effort has been dedicated to analyse the robustness of solutions ([14], [6]). Here, we propose a new method to study robustness for the fuzzy job shop problem, based on a numerical analysis and inspired by the semantics for fuzzy schedules from [7].

3.1   Semantics of Fuzzy Schedules

In [7] solutions to the fuzzy job shop are interpreted as *a-priori solutions*, found when the duration of tasks is not exactly known. In this setting, it is impossible to predict what the exact time-schedule will be, because it depends on the realisation of the task's durations, which is not known yet. Each fuzzy schedule corresponds to a crisp ordering of tasks and it is not until tasks are executed according to this ordering that we know their real duration and, hence, know the exact schedule, the *a-posteriori solution* with crisp job completion times and makespan. The practical interest of a solution to the fuzzy job shop would lie in the ordering of tasks that it provides a priori using the available incomplete information, which should yield good schedules in the moment of its practical use. Its behaviour could therefore be evaluated on a family of N crisp job shop problems, representing a posteriori realisations of the fuzzy problem. Such possible realisations are simulated by generating an exact duration for each task at random according to a probability distribution which is coherent with the fuzzy duration (namely the possibility distribution it provides normalised so the additivity axiom holds).

Given a solution to the fuzzy job shop, consider the task processing order it provides σ_F. For a crisp version of the problem, let η be the matrix of crisp durations, such that η_{ij}, the a-posteriori duration of task θ_{ij} is coherent with the constraint imposed by the fuzzy duration p_{ij}. The ordering σ_F can be used by an algorithm of semiactive schedule building as presented above, using the exact durations η instead of fuzzy ones, to obtain a time-schedule with a crisp makespan $C_{max}(\sigma_F, \eta, \nu)$. If instead of a single crisp instance we consider the whole family of N crisp problems, each with a duration matrix, we obtain N makespan values, and its average gives a measure of the overall performance of the fuzzy solution across the family of N crisp problems.

3.2   A Methodology for Robustness Analysis

In [2], the authors distinguish between five approaches to dealing with uncertainty in a scheduling environment where the evolution structure of the precedence network is deterministic: reactive scheduling, stochastic scheduling, scheduling under fuzziness, proactive (robust) scheduling, and sensitivity analysis. The fuzzy job shop approach falls clearly into the third category. However, we shall argue that it also falls in the proactive or robust scheduling category. *Proactive scheduling* constructs a predictive schedule that accounts for statistical knowledge of uncertainty, used to make the predictive schedule more robust, i.e., insensitive to disruptions. Even if the information about the uncertainty is not of stochastic nature, the fuzzy job shop approach is still proactive in the sense that the built schedule (the obtained task processing order) also accounts for the uncertain knowledge available and should therefore be less sensitive to perturbations in task durations. Hence we propose to test such robustness in comparison to a simpler approach which does not take into account the available albeit uncertain knowledge.

The uncertainty in processing times is modelled using TFNs with a single modal value. Provided that the membership function is symmetric, this value coincides with the TFN's expected value. This suggests reducing the fuzzy problem to a crisp one where task durations are given by their most typical value. This approach, based on defuzzification, is pretty standard and has the advantage of reducing the problem to a less complex and better known one. It also has the potential disadvantage of losing some information, which may reflect in a loss of robustness.

Let σ_F and σ_C denote feasible task processing orders obtained respectively for the fuzzy job shop problem and the crisp one where each task is allocated its most typical duration. We propose to compare both orderings in terms of robustness, when durations are subject to perturbations, independently of the method of resolution used. The comparison will take place under four different situations. The first one corresponds to the above semantics, testing their performance on a set T_1 of N crisp instances (possible realisations) obtained as a random sample of the probability distributions derived from the TFNs. The remaining situations correspond to "extreme" crisp instances, modelling situations where, either the expert has been very conservative when estimating the most typical duration, so the actual processing time is in general lower, or the expert has been too optimistic, so there are significant delays w.r.t. the most typical duration. First, we generate a set T_2 of N crisp instances where, for each task with fuzzy duration (p^1, p^2, p^3), its realisation (crisp duration) is selected at random from the interval $[p^1, p^1 + 0.25(p^3 - p^1)]$ (i.e. the first "quarter" of all possible durations). Analogously, another set T_3 of N crisp instances is generated so, for each task, its possible crisp duration is selected at random from $[p^1 + 0.75(p^3 - p^1), p^3]$. A final set T_4 of N crisp instances is obtained as a mixture of conservative and optimistic estimations, with each task duration selected at random from $[p^1, p^1 + 0.25(p^3 - p^1)] \cup [p^1 + 0.75(p^3 - p^1), p^3]$. For every crisp instance, both task orderings σ_F and σ_C can be applied to obtain a makespan value; the average and standard deviation of these values across each set of N crisp instances will provide a means of comparing both orderings. If the use of TFNs throughout the solving process is an adequate approach to taking into account uncertain information, then solution σ_F should behave better when faced with these perturbations than σ_C and, hence, it would be considered robust.

4 Experimental Results

For the experimental results, we consider 12 well-known benchmark problems for job shop: FT10 (size 10×10), FT20 (20×5), La21, La24 and La25 (15×10), La27 and La29 (20×10), La38 and La40 (15×15), and ABZ7, ABZ8 and ABZ9 (20×15). Fuzzy versions of each benchmark are generated following [8] and [9], so task durations become symmetric TFNs where the modal value is the original duration, ensuring that the optimal solution to the crisp problem provides a lower bound for the fuzzified version. The hybrid genetic algorithm is run 30 times for each of the 12 fuzzy job shop instances with population size 100 and for 200 generations. Another 30 runs are performed for each of the 12 crisp job shop instances, with the same population size and an extended number of generations to obtain equivalent CPU times and allow for comparisons.

Table 1 presents a first comparison between both approaches, showing the fuzzy makespan values $C_{max}(\sigma_F^*, \boldsymbol{p})$ and $C_{max}(\sigma_C^*, \boldsymbol{p})$ obtained with both orderings on the problem with fuzzy durations. It illustrates the convergence of the

Table 1. Initial comparison between σ_F^* and σ_C^*

Problem	$C_{max}(\sigma_F^*, \boldsymbol{p})$	$E[C_{max}(\sigma_F^*, \boldsymbol{p})]$	$C_{max}(\sigma_C^*, \boldsymbol{p})$	$E[C_{max}(\sigma_C^*, \boldsymbol{p})]$
FT10	(874, 935, 1003)	936.7	(893, 930, 999)	938.0
FT20	(1090,1165,1241)	1165.2	(1094,1165,1243)	1166.7
La21	(988,1052,1130)	1055.5	(992,1053,1135)	1058.2
La24	(872,939,1012)	940.5	(894,938,1007)	944.2
La25	(919,977,1059)	983	(923,977,1076)	988.2
La27	(1171,1249,1340)	1252.2	(1176,1254,1362)	1261.5
La29	(1107,1183,1262)	1183.7	(1112,1175,1264)	1181.5
La38	(1135,1215,1303)	1217	(1148,1215,1312)	1222.5
La40	(1145,1233,1324)	1233.7	(1160,1228,1328)	1236
ABZ7	(645, 675, 715)	677.5	(646, 680, 732)	684.5
ABZ8	(652,684,728)	687	(656,688,731)	690.7
ABZ9	(672,704,742)	705.5	(669,704,749)	706.5

hybrid algorithm minimising the expected makespan, since the solution found with this method for the fuzzy problem (σ_F^*) does obtain lower expected makespan than a different ordering σ_C^*, even if in some cases the most typical makespan value C_{max}^2 is greater for σ_F^* than for σ_C^*.

Following the proposed methodology, for each fuzzy problem instance and each execution of the algorithm, the obtained task processing order σ_F is tested on the four sets T_1 to T_4 of perturbations, with $N = 1000$. We proceed analogously, for the ordering σ_C for the corresponding crisp problem. Figure 2 presents a boxplot of the makespan values obtained using both σ_F and σ_C on each set of 1000 perturbations for instance ABZ9, averaged across the 30 runs of the hybrid algorithm. It shows that σ_F compares favourably to σ_C. Similar plots are obtained for all large problems.

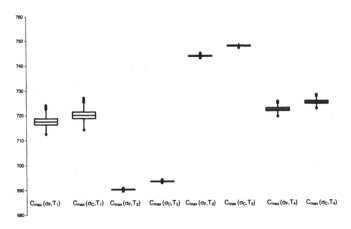

Fig. 2. Boxplot of crisp makespan values obtained with σ_F and σ_C on the four sets of possible perturbations of ABZ9

Table 2. Results for the robustness analysis

		T_1	T_2	T_3	T_4
FT10	σ_F	943.8±5.34	891.7±0.41	960.8±1.37	951.0±2.21
	σ_C	941.6±4.70	901.3±0.39	988.5±0.60	949.5±2.00
FT20	σ_F	1178.9±6.29	1117.3±0.50	1198.8±1.40	1185.4±2.38
	σ_C	1179.4±5.84	1117.9±0.50	1234.3±0.56	1186.6±2.38
La21	σ_F	1064.0±6.22	1003.3±0.51	1114.8±0.57	1073.9±2.30
	σ_C	1064.6±6.15	1008.5±0.43	1118.8±0.66	1075.3±2.31
La24	σ_F	951.4±4.47	901.2±0.45	967.7±1.16	959.0±1.86
	σ_C	955.7±3.99	906.9±0.41	1000.0±0.52	964.0±1.84
La25	σ_F	990.1±5.32	941.2±0.47	1038.7±0.60	999.8±2.23
	σ_C	991.6±6.06	945.9±0.43	1045.8±0.69	1000.6±2.30
La27	σ_F	1269.6±3.37	1193.8±0.58	1337.2±0.67	1280.9±2.36
	σ_C	1274.4±5.48	1203.0±0.48	1345.1±0.72	1286.3±2.26
La29	σ_F	1205.7±5.13	1145.6±0.46	1261.3±0.58	1215.8±2.11
	σ_C	1211.6±5.27	1153.3±0.42	1272.1±0.69	1222.6±2.14
La38	σ_F	1235.1±6.19	1170.6±0.56	1293.4±0.39	1245.8±2.56
	σ_C	1239.2±5.44	1177.4±0.50	1301.3±0.52	1251.6±2.53
La40	σ_F	1246.0±5.68	1173.5±0.53	1306.4±0.59	1256.9±2.19
	σ_C	1247.9±5.09	1179.7±0.52	1313.6±0.71	1260.1±2.26
ABZ7	σ_F	687.6±2.35	655.4±0.23	717.6±0.27	692.2±1.00
	σ_C	690.2±2.06	661.3±0.20	721.3±0.28	695.2±0.98
ABZ8	σ_F	701.4±2.17	671.9±0.23	729.3±0.33	706.4±1.01
	σ_C	704.1±2.12	677.0±0.20	733.6±0.33	709.9±0.97
ABZ9	σ_F	717.6±1.82	690.3±0.22	743.8±0.25	722.3±0.91
	σ_C	720.2±1.93	693.5±0.21	747.9±0.28	725.2±0.92

Table 2 contains a summary of results obtained with both processing orders σ_F and σ_C for each of the twelve problems with the average and standard deviation of makespan values across each set of 1000 perturbations, also averaged across the 30 runs of the hybrid algorithm. Overall, it is clear that the task ordering produced using fuzzy durations, σ_F, performs better than the task ordering σ_C found when only the most typical duration was considered.

By using TFNs, the hybrid algorithm, makes a joint search effort, trying to optimise makespan values across the three solution graphs $G^i(\sigma)$ in parallel. In some problem instances (such as ABZ or La29), the consequence is that the value of $E[C_{max}(\sigma_F)]$ is lower than the crisp makespan $C_{max}(\sigma_C)$ obtained with the defuzzified problem. In other instances (FT20, La21, La38), this is not the case; it could be thought that optimising three components in parallel penalises the global solution when compared to optimising only the most likely duration. In the first case, the improvement in terms of robustness of the solution when TFNs are used instead of crisp defuzzified durations is clear. Most interestingly, in the second case the experimental results in Table 2 show that the effort in maintaining an equilibrium among the three components of the TFNs has translated in greater robustness compared to the solution offered by the defuzzified problem.

5 Conclusions

We have considered a job shop problem with uncertain durations modelled as TFNs and have proposed to analyse the robustness of the solution based on its sensitivity to posterior perturbations in task durations. We have proposed a methodology based on a numerical analysis of the performance of the solution subject to different types of changes in task durations. This methodology has been applied to obtain experimental results on twelve problem instances. The results show that using fuzzy numbers to represent task durations and taking into account this information about uncertainty in the solving process produces proactive solutions, robust to possible changes in task processing times.

Acknowledgements. All authors are supported by MEC-FEDER Grant TIN2007-67466-C02-01.

References

1. Brucker, P., Knust, S.: Complex Scheduling. Springer, Heidelberg (2006)
2. Herroelen, W., Leus, R.: Project scheduling under uncertainty: Survey and research potentials. European Journal of Operational Research 165, 289–306 (2005)
3. Dubois, D., Fargier, H., Fortemps, P.: Fuzzy scheduling: Modelling flexible constraints vs. coping with incomplete knowledge. European Journal of Operational Research 147, 231–252 (2003)
4. Słowiński, R., Hapke, M. (eds.): Scheduling Under Fuzziness. Studies in Fuzziness and Soft Computing, vol. 37. Physica-Verlag (2000)
5. Sakawa, M., Kubota, R.: Fuzzy programming for multiobjective job shop scheduling with fuzzy processing time and fuzzy duedate through genetic algorithms. European Journal of Operational Research 120, 393–407 (2000)
6. Petrovic, S., Fayad, S., Petrovic, D.: Sensitivity analysis of a fuzzy multiobjective scheduling problem. Int. Journal of Production Research 46(12), 3327–3344 (2007)
7. González Rodríguez, I., Puente, J., Vela, C.R., Varela, R.: Semantics of schedules for the fuzzy job shop problem. IEEE Transactions on Systems, Man and Cybernetics, Part A 38(3), 655–666 (2008)
8. Fortemps, P.: Jobshop scheduling with imprecise durations: a fuzzy approach. IEEE Transactions of Fuzzy Systems 7, 557–569 (1997)
9. González Rodríguez, I., Vela, C.R., Puente, J.: A memetic approach to fuzzy job shop based on expectation model. In: Proceedings of IEEE International Conference on Fuzzy Systems, FUZZ-IEEE 2007, London, pp. 692–697 (2007)
10. Liu, B., Liu, Y.K.: Expected value of fuzzy variable and fuzzy expected value models. IEEE Transactions on Fuzzy Systems 10, 445–450 (2002)
11. Jin, Y., Branke, J.: Evolutionay optimization in uncertain environments–a survey. IEEE Transactions on Evolutionary Computation 9, 303–317 (2005)

12. Ishibuchi, H., Murata, T.: A multi-objective genetic local search algorithm and its application to flowshop scheduling. IEEE Transactions on Systems, Man, and Cybernetics–Part C 67(3), 392–403 (1998)
13. Van Laarhoven, P., Aarts, E., Lenstra, K.: Job shop scheduling by simulated annealing. Operations Research 40, 113–125 (1992)
14. Branke, J., Mattfeld, D.: Anticipation and flexibility in dynamic scheduling. International Journal of Production Research 43, 3103–3129 (2005)

A Synergy of Planning and Ontology Concept Ranking for Semantic Web Service Composition

Ourania Hatzi[1], Georgios Meditskos[2], Dimitris Vrakas[2], Nick Bassiliades[2], Dimosthenis Anagnostopoulos[1], and Ioannis Vlahavas[2]

[1] Department of Informatics and Telematics, Harokopio University of Athens, Greece
{raniah,dimosthe}@hua.gr
[2] Department of Informatics, Aristotle University of Thessaloniki, Greece
{gmeditsk,dvrakas,nbassili,vlahavas}@csd.auth.gr

Abstract. This paper presents a prototype system that exploits planning and an ontology concept ranking algorithm for composing semantic Web services (PORSCE). The system exploits the inferencing capabilities of a Description Logics Reasoner in order to compute the subsumption hierarchy of the ontologies whose concepts are used in the OWL-S Profile descriptions as input and output concepts. The concept ranking algorithm is applied over this hierarchy in order to determine similar concepts based on different degrees of semantic matching relaxation, such as subclass or sibling hierarchical relationships. The domain independent planning system's role is to semantically search the space of possible compositions of Web services, generating plans according to the desirable level of relaxation.

Keywords: Semantic Web Service Composition, Planning, Ontology Concept Ranking, Semantic Matching Relaxation.

1 Introduction

The advent of web services (WS) is a proof that nowadays the need for communication among loosely coupled distributed systems is bigger than ever. Web services offer a well-defined interface through which the major problem of interoperability on the Web can be dealt with. In order to exploit the web service technology to its full extent, Semantic Web languages, such as OWL-S [11], WSDL-S [12] SAWSDL [14], and tools, such as ontology reasoners [7], are used for the semantic annotation and processing of WS, leading to a new notion of web services, referred to as Semantic Web Services (SWS). The SWS paradigm is motivated by the fact that while the XML representation of services' characteristics (WSDL [15]) guarantees syntactic interoperability, it is unable to capture the semantics of information, which is essential for the automation of WS-related procedures.

The procedure of combining simple WS in order to create a complex service of enhanced functionality is fundamental. Composition can be either manual, where the user participates by selecting appropriate Web services from a set of available ones,

H. Geffner et al. (Eds.): IBERAMIA 2008, LNAI 5290, pp. 42–51, 2008.

or automated, where the composition plan is generated automatically, based on initial requirements about functional and non-functional properties.

In this paper the automated web service composition paradigm is approached as a planning problem over the OWL-S profile descriptions of web services. More specifically, PORSCE is proposed; a combination of a domain-independent planning system and a concept ranking module for computing similarities among OWL ontology concepts. The planning module searches for composition plans by matching OWL-S Profile input and output (I/O) parameters, while the concept ranking module semantically alters the I/O requirements of the Web services, selecting semantically related ontology concepts based on different notions of concept similarity.

The rest of the paper is organized as follows: Section 2 outlines the system architecture and points out the way the various modules cooperate. Sections 3 and 4 elaborate on the core of the system, namely the OWL Ontology Manager and the Planning System respectively. Section 5 presents some experimental results, while Section 6 concludes the paper and poses future directions.

2 System Architecture

PORSCE is a synergy of an OWL-S parser utilizing the OWL API [16], the OWL Ontology Manager, the PDDL Converter and an external planning system. The OWL-S Parser parses OWL-S profiles that correspond to a set of SWS. The output of the OWL-S Parser is a description of the WS which is provided to the PDDL converter and the domain ontologies which are forwarded to the OWL Ontology Manager (OOM). The OOM, utilizing the DL reasoner, applies the algorithm of Section 3.2 for determining similar concepts to a query concept q. The PDDL converter is responsible for expressing the problem of SW composition as a planning problem, interacting with the user in order to set the required threshold of conceptual similarities, enhancing the planning problem with semantic information retrieved from OOM and cooperating with the external planning system in order to acquire a solution to the problem. More details on both the OOM and the Planning System are provided in Sections 3 and 4 respectively.

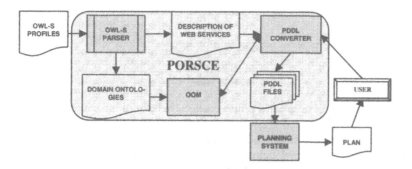

Fig. 1. The architecture of PORSCE

3 OWL Ontology Manager

The OWL Ontology Manager (OOM) is responsible for retrieving "similar" ontology concepts to a specific query concept, according to a degree of relaxation that is defined based on the hierarchical relationship H and the distance D between the concepts. OOM utilizes the inferencing capabilities of the Pellet DL Reasoner [7] in order to compute the subsumption relationships among the concepts. The general idea is to relax the concept matching criterion in order to obtain plans that might be useful, especially in cases where an exact input/output matching plan is not available.

3.1 Hierarchical Relationships

OOM utilizes three logic-based types of concept match [13] between a query q and an ontology concept C, and extends them by also introducing the *sibling* match:

- **exact.** The two concepts are inferred to be equivalent or have the same URI.
- **plugin.** This type of match holds when q is superclass of C.
- **subsume.** This type of match holds when the q is subclass of C.
- **sibling.** The two concepts have a common superclass T.
- **fail.** Nothing of the above holds, for example in the case of disjoint concepts.

These matching types represent the hierarchical relationships that two concepts could have in a hierarchy.

3.2 Concept Distance

Apart from the hierarchical relationships, the degree of relaxation is defined based on the distance D of two concepts, following the logical assumption that the more concepts exist between two concepts, the less "similar" they are. In simple subclass relationships, the distance between two concepts is defined as the sum of the concepts that exist between them, also including in the sum the two concepts themselves. For example, the distance between two concepts with a direct subclass relationship is 2. In the case of a sibling relationship between two concepts q and C with a common superclass T, the distance is defined as $D = d_{q,T} + d_{T,C} - 1$. For example, the distance of two concepts B and C with a direct common superclass A is 3, as Fig 2 depicts.

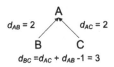

Fig. 2. An example of a sibling relationship between two concepts

The algorithm for determining all the concepts of an ontology that are similar to a query concept q is presented below. The listSubclasses(C) and listSuperclasses(C) notations are used to denote the set of subclasses and superclasses of an ontology concept C, and dist(C, C′) to denote the distance between the concepts C and C′. In case of exact matches, the algorithm returns only the equivalent to q concepts, while in the case of plugin matches, the algorithm finds the subclasses of the concept q and returns as a result each concept in the subclass list that satisfies the distance threshold. A similar approach is followed in the case of subsume matches where the superclasses of q are retrieved. Finally, in the case of sibling matches, the superclasses of q are retrieved, and for each of them, its subclasses are retrieved. The goal is to determine concepts in the subclass lists which satisfy the distance threshold.

Algorithm: Finds the similar concepts to the query concept q according to the hierarchical relationship H and the distance threshold D.
Input: Query concept q, Hierarchical relationship H, Distance threshold D.
Output: A list with the similar concepts to q.

```
function similarConcepts(q, H, D) {
    var result = ∅
1     if H = exact then
2         for each concept C | C ≡ q do
3             result ← add(C)
4     else if H = plugin then
5         subclasses ← listSubclasses(q)
6         for each C ∈ subclasses | dist(q, C) ≤ D do
7             result ← add(C)
8     else if H = subsume then
9         superclasses ← listSuperclasses(q)
10        for each C ∈ superclasses | dist(q, C) ≤ D do
11            result ← add(C)
12    else if H = sibling then
13        superclasses ← listSuperclasses (q)
14        for each T ∈ superclasses do
15            subclasses ← listSubclasses (T) - listSubclasses(q)
16            for each C' ∈ subclasses do
17                if dist(q, T) + dist(T, C') -1 ≤ D then
18                    result ← add(C')
19    return result  }
```

4 Problem Representation and Solving

The problem of composing simple web services in order to come up with a complex one that fulfills the user's needs can be easily transformed into a planning problem and solved using a domain independent planning system. A planning problem is usually modelled according to STRIPS (Stanford Research Institute Planning System) notation [9]. A planning problem in STRIPS is a tuple <I,A,G> where I is the Initial state, A is a set of available actions and G is a set of goals. States in STRIPS are represented as sets of atomic facts.

Set A contains all the actions that can be used to modify states. Each action A_i has three lists of facts containing the preconditions of A_i (noted as prec(A_i)), the facts that are added to the state (noted as add(A_i)) and the facts that are deleted from the state (noted as del(A_i)).

The following formulae hold for the states in the STRIPS notation:

- An action A_i is applicable to a state S if $prec(A_i) \subseteq S$.
- If A_i is applied to S, the successor state S' is calculated as S' = S \ $del(A_i) \cup add(A_i)$
- The solution to a planning problem is a sequence of actions, which, if applied to I, lead to a state S' such that $S' \supseteq G$.

The representation of a WS composition problem in planning terms requires simple WS to be viewed as actions, and complex WS to be viewed as plans. More details of the representation in the proposed system will be discussed in the following sections.

4.1 Problem Representation

Consider the case were a user wishes to use a complex web service which, when provided with some input data, will return some required information. There may be a number of alternatives when formalizing the problem of web service composition as a planning problem. A straightforward solution adopted by PORSCE is the following: The inputs provided by the user form the initial state of the problem, while the desired outputs form the goals of the problem. The available OWL-S profiles are used to obtain the actions available in the planning domain. For each action the following statements hold: a) its name is the same as the name of the corresponding web service, b) its preconditions list is formed by the inputs of the service, c) the add effects of the actions are the outputs of the service and d) the delete list is left empty.

The formalization presented above requires the planning system to be aware of possible semantic similarities among syntactically different concepts. This situation can be dealt with in two ways. The first solution is to alter the planning system in order to constantly advise the OWL Ontology Manager (OOM), whenever it is required, such as to determine the applicability of an action in a given state. The second solution is to enhance the problem description given above with all the required semantic information in a pre-processing phase.

In order to maintain the independency of the planner from the rest of the PORSCE system, the second solution was adopted. Therefore, the planning module can be replaced by any planning system compliant with PDDL [10] input files. In the pre-processing phase, the system uses the OOM in order to return all the semantically similar concepts for both the facts of the initial state and the preconditions of the available actions. The original concepts of the initial state together with the semantic equivalent and similar concepts form a new set of facts noted as the Expanded Initial State (EIS) (note that the term *state* is used improperly). Moreover, for each action the pre-processor creates all the possible combinations of the original preconditions and their semantically equivalents in order to form the Extended Action Set (EAS). Suppose, for example, that the initial state I of the problem is the following

$$I = \{Sightseeing, Dates\}$$

There are two available actions:

```
CityHotelMapService: prec={City, LuxuryHotel}
SightSeeingAreaService: prec={Sightseeing}
```
The OOM for a given threshold discovers the following similarities:

```
Dates≡Duration, Hotel≡Motel, Hotel≡LuxuryHotel
```

The pre-processor alters the problem definition to the following:

```
EIS = {Sightseeing, Dates, Duration}
EAS:    CityHotelMapService: prec={City, LuxuryHotel}
        CityHotelMapService1: prec={City, Hotel}
        CityHotelMapService2: prec={City, Motel}
        SightSeeingAreaService: prec={Sightseeing}
```

The new problem, namely <EIS,EAS,G> is then encoded into PDDL and is forwarded to the planning system in order to acquire a solution.

4.2 The Planning System

The planner module incorporated in the system is JPlan [1], an open-source implementation of Graphplan in Java. Graphplan [2] is a general-purpose planner for STRIPS-like domains, which exploits the benefits of graph algorithms in order to reduce search space and provide better solutions.

JPlan proved to be remarkably fast and can handle a respectable number of operators, unlike other implementations of Graphplan. Currently, it has been tested for more than 2000 operators in a single planning domain. This is very important as the number of operators increases significantly when equivalent or similar concepts are taken into account. After the planning process is completed, JPlan provides not only the plan, if found, but also the mutual exclusion description of the leveled graph.

JPlan supports predicates with an arbitrary number of arguments, but not predicates without arguments, a disadvantage which had to be overcome in order to be adopted for the web service case by adding a "dummy" argument, as web service inputs and outputs are usually represented as predicates without arguments. Another technical issue that had to be dealt with is the fact that JPlan does not support PDDL, but text files with a similar structure. Finally, JPlan does not seem to offer a way to supply alternative plans, if there are any, as it expands the graph to a predefined level and does only one search through it. Despite its disadvantages, JPlan proved to be efficient and serve the purposes of testing the system.

5 Experimental Results

In this section, the experiments performed and a specific example will be presented in order to illuminate the aspects of this approach. The test sets used to perform experiments were obtained from the OWLS-TC version 2.2 revision 1 [8] and included SWS descriptions in OWL-S from various domains such as travel, food and economy, and the corresponding ontologies. Initially, attempts were made to obtain all possible plans that could be produced from each domain, using only one concept of the domain as input and another concept as output, in order to familiarize with the domains and detect the flow of information among the various services. The results included only plans of length 1, namely the simple web services that had these exact concepts as input and output, and some plans of length 2. Unfortunately, the nature of these domains did not permit the creation of longer plans, and therefore more complex web services. Using more relaxed restrictions on the similarity of concepts did not alter the results. Using more than one concept in the inputs and outputs sets increased the length of the produced plans, however, this case was not examined further because the produced plans represented more likely collections of independent web services, rather than in fact complex web services.

In order to test the abilities of the system in managing simple web services that can be composed into longer plans, therefore more complex web services, some of the service descriptions were modified. The scenario that was chosen to implement referred to the travel domain, and included a user who wants to go sightseeing at some specific dates. The user requires to know the price of the hotel, place a reservation and be presented with a map of the area. As there is no simple web service that has such functionality, but there are web services that provide this functionality partially, the problem must be solved through composition.

In order to demonstrate the dependence of the solution on the distance between concepts in the ontology we permit, we added to the domain the following service descriptions:

1. SightseeingAreaService: A service that accepts as input the activity Sightseeing and returns areas of a city that offer this activity.
2. DatesToDurationService: A service that accepts as input dates and supplies the duration of the time period specified by these dates.
3. AreaCityService: A service that accepts as input areas of a city and returns the city they belong to.
4. CityLuxuryHotelService: A service that accepts as input a city name and returns luxury hotels in this city. Luxury hotel is a subclass of Hotel.
5. CityHotelMapService: A service that accepts as inputs a city and a hotel name, and presents a map of the area of the city the hotel resides.
6. HotelPriceInfoService: A service that accepts as input a hotel name and provides information about its prices.
7. HotelReserveService: A service that accepts as inputs a city and a hotel name, as well as a duration, and places a reservation at this hotel for the specified dates.

For the sake of the example, we assume that there are no other web services in the domain that interfere with these in any way. However, the descriptions of the rest domain services are still parsed and turned into operators, in order to maintain the size of the domain in realistic levels, and therefore obtain plausible time measurements.

When no equivalent concepts are allowed in the planning process, is it obvious that these web services will not be composed to form a complex web service with the desired results, because the CityLuxuryHotelService yields an object of the class LuxuryHotel, while all other services accept objects of the class Hotel. While LuxuryHotel is a subclass of Hotel, a planner without the help of a reasoner perceives them as two totally separate concepts.

This restriction can be relaxed by taking into account concepts with distance 1 from the concept at hand. In that case, planning can match concepts with other concepts which are direct subclasses and superclasses in some specified ontology. Thus, the result set is expanded and a plan involving all 7 web services presented above is produced. (Fig. 3).

If the restrictions are relaxed even more, by increasing the distance to 2 or more, concepts can be matched with other concepts that are even further, in ontology terms. This could potentially provide more plans, and in several cases shorter plans,

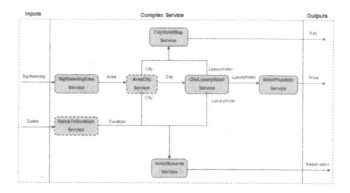

Fig. 3. A Plan of 7 steps for the Travel domain

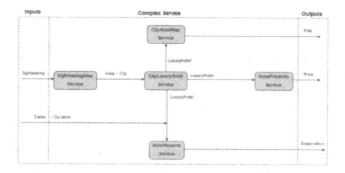

Fig. 4. A Plan of 5 steps for the Travel domain

as Fig. 4 depicts. However, the more relaxed the restrictions are, the less accurate the results become, and the complex WS provided might not fulfill the prospects of the user.

Experiments were run on a machine with an Inter Core2 CPU at 1.66GHz, with 2 GB or RAM memory. In all cases, the preprocessing step took approximately 14 seconds to parse and process 23 ontologies. However, this is a step that has to be performed only once, as long as the ontologies remain unchanged. In the first case, when the acceptable distance between concepts that can be considered equivalent is 1, the step where service descriptions are parsed and operators are generated for each service lasted approximately 47 seconds. This time includes the invocation of the object ranker module to provide equivalent and similar concepts, and the generation of additional operators for each combination of these concepts. In the travel domain, 150 web service descriptions were parsed, while the number of operators that were produced eventually was 690. In the case of distance 2, which is still considered a close relation, this time increased to approximately 97 seconds, while the number of operators was 2010. Finally, planning time was insignificant compared to parsing time, as in both cases the planner produced the desired result in less than a second.

6   Related Work

Other efforts that attempt to exploit the benefits of planning techniques to tackle the problem of automatic web service composition will be presented in this section.

One of the first systems that attempted automatic web service composition was SHOP-2 [3]. The system uses services descriptions in DAML-S, the predecessor of OWL-S, and performs HTN planning to solve the problem. The disadvantage of this approach lies in the fact that the planning process, due to its hierarchical nature, requires given decomposition rules, or *methods*, as they are referred to, which have to be encoded in advance with the help of a DAML-S process ontology.

OWLS-Xplan [4] uses semantic descriptions of web services in OWL-S to derive planning domains and problems, and then invokes a planning module called Xplan to generate the complex services. The system is PDDL compliant, as the authors have developed an XML dialect of PDDL called PDDXML. However, semantic information provided from domain ontologies is not utilized, therefore the planning module requires exact matching for service inputs and outputs.

Other approaches that use knowledge-based planning include the system described in [5] which composes web services with the PKS planning system. However, this effort does not deal with the important issue of translating semantic web service descriptions into planning terms. The work in [6] also uses knowledge-level planning to approach the automated web service composition problem. The web service descriptions in this case have to be expressed in some standard process modeling and execution language, such as BPEL4WS, therefore some prior, domain-specific knowledge of the composition issues is required.

The advantages of the proposed framework lie in the fact that the OWL-S descriptions of the web services and the corresponding ontologies are adequate information for the system to determine how to form valid complex services that satisfy given goals. Even in the case that no exact match can be found, the system is still able to find a complex service that approximates best the desired goal. No prior or additional knowledge is demanded since the ontologies capture the semantics of the concepts used, while the trade-off between the quantity and quality of the results, i.e. between the number of complex services produced and their accuracy in achieving the given goals, is up to the user to decide, by selecting desirable concept distances.

7   Conclusions and Future Work

The work presented in this paper concerns the development of a prototype system that combines planning with object ranking in order to approach the semantic web service composition problem. Each web service composition problem is mapped into a planning problem by representing simple web services as operators, inputs as the initial state of the planning problem and outputs as the goal state. Such representations are derived from the OWL-S descriptions of the web services. However, before the planning problem is fed into to planning module in order to obtain a plan, which will represent the description of the desired complex web service, the object ranker module is utilized. The object ranker exploits knowledge contributed by domain ontologies, and returns semantically equivalent or similar concepts, which are in turn used to form an extended initial state and set of actions. As a result, the requirement for exact matching of the service inputs and outputs is eliminated, and the planning procedure can be performed with the desired degree of semantic relaxation. The system was implemented and tested with different web service domains, and experimental results were presented.

Future goals include the extension of the system in order to cooperate with different planners which are capable of providing alternative plans. Moreover, the possibility of experimenting with different metrics for semantic similarity, other than distance, should be explored, and their effect on the planning procedure and the produced plans should be examined.

References

1. JPlan: Java Graphplan Implementation,
   http://sourceforge.net/projects/jplan
2. Blum, A.L., Furst, M.L.: Fast Planning Through Planning Graph Analysis. Artificial Intelligence 90, 281–300 (1997)
3. Sirin, E., Parsia, B., Wu, D., Hendler, J., Nau, D.: HTN planning for web service composition using SHOP2. Journal of Web Semantics 1(4), 377–396 (2004)
4. Klusch, M., Gerber, A., Schmidt, M.: Semantic Web Service Composition Planning with OWLS-XPlan. In: AAAI Fall Symposium on Semantic Web and Agents, USA (2005)
5. Martinez, E., Lesperance, Y.: Web service composition as a planning task: Experiments using knowledge-based planning. In: Proceedings of the ICAPS 2004 Workshop on Planning and Scheduling for Web and Grid Services, pp. 62–69 (2004)
6. Pistore, M., Marconi, A., Bertoli, P., Traverso, P.: Automated Composition of Web Services by Planning at the Knowledge Level. In: Proceedings of the 19th International Joint Conference on Artificial Intelligence (IJCAI 2005), Edinburgh, UK (August 2005)
7. Sirin, E., Parsia, B., Grau, B., Kalyanpur, A., Katz, Y.: Pellet: A Practical OWL DL Reasoner. J. Web Semantics (2007)
8. OWLS-TC version 2.2 revision 1,
   http://projects.semwebcentral.org/projects/owls-tc/
9. Fikes, R., Nilsson, N.J.: STRIPS: A new approach to the application of theorem proving to problem solving. Artificial Intelligence 2, 189–208 (1971)
10. Ghallab, M., Howe, A., Knoblock, C., McDermott, D., Ram, A., Veloso, M., Weld, D., Wilkins, D.: PDDL – the Planning Domain Definition Language. Technical report, Yale University, New Haven, CT (1998)
11. OWL-S 1.1 Release, http://www.daml.org/services/owl-s/1.1/
12. WSDL-S, http://www.w3.org/Submission/WSDL-S/
13. Paolucci, M., Kawmura, T., Payne, T., Sycara, K.: Semantic Matching of Web Services Capabilities. In: First International Semantic Web Conference (2002)
14. Semantic Annotations for WSDL, http://www.w3.org/2002/ws/sawsdl/
15. Booth, D., et al.: Web Services Architecture. W3C Working Draft (August 2003),
    http://www.w3.org/TR/ws-arch/
16. The OWL API, http://owlapi.sourceforge.net/

Towards the Use of XPDL as Planning and Scheduling Modeling Tool: The Workflow Patterns Approach

Arturo González-Ferrer, Juan Fdez-Olivares, Luis Castillo, and Lluvia Morales

Departamento de Ciencias de la Computación e IA
University of Granada, Spain

Abstract. This paper presents a transformation from a business process model diagram stored in XPDL format, into a hierarchical extension of the PDDL planning language, using the concept of workflow patterns as base of the translation process. The proposed architecture is evaluated within a specific teamwork project management scenario: the allocation of human resources and web services for the cooperative development of on-line courses in an e-learning center.

1 Introduction

The integration of Planning and Scheduling (P&S) and Business Process Management (BPM) is a significant challenge for enterprise environments. On the one hand, BPM tools are able to deal with goals specification, environmental analysis, design, implementation, enactment, monitoring and evaluation of business processes[7], and they are acquiring an increasing business value for the efficient and intelligent knowledge management on these organisations. However, they lack of power for the anticipated planning and decision making of organisational processes. On the other hand, automated P&S, defined as "the process of generating possible representations of future behaviour *prior to the use of such plans* to constrain or control that behaviour"[16], is a technology that, due to the absence of simple modeling tools, has not explode its great potential in enterprise environments. Therefore, a common framework including these technologies would be interesting from both points of view.

Introducing an automated P&S system into the BPM life cycle[7] of a company, capable of both interpreting and reasoning about an initial workflow model representation, would contribute to cover these missing goals, as it provides support for the generation of action plans, whatever these actions are carried out by humans or by remote calls to web services[5], as well as support for decision-making on key issues like tasks organization and resources allocation. Furthermore, if we were able to automatically transform the information present in a process model (usually described by a BPM diagram created by business analysts) to its corresponding P&S representation, we would overcome the traditional obstacle for P&S technology: the use of complex languages to model a planning domain. This paper gives further insights into this integration process.

H. Geffner et al. (Eds.): IBERAMIA 2008, LNAI 5290, pp. 52–61, 2008.

Prior work on the use of P&S for the automatic generation of business process models is exposed in [10] (using an augmentation of STRIPS representation). As opposite to this work, our approach shows how to use an existing process model diagram stored in a standard BPM language, to automatically generate P&S representations using the HTN[12] planning paradigm (detailed later in this paper). Afterwards, we use the output of this transformation as input of an intelligent planner in order to prepare action plans and resources allocation that, after the corresponding validation by a business manager, would be helpful for decision making on risk management[7], mainly to avoid unwanted situations, like the detection of high loads of work in a specific period, or the incapacity to complete a project before a deadline, which is specially useful in ad-hoc workflows with human intervention. Some authors worked in similar problems as coordinating the design of airplanes[1], or workflow coordination in a mobile environment[11].

So, the main contributions of this paper can be summarized as:

1. To stablish the cornerstone for a new way to model P&S problems using a standard business process modeling tool, overcoming the need of new ad-hoc tools or languages[15] as well as the need for staff training on P&S languages.
2. To introduce the concept of workflow patterns decomposition for the automatic transformation of BPM diagrams into HTN planning representations.
3. To show how to integrate P&S technology at a low cost within a BPM framework, to make the most of an existing process model for anticipated management planning and resources allocation.

The paper is structured as follows. Section 2 describe the real case the paper is focused on. Section 3 provides an overview of the technologies used. Section 4 details the architecture overview and the mapping algorithm. Section 5 expose some results and Section 6 contains a conclusion of the contribution made and future work.

2   E-Learning Management Scenario

In order to expose the contributions mentioned before, the paper is centered around the process of creating an online course within a Learning Management System. This process implies the participation and the correct interaction of different roles (instructional designers, graphic designers, HTML developers, sysadmins, tutors, students, etc). The corresponding process model will be customised accordingly to the operation of an specific e-learning center. In this case we have been supported by the teamwork experience of CEVUG[1]. The resulting process model diagram can be observed at Figure 1.

Note that some of the tasks needed to complete the process can only be done by a specific worker/role, and they can have some previous dependencies. For example, the task "content authoring" (A2) could only be completed by a content author and the task of "training authors on instructional design" (A1) had to be

---

[1] University of Granada E-learning Center, http://cevug.ugr.es

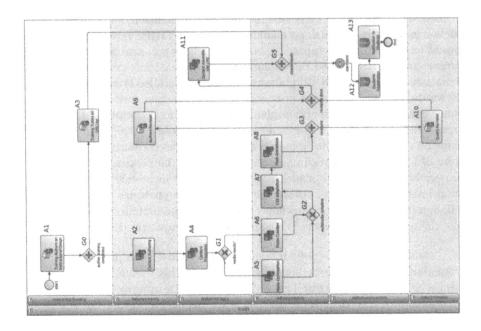

Fig. 1. BPM representation for "e-learning course creation" process (rotated)

previously completed by the training department. So, the election of a specific worker for a specific task will be conditioned by his *ability* to complete it, and possibly by his temporal *availability* (or any implicit condition of the problem, i.e. the worker cannot work in more that n courses simultaneously).

Note that almost all the activities described can be considered as subflows themselves (i.e. they might be decomposed in sub-activities and so on recursively), so the subprocess diagram should be also specified for every of them. This decomposition-based representation of tasks make the HTN planning paradigm very appropriate in order to capture the model information on a BPM diagram, as better explained in Section 4. Thus, the proposed scenario considers different workers that have to cooperate together to achieve a final goal.

For each **activity** we could identify

- Duration: Estimated duration for the activity to be completed.
- Web Service: web service associated to the automated execution of the activity (in case it is needed).
- Dependencies and requirements: activities to be completed before the possible execution of the activity, as well as other requirements stablished (i.e. a specific worker ability).

For each **worker** we could identify

- Abilities: a list of abilities to achieve the requirements mentioned before.
- Lane: The department or lane the worker belongs to.

- Number of courses: number of courses the worker is working on.
- Availability dates: dates in which the worker is available to be assigned a task.

This information will help us to establish the preconditions for the execution of actions, and to represent temporal knowledge associated to the problem (that might also be automatically generated[2], though not addressed in this paper). The BPM language chosen in order to capture all the mentioned information is XPDL[3], which is detailed in the next section.

3 Technical Background

In this section XPDL and the concept of workflow patterns are defined. We also introduce the HTN planning paradigm, as well as some equivalences with BPM.

3.1 XPDL and Workflow Patterns

The goal of XPDL[3] language is to store and exchange the process diagram. An XPDL file offers a one-to-one representation of the original Business Process Management Notation (BPMN)[8] process diagram. The main advantage of using XPDL as modeling language is that it is a common language used among business analysts, and it can be used to represent the organisation activity easily, storing it in an XML standard format. There are a lot of modeling tools that already incorporate XPDL natively or as an additional plug-in. Some of the tools evaluated store process models either using a proprietary format or directly BPEL[8], but ideally this should be done in XPDL, as it was thought for modeling, not for execution[9]. We have used "TIBCO Business Studio"[2], since it supports XPDL v2.0 and it is offered for free.

XPDL offers some standard **tags** to represent business processes. The definition of a **WorkflowProcess** consists of one or more **Activities** (also called Implementation Activities), each comprising a logical, self-contained unit of work, which will be carried out by **Participants** and/or computer **Applications**. Activities are related to one another via **Transitions**. Transitions may be conditional (involving expressions which are evaluated to permit or inhibit the transition) or unconditional, and may result in the sequential or parallel operation of individual activities within the process. In graphical terms, a transition is a connection between two nodes. Special activities, referred to as **Route Activities**, are used to implement decisions that affect the sequence flow path through the process. An activity may also be a subflow (**ActivitySet**), being itself a container for the execution of a (separately specified) process. **Lanes** are used to organise and categorise activities, often used for specifying roles, departments, etc. XPDL assumes a number of standard **DataTypes** (string, integer, float, date, etc) that are relevant to **DataFields**, environmental or participant data, and that may be used to define expressions, to support conditional evaluations and

---

[2] Available at http://www.tibco.com

assignment of new values to DataFields or **Parameters**. In case these tags are not expressive enough to represent all the information wanted, XPDL provides the **extendedAttribute** element, that can be appropriate in most cases. For further details about XPDL, refer to its specification[3].

On the other hand, Workflow Patterns[14] are those generic structures that represent frequently-used relationships between tasks in a process, and that are typically nested to form the whole process model[4]. As clearly exposed in the next subsection, a workflow pattern decomposition of any XPDL process can be easily converted into an HTN domain definition. However, XPDL lacks of some power for the correct representation of some complex patterns[13]. Therefore, only the most basic ones has been studied in this paper, those that can be well represented and are expressive enough for the definition of most processes.

3.2   HTN Planning

The Hierarchical Task Network (HTN) planning paradigm was developed in order to express planning problems in a structured way, by means of the definition of compound tasks that are reduced into a network of lowest level activities, or primitive non-decomposable actions whose execution represents a state change. HTN planners use as input two different files:(a) the **problem**, which encodes the *initial state* (literals that are true at the beginning of the problem) and the *task-goal* (a partially ordered set of tasks that need to be carried out), and (b) the **domain**, which encodes reduction schemes for compound *tasks* as (possibly alternative) decomposition methods through the definition of (compound and primitive) tasks and the order in which they should be decomposed, as well as a set of *predicates* and *constants* definitions.

HTN-PDDL Notation. The HTN planning domain language used in this work is a hierarchical extension of PDDL[2], and it use the following notation:

- (:types), (:constants), (:predicates) and (:functions).
- (:task) to express compound tasks. Its definition can include *:parameters*, and different *(:methods* with associated *:preconditions* and *:tasks* that represents its corresponding lowest level task decomposition.
- (:durative-action) to express primitive actions, composed of *:parameters*, *:duration*, *:condition* and *:effects* caused by the execution of this action.
- (:objects) to define objects that are present in the problem.
- (:init) to define the set of literals that are initially true.
- (:task-goals) to define the set of high level tasks to achieve.

Therefore, the HTN paradigm is able to represent the hierarchical structure of the domain and it is also expressive enough to capture the expert knowledge in order to drive the planner to a desirable solution. We have used the HTNP[3] planner for this paper, as it is already known how to translate workflow patterns for semantic web services composition[5], as well as its adaptation to temporal knowledge[2]. Therefore, plans obtained using the task representation described above could be interpreted as workflow instances.

---

[3] Formerly named SIADEX, refer to [2] for details.

4   Architecture Overview

A sketch of the proposed architecture can be observed in Figure 2. Firstly, we have to draw the model for a specific process of the company in close cooperation with its managers, specifying all the needed information (in our case mentioned on Section 2) and storing it in XPDL. Afterwards, the basic workflow patterns present in that model are analysed, finding a decomposition tree for them (Fig. 3) that will be automatically mapped into an HTN-PDDL task network, taking into account the transformations mentioned in next subsection.

The generated code is used as input of the HTNP planner triggering a reasoning and search process that, guided by the knowledge included in the domain, finally returns a workers allocation and an action plan, to carry out the tasks defined as goal. Finally, the resulting plans could also be converted again into BPEL, a language which is readable by most BPM engines, developed for the execution of processes and web services composition, and that has been subject of prior research related to our work[8]. This would help to complete the cycle, seamlessly introducing P&S technology within the BPM life cycle.

The underlying idea of the proposed architecture is that outcomes could be easily applied to different domains, developing a solution that maintains consistency and completeness for a wide subset of the possible inputs, as well as readability of the generated code. That is one of the reasons for the prior workflow patterns recognition phase[4], as well as the existing equivalences between both the decomposition tree and the HTN paradigm, detailed in next subsection.

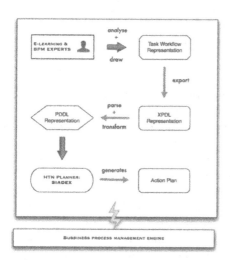

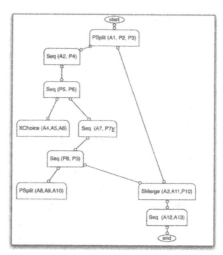

Fig. 2. Architecture for business anticipated management planning

Fig. 3. Workflow Patterns decomposition for the business process shown at Fig. 1

4.1   XPDL to HTN-PDDL Mapping

What drives us to propose the use of XPDL to model P&S problems following the HTN paradigm, is the existing equivalence between both. The basis for this statement is the fact that most business processes modeled under XPDL can be decomposed as a set of related workflow patterns (defined in Section 3.1). This set is what we call a *workflow patterns decomposition tree*. For example, the process diagram of Figure 1 can be expressed as the decomposition tree shown in Figure 3. As we can observe, the root node is a "Parallel Split" in which, after the execution of activity A1, the blocks P2 and P3 are executed in parallel. At the same time, block P2 is defined as `Sequence(A2, P4)` (left child node) and block P3 is defined as `SimpleMerge(A3,A11,P10)` (right child node) . Subsequently, every of the existing blocks, P$_x$, are recursively defined as a new decomposition, until we complete the whole diagram. This finally forms the decomposition tree shown at Figure 3. The mapping of this structure into an HTN-PDDL domain is intuitive, as detailed next.

Workflow activities as durative-actions. The execution of an activity in a workflow corresponds to the execution of a primitive action in an HTN-PDDL domain. XPDL Activity names should also be mapped as HTN-PDDL constants, used as parameters of a predicate (`completed ?a -activity`), that indicates the completion of this activity upon its execution (defined as an :effect), and that can also be used in preconditions statements needed for the execution of other tasks. XPDL Participants and Lanes will be mapped as objects, making possible the allocation of participants to activities through the inclusion of a parameter (`?p - participant`) in the durative-action definition. Furthermore, the membership of a Participant P$_x$ to a Lane L$_y$ will be mapped as an init condition of the problem, using the previously defined predicate (`belongstolane P$_x$ L$_y$`). This predicate can also be used as precondition (i.e. the activity A3 can only be done by participants that belongs to the training department). The duration of an activity is modeled using the XPDL *extendedAttribute* tag.

Workflow patterns and subprocesses as composed tasks. A workflow pattern present in the XPDL representation will be mapped as an HTN-PDDL task (Table 1 shows the translation for the patterns considered). Furthermore, Activity-Sets (subprocesses embedded into an XPDL description) will also be mapped as compound tasks. The main advantage of using the HTN-PDDL knowledge representation is that decomposition methods provide a great expressivity to describe order constraints between subtasks. To do so, HTN-PDDL use the symbols () to express *sequencing* (see Table 1(a)), and the symbols [] to express *parallelism* (see Table 1(b)). Therefore, control structs found in a workflow pattern decomposition tree that define the execution order and control flow between processes can be almost directly translated into HTN decomposition methods."

We will also map XPDL DataTypes as custom HTN-PDDL types, and XPDL Parameters and DataFields can be used in preconditions statements for the definition of conditional workflow patterns (see Table 1(c)), to define the control

Table 1. Definition for the basic workflow patterns on the left side. A corresponding HTN-PDDL representation on the right side, using data from some of the patterns found on Figure 1. Note in (c) that a workflow pattern as XChoiceG1 is decomposed using two methods, executing a primitive task and afterwards the next worfklow pattern found (SeqA7A8), which will be also decomposed using a similar transformation to that found in (a). This transformation process continue until all the diagram is represented.

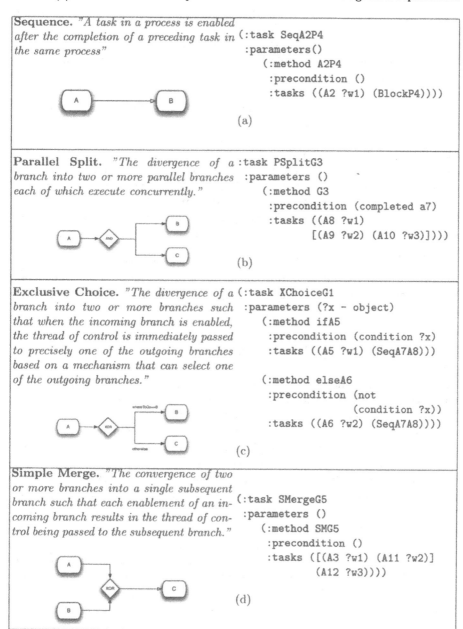

Sequence. *"A task in a process is enabled after the completion of a preceding task in the same process"*

```
(:task SeqA2P4
    :parameters()
        (:method A2P4
            :precondition ()
            :tasks ((A2 ?w1) (BlockP4))))
```

(a)

Parallel Split. *"The divergence of a branch into two or more parallel branches each of which execute concurrently."*

```
:task PSplitG3
    :parameters ()
        (:method G3
            :precondition (completed a7)
            :tasks ((A8 ?w1)
                    [(A9 ?w2) (A10 ?w3)])))
```

(b)

Exclusive Choice. *"The divergence of a branch into two or more branches such that when the incoming branch is enabled, the thread of control is immediately passed to precisely one of the outgoing branches based on a mechanism that can select one of the outgoing branches."*

```
(:task XChoiceG1
    :parameters (?x - object)
        (:method ifA5
            :precondition (condition ?x)
            :tasks ((A5 ?w1) (SeqA7A8)))

        (:method elseA6
            :precondition (not
                            (condition ?x))
            :tasks ((A6 ?w2) (SeqA7A8))))
```

(c)

Simple Merge. *"The convergence of two or more branches into a single subsequent branch such that each enablement of an incoming branch results in the thread of control being passed to the subsequent branch."*

```
(:task SMergeG5
    :parameters ()
        (:method SMG5
            :precondition ()
            :tasks ([(A3 ?w1) (A11 ?w2)]
                    (A12 ?w3))))
```

(d)

flow between two activities. Finally, the task goal for the planning problem correspond to the root node of the workflow patterns decomposition tree.

5   Results

We have used the process model shown at Figure 1 for the experimentation results. We achieved to transform this model into HTN-PDDL domain and problem files, using the workflow patterns decomposition shown at Figure 3, the transformations proposed at Table 1, and estimated durations for the activities.

The following action plan (that could also be generated as a gantt diagram) was returned by the planner, being (A_x P_y) the corresponding allocation of activity A_x to participant P_y, and "Day1 Month1-Day2 Month2" the timeframe where that activity should be executed:

```
(A1 Emilio) 1st Jun-10th Jun  -> (A2 Storre) 10th Jun-15th Jun ->
(A4 Miguel) 15th Jun-20th Jun -> (A5 JoseBa) 20th Jun-22nd Jun ->
(A7 JoseBa) 22nd Jun-25th Jun -> (A8 JoseBa) 25th Jun-28th Jun ->
(A9 Storre) 28th Jun-1st Jul  -> (A10 FMoren) 1st Jul-3rd Jul  ->
(A3 Emilio) 10th Jun-8th Jul  -> (A11 Miguel) 8th Jul-14th Jul ->
(A12 Artur) 14th Jun-15th Jul -> (A13 Artur) 15th Jul-16th Jul ->
```

Results were evaluated by the manager of the e-learning center, outperforming the expected. However, some improvements are still necessary for the implementation of temporal restrictions[2], stressing on the translation of synchronization/merge route gateways.

6   Conclusions and Future Work

Designing Planning and Scheduling scenarios manually through the use of complex languages as PDDL[6] is a very difficult task, even for well-trained engineers. This has been a traditional drawback for the introduction of P&S techniques in enterprise environments. Therefore, given the absence of simple tools for modeling P&S problems, as well as the inability of Business Process Management for the anticipated planning of processes, we present some significative contributions in this paper. Firstly, we introduced a new and easy way to model P&S problems using existing BPM tools, that are commonly used among business analysts, and that, furthermore, already consider the significance of web services for a new age of interconnected organisations. To achieve this goal, a transformation from the standard XPDL language is proposed, through the decomposition of the input diagram into basic workflow patterns, that are directly mapped into an HTN-PDDL domain, supplying consistency and completeness to our process. The generated domain will be later used as input of an intelligent planner. This triggers a reasoning process that finally offers the automatic generation of action plans and resources allocation, introducing Planning and Scheduling techniques within the traditional BPM life cycle at a low cost.

Future work will explore the HTN-PDDL representation of complex workflow patterns and will also study how to represent more demanding temporal restrictions that are usually present in business processes, so that we can increase the capacity of the business analyst to represent real planning domains through the use of the same business modeling tools.

Acknowledgments. We would like to be specially grateful to CEVUG staff, specially to F. Moreno Ruiz and M. González Laredo for their invaluable help.

References

1. Bahrami, A.: Integrated Process Management: From Planning to Work Execution. In: IEEE Workshop on Business Service Networks, pp. 11–18 (2005)
2. Castillo, L., Fdez-Olivares, J., García-Pérez, O., Palao, F.: Efficiently handling temporal knowledge in an HTN planner. In: 16th ICAPS Conf., pp. 63–72 (2006)
3. Workflow Management Coalition. XML Process Definition Language Specification, v2.1. WFMC-TC-1025, pp. 1–216 (2008)
4. Dirgahayu, T., Quartel, D.A.C., van Sinderen, M.J.: Development of transformations from business process models to implementations by reuse. In: 3rd International Workshop on Model-Driven Enterprise Information Systems, pp. 41–50 (2007)
5. Fdez-Olivares, J., Garzón, T., Castillo, L., García-Pérez, O., Palao, F.: A Middleware for the automated composition and invocation of semantic web services based on HTN planning techniques. In: Borrajo, D., Castillo, L., Corchado, J.M. (eds.) CAEPIA 2007. LNCS (LNAI), vol. 4788, pp. 70–79. Springer, Heidelberg (2007)
6. Long, D., Fox, M.: PDDL2.1: An Extension to PDDL for Expressing Temporal Planning Domains. Journal of Artificial Intelligence Research 20, 61–124 (2003)
7. Muehlen, M.Z., Ting-Yi Ho, D.: Risk Management in the BPM Lifecycle. In: Bussler, C.J., Haller, A. (eds.) BPM 2005. LNCS, vol. 3812, pp. 454–466. Springer, Heidelberg (2006)
8. Ouyang, C., Dumas, M., Hofstede, A., van der Aalst, W.M.P.: Pattern-based translation of BPMN process models to BPEL web services. International Journal of Web Services Research 5(1), 42–62 (2007)
9. Palmer, N.: Workflow and BPM in 2007: Bussiness Process Standards see a new global imperative. In: BPM and Workflow Handbook, pp. 9–14 (2007)
10. R-Moreno, M.D., Borrajo, D., Cesta, A., Oddi, A.: Integrating planning and scheduling in workflow domains. Expert Systems with Applications 33(2), 389–406 (2007)
11. Sen, R., Hackmann, G., Haitjema, M., Roman, G.C., Gill, C.: Coordinating Workflow Allocation and Execution in Mobile Environments. In: Murphy, A.L., Vitek, J. (eds.) COORDINATION 2007. LNCS, vol. 4467, pp. 249–267. Springer, Heidelberg (2007)
12. Sirin, E., Parsia, B., Wu, D., Hendler, J., Nau, D.: HTN planning for web services composition using shop2. Journal of Web Semantics 1(4) (2004)
13. van der Aalst, W.M.P.: Patterns and XPDL: A critical Evaluation of the XML Process Definition Language. QUT report FIT-TR-2003-06, pp. 1–30 (2003)
14. van der Aalst, W.M.P., ter Hofstede, A.H.M., Kiepuszewski, B., Barros, A.P.: Workflow Patterns. Distributed and Parallel Databases 14(1), 5–51 (2003)
15. Vaquero, T.S., Romero, V.M.C., Tonidandel, F., Silva, J.R.: itSIMPLE 2.0: An Integrated Tool for Designing Planning Domains. In: 17th ICAPS Conf. (2007)
16. Wilson, R., Keil, F.C.: MIT Encyclopedia of Cognitive Science, pp. 652–654. MIT Press, Cambridge (2001)

A Heuristic Method for Balanced Graph Partitioning: An Application for the Demarcation of Preventive Police Patrol Areas

Thiago Assunção and Vasco Furtado

University of Fortaleza (UNIFOR) – Graduate Program in Applied Informatics (MIA)
Av. Washington Soares, 1321 - Bloco M Sala 11 - 60.811-905 - Fortaleza – Brazil
thiagoaa_unifor@yahoo.com.br, vasco@unifor.br

Abstract. In this paper we describe a heuristic method, based on graph-partitioning algorithms, with the purpose of improving the demarcation of areas for police patrolling. This demarcation seeks to homogenize the number of crimes among the patrol regions. If the map of a particular region is taken as a graph, we can say that the problem faced by police forces (typically preventive police) is similar to the problem of finding balanced connected q partitions of graphs (BCPq). Since this is a problem belonging to the NP-Hard class, approximate algorithms are the most suitable for solving such a problem. The method described in this article obtains results nearest those considered optimal for the more general case of BCPq, for $q \geq 2$.

Keywords: approximate algorithm, graphs, heuristic method, balanced connected partition.

1 Introduction

In order to contain criminal activity, it is necessary to provide the organizations that act repressively or preventively with tools for the efficient performance of their actions. Preventive Police Force has the task of carrying out ostensible law enforcement. It is assumed, therefore, that this group's presence acts as a dissuasive force, thus preventing the occurrence of crimes.

The division of patrol areas is one of the basic activities of planning for the police patrol. One example of a project in which the issue of division of patrol areas causes a major impact is being developed in Brazil: the "Block Patrol" project.

This project intends to divide the city of Fortaleza (more than 2 million inhabitants) into patrol areas that would be covered by teams of police officers. This territorial division, in principle, is being done by means of an *ad hoc* criterion: fixed areas measuring 3 km² each. The search for efficient methods to carry out this division, based on criteria such as the crime rate of the areas, is the object of this work. It is easy to understand why the technicians of the Block Patrol chose such a simple method. The division of the city into variable areas considering different optimization criteria is not a trivial task. The difficulty of such an activity is evident in this scientific paper. For this work, we decided to model the problem of the optimized division

H. Geffner et al. (Eds.): IBERAMIA 2008, LNAI 5290, pp. 62–72, 2008.

of patrol areas as a problem of balanced connected partition of graphs in q partitions (BCPq). It can be perceived, by doing so, that the problem in question is presented as NP-Hard [4].

The optimization in demarcating the regions intends to achieve the maximum homogenization possible in the distribution of crimes among the areas. Doing so, the distribution of police patrol teams can be associated to a demarcated area (i.e. each area is associated to one team).

The first contribution of this article is, therefore, to supply a formal setting for the treatment of the problem and, for this reason, is inspired by works already developed by the scientific community for seeking an approximated and viable solution to the problem. In addition to the formal modeling of the problem, this paper proposes a heuristic method for efficient resolution (in comparative terms with the state of the art) for the problem of balanced graph partition. Finally, the application of such a method to partition the city of Fortaleza into patrol areas is the practical contribution provided herein.

The remainder of the article is structured in the following way: Initially, we present a short analysis of the problem of balanced connected partition of graphs and of the main algorithms related to this problem. Then, we show how modeling the problem of dividing the patrol areas was done to a graph partition problem, and we describe this article's objective heuristic method. In the fourth section, we evaluate the heuristic method and compare it with the algorithm proposed by Chlebíková [3], which is considered the algorithm that produces the best results for the specific case of BCPq, for q = 2. Finally, the last section brings final considerations and perspectives for future works.

2   Balanced Connected Partitions of Graphs

BCPq (Balanced Connected Partition of graphs for q partitions, where q ≥ 2) can be defined in the following way:

Given an integer number q and a connected graph G = (V, E), where its vertices possess weights, find a q-partition of G such that each subgraph associated to each partition is connected and the weight of the lightest one is the highest possible, i.e., the distribution of the weights among the subgraphs should be the most homogeneous possible.

This problem belongs to the class of the problems of graph partitioning and is classified as an NP-Hard problem, even for q-connected graphs [4]. Therefore, the most appropriate algorithms for solving this problem are approximation algorithms, which tend to find solutions nearest those considered optimal.

Several algorithms exist for the more general problem of graph partitioning. Among those, we can cite the following: the Cartesian Nested Dissection method [6], the Kernighan-Lin (KL) algorithm [1], the Fiduccia-Mattheyses (FM) algorithm [2], the multilevel methods [8] and [10], recursive coordinate bisection [11]. It is worthy of mention that the KL algorithm is one of the most widely referenced for solving this problem, since it produces a good local partitioning regarding the number of cut edges. For further information, we recommend reading [7].

There are few algorithms geared specifically toward the BCPq problem. For the particular case where q = 2, the algorithm proposed by Chlebíková [3] is the one that produces a partition nearest to what is considered optimal, i.e., the partitions are connected and possess weights whose values are approximations of the ideal result (each partition possesses half the weight of the graph). For the case where q ≥ 3, BCPq has not been widely investigated, in as much as—up to until 2007—no algorithms existed that resolved any problem for q ≥ 3 within the set of integer numbers [5]. Very recently, Pinheiro in [5] constructed several heuristics, based on spanning trees, which present good results for the general case of the problem. For further information regarding the BCPq problem and algorithms of approximation geared toward this problem, we recommend reading [9].

3 Description of the Solution

For solving the problem of optimization of patrol area demarcation, we use the graph data structure for the computer representation of geographical maps [12]. In this paper, we used the map that represents the district of *Aldeota*, located in the city of Fortaleza, Brazil. In order to explain this modeling, let's take this map as shown in Fig. 1.

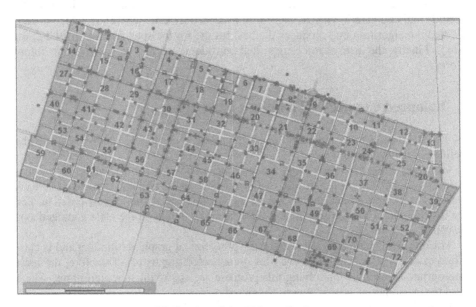

Fig. 1. Map of the Aldeota district

The map was divided into 72 parts called "blocks". One block is a sub-region of a district whose area includes about four city squares [area of buildings/lots surrounded by four streets], i.e., 0.04 km². Each block was numbered with a value from 1 to 72. The points in black indicate the occurrence of a crime at a particular location in the district.

The choice of small areas to delimit the blocks was arbitrary. However, this demarcation could be of another granularity; but—since specialists on the subject believe that this granularity is reasonable, because they would not constitute *per se* just one useful area of policing—we adopted this demarcation. Moreover, if we chose larger areas, the heuristic method would have to divide these blocks into sub-blocks in order to guarantee a greater homogeneity of crimes among the patrol areas, thus diminishing the performance of such a method.

Each block of this map was represented by a vertex on the graph. Additionally, each vertex possessed a weight, denoting the number of crimes within the region of the block represented by the vertex. The edges of the graph represent the idea of neighborhood between the blocks, i.e., two neighboring blocks on the map will be represented by an edge (u, v), where u and v are graph vertices associated to the blocks. For example, blocks 1 and 2 are neighbors on the map; therefore they will form an edge (v1, v2) on the graph. Observe that diagonal blocks are not considered neighbors. For example, blocks 1 and 15 are not neighbors. Fig. 2 illustrates the graph that results from the map in Fig. 1. The numbers in bold represent the weights of the vertices, i.e., the number of crimes that occurred within the limits of a particular block associated to the vertex.

Now that we already have the graph representing the geographical map of the Aldeota district, all we have to do is apply the method of balanced connected partitioning in order to produce the regions that will be patrolled by the police teams.

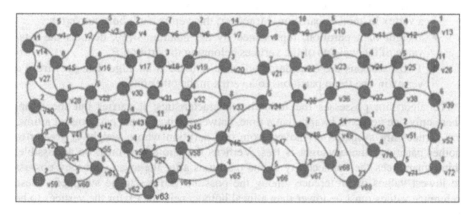

Fig. 2. Graph representing the map in Fig. 1

3.1 Description of the Heuristic Method

The method is comprised of two phases: initial partitioning and partition refinement. In the initial partitioning phase, we can use any method that partition a graph in two connected sub-graphs. Particularly, for the application in the demarcation of patrol areas we have chosen to use the Cartesian Parallel Nested Dissection algorithm [6]. The rationale behind this choice is two-fold. Such an algorithm assumes that the vertices possess geographical coordinates which it is the case in the patrol area domain where coordinate values are associated to each vertex according to the position of the block that this vertex represents on the map. Furthermore, the Cartesian Nested Dissection algorithm is simple to implement, efficient having low complexity.

In the partition refinement phase, we use a heuristic algorithm that we constructed based on the strategies of the KL algorithm [1]. This heuristic algorithm swaps the vertices between the partitions with the intent of maximizing the homogeneity of the weights between them. Such a refinement algorithm is this article's main contribution toward the BCPq problem.

3.2 Algorithm for Partition Refinement

The partition refinement algorithm is based on concepts adopted by the Kernighan-Lin method [1]. The KL algorithm executes swaps among partitions with the aim of minimizing the number of edges that will be cut. Similarly, our algorithm executes such swaps with the intent of better distributing the weights among the partitions. Both receive a graph and the partitions thereof as input and return the refined partitions according to their refinement criteria. Before detailing the algorithm, it is important to define some of the concepts:

- Cut vertex or articulation point is a vertex of a graph such that its removal causes an increase in the number of connected components. If the graph was connected before the removal of the vertex, it will be disconnected afterwards;
- A vertex of a partition is said to be admissible if there is an edge linking it to a vertex in another partition. Moreover, this vertex can't be a cut vertex;
- Weight of a partition, represented by the notation $w(P)$, denotes the total value of the weights of the vertices belonging to partition P;
- Two partitions are considered adjacent if there is an edge that goes from a vertex in one these partitions to a vertex in the other one.

The algorithm possesses the following characteristics: it carries out the swap, where only one vertex is swapped at a time, between two adjacent partitions at a time. The vertices are swapped or moved from one partition whose weight is greater to another partition whose weight is less. Vertices that are swept must be admissible, which guarantees the connectivity of the partitions after the swap, and they possess the lowest values of preference among the possible vertices to be swapped. These preference values must be lower than a local homogeneity index for the vertices to be transferred.

The local homogeneity index α indicates how far away the weights of both partitions are from a weight that is considered ideal. This ideal weight is the average among the weights of the partitions. The index is calculated according to the equation defined in (1), where:

$$\alpha = \left| w\left(P_1\right) - w\left(P_2\right) \right| \tag{1}$$

- $w\left(P_1\right)$ *denotes the weight of partition* P_1;
- $w\left(P_2\right)$ *denotes the weight of partition* P_2;

The preference criterion for a vertex $\gamma(v)$ represents the value of α after swapping this vertex. Such value is calculated according to the equation defined in (2), where:

$$\gamma(v) = \left|\left(w_{max}(P_1) - w_{vertex}(v)\right)\right| + \left|\left(w_{min}(P_2) + w_{vertex}(v)\right)\right| \qquad (2)$$

- $w_{max}(P_1)$ *denotes the weight of the partition with highest weight, i.e., that to which vertex v belongs;*
- $w_{vertex}(v)$ *denotes the weight of vertex v ;*
- $w_{min}(P_2)$ *denotes the weight of the partition adjacent to P_1 with the lowest weight;*

To optimize the swapping process, the algorithm prefers swaps between the partition with the highest weight and the partition adjacent thereto with the lowest weight in a given iteration of the algorithm. Following this preference criterion, the weights of the most valued partitions are first diminished and, consequently, the weights of their respective smaller valued adjacent partitions are increased, improving the homogeneity among the partitions. The process finishes when there is no vertex that can be swapped among adjacent partitions, i.e., the solution cannot be more refined according to the algorithm's criteria.

The algorithm of the GLOBALREFINEMENT procedure, which carries out the process described previously. See it below.

GLOBALREFINEMENT (Partitions[])

```
1     For each partition do
2        Attribute an optimal weight value to the partition;
3     INITIALIZEADJACENCYPARTITIONS (Partitions);
4     Place partitions in decreasing order according to their weights;
5     indexCurrentPartition ← 0;
6     numberIterations ← 0;
7     currentPartition ← null;
8     While (indexCurrentPartition = Partitions.length) do
9        currentPartition ← Partitions[indexCurrentPartition];
10       Place partitions adjacent to currentPartition in increasing order according to
11       their weights;
12       For each partition adjacent to currentPartition do
13          numberIterations ← LOCALREFINEMENT (adjacentPartition, currentPartition);
14          If (numberIterations = 0) then
15             stop;
16       If (numberIterations = 0) then
17          indexCurrentPartition ← indexCurrentPartition + 1;
18       Else
19          indexCurrentPartition ← 0;
20          numberIterations ← 0;
21       UPDATEADJACENCYPARTITIONS (Partitions);
22       Place partitions in decreasing order according to their weights;
```

The procedure begins by attributing an optimal weight value to each partition (lines 1 and 2). This optimal value is the result of the division between the weight of the graph and the number of partitions. Then, the procedure initializes the relations of adjacency among the partitions invoking the INITIALIZEADJACENCYPARTITIONS procedure (line 3). Immediately thereafter, the partitions are placed in decreasing order according to their weights (line 4), and the variables: indexCurrentPartition, numberIterations and currentPartition are initialized (lines 5, 6 and 7). The outermost loop repeats until all of the partitions have been tested for the swapping process (line 8). Within that loop, first the partition with the greatest weight is attributed to the currentPartition variable (line 9), and the partitions adjacent thereto are placed in increasing order according to their weights (line 10). Then, for each adjacent partition, the swapping process is executed by calling the LOCALREFINEMENT function (lines 12 and 13). If this method executes any swap, the innermost loop ends (lines 14 and 15). Otherwise, it continues until reaching the end of the list of adjacent partitions or until some swap is carried out. Right after this innermost loop, if no swap was made between the current partition with the highest weight and one of its adjacent partitions, the indexCurrentPartition variable is increased (line 17), and the outermost loop goes on to its next iteration. Otherwise, the indexCurrentPartition and numberIterations variables are again initialized (lines 19 and 20), the relations of adjacency among the partitions are updated (UPDATEADJACENCYPARTITIONS procedure) (line 21), the partitions are again placed in decreasing order according to their weights (line 22), and the outermost loop goes on to its next iteration.

4 Evaluation and Comparison with the Chlebíková Algorithm

In order to utilize an approximative method, we will use the approximation ratio or performance ratio (represented by the letter p) as a metric for evaluating the method described in the previous section. This measure informs how close the solution obtained by an algorithm is to the optimal solution.

Using equation (3), we can calculate the approximation ratio of an algorithm, where A(I) represents the value of a solution obtained by executing algorithm A for an instance I of the problem, and opt(I) represents the value of an optimal solution for instance I of the problem.

$$A(I) \leq p * opt(I) \tag{3}$$

Since—in our case—the partitioning method may produce partitions with weights above those considered optimal, the value of A(I) is calculated in the following manner: optimal weight for a partition (weight of the graph divided by the number of partitions) – the greatest difference in module between the weight of a partition and the optimal weight for a partition.

For example: suppose that the partitioning algorithm for a graph G with weight 30 produced three partitions with the following weights: 11, 11 and 8. The opt(I) value will be 10 (1/3 of the weight of the graph), and the A(I) value will be 8, i.e., (10 - |8 – 10|). Therefore, the approximation ratio (p) will be 0,8 (80%), i.e., the weights of the three partitions approximated the optimal weight by at least 80% for a partition of this graph.

4.1 Application and Evaluation of the Algorithm in the Graph of the Aldeota District

In order to verify the efficacy of the heuristic method that is the subject of this article, we applied it to the graph that represents the Aldeota district (Fig. 2) for a number q of partitions varying from 2 to 15. The results are presented in Table 1.

Observe that, for the most part, the results were good, with an approximation percentage greater than or equal to 80%, except for the case where the number of partitions is equal to 4, whose approximation percentage was 69.56%. This occurred due to the fact that the Initial Partitioning phase did not produce—for that case—partitions that better aided the Partition Refinement phase regarding adjacency among the partitions, in order to produce a solution with a higher approximation percentage. However, the greatest contribution of this article, i.e., the refinement algorithm that we constructed, applied in the Partition Refinement phase, showed that given an initial connected partitioning, one can produce good solutions for a number of partitions greater than or equal to two. Furthermore, for these tests, the partitioning method takes no more than 0.5s to produce the solutions.

It should be pointed out that we applied the method on a planar graph with coordinate values associated with its vertices. We were not able to affirm that the method described in this article produces solutions with the same percentage of approximation for all types of graphs. However, we believe that, given an initial connected partitioning, the heuristic algorithm (Partition Refinement phase) manages to produce connected partitions with good percentages of approximation.

Table 1. Results of the tests on the Aldeota graph

Number of Partitions	Percentage of Approximation
2	99.45%
3	99.18%
4	69.56%
5	97.26%
6	93.44%
7	86.53%
8	93.47%
9	87.50%
10	88.88%
11	90.90%
12	90%
13	82.14%
14	80.76%
15	87.50%

4.2 Comparison with the Chlebíková Algorithm

As already mentioned previously, the Chlebíková algorithm [3] is the one that produces a balanced connected partitioning closest to what is considered optimal for the BCP2 problem, where the input graph is 2-connected.

However, the algorithm proposed by Chlebíková, in certain situations, fails to produce better solutions because it always chooses the admissible vertex with the lowest weight among all admissible vertices.

Unlike Chlebíková's algorithm, the refinement algorithm that we constructed chooses admissible vertices that best balance the weights among the partitions in any given iteration. This difference makes the algorithm that we created produce solutions that are equal to or better than the solutions obtained by applying the algorithm proposed by Chlebíková.

We compared the two methods through several tests conducted by varying the number of vertices and the density (number of edges) of biconnected graphs. We have used the Jung electronic library [13], version 1.7.6, to randomly generate the graphs. The graph's vertex weighs are also randomly set up with values varying between one and the half of the graph size (total number of vertices).

We mean by initial partition the phase the returns two partitions in which one of them has the heaviest graph vertex and another has the rest of the vertices. This is the same strategy used in the initial phase of Chlebíková's algorithm. We have adopt it for comparison purposes since we keep the same conditions between our approach and Chlebíková`s one. Otherwise the results could be biased by the results obtained during the initial phase what would compromise the evaluation of the refinement phase which is our main goal. Moreover, the use of the Cartesian Dissection would require the association of coordinates for the vertices what would constraint the choice of graphs in the evaluation process. The test results are presented in Table 2. The first column and second columns show the graph edges and vertices number, respectively. For each test, ten graphs were used and we run the algorithm for each one of them. The third and fourth columns represent the average approximation ratio of our approach and Chlebíková`s, respectively. Finally, the fifth and sixth columns show, also for our approach and Chlebíková`s one, the average iteration number for finding a solution. Note thus that the average iteration number accounts the average of the number of times one vertex was transferred from one partition to another during the algorithm execution. According to these tests, the algorithm that we describe in

Table 2. Comparison between the Chlebíková algorithm and this article's method

Density	n	p Our Approach	p Chlebíková	Nb. Iteration Our Approach	Nb. Iteration Chlebíková
2n	10	0.95	0.89	2.9	4.5
	20	0.99	0.95	6.4	12
2.5n	10	0.98	0.94	3	4.7
	20	0.99	0.96	6.4	11.7
	30	0.99	0.98	9.4	18.1
	40	0.99	0.98	12.4	25.5
3n	10	0.95	0.92	2.9	4.8
	20	0.99	0.96	5.7	12.2
	30	0.99	0.97	9.3	18.6
	40	0.99	0.98	12.3	25.4
	50	0.99	0.98	15.1	33.1
	60	1	0.99	18.1	39.8
	70	1	0.99	21.7	46.3

section 3 produces solutions with an approximate ratio better than those proposed by Chlebíková. Note that these results were achieved in less iterations than Chlebíková`s.

The Chlebíková algorithm used in our tests was implemented by us in JAVA. In order to perform the tests presented in this section, we used an Intel Pentium 4 Processor with 512Mb of memory.

5   Final Considerations and Future Works

The intent of this article is to help preventive police forces. Such help consists of better delimiting the patrol areas and distributing the police teams among these areas. For such, we showed that the problem faced by the preventive police can be modeled as a problem of balanced connected partitioning of graphs (BCPq). Such a problem has not been widely investigated for its most general case, where the number of partitions is greater than 2.

We developed a heuristic method based on strategies pertaining to the foremost graph-partitioning algorithms. We applied it on a graph that represents the Aldeota district in the city of Fortaleza, Brazil. The results obtained from the tests on this graph showed that, in general, the approximation percentage was equal to or greater than 80% for a number of partitions varying from 2 to 15. Moreover, we compared this method to the approximation algorithm proposed by Chlebíková. Several tests were conducted, varying the number of vertices and of edges of the graphs. The results obtained showed that the algorithm proposed in this article possessed a degree of approximation equal to or higher than that obtained with the algorithm proposed by Chlebíková.

Based on this work, we show the feasibility, in the future, of delimiting patrol areas that obey certain limits of extension. In order for this to be possible, an area value would be associated with each vertex, and such value would represent the extension of the block associated therewith. Thus, the patrols would not be under-utilized, i.e., there would be no patrols in small regions. In the long term, it is also possible to envision the use of this algorithm to improve patrolling efforts in other districts of the city of Fortaleza, as well as in other cities.

References

1. Kernighan, B.W., Lin, S.: An efficient heuristic procedure for partitioning graphs. Bell Sys. Tech. J., 291–307 (1970)
2. Fiduccia, C.M., Matteyses, R.M.: A linear time heuristic for improving network partitions. In: 19th Design Automaton Conference, pp. 175–181 (1982)
3. Chlebíková, J.: Approximating the maximally balanced connected partition problem in graphs. Information Processing Letters 60, 225–230 (1996)
4. Chataigner, F., Salgado, L.R.B., Wakabayashi, Y.: Approximability and inaproximability results on balanced connected partitions of graphs. Discrete Mathematics and Theoretical Computer Science (DMTCS) 9, 177–192 (2007)
5. Lucindo, R.P.F.L.: Partição de Grafos em Subgrafos Conexos Balanceados. Dissertação de mestrado, Universidade de São Paulo (2007)

6. Heath, M.T., Raghavan, P.: A Cartesian Parallel Nested Dissection Algorithm. SIAM Journal on Matrix Analysis and Applications (1994)
7. Pereira, M.R.: Particionamento Automático de Restrições. Tese de Doutorado, Universidade Federal do Rio de Janeiro (COPPE) (2006)
8. Karypis, G., Kumar, V.: A Fast and High Quality Multilevel Scheme for Partitioning Irregular Graphs. Technical Report TR 95-035. Departament of Computer Science. University of Minnesota (1995)
9. Salgado, L.R.B.: Algoritmos de Aproximação para Partições Conexas em Grafos. Tese de doutorado, Universidade de São Paulo (2004)
10. Moretti, C.O., Bittencourt, T.N., André, J.C., Martha, L.F.: Algoritmos Automáticos de Partição de Domínio. Escola Politécnica da Universidade de São Paulo, Boletim Técnico, BT/PEF-9803 (1998) ISSN 0103-9822
11. Simon, H.D., Teng, S.H.: Partitioning of Unstructured Problems for Parallel Processing. Computing Systems in Engineering 2, 135–148 (1991)
12. Gersting, J.L.: Mathematical Structures for Computer Science, 6th edn. W.H. Freeman, New York (2006)
13. Jung. Java Universal Network/Graph Framework (2003) (Last access: February 14 , 2008), http://jung.sourceforge.net/index.html

Using Indexed Finite Set Variables for Set Bounds Propagation

Ruben Duarte Viegas, Marco Correia, Pedro Barahona, and Francisco Azevedo

CENTRIA
Departamento de Informática
Faculdade de Ciências e Tecnologia
Universidade Nova de Lisboa
{rviegas,mvc,pb,fa}@di.fct.unl.pt

Abstract. Constraint Programming (CP) has been successfully applied to numerous combinatorial problems such as scheduling, graph coloring, circuit analysis, or DNA sequencing. Following the success of CP over traditional domains, set variables were also introduced to more declaratively solve a number of different problems.

Using a bounds representation for a finite set variable allows one to compactly represent the solution set of a set constraint problem. Many consistency mechanisms for maintaining bounds consistency have been proposed and in this paper we propose to use delta domain variable information to speed up constraint propagation. Additionally, we propose the use of indexed set domain variable representations as a better means of improving the use, intuitiveness and efficiency of delta domain variables for propagation tasks.

Keywords: finite set constraint variables, graph constraint variables, constraint propagation, delta domain variables, indexation.

1 Introduction

Set variables and set constraints provide an intuitive and efficient way of modelling Constraint Satisfaction Problems's (CSP) over sets [1,2].

This paper addresses *Cardinal*, a state-of-the-art *bounds consistency* set solver (available in the *ECLiPSe Constraint System* distribution [3] and also with *CaSPER* [4,5]) which has already proved its efficiency in solving real-life set constraint problems [6,2]. More specifically, we improve over the version presented in [2] by lowering its worst-case complexity for most propagators. The improvement is based on the idea of exploring detailed information about past domain updates (delta domains), together with a new domain representation which allows us to take advantage of this information.

We define three new representations of finite set variables, combine them with delta information and compare them against the original *Cardinal* version, in *CaSPER*.

The structure of the paper is the following: in section 2 we present the formal notation we use throughout the paper. In section 3 we explain the usefulness of

H. Geffner et al. (Eds.): IBERAMIA 2008, LNAI 5290, pp. 73–82, 2008.

using delta domain variables and how we can use indexation to explore it. We test our indexation mechanisms in section 4 by solving some benchmarks and comparing results. Finally, we conclude in section 5 with our closing remarks and future work.

2 Preliminaries

We start by revising useful definitions while also introducing the notation used throughout the paper.

Definition 1. [CSP] *A constraint network consists of a set of variables $\mathcal{X}$, a set of domains $\mathcal{D}$, and a set of constraints $\mathcal{C}$. Every variable $X \in \mathcal{X}$ has an associated domain $D(X)$ denoting its possible values. The constraint satisfaction problem (CSP) consists in finding an assignment of values to variables such that all constraints are satisfied.*

For CSPs over set variables, each domain $D(X)$ therefore represents a set of possible sets for variable X. In *Cardinal* only the set bounds are explicitly maintained:

Definition 2. [Set variable] *A set variable X is represented by $[a_X, b_X]_{c_X}$ where a_X is the set of elements known to belong to X (its greatest lower bound, or glb), b_X is the set of elements not excluded from X (its least upper bound, or lub), and c_X its cardinality (a finite domain variable). We define $p_X = b_X \setminus a_X$ to be the set of elements, not yet excluded from X and that can still be added to a_X.*

Solving a CSP typically involves interleaving search with some kind of consistency enforcing which effectively narrows the search space. Consistency enforcement is accomplished by means of propagators:

Definition 3. [Propagator] *A propagator $\pi : \mathcal{D} \to \mathcal{D}, \pi(\mathcal{D}) \subseteq \mathcal{D}$ is a monotonically decreasing function from domains to domains, preserving the CSP solutions.*

The set of propagators associated with $\mathcal{C}$ are executed repeatedly until fixpoint, i.e., no further domain reduction is possible by an additional execution of any propagator. A propagator may, therefore, be executed several times between consecutive fixpoint operations. In the remaining of the paper, let π_i denote the i'th execution of propagator π.

3 Delta Domains and Indexation

Generally, a *delta domain* represents the set of updates on a variable's domain between two consecutive executions of some propagator at a given fixpoint operation. In the following, let $X \ominus Y = \langle a_X \setminus a_Y, b_X \setminus b_Y \rangle$ be the standard (bounds) difference between two set variables X and Y:

Definition 4. [Delta domain] *Let $D_I(X)$ and $D_F(X)$ denote respectively the initial domain of X (i.e. before any propagator is executed), and final domain of X (i.e. after fixpoint is reached). The delta domain of variable X is $\Delta(X) = D_I(X) \ominus D_F(X)$. Let $D_{\pi_i}(X)$ be the domain of variable X right after the i'th execution of propagator π. The delta domain of variable X with respect to propagator π_i is $\Delta_{\pi_i}(X) = D_{\pi_{i-1}}(X) \ominus D_{\pi_i}(X)$.*

Maintaining delta domains is a complex task. Delta domains must be collected, stored and made available later during a fixpoint operation. Moreover, each propagator has its own (possibly distinct) set of deltas which must be updated independently.

The basic idea is to store $\Delta(X) = \{\delta_1 \ldots \delta_n\}$ in each set variable X as the sequence (we use a singly-linked list) of every atomic operation δ_i applied on its domain since the last fixpoint. In this context, δ_i is either a removal or insertion of a range of contiguous elements respectively from the set *lub* or in the set *glb*. A delta domain with respect to some propagator execution $\Delta_{\pi_i}(X)$ is then just a subsequence from the current $\Delta(X)$. Although the full details of this task are out of the scope for this paper, we note that domains may be maintained almost for free on constraint solvers with a smart garbage collection mechanism.

The availability of delta information can speed up constraint propagation for integer domains [7]. As noted in [2], it can also be very useful for set variables.

However, using delta information with *Cardinal* domain representation (a pair of lists for a_X and b_X) does not help reducing complexity in most cases. The reason is that in addition to finding what has changed, propagators need to perform domain pruning as well, and usually these operation may be combined.

As explained, $\Delta(X)$ is a list of contiguous range updates on the domain of X. However, since propagators are not executed in any specific order, the list of ranges is not necessarily sorted. Unfortunately, this means that using delta domains even increases the worst-case complexity. Consider the previous example, but where elements $e_1 \ldots e_n$ were inserted in reverse order. The delta domain is now $\Delta_\pi(X) = \{(e_n, e_n), \ldots, (e_1, e_1)\}$ instead of $\Delta_\pi(X) = \{(e_1, e_n)\}$ as previously. The complexity for the contained propagator execution is therefore $O(n \times \#b_Y)^1$. Although in practice $|\Delta_\pi(X)|$ is typically small, we can effectively improve this theoretic worst case bound by indexing the set variable domain.

Since delta domain variables are independent of the data structures used for the domain variables themselves, this enables the development of alternative data structures for storing the domain information and which may make a more efficient use of delta domain information. Note that the same could be achieved with other domain representations (e.g. trees) since in our implementation, delta domain variables are orthogonal to the data structures used for the domain variables themselves.

---

[1] Note that this could possibly be improved by first sorting $\Delta_\pi(X)$, yielding $O(n \log n + n + \#b_Y)$.

3.1   Indexation

Indexation is a well known mechanism for allowing direct access of elements in constant time. It is not hard to see that with constant access to elements in the domain of X most operations can be done in optimal time. In the running example, the insertion of $e_1 \ldots e_n$ in a_X (in any ordering) requires the insertion of $\Delta(X)$ in the domain of Y, which can be done optimally in $O(n)$. Finally, note that indexation *without* delta domains would still require the inspection of $a_X \setminus a_Y$, and thus does not improve over the *Cardinal* domain representation.

In the next sections we introduce three different indexation mechanisms for finite set variables upon which these finite sets domain variables and the *Cardinal* filtering rules can be implemented and which we will evaluate in section 4.

Hash Implementation. The first indexation mechanism uses a list for storing, in sorted order, the elements that constitute the finite set variable (*lub*) and an hash-table to directly access them. At any given time an element may either be in the set's *glb*, *poss* (= *lub* \ *glb*) or may even be removed from the set. For this purpose every node in the hash-table will have both the represented element and an indicator of where the element currently is (*glb*,*poss* or *out*). This implementation will henceforth be called *Hash*.

In Figure 1 we represent the internal structure of a *Cardinal* finite set variable, using the *Hash* implementation, with $glb = \{a\}$ and $poss = \{f, p, z\}$ and having removed the element p. In it, *index* represents our indexing mechanism for efficiently accessing the elements while *elementsHead* and *elementsTail* represent the limits of the list of all elements in sorted order for iteration purposes.

Hash-1 Implementation. This implementation inherits the same structure and functionality as the *Hash* implementation. The only modification is in how the delta domain events are stored. In the *Hash* implementation, deltas are stored as ranges allowing to store in one single delta a complete set of elements that

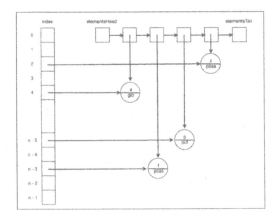

Fig. 1. Hash complete structure

had been either removed from or inserted into the finite set domain variable at a given time. In the *Hash-1* implementation, even though a change in the domain may be caused by a set of elements, these elements are stored individually as deltas, i.e., each delta contains only one of those elements.

Hash+Poss Implementation. The third and final indexation mechanism, in addition to the structures used by both the *Hash* and the *Hash-1* implementations uses a list to store only the elements in the set's *poss*. This is important since many dynamic heuristics reason only about elements which are in the set's *poss* and both the *Hash* and the *Hash-1* implementations do not have a dedicated structure for efficiently accessing it.

If we disregard the indexation used, the main difference between this implementation and the original *Cardinal* implementation is that *Hash+Poss* does not use a structure for the set's *glb* thus theoretically outperforming the original *Cardinal* version for insertion operations since it does not have to sweep the entire set's *glb* in order to find the position where to insert the element, instead it just removes the element from the *poss* structure and updates the indicator to *glb*.

In Figure 2 we represent the internal structure of a *Cardinal* finite set variable, using the *Hash+Poss* implementation, with *glb* = {a} and *poss* = {f, p, z} and having removed the element *p*. In it, *index* represents our indexing mechanism for efficiently accessing the elements, *elementsHead* and *elementsTail* represent the limits of the list containing all elements in sorted order for iteration purposes and finally, *possHead* and *possTail* represent the limits of the list containing only the elements belonging to the variable's *poss*, in sorted order, for set *poss*'s iteration purposes.

3.2 Complexity Analysis

In order to assess the theoretical efficiency of the different *Cardinal* indexed implementations we introduce the following operations, which represent the most

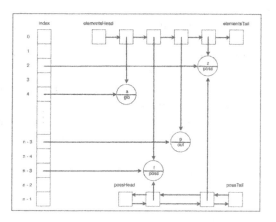

Fig. 2. Hash+Poss complete structure

Table 1. Worst-case temporal complexity of the *hash+poss Cardinal* implementation

Operation	Complexity			
	Cardinal	*Hash*	*Hash-1*	*Hash+Poss*
inGlb(e):	$O(\#a_S)$	$O(1)$	$O(1)$	$O(1)$
inPoss(e):	$O(\#p_S)$	$O(1)$	$O(1)$	$O(1)$
inLub(e):	$O(\#b_S)$	$O(1)$	$O(1)$	$O(1)$
ins(e):	$O(\#b_S)$	$O(1)$	$O(1)$	$O(1)$
ins(*e):	$O(1)$	$O(1)$	$O(1)$	$O(1)$
insRg(b,e):	$O(\#b_S)$	$O(\#(e-b))$	$O(\#(e-b))$	$O(\#(e-b))$
insRg(*b,*e):	$O(\#a_S)$	$O(\#(*e-*b))$	$O(\#(*e-*b))$	$O(\#(*e-*b))$
rem(e):	$O(\#p_S)$	$O(1)$	$O(1)$	$O(1)$
rem(*e):	$O(1)$	$O(1)$	$O(1)$	$O(1)$
remRg(b,e):	$O(\#p_S)$	$O(\#(e-b))$	$O(\#(e-b))$	$O(\#(e-b))$
remRg(*b,*e):	$O(1)$	$O(\#(*e-*b))$	$O(\#(*e-*b))$	$O(\#(*e-*b))$
iterateGlb():	$O(\#a_S)$	$O(\#b_S)^2$	$O(\#b_S)^2$	$O(\#b_S)^2$
iteratePoss():	$O(\#p_S)$	$O(\#b_S)^2$	$O(\#b_S)^2$	$O(\#p_S)$
iterateLub():	$O(\#b_S)$	$O(\#b_S)^2$	$O(\#b_S)^2$	$O(\#b_S)^2$

common operations performed on *Cardinal*'s underlying structure, all other set operations being decomposable into these more simple ones.

- **inGlb**(e): Consists of verifying if e is in the set's *glb*
- **inPoss**(e): Consists of verifying if e is in the set's *poss*
- **inLub**(e): Consists of verifying if e is in the set's *lub*
- **ins**(e): Consists of moving e from the set's *poss* to the set's *glb*
- **ins**(*e): Consists of moving the element pointed by e from the set's *poss* to the set's *glb*
- **insRg**(b,e): Consists of moving the range of elements between b and e from the set's *poss* to the set's *glb*
- **insRg**(*b,*e): Consists of moving the range of elements between the one pointed by b and the one pointed by e from the set's *poss* to the set's *glb*
- **rem**(e): Consists of removing e from the set's *poss*
- **rem**(*e): Consists of removing the element pointed by e from the set's *poss*
- **remRg**(b,e): Consists of removing the range of elements between b and e from the set's *poss*
- **remRg**(*b,*e): Consists of removing the range of elements between the element pointed by b and the element pointed by e from the set's *poss*
- **iterateGlb**(): Consists of iterating through all the elements in the set's *glb*
- **iteratePoss**(): Consists of iterating through all the elements in the set's *poss*
- **iterateLub**(): Consists of iterating through all the elements in the set's *lub*

---

[2] For the indexed versions, elements are not removed from the index, but marked with the *out* indicator and therefore the cost increases for having to pass through these elements.

In Table 1, we present the worst-case temporal complexity analysis for the operations summarised at the beginning of the section for a set variable S and using the original *Cardinal* implementation as well as the 3 indexed implementations.

From Table 1 we conclude that all the indexed versions outperform the original version for access operations, inserting elements and ranges of elements by value and removing elements and ranges of elements by value. On the other hand the original version outperforms the indexed versions for the insertion and removal of ranges of elements by pointer and for the *glb* and *poss* iteration operations, being *Hash+Poss* the exception for this last operation.

At this time, indexed versions provide a more efficient framework than the original version for a considerable part of the operations considered, albeit the original one still manages to present better results then the indexed versions for some of the operations. In the next section and in order to clearly determine the benefit of these indexation mechanisms, we introduce two problems able to be directly encoded, into *CaSPER* [4], as set constraint problems and as graph constraint problems (graphs which in turn are decomposable into sets as explained in [8,9,10,11]) and compare results between all these implementations.

4   Benchmarks

In this section we present the results obtained for our *Cardinal* versions for three different benchmarks. All results were obtained using an Intel Core 2 Duo 2.16 GHz, 1.5 Gb of RAM, 4MB L2 cache.

4.1   Set Covering Problem

In the set-covering problem [12,13,14], we are given a set $U = \{1, 2, \ldots, n-1, n\}$ of elements and a set $X = \{S_1, S_2, \ldots, S_{k-1}, S_k\}$ of sets where each S_i ($1 \leq i \leq k$) is contained in U and the objective is to determine the smallest subset S of X such that $U = \bigcup_{S_i \in S} S_i$.

We tested a solution for the set covering problem for our set implementations with the benchmarks used in [13,15]. A time limit of 300 seconds was imposed. We ran the application for each of the *Cardinal* versions and using each of the problem instances. In Table 2 we present the results, in seconds, obtained for the instances presenting the most variance, where *Size* is the cardinality of the best solution found.

In Table 2 we can see that for some of the instances the *Hash-1* version could not even manage to obtain a solution as good as the others and when it did it usually was far more inefficient in the task. In turn, *Hash* always obtained the same best solution, being able to outperform the original *Cardinal* version for some of these instances. Additionally, *Hash+Poss* achieved the same results as the original and the *Hash* versions albeit taking slightly more time than the latter to find them. It seems clear that, for this problem, the *Hash Cardinal* version was the best one and there was benefit in using an indexed representation.

Table 2. Comparison between *Cardinal* versions for the set-covering problem

Problem	Size	Cardinal	Hash	Hash-1	Hash+Poss
scp46	42	154.210	124.330	—	131.640
scp56	39	33.900	34.620	133.380	47.020
scp58	38	24.570	20.390	83.620	26.070
scpa3	42	1.230	1.220	5.090	1.930
scpa4	40	93.480	82.890	—	118.770
scpc1	47	0.110	0.130	0.210	0.150
scpd1	26	57.590	33.640	187.720	41.560

4.2   Metabolic Pathways

Metabolic networks [16,17] are biochemical networks which encode information about molecular compounds and reactions which transform these molecules into substrates and products. A pathway in such a network represents a series of reactions which transform a given molecule into others. An application for pathway discovery in metabolic networks is the explanation of DNA experiments.

Constraints in metabolic networks pathway finding include the preferable avoidance of highly connected molecules (since they do not bring additional pathway information), the safeguard that reactions are observed in a single direction (to ignore a reaction from the metabolic network when the reverse reaction is known to occur, so that both do not occur simultaneously) and the obligation to visit a given set of mandatory molecules (when, for instance, biologists already know some of the products which are in the pathway but do not know the complete pathway). In [8,9,10,11] a complete modelling for this problem is presented.

A possible heuristic for search, adapted from [18], is to iteratively extend a path (initially formed only by the starting vertex) until reaching the final vertex. At every step, we determine the next vertex which extends the current path to the final vertex minimizing the overall path cost. Having this vertex we obtain the next edge to label by considering the first edge extending the current path until the determined vertex. The choice step consists in including/excluding the edge from the graph variable. If the edge is included the current path is updated and the last vertex of the path is the out-vertex of the included edge, otherwise the path remains unchanged and we try another extension. The search ends as soon as the final vertex is reached and the path is minimal. This heuristic shall be referred as *shortest-path*.

We present the results obtained for the problem of solving the shortest metabolic pathways for three metabolic chains (*glyco*, *heme* and *lysine*) and for increasing graph orders (the order of a graph is the number of vertices that belong to the graph).

Table 3 presents the results, in seconds, obtained using the *shortest-path* heuristic using instances obtained from [19].

In Table 3 we can observe that the original *Cardinal* version was consistently worse than the three indexed versions. In what regards the three indexed

Table 3. Comparison between *Cardinal* versions for the Metabolic Pathways problem

Order	Cardinal			Hash			Hash-1			Hash+Poss		
	Glyco	Lysine	Heme	Glyco	Lysine	Heme	Glyco	Lysine	Heme	Glyco	Lysine	Heme
200	0.2	0.4	0.2	0.1	0.3	0.1	0.1	0.3	0.1	0.1	0.3	0.1
400	1.2	1.4	0.6	0.8	1.0	0.5	0.8	1.0	0.4	0.8	1.1	0.5
600	1.9	2.2	1.1	1.6	1.6	0.9	1.6	1.7	1.0	1.6	1.7	1.0
800	3.1	2.9	1.8	2.5	2.6	1.6	2.6	2.6	1.5	2.6	2.6	1.6
1000	5.2	4.0	3.1	4.5	3.6	2.6	4.4	3.5	2.5	4.5	3.6	2.5
1200	7.6	6.5	4.4	6.1	5.5	3.5	6.2	5.4	3.5	6.4	5.7	3.6
1400	10.2	9.6	6.0	8.7	7.9	4.9	8.5	7.9	4.9	8.7	7.9	5.1
1600	13.8	10.8	8.0	11.9	9.5	6.2	11.7	9.6	6.3	12.2	9.9	6.5
1800	18.5	13.9	10.7	16.2	11.9	8.4	16.0	11.7	8.2	16.5	12.1	8.6
2000	21.7	17.6	13.5	18.8	15.5	11.0	18.6	15.4	10.6	18.7	15.8	11.3

versions, this benchmark does not present a clear means of distinction in terms of efficiency, since all of them present similar results. Despite this fact, the indexed versions improve the results of the original *Cardinal* version and again bring a benefit in using indexation for finite sets and graph domain variables.

5 Conclusions and Future Work

In this paper we explained the usefulness in combining delta domain variables and indexation for defining more intuitive and efficient propagators. We tested three different indexed finite set representations with two benchmarks which presented us a grounds for comparing these indexed versions with the original *Cardinal* version.

By considering the results obtained, the indexed versions with delta domains appear as a competitive alternative to the original *Cardinal* version. However, the indexed versions did not provide a considerable speed-up. We think that this may be due to the increase of the number of copy operations necessary for storing and restoring the state of the indexed set domains, compared with the original *Cardinal* version. For instance, the removal of a range of n contiguous elements requires $O(n)$ trailing operations in the indexed domains version, while it is $O(1)$ in the original *Cardinal* version (only 2 pointers in the list are modified).

As shown, the indexed representations are better than the original version for some class of constraints problems. Currently we are trying to identify the special features which characterise this class. We also intend to study other finite set representations, of which we highlight the use of delta domain information with the original *Cardinal* version. While the worst-case runtime cannot be improved with this combination (as pointed in section 3), the availability of delta information may be exploited only when it effectively decreases the required number of operations compared to sweeping the variable's domain.

References

1. Gervet, C.: Interval Propagation to Reason about Sets: Definition and Implementation of a Practical Language. Constraints journal 1(3), 191–244 (1997)
2. Azevedo, F.: Cardinal: A finite sets constraint solver. Constraints journal 12(1), 93–129 (2007)
3. ECLiPSE Constraint System, http://eclipse.crosscoreop.com/
4. Correia, M., Barahona, P., Azevedo, F.: Casper: A programming environment for development and integration of constraint solvers. In: Azevedo, F., Gervet, C., Pontelli, E. (eds.) Proceedings of the First International Workshop on Constraint Programming Beyond Finite Integer Domains (BeyondFD 2005), pp. 59–73 (2005)
5. CaSPER: Constraint Solving Programming Environment for Research, http://proteina.di.fct.unl.pt/casper/
6. Azevedo, F.: Constraint Solving over Multi-Valued Logics. Frontiers in Artificial Intelligence and Applications, vol. 91. IOS Press, Amsterdam (2003)
7. Lagerkvist, M., Schulte, C.: Advisors for incremental propagation. In: Bessière, C. (ed.) CP 2007. LNCS, vol. 4741, pp. 409–422. Springer, Heidelberg (2007)
8. Viegas, R.D., Azevedo, F.: GRASPER: A Framework for Graph CSPs. In: Lee, J., Stuckey, P. (eds.) Proceedings of the Sixth International Workshop on Constraint Modelling and Reformulation (ModRef 2007), Providence, Rhode Island, USA (September 2007)
9. Viegas, R.D., Azevedo, F.: GRASPER: A Framework for Graph Constraint Satisfaction Problems. In: Analide, C., Novais, P., Henriques, P. (eds.) Simpósio Doutoral em Inteligência Artificial, Guimarães, Portugal (December 2007)
10. Viegas, R.D., Azevedo, F.: GRASPER: A Framework for Graph Constraint Satisfaction Problems. In: Azevedo, F., Lynce, I., Manquinho, V. (eds.) Search Techniques for Constraint Satisfaction, Guimarães, Portugal (December 2007)
11. Viegas, R.D.: Constraint Solving over Finite Graphs. Master's thesis, Faculdade de Ciências e Tecnologia, Universidade Nova de Lisboa (2008)
12. Padberg, M.W.: Covering, Packing and Knapsack Problems. Annals of Discrete Mathematics, vol. 4 (1979)
13. Beasley, J.: An algorithm for set covering problems. European Journal of Operational Research 31, 85–93 (1987)
14. Cormen, T., Leiserson, C., Rivest, R., Stein, C.: Introduction to Algorithms, 2nd edn. MIT Press, Cambridge (2001)
15. Beasley, J.: A Lagrangian Heuristic for Set-Covering problems. Naval Research Logistics (NRL) 37(1), 151–164 (1990)
16. Mathews, C., van Holde, K.: Biochemistry, 2nd edn. Benjamin Cummings (1996)
17. Attwood, T., Parry-Smith, D.: Introduction to Bioinformatics. Prentice-Hall, Englewood Cliffs (1999)
18. Sellmann, M.: Cost-based filtering for shorter path constraints. In: Rossi, F. (ed.) CP 2003. LNCS, vol. 2833, pp. 694–708. Springer, Heidelberg (2003)
19. Dooms, G.: The CP(Graph) Computation Domain in Constraint Programming. PhD thesis, Faculté des Sciences Appliquées, Université Catholique de Louvain (2006)

Extension of Bayesian Network Classifiers to Regression Problems*

Antonio Fernández and Antonio Salmerón

Department of Statistics and Applied Mathematics, University of Almería,
Carrera de Sacramento s/n, E-04120 Almería, Spain
{afalvarez,antonio.salmeron}@ual.es

Abstract. In this paper we explore the extension of various Bayesian network classifiers to regression problems where some of the explanatory variables are continuous and some others are discrete. The goal is to compute the posterior distribution of the response variable given the observations, and then use that distribution to give a prediction. The involved distributions are represented as Mixtures of Truncated Exponentials. We test the performance of the proposed models on different datasets commonly used as benchmarks, showing a competitive performace with respect to the state-of-the-art methods.

Keywords: Bayesian networks, Regression, Mixtures of truncated exponentials.

1 Introduction

Bayesian network classifiers [4] constitute one of the most successful applications of Bayesian networks. Recently, Bayesian networks have been proposed as a tool for solving regression problems [2,3,7]. The main advantage with respect to other regression models is that it is not necessary to have a full observation of the explanatory variables to give a prediction for the response variables. Also, the model is usually richer from a semantic point of view. The most recent advances considering the application of Bayesian networks to regression problems, came through the extension of models that had been originally proposed as classifiers, as the so-called *naive Bayes (NB)* [7] and *tree augmented naive Bayes (TAN)* [2]. In both cases, an interesting feature of the proposed solutions is that they can handle problems in which the explanatory variables are discrete or continuous. This is achieved by modelling the joint distribution of the variables involved in the problem, as a mixture of truncated exponentials (MTE) [6].

The fact that models as NB and TAN are appropriate for classification as well as regression is not surprising, as the nature of both problems is similar: the goal is to predict the value of a response or class variable given an observation over the explanatory variables. Therefore, the aim of this paper is to

---

* This work has been supported by the Spanish Ministry of Education and Science, project TIN2007-67418-C03-02 and by Junta de Andalucía, project P05-TIC-00276.

H. Geffner et al. (Eds.): IBERAMIA 2008, LNAI 5290, pp. 83–92, 2008.

investigate the behaviour of different Bayesian network classifiers when applied
to regression problems. In all the cases we will consider problems where some
of the independent variables are continuous while some others are discrete, and
therefore we will concentrate on the use of MTEs, since this distribution has
shown to be an appropiate tool for handling discrete and continuous variables
simultaneously. More precisely, the starting point is the NB and TAN models
for regression proposed in [2,7].

2   Bayesian Networks and Regression

We will denote random variables by capital letters, and their values by lowercase
letters. Random vectors will be denoted by boldfaced characters. We will use $\Omega_{\mathbf{X}}$
to indicate the support of a random vector $\mathbf{X}$. A *Bayesian network* for variables
$\mathbf{X} = \{X_1, \ldots, X_n\}$ is a directed acyclic graph where each X_i is assigned to
one node, which has associated a conditional distribution given its parents [8].
An arc linking two variables indicates the existence of probabilistic dependence
between both of them. A fundamental property of Bayesian networks is that
the joint distribution over $\mathbf{X}$ factorises according to the d-separation criterion
as $p(x_1, \ldots, x_n) = \prod_{i=1}^{n} p(x_i|pa(x_i))$, where $Pa(X_i)$ is the set of parents of X_i
and $pa(x_i)$ is a configuration of values of them. The factorisation induced allows
to represent complex distributions by a set of simpler ones, and therefore the
number of parameters needed to specify a model is lower in general.

A Bayesian network can be used as a regression model. Assume that Y is the
response variable and $X_1, \ldots, X_n$ are the explanatory variables. Then, in order to
predict the value for Y for the observations $x_1, \ldots, x_n$, the conditional density
$f(y|x_1, \ldots, x_n)$, is computed and a numerical prediction for Y is given using
the corresponding mean or the median. As $f(y|x_1, \ldots, x_n)$ is proportional to
$f(y) \times f(x_1, \ldots, x_n|y)$, solving the regression problem would require to specify an
n dimensional density for $X_1, \ldots, X_n$ given Y. However, using the factorisation
encoded by the Bayesian network, this problem is simplified depending on the
structure of the network. The extreme case is the NB structure, where all the
explanatory variables are considered independent given Y (see Fig. 1(a)).

The strong independence assumption behind NB models is somehow com-
pensated by the reduction of the number of parameters to be estimated from
data, since in this case, it holds that $f(y|x_1, \ldots, x_n) \propto f(y) \prod_{i=1}^{n} f(x_i|y)$, which

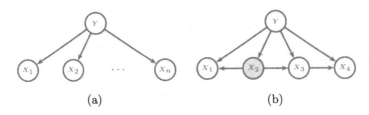

(a)   (b)

Fig. 1. Structure of a *naive Bayes* model (a) and a TAN model (b)

means that, instead of one n-dimensional conditional density, n one-dimensional conditional densities are estimated.

The impact of relaxing the independence assumption has been studied for classification oriented Bayesian networks. One step beyond NB we find the so-called *tree augmented naive Bayes* (TAN) [4] and *forest augmented naive Bayes* (FAN) [5]. In these models, some more dependencies are allowed, expanding the naive Bayes structure by permitting each feature to have one more parent besides Y. Some more complex is the *kDB classifier* [12]. This last model establishes an upper limit of k parents per variable plus the class. The detailed construction of regression models based on these classifiers is described in the next sections.

In any case, regardless of the structure employed, it is necessary that the joint distribution for $Y, X_1, \ldots, X_n$ follows a model for which the computation of the posterior density for Y can be carried out efficiently. Furthermore, we are interested in models able to simultaneously handle discrete and continuous variables. We think that the model that best meets these requirements is the MTE model, explained next. We refer to [7] for a more detailed explanation on the reasons to choose the MTE model for regression.

3   Regression Based on the MTE Model

The MTE model is characterised by a potential defined as follows [6]:

Definition 1. (MTE potential) *Let* $\mathbf{X}$ *be a mixed n-dimensional random vector. Let* $\mathbf{Y} = (Y_1, \ldots, Y_d)$ *and* $\mathbf{Z} = (Z_1, \ldots, Z_c)$ *be the discrete and continuous parts of* $\mathbf{X}$, *respectively, with* $c + d = n$. *We say that a function* $f : \Omega_{\mathbf{X}} \mapsto \mathbb{R}_0^+$ *is a Mixture of Truncated Exponentials potential (MTE potential) if for each fixed value* $\mathbf{y} \in \Omega_{\mathbf{Y}}$ *of the discrete variables* $\mathbf{Y}$, *the potential over the continuous variables* $\mathbf{Z}$ *is defined as:*

$$f(\mathbf{z}) = a_0 + \sum_{i=1}^{m} a_i \exp\left\{\sum_{j=1}^{c} b_i^{(j)} z_j\right\} \tag{1}$$

for all $\mathbf{z} \in \Omega_{\mathbf{Z}}$, *where* a_i, $i = 0, \ldots, m$ *and* $b_i^{(j)}$, $i = 1, \ldots, m$, $j = 1, \ldots, c$ *are real numbers. We also say that f is an MTE potential if there is a partition* $D_1, \ldots, D_k$ *of* $\Omega_{\mathbf{Z}}$ *into hypercubes and in each* D_i, *f is defined as in Eq. (1).*

An MTE potential f is an *MTE density* if $\sum_{\mathbf{y} \in \Omega_{\mathbf{Y}}} \int_{\Omega_{\mathbf{Z}}} f(\mathbf{y}, \mathbf{z}) d\mathbf{z} = 1$. A *conditional MTE density* can be specified by dividing the domain of the conditioning variables and giving an MTE density for the conditioned variable for each configuration of splits of the other variables. An example of conditional MTE density for a continuous variable Y given a continuous variable X is

$$f(y|x) = \begin{cases} 1.26 - 1.15e^{0.006y} & \text{if } 0.4 \leq x < 5, \ 0 \leq y < 13 \ , \\ 1.18 - 1.16e^{0.0002y} & \text{if } 0.4 \leq x < 5, \ 13 \leq y < 43 \ , \\ 0.07 - 0.03e^{-0.4y} + 0.0001e^{0.0004y} & \text{if } 5 \leq x < 19, \ 0 \leq y < 5 \ , \\ -0.99 + 1.03e^{0.001y} & \text{if } 5 \leq x < 19, \ 5 \leq y < 43 \ . \end{cases}$$

In this work we follow the approach in [7], where a 5-parameter MTE is fitted to each split of the support of the variable, which means that in each split there will be 5 parameters to be estimated from data: $f(x) = a_0 + a_1 e^{a_2 x} + a_3 e^{a_4 x}$, $\alpha < x < \beta$. As explained in [7], the reason to use the 5-parameter MTE is that it has shown its ability to fit the most common distributions accurately, while the model complexity and the number of parameters to estimate is low [1]. The estimation procedure is described in [11].

The general procedure for obtaining a regression model is, therefore, to choose one of the structures mentioned in section 2 and to estimate the corresponding conditional distributions using 5-parameter MTEs. Once the model is constructed, it can be used to predict the value of the response variable given that the values of the explanatory variables are observed. The forecasting is carried out by computing the posterior distribution of the response variable given the observed values for the others. A numerical prediction can be obtained from the posterior distribution, through its mean or its median. The posterior distribution can be computed using the algorithm introduced in [10].

4   Filtering the Explanatory Variables

It is a well known fact in classification and regression that, in general, it is not true that including more variables increases the accuracy of the model, because unnecessary may provide noise to other variables in the model and increase in the number of parameters that need to be determined from the data.

The problem of selecting the independent variables to be included in the model was addressed in [7] following a *filter-wrapper* approach described in [9]. It consists of first ordering the independent variables according to a measure of association with respect to the class (more precisely, the *mutual information* is used) and then try to include the independent variables one by one according to the initial ranking, whenever the inclusion of a new variable increases the accuracy of the preceding model. The accuracy of the model is measured by the *root mean squared error* between the actual values of the response variable and those ones predicted by the model for the records in a test database. If we call $\hat{y}_1, \ldots, \hat{y}_n$ the corresponding estimates provided by the model, the root mean squared error is obtained by

$$rmse = \sqrt{\frac{1}{n} \sum_{i=1}^{n} (y_i - \hat{y}_i)^2} \ . \tag{2}$$

5   The TAN Regression Model

The application of the TAN model to regression was proposed in [2]. A TAN for regression is a Bayesian network where the response variable is the root and the explanatory variables conform a directed tree. Besides, there is an arc from the root to all of the other variables (see Fig. 1(b)).

There are several possible TAN structures for a given set of variables. Usually, the dependence structure among the explanatory variables is obtained by constructing a tree of maximum weight, using some measure of association between variables for labelling the arcs. A sensible choice for this measure is the mutual information conditional on the response variable [4,2]. The conditional mutual information between two explanatory variables X_i and X_j given Y is

$$I(X_i, X_j|Y) = \iiint f(x_i, x_j, y) \log \frac{f(x_i, x_j|y)}{f(x_i|y)f(x_j|y)} dx_i dx_j dy \; . \tag{3}$$

If we consider MTE densities, the integral above cannot be obtained in closed form, and therefore it has to be approximated. The solution proposed in [2], consists of estimating it, from a sample of size m drawn from the joint distribution of X_i, X_j and Y, as

$$\hat{I}(X_i, X_j|Y) = \frac{1}{m} \sum_{k=1}^{m} \left(\log f(X_i^{(k)}|X_j^{(k)}, Y^{(k)}) - \log f(X_i^{(k)}|Y^{(k)}) \right) \tag{4}$$

As we are not using the exact value of the mutual information, it is sensible to compute a bound on the sample size m that should be used to reach some preset accuracy. Assume, for instance, that we want to estimate I with an error lower than $\epsilon > 0$ with probability not lower than δ, that is, $P\{|\hat{I} - I| < \epsilon\} \geq \delta$. Using this expression, we can find a bound for m using Tchebyshev's inequality:

$$P\{|\hat{I} - I| < \epsilon\} \geq 1 - \frac{\text{Var}(\hat{I})}{\epsilon^2} \geq \delta \; . \tag{5}$$

We only need to relate m with $\text{Var}(\hat{I})$, which is $\text{Var}(\hat{I}) = \frac{1}{m}\text{Var}(\log f(X_i|X_j, Y) - \log f(X_i|Y))$. Therefore, $\text{Var}(\hat{I})$ depends on the discrepancy between $f(X_i|X_j, Y)$ and $f(X_i|Y)$. As these distributions are unknown beforehand, we will compute a bound for m using two fixed distributions with very different shape, in order to simulate a case of extreme discrepancy. If we choose $f(x_i|x_j, y) = ae^{-x_i}$ and $f(x_i|y) = be^x$, with $\alpha < x_i < \beta$ and a, b normalisation constants, we find that

$$\text{Var}(\hat{I}) = \frac{1}{m}\text{Var}\left(\log ae^{-x_i} - \log be^{x_i}\right) = \frac{1}{m}\text{Var}\left((\log a) - x_i - (\log b) - x_i\right)$$

$$= \frac{1}{m}\text{Var}(-2X_i) = \frac{4}{m}\text{Var}(X_i) \; .$$

Plugging this into Eq. (5), we obtain $1 - \frac{\text{Var}(\hat{I})}{\epsilon^2} \geq \delta \Rightarrow 1 - \frac{4\text{Var}(X_i)}{m\epsilon^2} \geq \delta \Rightarrow$ $m \geq \frac{4\text{Var}(X_i)}{(1-\delta)\epsilon^2}$. If we assume, for simplicity, that X_i follows a distribution with standard deviation 1, and set $\delta = 0.9$ and $\epsilon = 0.1$, we obtain $m \geq \frac{4}{0.1 \times 0.01} = 4000$. Thus, in all the experiments described in this work we have used a sample of size $m = 4000$.

The TAN regression model described in [2] incorporate all the explanatory variables available in the database from which it is learnt. Here we propose

---

Algorithm 1. Selective MTE-TAN regression model

Input: Variables $X_1, \ldots, X_n, Y$ and a database D for variables $X_1, \ldots, X_n, Y$.
Output: Selective TAN regression model for variable Y.
1 **for** $i \leftarrow 1$ to n Compute $\hat{I}(X_i, Y)$.
2 Let $X_{(1)}, \ldots, X_{(n)}$ a decreasing order of the independent variables according to $\hat{I}(X_i, Y)$.
3 Divide D into two sets: D_l, for learning the model, and D_t for testing its accuracy.
4 Let M be a TAN with variables Y and $X_{(1)}$ learnt from D_l using the algorithm in [2].
5 Let $rmse(M)$ the estimated accuracy of model M using D_t.
6 **for** $i \leftarrow 2$ to n **do**
7 $\quad$ Let M_1 be the TAN regression model for the variables in M and $X_{(i)}$.
8 $\quad$ Let $rmse(M_1)$ be the estimated accuracy of model M_1 using D_t.
9 $\quad$ **if** $(rmse(M_1) \leq rmse(M))$ $M \leftarrow M_1$.
10 **end**
11 **return** M.

---

to improve it by introducing a variable selection scheme analogous to the one used by the selective naive Bayes [7], described in section 4. The steps for its construction are presented in Algorithm 1. The main idea is to start with a model containing the response variable and one explanatory variable, which is the node with the highest mutual information with the dependent variable. Afterwards, the rest of the variables are included in the model in sequence, according to their mutual information with Y. In each step, if the included variable increases the accuracy of the model, it is kept. Otherwise, it is discarded.

6 Forest Augmented Naive Bayes Regression Model

A problem of the TAN model is that some of the introduced links between explanatory variables may not be necessary. This fact was pointed out in [5] within the context of classification problems, proposing to discard unnecessary links, obtaining a structure as the one displayed in Fig. 2, where, instead of a tree, the features conform a forest of directed trees. The resulting model is called a *forest augmented naive Bayes (FAN)*. We will consider in this section how to construct a regression model following the FAN methodology. The first step is to create a *forest of maximum weight* with an input paremeter k that represents

---

Algorithm 2. MTE-FAN regression model

Input   : A database D with variables $X_1, \ldots, X_n, Y$ and an integer value $k \in [1, n-2]$, that represents the number of links that will contain the maximum spanning forest
Output: A FAN model with root variable Y and features $X_1, \ldots, X_n$, with joint distribution of class MTE.
1 Construct a complete graph C with nodes $X_1, \ldots, X_n$.
2 Label each link (X_i, X_j) with $\hat{I}(X_i, X_j | Y)$.
3 Let $\mathcal{F}$ be the maximum spanning forest obtained from C with exactly k links and using the method described in [5].
4 For each connected component $\mathcal{F}_i \in \mathcal{F}$, choose a root at random and direct the links starting from the root to form a directed tree.
5 Construct a new network $\mathcal{G}$ with nodes $Y, X_1, \ldots, X_n$ and the links computed in each connected component $\mathcal{F}_i$.
6 Insert the links $Y \rightarrow X_i$, $i = 1, \ldots, n$ in $\mathcal{G}$.
7 Estimate a set P of conditional MTE densities for the variables in $\mathcal{G}$.
8 **return** a Bayesian network with structure $\mathcal{G}$ and distributions P.

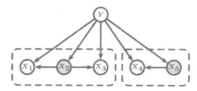

Fig. 2. A *forest augmented naive Bayes* structure with $k = 3$ and 2 forests

the number of links included among the explanatory variables. The construction of each tree inside the forest is carried out as in the TAN. As in the construction of the TAN, the links are labeled with the conditional mutual information when computing the forest of maximum weight. The details are given in Algorithm 2. The selective version of the FAN regression model is totally analogous to the selective TAN. Due to space limitations, we skip the detailed algorithm.

7   Regression Model Based on kDB Structure

Our last proposal consists of extending the kDB structure, already known in classification contexts [12], to regression problems. The kDB structure is obtained by forcing the explanatory variables to conform a directed acyclic graph where each variable has at most k parents besides the response variable. An example can be found in Fig. 3. The method proposed in [12] for obtaining such structure ranks the explanatory variables according to their mutual information with respect to the dependent variable. Then, the variables are inserted in the directed acyclic graph following that rank. The parents of a new variable are selected among those variables already included in the graph, so that the k variables with higher conditional mutual information with the new variable given the response are chosen.

The regression model we propose here is constructed in an analogous way, but estimating the mutual information and the conditional mutual information as described in section 4. The details can be found in algorithm 3. Note that the complexity of constructing a kDB model is much higher than the complexity for NB, TAN and FAN. The complexity is in the selection of the parent of a variable and also in the estimation of the parameters, since their number is much higher than in the other cases. For this reason, we do not propose a selective version

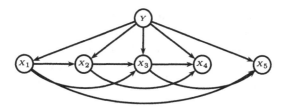

Fig. 3. A sample kDB regression model

Algorithm 3. MTE-kDB regression model

Input: Variables $X_1, \ldots, X_n, Y$ and a database D for them. An integer value k, which is the maximum number of parents allowed.

Output: kDB regression model for variable Y, with a joint distribution of class MTE.

1 Let $\mathcal{G}$ a graph with nodes $Y, X_1, \ldots, X_n$ and a empty set of arcs.
2 Let $X_{(1)}, \ldots, X_{(n)}$ be a decreasing order of the independent variables according to $\hat{I}(X_i, Y)$.
3 $S \leftarrow \{X_{(1)}\}$.
4 **for** $i \leftarrow 2$ *to* n **do**
5 $\quad$ $S \leftarrow S \cup \{X_{(i)}\}$.
6 $\quad$ **for** $j \leftarrow 1$ *to* k **do**
7 $\quad\quad$ Select the variable $Z \in S \setminus Pa(X_{(i)})$ with higher $\hat{I}(X_{(i)}, Z|Y)$.
8 $\quad\quad$ Add the link $Z \rightarrow X_{(i)}$ to $\mathcal{G}$.
9 $\quad$ **end**
10 **end**
11 Insert the links $Y \rightarrow X_i$, $i = 1, \ldots, n$ in $\mathcal{G}$.
12 Estimate a set P of conditional MTE densities for the variables in $\mathcal{G}$.
13 **return** *a Bayesian network with structure $\mathcal{G}$ and distributions P.*

---

of this regression model, since the selection scheme used for the other models is too costly from a computational point of view.

8   Experimental Evaluation

We have implemented all the models proposed in this paper in the Elvira platform, which is available at `leo.ugr.es/elvira`. For testing the models we have chosen a set of benchmark databases borrowed from the UCI and StatLib repositories. A description of the used databases can be found in table 1. In all the cases, we have considered the options of predicting with the mean and the median of the posterior distribution of the dependent variable. Regarding the kDB model, we have restricted the experiments to $k = 2$.

It was shown in [7] that the selective naive Bayes regression model was competitive with the so far considered state-of-the-art in regression problems using graphical models, namely the so-called M5' algorithm [13]. Therefore, we have compared the new models with the NB and the M5' methods. For the M5' we have used the implementation in software Weka. The results of the comparison are shown in table 2, where the values displayed correspond to the root mean squared error for each one of the tested models in the different databases, computed through 10-fold cross validation. The boldfaced numbers represent the best value obtained among all the models, while the underlined ones are the worst.

We have used Friedman's test to compare the experimental results, obtaining that there are not significant differences among the analysed algorithms (p-value of 0.9961). However, a more detailed analysis of the results in table 2, show how in general the more simple models (NB, TAN, FAN) have a better performance than the more complex (2DB). We believe that this is due to increase on the

Table 1. A description of the databases used in the experiments

Database	# records	# Cont. vars.	# Discr. and qualit. vars.
abalone	4176	8	1
bodyfat	251	15	0
boston_housing	452	11	2
cloud	107	6	2
disclosure	661	4	0
halloffame	1340	12	2
mte50	50	3	1
pollution	59	16	0
strikes	624	6	1

Table 2. Results of the experiments in terms of *rmse*

Model	abalone	bodyfat	boston	cloud	disclosure	halloffame	mte50	pollution	strikes
NB(mean)	2.8188	6.5564	6.2449	0.5559	196121.4232	186.3826	1.8695	43.0257	503.5635
NB(med.)	2.6184	6.5880	6.1728	0.5776	792717.1428	187.6512	2.0224	44.0839	561.4105
SNB(mean)	2.5307	5.1977	4.6903	0.5144	93068.5218	160.2282	1.5798	**31.1527**	**438.0894**
SNB(med.)	2.4396	5.2420	4.7857	0.5503	797448.1824	170.3880	1.6564	31.2055	582.9391
TAN(mean)	2.5165	5.7095	6.9826	0.5838	250788.2272	165.3717	2.6251	48.4293	571.9346
TAN(med.)	2.4382	5.8259	6.8512	0.6199	796471.2998	166.5050	2.6718	48.8619	584.9271
STAN(mean)	2.4197	4.5885	4.5601	0.5382	108822.7386	147.2882	**1.5635**	38.1018	447.2259
STAN(med.)	2.3666	**4.5820**	4.3853	0.5656	794381.9068	153.1241	1.6458	36.8456	596.6292
FAN(mean)	2.6069	6.0681	6.5530	0.5939	228881.7789	179.8712	2.0990	43.9893	525.9861
FAN(med.)	2.4908	6.1915	6.5455	0.5957	<u>798458.2283</u>	181.8235	2.2037	44.2489	560.7986
SFAN(mean)	2.4836	4.9123	4.2955	0.5253	97936.0322	150.0201	1.5742	36.3944	449.8657
SFAN(med.)	2.4037	4.9646	4.4376	0.5623	794825.1882	157.6618	1.6707	35.6820	597.7038
2DB(mean)	<u>3.1348</u>	8.2358	<u>8.4179</u>	<u>1.0448</u>	23981.0983	293.8374	2.7460	58.5873	516.2400
2DB(med.)	3.0993	8.2459	8.3241	1.0315	793706.7221	<u>301.4728</u>	<u>2.7598</u>	<u>58.9876</u>	<u>715.0236</u>
M5'	**2.1296**	<u>23.3525</u>	**4.1475**	**0.3764**	**23728.8983**	**35.3697**	2.4718	46.8086	509.1756

number of parameters to estimate from data. Also, the selective versions are usually more accurate than the models including all the variables. The behaviour of the SNB model is remarkable, as it gets the best results in two experiments and is never the worst. M5' also shows a very good performance, obtaining the best results in 5 databases, though in one it is the worst model.

9   Concluding Remarks

In this paper we have analysed the performance of well known Bayesian networks classifiers when applied to regression problems. The experimental analysis shows that all models considered are comparable in terms of accuracy, even with the very robust M5' method. However, in general we would prefer to use a Bayesian network for regression rather than the M5', at least from a modelling point of view. In this way, the regression model could be included in a more general model as long as it is a Bayesian network, and the global model can be used for other purposes different from regression. However, the M5' provides a regression tree, which cannot be used for reasoning about the model it represents. We think that the methods studied in this paper can be improved by considering more elaborate variable selection schemes, and this is our ongoing work now.

References

1. Cobb, B., Shenoy, P.P., Rumí, R.: Approximating probability density functions with mixtures of truncated exponentials. Stat. and Computing 16, 293–308 (2006)
2. Fernández, A., Morales, M., Salmerón, A.: Tree augmented naive Bayes for regression using mixtures of truncated exponentials: Applications to higher education management. In: R. Berthold, M., Shawe-Taylor, J., Lavrač, N. (eds.) IDA 2007. LNCS, vol. 4723, pp. 59–69. Springer, Heidelberg (2007)
3. Frank, E., Trigg, L., Holmes, G., Witten, I.H.: Technical note: Naive Bayes for regression. Machine Learning 41, 5–25 (2000)
4. Friedman, N., Geiger, D., Goldszmidt, M.: Bayesian network classifiers. Machine Learning 29, 131–163 (1997)
5. Lucas, P.: Restricted Bayesian network structure learning. In: Proceedings of the 1st European Workshop on Probabilistic Graphical Models (PGM 2002) (2002)
6. Moral, S., Rumí, R., Salmerón, A.: Mixtures of truncated exponentials in hybrid Bayesian networks. In: Benferhat, S., Besnard, P. (eds.) ECSQARU 2001. LNCS(LNAI), vol. 2143, pp. 135–143. Springer, Heidelberg (2001)
7. Morales, M., Rodríguez, C., Salmerón, A.: Selective naive Bayes for regression using mixtures of truncated exponentials. International Journal of Uncertainty, Fuzziness and Knowledge Based Systems 15, 697–716 (2007)
8. Pearl, J.: Probabilistic reasoning in intelligent systems. Morgan-Kaufmann, San Francisco (1988)
9. Ruiz, R., Riquelme, J., Aguilar-Ruiz, J.S.: Incremental wrapper-based gene selection from microarray data for cancer classification. Pattern Recognition 39, 2383–2392 (2006)
10. Rumí, R., Salmerón, A.: Approximate probability propagation with mixtures of truncated exponentials. Int. Jnl. of Approximate Reasoning 45, 191–210 (2007)
11. Rumí, R., Salmerón, A., Moral, S.: Estimating mixtures of truncated exponentials in hybrid Bayesian networks. Test 15, 397–421 (2006)
12. Sahami, M.: Learning limited dependence Bayesian classifiers. In: Second International Conference on Knowledge Discovery in Databases, pp. 335–338 (1996)
13. Wang, Y., Witten, I.H.: Induction of model trees for predicting continuous cases. In: Procs. of the Poster Papers of the European Conf. on Machine Learning, pp. 128–137 (1997)

Transfer Learning for Bayesian Networks

Roger Luis, L. Enrique Sucar, and Eduardo F. Morales

National Institute of Astrophysics, Optics and Electronics,
Computer Science Department,
Luis Enrique Erro 1, 72840 Tonantzintla, México
{roger_luve,esucar,emorales}@inaoep.mx
http://ccc.inaoep.mx

Abstract. In several domains it is common to have data from different, but closely related problems. For instance, in manufacturing many
products follow the same industrial process but with different conditions;
or in industrial diagnosis, where there is equipment with similar specifications. In these cases, it is common to have plenty of data for some
scenarios but very little for other. In order to learn accurate models
for rare cases, it is desirable to use data and knowledge from similar
cases; a technique known as "transfer learning". In this paper, we propose a transfer learning method for Bayesian networks, that considers
both, structure and parameter learning. For structure learning, we use
conditional independence tests, by combining measures from the target
domain with those obtained from one or more auxiliary domains, using a
weighted sum of the conditional independence measures. For parameter
learning, we compared two techniques for probability aggregation that
combine probabilities estimated from the target domain with those obtained from the auxiliary data. To validate our approach, we used three
Bayesian networks models that are commonly used for evaluating learning techniques, and generated variants of each model by changing the
structure as well as the parameters. We then learned one of the variants with a small data set and combined it with information from the
other variants. The experimental results show a significant improvement
in terms of structure and parameters when we transfer knowledge from
similar problems.

1 Introduction

For many machine learning applications, it is assumed that a sufficiently
large data set is available from which a reliable model can be induced. In some
domains, however, it is difficult to gather enough data, for instance, in manufacturing some products are rarely produced. Experts, when confronted with a
problem in a novel domain, use their experience from related domains to solve the
problem. Recently, there has been an increasing interest in the machine learning
community for using data from related domains, in particular when the available
data is not enough [2,11,1], an approach known as *transfer learning*. However,
this has not been explored for learning Bayesian networks. In this paper we
propose transfer learning for Bayesian networks.

H. Geffner et al. (Eds.): IBERAMIA 2008, LNAI 5290, pp. 93–102, 2008.

Learning a Bayesian network (BN) involves two main aspects: structure learning and parameter learning. Our structure learning algorithm combines the dependency measure obtained from data in the target domain, with those obtained from data in the auxiliary domains. We propose a combination function that takes into account the consistency between these measures, based on a variant of the PC algorithm [9].

The parameter learning algorithm uses an aggregation process, combining the parameters estimated from the target domain, with those estimated from the auxiliary data. Based on previous linear combination techniques, we propose two variants: (i) Distance–based linear pool (DBLP), which takes into account the distance of the auxiliary parameters to the target parameters, and (ii) Local linear pool (LoLP), which only includes auxiliary parameters that are *close* to the target one, weighted by the amount of data in each auxiliary domain. In the experiments we compare both methods, and also the basic linear pool as a baseline.

We evaluated experimentally the structure and parameter transfer learning techniques and compared the results vs. using only the data from the target domain. For this we considered 3 BNs commonly used for benchmarking learning algorithms (Alarm, Boblo and Insurance), and generated auxiliary models by changing the structure and parameters of the original model. We generated data from the original net and its variants, and then tested our method by combining these data sets. We evaluated both, the structure (in terms of edit distance) and parameters (in terms of the average square error), comparing the models obtained against the original model. Both aspects, structure and parameters, show a significant improvement when the amount of data for the target network is *small*. Also, the amount of improvement increases as the size of the auxiliary data increases. These results indicate that transfer learning can be a very useful approach for learning BNs.

The paper is structured as follows. Section 2 provides an overview of learning techniques for Bayesian networks. Section 3 describes relevant related work. Sections 4 and 5 introduce the structure and the parameter learning algorithms, respectively. The experiments and results are presented in Section 6. Finally, conclusions and future research directions are given in Section 7.

2   Learning Bayesian Networks

A Bayesian network (BN) [7] represents the joint distribution of a set of n (discrete) variables, $x_1, x_2, \ldots, x_n$, as a directed acyclic graph and a set of conditional probability tables (CPTs). Each node, that corresponds to a variable, has an associated CPT that contains the probability of each state of the variable given its parents in the graph. The structure of the network implies a set of conditional independence assertions, which give its power to this representation.

Learning a BN includes two aspects: learning the structure and learning the parameters. When the structure is known, parameter learning consists on estimating the CPTs from the data. For structure learning there are two main types of methods: (i) search and score, and (ii) conditional independence tests. The first class of methods [3] perform a heuristic search over the space of network structures, starting for some initial structure, and generating variation of the structure at each step. The *best* structure is selected based on a score that measures how well the model represents the data, common scores are BIC [3] and MDL [5]. The second class of methods are based on testing conditional independence between variables, and in this way adding or deleting arcs in the graph. A popular method of this type is the PC algorithm [9].

The PC algorithm starts from a fully connected undirected graph, and measures conditional independence of each pair of variables given some subset of the other variables, using the conditional cross entropy measure. If this measure is below a limit set according to certain confidence level, the arc between the pair of variables is eliminated. These tests are iterated until no more arcs can be eliminated. The direction of the remaining arcs are set based on conditional independence tests between variable triplets.

Both structure learning methods, including their variants, require *enough* data to produce accurate results. For instance, the PC algorithm assumes that there is sufficient data for accurate statistical tests; and the scores such as BIC and MDL require also a representative data set to provide good estimates.

3   Related Approaches

An alternative to compensate for the lack of data is to incorporate expert knowledge. A recent approach in this direction is proposed in [8], and considers the combination of multiple experts. They developed a Bayesian approach in which the knowledge of several experts is encoded as the prior distribution of possible structures, and the data is used to refine this structure and learn the parameters. The expert knowledge is represented as a "meta" Bayesian network, where the expert assertions are codified as the probability that an arc exists (and its direction) between two variables. In this way, the experts' knowledge is used to obtain a probability distribution over structures. The *best* structure is obtained by using a hill–climbing search method. Then, the parameters for this structure are estimated from data. In our work, we only use data and we do not include expert knowledge. In their work they combine several "weak" experts to obtain, in principle, a "strong" model; while we transfer knowledge (based on data) from a strong model(s) to improve a weak one.

Other work [6] considers the problem of learning Bayesian nets structures for related tasks. They consider that there are k data sets for related problems, and they propose a score and search method to learn simultaneously the BNs structures, one for each task. Assuming that the parameters of the different nets are independent, they define the joint probability distribution of the k structures, given the k data sets. The prior is defined such that it penalizes structures that are different for each other. Based on this score, they define a greedy search algorithms to find the best structures, where a new configuration is obtained by adding/deleting/reversing links for each structure. In contrast to this approach, our proposal is based on independence tests that are obtained separately for each data set, and then combined, resulting in a simpler and more efficient method. Again, the goal is different, we use data from one domain to improve the model in other, related domain; while they learn simultaneously the models for different problems. Our approach is divided into two phases, structure learning (Section 4) and parameter learning (Section 5), as described below.

4   Structure Learning

In this paper we propose an algorithm for structure learning of BN that incorporates information from auxiliary data sets in related domains, implementing a knowledge transfer approach based on dependency tests. The method can be seen as an extension of the PC algorithm for learning a BN when we have a small data set, and auxiliary data from related problems. Let us assume that there is a domain of interest with a *small* data set, D_0; and n larger data sets, $D_1, \ldots, D_n$, from auxiliary domains. The set of variables is the same for all the domains, $X_1, \ldots, X_m$. This is a reasonable assumption for manufacturing process, such as steel tube production, where each tube follows the same manufacturing process but with different furnace conditions or chemical components. As future work we will explore how to combine data with different, although similar, sets of variables.

Associated with the domain of interest there is a BN model, BN_0, with structure G_0 and parameters P_0. Then the problem is to obtain BN_0 from $D_0, D_1, \ldots, D_n$ so that it approximates the model that we will obtain if we had a *large* data set D_0. We start by learning the structure of the BN.

Following the PC algorithm we start with a fully connected undirected graph, and measure conditional independence values of each pair of variables given some subset of the other variables, using the conditional cross entropy measure. We obtain a set of measures for each pair of variables in the target domain, I_0, and in a similar way for each of the auxiliary domains, $I_1, \ldots, I_n$. Then, we combine these measures to build the structure for the target domain, G_0.

Before we see how we combine the results from the independency tests, we define a confidence measure for these tests. The cross entropy measure used in the PC algorithm depends on the size of the data set; it can be shown that the error of this test is asymptotically proportional to $logN/N$, where N is the size of the data set [10]. Based on this, we define the following function to estimate the confidence of the independency test between two variables X and Y given the conditioning set S:

$$\alpha(X, Y \mid S) = 1 - (logN/2 \times N) \times T \qquad (1)$$

where $T = |X| \times |Y| \times |S|$. If the difference becomes negative, we set $\alpha = 0.005$. This function is proportional to the confidence of the test (inversely proportional to the size of the data set). We use this term to quantify the independency measures for the target and auxiliary data, before we combine them.

First we estimate how similar are the independency tests of each auxiliary data set with the target domain. The most similar domain is selected, say I_j. Then we combine the independence measures of this domain with those of the target domain using the following equation:

$$I_c(X, Y|S) = sgn(I_0(X, Y|S)) \times \alpha_0(X, Y|S) + w \times sgn(I_j(X, Y|S)) \times \alpha_j(X, Y|S)$$
(2)

where $sgn(I)$ is $+1$ if the independence test is positive (the variables are independent) and -1 otherwise. w is 1 if the result of the test is the same for the auxiliary data and the target data, 0.5 otherwise. Finally we use the results of the combined independency measure (I_c) to build the structure of the BN.

For efficiency reasons we currently restrict the conditioning set S to dimension one. Even with this restriction we obtain good results as described in the experiments. Once we have the structure of the model, we estimate the parameters also using the information from the auxiliary domains.

5 Parameter Learning

Given a Bayesian network structure, we need to specify all the conditional probability tables. The idea in this paper is to fill all the conditional probability tables using aggregation functions between several sources. There are several cases to consider when we want to combine conditional probabilities from different Bayesian networks:

- Combine CPTs that have the same variables, i.e., the same substructure. This is the simplest case and we do not need to do any transformation in the CPTs to apply an aggregation function.
- Combine CPTs with more parents in the auxiliary substructures. In this case we can marginalize over the additional variable to obtain the required conditional probability value in the target substructure. E.g., if we want to combine $P(X|Y, Z)$ of the target network with $P(X|Y, Z, W)$ of an auxiliary network, we can obtain $P(X|Y, Z)$ from the auxiliary substructure by marginalizing over W, i.e., $P(X|Y, Z) = \sum_i P(X|Y, Z, W_i)P(W_i)$.
- Combine CPTs with less parents in the auxiliary substructure. In this case, we can duplicate the CPTs of the auxiliary substructure for all the values of the additional variable in the target network.

Once we have a set of CPTs in terms of the CPTs of the target network, i.e., involving the same variables, we can proceed to combine them. There are several aggregation functions that have been proposed in the literature. Two commonly used functions are:

- Linear aggregation (lineal pool): a weighted sum of the different conditional probabilities, expressed as follows:

$$P(X) = k \times \sum_{i=1}^{n} w_i P_i(X)$$

where $P_i(X)$ represents the conditional probability of the i-th network in-volving X variables, w_i is the weight associated with that probability and k is a normalization factor.

-   Logarithmic aggregation: a weighted product of the different conditional probabilities, expressed as follows:

$$P(X) = k \times \prod_{i=1}^{n} P_i(X)^{w_i}$$

The associated weight of the conditional probabilities, in our approach, de-pends on the confidence assigned to that probability. We proposed two novel aggregation methods: (i) using a weighted average and (ii) using a weighted average only over similar probabilities.

Our first aggregation method, called DBLP, involves the following steps:

1. Obtain the average probabilities of all the data sets:

$$\overline{P} = \frac{1}{n} \sum_{i=1}^{n} P_i$$

2. Obtain the minimum (d_{min}) and maximum (d_{min}) difference between the probability of the target data set and the above average.
3. Evaluate the new conditional probabilities of the target network as follows:

$$P_{target} = (1 - c_i) \times P_{target} + c_i \times \overline{P}$$

where the aggregation coefficients, c_i, express how much to consider from the CPTs of the other networks. The coefficients c_i basically express the following: if the CPTs of the target network are similar to the average of all the CPTs, then give more weight to the average, otherwise give more weight to the target CPT. This is expressed as follows:

$$c_i = (d_i - d_{min}) \times \left(\frac{c_{max} - c_{min}}{d_{max} - d_{min}} \right) + c_{min}$$

where c_{max} and c_{min} are parameters to indicate how close we want to con-sider the influence of the other CPTs. In our case we used $c_{max} = 0.75$ and $c_{min} = 0.25$.

The idea in our other aggregation function, called LoLP, is to use only the most similar or local probabilities and weight them according to the amount of data used in the target data set. This strategy has the following steps:

1. Obtain the average of the probabilities of the large data sets, but only be-tween the most similar probabilities, in our case, those that are within the difference between the target probability and the overall average probability:

$$\overline{P}_{local} = \frac{1}{n} \sum_{i=1}^{n} P_i \ \forall P_i \ \text{s.t.} \ P_i \in \{P_{target} \pm (P_{target} - \overline{P})\}$$

2. Obtain the new conditional probabilities of the target network as follows:

$$P_{target} = (1 - e_i) \times P_{target} + e_i \times \overline{P}_{local}$$

where e_i represents how much error we can expect from the CPTs.

$$e_i = \begin{cases} 1 - \frac{log(c_f)}{c_f} & \text{if } c_f \geq 3 \\ 1 - \frac{c_f \times log(3)}{3} & \text{if } c_f < 3 \end{cases}$$

where $c_f = \frac{N}{T_{i,j} \times 2}$ gives us a confidence value over the CPTs, that depends on $T_{i,j}$, the size of the CPT (number of possible values) and on N, the number of cases.

6 Experiments

The aim of the experiments is to show that by considering additional data sets from related problems it is possible to improve the performance of a model constructed with a small data set.

We consider in the experiments three commonly used data sets for evaluating Bayesian networks, namely, *Alarm, Boblo* and *Insurance*. Table 1 provides a short description of them.

Table 1. Description of the data sets used in the experiments

Name	Description	Num. Attrib.
Alarm	Dataset in medical diagnosis for monitoring patients in intensive care units	37
Boblo	Data to identify cattle using blood type information	23
Insurance	Data used to classify insurance policies	27

We perform two main types of experiments to show the improvements in the structure/parameter learning algorithms when information from related problems is taken into account. The original data set is taken as our target network. We first build a Bayesian network with all the data using the PC algorithm as implemented in Elvira [4] with a 90% of significance value. We created new related problems by changing the original network and introducing Gaussian noise into the CPTs. We deleted links from the original network and altered the CPTs by introducing Gaussian noise with mean = 0 and different values of standard deviation. These altered networks are used as our auxiliary networks to try to reproduce the original network using only a subset of the original data. We created two related networks: (i) a similar network by randomly adding 5% of the links followed by randomly deleting 5% of the links and then introducing 5% of noise into the CPTs by multiplying them by a random noise, and (ii) a less similar network by adding and deleting 20% of the links and introducing 20% of

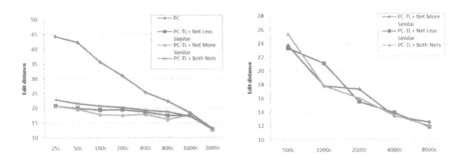

Fig. 1. Comparison between PC and PC-TL considering different number of cases for the Alarm data set with two auxiliary data sets. With increasing number of cases of the target network (left) and with increasing number of cases on the auxiliary networks (right).

noise into the CPTs. All the experiments were repeated 15 times and the figures show only the average values.

Figure 1 shows to the left, the behavior of the structure learning algorithm (PC-TL) considering auxiliary data sets against PC as more cases are considered from the the Alarm data set. The number of examples from the auxiliary data sets is fixed to 1,000. The figure on the right shows the behavior of the structure learning algorithm (PC-TL) considering auxiliary data sets against PC as more cases are considered from the auxiliary data set. The number of examples from the target data set is fixed to 100. Similarly the results for the Boblo data set are shown in Figure 2. Due to space limitations we do not present all the results from all the data sets, but they all show similar behavior.

From the figures it can be seen the expected behavior. The proposed approach performs better than PC, specially with small data sets, and they tend to converge to the same results as we increase the size of the training data set. Additional tests are required to observe how the algorithm degrades with very different data sets.

Similarly, we performed experiments for the parameter learning algorithms. Figure 3 shows a comparison between the errors in the CPTs from the conditional probabilities constructed only with the target data (Base), with the linear aggregation algorithm (LP) and with two proposed algorithms (DBLP and LoLP). The figure to the left shows the behavior of the algorithms when increasing the number of data of the target network. The figure to the right shows the behavior with an increasing number of data on the auxiliary data sets. Here, the number of examples from the target data set is fixed to 100.

From the figures we can see that in general the proposed algorithms perform better than the base case, so the use of additional data sets can also improve the parameters of the Bayesian networks. There is however, a very slight improvement over the lineal aggregation approach. As future work we will study more carefully the proposed aggregation functions to try to obtain bigger improvements.

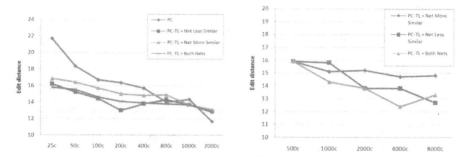

Fig. 2. Comparison between PC and PC-TL considering different number of cases for the Boblo data set with two auxiliary data sets. With increasing number of cases of the target network (left) and with increasing number of cases on the auxiliary networks (right).

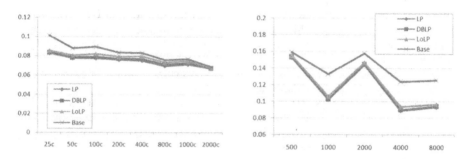

Fig. 3. Comparison between parameter learning considering different number of cases for the Alarm data set with two auxiliary data sets. Increasing the number of cases from the target data set (left) and increasing the number of cases of the auxiliary data sets (right).

7   Conclusions and Future Work

In this paper we have presented three algorithms for transfer learning in Bayesian networks, one for structure learning and two for parameter learning. The idea behind this research is to use information from related data sets in order to improve the performance of networks constructed with small data sets. This is common is several domains, where there can be rare cases, that nevertheless share some similarities with more common cases. From the experiments it is shown that using additional information can improve the accuracy of the constructed model. As future work, we plan to apply this technique to a manufacturing problem that originate the ideas developed in this work. We will also study the effect of increasingly dissimilar databases in the performance of the algorithms.

Acknowledgments

This work was supported in part by CONACyT, project 47968.

References

1. Baxter, J.: A bayesian/information theoretic model of learning to learn via multiple task sampling. Machine Learning 28(1), 7–39 (1997)
2. Caruana, R.: Multitask learning. Machine Learning 28(1), 41–75 (1997)
3. Cooper, G., Herskovitz, E.: A bayesian method for the induction of probabilistic networks from data. Machine Learning 9(4), 309–348 (1992)
4. Elvira: Elvira: An environment for creating and using probabilistic graphical models. In: Gámez, J.A., Salmerón, A. (eds.) First European Workshop on Probabilistic Graphical Models (2002)
5. Lam, W., Bacchus, F.: Learning bayesian belief networks: An approach based on the mdl principle. Computational Intelligence 10, 269–293 (1994)
6. Niculescu-Mizil, A., Caruana, R.: Inductive Transfer for Bayesian Network Structure Learning. In: Marina, M., Shen, X. (eds.) Proceedings of the 11th International Conference on AI and Statistics (AISTATS 2007), vol. 2, pp. 339–346 (2007), issn1938-7228
7. Pearl, J.: Probabilistic reasoning in intelligent systems: networks of plausible inference. Morgan Kaufmann, San Francisco (1988)
8. Richardson, M., Domingos, P.: Learning with knowledge from multiple experts. In: Fawcett, T., Mishra, N. (eds.) Proc. of the Twentieth Intl. Machine Learning Conf (ICML 2003), pp. 624–631. AAAI Press, Menlo Park (2003)
9. Spirtes, P., Glymour, C., Scheines, R.: Causation, prediction, and search. Springer, Berlin (1993)
10. Su, J., Zhang, H.: Full bayesian network classifiers. In: Cohen, W.W., Moore, A. (eds.) Proc. Twenty-Third Intl. Machine Lerning Conference (ICML 2006), vol. 148, pp. 897–904. ACM, New York (2006)
11. Thrun, S.: Is learning the n-th thing any easier than learning the first? In: Touretzky, D.S., Mozer, M.C., Hasselmo, M.E. (eds.) Advances in Neural Information Processing Systems, vol. 8, pp. 640–646. The MIT Press, Cambridge (1996)

A Dipolar Competitive Neural Network for Video Segmentation

R.M. Luque[1], D. López-Rodríguez[2], E. Dominguez[1], and E.J. Palomo[1]

[1] Department of Computer Science, University of Málaga, Málaga, Spain
{rmluque,enriqued,ejpalomo}@lcc.uma.es
[2] Department of Applied Mathematics, University of Málaga, Málaga, Spain
dlopez@ctima.uma.es

Abstract. This paper present a video segmentation method which separate pixels corresponding to foreground from those corresponding to background. The proposed background model consists of a competitive neural network based on dipoles, which is used to classify the pixels as background or foreground. Using this kind of neural networks permits an easy hardware implementation to achieve a real time processing with good results. The dipolar representation is designed to deal with the problem of estimating the directionality of data. Experimental results are provided by using the standard PETS dataset and compared with the mixture of Gaussians and background subtraction methods.

1 Introduction

The aim of moving object segmentation is to separate pixels corresponding to foreground from those corresponding to background. This task is complex by the increasing resolution of video sequences, continuing advances in the video capture and transmission technology.

The process of background modeling by comparison with the frames of the sequence is often referred to as background subtraction. These methods are widely exploited in videos for moving object detection. Adaptive models are typically used by averaging the images over time [1,2,3] creating a background approximation. While these method are effective in situations where objects move continuously, they are not robust in scenes with many moving objects, particularly if they move slowly.

Wren et al. [4] used a multiclass statistical representation based on Gaussian distributions, in which the background model is a single Gaussian per pixel. A modified version modeling each pixel as a mixture of Gaussians is proposed by Stauffer and Grimson [5]. This statistical approach is robust in scenes with many moving objects and lighting changes, and it is one of the techniques most cited in the literature.

Several steps are required for a typical video surveillance system to reach the objective. At first, a video object segmentation method is required to obtain the objects in motion of the stream. Subsequently, a tracking algorithm is applied to identify the objects in several frames of the sequence. A matching between each blob (or set of blobs) and an object previously recognized has to be done. Finally, an algorithm to detect the object behavior it is used to understand and analyze everything what it is happening in

H. Geffner et al. (Eds.): IBERAMIA 2008, LNAI 5290, pp. 103–112, 2008.

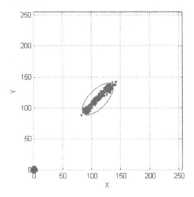

Fig. 1. A dipole is able to capture the intrinsic directionality of a set of data points

a scene. Therefore, low time complexity is required at the object segmentation stage in order to carry out the entire process in real time.

In this work an unsupervised competitive neural network is proposed for object segmentation in real time. The proposed neural approach is based on a dipolar representation in order to achieve a better representation of data since it is able to capture the intrinsic directionality of data at a low computational cost. Although the mixture of Gaussians model can obtain the directionality of data, the process of computing the covariance matrix is highly expensive from the computational point of view. Thus, in practice, it is usually assumed the independence of the RGB components, then all information relative to directionality is lost in this simplified model [6].

Dipolar competitive neural networks (DCN) [7] differ from traditional competitive networks [8,9,10] in that every prototype w_j is now represented by a segment formed of two distinct vectors $w_j^{(1)}$ and $w_j^{(2)}$. These two vectors represent the end-points of a segment in the input space. Note that $w_j^{(1)}$ and $w_j^{(2)}$ can also be interpreted as the two foci of an ellipsoid. The classical competitive learning rule can be applied to this model to make this segment adjust to data, obtaining the directionality of patterns activating that dipole (that is, patterns whose nearest dipole is the given one), see Fig. 1.

2   A Neural Model for Color Video Segmentation

In this work, a classification task is locally performed, for each pixel in the video sequence, in parallel. The classification algorithm used is a competitive network based on dipoles.

Let us consider a DCN for each pixel in the video. Each of these networks models the RGB space associated to the corresponding pixel, that is, training patterns are formed by the three values (R,G,B) for the pixel.

The target of the network is to classify the input pattern (for the specified pixel) at each frame as foreground or background. It can be noted that our model allows the use of many neurons (also called dipoles in this particular case) to represent multimodal classes. In our case, three neurons have been used to model the scene including both background and foreground. The B most activated neurons are used to model the background, whereas the rest of neurons correspond to foreground objects. This value B is computed as the amount of neurons whose number of activations $n_{a_1}, \ldots, n_{a_B}$ verify $\frac{n_{a_1} + \ldots + n_{a_B}}{N} > T$ for a prefixed threshold T, where N is the total number of activations of all neurons, as proposed in [6]. In this work, we have used $T = 0.7$.

The use of dipoles has an additional advantage for the classification task: the directionality of data is learned, thus obtaining extra information about the shape of clusters.

A detailed description of this model is presented in the next two subsections. There, we study the activation of the winning dipole by defining an adequate synaptic potential for each dipole, and the learning rule used to update each of the foci of the ellipsoids.

2.1   Definition of Synaptic Potentials

The computation of the synaptic potential received by each dipole is based on a crisp-fuzzy hybrid neighborhood, which enables to define certain mechanisms that improve the performance of the neural model.

For each neuron, there is a value r_j, defining the crisp neighborhood of the corresponding prototype $w_j = (w_j^{(1)}, w_j^{(2)})$: $\mathcal{N}_j = \{x : \|x - w_j^{(1)}\| + \|x - w_j^{(2)}\| \leq 2r_j\}$. This definition corresponds to an ellipsoid whose foci are $w_j^{(1)}$ and $w_j^{(2)}$ and such that the length of the main semi-axis is r_j. Note that the main direction of the ellipsoid corresponds to the direction of the dipole $w_j = (w_j^{(1)}, w_j^{(2)})$.

The fuzzy neighborhood of neuron j is given by a membership function μ_j defined over points not belonging to $\mathcal{N}_j$, and taking values in the interval $(0, 1)$. Usually, the membership function present in this model is of the form:

$$\mu_j(x) = e^{-k_j \left(\|x - w_j^{(1)}\| + \|x - w_j^{(2)}\| - 2r_j \right)}, \quad \text{for } x \notin \mathcal{N}_j \tag{1}$$

The items above provide us with a reasonable way to select the winning dipole for each input pattern, which is the one to be updated at the current iteration, after the input pattern is received by the network. We define the synaptic potential received by dipole j when pattern x is presented to the network as $h_j(x) = 1$ if $x \in \mathcal{N}_j$ and $h_j(x) = \mu_j(x)$ otherwise.

The winning dipole (with index denoted as $q(x)$) is the one receiving the maximum synaptic potential: $h_{q(x)} = \max_j h_j(x)$.

To break ties (more common when two crisp neighborhoods, corresponding to different dipoles, are overlapped), we consider the dipole which has been activated more times as the winning dipole. That is, if, for every j, n_j counts the number of times dipole j has been winner, and pattern x belongs to $\mathcal{N}_{j_1} \cap \mathcal{N}_{j_2}$ (overlapped neighborhoods), then $q(x)$ is defined as k for which $n_k = \max\{n_{j_1}, n_{j_2}\}$. In case $n_{j_1} = n_{j_2}$, a random dipole in $\{j_1, j_2\}$ is selected as winner.

The use of this hybrid neighborhood allows us to better assign an input pattern to a class:

- If input pattern x belongs to $\mathcal{N}_j$, the network assumes that the best matching class for x is the associated to dipole w_j.

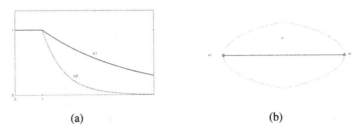

(a)   (b)

Fig. 2. (a) Comparison between the synaptic potentials h_1 and h_2 of two dipoles, such that $k_2 > k_1$, supposing $r_1 = r_2 = r$. (b) R represents the area of the input space well-represented by the dipole.

– If input pattern x does not belong to any crisp neighborhood, its most likely class is represented by the dipole achieving the maximum value of the membership function for this particular input.

The value of the parameter k_j is related to the slope of the function. The higher its value, the higher the slope is. For a great value of k_j, the fuzzy neighborhood of w_j will be more concentrated around $\mathcal{N}_j$. The effect (on the corresponding h_j) of increasing the value of k_j is shown in Fig. 2(a).

With the help of this parameter, we can model a mechanism of consciousness, necessary to avoid dead neurons. When a neuron is activated and updated many times, its crisp neighborhood usually englobes a very high percentage of the patterns associated to the neuron. In this case, patterns outside this neighborhood are not likely to belong to the corresponding category. Thus, the membership function of the fuzzy neighborhood should be sharp, with a high slope.

If a dipole, j, is rarely activated, then the ellipsoid $\mathcal{N}_j$ does not represent accurately the patterns associated to the dipole. Thus, the membership associated to the fuzzy neighborhood should express the actual fuzziness present in the data and therefore assign higher values to patterns outside $\mathcal{N}_j$.

From all this we can deduce that a good way to define k_j is proportional to the number of times that neuron j has been activated, n_j.

2.2   The Learning Rule

In what follows, let us suppose that the winning dipole is $w = (w^{(1)}, w^{(2)})$.

The purpose of the learning rule described in this section is to make each dipole, and the associated ellipsoid, represent both the location and distortion (with respect to the centroid of the dipole) of its corresponding data as accurately as desired.

Let us denote $R = \{x : \|x - w^{(1)}\|, \|x - w^{(2)}\| < \|w^{(1)} - w^{(2)}\|\}$. R denotes the set of points whose distance to each focus is lower than the distance between foci. A reasonable criterion to determine whether a given data point x is well-represented by the ellipsoid, is that $x \in R$, see Fig. 2(b) for a graphical representation of this situation. In this case, the dipole has just to be adjusted to better represent data location, trying to minimize the distance from x to the dipole centroid $\overline{w} = \frac{w^{(1)} + w^{(2)}}{2}$, $\|x - \overline{w}\|^2$.

The updating scheme in this case, at iteration step t, is therefore:

$$w^{(i)}(t+1) = w^{(i)}(t) + \lambda(x - \overline{w}(t))$$

for $i \in \{1,2\}$, λ being the learning rate parameter. This means that the centroid is updated as follows: $\overline{w}(t+1) = \frac{w^{(1)}(t+1)+w^{(2)}(t+1)}{2} = \overline{w}(t) + \lambda(x - \overline{w}(t))$ that is, the ellipsoid is able to better capture the location of x.

When $x \notin R$, the situation changes. It does not seem reasonable to update the dipole as in the previous case. In this paper, we propose an updating scheme based on how well points activating the dipole are represented by the latter.

To this end, let us define n_{in} as the number of points activating the dipole that belong to R at current iteration. Analogously, n_{out} is the number of points activating the dipole which do not belong to R.

A measure of how well points are represented by the dipole is given by the quotient $\frac{n_{out}}{n_{in}} = \rho$. Given $c \in (0,1]$, we say that the dipole represents accurately the data points activating it if, at least, a $100c\%$ of these points belongs to R, that is, c is the fraction of points activating the dipole and belonging to R. This means that $100(1-c)\%$ of the points does not belong to R, so $\rho \leq \frac{1-c}{c}$. Let us denote $\rho_0 = \frac{1-c}{c}$ the maximum desired value for ρ. Note that c is an user-defined parameter.

Then, there are two cases if $x \notin R$:

- If $\rho > \rho_0$, then there are many data points outside R comparing with the number of points that belong to R, so the dipole does not represent well the dataset. In order to improve this representation, the two foci will be updated towards the input data x, as in the standard competitive learning rule:

$$w^{(i)}(t+1) = w^{(i)}(t) + \lambda(x - w^{(i)}(t))$$

for $i \in \{1,2\}$.
- If $\rho \leq \rho_0$, then points are very well-represent by the ellipsoid, according to our definition. Thus, it suffices to update the focus nearest to x, denoted by $w^{(s(x))}$:

$$w^{(s(x))}(t+1) = w^{(s(x))}(t) + \lambda(x - w^{(s(x))}(t))$$

This transition allows to capture the actual directionality of data associated to the dipole.

This complex updating scheme helps the network to reduce the dispersion of the data points with respect to the dipole centroid.

On the other hand, our main concern is to detect the main directionality of data which is given by the main direction of the dipoles. Empirical studies have revealed an underlying ellipsoidal structure of data in the RGB color space, with a clearly predominant main direction. Since non-principal directions are not of importance in this problem we consider the corresponding semi-axes fixed. Therefore, only r_j, the major semi-axis, is updated accordingly in each step.

3   Improving the Segmentation

In this work, we have studied two improvements of the segmentation process:

Spurious Object Detection. In most real-life situations, some processes, such as compression, decrease the sharpness of the video sequence. For this reason, many objects consisting in a single and separated pixel are detected by segmentation methods (spurious objects). To solve this issue, we propose the use of a post-processing method, which consists in finding those isolated pixels representing objects and marking them as background. After this process, for each of those pixels, the corresponding dipole representing background is updated (by using the proposed learning rule), whereas the dipole which had been updated (representing foreground), returns to its state previous to the processing of the current frame.

Shadow Detection. Objects in motion probably cast shadow on the background, confusing with foreground pixels and interfering the correct detection of the scene objects. In our system, we develop the technique proposed in [11], based on the proportionality property between the shadow and the background in the RGB color space.

With these enhancements, we obtain better segmentation results, as will be shown in next section.

4   Results

In this section a comparison between our proposed neural approach and other techniques mentioned in the literature is done. We use different video sequences obtained from Internet to demonstrate the effectiveness of our algorithm for background subtraction and foreground analysis in a variety of environments. These sequences also present different features, from diverse kind of lighting to distinct objects in motion (people, vehicles) in order to conduct a more comprehensive study of the proposed method. Note that same parameters were used for all scenes.

Figure 3 shows the results obtained after applying the studied techniques. Our DCN model is compared with the mixture of Gaussians model (MoG) [6] and with another typical algorithm of background subtraction [3], consisting of subtracting the processed frame from a background model previously computed. A fixed threshold value has been established to get the objects segmented. In MoG we have set the number of normal distributions to $K = 3$, the mean of each distribution is initially computed as the gray-level value of the corresponding pixel in the first frame of the sequence, and the standard deviation is initialized to 25.

In our neural approach, fine-tuning of the model initial parameters (number of dipoles, learning rates, initial major semi-axis r_j) is made before the segmentation

Table 1. Comparative analysis of the success rate among the studied methods for the sequence observed in Fig. 4

Method	% Matching	% FP	% FN
DCN+	99.6957	0.07068	3.408
DCN	99.4387	0.2895	4.8602
MoG	98.7639	1.0967	1.3939
BS	98.6636	0.28041	30.1686

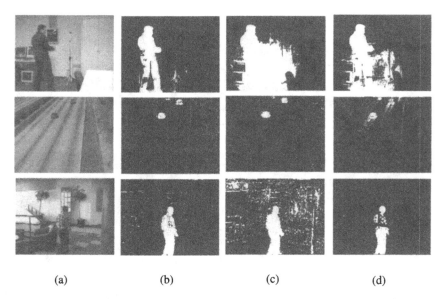

(a)   (b)   (c)   (d)

Fig. 3. Results of applying three segmentation methods to several frames. (a) column shows the capture frames for each scene in raw form; (b) proposed method; (c) mixture of Gaussians method; (d) background subtraction.

process. Three dipoles have been used to model the scene including both background and foreground, although more dipoles can be added for a better representation of multimodal backgrounds. The learning rate is decreased after each frame until stabilizing at a fixed value, while the major semi-axis is initialized to 15. Both the simple model with neighborhoods (DCN) and the extended model (DCN+), in which a mechanism to correcting the model and to avoid spurious pixels is applied, have been tested.

Figure 3 shows an example result on one PETS 2001 (IEEE Performance Evaluation of Tracking and Surveillance Workshops) sequence. A quantitative comparison among the different algorithms is shown in Tables 1 and 2. Three measures have been defined to evaluate the performance of each method. A false positive rate (FP) shows the number of wrong background pixels and a false negative rate (FN) is used to show the number of misleading foreground pixels. The success rate, indicating the accuracy of the corresponding algorithm, is presented in the column labelled '% Matching'. By observing these results, it can be noted that in general, our method gets better segmentation than the rest of analyzed methods, when we compare with a ground truth image. It is remarkable the ability of our neural approach to efficiently adapt to diverse scenes, without any modification of the mentioned parameters. Another comparison can be showed in Fig. 5 by using the intelligent room sequence, available at http://cvrr.ucsd.edu/aton/shadow.

Figure 6 shows the final result of our approach, after applying a shadow detection method and enhancing the obtained frame removing spurious objects. As we can observe, this segmentation is effective enough to be used in a subsequent tracking phase.

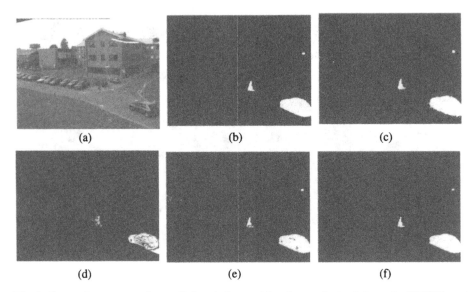

(a)   (b)   (c)

(d)   (e)   (f)

Fig. 4. Comparison among the studied techniques: (a) a frame obtained from the PETS01 sequence in raw form; (b) ground truth; (c) mixture of gaussians method; (d) background subtraction method; (e) DCN; (f) DCN+

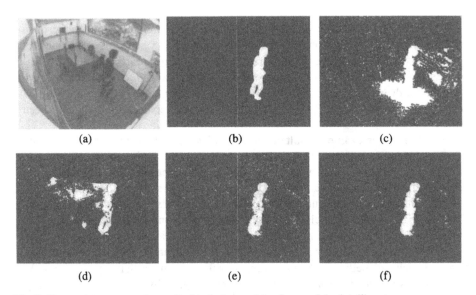

(a)   (b)   (c)

(d)   (e)   (f)

Fig. 5. Comparison among the studied techniques: (a) a frame of the intelligent room sequence; (b) ground truth; (c) mixture of gaussians method; (d) background subtraction method; (e) DCN; (f) DCN+

Table 2. Comparative analysis of the success rate among the studied methods for the sequence observed in Fig. 5

Method	% Matching	% FP	% FN
DCN+	98.9388	0.86961	6.7224
DCN	97.2409	2.5846	7.9157
MoG	87.9193	12.0628	12.6094
BS	95.4362	4.1031	18.1782

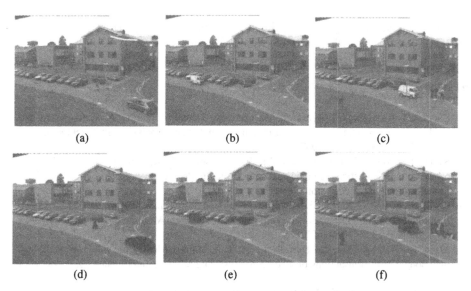

(a)   (b)   (c)

(d)   (e)   (f)

Fig. 6. Final results of the proposed method. In (a), (b) and (c) we can observe three frames (500, 750, 867) of a scene from PETS01 in raw form. (d), (e) and (f) show the segmentation results using our neural approach (DCN+), after applying shadow detection.

5   Conclusions and Future Work

In this work a new competitive neural network based on dipoles for video object detection and segmentation is presented. An unsupervised learning is performed to model the RGB space of each pixel together with the directionality of data using a dipolar representation.

The idea of using dipoles instead of a single point in the RGB color space permits to obtain the direction of the input pixel data. In this sense, experimental results have shown that the background model composed of ellipsoidal shapes (represented by the dipoles) outperforms the accuracy of other methods.

The segmentation accuracy of the proposed neural network is compared to mixture of Gaussian (MoG) and background subtraction (BS) models. In all the performed comparisons, our model achieved better results in terms of success rate and false positive rate, whereas the false negative rate is, at least, comparable to the obtained by the other studied methods.

Moreover, the proposed algorithm can be parallelized on a pixel level and designed to enable efficient hardware implementation to achieve real-time processing at great frame rates.

Other applications of this model will be studied, including the incorporation of this neural network to a remote sensing system performing people and vehicles tracking on closed scenes.

Acknowledgements

This work is partially supported by Junta de Andalucía (Spain) under contract TIC-01615, project name Intelligent Remote Sensing Systems.

References

1. Cucchiara, R., Grana, C., Piccardi, M., Prati, A.: Detecting moving objects, ghosts, and shadows in video streams. IEEE Transactions on Pattern Analysis and Machine Intelligence 25(10), 1337–1342 (2003)
2. Koller, D., Weber, J., Huang, T., Malik, J., Ogasawara, G., Rao, B., Russell, S.: Towards robust automatic traffic scene analysis in real-time. In: Proceedings of the International Conference on Pattern Recognition (1994)
3. Lo, B., Velastin, S.: Automatic congestion detection system for underground platforms. In: Proceedings of 2001 International Symposium on Intelligent Multimedia, Video and Speech Processing, pp. 158–161 (2001)
4. Wren, C., Azarbayejani, A., Darrell, T., Pentl, A.: Pfinder: Real-time tracking of the human body. IEEE Transactions on Pattern Analysis and Machine Intelligence 19(7), 780–785 (1997)
5. Stauffer, C., Grimson, W.: Adaptive background mixture models for real-time tracking. In: IEEE Computer Society Conference on Computer Vision and Pattern Recognition (1999)
6. Stauffer, C., Grimson, W.: Learning patterns of activity using real-time tracking. IEEE Transactions on Pattern Analysis and Machine Intelligence 22(8), 747–757 (2000)
7. García-Bernal, M., Muñoz, J., Gómez-Ruiz, J., Ladrón De Guevara-Lopez, I.: A competitive neural network based on dipoles. In: Mira, J., Álvarez, J.R. (eds.) IWANN 2003. LNCS, vol. 2686. Springer, Heidelberg (2003)
8. Oliveira, P., Romero, R.: Improvements on ica mixture models for image pre-processing and segmentation. Neurocomputing (in press, 2008)
9. Mu-Chun, S., Hung, C.H.: A neural-network-based approach to detecting rectangular objects. Neurocomputing 71(1-3), 270–283 (2007)
10. Meyer-Base, A., Thummler, V.: Local and global stability analysis of an unsupervised competitive neural network. IEEE Transactions on Neural Networks 19(2), 346–351 (2008)
11. Horprasert, T., Harwood, D., Davis, L.S.: A statistical approach for real-time robust background subtraction and shadow detection. In: Proceedings of International Conference on Computer Vision (1999)

Geodesic Generative Topographic Mapping

Raúl Cruz-Barbosa[1,2] and Alfredo Vellido[1]

[1] Universitat Politècnica de Catalunya, 08034, Barcelona, Spain
{rcruz,avellido}@lsi.upc.edu
[2] Universidad Tecnológica de la Mixteca, 69000, Huajuapan, Oaxaca, México

Abstract. Nonlinear dimensionality reduction (NLDR) methods aim to provide a faithful low-dimensional representation of multivariate data. The manifold learning family of NLDR methods, in particular, do this by defining low-dimensional manifolds embedded in the observed data space. Generative Topographic Mapping (GTM) is one such manifold learning method for multivariate data clustering and visualization. The non-linearity of the mapping it generates makes it prone to *trustworthiness* and *continuity* errors that would reduce the faithfulness of the data representation, especially for datasets of convoluted geometry. In this study, the GTM is modified to prioritize neighbourhood relationships along the generated manifold. This is accomplished through penalizing divergences between the Euclidean distances from the data points to the model prototypes and the corresponding geodesic distances along the manifold. The resulting Geodesic GTM model is shown to improve not only the *continuity* and *trustworthiness* of the representation generated by the model, but also its resilience in the presence of noise.

1 Introduction

The NLDR methods belonging to the manifold learning family model high-dimensional multivariate data under the assumption that these can be faithfully represented by a low-dimensional manifold embedded in the observed data space. This simplifying assumption may, at worst, limit the faithfulness of the generated data mapping due to either data point neighbourhood relationships that do not hold in their low-dimensional representation, hampering its *continuity*, or spurious neighbouring relationships in the representation that do not have a correspondence in the observed space, which limit the *trustworthiness* of the low-dimensional representation.

Generative Topographic Mapping (GTM) [1] is a flexible manifold learning NLDR model for simultaneous data clustering and visualization whose probabilistic nature makes possible to extend it to perform tasks such as missing data imputation [2], robust handling of outliers and unsupervised feature selection [3], or time series analysis [4], amongst others.

In the original formulation, GTM is optimized by minimization of an error that is a function of Euclidean distances, making it vulnerable to the aforementioned *continuity* and *trustworthiness* problems, especially for datasets of convoluted geometry. Such data may require plenty of folding from the GTM

H. Geffner et al. (Eds.): IBERAMIA 2008, LNAI 5290, pp. 113–122, 2008.

model, resulting in an unduly entangled embedded manifold that would hamper both the visualization of the data and the definition of clusters the model is meant to provide. Following an idea proposed in [5], the learning procedure of GTM is here modified by penalizing the divergences between the Euclidean distances from the data points to the model prototypes and the corresponding approximated geodesic distances along the manifold. By doing so, we prioritize neighbourhood relationships between points along the generated manifold, which makes the model more robust to the presence of off-manifold noise. In this paper, we first assess to what extent the resulting Geodesic GTM (or Geo-GTM) model (which incorporates the data visualization capabilities that the model proposed in [5] lacks) is capable of preserving the *trustworthiness* and *continuity* of the mapping. Then we assess whether Geo-GTM shows better behaviour in the presence of noise than its standard GTM counterpart.

2   Manifolds and Geodesic Distances

Manifold methods such as ISOMAP [6] and Curvilinear Distance Analysis [7] use the geodesic distance as a basis for generating the data manifold. This metric favours similarity along the manifold, which may help to avoid some of the distortions that the use of a standard metric such as the Euclidean distance may introduce when learning the manifold. In doing so, it can avoid the breaches of topology preservation that may occur due to excessive folding.

The otherwise computationally intractable geodesic metric can be approximated by graph distances [8], so that instead of finding the minimum arc-length between two data points lying on a manifold, we would set to find the shortest path between them, where such path is built by connecting the closest successive data points. In this paper, this is done using the K-rule, which allows connecting the K-nearest neighbours. A weighted graph is then constructed by using the data and the set of allowed connections. The data are the vertices, the allowed connections are the edges, and the edge labels are the Euclidean distances between the corresponding vertices. If the resulting graph is disconnected, some edges are added using a minimum spanning tree procedure in order to fully connect it. Finally, the distance matrix of the weighted undirected graph is obtained by repeatedly applying Dijkstra's algorithm [9], which computes the shortest path between all data samples.

3   GTM and Geo-GTM

The standard GTM is a non-linear latent variable model defined as a mapping from a low dimensional latent space onto the multivariate data space. The mapping is carried through by a set of basis functions generating a constrained mixture density distribution. It is defined as a generalized linear regression model:

$$\mathbf{y} = \phi(\mathbf{u})\mathbf{W}, \tag{1}$$

where ϕ are R basis functions, Gaussians in the standard formulation; $\mathbf{W}$ is a matrix of adaptive weights w_{rd}; and $\mathbf{u}$ is a point in latent space. To avoid computational intractability, a regular grid of M points $\mathbf{u}_m$ can be sampled from the latent space, which acts as visualization space. Each of them, which can be considered as the representative of a data cluster, has a fixed prior probability $p(\mathbf{u}_m) = 1/M$ and is mapped, using (1), into a low-dimensional manifold non-linearly embedded in the data space. A probability distribution for the multivariate data $\mathbf{X} = \{\mathbf{x}_n\}_{n=1}^N$ can then be defined, leading to the following expression for the log-likelihood:

$$L(\mathbf{W}, \beta | \mathbf{X}) = \sum_{n=1}^{N} \ln \left\{ \frac{1}{M} \sum_{m=1}^{M} \left(\frac{\beta}{2\pi} \right)^{D/2} \exp \left\{ -\beta/2 \|\mathbf{y}_m - \mathbf{x}_n\|^2 \right\} \right\} \qquad (2)$$

where $\mathbf{y}_m$, usually known as *reference* or *prototype* vectors, are obtained for each $\mathbf{u}_m$ using (1); and β is the inverse of the noise variance, which accounts for the fact that data points might not strictly lie on the low dimensional embedded manifold generated by the GTM. The EM algorithm is an straightforward alternative to obtain the Maximum Likelihood (ML) estimates of the adaptive parameters of the model, namely $\mathbf{W}$ and β. In the E-step, the responsibilities z_{mn} (the posterior probability of cluster m membership for each data point $\mathbf{x}_n$) are computed as

$$z_{mn} = p(\mathbf{u}_m | \mathbf{x}_n, \mathbf{W}, \beta) = \frac{p(\mathbf{x}_n | \mathbf{u}_m, \mathbf{W}, \beta) p(\mathbf{u}_m)}{\sum_{m'} p(\mathbf{x}_n | \mathbf{u}_{m'}, \mathbf{W}, \beta) p(\mathbf{u}_{m'})}, \qquad (3)$$

where $p(\mathbf{x}_n | \mathbf{u}_m, \mathbf{W}, \beta) = \mathcal{N}(\mathbf{y}(\mathbf{u}_m, \mathbf{W}), \beta)$.

3.1   Geo-GTM

The Geo-GTM model is an extension of GTM that favours the similarity of points along the learned manifold, while penalizing the similarity of points that are not contiguous in the manifold, even if close in terms of the Euclidean distance. This is achieved by modifying the standard calculation of the responsibilities in (3) proportionally to the discrepancy between the geodesic (approximated by the graph) and the Euclidean distances. Such discrepancy is made operational through the definition of the exponential distribution

$$\mathcal{E}(d_g | d_e, \alpha) = \frac{1}{\alpha} \exp \left\{ -\frac{d_g(\mathbf{x}_n, \mathbf{y}_m) - d_e(\mathbf{x}_n, \mathbf{y}_m)}{\alpha} \right\}, \qquad (4)$$

where $d_e(\mathbf{x}_n, \mathbf{y}_m)$ and $d_g(\mathbf{x}_n, \mathbf{y}_m)$ are, in turn, the Euclidean and graph distances between data point $\mathbf{x}_n$ and the GTM prototype $\mathbf{y}_m$. Responsibilities are redefined as:

$$z_{mn}^{geo} = p(\mathbf{u}_m | \mathbf{x}_n, \mathbf{W}, \beta) = \frac{p'(\mathbf{x}_n | \mathbf{u}_m, \mathbf{W}, \beta) p(\mathbf{u}_m)}{\sum_{m'} p'(\mathbf{x}_n | \mathbf{u}_{m'}, \mathbf{W}, \beta) p(\mathbf{u}_{m'})}, \qquad (5)$$

where $p'(\mathbf{x}_n|\mathbf{u}_m, \mathbf{W}, \beta) = \mathcal{N}(\mathbf{y}(\mathbf{u}_m, \mathbf{W}), \beta)\mathcal{E}(d_g(\mathbf{x}_n, \mathbf{y}_m)^2|d_e(\mathbf{x}_n, \mathbf{y}_m)^2, 1)$. When there is no agreement between the graph approximation of the geodesic distance and the Euclidean distance, the value of the numerator of the fraction within the exponential in (4) increases, pushing the exponential and, as a result, the modified responsibility, towards smaller values, i.e., punishing the discrepancy between metrics. Once the responsibility is calculated in the modified E-step, the rest of the model's parameters are estimated following the standard EM procedure.

3.2   Data Visualization Using Geo-GTM

The GTM was originally defined as a probabilistic alternative to Self-Organizing Maps (SOM). As a result, the data visualization capabilities of the latter are fully preserved and even augmented by the former. The main advantage of GTM and any of its extensions over general finite mixture models consists precisely on the fact that both data and results can be intuitively visualized on a low dimensional representation space.

Each of the cluster representatives $\mathbf{u}_m$ in the latent visualization space is mapped, following Eq. (1), into a point $\mathbf{y}_m$ (the center of a mixture component) belonging to a manifold embedded in data space. It is this mapping (and the possibility to invert it) what provides Geo-GTM with the data visualization capabilities that the alternative Manifold Finite Gaussian Mixtures model proposed in [5] lacks. Given that the posterior probability of every Geo-GTM cluster representative for being the generator of each data point, or responsibility z_{mn}^{geo}, is calculated as part of the modified EM algorithm, both data points and cluster prototypes can be visualized as a function of the latent point locations as the mean of the estimated posterior distribution:

$$\mathbf{u}_n^{mean} = \sum_{m=1}^{M} \mathbf{u}_m z_{mn}^{geo}, \tag{6}$$

4   Experiments

Geo-GTM was implemented in MATLAB®. For the experiments reported next, the adaptive matrix $\mathbf{W}$ was initialized, following a procedure described in [1], as to minimize the difference between the prototype vectors $\mathbf{y}_m$ and the vectors that would be generated in data space by a partial Principal Component Analysis (PCA). The inverse variance β was initialised to be the inverse of the 3rd PCA eigenvalue. This initialization ensures the replicability of the results. The latent grid was fixed to a square layout of approximately $(N/2)^{1/2} \times (N/2)^{1/2}$, where N is the number of points in the dataset. The corresponding grid of basis functions was equally fixed to a 5×5 square layout for all datasets.

The goal of the experiments is threefold. Firstly, we aim to assess whether the proposed Geo-GTM model could capture and visually represent the underlying structure of datasets of smooth but convoluted geometry better than the

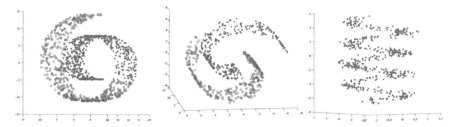

Fig. 1. The three datasets used in the experiments. (Left): *Swiss-Roll*, where two contiguous fragments are identified with different symbols in order to check manifold contiguity preservation in Fig. 3. (Center): *Two-Spirals*, again with different symbols for each of the spiral fragments. (Right): *Helix*.

standard GTM. Secondly, we aim to quantify the faithfulness of the generated mappings. Finally, we aim to evaluate the capability of Geo-GTM to uncover the underlying structure of the data in the presence of noise, and compare its performance with that of the standard GTM.

4.1 Results and Discussion

Three artificial 3-dimensional datasets, represented in Fig. 1, were used in the experiments that follow. The first one is *Swiss-Roll*, consisting on 1000 randomly sampled data points generated by the function: $(x_1, x_2) = (t\cos(t),\ t\sin(t))$, where t follows a uniform distribution $\mathcal{U}(3\pi/2, 9\pi/2)$ and the third dimension follows a uniform distribution $\mathcal{U}(0, 21)$. The second dataset, herein called *Two-Spirals*, consists of two groups of 300 data points each that are similar to *Swiss-Roll* although, this time, the first group follows the uniform distribution $\mathcal{U}(3\pi/4, 9\pi/4)$, while the second group was obtained by rotating the first one by 180 degrees in the plane defined by the first two axes and translating it by 2 units along the third axis. The third dataset, herein called *Helix*, consists of 500 data points that are images of the function $\mathbf{x} = (\sin(4\pi t), \cos(4\pi t), 6t - 0.5)$, where t follows $\mathcal{U}(-1, 1)$. These data are contaminated with a small level of noise. Also, and specifically for the experiments to assess the way the models deal with the presence of noise, Gaussian noise of zero mean and increasing standard deviation, from $\sigma = 0.1$ to $\sigma = 0.5$, was added to a noise-free version of *Helix* to produce the 5 datasets represented in Fig. 2.

The posterior mean distribution visualization maps for all datasets are displayed in Figs. 3 to 5. Geo-GTM, in Fig. 3, is shown to capture the spiral structure of *Swiss-Roll* far better than standard GTM, which misses it at large and generates a poor data visualization with large overlapping between non-contiguous areas of the data.

A similar situation is reflected in Fig. 4: The two segments of *Two-Spirals* are neatly separated by Geo-GTM, whereas the standard GTM suffers a lack of contiguity of the segment represented by circles as well as overlapping of part of the data of both segments.

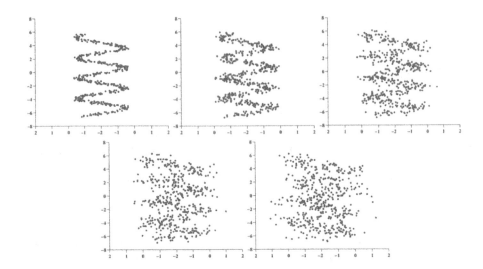

Fig. 2. The five noisy variations of *Helix* used in the experiments. From left to right and top to bottom, with increasing noise of standard deviation from $\sigma = 0.1$ to $\sigma = 0.5$.

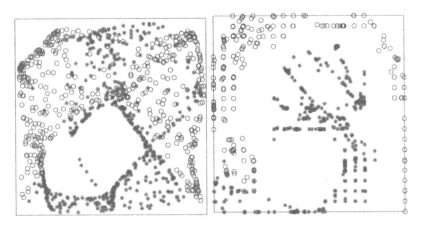

Fig. 3. Data visualization maps for the *Swiss-Roll* set. (Left): standard GTM; (right): Geo-GTM.

The results are even more striking for *Helix*, as shown in Fig. 5: the helicoidal structure is neatly revealed by Geo-GTM, whereas it is mostly missed by the standard GTM. The former also faithfully preserves data continuity, in comparison to the breaches of continuity that hinder the visualization generated by the latter.

In order to evaluate and compare the mappings generated by GTM and Geo-GTM, we use the *trustworthiness* and *continuity* measures developed in [10]. *Trustworthiness* is defined as:

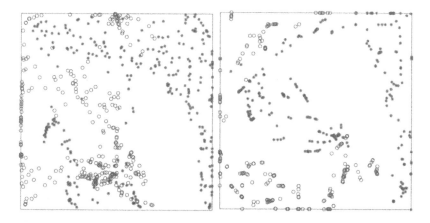

Fig. 4. Visualization maps for the *Two-Spirals* set. (Left): standard GTM; (right): Geo-GTM.

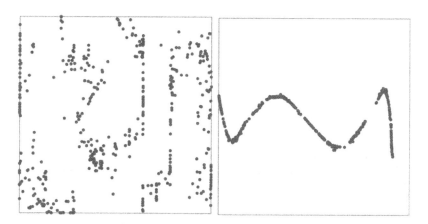

Fig. 5. Data visualization maps for the *Helix* set. (Left): standard GTM; (right): Geo-GTM.

$$T(K) = 1 - \frac{2}{NK(2N - 3K - 1)} \sum_{i=1}^{N} \sum_{x_j \in U_K(x_i)} (r(x_i, x_j) - K), \qquad (7)$$

where $U_k(x_i)$ is the set of data points x_j for which $x_j \in \hat{C}_K(x_i) \wedge x_j \notin C_K(x_i)$ and $C_K(x_i)$ and $\hat{C}_K(x_i)$ are the sets of K data points that are closest to x_i in the observed data space and in the low-dimensional representation space, respectively. *Continuity* is in turn defined as:

$$Cont(K) = 1 - \frac{2}{NK(2N - 3K - 1)} \sum_{i=1}^{N} \sum_{x_j \in V_K(x_i)} (\hat{r}(x_i, x_j) - K), \qquad (8)$$

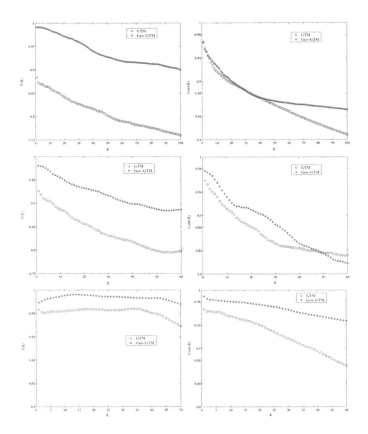

Fig. 6. Trustworthiness (left column) and continuity (right column) for (top row): *Swiss-Roll*, (middle row): *Two-Spirals*, and (bottom row): *Helix*, as a function of the neighbourhood size K

where $V_K(x_i)$ is the set of data points x_j for which $x_j \notin \hat{C}_K(x_i) \wedge x_j \in C_K(x_i)$. The terms $r(x_i, x_j)$ and $\hat{r}(x_i, x_j)$ are the ranks of x_j when data points are ordered according to their distance from the data vector x_i in the observed data space and in the low-dimensional representation space, respectively, for $i \neq j$.

The measurements of *trustworthiness* and *continuity* for all datasets are shown in Fig. 6. As expected from the visualization maps in Figs. 3-5, the Geo-GTM mappings are far more trustworthy than those generated by GTM for neighbourhoods of any size across the analyzed range. The differences in continuity preservation are smaller although, overall, Geo-GTM performs better than GTM model, specially with the noisier *Helix* dataset.

We finally evaluate, through some preliminary and illustrative experiments, the capability of Geo-GTM to uncover the underlying structure of the data in the presence of noise, comparing it with that of the standard GTM. We quantify it using the log-likelihood (2), as applied to a test dataset consisting of 500 randomly sampled data points from a noise-free version of *Helix*. For further

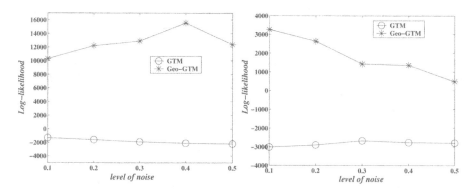

Fig. 7. Test log-likelihood results for the *Helix* (left) and *Two-Helix* (right) datasets, for increasing levels of added uninformative noise

testing, we repeat the experiment with noisy variations of a basic dataset, herein called *Two-Helix* consisting of two sub-groups of 300 data points each, which are, in turn, images of the functions $x1 = (sin(4\pi t), cos(4\pi t), 6t - 0.5)$ and $x2 = (-sin(4\pi t), -cos(4\pi t), 6t - 0.5)$, where t follows $\mathcal{U}(-1, 1)$. This is, in fact, a DNA-like shaped duplication of the *Helix* dataset. The corresponding results are shown in Fig. 7.

Remarkably, Geo-GTM is much less affected by noise than the standard GTM, as it recovers with much higher likelihood the underlying noise-free functions. This corroborates the visualization results reported in Fig. 5, in which the standard GTM generates a far less faithful representation of the underlying form and with breaches of continuity. This is probably due to the fact that Geo-GTM favours directions along the manifold, minimizing the impact of off-manifold noise.

5   Conclusion

A variation of the NLDR manifold learning GTM model, namely Geo-GTM, has been shown in this study to be able to faithfully recover and visually represent the underlying structure of datasets of smooth but convolute geometries. It does so by limiting the effect of manifold folding through the penalization of the discrepancies between inter-point Euclidean distances and the approximation of geodesic distances along the model manifold. As a byproduct of this approach, Geo-GTM avoids, at least partially, the problem of overfitting by penalizing off-manifold neighbouring relationships between data points. The reported experiments also show that Geo-GTM has recovered the true underlying data structure far better than the standard GTM, even in the presence of a considerable amount of noise. Future research should extend these experiments to a wider selection of datasets, both synthetic and real. It should also investigate, in wider detail, alternative approaches to graph generation as an approximation to geodesic distances. For this, we resorted in this paper to the K-rule, but other approaches could be considered, such as the ϵ-rule, the τ-rule, or even the more sophisticated Data- and Histogram- rules [11].

Acknowledgements. Alfredo Vellido is a researcher within the Ramón y Cajal program of the Spanish MICINN and acknowledges funding from the CICyT research project TIN2006-08114. Raúl Cruz-Barbosa acknowledges SEP-SESIC (PROMEP program) of México for his PhD grant.

References

1. Bishop, C.M., Svensén, M., Williams, C.K.I.: The Generative Topographic Mapping. Neural Computation 10(1), 215–234 (1998)
2. Vellido, A.: Missing data imputation through GTM as a mixture of t-distributions. Neural Networks 19(10), 1624–1635 (2006)
3. Vellido, A., Lisboa, P.J.G., Vicente, D.: Robust analysis of MRS brain tumour data using t-GTM. Neurocomputing 69(7-9), 754–768 (2006)
4. Olier, I., Vellido, A.: Advances in clustering and visualization of time series using GTM Through Time. Neural Networks (accepted for publication)
5. Archambeau, C., Verleysen, M.: Manifold constrained finite Gaussian mixtures. In: Cabestany, J., Gonzalez Prieto, A., Sandoval, F. (eds.) IWANN 2005. LNCS, vol. 3512, pp. 820–828. Springer, Heidelberg (2005)
6. Tenenbaum, J.B., de Silva, V., Langford, J.C.: A global geometric framework for nonlinear dimensionality reduction. Science 290, 2319–2323 (2000)
7. Lee, J.A., Lendasse, A., Verleysen, M.: Curvilinear Distance Analysis versus Isomap. In: Proceedings of European Symposium on Artificial Neural Networks (ESANN), pp. 185–192 (2002)
8. Bernstein, M., de Silva, V., Langford, J., Tenenbaum, J.: Graph approximations to geodesics on embedded manifolds. Technical report, Stanford University, CA (2000)
9. Dijkstra, E.W.: A note on two problems in connection with graphs. Numerische Mathematik 1, 269–271 (1959)
10. Venna, J., Kaski, S.: Neighborhood preservation in nonlinear projection methods: An experimental study. In: Dorffner, G., Bischof, H., Hornik, K. (eds.) ICANN 2001. LNCS, vol. 2130, pp. 485–491. Springer, Heidelberg (2001)
11. Lee, J.A., Verleysen, M.: Nonlinear Dimensionality Reduction. Springer, New York (2007)

Rough Evolutionary Fuzzy System Based on Interactive T-Norms

Graciela L. Meza Lovón and Maria Bernadete Zanusso

Universidade Federal do Mato Grosso do Sul
Departamento de Computação e Estatística
Campo Grande - MS - Brasil
gmezal@ucsp.edu.pe, mzanusso@dct.ufms.br

Abstract. A rough evolutionary neuro-fuzzy system for classification and rule generation is proposed. Interactive and differentiable t-norms and t-conorms involving logical neurons in a three-layer perceptron are used. This paper presents the results of application of the methodology based on rough set theory, which initializes the number of hidden nodes and some of the weight values. In search of the smallest network with a good generalization capacity, the genetic algorithms operate on population of individuals composed by integration of dependency rules that will be mapped on networks. Justification of an inferred decision was produced in rule form expressed as the disjunction of conjunctive clauses. The effectiveness of the algorithm is demonstrated on a speech recognition problem. The results are compared with those of fuzzy-MLP and Rough-Fuzzy-MLP, with no logical neuron; the Logical-P, which uses product and probabilistic sum; and other related models.

Keywords: T-norms, Classification, Rule Generation, Hybrid System.

1 Introduction

One of the objective of this work is to present the t-norms-based Interactive and Differentiable Neuro-Fuzzy System (IDNFS). This system has as nucleus a multilayer perceptron with three layers in which its neurons carry out logical operations *And* and *Or* and are trained with the backpropagation algorithm. Sec.2 presents the IDNFS with t-norms defined on [-1,1] following the L-fuzzy set concept [8].

The differentiability is an important characteristic in neuro-fuzzy systems because it allows the direct application of the training algorithms based on the descendant gradient [17]. In a data domain with different degrees of granularity among the attributes the interactivity has advantages on the min and max operators that are completely noninteractive [1].

When applied on a data set, the efficiency of the learning of a network measured in terms of its generalization capacity depends on the number of layers, and neurons and on the weights of connections among its neurons. On a symbolic knowledge-based neural networks these parameters can be determined by mapping rules. In order to solve this problem, the initialization methodology based

H. Geffner et al. (Eds.): IBERAMIA 2008, LNAI 5290, pp. 123–132, 2008.

on Rough Set (RS) theory and Genetic Algorithm (GA) is proposed in Sec. 3. RS is based on the application of mathematical concepts of equivalency classes and quotient set in an environment of uncertainty to generate dependency rules from a data set that will be mapped on the neuro-system. GA is introduced to determine the dependency rule combination that results in a IDNFS with the best generalization capacity. Many of the ideas and procedures of our methodology were previously proposed in [3][16]. However, there has been some attempts to overcome some of the limitations found in their methodology, mainly with the advantages offered by GA and other aspects of RS not considered previously.

The model proposed in this paper performs two main tasks. First we construct the three-layered fuzzy logical network for classifying multiclass patterns. Next, the trained network is used to generate rules. The connection weight in this stage constitutes the knowledge base (in embedded form) for the classification problem under consideration. The model is now capable of inferring the output decision for complete and/or partial quantitative inputs and provide justification for any conclusion. If asked by the user, the proposed model is capable of justifying its decision in rule form (in terms of the salient features) with the antecedent and consequent parts produced in linguistic and natural terms.

Sec. 4 shows that on a speech recognition problem the IDNFS with 17 nodes in the hidden layer, even without the fuzzification at the output, gave the best performance between other logical classifiers with 20 or 22 nodes. The results were very promising not only because the process of initialization was partially automatized but also because the generalization capacity was improved in the data set used in our experiments. The preliminary results about the rule generation for speech data are shown in Sec. 3.

2   Neuro-fuzzy System

In [15][17] several distinct types of fuzzy neurons were proposed, which could potentially give rise to many fuzzy neural networks. Our goal in this work is to use the interactive and differentiable t-norms defined by Zanusso [4][14] and to show that the classification results and the rules generated by the system are satisfactory and sometimes better than [2][10][3].

In the literature, the more frequent t-norms are those from *min* and *max*. However, the lattice operations are completely non interactive. The lack of interaction is well represented by the *min* and *max* operations: note that $min(x,a)$ returns x once x is less than a and this result does not reflect the value of a. If there is an interaction, one should favor some other t- and s-norms that are interactive [1].

The definition of a learning algorithm for a fuzzy perceptron using *min* and *max* is not as straightforward as for its neural counterpart because of the usually non-differentiable t-norms and t-conorms used as activation functions for the units. So a gradient descent method cannot be used. [17] discussed some neuro-fuzzy approaches that use special soft-min/soft-max functions to solve this problem. Another approach to solve it is GA.

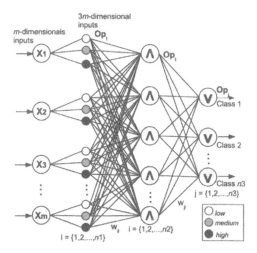

Fig. 1. Architecture of IDNFS

The IDNFS is defined in Fig. 1. This architecture is equal to KDL and Logical-P in [2]. Those models use the conjugate pair *min-max* or the *product-probabilistic sum* operators to represent the *And* and *Or* nodes, respectively. To solve the non interactivity problem, KDL uses various implication operators to introduce different amounts of interaction during back propagation of errors; the results of this are shown in Table 1, Section 4.

2.1 Interactive T-Norm and T-Conorm

[4][14] presents the characterization theorems of t-norm and t-conorm defined on $[-1, 1]$ (observing the extremes) using the axiomatic skeletons defined by Schweizer [7] and the concept of *L-fuzzy set* by Klir [8][9]. The t-norm, which performs the operation *And* among fuzzy sets, is denoted by C and the t- conorm, which carries out the operation *Or*, by D. These are defined via:

$$C(x_1, x_2, \ldots, x_k) = G_1(G_1(x_1) + G_1(x_2) + \ldots + G_1(x_k)) \tag{1}$$

and

$$D(x_1, x_2, \ldots, x_k) = G_3(G_2(x_1) + G_2(x_2) + \ldots + G_2(x_k)), \tag{2}$$

where $G_1(x)$ is the decreasing generator with $G_1^{-1}(x) = G_1(x)$ and $G_2(x)$ is the increasing generator with $G_2^{-1}(x) = G_3(x)$ being defined via:

$$G_1(x) = \frac{1-x}{1+x},$$

$$G_2(x) = \frac{1+x}{1-x},$$

$$G_3(x) = \frac{x-1}{x+1}.$$

In the logical neurons in Fig.1 C and D were used to calculate $\wedge = And$ and $\vee = Or$, respectively. The IDNFS has $n_1 = 3m$ neurons in the input layer, n_2 in the hidden and n_3 in output.

2.2   Input/Output Vector Representation and the LMS Error

The p-esimal m-dimensional pattern (or example)
$X_p = [X_{p1}, X_{p2}, \ldots, X_{pm}]$ is represented as $3m$-dimensional vector:

$$O_p = [\mu_{low}(x_{p1}), \mu_{medium}(x_{p1}),$$
$$\mu_{high}(x_{p1}), \ldots, \mu_{low}(x_{pm}), \mu_{medium}(x_{pm}), \mu_{high}(x_{pm})], \qquad (3)$$

where $\mu_{low}(x_{pi})$, $\mu_{medium}(x_{pi})$ and $\mu_{high}(x_{pi})$, for $i = 1, \ldots, m$ indicate the membership degrees for the value x_{pi} of the input feature X_{pi} to the low, medium and high fuzzy sets, respectively.

The membership function μ, assuming values in $[-1, 1]$, is defined via:

$$\mu(x) = \begin{cases} 2(2(1 - \frac{|x-c|}{\lambda})^2) - 1 & \text{if } \frac{\lambda}{2} \leq |x - c| \leq \lambda \\ 2(1 - 2(\frac{|x-c|}{\lambda})^2) - 1 & \text{if } 0 \leq |x - c| \leq \frac{\lambda}{2} \\ -1 & \text{otherwise} \end{cases}, \qquad (4)$$

where $\lambda > 0$, the radius and c, the central point, are calculated using the minimum and maximum values of the X attribute in the training set and depends on the parameter $0 < s \leq 1$ which controls the extension of overlapping.

In the neurons of the And layer the activation functions used are

$$net_{pi} = \bigwedge_{l=1}^{n_1} (O_{pl} \vee w_{il}), \qquad (5)$$

whose outputs are $O_{pi} = net_{pi}$, for input-output case p and $i = 1, \ldots, n_2$.
To the neurons from the Or layer, the activation functions used are,

$$net_{pj} = \bigvee_{i=1}^{n_2} (O_{pi} \wedge w_{ji}), \qquad (6)$$

whose outputs are $O_{pj} = net_{pj}$, for input-output case p and $j = 1, \ldots, n_3$.

The Least Mean Square (LMS) error was minimized by gradient-descent technique using η (learning-rate) and α (momentum constant) parameters. It is important to mention that after the updating of the weights, a truncation procedure is carried out, aiming to guarantee that their values belong to the interval (-1,1). The derivation of the error is shown in [5][6].

3   The Initialization Methodology

This section presents a summary of the initialization methodology. [11][12] has included more explanatory figures and the pseudocode of the Genetic Algorithm (GA).

The fuzzified training data (Sec. 2.2) is used by the RS theory. It includes tasks such as the binarization which creates granules of information through the application of a cut point (pc) over the data. Values higher than pc become 1, otherwise they become 0. In the theory of RS [13], the information in a data set are considered in a table named Information System (IS). The application of the RS theory allows discovering minimum subsets of attributes named *reducts* whose equivalence classes are the same as those produced by the whole set of attributes. A Decision System (DS) is a IS, which has a decision attribute d, and from which the d-reducts are determined .

For every d-reduct of the DS a dependency rule is generated: the antecedent is determined by conjunction of the attributes of a d-reduct; the consequent is d. These rules indicate the conditional attributes which discriminate the DS classes. They are denoted by RDS_q, $q = 1, 2, \ldots, Q$, where Q is the number of d-reducts. An example for the *Iris* dataset [19] is $high_3 \wedge low_1 \rightarrow specie$, where the subindex refers to the crisp attribute that was fuzzified. This rule discriminates a class representatives from other different class representatives.

Another type of dependency rule allows distinguishing the representatives of a given class. The DS is divided into n subsystems, one for each class, and their reducts are found. From those, the rules are generated: the antecedents like those of RDS, whereas the consequents are determined by the class. These rules are denoted by R_{jq_j}, $j = 1, 2, \ldots, n$, n is the number of classes and $q_j = 1, 2, \ldots, Q_j$, Q_j is the number of reducts of the j-esimal class. An example for the *Iris setosa* is $high_2 \wedge medium_2 \wedge low_1 \rightarrow I.setosa$.

In this work an integration of one RDS, randomly chosen from the set of Q rules, with one R rule, is proposed; named *class rule* and denoted by $R\text{-}RDS$. The antecedent is the conjunction of the antecedents of both rules and the consequent is the same as that of the rule R. [3] did not take into consideration the integration of rules which has the advantage of distinguishing the representatives of a given class and, at the same time, distinguishing those representatives from other of different classes.

The Genetic Algorithm (GA) is applied over a IDNFS's population. The aim is to find the IDNFS with the smallest number of neurons in the hidden layer and the highest hit rate on the test set.

The individual representation for GA considers that the antecedents of several class rule with the same consequent can be connected by disjunctions forming a rule $\Re$ whose antecedent is in the Disjunctive Normal Form. An individual is a combination of $\Re_j$, $j = 1, 2, \ldots n$, which defines n regions in the chromosome. Each region is formed by positions (genes) of type $R - RDS$. The individual has $Q_1 + Q_2 + \ldots + Q_n$ positions of the type $R - RDS$. One IDNFS is obtained by mapping an individual.

To define the initial population creation and to diversify the population a policy of $R - RDS$ activation is employed. An active gene participates in the mapping but an inactive one does not. The initial population is created in a way that on a quarter of the individuals all the genes are inactive, consequently, the mapping of those will build architectures with $Q_1 + Q_2 + \ldots + Q_n$ neurons in the hidden layer (the highest possible number). In another quarter, just one gene in the region of each class is randomly chosen to be activated.

The genetic operators are defined in a way different from the traditional GA, all the individuals from the population $P(t)$, in the t-th generation will cross with another individual randomly chosen. The crossover operator is applied by randomly choosing, for each class region, a crossover point from which there will be a change of subsets of $R - RDS$ rules. The sons and their progenitors compose the intermediary population, $IP(t)$ in the t-th generation. The mutation operator is applied over an individual of $IP(t)$, randomly choosing a region in the individual.

The genetic operators do not change the structure of the antecedents and consequents of the rules $R - RDS$ represented in the individuals. Later, the individuals of $IP(t)$ will be mapped over an IDNFS, as reported in [11][12]. The evaluation consists of training and testing each IDNFS from $IP(t)$. The fitness function is defined in terms of n_2, which is the number of neurons in the hidden layer, and hr, hit rate from the test. hr is the mean from the diagonal of confusion matrix. The output of the GA is the IDNFS with a higher hit rate.

The experiments were carried out making learning rate η and the momentum constant α decreases as the number of epochs increases. The methodology of K-fold Cross Validation (CV) for training and testing neural networks was used to determine the best combination from the parameter values. The mutation rate was fixed on 0.10; $s, pc \in \{0.2, 0.4, 0.6, 0.8\}$; ϵ, $\rho \in \{10, 15, 20\}$, that is, the number of evolutions and the number of the best individuals selected after evaluation of IP, respectively. By crossing these parameters, we get the largest mean hr between all folds. These K systems are called evolved-IDNFS.

From K evolved-IDNFS, those that get the largest hr's were chosen. The basic-IDNFS was created fixing s, n_2. The CV methodology, with the former folds, was applied on each basic-IDNFS (aleatory initial weights) and evolved-IDNFS (we have fixed s, n_2 and the initial weights). It is possible, then, to compare the initialization methodology effect when applied on IDNFS.

4   Implementation and Results

The proposed IDNFS with the initialization and rule generation methodology was used on vowel data. These data consist of a set of 871 Indian Telugu vowel sounds [18]; three features: F_1, F_2 and F_3 corresponding to the first, second and third formant frequencies obtained through spectrum analysis of the speech data. There is a 3-dimensional feature space of the six vowel classes $\partial(72$ examples$)$, $a(89)$, $i(172)$, $u(151)$, $e(207)$ or $o(180)$. This data set has overlapping and nonlinear class boundary. The goal is to compare all the results with [2][3][10][16].

Classification: At first the results from IDNFS without the application of the initialization methodology will be presented. The network was trained with the following parameters: $\eta = 0.01$ (fixed), $\alpha = 0.01$ (fixed), $maxepoch = 4500$,

Table 1. Output Performance for Vowel Data

Model Used	Fuzzy-MLP		KDL	Logical Logical-P		IDNFS	
Hidden nodes n_2	20	22	20	20	22	15	17
∂	44.6	69.8	9.3	31.2	24.6	4.6	4.6
α	65.4	72.8	97.5	76.5	93.8	95.1	93.8
i	79.2	81.8	96.7	90.2	92.2	90.3	88.4
u	88.3	85.9	85.9	80.0	93.5	91.2	91.2
e	75.0	75.0	15.8	75.1	62.3	73.3	76.5
o	85.7	87.2	3.0	86.5	77.9	91.4	91.4
Overall	76.8	80.1	48.8	77.8	77.1	80.0	80.3

$n_2 = 17$ and $s = 1.0$. The last weights from the train are clamped on the neuron connections. In all cases 10% of the samples are used as training set, and the remaining samples are used as a test set. The test examples are fuzzified with the same membership functions as the train examples to enter in the net.

Table 1 compares the average percent of the correct recognition score (on the test set using the best match criterion, both classwise and overall) of the proposed IDNFS model with that of Fuzzy-MLP, KDL and Logical-P. The best match criterion tests whether the jth neuron output has the maximum O_{pj} when the jth component of the desired output vector also has the highest value.

In Table 1 the non logical model Fuzzy-MLP [10] is defined by using weighted sum and sigmoid functions. The logical model KDL uses implication operator of Kleene-Dienes-Lukasiewicz [2] to introduce interaction during back propagation of errors with the non interactive standard min-max operators. The model Logical-P uses the product and probabilistic sum operators [10]. In all these models the input vector consists of membership values for linguistic properties as in Sec. 2.2 with μ transformed into [0,1] while the output vector is fuzzy class membership values. The logical model IDNFS gave the best performance between them with 17 nodes in the hidden layer while the other models had 20 and 22 nodes without implementing the fuzzification at the output.

Table 2 was gotten from application of experiments in Sec. 3 and shows the mean hr for the basic and evolved-IDNFS together with the standard deviation S. The results were attained with $s = 0.8$, $pc = 0.7$, $\epsilon = 15$, $\rho = 15$ and 550 epochs for training during the evolutive process and 4500 epochs on the last

Table 2. Basic-IDNFS and Evolved-IDNFS for the vowel dataset on the test set

n_2	Basic-IDNFS mean $hr \pm S$	Evolved-IDNFS mean $hr \pm S$
21	0.7797 ± 0.039	0.8162 ± 0.020
22	0.7934 ± 0.036	0.8139 ± 0.025
23	0.8071 ± 0.036	0.8151 ± 0.020

Table 3. Rule Generation for Vowel Data with IDNFS

Serial	Input Features			Justification/Rule Generation	
No.	F_1	F_2	F_3	If Clause	Then Conclusion
1	900	1400	*unobt*	F_2 is very medium	Mol likely class a
2	700	2300	3100	F_1 is high *And* F_3 is very high	Very likely class e
4	700	1100	2200	F_1 is very medium *And* F_3 is very medium	Likely class a
5	700	1000	2600	F_1 is very medium *And* F_3 is very medium *Or* F_3 is mol high	Likely class a
6	700	1000	*unobt*	F_1 is very medium	Likely class a
8b	700	*Unobt*	*unobt*	F_1 is very medium	Not unlikely class a
9a	600	1600	*unobt*	F_1 is mol high *And* F_2 is very medium *And* F_2 is mol low	Not unlikely class e *Or o*
10a	600	1200	*unobt*	F_1 is very medium *And* F_2 is very medium	Not unlikely class a
10b	600	1200	*unobt*	F_1 is mol high *And* F_2 is very medium	Not unlikely class o
11	50	2400	*unobt*	F_1 is low *Or* F_1 is very medium	Likely class e, but not unlikely class i
13	400	*unobt*	*unobt*	F_1 is very low	Not unlikely class e
15b	250	1550	*unobt*	F_2 is very medium *And* F_2 is mol low	Mol likely class i

train. Note that the increase on the mean hit rates from evolved-IDNFS are larger than those found from basic-IDNFS in average about 2%.

Rule Generation from the Trained Best IDNFS: The rules on Table 3 were generated from the learned knowledge base embedded among the connection weights using the *path generation by backtracking* and the same *certainty measure* for linguistic output as reported in [2].

The magnitudes of the connection weights of trained network were used in every stage of the inferencing procedure. The input feature values of a test pattern, presented in quantitative form, influence the generation of the rule from the trained set of connection weights. This helps extract rules relevant to that region of the feature space that is local to the area pointed to by the feature values of the pattern. On the table, *mol* stands for more or less and *unobt* means that the membership value of that feature value to *low, medium* and *high* will be equal to 0, the most ambiguous value. The consequent part clauses were generated for all output neurons that had certainty measure larger than 0.1.

5   Conclusion and Discussion

A three-layered rough evolutionary neuro fuzzy system has been presented. Interactive and differentiable conjugate pair of t-norms was used to perform the logical operations in the neurons. It could be seen in Table 1, the performance of IDNFS classification showed to be comparable to those obtained by models Fuzzy-MLP, KDL and Logical-P. It is important to point out that this performance was obtained by using a network with less neurons in the hidden layer and not yet introducing the fuzzyfication in the net output. [2] introduced different amounts of fuzziness at the output on model Logical-P; the performance increased from 77.8% to 86.1%, that is, 8.3% above. With further development of this work, a comparison is expected between the results of the applications of differentiable and interactive t-norms, proposed in Sec. 2, and the t-norms of max and min and other t-norms proposed in the literature in a data set with different levels of granularity.

The use of rough set theory, which also deals with "information granules", has been used to optimize the number of neurons in the hidden layer and to initialize the weights for some connections between the layers characterizes a knowledge-based network. Note that we have attained satisfactory results when comparing the performance on the test set from speech data between the evolved-IDNFS (Table 2) and various neural net models. [3] has introduced the RS-initialization in Fuzzy-MLP (3 hidden layer, 22 nodes) and renamed it Rough-Fuzzy-MLP. The performance increased from 83.6% to 85.1%, that is, 1.5% better; while the evolved-IDNFS is better than basic-IDNFS in average 2.0% and with one hidden layer. Perhaps if we implement the fuzzification at the output in the IDNFS model we can increase its performance.

After the design, training and test of the network is complete, it is expected the learned hypothesis be able to infer the correct classification for future examples and, if asked by the user, the proposed model is capable of justifying its decision in rule form with the antecedent (in terms of the salient features) and the consequent parts produced in linguistic terms. The IDNFS model generates a number of such rules in If-Then form corresponding to each presentation of examples extracted from the same population of the train and test sets. The rules generated by IDNFS (Table. 3) showed to be satisfactory in relation to the classification given to test input feature and consistent with the rules generated by Logical-P and FUZZY-MLP models [2] (Tables 9,10), when the same set of test input feature was presented. It is still necessary to apply some measures in order to evaluate the performance of the rules.

Acknowledgments. The authors acknowledge CAPES-Brazil for the scholarship.

References

1. Klösgen, W., Zytkow, J.M.: Handbook of Data Mining and Knowledge Discovery. Cap. 10 by Witold Pedrycz, 1st edn. Oxford University Press, New York (2002)
2. Mitra, S., Pal, S.K.: Logical Operation Based Fuzzy MLP for Classification and Rule Generation. Neural Networks 7(2), 683–697 (1994)
3. Banerjee, M., Mitra, S., Pal, S.K.: Rough Fuzzy MLP: Knowledge Encoding and Classification. IEEE Transactions On Neural Networks 9(6), 1203–1216 (1998)
4. Zanusso, M.B.: Familias de T-Normas Diferenciáveis, Funções de Pertinência Relacionadas e Aplicações. Universidade Federal de Santa Catarina. Tese de Doutorado, Brasil (November 1997)
5. Oliveira, F.R., Zanusso, M.B.: A Fuzzy Neural Network with Differentiable T-Norms: Classification and Rule Generation. In: International Conference on Artificial Intelligence(ICAI), Las Vegas, Nevada, June 27-30, vol. I(1), pp. 195–201 (2005)
6. Oliveira, F.R.: Rede Neural Difusa com T-normas Diferenciáveis e Interativas. Universidade Federal de Mato Grosso do Sul, Dissertação de Mestrado, Brasil, Novembro (2006)
7. Schweizer, B., Sklar, M.: Associative Functions and Statistical Inequalities. Publ. Math. Debrecen 8(1), 169–186 (1961)
8. Klir, G.J., Folger, T.A.: Fuzzy Sets, Uncertainty and Information. Prentice Hall, New Jersey (1988)
9. Klir, G.J., Yuan, B.: Fuzzy Sets and Fuzzy Logic: Theory and Applications. Prentice Hall, New Jersey (1995)
10. Pal, S.K., Mitra, S.: Multilayer Perceptron, Fuzzy Sets, and Classification. IEEE Transactions on Neural Networks 3(5), 683–697 (1992)
11. Lovón, G.L.M.: Rough Sets e Algoritmo Genético para Inicializar um Sistema Neuro-Fuzzy. Universidade Federal de Mato Grosso do Sul. Dissertação de Mestrado, Brasil (April 2007)
12. Lovón, G.L.M., Zanusso, M.B.: Rough Sets e Algoritmo Genético para Inicializar um Sistema Neuro-Fuzzy. In: XXXIII Conferencia Latinoamericana en Informática, San José, Costa Rica (2007)
13. Pawlak, Z.: Rough Sets - Theoretical Aspects of Reasoning about Data. Kluwer Academic Publishers, Dordrecht (1991)
14. Zanusso, M.B., Araújo, A.: Differentiable T-Norms and Related Membership Functions Families and their Applications. In: IBERAMIA-SBIA, November 19-22, vol. 2, pp. 294–303 (2000)
15. Pedrycz, W., Gomide, F.: An Introduction to Fuzzy Sets - Analysis and Designs, 1st edn. MIT Press, Cambridge (1994)
16. Pal, S.K., Mitra, P.: Pattern Recognition Algorithms for Data Mining. Chapman/Hall-CRC, New York (2004)
17. Nauck, D., Klawonn, F., Kruse, R.: Neuro-Fuzzy Systems. John Wiley and Sons, New York (1997)
18. Indian Statistical Institute, Calcutta, http://www.isical.ac.in/~miu
19. Fisher, R.A. (1936), http://archive.ics.uci.edu/ml/datasets/Iris

K-Means Initialization Methods for Improving Clustering by Simulated Annealing

Gabriela Trazzi Perim, Estefhan Dazzi Wandekokem, and Flávio Miguel Varejão

Universidade Federal do Espírito Santo - Departamento de Informática, Av. Fernando Ferrari, s/n, Campus de Goiabeiras, CEP 29060-900, Vitória-ES, Brasil
{gabrielatp,estefhan}@gmail.com, fvarejao@inf.ufes.br

Abstract. Clustering is defined as the task of dividing a data set such that elements within each subset are similar between themselves and are dissimilar to elements belonging to other subsets. This problem can be understood as an optimization problem that looks for the best configuration of the clusters among all possible configurations. K-means is the most popular approximate algorithm applied to the clustering problem, but it is very sensitive to the start solution and can get stuck in local optima. Metaheuristics can also be used to solve the problem. Nevertheless, the direct application of metaheuristics to the clustering problem seems to be effective only on small data sets. This work suggests the use of methods for finding initial solutions to the K-means algorithm in order to initialize Simulated Annealing and search solutions near the global optima.

Keywords: Combinatorial Optimization, Metaheuristics, K-means, Simulated Annealing.

1 Introduction

The fundamental problem of clustering consists on grouping elements that belong to a data set, according to the similarity between them [1]. Given the data set, defined as $X = \{\mathbf{x_1}, ..., \mathbf{x_N}\}$, with N elements, and each element $\mathbf{x_i} = [x_{i1}, ..., x_{id}]^t$ having d attributes, the goal is to find K groups ($C_1, ..., C_K$), such that elements within each cluster are similar between themselves and are dissimilar to elements belonging to the other clusters.

This problem can be formulated as the combinatorial optimization task of finding the best configuration of partitions among all possible ones, according to a function that assesses the quality of partitions. With this formulation, the problem is known to be NP-Hard.

Partitional algorithms are often used for solving this problem. The most common example of this class of algorithms is K-means [2], which is applied to data with numerical attributes. Simplicity and fast convergence to the final solution are the main features of this algorithm. However, the K-means algorithm is very sensitive to the choice of the initial solution, used as a starting element for the searching process. Furthermore, the algorithm is subject to achieve local optima as a solution, according to Selim and Ismail [3].

H. Geffner et al. (Eds.): IBERAMIA 2008, LNAI 5290, pp. 133–142, 2008.

Another approach for solving the clustering problem is the use of metaheuristics, which combine techniques of local search and general strategies to escape from local optima, broadly searching the solution space. However, Rayward-Smith [4] indicates that the direct application of metaheuristics to the problem seems to be more effective in smaller sets (with a small number of elements and partitions).

Based on the tendency of the K-means algorithm to obtain local optima, this work investigates a new approach to solve the clustering problem, using initialization methods originally defined to K-means, PCA-Part [14] and K-means++ [15], together with the metaheuristic Simulated Annealing. The objective of this combination is to obtain solutions that are closer to the global optima of the problem.

Experiments were performed using a procedure based on the cross-validation technique in order to avoid bias on the results. This procedure uses different subsets of the available data to search the best values of the parameters of Simulated Annealing algorithm (initial temperature, number of iterations without improvement and the temperature decreasing rate) and to estimate the objective function. In addition, a statistical approach was adopted to analyze the results of the experiments. The results were obtained with eight real databases and the proposal approach was generally better than the other combinations of algorithms tried on the experiments.

Section 2 presents the K-means and Simulated Annealing approaches. Section 3 introduces two initialization methods, and proposes the use of these methods together with the metaheuristic Simulated Annealing. Section 4 shows the experimental results, and compares the performance of combinations of the initialization methods with K-means and Simulated Annealing. Finally, Section 5 presents the conclusions and future work.

2   Clustering with K-Means and Metaheuristics

The K-means algorithm performs the search using an iterative procedure which associates the elements to its closest partition, aiming to minimize an objective function. This function is calculated by taking the sum of the square of the Euclidian distance between each element and the centroid of the partition to which it belongs. The centroid is the representative element of the partition and is calculated as the mass center of its elements. The function which evaluates the partitions in this way is called Sum of the Squared Euclidian distances (SSE).

The classical version of K-means, according to Forgy [2], initially chooses a random set of K elements to represent the centroids of the initial solution. Each iteration generates a new solution, associating every element to the closest centroid in the current solution and recalculating the centroids after all elements are associated. This procedure is performed while convergence is not achieved.

Despite the simplicity and rapid convergence of the algorithm, K-means may be the highly sensitive to the choice of the initial solution. If that choice is bad, the algorithm may converge to a local minimum of the objective function.

Initialization methods may be used to improve the chances of a search finding a solution that is close to the global optima. The next section presents two initialization methods for choosing the initial solution of the problem. One of them, PCA-Part, represents a deterministic procedure with good results compared to other methods, and the other, K-means++, is a stochastic procedure that guarantees that the solution is close to the global optima.

Even with the use of a meticulous initialization method, the K-means algorithm may still not escape from local optima. If the initialization leads to a solution that is also close to local optima, the result of the algorithm could be a local optimum solution.

An alternative approach for solving the problem is to apply metaheuristics, which are heuristic procedures with more general characteristics that have mechanisms to escape from locally optimal solutions.

The algorithm Simulated Annealing [5] is an example of metaheuristics that can be applied to this problem. Klein and Dubes [6] present an implementation of the Simulated Annealing algorithm for solving the clustering problem, and analyzes the appropriate values for the parameters of the algorithm, as well as the appropriate neighborhood function. Selim and Alsultan [7] also suggest an adaptation of Simulated Annealing to the clustering problem, besides conducting a detailed assessment and interpretation of the parameters. Both works were successful with simple databases.

Other works apply different metaheuristics for the problem. For example, Murty and Chowdhury [8] and Hall et al. [9] use genetic algorithms for finding solutions that are closer to the global optima. Tabu Search [10], Particle Swarm [11] and Ant Colony Optimization [12] were also used for the same purpose.

However, as indicated by Rayward-Smith [4], the direct application of metaheuristics to the clustering problem seems to be more effective in small databases.

Hybrid approaches have achieved more promising results in this case. One possible hybrid approach is the use of metaheuristics to find promising solutions in the search space and then use partitional algorithms to explore these solutions and find better ones. The work presented by Babu and Murty [13] proposes the implementation of Simulated Annealing to choose the initial solution of the K-means algorithm.

Another example of a hybrid approach is the application of partitional algorithms for generating the initial solution of some metaheuristic. For instance, Merwe and Engelbrecht [11] shows that the performance of the Particle Swarm algorithm applied to the clustering problem can be enhanced by an initial solution found by K-means.

3 K-Means Initialization Methods with Simulated Annealing

This paper proposes using the methods PCA-Part and K-means++ to choose the initial solution of the Simulated Annealing algorithm applied to the clustering problem in order to increase the chances of finding solutions that are closer to the global optima.

The proposed approach aims to obtain better results, especially in larger data sets of the problem, than those obtained with the classical version of Simulated Annealing (where the original solution is randomly chosen) and also those achieved by the K-means algorithm using random, PCA-Part and K-means++ initialization methods.

The PCA-Part method uses a hierarchical approach based on the PCA (Principal Component Analysis) technique [16]. This method aims to minimize the value of the SSE function for each iteration. Initially, the method considers that the entire data set forms a single partition. Then, the algorithm iteratively selects the partition with the highest SSE and divides it into two, in the direction that minimizes the value of SSE after the division. This is the same direction that maximizes the difference between the SSE before and after the division. This problem is simplified to find the direction that contributes to the highest value of SSE before the division, which is determined by the direction of the largest eigenvector of the covariance matrix. The process is repeated until K partitions are generated.

The interesting aspect of this method is that, besides it potentially provides better results than those obtained with the traditional random initialization, it also performs a deterministic choice of the start solution, therefore removing the random nature of K-means.

The method K-means++ is based on a random choice of centroids, with a specific probability. Initially, the method selects a random element of the data set to represent the first centroid. The other $K-1$ centroids are chosen iteratively by the selection of elements of the data set with probability proportional to its contribution to the SSE function. Thus, the higher is the contribution of a element to the function, the greater will be the chances of that element to be chosen as centroid. Besides being fast and simple, this method improves the quality of the K-means results, assuring that the SSE of the solution will be proportional to the SSE of the optimal solution by a constant in $O(log (K))$.

The algorithm used in this work for searching the final solution of the clustering problem was Simulated Annealing. This metaheuristic was chosen because it is a traditional algorithm and it has also been effective in a large number of optimization problems. Moreover, it is a conceptually simple procedure. Indeed, its procedure is equally simple as the K-means procedure.

The Simulated Annealing algorithm is an iterative search method based on the annealing process. The algorithm starts from an initial solution (either randomly or heuristically constructed) and an initial temperature T_0. Then, the procedure takes iterations until it achieves a stopping criterion, that is, in most implementations, the achievement of very small values of temperature, lower than a final temperature T_f.

The algorithm performs, for each value of temperature, a perturbation at the current solution until the thermal equilibrium is achieved. That equilibrium is usually implemented as a fixed number of iterations N_{iter} without improvements in the visited solutions. The algorithm randomly generates a neighbor of the current solution for performing the perturbations. If the objective function evaluation improves, the new solution is accepted. Otherwise, the solution is accepted with a probability that is directly proportional to the temperature, allowing the algorithm to escape from local optima.

Once the thermal equilibrium is reached, the temperature is reduced by a rule of cooling and the algorithm can continue doing perturbations in the solutions until a stopping criterion is achieved. One of the most common cooling rules follows a geometric form wherein the temperature decreases exponentially by a rate r, such that $T = r \, x \, T$, with $0 < r < 1$.

Besides this basic procedure, the implemented version of the Simulated Annealing presents some characteristics that are listed as following:

The representation of the solution of the clustering problem, based on a proposal of Murty and Chowdhury [8], is given by an array of size N, with each position i of the vector representing a element x_i of the data set and having values in the range $1..K$, indicating which partition the element x_i belongs. For example, if the solution of a specific clustering problem is $C_1 = \{x_1, x_4\}$, $C_2 = \{x_3, x_5\}$, $C_3 = \{x_6, x_7\}$ and $C_4 = \{x_2\}$, then this solution is represented by the array [1 4 2 1 2 3 3]. This representation makes the calculation of the objective function and the centroids of the clusters easier.

The proposed algorithm, like K-means, uses the SSE criterion as objective function in order to make a consistent comparison between the algorithms.

The neighborhood function follows the proposal of Klein and Dubes [6]. It makes a random choice of an element in the data set to be moved to a random partition that is different of the current one. With this function, the new solution will be in a neighborhood that is close to the current solution.

4 Experiments and Results

The experiments evaluated the use of Simulated Annealing and K-means, both initial-ized with random, PCA-Part and K-means++ methods, with the goal of finding the best configuration of partitions in eight real data bases. Table 1 shows the characteris-tics of these databases, all of them being available in public repositories.

In these experiments, the search for the best parameters of Simulated Annealing and the estimated value of SSE were based on the cross-validation technique. The adopted procedure divides randomly the data set in q independent subsets, and takes q iterations. Iteratively one of the q subsets (Y_i) is used as a test set to estimate the out-come of the algorithm, using the best parameters found with the other $(q-1)$ subsets, which are forming a training set (T_i). The final estimate of the value of SSE is the average of the results obtained in the q iterations.

Table 1. Data sets descriptions used in the experiments

Data Set	Number of Elements	Number of Attributes	Number of Classes
Iris	150	4	3
Wine	178	13	3
Vehicle	846	18	4
Cloud	1024	10	10
Segmentation	2310	19	7
Spam	4601	57	2
Pen digits	10992	16	10
Letter	20000	16	26

The search for the best parameters is made with the use of a second cross-validation procedure, in which the set T_i is randomly divided into m independent sub-sets and the combination of values of the parameters that minimizes the function SSE is set to be applied in Y_i. This second cross-validation procedure was used because it is necessary training the algorithm in a subset different of the subset used to estimate the SSE criterion. We assumed that another cross-validation procedure would produce a more general clustering method than the one obtained by simply finding the parame-ters values that optimize the SSE function in the whole partition. The two-step cross-validation procedure was performed with small values of q and m ($q = 10$ and $m = 3$) due to the exhaustive adjustment adopted.

Since the parameter value space is vast and the search performed by the algorithm is a time consuming task, the procedure evaluates all possible combinations of discrete values for the parameters. These values were chosen based on the analysis of Selim and Alsultan [7] and were equal to: T_0 = (500; 5500, 10500, 15500, 20500), T_f = (0.1), r = (0.85, 0.90, 0.95) and N_{iter} = (1000, 2000, 3000).

The combination of these methods (random, PCA-Part and K-means++) were also applied to K-means for the same subsets Y_i used with Simulated Annealing.

Table 2 presents the experimental results using the combination of different initialization methods (random, PCA-Part and K-means++) and search algorithms (K-means and Simulated Annealing). For each base, three experiments with different values of K were performed, one of them equal to the original number of classes of the data set. The best results of each test are emphasized in bold. It is worth to notice that the SSE objective function monotonically decreases when the value of K increases.

Analyzing the results of Table 2, we may notice that, in 14 of the 24 tests, the K-means initialized with PCA-Part obtained better results than K-means++, indicating that the PCA-Part may be generally better than the initialization method of K-means++ (which has the property of assuring closeness to the global optima).

Another observation is that the best result with the Simulated Annealing was greater or equal to the best result with the K-means in 20 of the 24 tests.

It was also noticed that the best results were obtained by the Simulated Annealing initialized with PCA-Part method, which got the best result in 14 of the 24 tests.

Moreover, Simulated Annealing with PCA-Part and K-means++ methods achieved greater or equal results than the K-means initialized with the K-means++ method in 20 of the 24 tests. This indicates that the metaheuristics initialized with these methods may get even closer to the global optima.

It was also observed that, in 17 of the 24 tests, the Simulated Annealing initialized with PCA-Part was better or equal to the same metaheuristic combined to the initialization method of K-means++, reinforcing the indication that the first combination is better than the second.

We applied statistical methods adapted for algorithm comparison in multiple domains (different databases). These methods show if there are differences between the algorithms with the significance level of $a\%$. The significance level indicates the probability of a random data sample generates the result, assuming that the algorithms are equivalent (null-hypothesis). Whenever the random sample produces the result with a probability that is lower than the desired significance level (generally is used $a = 5\%$), then the null-hypothesis is rejected.

The most appropriate method for comparison of multiple algorithms is the Friedman test [17, 18]. This method verifies if in c different, dependent experiments, $c > 1$, at least two are statistically different. The test makes the ordering of the algorithms for each problem separately, giving a rank to each of them with values of 1 to c. The best algorithm receives the rank 1, the second best receives the rank 2, and so on. In case of ties the algorithms receive the average of ranks that would be

Table 2. Experimental Results – SSE Average

Data Set	K	K-means			Simulated Annealing		
		Random	PCA-Part	K-means++	Random	PCA-Part	K-means++
Iris	2	13.9491	13.9491	**13.8699**	**13.8699**	**13.8699**	**13.8699**
	3	9.96375	6.7914	6.75412	**5.98379**	**5.98379**	**5.98379**
	4	5.00787	4.23722	3.87814	**3.46131**	**3.46131**	**3.46131**
Wine	2	369267	364926	368955	**362683**	**362683**	**362683**
	3	159229	154158	155967	151839	**145690**	150402
	4	93706.8	86061.1	107483	**76841.1**	79477.1	83833.8
Vehicle	3	**463986**	471304	481356	482624	466703	480391
	4	324726	290645	318651	286907	**283006**	294798
	5	242253	221410	234724	222688	**216325**	220228
Cloud	9	834627	504282	569423	678689	**477777**	525079
	10	669664	421224	448449	451459	**392694**	397056
	11	659576	377512	388657	393348	**345548**	347743
Segm.	6	1.44e+06	1.25e+06	1.246e+06	1.36e+06	**1.17e+06**	1.22e+06
	7	1.17e+06	1.11e+06	1.08e+06	1.14e+06	1.07e+06	**1.05e+06**
	8	1.12e+06	976326	969249	943673	**921804**	937324
Spam	2	9.00e+07	9.00e+07	8.32e+07	8.07e+07	8.07e+07	**7.07e+07**
	3	5.39e+07	5.39e+07	3.0754e+07	4.17e+07	4.17e+07	**3.0753e+07**
	4	2.59e+07	2.52e+07	2.04e+07	2.40e+07	2.34e+07	**2.01e+07**
Pen digits	9	5.49e+06	5.32e+06	5.38e+06	5.35e+06	**5.28e+06**	5.33e+06
	10	5.03e+06	5.02e+06	4.988e+06	**4.95e+06**	5.04e+06	4.99e+06
	11	4.91e+06	4.73e+06	4.82e+06	4.70e+06	**4.69e+06**	4.75e+06
Letter	25	62001	**61791.9**	62543.7	65033.3	63663	63532.4
	26	61347.2	**60979.2**	61519.8	63274.1	64721.6	67876.8
	27	60509.6	**60053**	60386.5	62428.4	62173.2	61355

assigned to them. The hypothesis that the algorithms are equal is rejected if the value of Friedman statistic indicates a probability that is lower than the desired significance level.

Whenever the null-hypothesis is rejected, the alternative hypothesis is accepted, indicating that at least two algorithms are statistically different. In this case, the analysis continues to find out which pairs of algorithms are different. The Nemenyi test [19] is used to identify the difference between the algorithms. Every algorithm is compared to each other. It means that there is not an algorithm of reference to which the others should be compared. With this test, two algorithms are considered significantly different if the corresponding average ranks differ by the critical difference $CD = q_a [c(c+1)/6n]^{1/2}$, at least, where the critical values q_a are based on the t distribution divided by $2^{(1/2)}$.

In the statistical analysis we have only used the results obtained from each base when K is equal to the number of classes of data, because if more than one test were used on the same data set, even with different values of K, the problems would not represent independent samples, violating the preconditions of the statistical test. Moreover, once the algorithms are executed on the same subsets obtained by the cross-validation division, the experiments are considered dependent, satisfying the required restrictions of the Friedman test.

Table 3. Statistical comparison algorithms over multiple data sets using Friedman Test

Data Set	K-means			Simulated Annealing		
	Random	PCA-Part	K-means++	Random	PCA-Part	K-means++
Iris	6	5	4	2	2	2
Wine	6	4	5	3	1	2
Vehicle	6	3	5	2	1	4
Cloud	6	3	4	5	1	2
Segm.	6	4	3	5	2	1
Spam	5.5	5.5	4	2.5	2.5	1
Pen dig.	5	4	2	1	6	3
Letter	2	1	3	4	5	6
p.m.	5.3	3.7	3.8	3.1	2.6	2.6

Table 3 shows the ranks assigned by the Friedman test and the average of posts (in the last line of the table).

The Friedman test reports a probability of 2.04% that the null-hypothesis is true. This hypothesis may therefore be rejected with 5% significance level. The result of the test indicates that there is at least one pair of statistically different algorithms.

Considering the Nemenyi test, two algorithms are different if their average ranks differ by at least CD = $2.85[(6x7)/(6x8)]^{1/2}$ = 2.67. Thus, the test reports that Simulated Annealing initialized with both PCA-Part and K-means++ are significantly better than the random K-means (5.3125 - 2.5625 = 2.75 > 2.67). Concerning the other algorithms, the analysis couldn't conclude whether there is a difference between them.

5 Conclusions and Future Work

We investigated the use of initialization methods, PCA-Part and K-means++, combined to Simulated Annealing to obtain better results for the clustering problem. The objective of this combination is to find initial solutions that are closer to the global optima, guiding the search algorithm to find the best solution according to the SSE objective function.

In order to analyze the performance of these combinations, experiments were performed in eight databases available in public repositories. The experimental evaluation indicated that the proposed approach performs better than K-means and the classical Simulated Annealing algorithm.

Statistical analysis showed that the Simulated Annealing algorithm initialized with the method PCA-Part and the method of K-means++ has a better performance than the random K-means.

As possible future work, we could extend the statistical analysis by conducting experiments with new bases. We could also try out other initialization methods and metaheuristics to verify if better results are obtained.

Simulated Annealing got bad results in the Letter data set (the largest one) in our experiments, presenting a different behavior of what we expected. Thus, another future work is to analyze the reason of this result and verify if there is some feature of this data set that justifies this behavior.

In addition, the execution time of the algorithms should be analyzed in order to compare the time performance of K-means and Simulated Annealing algorithms. Although this result were not shown here, the experiments showed that K-means had a more efficient time performance than Simulated Annealing because it needs less iterations to reach the final solution.

Acknowledgments. Authors thank the financial support of Conselho Nacional de Desenvolvimento Científico e Tecnológico – CNPq (process 620165/2006-5).

References

1. Jain, A.K., Murty, M.N., Flynn, P.J.: Data Clustering: A Review. ACM Computing Surveys 31, 264–323 (1999)
2. Forgy, E.W.: Cluster Analysis of Multivariate Data: Efficiency vs. Interpretability of Classifications. Biometrics 21, 768–780 (1965)
3. Selim, S.Z., Ismail, M.A.: K-means-type Algorithms: A Generalized Convergence Theorem and Characterization of Local Optimality. IEEE Transaction on Pattern Analysis and Machine Intelligence 6, 81–87 (1984)
4. Rayward-Smith, V.J.: Metaheuristics for Clustering in KDD. In: IEEE Congress on Evolutionary Computation, vol. 3, pp. 2380–2387 (2005)
5. Kirkpatrick, S., Gelatt, C.D., Vecchi, M.P.: Optimization by Simulated Annealing. Science 220, 671–680 (1983)
6. Klein, R.W., Dubes, R.C.: Experiments in Projection and Clustering by Simulated Annealing. Pattern Recognition 22, 213–220 (1989)
7. Selim, S.Z., Alsultan, K.: A Simulated Annealing Algorithm for the Clustering Problem. Pattern Recognition 24, 1003–1008 (1991)
8. Murty, C.A., Chowdhury, N.: In Search of Optimal Clusters using Genetic Algorithms. Pattern Recognition Letter 17, 825–832 (1996)
9. Hall, L.O., Özyurt, I.B., Bezdek, J.C.: Clustering with a Genetically Optimized Approach. IEEE Transaction on Evolutionary Computation 3, 103–112 (1999)
10. Alsultan, K.: A Tabu Search Approach to the Clustering Problem. Pattern Recognition 28, 1443–1451 (1995)
11. Merwe, D.W., Engelbrecht, A.P.: Data Clustering using Particle Swarm Optimization. In: Congress on Evolutionary Computation, vol. 1, pp. 215–220 (2003)
12. Kanade, P.M., Hall, L.O.: Fuzzy Ants Clustering by Centroid Positioning. In: IEEE International Conference on Fuzzy Systems, vol. 1, pp. 371–376 (2004)
13. Babu, G.P., Murty, M.N.: Simulated Annealing for Optimal Initial Seed Selection in K-means Algorithm. Indian Journal of Pure and Applied Mathematics 3, 85–94 (1994)
14. Su, T., Dy, J.: A Deterministic Method for Initializing K-means Clustering. In: IEEE International Conference on Tools with Artificial Intelligence, pp. 784–786 (2004)
15. Arthur, D., Vassilvitskii, S.: K-means++: The Advantages of Careful Seeding. In: Symposium on Discrete Algorithms (2007)
16. Jolliffe, I.T.: Principal Component Analysis. Springer, New York (1986)

17. Friedman, M.: The Use of Ranks to Avoid the Assumption of Normality Implicit in the Analysis of Variance. Journal of the American Statistical Association 32, 675–701 (1937)
18. Friedman, M.: A Comparison of Alternative Tests of Significance for the Problems of m Rankings. Annals of Mathematical Statistics 11, 86–92 (1940)
19. Nemenyi, P.B.: Distribution-free Multiple Comparisons. PhD thesis. Princeton University (1963)

Data Reduction Method for Categorical Data Clustering

Eréndira Rendón[1], J. Salvador Sánchez[2], Rene A. Garcia[1], Itzel Abundez[1],
Citlalih Gutierrez[1], and Eduardo Gasca[1]

[1] Lab. Reconocimiento de Patrones, Instituto Tecnológico de Toluca
Av. Tecnológico s/n, 52140 Metepec (México)
`erendon@ittoluca.edu.mx`
[2] Dept. Llenguatges i Sistemes Informtics, Universitat Jaume I
Av. Sos Baynat s/n, E-12071 Castell de la Plana (Spain)
`sanchez@uji.es`

Abstract. Categorical data clustering constitutes an important part of data mining; its relevance has recently drawn attention from several researchers. As a step in data mining, however, clustering encounters the problem of large amount of data to be processed. This article offers a solution for categorical clustering algorithms when working with high volumes of data by means of a method that summarizes the database. This is done using a structure called CM-tree. In order to test our method, the K-Modes and Click clustering algorithms were used with several databases. Experiments demonstrate that the proposed summarization method improves execution time, without losing clustering quality.

Keywords: Categorical Attributes, K-modes Clustering Algorithm, Reduced database.

1 Introduction

Finding a database object homogeneous partition (tuple) constitutes a fundamental data mining task. This task is referred to as clustering, defined by [1] [2] as a method to partition a set of objects in clusters so that objects in the same cluster are more similar between them than objects from other clusters, according to a previously established criterion, and in order to maximize intra-cluster similarity and minimize inter-cluster similarity. Most of the existing clustering algorithms can be classified into two main categories, namely hierarchical(agglomerative or divisive) and partitioning algorithms [1]. Most clustering algorithms in literature must keep the set of data in the main memory, so not every clustering algorithm can be applied directly when the set of data cannot be stored in the memory. This constitutes a frequent problem in data mining applications, which work with high volumes of data. The presence of categorical data is also frequent.There are clustering algorithms [3] [4] [5] that work with

H. Geffner et al. (Eds.): IBERAMIA 2008, LNAI 5290, pp. 143–152, 2008.

large databases and categorical data, like ROCK [6] clustering algorithm, which deals with the size of databases by working with a database random sample. However, the algorithm is highly impacted by size of the sample and randomness. In this paper, we offer a solution that consists in reducing the size of a categorical-type database, therefore it possible to used any clustering algorithm. In our case, we use the clustering algorithm K-Modes and CLICK [8]. Several scalable clustering algorithms have been recently reported [8] [3] [4]. One of them is the K-Modes algorithm [4], which is the version of the K-means algorithm for categorical data. Although K-Modes is a scalable algorithm, some problems still arise from it. The data mining community has carried out efforts to develop quick and scalable clustering algorithms for large databases and to make them work with categorical data; some of them are described as follows: The ROCK [6] algorithm is an adaptation of an agglomerative hierarchical algorithm. The algorithm attempts to maximize a goodness measure that favors merging pairs with a large number of Links. Two objects are called neighbors if their similarity exceeds a certain threshold θ given by the user. The number of Links between two objects is the number of common neighbors. The Rock algorithm selects a random sample from the databases after a clustering algorithm employing Links is applied to the sample. Finally, the resulting clusters are used to assign the remaining objects on the disk to the appropriate clusters. CACTUS [5] is an agglomerative algorithm that uses data summarization to achieve linear scaling in the number of rows. It requires only two scans of the data. The CACTUS algorithm is based on the idea of co-occurrence for attributes-values pairs and consists of three phases: summarization, clustering and validation. The COOL-CAT clustering algorithm presented by Barbará in [7] is very similar to the K-means algorithm. Unlike K-means, it includes a step that has the purpose of selecting the most adequate representative clusters. It uses entropy as a measure to compute similarity between objects and, as criterion function, it uses minimization of entropy between clusters. The COOLCAT algorithm depends on a sample and it is a hierarchical algorithm. It assumes features are independent from each other. COOLCAT defines a cluster's entropy and starts with a sample of objects; it uses a heuristic method to identify the number of initial clusters, which are the objects with higher entropy. COOLCAT requires as entrance parameters the number of clusters to be formed and the sample size. The CLICK clustering algorithm [8] finds clustering in categorical datasets using a seach method for K- partite maximal cliques. This paper is organized as follows: section 2 provides definitions used by the proposed method; section 3 contains a brief explanation of the K-Modes algorithm; section 4 has the proposed model to summarize the database. Section 5 offers results obtained and, finally, section 6 contains the analysis of results. This paper is organized as follows: section 2 provides definitions used by the method proposed; section 3 contains a brief explanation of the K-Modes algorithm; section 4 has the model proposed to summarize the database. Section 5 offers results obtained and, finally, section 6 contains the analysis of results.

2   Definitions

This section defines concepts that will be used in the rest of this paper. Let D be a database described by a set of records (Tuples), where each tuple $t : t \in D_1 \times \ldots \times D_n$ and a tuple t is represented by $t.A_1, t.A_2, \ldots, t.A_m$; each feature $t.A_i$ takes values in domain D. In clustering, data may be of different types, numeric and non-numeric; non-numeric are frequently referred to as categorical. The first use continuous values and, with categorical data, their domain D_i takes values in a finite, disarranged set; therefore, a feature $t.A_i$ only takes one value from D . Like in [9] an object is a logical conjunction of events. An event is a pair relating features with a value, as follows:

$$[t.A_1 = x_1] \wedge \ldots \wedge [t.A_2 = x_2] \wedge \ldots \wedge [t.A_m = x_m]$$

Where $x_j \in D_j$ for $1 \leq j \leq m$. Then, we define a categorical object as a logical conjunction of events as follows:

$$X = [t.A_1 = x_1] \wedge \ldots \wedge [t.A_2 = x_2] \wedge \ldots \wedge [t.A_m = x_m]$$

For simplicity purposes, an event will be referred to as feature to an event.

2.1   Dissimilarity Measure

The similarity measure used in this paper is described in [4]. Let us take two categorical objects X and Y described in m features. The dissimilarity measure between the objects X and Y is defined by the number of feature-to-feature non-coincidences of objects, formally defined as follows:

$$d_1(X, Y) = \sum_{j=1}^{m} \delta(x_j, y_j) \tag{1}$$

where:

$$\delta(x_j, y_j) = \begin{cases} 1 \ if \ x_j \neq y_j \\ 0 \ if \ x_j = y_j \end{cases} \tag{2}$$

2.2   Frecuency and Mode Vectors

Definition 1. *Let* $C = (t.A_i, t.A_{i+1}, \ldots, t.A_m)$ *be a frecuency vector, where* $i = 1, \ldots, m$; $m = $ *number of attributes and* $t.A_i$ *is defined as follows:* $t.A_i = (x_{i,j}|f_{i,j}| \rightarrow, x_{i,j+1}|f_{i,j+1}| \rightarrow, \ldots, x_{i,d}|f_{i,d}|null)$; *where* $d = |D_i|, x_{i,j}$ *is some value of* A_i; $f_{i,j}$ *is the relative frecuency of* $x_{i,j}$ *and* $\rightarrow$ *is a link to* $x_{i,j+1}$

Definition 2. *Let* $\tilde{F}C = \left(\tilde{f}_j.A_1, \tilde{f}_j.A_2, \ldots, \tilde{f}_j.A_m \right)$ *be a mode vector from* C, *where* $\tilde{f}_i.A_i$ *is* $x_{i,j}$ *value from* A_i *with the highest relative frecuency, which we calculated as follows:* $\tilde{f}_j.Ai = Max \, [x_{i,j}|f_{i,j}| \rightarrow, x_{i,j+1}|f_{i,j+2}| \rightarrow, \ldots, x_{i,d}|f_d|Null]$.

2.3 CM Structure

A CM structure is a pair for summarizing the information that we maintain about a subcluster of objects.

Definition 3. *Given N m − Dimensional categorical objects in a cluster:*$[N_i]$ *where* $i = 1, 2, \ldots, N$, *the structure CM entry of the cluster is defined as a pair* $CM = \left(C, \tilde{F}C \right)$, *where C is a frecuency vector and $\tilde{F}C$ is a mode vector from C.*

2.4 Definition of $CM − Tree$

A $CM − tree$ is a tree balanced by height (see Fig. 1); it is formed by two types of nodes: non-leaf nodes and leaf nodes. These nodes have, in turn, a number of entries, B for the non-leaf nodes and L for leaf nodes, which determine the tree expansion factor, and an absorption threshold T that should meet entries of leaf nodes. Leaf and non-leaf node entries store CM's. At a certain point of the tree construction, leaf nodes contain vector $\tilde{F}C$ representing the cluster of objects that have been absorbed in this entry. Non-leaf nodes store CMs formed by CMs of children nodes (leaf or non-leaf nodes). The construction algorithm is described hereinbelow. Each entry of a leaf and non-leaf node (see Fig.3) stores CMs

2.5 Calculation of Threshold T

To compute T, a heuristic function is proposed to go from T_i to T_{i+1} , which depends on the number of rebuilding and features:

$$T_{i+1} = \frac{m - dec}{m} \tag{3}$$

where m is the number of features, dec is a constant taking values between 0 and m, which may be increased in 1 at each rebuilding to obtain a more compact $CM − tree$.

3 K-Modes Algorithm

The K-Modes [3] algorithm is an extension of the K- means algorithm for categorical data.

General description: The K-Modes algorithm was designed to group large sets of categorical data and its purpose is to obtain K-modes representing the data set and minimizing the criterion function. Three modifications are carried out in the K-modes algorithm with respect to the K-means algorithm:

1. It uses different dissimilarity measures,
2. It substitutes K means by K modes to form centers and
3. It uses a method based in frequencies of attribute values to update modes.

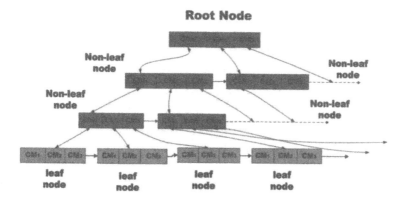

Fig. 1. CM-Tree with L=3 and B=3

Mode update is carried out at each allotment of an object to its set. The K-Modes algorithm produces local optimum solutions depending on initial modes and the objects' entrance order.

4   Proposed Method

The method proposed to reduce the database consists in building a CM-tree that allows obtaining a database summarization.

4.1   Method Overview

Figure 2 shows the details of the summary method. Assume that we know values L, B, T_i and M bytes of memory available for building the $CM - tree$. Summary starts with a $CM - tree$ of a small initial threshold value, say 1, scans the data and inserts objects into the $CM - tree$ t_i using the insertion algorithm described in Section 4.3. If it runs out of memory before it finishes scanning the data, it then increases the threshold value (T_i) and rebuilds a new $CM - tree$ t_{i+1} from $CM - tree$ t_i and T_{i+1}, using the rebuilding process described in Section 4.2. When all objects in the database have been scanned, it has the reduced database into the entry leaves $(\tilde{F}C)$ of the last formed $CM - tree$.

4.2   Rebuilding Process

Assume t_i is a $CM - tree$ of threshold T_i. Its height is h and its size (number of nodes) is S_i. Given $T_{i+1} \geq T_i$, we use all the leaf node entries of $CM - tree$ t_i to rebuild a $CM - tree$ t_{i+1} of threshold T_{i+1} such that the size of t_{i+1} should not be larger than S_i. The building process obtains a $CM - tree$ t_{i+1} from $CM - tree$ t_i using the CM structure from entry leaf nodes of $CM - tree$ t_{i+1}

```
BEGIN
READ L, B, T;
M= MEMORY AVAILABLE
WHILE (EOF)
    {
            SCAN DATA (ent)
            IS THERE MEMORY?
            {
                INSERT (ent) TO CM-TREE t;
            }
            ELSE
            { T_{i+1} = T_i +1;
            EBUILDING (CM-TREE t; ,T_{i+1});
            DELETE CM-TREE t;
            CM-TREE t; CM-TREE t_{i+1};
                T_i =T_{i+1};
            }
    }
```

Fig. 2. Overview of reduced method

4.3 Insertion Algorithm

The insertion algorithm offered here is very similar to the one presented in [10]; the main difference is node entries.

1. Identifying the appropriate leaf: starting from the root, it recursively descends the CM-tree by choosing the closest child node according to the similarity metric given in Sect. 2.1.
2. Updating the leaf: when a leaf node is reached, it finds the closest leaf entry, say L_i, and then tests whether L_i can absorb *ent* without violating the threshold condition. If so, the new entry is absorbed by L_i. If not, it tests whether there is space for this new entry on the leaf. If so, a new entry for *ent* is added to the leaf. Otherwise, the leaf node must be split. Splitting is done by choosing the farthest pair of entries as seeds and redistributing the remaining entries based on the closest criteria.
3. Updating the path to the leaf: after inserting *ent* into a leaf, the information for each non-leaf entry must be updated on the path from the root to the leaf. If no splitting was done, this simply involves the leaf entry that absorbed *ent*. Conversely, a leaf split means that a new non-leaf entry has to be inserted into the parent. If the parent has space for this new entry, at all higher levels, it is only necessary to update the corresponding entries to reflect the addition of *ent*. However, it may be required to split the parent as well, and so on up to the root. If the root is split, the tree height increases by one.

5 Experimental Evaluation

This section offers the results of applying our database reduction method, for which we selected the K-Modes and Click clustering algorithms. Experiments were carried out to test that, when reducing the database, clustering quality is not impacted and execution time is improved. The main task of clustering algorithms is to discover the grouping structures inherent in data. For this purpose, the assumption that a certain structure may exist in a given database is first made and, then, a clustering algorithm is used to verify the assumption

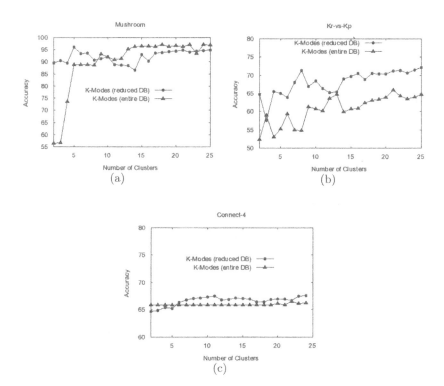

Fig. 3. Accuracy vs Number of clusters (K-Modes)

and recover the structure. [2] presents three types of criteria used to evaluate the performance of clustering algorithms. In evaluating our database reduced method, we chose an external criterion, which measures the degree of correspondence between the clusters obtained from clustering algorithms and the classes assigned a priori. We have used the clustering accurancy as a measure of a clustering result. Clustering algorithms were run in two ways: first, we ran them throughout the entire database; the clustering results obtained are called *Entire DB*; when we ran algorithms throughout the reduced database (using our method), the clustering results are called *Reduced DB*.

5.1 Set of Data Used

Our experiments were carried out with data sets taken from UCI achina Learning Repository: http://www.ics.uci.edu/ mlearn/MLRepository.html. The data sets used were Kr-vs-Kp with 3198 objects, Connect-4 with 67557 and Mushroom with 8124, all of them with categorical data.

5.2 Tests

To measure the results of our model, the k-Modes and Click clustering algorithms were both executed with the reduced and the entire database for different values

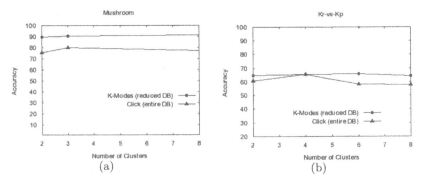

Fig. 4. Accuracy vs Number of clusters (Click)

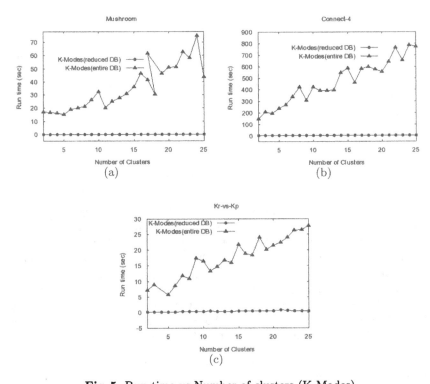

Fig. 5. Run time vs Number of clusters (K-Modes)

of K. The execution time and clustering quality (accuracy) were compared, as shown in Figs. 3 and 5.

5.3   Discussion

– About the K-Modes Algorithm: Figure 3.a presents both clustering results, with the mushroom entire and reduced database for different values of K.

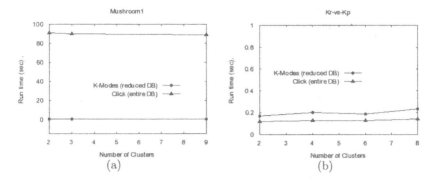

Fig. 6. Run time vs Number of clusters (Click)

On the Reduced DB clustering results, we can see that accuracy was better when K took values between 2-10; however, when K took values between 11 to 25, both clustering results were almost similar. Figure 3.b shows clustering results of the Kr-vs-Kp database, with the Reduced DB clustering results accuracy being slightly better than with the Entire DB clustering results. Figure 3.c shows the Entire DB and Reduced DB clustering results of the Connect-4 database. In this case, accuracy reported on the Reduced DB clustering results was better than with the Entire DB clustering results when K took values between 6 to 23. Figure 5 presents execution times obtained by means of the K-Modes algorithm for both the entire and reduced database. When the K-Modes algorithm was run with the reduced database, better run times were obtained than with the K-modes algorithm and the entire database. We can therefore state that the proposed database reduction method considerably improves the efficiency of the K-Modes algorithm due to the reduction of execution times and because the clustering quality is not affected by this reduction.

– About the Click Algorithm: Figure 4 presents the results obtained by the Click and K-Modes algorithms. The first was run with the reduced DB and the second with the entire DB, using different values of K. For the mushroom dataset, accuracy obtained with K-Modes (Reduced DB) was better than with the Click algorithm (Entire DB). Results obtained with the Kr-vs-Kp dataset were similar (see Figure 4a and Figure 4b). Figure 6 shows the time run, evidencing its decrease when using the reduced DB.

6 Conclusions and Future Works

We offer a solution for categorical data clustering algorithms considering the size of data sets. This solution consists in a database reduction method using a tree-type structure balanced by the height of the CM-tree; it adjusts to the memory availability and, as it reduces the data set, it also carries out semi-clustering. When reducing the data set, tests demonstrated that clustering quality is not affected and execution time decreases considerably. We consider applying this method to other clustering algorithms in the future.

References

1. Kaufman, L., Rousseeuw, P.J.: Finding Groups in Data: An Introduction to Cluster Analysis. John Wiley and Sons, New York (1990)
2. Jain, A.K., Dubes, R.C.: Algorithm for Clustering Data. Prentice-Hall, Englewood Cliffs (1988)
3. Andritsos, P., Tsaparas, P., Miller, R.J., Sevcik, K.C.: LIMBO: A scalable Algorithm to Cluster Categorical Data. Technical report, University of Toronto, Department of Computer Science, CSRG-467 (2004)
4. Huang, Z.: A Fast Clustering Algorithm to Cluster Very Large Categorical Data Sets in Data Mining. In: Sigmod Workshop on Research Issues on Data Mining and Knowledge Discovery, pp. 1–8 (1997)
5. Ganti, V., Gehrkeand, J., Ramakrishanan, R.: CACTUS-Clustering Categorical Data Using Summaries. In: Proceeding of the 5th ACM Sigmod International Conference on Knowledge Discovery in Databases, San Diego, California, pp. 73–83 (1999)
6. Guha, S., Rastogi, R., Shim, K.: Rock: A robust clustering algorithm for categorical attributes. In: Proceeding of the 15th International Conference on Data Engineering (ICDE), Sydney, pp. 512–521 (1999)
7. Barbará, D., Li, Y., Couto, J.: Coolcat: an entropy-based algorithm for categorical clustering, pp. 582–589. ACM Press, New York (2002)
8. Zaki, M.J., Peters, M., Assent, I., Seidl, T.: CLICK: An Effective algorithm for Mining Subspace Clustering in categorical datasets. In: Proceeding of the eleventh ACM SIGKDD International Conference on Knowledge Discovery in Data Mining, pp. 733–742 (2005)
9. Gowda, K., Diday, E.: Symbolic Clustering Using a New Dissimilarity Measure. Pattern Recognition 24(6), 567–578 (1991)
10. Rendón, E., Sánchez, J.S.: Clustering Based on Compressed Data for Categorical and Mixed Attibutes. In: Yeung, D.-Y., Kwok, J.T., Fred, A., Roli, F., de Ridder, D. (eds.) SSPR 2006 and SPR 2006. LNCS, vol. 4109, pp. 817–825. Springer, Heidelberg (2006)

A Multi-measure Nearest Neighbor Algorithm for Time Series Classification

Fábio Fabris, Idilio Drago, and Flávio M. Varejão

Federal University of Espírito Santo, Computer Science Department,
Goiabeiras, 29060900, Vitória–ES, Brazil
{ffabris,idrago,fvarejao}@inf.ufes.br

Abstract. In this paper, we have evaluated some techniques for the time series classification problem. Many distance measures have been proposed as an alternative to the Euclidean Distance in the Nearest Neighbor Classifier. To verify the assumption that the combination of various similarity measures may produce a more accurate classifier, we have proposed an algorithm to combine several measures based on weights. We have carried out a set of experiments to verify the hypothesis that the new algorithm is better than the classical ones. Our results show an improvement over the well-established Nearest-Neighbor with DTW (Dynamic Time Warping), but in general, they were obtained combining few measures in each problem used in the experimental evaluation.

Keywords: Data Mining, Machine Learning, Time Series Classification, Multi-Measure Classifier.

1 Introduction

A time series is a sequence of data points taken at regular intervals. Supervised classification is defined as the task of assigning a label to cases, based on the information learned from examples with known labels. Special algorithms are needed when temporal features represent the examples. The Nearest Neighbor Algorithm with some specialized measure has been the main approach to deal with this kind of classification problem. Several measures have been proposed to this task throughout the years. [1,2] describe some of them without any practical accuracy evaluation. [3] evaluates empirically a set of measures and shows poor classification results in a couple of time series classification problems. [4] shows an extensive experimental evaluation about DTW and concludes that the measure is superior to the basic Euclidean.

In this work, we evaluated if combining measures can improve classification accuracy. We proposed a new heuristic based on weights to combine measures in the nearest neighbor decision rule and carried out a set of experiments to verify our algorithm.

In the next section, we briefly describe the Nearest Neighbor Algorithm and some similarity measures commonly used. Next, we describe the algorithm proposed to search the best weights combination. In Section 4, we showed the

H. Geffner et al. (Eds.): IBERAMIA 2008, LNAI 5290, pp. 153–162, 2008.

testing method, the data sets and our experimental results. Finally, in Section 5, we pointed out our conclusions.

2   1NN Algorithm and Similarity Measures

The traditional approach to classify a given time series uses the Nearest Neighbor Algorithm (1NN) with some similarity measure suitable for temporal data. In this section, we present the nearest neighbor decision rule and several similarity measures that are able to work with time series.

2.1   1NN Algorithm

In the context of classification, the 1NN Algorithm was first introduced by [5]. The algorithm idea rests in the fact that close samples (given some similarity measure) should belong to the same class if they are well distributed and there is enough correlation between the time series and the classes.

We can define formally the 1NN Algorithm given $S = \{(\mathbf{x_1}, \theta_1), \ldots, (\mathbf{x_n}, \theta_n)\}$ as a set of pairs containing n time series $\mathbf{x_i}$ and their classes θ_i. For the sake of our discussion, $\theta_i \in \{\theta^1, \ldots, \theta^c\}$. We wish to ascertain the class of a new sample when introduced its correspondent $\mathbf{x}$. We call $\mathbf{x}' \in \{\mathbf{x_1}, \mathbf{x_2}, \ldots, \mathbf{x_n}\}$ the nearest neighbor of $\mathbf{x}$ if

$$\delta(\mathbf{x}', \mathbf{x}) = min \; \delta(\mathbf{x_i}, \mathbf{x}) \quad i = 1, 2, ..., n \; , \tag{1}$$

where $\delta(\mathbf{y}, \mathbf{z})$ measures the similarity between two time series $\mathbf{y}$ and $\mathbf{z}$. The θ of the new sample is set to its nearest neighbor class. If more than one such neighbor exist, θ is set to the most frequent class.

2.2   Similarity Measures

In order to classify an unlabeled time series using the 1NN Algorithm, we must use some kind of similarity measure $\delta(\mathbf{y}, \mathbf{z})$. Many measures have been proposed throughout the years. In this section, we shall expose a brief description of the most used ones together with some well-known remarks about them.

Euclidean Distance. Probably the first choice of measurement between two time series $\mathbf{y}$ and $\mathbf{z}$, both with size d, is to consider the series as a vector in a d-dimensional space and ascertain the Euclidean Distance between them. [6] defines the distance as

$$\delta(\mathbf{y}, \mathbf{z}) = [(\mathbf{y} - \mathbf{z})^t (\mathbf{y} - \mathbf{z})]^{1/2} = \left[\sum_{i=1}^{d} (y_i - z_i)^2 \right]^{1/2} . \tag{2}$$

There are several drawbacks using Euclidean Distance we have to consider. For instance, the distance is very sensitive to noise, translations, scaling, and small phase differences [7]. To solve vertical translation and scaling problems, an accepted solution is to normalize the curves before measuring [3]. [6] shows many other similarity measures, for example Manhattan Distance, however the same noise, scaling, translation and phase difference problems apply to them.

Edit Distance. The Edit Distance [8] is defined as the minimum set of operations required to change a string into another. The allowed operations are characters deletion, insertion, and substitution. In order to use the Edit Distance, we first have to discretize the data to create a finite set of symbols. [9] defines the Edit Distance of two strings $\mathbf{y}$ and $\mathbf{z}$ as follows:

$$\mathcal{D}(i,0) = s_w \times i \tag{3}$$

$$\mathcal{D}(0,j) = s_w \times j \tag{4}$$

$$\mathcal{D}(i,j) = min \begin{cases} \mathcal{D}(i, j-1) + d_w \\ \mathcal{D}(i-1, j) + d_w \\ \mathcal{D}(i-1, j-1) + t(i,j) \end{cases} \tag{5}$$

where $\mathcal{D}(i,j)$ means the minimum operation cost needed to change the first i symbols of the string $\mathbf{y}$ into the first j symbols of the string $\mathbf{z}$, $t(i,j)$ equals m_w (matching weight) if $y_i = z_j$ and s_w (substitution weight) otherwise, and finally d_w means the character insertion or deletion weight.

In particular, we are interested in the original Edit Distance formulation, with $m_w = 0$ and $s_w = d_w = 1$. The Edit Distance has two main advantages over Euclidean Distance: the character deletion and insertion remove distortions in the series and correct local misalignment; the discretizing process acts as a noise filter.

A common variation of the Edit Distance ($s_w = 1$, $d_w = \infty$, and $m_w = 0$) is the Hamming Distance [10], defined as the number of positions with different symbols in two strings. This variation does not keep the desirable property of distortion removal. The noise filter, however, is still present since the data must be discretized before Hamming Distance calculation.

Another common variation is the *Longest Common Subsequence* (LCSS [9]), defined as the size of the longest ordered sequence of symbols (not necessarily contiguous) appearing in both sequences $\mathbf{y}$ and $\mathbf{z}$. We can define LCSS as

$$\mathcal{L}(i,j) = \begin{cases} \mathcal{L}(i-1, j-1) + 1 & y_i = z_i \\ \mathcal{L}(i-1, j) & \mathcal{L}(i-1, j) \geq \mathcal{L}(i, j-1) , \\ \mathcal{L}(i, j-1) & \text{otherwise} \end{cases} \tag{6}$$

where $\mathcal{L}(i,0) = \mathcal{L}(0,j) = 0$, and use the LCSS as a similarity measure by the relation

$$\delta(\mathbf{y}, \mathbf{z}) = d - \mathcal{L}(d, d) , \tag{7}$$

where d is the series size. If we consider the Edit Distance formulation with $s_w = \infty$, $d_w = 1$, and $m_w = 0$, [11] shows the following relation

$$\mathcal{D}'(d, d) = 2[d - \mathcal{L}(d, d)] , \tag{8}$$

where $\mathcal{D}'(d, d)$ is the Edit Distance particular case.

Dynamic Time Warping. Dynamic Time Warping (DTW) is often used to classify continuous time series [12,4]. The goal is to calculate the minimum distance (often Euclidean) between two series after aligning them. The concept is similar to Edit Distance's but while the Edit Distance only outputs the number of operations made in a reduced set of symbols, DTW outputs the actual distance between the aligned curves. Therefore, it appears that DTW is more prone to deal with time series because no information is lost. On the other hand, we probably do not get the desirable noise reduction from discretization.

The recurrence relation to calculate DTW Distance of two series $\mathbf{y}$ and $\mathbf{z}$ can be written as

$$DTW(i,j) = \gamma(y_i, z_j) + min \begin{cases} DTW(i, j-1) \\ DTW(i-1, j) \\ DTW(i-1, j-1) \end{cases} \tag{9}$$

where $DTW(i,j)$ is the aligned distance of the first i points in $\mathbf{y}$ and the first j points in $\mathbf{z}$. $\gamma(y_i, z_j)$ is the coordinate distance of points y_i and z_j.

DTW has an integer non-negative parameter r (also known as *warping window*) that fixes the greatest modular difference between i and j. If $r = 0$ we are merely calculating the Euclidean Distance of two series. Other values of r limit the maximum possible distortion allowed to match the series.

The value of r affects the classification performance. If r is too big, the alignment could distort too much the series involved, resulting in poor classification performance (see [4]). We can extend the concept of r to Edit Distance and its variations as well. We have considered r as a parameter of these measures during the experimental evaluation.

Transformation based measures. A common approach to measure time series distance requires transforming the series to a new domain and then perform calculation. The Edit Distance, for instance, does exactly that by changing continuous time series to simple discrete strings of symbols. We can use various mathematical transformations to change the series format before measuring.

The Discrete Fourier Transform (DFT) and the Discrete Wavelet Transform (DWT) have been used frequently as a pre-processing step in measure calculation. The amplitude of Fourier coefficients, for example, has the attractive property of been invariant under shifts. Moreover, for some kind of time series, they concentrate major signal energy in few low frequency coefficients [1].

We can generate the Fourier coefficients using the well-known relation [13]

$$X_k = \frac{1}{\sqrt{d}} \sum_{t=0}^{d-1} x_t e^{\frac{-i2\pi tk}{d}} \quad k = 0, 1, \ldots, d-1 , \tag{10}$$

and use the k first coefficients distance as a similarity measure. In this case, k is a parameter to tune and small values will filter high frequencies components (probably noise). In the same way, the Discrete Wavelet Transform can be used as the pre-processing step. The following relation calculates the DWT coefficients

$$c_{j,k} = \frac{1}{d} \sum_{t=0}^{d-1} x_t \psi_{j,k}(t) , \tag{11}$$

where the Mother Wavelet $\psi_{j,k}(t)$ will be scaled and translated by the following relation

$$\psi_{j,k}(t) = 2^{j/2}\psi(2^j t - k) , \qquad (12)$$

where j is a scale factor, k determines the translation and several basis are available, for instance, Haar and Daubechies basis [14]. In this case, we can only use the first j scales in the measuring in order to obtain a noise free distance between two time series.

Discretization Process. When the measure needs to convert series to strings, a discretizing step is needed. The usual method is defining a (fixed) number of intervals and mapping the real numbers to some of them. The intervals limits are chosen equally spaced to divide the values in a homogeneous way.

This method has however a weakness in the boundaries: when two values are near to the limits they may be mapped to different symbols. For instance, the Edit Distance will be increased in that situation, when the series in fact may be very similar.

An alternative is matching points based on proximity [11]. In this case, two points are considered the same symbol if they are closer than a limit β. The value of β must be adjusted, and will deeply affect the classification accuracy.

3   Combining Measures

In the previous section, we have defined several similarity measures. When it comes to classification using the 1NN Algorithm, the traditional approach is to select one measure at a time. We want to evaluate if the use of several measures will extract more useful information from data, improving the overall classification accuracy.

Therefore, a way for selecting or combining measures is necessary. We have created a weighting algorithm to assign a real number for each measure. In our approach, the nearest neighbor is defined as a weighted sum of all measures. We have proposed a new heuristic to search for the best weights, based on a method for the feature selection problem. In this context, [15] proposed the following strategy: divides the interval $[0,1]$ in k equally spaced sub-intervals, uses the middle of the interval as starting point in the search, moves through space replacing weights by their next larger or smaller values in a greedy way, and uses the estimated error rate in the training set as evaluation function. The search stops when successive moves do not produce better results.

In some situations, this approach may generate redundant weights. For example, if $k = 10$ and we have two measures (or features), the combinations $(0.2, 0.8)$ and $(0.1, 0.4)$ produce the same classification results. We have proposed a new approach to avoid generating redundant values and to reduce the search space size: the sum of all values must be always 1. This restriction has led us to the following number of possible weights:

$$C^k_{m+k-1} = \binom{m+k-1}{k} , \qquad (13)$$

where m is the number of measures. For small values of k and m, we can check exhaustively all combinations. In the experimental evaluation presented in the next section, we have $m = 8$ and $k = 10$, so the exhaustive enumeration is feasible.

Algorithm 1 shows the steps to generate all C^k_{m+k-1} weights combinations. It enumerates all possibilities using the lexicographic order and estimates the error rate for each distribution using only the training set and the *leave-one-out* procedure [16].

Algorithm 1. Searches for the combination of weights that maximize the classification performance using several measures

---

Require: S, training examples;
     M, similarity measures;
     d, the step for weight distribution $(1/k)$.
Ensure: **P**, array of size m containing the best weight distribution found.
  1: $se \leftarrow sd \leftarrow \infty$ {se - smallest error found. sd - average distance between samples on the best combination.}
  2: $Q_0 \leftarrow 1$ e $Q_{1...m-1} \leftarrow 0$ {Initializes the weight array for evaluation.}
  3: **repeat**
  4:   $e \leftarrow ascertain\_error(\mathbf{Q}, M, S)$ {Evaluates the current weight distribution.}
  5:   $dist \leftarrow ascertain\_distance(\mathbf{Q}, M, S)$
  6:   **if** $(e < se) \vee [(e = se) \wedge (dist < sd)]$ **then**
  7:     Updates **P**, se and sd;
  8:   **end if**
  9:   $i \leftarrow m - 1$ {i determines if there are more combinations to evaluate.}
10:   **repeat**
11:     $i \leftarrow i - 1$
12:   **until** $[(i \geq 0) \wedge (Q_i = 0)]$
13:   **if** $i \geq 0$ **then** {There are more valid configurations yet.}
14:     $tmp \leftarrow Q_{m-1}$
15:     $Q_{m-1} \leftarrow 0$
16:     $Q_{i+1} \leftarrow tmp + d$
17:     $Q_i \leftarrow Q_i - d$
18:   **end if**
19: **until** $[(i \geq 0)]$

As an example of Algorithm 1 steps, suppose $d = 0.5$ and 3 similarity measures. The algorithm will generate weights as showed in Table 1 and use the *ascertain_error* function to estimate the classification error for each combination.

The algorithm solves ties by preferring combinations where the average distance from samples to their nearest neighbors is minimal (line 1 and variable sd), i.e. we are looking for a selection that keeps neighbors as close as possible.

Another important remark about this algorithm is that it does not tune each measure during the search. It is well known in the literature that some measure parameters affect the classification accuracy - for instance, see [4] where

Table 1. Weights sequence generated by Algorithm 1 when $d = 0.5$ and there are 3 metrics

Step	Q_0	Q_1	Q_2	Step	Q_0	Q_1	Q_2
0	1.0	0.0	0.0	3	0.0	1.0	0.0
1	0.5	0.5	0.0	4	0.0	0.5	0.5
2	0.5	0.0	0.5	5	0.0	0.0	1.0

the authors present such evaluation, about the parameter *warping window* in DTW. We have chosen to work only with the best individual measure setup to restrict the search space size in Algorithm 1. In the experimental evaluation, we have adjusted each measure separately with the training set before running the algorithm.

4 Experimental Evaluation

Our goal is to determine if combining measures in the classification is better than using always the same one. We have compared the new classifier against a "classical option". Normally the Euclidean Distance is used in the baseline classifier when someone wants to advocate the utility of a novel measure, however many works already had showed various weakness related with this measure [7]. We have chosen DTW because it is certainly better than Euclidean Distance, when implemented with *warping window* and tuned with a sufficiently large training set (see [4]).

We want to ascertain if Algorithm 1 yields an improved performance over 1NN-DTW in general, and not only in a special problem. According [17], what we need is a technique to compare two classifiers on multiple data sets. The *Wilcoxon Signed-Rank Test* is suitable for this task, if a random set of time series classification problems is available. The test ranks the difference between the two algorithms and computes the rank sums where each algorithm wins. Under the *null hypothesis*, the algorithms are equal and the sums will be the same. If the data indicate low probability of the result, we can reject the *null hypothesis*. A complete description about that test can be found in [18].

4.1 Data Sets

In order to compare the accuracy of two algorithms on multiple domains, we need a random sample of time series classification problems. There is a great difficulty in obtaining such sample - for instance, [3] shows how the absence of database benchmarks causes erroneous conclusions in data mining community.

We have used 20 problems available in [19], probably the biggest public repository of time series classification data. Even with a reasonable number of examples (in this case, different classification problems), the lack of randomness is a serious drawback to this kind of experimental essay, as described in [20]. Although this weakness reduces the quality of our results, we have used a very safe statistic method (according [17]) and the best sample available, so our conclusions are supported at least by good evidences.

All data sets in the repository were normalized to standard deviation 1 and average 0 in order to mitigate vertical translations and scales issues. Each data set were originally split in two disjoint files for training and independent test. We have merged the two files, randomized their examples, and estimated the error rate by cross-validation, as described in the next section.

4.2   Experimental Results

In order to apply the *Wilcoxon Signed-Rank Test* we have to estimate the error rate for each domain in the experimental sample. We have used the recommended approach in [20]: we have conduced a 10-fold cross-validation, where for each fold only the training set was used to tune the measures and to estimate the weight distribution that minimizes the error rate. In both cases, the *leave-one-out* procedure was used. We have ascertained the round errors with the test sets and the final error rate was the average across 10 repetitions. As noted in [17], individual variances are not needed, since it comes from the different (and ideally independent) problems in the sample.

Table 2 summarizes the results. It shows 1NN-DTW and Algorithm 1 results and marks (boldface) the best result for each problem. The errors for both algorithms were obtained using the same random split during the cross-validation. For this table, the *Wilcoxon Signed-Rank Test* reports *p-value* equal to 2.2% and we were able to reject the null hypothesis that the algorithms have the same accuracy, with 5% significance level.

We now must point out some details about the results in Table 2. Firstly, Algorithm 1 searches exhaustively for the best weight distribution, so the combinations where just one measure receives all weights (all others with zero weight) were checked. We expected at least the same results for both algorithms, because the 1NN-DTW was a special case tested by Algorithm 1, but in 5 problems 1NN-DTW has got better results. This might have occurred in some cases due to the

Table 2. Comparison of error rates for 1NN-DTW and measures combined as in the Algorithm 1

Database	1NN-DTW	Comb. Measures	Database	1NN-DTW	Comb. Measures
50 Words	20.87	**17.12**	*Adiac*	**33.17**	33.30
Beef	43.33	**33.33**	*CBF*	**0.00**	**0.00**
Coffee	**0.00**	1.67	*ECG200*	11.00	**1.00**
Face/All	2.70	**1.40**	*Face/Four*	6.36	**1.82**
Fish	14.57	**8.86**	*Gun/Point*	**2.00**	3.00
Lighting 2	13.01	**11.35**	*Lighting 7*	**22.38**	22.43
Olive Oil	**11.67**	**11.67**	*OSU Leaf*	26.22	**13.15**
S. Leaf	12.89	**8.27**	*S. Control*	1.00	**0.67**
Trace	**0.50**	**0.50**	*Two Pat.*	**0.00**	**0.00**
Wafer	**0.50**	0.60	*Yoga*	15.67	**13.00**

small data set size - for instance, in *Coffee* database we had about 50 examples for round training, almost all measures alone got 100% of correct classification, and the final error difference (1.67%) was caused by 1 mistake. The small database size prevented us from finding the true best measure. In other cases, the weight distribution was very unstable across the cross-validation rounds and probably Algorithm 1 has suffered from overfitting.

In 8 out 11 problems where Algorithm 1 was better, the weights were very concentrated on measures derived from Edit Distance. These measures are much related to DTW. In those problems, probably the noise filter makes the difference.

5   Conclusions

In this work, we presented some measures typically used in time series classification problems. To verify if using different measures together improves the classification accuracy, we proposed an algorithm that combines several measures by assigning weights to them. We conduced a set of experiments and we compared the accuracy of the new algorithm against 1NN-DTW. The *Wilcoxon Signed-Rank Test* reported results with 5% significance level. Our results show that DTW is certainly the first good choice in this kind of problems, but another measures, specially the string ones, must be checked. In some cases, combining metrics brought a good accuracy gain, but in most cases the weights were concentrated in the few best metrics to each problem.

Acknowledgments. We would like to thank CNPq (Grant N° 620165/2006-5) for the financial support given to the research from which this work originated, and Dr. Eamonn Keogh from University of California - Riverside for providing the data used in the experimental evaluation.

References

1. Antunes, C.M., Oliveira, A.L.: Temporal Data Mining: An Overview. In: Proceedings of the Workshop on Temporal Data Mining, San Francisco, EUA. Knowledge Discovery and Data Mining (KDD 2001) (2001)
2. Savary, L.: Notion of Similarity in (Spatio-)Temporal Data Mining. In: ECAI 2002 Workshop on Knowledge Discovery from (Spatio-)Temporal Data, pp. 63–71 (2002)
3. Keogh, E., Kasetty, S.: On the Need for Time Series Data Mining Benchmarks: A Survey and Empirical Demonstration. Data Mining and Knowledge Discovery 7(4), 349–371 (2003)
4. Xi, X., Keogh, E., Shelton, C., Wei, L., Ratanamahatana, C.A.: Fast Time Series Classification Using Numerosity Reduction. In: ICML 2006: Proceedings of the 23rd international conference on Machine learning, pp. 1033–1040. ACM Press, New York (2006)
5. Cover, T., Hart, P.E.: Nearest Neighbor Pattern Classification. IEEE Transactions on Information Theory 13(1), 21–27 (1967)

6. Devijver, P.A., Kittler, J.: Pattern Recognition: A Statistical Approach. Prentice Hall, London (1982)
7. Agrawal, R., Lin, K.I., Sawhney, H.S., Shim, K.: Fast Similarity Search in the Presence of Noise, Scaling, and Translation in Time-Series Databases. In: Proceedings of the 21st International Conference on Very Large Data Bases, pp. 490–501 (1995)
8. Levenshtein, V.I.: Binary Codes Capable of Correcting Deletions, Insertions and Reversals. Soviet Physics Doklady 10(8), 707–710 (1966)
9. Gusfield, D.: Algorithms on Strings, Trees, and Sequences: Computer Science and Computational Biology. Cambridge University Press, New York (1997)
10. Hamming, R.W.: Error Detecting and Error Correcting Codes. Bell System Technical Journal 29(2), 147–160 (1950)
11. Bozkaya, T., Yazdani, N., Özsoyoglu, M.: Matching and Indexing Sequences of Different Lengths. In: CIKM 1997: Proceedings of the Sixth International Conference on Information and Knowledge Management, pp. 128–135. ACM Press, New York (1997)
12. Sakoe, H., Chiba, S.: Dynamic Programming Algorithm Optimization for Spoken Word Recognition. IEEE Transactions on Acoustics, Speech, and Signal Processing 26(1), 43–49 (1978)
13. Agrawal, R., Faloutsos, C., Swami, A.: Efficient Similarity Search in Sequence Databases. In: Proceedings of the 4th International Conference on Foundations of Data Organization and Algorithms, pp. 69–84 (1993)
14. Daubechies, I.: Ten Lectures on Wavelets. In: CBMS-NSF Reg. Conf. Series in Applied Math. SIAM, Philadelphia (1992)
15. Kohavi, R., Langley, P., Yun, Y.: The Utility of Feature Weighting in Nearest-Neighbor Algorithms. In: 9th European Conference on Machine Learning, Prague, Czech Republic. Springer, Heidelberg (1997)
16. Duda, R.O., Hart, P.E., Stork, D.G.: Pattern Classification, 2nd edn. John Wiley and Sons, New York (2001)
17. Demšar, J.: Statistical Comparisons of Classifiers over Multiple Data Sets. Journal of Machine Learning Research 7(1), 1–30 (2006)
18. Sheskin, D.J.: Handbook of Parametric and Nonparametric Statistical Procedures, 2nd edn. Chapman & Hall/CRC, Boca Raton (2000)
19. Keogh, E., Xi, X., Wei, L., Ratanamahatana, C.A.: The UCR Time Series Classification/Clustering (2006), http://www.cs.ucr.edu/~eamonn/time_series_data
20. Salzberg, S.L.: On Comparing Classifiers: Pitfalls to Avoid and a Recommended Approach. Data Mining and Knowledge Discovery 1(3), 317–328 (1997)

Detection of Anomalies in Large Datasets Using an Active Learning Scheme Based on Dirichlet Distributions

Karim Pichara, Alvaro Soto, and Anita Araneda

Pontificia Universidad Católica de Chile
kpb@ing.puc.cl, asoto@ing.puc.cl, aaraneda@mat.puc.cl

Abstract. Today, the detection of anomalous records is a highly valuable application in the analysis of current huge datasets. In this paper we propose a new algorithm that, with the help of a human expert, efficiently explores a dataset with the goal of detecting relevant anomalous records. Under this scheme the computer selectively asks the expert for data labeling, looking for relevant semantic feedback in order to improve its knowledge about what characterizes a relevant anomaly. Our rationale is that while computers can process huge amounts of low level data, an expert has high level semantic knowledge to efficiently lead the search. We build upon our previous work based on Bayesian networks that provides an initial set of potential anomalies. In this paper, we augment this approach with an active learning scheme based on the clustering properties of Dirichlet distributions. We test the performance of our algorithm using synthetic and real datasets. Our results indicate that, under noisy data and anomalies presenting regular patterns, our approach significantly reduces the rate of false positives, while decreasing the time to reach the relevant anomalies.

1 Introduction

In this paper, we propose a new algorithm for the detection of anomalous records in large datasets. Depending of the domain, these anomalies may correspond to fraudulent transactions in a financial database, new phenomena in scientific information, or records of faulty products in a manufacturing database [6]. Our approach is based on the active learning paradigm. Under this scheme, our algorithm selectively asks a human expert for feedback searching for informative data points which, if labeled, would improve the performance of the overall process.

We build upon our previous work [4] [15] that allows us to efficiently find a Bayesian network (BN) [11] [10] to model the joint probability density function (pdf) of the attributes of records in a large database. This joint pdf provides a straight forward method to rank the records according to their oddness. In effect, while highly common records, well explained by the BN receive a high likelihood, strange records, poorly explained by the BN, receive a low likelihood.

Although our previous approach has shown to be effective in the detection of strange records, in practical applications the real relevance of an unusual record

H. Geffner et al. (Eds.): IBERAMIA 2008, LNAI 5290, pp. 163–172, 2008.

is highly dependent of the domain under consideration. For example, in a fraud detection application, an unusual business transaction might not correspond to a fraud but it can be just a legal and irrelevant operation. As suggested by this example, our experience indicates that the raw unsupervised BN, constructed only from the low level features stored in a database, usually provides a great number of false positives.

In this paper, we augment our previous approach with an active learning scheme that helps us to bridge the gap between the blind unsupervised results provided by the BN and the domain knowledge provided by an expert. Our rationale is that while computers can process huge amounts of low level data, an expert can provide high level semantic knowledge to efficiently lead the search. In this way, starting from an initial set of candidate anomalies provided by a BN, our active learning algorithm selectively asks the expert for data labeling, looking for relevant semantic feedback to improve its knowledge about what characterizes a truly relevant anomaly.

The basic ideas behind our active learning approach are based on two main observations:

1) Our first observation is that, usually, the anomalies present in large databases are not isolated points but they exhibit certain regularities or patterns that arise in selective subspaces. In effect, in many domains, it is possible to find "types" of anomalies that form microclusters characterized by specific subsets of attributes of the database. The main goal of our active learning approach is to use the feedback from the expert to rapidly discover these microclusters.

2) Our second observation is rooted in a key feature of our probabilistic model, that is, the factorization of the joint pdf provided by the BN. From a clustering point of view, this factorization can be understood as model fitting in selective dimensions or subspaces. In effect, each factor in the joint pdf is given by a local conditional pdf over a subset of variables. These subsets of variables correspond to relevant subspaces of the feature space. As we explain in Section 2, our active learning approach makes use of the relevant factors provided by the BN and the clustering properties of Dirichlet distributions as the guiding tools to use the feedback provided by the user to find the micro clusters with relevant anomalies.

This paper is organized as follows. Section 2 discusses the details of our approach. Section 3 shows the results of applying our methodology to synthetic databases. Section 4 briefly reviews relevant previous work. Finally, Section 5 presents the main conclusions of this work.

2   Our Approach

This section describes the main steps of our active learning approach. As mentioned before, this algorithm actively asks for feedback from the expert to efficiently explore an initial set of candidate anomalies provided by a BN. In this exploration, the algorithm uses the factorization provided by the BN to identify key subspaces to detect the anomalies. Within the most prominent subspaces, the algorithm identifies relevant microclusters that contain the anomalies. Our algorithms is based on three main steps: 1) Identification of initial set of candidate anomalies, 2) Selection of relevant subspaces using the factorization provided by a BN, and 3) Use of active learning to identify relevant microclusters. In the rest of this section, we refer to the details of these 3 steps.

In what follows, we use lowercase boldface letters, such as $\mathbf{x}$, to denote sets of single random variables, such as x_i. We use lowercase letters, such as x, to denote an instance of $\mathbf{x}$. We assume that the input database contains unlabeled observations and that there is no missing data.

2.1 Identification of Initial Set of Candidate Anomalies

As a first step of our algorithm, we fit a BN to the records in the database (see [4] for details). If the training of the BN is successful, most anomalies appear as low probability objects. Therefore, we use the likelihood values provided by the BN as an indicator of the degree of rareness of each record in the database. This helps us to filter the dataset by identifying as candidate anomalous records only the first τ records with lowest likelihood. Deciding the correct value of τ depends directly on the capacity of the BN to fit the data. In our experience, the anomalous records usually fall between the 5 to 10% of the records with lowest probability under the BN model.

The factorization of the joint pdf provided by the BN allows us to efficiently estimate the likelihood of a record x in the database, as

$$P(x) = \prod_i^n p(x_i | Pa^G(x_i)) \tag{1}$$

where G is the acyclic directed graph that defines the BN, $Pa^G(x_i)$ is the set of direct parents of x_i in G, and n is the total number of attributes in the database.

2.2 Selection of Relevant Subspaces

Our next step is to find the relevant subspaces, or sets of attributes, that we use to identify microclusters containing anomalies. Our intuition is that the target subspaces are closely related to the factors provided by the BN, as these factors model the most relevant relations or patterns arising from the data.

In most situations, as it is in our experiments, the anomalies in the database correspond to a very small fraction of the total number of records, so we do not expect that the initial set of factors found by the BN highlights the target subspaces. Therefore, we fit a second BN to the reduced set of candidate anomalies, with the goal of obtaining a set of factors with a closer relation to the subspaces that determine the patterns of the anomalies.

For a given record in the candidate set of anomalies, we define its relevant factors as the set of factors that contribute the most to its likelihood obtained from the new BN. In particular, let $\bar{p}_i$ be the mean value of factor $p(x_i | Pa^G(x_i))$ over the candidate anomalies k, $k = 1, \ldots, \tau$. Also, let S be the set of all records with values of the i-th factor greater than $\bar{p}_i$. Then, for a given record we define the factor $p(x_i|Pa^G(x_i))$ as relevant, if:

$$p(x_i^k|Pa^G(x_i)^k) \ > \ \bar{p}_i + \delta, \qquad (2)$$

$$\text{where} \qquad \delta = \frac{1}{|S|} \sum_{x^k \in S} (p(x_i^k|Pa^G(x_i)^k) - \bar{p}_i).$$

After obtaining the relevant factors, we relate them to the respective records. We visualize this as a bucket filling process. We represent each factor $p(x_i|Pa^G(x_i))$ of the joint pdf by a bucket i, $i = 1, \ldots n$. A record x from the set of candidate anomalies is included in that bucket, if the corresponding factor is relevant for that record. In this way, each record can be assigned to several buckets.

Given that our goal is to find microclusters with potential anomalies, we perform a clustering process within each bucket, using the elements inside the bucket. We use Gaussian Mixture Models (GMMs) to find the microclusters. Each GMM is trained with an accelerated version of the Expectation Maximization (EM) algorithm [15] that incorporates a model selection step to estimate a suitable number of Gaussians. When training the mixture in a given bucket, we use only the dimensions or attributes that identify that bucket. In this way, in bucket i the mixture is trained in the subspace generated by x_i and those attributes contained in $Pa^G(x_i)$.

After we find the microclusters, we assign to each datapoint a weight that is inverse to the initial joint probability value under the initial BN model. This ensures higher likelihood values to less probable elements according to the BN used to model all the data. As a result, the strangest records have a higher probability of being sampled in the next step the algorithm.

2.3 Use of Active Learning to Identify Relevant Microclusters

In this step of our algorithm, we implement the active learning scheme that uses the feedback from the expert to guide the search for anomalous records. The selection of candidate anomalous records shown to the expert is based on the buckets and microclusters found in the previous step. The selection is performed by a 3-step sampling process: 1) First, we select one of the buckets. 2) Then, from this bucket, we select a microcluster and, 3) Finally, from this microcluster, we select the candidate anomalous record that is shown to the expert. According to the classification assigned by the expert to the selected record, we refine our model, increasing or decreasing the likelihood of retrieving again a relevant anomaly from the same bucket and microcluster.

We perform the 3-step sampling process and model refinement using a probabilistic approach, where probabilities represent the uncertainty about whether or not a bucket or microcluster contains anomalous records. We model the problem using Dirichlet distributions [5], and take advantage of their clustering properties. In particular, our microcluster selection process corresponds to an instance of a Polya Urn model [3].

In the process of sampling buckets, we use a Multinomial distribution to model the probability of selecting each bucket. Initially, each bucket has the same probability p_i of being selected. Later, after receiving feedback from the expert, we update the parameters of the Multinomial distribution according to the equations of a Polya Urn process [5]. In this way, a successful bucket increases its own probability of been selected while an unsuccessful bucket decreases this probability.

Once a given bucket is selected, we sample an observation from the GMM used to model the microclusters inside that bucket. Given that we use Gaussian functions, it is possible that the sample from the Gaussian mixture does not correspond to the position of a real record inside the bucket. To solve this problem, we use Euclidean distance to select the record in the bucket that is closest to the sampled observation. As we do in the bucket selection process, we also use the feedback from the user and the equations of a Polya urn process to update the probabilities of selecting a given microcluster from the relevant GMM. Here, the Dirichlet distribution controls the parameters of a Multinomial distribution over the set of mixture weights of the GMM. In this way, a positive feedback from the user increases the probability of selecting again a record from the given microcluster.

3 Results

We test our algorithm under different conditions using synthetic and real datasets. Synthetic datasets correspond to samples from GMMs, where we artificially add anomalous records as datapoints in microcluster of low density areas. In the real case, we use a dataset from the UCI repository [2], corresponding to a pen-based recognition of handwritten digits.

In the experiments, we use as a baseline method an scheme that we called BN-detection. This scheme consists on showing sequentially to the experts, the records sorted in ascending order according to the likelihood values provided by the BN applied to the complete dataset. In this way, we can observe the advantages of adding the active learning scheme.

3.1 Anomaly Detection in Synthetic Datasets

To analyze the performance of our algorithm, we use synthetic datasets to conduct 3 main experiments: 1)Evaluation of anomaly detection, 2)Evaluation of capabilities to learn the relevant subspaces for the anomalous records, 3) Evaluation of sensibility under presence of noisy records.

The synthetic datasets contains 90.000 records and 10 attributes. We add to this dataset 2000 anomalous records, simulated on five different subspaces with 400 anomalies contained in each one. To build the BN that models the candidate set of anomalies, we use 10% of the records with lowest likelihood, i.e., $\tau = 9200$.

Figure 1 shows the number of anomalies detected by the algorithm in each of the 5 subspaces with anomalies versus the number of records shown to the expert.

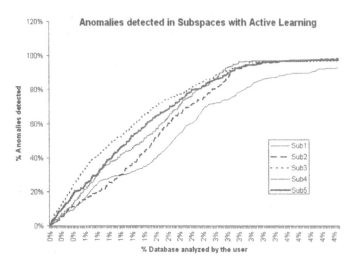

Fig. 1. Detection of anomalies in a database containing 90.000 records, 10 attributes, and 2000 anomalous records

We can see that the algorithm is able to detect around 90% of the anomalies when the expert has analyzed only 2% of the database.

In terms of the impact of our active learning scheme to speed up the detection of the anomalies, our tests indicate that the proposed approach speed up in 25% the anomaly detection rate with respect to the baseline method.

3.2   Detection of Relevant Subspaces for Anomalous Records

To test the effectiveness of our algorithm to detect relevant subspaces where anomalies are generated, we conduct the following experiment. We simulate a database containing 11.000 records and 8 attributes. We add to this dataset 249 anomalous records, simulated on five different subspaces with 83 anomalies contained on each one. The anomalies were simulated on subspaces $S_1 = \langle x_1, x_3, x_5 \rangle$, $S_2 = \langle x_2, x_4, x_6 \rangle$, and $S_3 = \langle x_8, x_7 \rangle$. To build the BN that models the candidate set of anomalies we used $\tau = 2000$.

Figure 2 shows the percentage of the anomalous records detected in the different buckets provided by the BN factorization. In the figure, most of the anomalies generated in subspace $S_1 = \langle x_1, x_3, x_5 \rangle$ are detected in the bucket related to subspace $\langle x_3, x_5 \rangle$. A similar situation occurs with anomalies generated in the subspace $S_2 = \langle x_2, x_4, x_6 \rangle$, which are mostly detected in the bucket related to subspace $\langle x_4, x_6 \rangle$. This result shows that indeed, there is a close relation between the factorization provided by the BN and the subspaces that are relevant for the anomalies.

In the case of subspace $S_3 = \langle x_8, x_7 \rangle$, there is an indication of some indirect relations occurring between variables in subspaces and buckets, where some variables are related with others subspaces through the BN structure. In effect, the

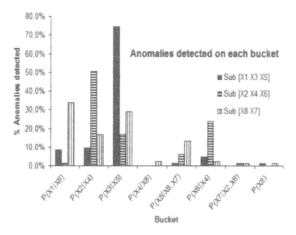

Fig. 2. Anomalies detected inside each bucket. Higher levels of detection are inside the buckets representing variables related to the subspaces where the anomalies are generated.

bucket related to the subspace $\langle x_2, x_4 \rangle$ detects almost 20% of the anomalies from subspace $S_3 = \langle x_8, x_7 \rangle$, whose variables are not included in the set of variables that represent the bucket. Following the BN structure, however, we see that x_4 is a parent of x_8 and x_2 is a direct descendant of x_7.

3.3   Sensibility under Presence of Noise

In this experiment we compared the performance of BN-detection versus our algorithm under databases containing different levels of noisy records. Figure 3 shows number of questions required to detect 100% of total number of anomalies for a synthetic database with 15.000 records and 10 attributes, where 400 frauds are simulated on five different subspaces under different level of noisy records. Noisy records were generated using samples from uniform distributions in the range of values of each attribute.

Figure 3 shows that the performance of BN-detection schemes does not scale well with level of noisy records. This result was expected because most of the noisy records appear as low likelihood points, then they are shown to the expert. In contrast, the clustering properties of our active learning scheme provides better scaling with level of noise because the search concentrates in buckets and microclusters with relevant anomalies.

It is relevant to note that previous experiments were conducted under different conditions of database size, dimension, and number of anomalies. In all tests, we observed similar results to the ones shown in this paper.

3.4   Anomaly Detection in a Real Dataset

We test our active learning approach and the BN-detection scheme with a real database containing 9000 records with 16 attributes. Each record corresponds

Noise level effect

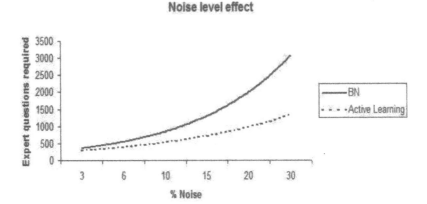

Fig. 3. How the Noise level increase the time required for anomaly detection. Active Learning is less sensible to noise.

to a handwritten character of one of 10 different classes. Here, two of these classes are considered as anomalous because they correspond to only 2% of the database. Figure 4 shows the number of detections with both approaches. Our algorithm detects 90% of the anomalies analyzing around 20% of the total dataset. Particularly, in the case of the first anomalous class, the number of anomalies detected is highly improved with the active learning scheme. For this case, the active learning based approach detects 150% more anomalies than the BN-detection scheme among the first 25% of the objects shown to the expert.

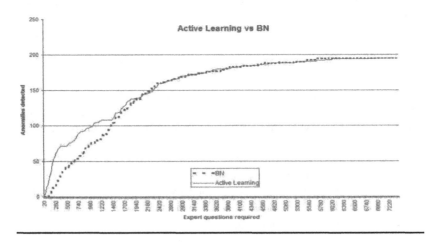

Fig. 4. Anomaly detection performance using the active learning scheme and the BN detection for both anomalous class on a real database

4   Previous Work

Given space constraints we just briefly review some relevant related work in the area of anomaly detection and active learning. The AI [7] [1] and the related Machine Learning communities [8] [6] have tackled the problem of anomaly detection, motivated mainly by applications on fraud detection. In contrast to our approach, most of these applications are based on supervised learning techniques. Unsupervised learning, such as clustering techniques, have also been used to detect anomalies. Using clustering, anomalies are detected as micro clusters or isolated points located in low density regions of the features space [8].

In the context of active learning, mainly in problems related to classification, there have been considerable research about the problem of deciding how to improve the accuracy of a classifier by actively deciding what instance to label [14] [9] [13] [16]. In a work closely related to our application domain, Pelleg and Moore [12] propose an active learning strategy to find anomalies in a database. The main difference with our approach is that they do not explicitly search for relevant anomalies in selective subspaces.

5   Conclusions

This work contributed with an algorithm based on the active learning paradigm that tackles the problem of detecting anomalous records in large datasets. Using the factorization of the joint pdf provided by a BN and the properties of Dirichlet distributions to model a Polya urn process, we were able to use the feedback from the user to speed up the selection of relevant anomalies that exhibit regularities or patterns in selective subspaces.

Our results indicated that with respect to a baseline method that do not incorporate active learning, the approach presented in this work was able to significantly decrease the time to reach the relevant anomalies. Furthermore, by providing a set of specific attributes corresponding to the subspace used to detect the anomaly, the method proposed here was also able to provide an explanation of the main sources of the anomaly.

As future work, we believe that the incorporation of previous knowledge in the modeling steps can improve the detection. Also a most exhaustive experimental analysis in datasets coming from different domains is also a valuable step forward. Given that the expert time is usually the most valuable resource in the loop, we believe that tools as the one presented here may be of great help as a filtering step to help and guide the search in datasets where an exhaustive analysis is not possible.

References

1. Aamodt, A., Plaza, E.: Case-based reasoning: Foundational issues, methodological variations, and system approaches. Artificial Intelligence Communications 7(1), 39–59 (1994)
2. Asuncion, A., Newman, D.J.: UCI machine learning repository (2007), http://www.ics.uci.edu/~mlearn/MLRepository.html

3. Blackwell, D., MacQueen, J.: Ferguson distribution via polya urn schemes. The Annals of Statistics 1(2), 353–355 (1973)
4. Cansado, A., Soto, A.: Unsupervised anomaly detection in large databases using bayesian networks. Applied Artificial Intelligence 22(4), 309–330 (2008)
5. Ferguson, T.: A bayesian analysis of some nonparametric problems. The Annals of Statistics 1(2), 209–230 (1973)
6. Hodge, V., Austin, J.: A survey of outlier detection methodologies. Artificial Intelligence Review 22(2), 85–126 (2004)
7. Jackson, P.: Introduction to Expert Systems. Addison-Wesley, Reading (1998)
8. Kou, Y., Lu, C., Sirwongwattana, S., Huang, Y.: Survey of fraud detection techniques. In: Proc. of the IEEE Int. Conf. on Networking, Sensing and Control, pp. 749–754 (2004)
9. Lewis, D., Gale, W.: A sequential algorithm for training text classifiers. In: Proc. of 17th Int. Conf. ACM SIGIR, pp. 3–12 (1994)
10. Neapolitan, R.: Learning Bayesian Networks. Prentice-Hall, Englewood Cliffs (2004)
11. Pearl, J.: Probabilistic Reasoning in Intelligent Systems: Networks of Plausible Inference. Morgan Kaufmann, San Francisco (1988)
12. Pelleg, D., Moore, A.: Active learning for anomaly and rare-category detection. In: Proc. of the 18th Conf. on Advances in Neural Information Processing Systems, NIPS (2004)
13. Roy, N., McCallum, A.: Toward optimal active learning through sampling estimation of error reduction. In: Proc. of 18th Int. Conf. on Machine Learning, ICML, pp. 441–448 (2001)
14. Seung, S., Opper, M., Sompolinski, H.: Query by committee. In: Proc. of 5th Annual ACM Workshop on Computational Learning Theory, pp. 287–294 (1992)
15. Soto, A., Zavala, F., Araneda, A.: An accelerated algorithm for density estimation in large databases using Gaussian mixtures. Cybernetics and Systems 38(2), 123–139 (2007)
16. Tong, S., Koller, D.: Active learning for parameter estimation in bayesian networks. In: Proc. of the 13th Conf. on Advances in Neural Information Processing Systems, NIPS, pp. 647–653 (2001)

The SKM Algorithm: A K-Means Algorithm for Clustering Sequential Data

José G. Dias[1] and Maria João Cortinhal[2]

[1] Department of Quantitative Methods,
ISCTE Business School and UNIDE,
Av. das Forças Armadas, Lisboa 1649–026, Portugal
jose.dias@iscte.pt

[2] Department of Quantitative Methods,
ISCTE Business School and CIO,
Av. das Forças Armadas, Lisboa 1649–026, Portugal
maria.cortinhal@iscte.pt

Abstract. This paper introduces a new algorithm for clustering sequential data. The SKM algorithm is a K-Means-type algorithm suited for identifying groups of objects with similar trajectories and dynamics. We provide a simulation study to show the good properties of the SKM algorithm. Moreover, a real application to website users' search patterns shows its usefulness in identifying groups with heterogeneous behavior. We identify two distinct clusters with different styles of website search.

Keywords: clustering, sequential data, K-Means algorithm, KL distance.

1 Introduction

Clustering is the partition of a data set into subsets (clusters), so that the data in each subset share similar characteristics. The application of clustering algorithms has been extensive. For example, in Marketing, market segmentation means the identification of groups of customers with similar behavior given a large database of customer data containing their properties and past buying records; in Biology, the taxonomical classification of plants and animals given their features; or, in earthquake studies in which clustering observed earthquake epicenters allows the identification of dangerous zones. In this research we focus on the clustering of sequential data.

Let us have a data set of n objects to be clustered. An object will be denoted by i ($i = 1, \ldots, n$). Each object is characterized by a sequence of states $\mathbf{x}_i$. Let $\mathbf{x} = (\mathbf{x}_1, \ldots, \mathbf{x}_n)$ denote a sample of size n. Let x_{it} denote the state of the object i at position t. We will assume discrete time from 0 to T_i ($t = 0, 1, \ldots, T_i$). Note that the length of the sequence may differ among objects. Thus, the vector $\mathbf{x}_i$ denotes the consecutive states x_{it}, with $t = 0, \ldots, T_i$. The sequence $\mathbf{x}_i = (x_{i0}, x_{i1}, \ldots, x_{iT_i-1}, x_{iT_i})$ can be extremely difficult to characterize, due to its possibly huge dimension $(T_i + 1)$. A common procedure to simplify the sequence

H. Geffner et al. (Eds.): IBERAMIA 2008, LNAI 5290, pp. 173–182, 2008.
© Springer-Verlag Berlin Heidelberg 2008

is by assuming the Markov property. It states that the occurrence of event x_t depends only upon the previous state x_{t-1}; that is, conditional on x_{t-1}, x_t is independent of the states at the other time points. From the Markov property, it follows that the probability of a sequence $\mathbf{x}_i$ is

$$p(\mathbf{x}_i) = p(x_{i0}) \prod_{t=1}^{T_i} p(x_{it}|x_{i,t-1}) \tag{1}$$

where $p(x_{i0})$ is the initial distribution and $p(x_{it}|x_{i,t-1})$ is the probability that object i is in state x_{it} at t, given that it is in state $x_{i,t-1}$ at time $t-1$ (For an introduction to Markov chains, see [9]). A first-order Markov chain is specified by its transition probabilities and initial distribution. Hereafter, we denote the initial and the transition probabilities as $\lambda_j = P(x_{i0} = j)$ and $a_{jk} = P(x_t = k|x_{t-1} = j)$, respectively. The parameters of the Markov chain can be estimated by

$$\hat{\lambda}_j = \sum_{i=1}^{n} I(x_{i0} = j) \tag{2}$$

$$\hat{a}_{jk} = \frac{\sum_{i=1}^{n} n_{ijk}}{\sum_{r=1}^{K} \sum_{i=1}^{n} n_{ijr}}, \tag{3}$$

where K denotes the number of states, $I(x_{i0} = j)$ is the indicator function at time point 0, and n_{ijk} is the number of transitions from state j to state k for object i.

This paper introduces a K-Means-type algorithm that allows the clustering of this type of data. Section 2 describes a K-means algorithm for sequential data. Section 3 analyzes the performance of the algorithm. Section 4 illustrates the application of the algorithm in clustering web users based on their longitudinal pattern of search. The paper concludes with a summary of main findings, implications, and suggestions for further research.

2   The SKM Algorithm

2.1   The K-Means Algorithm

The K-means algorithm [7] is one of the simplest unsupervised learning algorithms that solves the clustering problem. That is, this procedure defines a simple and fast way to determine a partition of a data set into a certain number of clusters (assume S clusters) fixed a priori so that the within group sum of squares is minimized. The K-means algorithm consists of the following steps:

1. Set the number of clusters, S;
2. Generate randomly initial cluster centroids;
3. Assign each object i to the cluster s that has the closest centroid;
4. Recalculate the positions of the centroids;
5. If the positions of the centroids did not change the algorithm ends, otherwise go to Step 2.

However, it has been shown that the conventional K-means algorithm is inappropriate for the discovery of similar patterns in sequential data (e.g., for web usage patterns, see [13]). For web mining purposes, [8] proposed clustering web users using a K-means algorithm based on the KL-divergence which measures the "distance" between individual data distributions. A similar approach is adopted by [16], who looked at the number of times a given user visited a given webpage. [12] suggested using self-organizing maps (SOMs) of user navigation patterns. On the other hand, [14] suggests the clustering of objects at different time points and then, the analyzes of the evolution of the clusters found. However, none of these approaches accounts for the sequential structure of data at the individual level. This means that consecutive states in a sequence are, in fact, treated as independent observations conditional on cluster membership, an assumption that is rather unrealistic. The proposed SKM algorithm circumvents this problem.

2.2   The SKM Algorithm

The SKM (Sequential K-Means) algorithm is a K-Means-based algorithm that uses the Kullback-Leibler distance [4] to cluster sequential data. Let us define some notation first. Let $z_{is} = 1$ if object i belongs to cluster s, and 0 otherwise. Then, transition probabilities within each cluster are the *centroids* and are defined by:

$$\hat{a}_{sjk} = \frac{\sum_{i=1}^{n} z_{is} n_{ijk}}{\sum_{r=1}^{K} \sum_{i=1}^{n} z_{is} n_{ijr}}. \tag{4}$$

Let d_{is} be a measure of distance of object i to the prototype of cluster s. Because we want to measure the distance or divergence of each object i to each centroid s, and provided that the centroid of each cluster is defined by the set of transition probabilities $\hat{a}_{sjk}$, the Kullback-Leibler (KL) distance is the appropriate distance for this type of centroids (probabilities or proportions) and yields[1]

$$d_{is} = \sum_{j=1}^{K} \sum_{k=1}^{K} \hat{a}_{sjk} \ln \left(\frac{\hat{a}_{sjk}}{p_{ijk}} \right), \tag{5}$$

---

[1] In our clustering procedure we do not compute the distance between objects i and j. In that case, it would be desirable to have a symmetric distance, i.e., the distance between objects i and j should be the same as the one between objects j and i ($d_{ij} = d_{ji}$). Because the KL distance between i and j is different from the KL distance between j and i, we could have obtained a symmetric KL distance by computing the mean of these two KL distances as in [8]. In our clustering procedure symmetry is not needed or even desirable. By computing the distance between each object i and the centroid of each cluster s, the KL distance uses as weight function $\hat{a}_{sjk}$ that is a more stable distribution than p_{ijk} as the former is based on all objects in cluster s (equation 4) and the latter is just based on observed transitions for object i.

where p_{ijk}, the transition probability from state j to state k for object i, is defined by

$$p_{ijk} = \frac{n_{ijk}}{\sum\limits_{k=1}^{K} n_{ijk}}. \tag{6}$$

The SKM is an iterative algorithm that starts from a randomly generated solution. Given the number of clusters, a randomly generated allocation of objects is generated, and at each iteration step objects are reallocated according to the Kullback-Leibler distance; that is, each object is assigned into the closest cluster's centroid. This process is repeated until some termination criterion is met. Moreover, two termination criteria are defined: the maximum number of iterations - $MaxIter$ - and the absence of change in the allocation of objects between two consecutive iterations. Because these K-Means type algorithms suffer from local optima, it is desirable to repeat the iterative process with different random starting values. Out of a set of R runs, we select the solution that maximizes the classification log-likelihood:

$$\ell = \sum_{i=1}^{n} \sum_{s=1}^{S} z_{is} \left[\log \pi_s + \sum_{j=1}^{K} I(x_{i0} = j) \log \lambda_{sj} + \sum_{j=1}^{K} \sum_{k=1}^{K} n_{ijk} \log a_{sjk} \right], \tag{7}$$

where $\hat{\lambda}_{sj}$ – the initial probabilities within each cluster – and $\hat{\pi}_s$ – the proportion of objects in cluster s – are defined by:

$$\hat{\lambda}_{sj} = \frac{\sum_{i=1}^{n} z_{is} I(x_{i0} = j)}{\sum_{i=1}^{n} z_{is}}, \tag{8}$$

$$\hat{\pi}_s = \frac{1}{n} \sum_{i=1}^{n} z_{is}. \tag{9}$$

The pseudo code for the SKM algorithm is:

SKM$(S, x_{i0}, n_{ijk}, MaxIter)$
1. $Iter \leftarrow 1$
2. Randomly generate a matrix Z such that:
3. $\quad z_{is} \in \{0,1\}, \sum_{s=1}^{S} z_{is} = 1$, and $\sum_{i=1}^{n} z_{is} > 0$
4. **REPEAT**
5. $\quad$ Update the previous allocation of objects:$Z\_Old \leftarrow Z$
6. $\quad$ Update the centroids $(\hat{a}_{sjk})$
7. $\quad$ Compute d_{is} for each object i and cluster s
8. $\quad$ Determine $s_i = \arg\min_{s \in \{1,...,S\}} d_{is}$, for each object i
9. $\quad$ Update $Z : z_{i,s_i} \leftarrow 1$ and $z_{is} \leftarrow 0$, for all $s \neq s_i$
10. $\quad$ $Iter \leftarrow Iter + 1$
11. **UNTIL** $(Iter = MaxIter$ or $Z\_Old = Z)$
12. Compute $\hat{\pi}_s$, $\hat{\lambda}_{sj}$, and the classification log-likelihood (ℓ)
13. **RETURN** $(\ell, \hat{a}_{sjk}, \hat{\pi}_s, \hat{\lambda}_{sj})$

where Z and Z_Old represent matrices with allocations z_{is}, and $Iter$ counts the number of iterations.

The SKM algorithm was implemented in MATLAB 7.0 [6].

3   Simulation Study

This section analyzes the performance of the proposed algorithm using synthetic data sets. We set:

1. Sample size: $n = 1200$;
2. Sequence length: $T = 50$;
3. Number of clusters: $S = 3$;
4. Number of states: $K = 3$;
5. Number of runs: $R = 50$.

The clusters' sizes (π_s) and initial probabilities (λ_{js}) are the same across clusters and states, respectively. They are defined as $\pi_s = S^{-1}$ and $\lambda_{js} = K^{-1}$. Thus, all cluster size proportions are 0.333 (π_s) and the probability of starting in a given state within each cluster is 0.333 (λ_{js}). In order to obtain different levels of separation of these three clusters, the transition probabilities are defined as

$$a_{sjk} = \begin{cases} \alpha_s & , j = k \\ (1 - \alpha_s)/(K - 1) & , j \neq k, \end{cases} \tag{10}$$

where

$$\alpha_s = \begin{cases} 0.5 - \delta & , s = 1 \\ 0.5 & , s = 2 \\ 0.5 + \delta & , s = 3. \end{cases} \tag{11}$$

The δ parameter is set to 0.4, 0.3, 0.2 and 0.1, which yields four data sets – Study1_40, Study1_30, Study1_20 and Study1_10 – with increasing cluster overlapping. For example, for Study1_40 the diagonal probabilities are 0.1, 0.5, and 0.9 for cluster 1, 2, and 3, respectively.

For each data set, the SKM algorithm was run with $R = 50$ different randomly generated initial solutions. The effect of the starting solutions on the results was analyzed by a percentage deviation based on the classification log-likelihood (ℓ). Let $Best_\ell$ be the maximum classification log-likelihood out of 50 and ℓ_r the classification log-likelihood obtained at run r.[2] The percentage deviation is defined by:

$$Dev_r = 100 \times \frac{\ell_r - Best_\ell}{Best_\ell} \tag{12}$$

Table 1 depicts the maximum (max), the mean, the minimum (min), and the standard deviation (stdev) values of the percentage deviation for each data set.

---

[2] To avoid the comparison of the best classification log-likelihood with itself only 49 runs are applied.

Table 1. Minimum, mean, maximum, and standard deviation values of percentage deviations for Study1 data sets

Data Set	min	mean	max	stdev
Study1_10	0.005	0.027	0.051	0.010
Study1_20	0.000	0.006	0.009	0.003
Study1_30	0.000	0.002	0.003	0.001
Study1_40	0.001	0.002	0.002	0.000

Exception made for minimum values, the percentage deviation increases as the level of separation decreases. However, the average and standard deviation values lead us to conclude that SKM algorithm is not significantly dependent of the initial solution.

Table 2 depicts the best result out of 50 runs of the SKM algorithm for each data set. Globally one concludes that the results are very close to the true values and the differences are due to sampling error in the simulation study. Indeed, in all four data sets the SKM algorithm is able to retrieve their cluster structure. As expected the Study1_10 is the most difficult one because the clusters are not very well separated as for example in Study1_40, where groups show very different dynamic behavior. For example, cluster 1 tends to move in a very fast way between states, whereas cluster 3 tends to stay in the same state. Because in Study1_10 clusters have more similar patterns of change the results are slightly more difficult to retrieve comparing to the remaining three data sets.

To compare the relative performance of the SKM algorithm for these four data sets we compute the Kullback-Leibler divergence between the true values and the SKM results (Table 3). We conclude that Study1_10 has the most difficult structure to be retrieved (0.050). Interestingly the cluster structure of Study1_40 is more difficult than Study1_30 structure. This has to do with the existence of rare transitions between states in cluster 3 of Study1_40 data set (the true value of the probability of transition between different states is 0.05) that introduces some instability in the computation of the centroids of the SKM algorithm. Setting Study_10 as the standard the KL proportion (Table 3) gives each distance as a proportion of the maximum distance (Study1_10). For instance, we infer that Study1_10 is more difficult comparing with Study1_20 than Study1_20 comparing with Study1_30.

4   Application

The analysis of the sequence of web pages requested by each web user visiting a web site allows a better understanding and prediction of users' behavior and further improvements of the design of the web site. For example, web mining of online stores may yield information on the effectiveness of marketing and web merchandizing efforts, such as how the consumers start the search, which products they see, and which products they buy [10,5]. Substantial effort has

Table 2. Best SKM results for Study1 data sets

Data set	Cluster								
	$s=1$			$s=2$			$s=3$		
	$k=1$	$k=2$	$k=3$	$k=1$	$k=2$	$k=3$	$k=1$	$k=2$	$k=3$
Study1_40									
π_s		0.338			0.316			0.347	
λ_{s1}		0.363			0.309			0.361	
λ_{s2}		0.338			0.330			0.341	
λ_{s3}		0.299			0.362			0.298	
a_{s1k}	**0.103**	0.456	0.442	**0.519**	0.242	0.239	**0.874**	0.063	0.063
a_{s2k}	0.458	**0.105**	0.437	0.258	**0.493**	0.249	0.058	**0.884**	0.058
a_{s3k}	0.439	0.451	**0.111**	0.246	0.256	**0.499**	0.056	0.059	**0.885**
Study1_30									
π_s		0.353			0.308			0.339	
λ_{s1}		0.331			0.314			0.344	
λ_{s2}		0.333			0.368			0.319	
λ_{s3}		0.336			0.319			0.337	
a_{s1k}	**0.213**	0.397	0.390	**0.505**	0.249	0.246	**0.787**	0.105	0.108
a_{s2k}	0.395	**0.216**	0.389	0.250	**0.503**	0.247	0.100	**0.796**	0.104
a_{s3k}	0.389	0.398	**0.213**	0.246	0.243	**0.511**	0.109	0.112	**0.779**
Study1_20									
π_s		0.359			0.293			0.348	
λ_{s1}		0.362			0.339			0.345	
λ_{s2}		0.350			0.345			0.325	
λ_{s3}		0.288			0.316			0.330	
a_{s1k}	**0.301**	0.342	0.357	**0.502**	0.249	0.249	**0.693**	0.158	0.150
a_{s2k}	0.338	**0.311**	0.351	0.246	**0.496**	0.258	0.156	**0.694**	0.151
a_{s3k}	0.347	0.350	**0.303**	0.246	0.250	**0.505**	0.151	0.149	**0.693**
Study1_10									
π_s		0.353			0.269			0.378	
λ_{s1}		0.312			0.344			0.330	
λ_{s2}		0.305			0.347			0.317	
λ_{s3}		0.383			0.310			0.352	
a_{s1k}	**0.395**	0.320	0.284	**0.486**	0.239	0.275	**0.606**	0.195	0.199
a_{s2k}	0.292	**0.417**	0.291	0.241	**0.450**	0.309	0.206	**0.613**	0.181
a_{s3k}	0.315	0.322	**0.364**	0.230	0.200	**0.569**	0.202	0.237	**0.561**

Table 3. KL divergence between true values and best SKM results and KL proportion using Study_10 as the standard one

Data Set	KL divergence	KL proportion
Study1_40	0.0170	0.23
Study1_30	0.0088	0.18
Study1_20	0.0195	0.39
Study1_10	0.0500	1.00

Table 4. Cluster sizes and initial proportions

Parameters	Cluster 1	Cluster 2
π_s	0.5890	0.4110
λ_{s1}	0.2350	0.5319
λ_{s2}	0.0981	0.0122
λ_{s3}	0.0625	0.0117
λ_{s4}	0.0278	0.0783
λ_{s5}	0.0105	0.0004
λ_{s6}	0.1674	0.0365
λ_{s7}	0.0071	0.0034
λ_{s8}	0.0251	0.1800
λ_{s9}	0.0547	0.1041
λ_{s10}	0.0177	0.0015
λ_{s11}	0.0170	0.0049
λ_{s12}	0.0750	0.0127
λ_{s13}	0.1178	0.0039
λ_{s14}	0.0747	0.0073
λ_{s15}	0.0068	0.0112
λ_{s16}	0.0017	0.0000
λ_{s17}	0.0001	0.0000

been put on mining web access logs in an attempt to discovering groups of users exhibiting similar browsing patterns [15].

We apply the SKM algorithm to the well-known msnbc.com anonymous web data in kdd.ics.uci.edu/databases/msnbc/msnbc.data.html. This dataset describes the page visits on msnbc.com on September 28, 1999. Each sequence in the data set corresponds to page views of a user during a twenty-four hour period. The original number of users is 989818 and each event in the sequence is classified into the following categories (states): 1) frontpage, 2) news, 3) tech, 4) local, 5) opinion, 6) on-air, 7) misc, 8) weather, 9) health, 10) living, 11) business, 12) sports, 13) summary, 14) bbs (bulletin board service), 15) travel, 16) msn-news, and 17) msn-sports. This dataset has been used by others [1,3]. In our study, we used a sample of 5000 sequences with at least one transition.

The SKM algorithm allows the clustering of the web users into S clusters, each of which contains individuals with similar browsing pattern. For K-Means-like algorithms the number of clusters is set a priori. In this application, we set the number of clusters based on the Bayesian Information Criterion (BIC) of Schwarz [11]. We set $S = 2$ (see, e.g., [1,3])[3].

Table 4 and Figure 1 provide a summary of the SKM algorithm's best results. The size of each cluster ($\hat{\pi}_s$) is provided in Table 4. Cluster 1, the largest (58.9%),

---

[3] One difficulty in applying K-means like algorithms is that the number of clusters has to be set in advance. Whenever the number of groups is not known *a priori* we suggest a BIC-like decision rule [11], i.e., we select the number of clusters S that minimizes $C_S = -2\ell + d \times log(n)$, where ℓ and d are the classification log-likelihood and the number of free parameters, respectively.

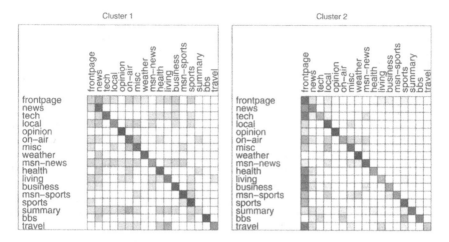

Fig. 1. Transitions matrix within each cluster. For the minimum and maximum values of the transitions probabilities (0 and 1), we use white and black, respectively. Values in between with a gray color which is obtained by a linear grading of colors between white and black. Note that the origin states are in the rows and the destination states in the column, which means that the row totals are equal to 1.

is still very heterogeneous with web users starting their browsing mainly from `frontpage` (23.5% of the web users in this cluster start their sequence in this state), `on-air` (16.7%), and `summary` (11.8%). Moreover, this cluster has a very stable pattern of browsing (Figure 1) almost absorbing for most of the states. Cluster 2 (41.1% of the sample) is rather stable. Indeed, most of them start their search from `frontpage` (53.2%) or `weather` (18.0%) states and tend to stay in these states. On the other hand, even users starting from other states tend to move to `frontpage` (Figure 1).

5   Conclusion

In this paper we provided a new K-Means algorithm for clustering sequential data. It is based on the Kullback-Leibler distance as an alternative to the standard Euclidean distance. We illustrate its performance based on synthetic data sets. The application of the algorithm in a web mining problem allows the identification of the clustering structure of web users using a well-known data set. Future research could extend our findings using synthetic data sets in such a way that can provide evidence of the performance of the SKM algorithm. In particular, the comparison between the SKM algorithm with the model-based clustering approach as in [1,2] would allow a better understanding of the statistical properties of the SKM algorithm. Another topic for further investigation is the definition of rules in the selection of the number of clusters to set *a priori*.

References

1. Cadez, I., Heckerman, D., Meek, C., Smyth, P., White, S.: Model-based clustering and visualization of navigation patterns on a web site. Data Mining and Knowledge Discovery 7(4), 399–424 (2003)
2. Dias, J.G., Willekens, F.: Model-based clustering of life histories with an application to contraceptive use dynamics. Mathematical Population Studies 12(3), 135–157 (2005)
3. Dias, J.G., Vermunt, J.K.: Latent class modeling of website users' search patterns: Implications for online market segmentation. Journal of Retailing and Consumer Services 14(4), 359–368 (2007)
4. Kullback, S., Leibler, R.A.: On information and sufficiency. The Annals of Mathematical Statistics 22(1), 79–86 (1951)
5. Lee, J., Podlaseck, M., Schonberg, E., Hoch, R.: Visualization and analysis of clickstream data of online stores for understanding Web merchandising. Data Mining and Knowledge Discovery 5(1-2), 59–84 (2001)
6. MathWorks.: MATLAB 7.0. Natick, MA: The MathWorks, Inc (2004)
7. MacQueen, J.B.: Some Methods for classification and Analysis of Multivariate Observations. In: Proceedings of 5-th Berkeley Symposium on Mathematical Statistics and Probability, vol. 1, pp. 281–297. University of California Press, Berkeley (1967)
8. Petridou, S.G., Koutsonikola, V.A., Vakali, A.I., Papadimitriou, G.I.: A divergence-oriented approach for web users clustering. In: Gavrilova, M.L., Gervasi, O., Kumar, V., Tan, C.J.K., Taniar, D., Laganá, A., Mun, Y., Choo, H. (eds.) ICCSA 2006. LNCS, vol. 3981, pp. 1229–1238. Springer, Heidelberg (2006)
9. Ross, S.M.: Introduction to Probability Models, 7th edn. Harcourt/Academic Press, San Diego (2000)
10. Shahabi, C., Zarkesh, A.M., Adibi, J., Shah, V.: Knowledge discovery from users Web-page navigation. In: Proceedings of the 7th International Workshop on Research Issues in Data Engineering (RIDE 1997). High Performance Database Management for Large-Scale Applications, pp. 20–29. IEEE Computer Society, Los Alamitos (1997)
11. Schwarz, G.: Estimating the dimension of a model. Annals of Statistics 6, 461–464 (1978)
12. Smith, K.A., Ng, A.: Web page clustering using a self-organizing map of user navigation patterns. Decision Support Systems 35(2), 245–256 (2003)
13. Spiliopoulou, M., Pohle, C.: Data mining for measuring and improving the success of Web sites. Data Mining and Knowledge Discovery 5(1-2), 85–114 (2001)
14. Spiliopoulou, M., Ntoutsi, I., Theodoridis, Y., Schult, R.: MONIC: modeling and monitoring cluster transitions. In: KDD 2006, pp. 706–711 (2006)
15. Vakali, A., Pokorny, J., Dalamagas, T.: An overview of web data clustering practices. In: Lindner, W., Mesiti, M., Türker, C., Tzitzikas, Y., Vakali, A.I. (eds.) EDBT 2004. LNCS, vol. 3268, pp. 597–606. Springer, Heidelberg (2004)
16. Yang, Y.H., Padmanabhan, B.: GHIC: A hierarchical pattern-based clustering algorithm for grouping Web transactions. IEEE Transactions on Knowledge and Data Engineering 17(9), 1300–1304 (2005)

Ensuring Time in Real-Time Commitments

Martí Navarro, Stella Heras, and Vicente Julián

Departamento de Sistemas Informáticos y Computación
Universidad Politécnica de Valencia
Camino de Vera S/N 46022 Valencia (Spain)
{mnavarro,sheras,vinglada}@dsic.upv.es

Abstract. This paper presents a framework for the estimation of the temporal cost of agent commitments. The work here presented focuses on the development of a commitment manager as a special module in a real-time agent. This manager has been constructed for the previous analysis of a commitment request in a temporal bounded way. The proposed commitment manager incorporates as CBR module whose aim is to decide if the agent will be able to perform a requested service without exceeding a specified deadline. The proposal has been tested over a mobile robot example and this paper presents the results obtained.

1 Introduction

Nowadays, a way of characterising MAS is to employ the notion of *commitments*. Commitments are viewed as responsibilities acquired by an agent for the fulfilment of some action under certain conditions concerning other agent [1]. If we apply the notion of commitments in real-time environments, the responsibility acquired by an agent for the accomplishment of some action under, possibly hard, temporal conditions increases the complexity of this kind of systems. So, we can define a *real-time commitment* as a commitment characterised by the fact that an agent delegates a task to another with a determined execution time or deadline. Therefore, the agent who commits itself to developing this task must not fail to fulfil this commitment on time. Otherwise, a deadline violation in real-time environments may cause serious or catastrophic effects in the system or produce an important decrease in the quality of the response.

This work proposes a commitment-based framework for real-time agents (agents specially designed for real-time environments –RT-Agents–) [2] based on the Case-Based Reasoning (CBR) methodology. To do this, our proposal includes bounded CBR techniques providing temporal estimations based on previous experiences. This temporal bounded CBR allows a feasibility analysis checking if the agent has enough time to do the commitment, while guaranteeing the possible real-time constraints of the agent. The rest of the paper is structured as follows: section 2 shows the main features of the commitment-based framework; section 3 presents the Temporal Constraints Manager; section 4 proposes the bounded CBR technique; section 5 summarises the results obtained in an application example based on mobile robots and finally, some conclusions are explained in section 6.

H. Geffner et al. (Eds.): IBERAMIA 2008, LNAI 5290, pp. 183–192, 2008.

2   Real-Time Commitment Management

The Commitment Manager is a module of a real-time agent aimed at improving the agent behaviour when it offers services in a real-time environment. This manager is integrated in the real-time agent and it is used to analyse whether or not the agent can satisfy the service requests of other agents before certain deadline. Once a service request is accepted, the agent is committed to its performance within the Multi-Agent System (MAS) where the agent is located. Also, the agent manages other different commitments that it has acquired before. As a last resort, if the agent integrity is in danger due to any unexpected error, the manager can cancel a commitment. The Commitment Manager is composed of two independent modules:

- **The Resource Manager:** with this module the agent can check if it has the necessary resources to execute the related tasks to achieve the goal associated to the service when its request arrives. Otherwise, the module can determine when the agent would have the resources available. This analysis calculates when the agent should start the task execution with all the available resources.
- **The Temporal Constraint Manager (TCM):** before the agent is committed to performing a service, verifying if it can complete the service before its deadline is necessary. The TCM module performs this verification. This module uses dynamic real-time scheduler techniques to determine if executing the task ensuring its temporal constraints is feasible.

The real-time agent uses the Resources Manager and the Temporal Constraint Manager modules to determine if it can commit to performing the service on time. Due to space restrictions, this paper is focused on the temporal analysis performed by the TCM.

3   Temporal Constraint Manager

As pointed out before, the TCM is in charge of deciding if an agent can commit itself to performing some service without exceeding the maximum time that it has been assigned for performing that service.

To determine whether a service can be executed on time, knowing the worst-case execution time (WCET) for each service to complete its execution is necessary. In some cases, the execution time of the service is known and limited. In these bounded services to determine the necessary tasks to fulfil the service and the maximum time needed to perform it is relatively easy.

Moreover, there are services whose number of necessary tasks to complete them cannot be determined, and therefore, to calculate the needed time to execute those services is not possible. In this type of services, a time estimation is the unique time measure that can be made. Figure 1 shows the execution phases of the TCM. The module is launched when the agent begins its execution. At the begining, the manager controls if a new service request has arrived

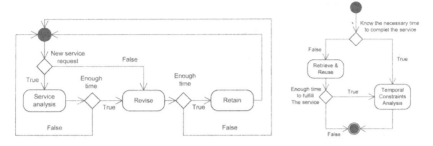

Fig. 1. Temporal Constraints Manager Algorithm

Fig. 2. Service Analysis state

(Figure 2). If the new request is an unbounded service request, the manager must estimate the time required to execute that service. As explained in section 4, to determine if the service can be completed before the deadline specified in the request is necessary. When the estimated time is obtained and the service execution is possible, the necessary tasks to perform the service are analysed at low-level using a real-time scheduler. The WCET of each phase of the TCM is known and therefore the phases are temporally bounded. This feature is crucial to allow the TCM to have a precise time control of each execution phase. As can be seen in Figure 1, the TCM execution is cyclical. When there is no request, the manager can employ its time to perform the revision and retention phases (below commented). The CBR methodology employed to obtain the temporal estimations is explained in the following section.

4   RT-CBR

As shown in the previous section, the TCM must decide if an agent can commit itself to performing a specific service. A possible way of performing such decision-making functionality is to use the knowledge that the manager has gained about previous commitments that it undertook in the past. This fits the main assumption of Case-Based Reasoning systems, which adapt previous problem solving cases to cope with current similar problems [3]. Therefore, in the absence of unpredictable circumstances, we assume that an agent can commit itself to performing a service within certain time if it has already succeeded in doing so in a similar situation.

To carry out the decision-making about contracting or not a commitment, the TCM has been enhanced with a RT-CBR module, following a soft Real-Time approach. This module estimates the time that the performance of a service could entail by using the time spent in performing similar services. With this aim, the RT-CBR module follows the typical steps of the CBR methodology: *retrieve* similar experiences from a *case-base*, *reuse* the knowledge acquired in them, *revise* such knowledge to fit the current situation and finally, *retain* the knowledge learnt from this problem-solving process.

The cases of the RT-CBR module have the following general structure:

$$C = < S, \{T\} >$$ (1)

where S represents the features that characterise a service (or one of its sub-tasks) that the agent performed in the past and T is the time that the agent spent in the execution of that previous service. In addition, since the same task could be executed several times with different duration, this value T can also be a series of temporal values. Therefore, the RT-CBR module estimates the duration of new services by means of a function $t : T \rightarrow f(T)$ computed over the temporal values that last similar previous services. The expected time T_s to perform a service that consists of a set of tasks is the aggregation of the estimated time for each of its tasks:

$$T_s = \sum_{i=0}^{I} t_i$$ (2)

Finally, the series of observed execution times could also allow the RT-CBR module to estimate a *success probability* $P(T_s)$ for a service to be performed within a specified time. This is an interesting data for agents, which could use this probability to make strategic decisions about their potential commitments. Setting a *confidence factor* (CF) that represents a minimum threshold for the success probability, agents would commit themselves to fulfilling a service if:

$$\exists T_s / P(T_s) \geq CF \land Ts \leq deadline$$ (3)

Thus, agents with more risky strategies could undertake commitments with lower confidence values than more cautious agents.

4.1   Real-Time Case-Based Commitment Management

As commented before, the CBR cycle consists of four steps: *Retrieve, Reuse, Revise* and *Retain*. After the first two steps, a case-based answer to the query that started the reasoning cycle can be proposed. The last two steps are more related with the learning ability of the system, that revises the devised answer and learns from the experience. In our framework, the retrieve and reuse phases must observe soft real-time constraints and thus, its execution time must be bounded. Otherwise, the RT-CBR module could provide the TCM with useless time estimations about services whose deadline have already expired.

To bound the response time of the module, the RT-CBR case-base must have a structure that eases the cases retrieval (e.g. indexing the case-base as a *Hash Structure* with a worst case temporal cost for the search linear with the number of cases stored). Anyway, independently of the choice made about the indexation of the case-base, the temporal cost of most retrieval (and reuse) algorithms depend on its size. This entails to specify a maximum number of cases that can be stored in the case-base and to perform a constant maintenance and updating of the information stored. However, the revise and retain phases can be performed off-line, since their execution does not hinder RT-CBR in providing the TCM with an estimation about the service duration.

5   Application Example

A prototype of a mail robot example has been developed for our proposal. The problem to solve consists in the automated management of the internal and external mail (physical mail, non-electronic) in a department plant. The system created by this automation must be able to request the shipment of a letter or package from an office on one floor to another office on the same floor, as well as the reception of external mail at a collection point for later distribution. Once this service has been requested, a Pioneer 2 mobile robot must gather the shipment and direct it to the destination. Note that each mail or package distribution must be finalised before a maximum time, specified in the shipment request. One of the services offered by the robot agent is mail delivery, which involves its movement from an initial to a final position. In order for an agent to commit itself to that delivery in a bounded time, a temporal estimation, as accurate as possible, is required. In this system, the TCM makes use of the CBR methodology to deal with this requirement.

5.1   RT-CBR Reasoning Cycle

In the previous example, the RT-CBR module has been integrated in the TCM of the robot agent. By means of this module, the manager can decide if an agent could perform a specific service before a deadline and hence, to commit the robot agent to the execution of that service. Therefore, the cases of the module store the information about previous shipment experiences. This information will be used to decide if the agent should undertake a new commitment. The cases are structured as follows:

$$C = < I, F, N_t, N_s, \{T\} > \qquad (4)$$

where I and F represent the coordinates of a path from the initial position I to the final position F that the robot travelled (one or several N_t times) straight ahead in the past, N_s stands for the number of times that the robot successfully completed the path within the case-based estimated time. These features define the service. In addition, T shows the series of time values that the robot spent to cover that route. Note that only straight routes are stored as cases, since we assume that it is the quickest way between two points. This design decision should minimise the time for travelling an unvisited route that the RT-CBR module would try to compose by reusing several known routes (old cases).

The RT-CBR reasoning cycle starts when the TCM must decide if an agent could fulfil a shipment service within the time assigned to do it. In that case, the manager is also in charge of checking if the agent has enough power resources to travel the path. In what follows the operation of each reasoning phase of the module is described.

Retrieval and Reuse: Due to the temporal constraints that the CBR process has to keep, we have followed an anytime approach [4] in the design of the algorithm that implements the retrieval and reuse phases of the RT-CBR module. In

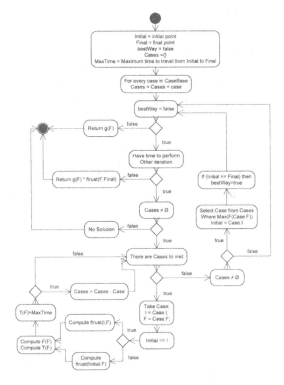

Fig. 3. Retrieval-Reuse Diagram

our design, both phases are coupled in the algorithm, reusing the time estimations about several paths to retrieve the most suitable case(s) to travel current routes (the composition of cases that minimises the travelling time). At the end of each iteration, the algorithm provides the manager with a probability of being able to perform the shipment service on time. If more time is still available, the algorithm computes better estimations on subsequent iterations. In Figure 3 a diagram of the RT-CBR retrieval-reuse algorithm is shown.

First, the RT-CBR module searches its case-base to retrieve a case that represents a similar path that the robot agent travelled in the past. Then, for each retrieved case, the algorithm uses a *confidence function* to compute the probability of travelling from an initial to a final point in an area without diverting the agent's direction. Shortest paths are assumed to have less probability that an unpredictable circumstance could deviate the agent from its route and hence, they are preferred from longer ones. In the best case, there will be a case in the case-base that exactly or very approximately covers the same path that the agent must travel. Then, the necessary time to perform the shipment can be estimated by using the time spent in that previous case. Otherwise, the route could be covered by aggregating a set of cases and estimating the global time by adding the time estimation for each case. If the route can be composed with the cases of the case-base, the following confidence function will be used:

$$f_{trust}(i,j) = 1 - \frac{dist_{ij}}{maxDist} * \frac{N_s}{N_t} \text{ where } dist_{ij} \leq maxDist \qquad (5)$$

being $dist_{ij}$ the distance travelled, N_t times between the points $<i,j>$, N_s the number of times that the robot has travelled the path within the case-based estimated time and $maxDist$ the maximum distance above which the agent is unlikely to reach its objective without finding obstacles. In the worst case, the agent will not ever travelled a similar path and hence, it cannot be composed with the cases stored. Then, a confidence function that takes into account the distance that separates both points will be used:

$$f_{trust}(i,j) = \begin{cases} 1 - \frac{dist_{ij}}{const_1} & \text{if } 0 \leq dist \leq dist_1 \\ 1 - const_2 * dist_{ij} & \text{if } dist_1 < dist \leq dist_2 \\ \frac{dist_{ij}}{dist_{ij}^2} & \text{if } dist_2 < dist \end{cases} \qquad (6)$$

where $const1$ and $const2$ are normalisation parameters defined by the user, $dist_{ij}$ is the Euclidean distance between the initial and final points of the path $<i,j>$ and $dist_1$ and $dist_2$ are distance bounds that represent the thresholds that delimit near, medium and far distances from the initial point. This function computes a smoothed probability that the robot can travel its path straight ahead. As the distance between the initial and the final point increases, the confidence on travelling without obstacles decreases.

Once the probability to reach the robot's objective is computed for each case, the complete route from the initial to the final position with the maximum probability of success must be selected. This route is composed by using a selection function $F(n)$ (7), which follows an $A*$ heuristic search approach [5]. The function consists of two sub-functions: $g(n)$ (8) that computes the case-based confidence of travelling from the initial point to a certain point n and $h(n)$ (9) that computes an estimated confidence of travelling from the point n to the final point (always better than the real confidence). Finally, the function $T(n)$ (10) checks if the robot agent has enough time to complete the shipment service by travelling across this specific route. Else, the algorithm prunes the route. The function consists of two sub-functions: $time(n)$ (11) that computes the case-based time of travelling from the initial point to a certain point n and $E(n)$ (12) that computes an estimated time of travelling from the point n to the final point. In (11) $dist_{mn}$ represents the distance between the last point m visited by the algorithm to the current point n, V_{robot} is the speed of the robot, $f_{trust}(m,n)$ corresponds to (5) or (6) (depending on the possibility of composing the route by using the cases of the case-base) and the constant $const_{trust} \in [0,10]$ shows the caution degree of the robot agent. Bigger values of this constant are chosen for more cautious agents.

Finally, if the RT-CBR algorithm is able to compose the entire route with the information stored in the case-base, it returns the case-based probability to perform the shipment service on time. Otherwise, it returns the product of the probability accumulated to that moment and a pessimistic probability to travel from the last point that could be reached by using the cases of the case-base to the final point of the route. Finally, in case that all possible solutions computed by the algorithm exceed the time assigned to fulfil the commitment, it returns a null probability to perform successfully the service.

$$F(n) = g(n) * h(n) \tag{7}$$

$$g(n) = g(m) * f_{trust}(m, n) \tag{8}$$

$$h(n) = 1 - \frac{dist_{nf}}{maxDist} \text{ where } dist \leq maxDist \tag{9}$$

$$T(n) = time(n) + E(n) \tag{10}$$

$$time(n) = time(m) + \frac{dist_{mn}}{V_{robot}} + \frac{const_{trust}}{f_{trust}(m, n)} \tag{11}$$

$$E(n) = \frac{dist_{nf}}{V_{robot}} \tag{12}$$

Revision. Once the robot agent has finished the shipment service, it reports to the TCM the coordinates of each path that it finally travelled straight ahead and the time that it spent in doing so. In that way, the manager can check the performance of the RT-CBR module by comparing the time estimated by the module and the real time that finally took the service. Note that if the agent has not changed its navigation algorithm, it will likely try to perform the shipment by following the same route that ended in a success in the past. However, due to that some new obstacles could be found during the route, the design decision of reporting the specific paths that the robot agent has travelled has been taken.

Retention. The last step of the reasoning cycle considers the addition of new knowledge in the case-base of the RT-CBR module. As pointed out before, the size of the case-base must be controlled and therefore, only useful cases must be added (and correspondingly, out-of-date cases must be eliminated). Therefore, the decision about the addition of a new case in our model is crucial. At the moment, we have taken a simple but effective procedure by defining a threshold α below which two points must be considered as nearby in our shipment domain. Let us consider a new case c with coordinates (x_i^c, y_i^c) (initial point) and (x_f^c, y_f^c) (final point) to be added in the case-base. Following an *Euclidean* approach, the distance (dissimilarity) between the case c and each case z of the case-base can be computed with the formula:

$$dist(c, z) = max(\sqrt{(x_i^c - x_i^z)^2 + (y_i^c - y_i^z)^2}, \sqrt{(x_f^c - x_f^z)^2 + (y_f^c - y_f^z)^2}) \tag{13}$$

Therefore, the new case will be included in the case-base iff:

$$\forall z \in caseBase \ / \ dist(c, z) < \alpha \tag{14}$$

In that case, the new case $< (x_i^c, y_i^c), (x_f^c, y_f^c), 1, 1, time >$ will be added in the case-base (1 values stand for this first time that the path has been travelled and that it was done within the case-based estimated time). Note that the addition of new cases is always conditioned at the existence of 'free space' to add cases in the case-base. Otherwise, a maintenance cycle will be triggered, deleting, for instance, those old cases that have low use ratings. Else, if a similar case has been identified, the number of times that the agent has travelled the path that represents the case (N_t) will be increased by 1 and the time spent in travelling the current path will be added to the time series of that case.

5.2   Tests and Results

To develop and execute the proposed real-time MAS, we have use the jART platform [6] that is especially designed for systems of this type and RT-Java [7] as the programming language. Once the example was implemented over the jART platform, several simulation experiments were conducted to evaluate different parameters in order to verify the use of the proposed commitment framework. A simulation prototype was implemented using a Pioneer 2 mobile robot simulation software (specifically, the Webots simulator [8]). The simulation experiments were conducted to evaluate different aspects and to try to show the benefits of the integration of the commitment framework in a real-time agent. A series of tests to check the proper operation of the TCM have been performed. The first test analyses the behaviour of the TCM as it receives new requests by increasing the number of queries. As shown in figure 4, the number of estimations that the TCM performs decreases as new requests are queried. This demonstrates

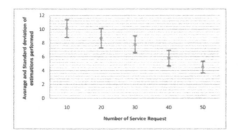
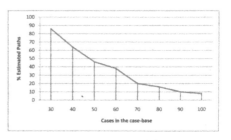

Fig. 4. Average and standard deviation of the number of estimations performed vs number of service requests

Fig. 5. Percentage of estimated paths in a complete route vs number of cases in the case-base

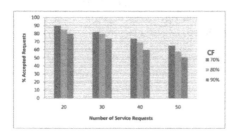
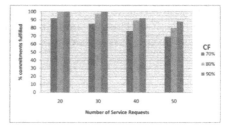

Fig. 6. Percentage of accepted requests vs number of service requests

Fig. 7. Percentage of commitments fulfilled vs number of service requests

that as the number of requests increases, the case-base learns properly the new information and hence, the number of routes that can be composed with the cases increases (and an estimation is not necessary). Figure 5, which shows the relation between the number of cases in the case-base and the percentage of estimated routes, also supports this conclusion. Finally, the percentage of distrust from which an agent can commit itself to performing a service was also checked (modifying the confidence values from 70%, 80% and 90%). As expected, bigger confidence percentages resulted in agents committing themselves to performing more tasks (Figure 6). However, in such cases the percentage of services accepted and completed on time decreases, since the agent committed itself to the performance of a big amount of services (Figure 7).

6   Conclusions

A module to analyse whether an agent has enough time to perform a service has been developed. A CBR approach for deciding if an agent can commit itself to performing some service without exceeding the maximum time assigned for performing that service has been used. From now, we have focused our work on the design and implementation of the different phases of the CBR cycle for the mobile robot problem. This work has been tested and evaluated by using a simulated scenario. The results obtained support the expectations.

References

1. Winikoff, M.: Designing commitment-based agent. In: International Conference on Intelligent Agent Technology, pp. 18–22 (2006)
2. Julián, V., Botti, V.: Developing Real-Time Multi-agent Systems. Integrated Computer-Aided Engineering 11(2), 135–149 (2004)
3. Aamodt, A., Plaza, E.: Case-based reasoning; Foundational issues, methodological variations, and system approaches. AI Comm. 1(7), 39–59 (1994)
4. Dean, T., Boddy, M.: An analysis of time-dependent planning. In: Proceedings of the seventh National Conference on AI, pp. 49–54 (1988)
5. Hart, P.E., Nilsson, N.J., Raphael, B.: A formal basic for the heuristic determination of minimum cost paths. IEEE Transactions on SSC 4, 100–107 (1968)
6. Navarro, M., Julián, V., Soler, J., Botti, V.: jART: A Real-Time Multi-Agent Platform with RT-Java. In: Proc. 3rd IWPAAMS 2004, pp. 73–82 (2004)
7. RTJ: The Real-Time for Java Expert Group, http://www.rtsj.org
8. Webots: http://www.cyberbotics.com/

Hybrid Multi-agent Architecture (HoCa) Applied to the Control and Supervision of Patients in Their Homes

Juan A. Fraile[1], Javier Bajo[1], and Juan M. Corchado[2]

[1] Pontifical University of Salamanca, Compañía 5, 37002 Salamanca, España
[2] Departamento de Informática y Automática, Universidad de Salamanca,
Plaza de la Merced s/n, 37008 Salamanca, España
{jafraileni,jbajope}@upsa.es, corchado@usal.es

Abstract. This paper presents a Hybrid Multi-Agent Architecture for the control and supervision of dependent environments. HoCa (Home health Care) integrates various modules to allow an agile exchange of information, minimizing the necessary message traffic and optimizing the efficiency. HoCa is based on an Ambient Intelligence model and integrates a management system of alerts and an automated identification, localization, and movement control system. The core of the architecture is formed by both deliberative agents and reactive agents that interact to offer efficient services. The architecture has been successfully tested in a real environment.

Keywords: Dependent environments, Ambient Intelligence, Multiagent Systems, Home Care.

1 Introduction

In recent years, there has been an important growth in the field of Ambient Intelligence (AmI) [1] [13], involving major changes in the daily lives of people. The vision of Ambient Intelligence implies the creation of intelligent spaces where users interact in a natural way with computational systems and communication technologies, which become invisible and ubiquitous. The technology is adapted to individuals and their context, acting autonomously, and facilitating their daily tasks. One of the main aims of Ambient Intelligence focuses in building systems that support the activities of daily living in an efficient way. For example, activities related to the home automation. These systems can be developed under various scenarios and are known as "ubiquitous intelligent environments" [9], where it is possible to solve the challenge of developing strategies for early problems detection and prevention in automated environments. The society will benefit from the technological advances provided by the AmI, but particularly dependent people will see more improved their quality of life, thanks to future generations of products based on these advances.

The complexity of these systems requires advanced control architectures, which have gained increasing importance in recent years. These architectures must provide novel structures, information exchange mechanisms and computer resources management. Besides, most of the current systems require concurrent work to provide real

H. Geffner et al. (Eds.): IBERAMIA 2008, LNAI 5290, pp. 193–202, 2008.

time solutions. This paper presents Home Care architecture (HoCa), a novel architecture specifically designed to be implemented in Ambient Intelligence environments. HoCa integrates an alert management system and an identification, location and movement control mechanism based on a multi-agent system. These mechanisms facilitate most of the common tasks required in home care environments, as patients monitoring and tracking, as well as quick response to problematic situations. HoCa must be flexible enough to allow communication between remote modules, adaptation to computational requirements as well as to support the rapid integration of new modules and sensors. Multi-agent systems are very appropriate to satisfy these needs, due to their characteristics [14]. A multiagent system consists of a software agent's networks that interact to solve problems that are beyond individual capabilities. One of the main contributions of HoCa is the use of both reactive and deliberative agents, which facilitates advanced reasoning capabilities together with real-time reactive behaviours. These are two important characteristics that must be taken into account in the development of intelligent environmets.

The paper is organized as follows: The first section presents the problem that prompted this work. The third section presents the proposed architecture, and the fourth section gives the results and conclusions obtained after applying the proposed architecture to a real case in an environment of dependence.

2   General Description of the Problem

The use of intelligent agents is an essential component for analyzing information on distributed sensors [14]. These agents must be capable of both independent reasoning and joint analysis of complex situations in order to be able to achieve a high level of interaction with humans [3]. Although multi-agent systems already exist and are capable of gathering information within a given environment in order to provide medical care [6], there is still much work to be done. It is necessary to continue developing systems and technology that focus on the improvement of services in general. After the development of the internet there has been continual progress in new wireless communication networks and mobile devices such as mobile telephones and PDAs. This technology can help to construct more efficient distributed systems capable of addressing new problems [7].

Hybrid architectures try to combine deliberative and reactive aspects, by combining reactive and deliberative modules [5]. The reactive modules are in charge of processing stimuli that don't need deliberation, whereas the deliberative modules determine which actions to take in order to satisfy the local and cooperative aims of the agents. The aim of modern architectures like Service Oriented Architecture (SOA) is to be able to interact among different systems by distributing resources or services without needing to consider which system they are designed for. An alternative to these architectures are the multi-agent systems, which can help to distribute resources and to reduce the centralization of tasks. Unfortunately the complexity of designing multi-agent architecture is great since there are not tools to either help programme needs or develop agents.

Multi-agent systems combine aspects of both classic and modern architectures. The integration of multi-agent systems with SOA has been recently investigated [2]. Some researchers focus on the communication among these models, whereas others focus on the integration of distributed services, especially web services, in the agents' structure [4] [12]. These works provide a good base for the development of multi-agent systems. Because the majority of them are in the development stage, their full potential in a real environment is not known. HoCa has been implemented in a real environment and not only does it provide communication and integration among distributed agents, services and applications, but it also provides a new method for facilitating the development of multi-agent systems, thus allowing the agents and systems to function as services. HoCa also implements an alert and alarm system across the agent's platform, specially designed to be used by mobile devices. The platform agents manage this service and determine the level of alert at every moment so that they can decide who will receive the alert and when. The alerts are received by the subscribed in the system that have associated such alerts. Hours sending alerts depend on the system parameters and the urgency of the warning. In order to identify each user, HoCa implements a system based on Java Card [15] and RFID (Radio Frequency IDentification) microchip technology in which there will be a series of distributed sensors that provide the necessary services to the user.

3 HoCa Architecture

The HoCa model architecture uses a series of components to offer a solution that includes all levels of service for various systems. It accomplishes this by incorporating intelligent agents, identification and localization technology, wireless networks and mobile devices. Additionally, it provides access mechanisms to multi-agent system services, through mobile devices, such as mobiles phones or PDAs.

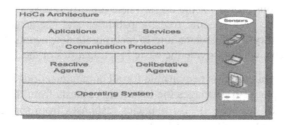

Fig. 1. HoCa Framework

Access is provided via wi-fi wireless networks, a notification and alarm management module based on SMS (Short Message Service) and MMS (Multimedia Messaging System) technologies, and user identification and localization system based on Java Card and RFID technologies. This system is dynamic, flexible, robust and very adaptable to changes of context.

HoCa architecture describes four basic blocks that can be seen in Figure 1: Applications, Services, Agents Platform and Communication Protocol. These blocks constitute the whole functionality of the architecture. The applications represent all programs that can be used to exploit the system functionalities. The services represent the functionalities that the architecture offers. The Agents Platform and the

Communication Protocol are explained in detail in the following subsections. Moreover, the identification and alert systems integrated within HoCa are also described, presenting their appropriateness for home care environments.

3.1 Agents Platform in HoCa

The agents platform is the core of the architecture and integrates two types of agents, each of which behaves differently for specific tasks, as shown in Figure 2.

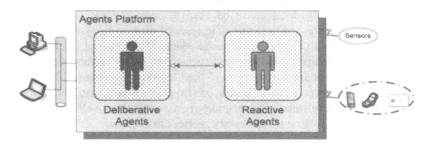

Fig. 2. Agents platform structure in the HoCa architecture

The first group of agents is made up of deliberative BDI agents, which are in charge of the management and coordination of all system applications and services. These agents are able to modify their behaviour according to the preferences and knowledge acquired in previous experiences, thus making them capable of choosing the best solution. Deliberative agents constantly deal with information and knowledge. Because they can be executed on mobile devices, they are always available and they provide ubiquitous access for the users. There are different kinds of agents in the architecture, each one with specific roles, capabilities and characteristics. This fact facilitates the flexibility of the architecture to incorporate new agents. However, there are pre-defined agents which provide the basic functionalities of the architecture:

- CoAp Agent: This agent is responsible for all communications between applications and the platform. Manages the incoming requests from the applications to be processed by services. It also manages responses from services to applications. CoAp Agent is always on listening mode. Applications send XML messages to the agent requesting for a service.
- CoSe Agent: It is responsible for all communications between services and the platform. The functionalities are similar to CoAp Agent but backwards. This agent is always on listening mode waiting for responses of services. Manager Agent indicates CoSe Agent the service that must be invoked. Then, CoSe Agent sends an XML message to the service.
- Directory Agent. Manages the list of services that can be used by the system. For security reasons, the list of services is static and can only be modified manually, however services can be added, erased or modified dynamically. The list contains the information of all trusted available services.
- Supervisor Agent. This agent supervises the correct functioning of the agents in the system. Supervisor Agent verifies periodically the status of all agents

registered in the architecture by means of sending ping messages. If there is no response, the agent kills the agent and creates another instance of that agent.

- Security Agent. This agent analyzes the structure and syntax of all incoming and outgoing XML messages. If a message is not correct, the Security Agent informs the corresponding agent that the message cannot be delivered.
- Manager Agent. Decides which agent must be called taking into account the users preferences. Users can explicitly invoke a service, or can let the Manager Agent decide which service is better to accomplish the requested task. If there are several services that can resolve the task requested by an application, the agent selects the optimal choice using a strategy based on the analysis of the efficiency of the services. An optimal choice service has higher and better performance that other. Manager Agent has a routing list to manage messages from all applications and services.
- Interface Agent. This kind of agent has been designed to be embedded in users' applications. Interface agents communicate directly with the agents in HoCa so there is no need to employ the communication protocol, but FIPA ACL specification. The requests are sent directly to the Security Agent, which analyzes the requests and sends them to the Manager Agent.

The second group is made up of reactive agents. Most of the research conducted within the field of multi-agent systems focuses on designing architectures that incorporate complicated negotiation schemes as well as high level task resolution, but don't focus on temporal restrictions. In general, the multi-agent architectures assume a reliable channel of communication and, while some establish deadlines for the interaction processes, they don't provide solutions for limiting the time the system may take to react to events. It is possible to define a real-time agent as an agent with temporal restrictions for some of its responsibilities or tasks [11]. From this definition, we can define a real-time multi-agent system (Real Time Multi-Agent System, RT-MAS) as a multi-agent system in which at least one of the agents is a real-time agent. The use of RT-MAS makes sense within an environment of critical temporal restrictions, where the system can be controlled by autonomous agents that need to communicate among themselves in order to improve the degree of system task completion. In this kind of environments every agent requires autonomy as well as certain cooperation skills to achieve a common goal.

3.2 HoCa Communication Protocol

Communication protocol allows applications, services and sensors to be connected directly to the platform agents. The protocol presented in this work is open and independent of programming languages. It is based on the SOAP standard and allows messages to be exchanged between applications and services as shown in Figure 3.

However, interaction with environmental sensors requires Real-time Transport Protocol (RTP) [10] [5] which provides transport functions that are adapted for applications that need to transmit real-time data such as audio, video or simulation data, over multicast or unicast network services. The RTCP protocol is added to RTP, allowing a scaleable form of data supervision. Both RTP and RTCP are designed to work independently from the transport and lower network services. They

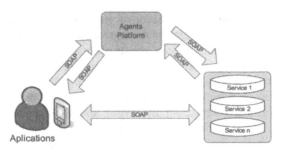

Fig. 3. Communication using SOAP messages in HoCa

are in charge of transporting data with real-time characteristics, and of supervising the quality of service, managing the information for all the entities taking part in the current session.

The communications between agents within the platforms follows the FIPA ACL (Agent Communication Language) standard. This way, the applications can use the platform to communicate directly with the agents.

3.3 Location and Identification System in HoCa

This system incorporates Java Card [15] and RFID [8] technologies. The primary purpose of the system is to convey the identity of an object or person, as with a unique serial number, using radio waves. Java Card is a technology that permits small Java applications (applets) to be run safely in microchip smart cards and similar embedded devices. Java Card gives the user the ability to program applications that can be run off a card so that it has a practical function in a specific application domain. The main features of Java Card are portability and security; it is described in ISO 7816. The data are stored in the application and the Java Card applications are executed in an isolated environment, separated from the operating system and from computer that reads the card. The most commonly used algorithms, such as DES, 3DES, AES, and RSA, are cryptographically implemented in Java Card. Other services such as electronic signature or key generation are also supported.

RFID technology is grouped into the so-called automatic identification technologies. But RFID provides more information than other auto-identification technologies, speeds up processes without losing reliability, and requires no human intervention.

The combination of these two technologies allows us to both identifiable element, and to locate it, by means of sensors and actuators, within the environment, at which time we can act on it and provide services. The microchip, which contains the identification data of the object to which it is adhered, generates a radio frequency signal with this data. The signal can be picked up by an RFID reader, which is responsible for reading the information and sending it, in digital format, to the specific application.

3.4 Alert System in HoCa

The alert system is integrated into the HoCa architecture and uses mobile technology to inform users about alerts, warnings and information specific to the daily routine of the application environment. This is a very configurable system that allows users to select the type of information they are interested, and to receive it immediately on their mobile phone or PDA. It places the information to be sent into information categories. The users determine the information they are interested in. The system automatically sends the information to each of the users as soon as it is available.

4   Using HoCa to Develop a Multi-agent System for a Home Care Dependent Environment

Ambient Intelligence based systems aim to improve people quality of life, offering more efficient and easy to use services and communication tools to interact with other people, systems and environments. One of the most benefited segments of population with the development of these systems is elderly and dependent people. Agents and multi-agent systems in dependency environments are becoming a reality, specifically on health care. Most agents-based applications are related to the use of this technology in patients monitoring, treatment supervision and data mining.

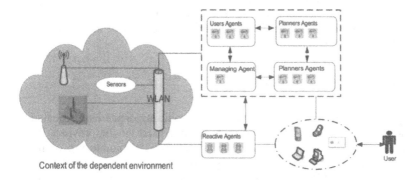

Fig. 4. HoCa structure in a dependent environment

HoCa has been employed to develop a multi-agent system aimed to enhance assistance and care for low dependence patients at their homes. Main functionalities in the system include reasoning, planning mechanisms, management alerts and responses in execution time offered to certain stimuli, as shown in Figure 4. These functionalities allow the system the use of several context-aware technologies to acquire information from users and their environment. Among the technologies used are mobile systems for alerts service managing across PDA and mobile phones, Java Card elements for identification and presence detectors and access control.

Each agent in the system has its own functionalities. If an agent needs to develop a task in collaboration with other agent a request form is sent. There are priority tasks that a set of agents can perform. This ensures that the priority tasks are always available. There are four specific types of deliberative BDI [14] agents included in the case study which collaborate with the predefined agents in the HoCa platform:

- User Agent manage user personal data and their behavior. They are responsible through the system, identify and locate implemented by the architecture. They determine the status of the user and offering services in the environment as a correct temperature, automatic lighting, access blocking or opening, etc.

- SuperUser Agent runs on mobile devices and inserts new tasks into the ManagerALZ Agent to be processed by a reasoning mechanism. It also needs to interact with the User Agents to impose new tasks and receive periodic reports, and with the ScheduleUser Agents to ascertain plans' evolution.
- SheduleUser Agent schedules the users' daily activities obtaining dynamic plans depending on the tasks needed for each user. It manages scheduled-users profiles, tasks, available time and resources. Every agent generates personalized plans depending on the scheduled-user profile.
- ManagerALZ Agent runs on a Workstation and plays two roles: the physical security role that monitors the users and the managerAlz role that handle the data and the tasks assignment for the medical staff. It must provide security for the users and ensure the tasks assignments are efficient.

On the other hand there are a number of reactive agents that work in collaboration with the deliberative agents. These agents are in change of control devices interacting with sensors (access points, lights, temperature, alarms detection, etc.). They receive information, monitor environment services and also check the devices status connected to the system. All information is treated by the reactive agent and it is sent to the manager agent to be processed.

5 Results and Conclusions

HoCa has been used to develop a system for monitoring dependent patients at home. The testing environment has evolved from the one used for the previous ALZ-MAS architecture [6]. The ALZ-MAS architecture allows the monitoring of patients in geriatric residences, but home care is carried out through traditional methods. As mentioned in [6], ALZ-MAS present certain advantages with respect to previous architectures. However, one of the problems of ALZ-MAS was the number of agents crashed during tests. HoCa solves this problem using replicated services and reducing the crashes an average of 9%. Moreover, HoCa incorporates mobile SMS technology for managing service alerts through PDAs and mobile phones, which provides a remote alert system, and Java Card technology for identification and access control, which improves the previous RFID location technology. The environment includes reasoning and planning mechanisms, and alert and response management. Most of these responses are reactions in real time to certain stimuli, and represent the abilities that the reactive agents have in the HoCa architecture based platform. Real-time systems require an infrastructure characterized by their response time for computing and communication processes [5]. The time is considered as a critical parameter [10] to react to sensor values, i.e. when a door has to be automatically open or closed after detecting a patient identification. In this kind of situations the reactive agents receive behaviors from the deliberative agents and take control of the actions carried out.

One of the main contributions of the HoCa architecture is the remote alert system. We implemented several test cases to evaluate the management of alerts integrated into the system. This allowed us to determine the response time for warnings generated by the users, for which the results were very satisfactory, with response times shorter than those obtained prior to the implementation of HoCa. The system studies the information collected, and applies a reasoning process which allows alerts to be automatically generated, trying to avoid false alarms. For these alerts, the system does not only take response time into account, but also the time elapsed between alerts, and the user's profile and reliability, in order to generalize reactions to common situations. The results show that HoCa fits perfectly within complex systems by correctly exploiting services and planning mechanisms.

Table 1. Comparison between the HoCa and the ALZ-MAS architectures

Factor	HoCa	ALZ-MAS
Average Response Time to Incidents(min.)	8 minutes	14 minutes
Assisted Incidents	12	17
Average number of daily planned tasks	12	10
Average number of services completed daily	46	32
Time employed by the medical staff to attend to an alert (min.)	75 minutes	90 minutes

Table 1 presents the results obtained after comparing the HoCa architecture to the previously developed ALZ-MAS architecture [6] in a case study on medical care for patients at home. The case study presented in this work consisted of analysing the functioning of both architectures in a test environment. The HoCa architecture was implemented in the home of 5 patients and was tested for 30 days. The results were promising. The data shown in Table 1 are the results obtained from the test cases. They show that the alert system improved the communication between the user and the dependent care services providers. The user identification and location system in conjunction with the alert system has helped to notably reduce the percentage of incidents in the environment under study. Moreover, in addition to a reduction in the number of incidents, the time elapsed between the generation of a warning and solution decreased significantly. Finally, due to the many improvements, the level of user satisfaction increased with the introduction of HoCa architecture since patients can live in their own homes with the same level of care as those offered at the residence.

References

1. Anastasopoulos, M., Niebuhr, D., Bartelt, C., Koch, J., Rausch, A.: Towards a Reference Middleware Architecture for Ambient Intelligence Systems. In: ACM Conference on Object-Oriented Programming, Systems, Languages, and Applications (2005)
2. Ardissono, L., Petrone, G., Segnan, M.: A conversational approach to the interaction with Web Services. Computational Intelligence 20, 693–709 (2004)
3. Bahadori, S., Cesta, A., Grisetti, G., Iocchi, L., Leone1, R., Nardi, D., Oddi, A., Pecora, F., Rasconi, R.: RoboCare: Pervasive Intelligence for the Domestic Care of the Elderly. AI*IA Magazine Special Issue (January 2003)

4. Bonino da Silva, L.O., Ramparany, F., Dockhorn, P., Vink, P., Etter, R., Broens, T.: A Service Architecture for Context Awareness and Reaction Provisioning. In: IEEE Congress on Services (Services 2007), pp. 25–32 (2007)

5. Carrascosa, C., Bajo, J., Julian, V., Corchado, J.M., Botti, V.: Hybrid multi-agent architecture as a real-time problem-solving model. Expert Systems With Applications 34(1), 2–17 (2008)

6. Corchado, J.M., Bajo, J., de Paz, Y., Tapia, D.: Intelligent Environment for Monitoring Alzheimer Patients, Agent Technology for Health Care. Decision Support Systems 34(2), 382–396 (2008)

7. Corchado, J.M., Bajo, J., Abraham, A.: GERAmI: Improving the delivery of health care. IEEE Intelligent Systems. Special Issue on Ambient Intelligence (March/April 2008)

8. ITAA. Radio Frequency Identification. RFID...coming of age. Information Technology Association of America (2004), http://www.itaa.org/rfid/docs/rfid.pdf

9. Kleindienst, J., Macek, T., Seredi, L., Sedivy, J.: Vision-enhanced multi-modal interactions in domotic environments. IBM Tecnologías de Voz y Sistemas. República Checa (2004)

10. Jacobsen, V., Fredrick, R., Casner, S., Schulzrinne, H.: RTP: A transport Protocol for Real-Time Applications. RFC 1889. Lawrence Berkeley National Laboratory, Xerox PARC, Precept Software Inc., GMD Fokus (January 1996), http://www.connect.org.uk/teckwatch/cgi-bin/rfcshow?1889 (accessed October 16, 1996)

11. Julian, V., Botti, V.: Developing real-time multi-agent systems. In: Proceedings of the Fourth Iberoamerican Workshop on Multi-Agent Systems (Iberagents 2002), Málaga (2004)

12. Ricci, A., Buda, C., Zaghini, N.: An agent-oriented programming model for SOA & web services. In: 5th IEEE International Conference on Industrial Informatics (INDIN 2007), Vienna, Austria, pp. 1059–1064 (2007)

13. Richter, K., Hellenschmidt, M.: Interacting with the Ambience: Multimodal Interaction and Ambient Intelligence. In: W3C Workshop on Multimodal Interaction, July 19-20 (2004) (position paper)

14. Tapia, D.I., Bajo, J., De Paz, F., Corchado, J.M.: Hybrid Multiagent System for Alzheimer Health Care. In: Rezende, S.O., da Silva Filho, A.C.R. (eds.) Proceedings of HAIS 2006. Ribeirao Preto, Brasil (2006)

15. ZhiqunChen (Sun Microsystems). Java Card Technology for Smart Cards. Addison Wesley/Longman ISBN 0201703297

Mixing Greedy and Evolutive Approaches to Improve Pursuit Strategies

Juan Reverte, Francisco Gallego, Rosana Satorre, and Faraón Llorens

Department of Computer Science and Artificial Intelligence
University of Alicante
{jreverte,fgallego,rosana,faraon}@dccia.ua.es

Abstract. The prey-predator pursuit problem is a generic multi-agent testbed referenced many times in literature. Algorithms and conclusions obtained in this domain can be extended and applied to many particular problems. In first place, greedy algorithms seem to do the job. But when concurrence problems arise, agent communication and coordination is needed to get a reasonable solution. It is quite popular to face these issues directly with non-supervised learning algorithms to train prey and predators. However, results got by most of these approaches still leave a great margin of improvement which should be exploited.

In this paper we propose to start from a greedy strategy and extend and improve it by adding communication and machine learning. In this proposal, predator agents get a previous movement decision by using a greedy approach. Then, they focus on learning how to coordinate their own pre-decisions with the ones taken by other surrounding agents. Finally, they get a final decission trying to optimize their chase of the prey without colliding between them. For the learning step, a neuroevolution approach is used. The final results show improvements and leave room for open discussion.

Keywords: Multi-agent systems, communication, coordination, neuroevolution.

1 Introduction

The Predator-prey problem (or pursuit domain) is a well-known testbed for multi-agents systems. It consists of world where a group of agents (called predators) aim to chase and surround another agent (called prey) that tries to evade them [1]. The goal of predator agents is to surround (capture) prey without touching it (i.e. occuping the adjacent cells), whilst the goal of the prey, as expected, is not to be captured.

This problem has been adressed many times in literature. Initially, Korf [7] proposed a greedy without inter-agent communication. His approach was to use a fitness function that combined 2 forces: each predator was "attracted" by the prey and "repelled" from the closest other predator. This solution kept predators away from other predators while they got closer to the prey; the idea

H. Geffner et al. (Eds.): IBERAMIA 2008, LNAI 5290, pp. 203–212, 2008.

was to chase the prey arranging predators in an stretching circle. Korf concluded that the pursuit domain was easily solved with local greedy heuristics.

A great number of alternatives have emerged since Korf's. Haynes and Sen [3] used genetic programming to evolve coordinated predators. Haynes compared differences between communicating and non-communicating predators with respect to their success in capturing the prey. He also co-evolved predators and the prey and found that a prey following a straight, diagonal line in an infinite world was never captured unless it was slower than its pursuers. This demonstrated that for certain instantiations of the domain, Korf's heuristic was not enough. Next, Chainbi et al. [2] used petri nets to coordinate predators while solving concurrency problems between them. Tan [10] used Reinforcement Learning to improve cooperation in three ways: (1) sharing instantaneous information (sensation, action, rewards obtained), (2) sharing episodes of instantaneous information, and (3) sharing learnt policies. Tan showed that agents learn faster when they learn cooperatively than when they learn individually. Later, Jim and Giles [4] proposed a genetic algorithm and multi-agent communication through a blackboard. A really interesting alternative was proposed by Katayama et al. [5]. They developed a way to integrate Analytic Hierarchy Process (AHP) into a Profit-Sharing algorithm. They gave primary knowledge to agents when they start their learning process. As they say, it does not seem reasonable to continue giving "hints" to grown agents that have developed their own knowledge, so Katayama et al. proposed a way to progresively stop providing "hints" to agents.

Despite the great number of proposed solutions, there is still room for improvements in different instantiations of the pursuit domain. As Tan stated in his work [10], coordination algorithms or protocols tested under the pursuit domain may easily be ported to other autonomous agents domains in general. This paper presents a new proposal for improving cooperation between predators in the pursuit domain. The idea presented here is to mix the efficiency of greedy approaches with two coordination proposals: a simple sight notice protocol and an evolutionary coordination system based on Neuroevolution [8]. Results show that this is a promising approach that develops a very efficient coordination mechanism, with still room for more improvements.

2 The Pursuit Domain

Stone&Veloso [9] considered the pursuit domain to be a toy problem with respect to multi-agent systems. However, it is an interesting start point because it is easy to understand, easy to play around with and difficult to master. Moreover, it is still popular because it is possible to create many different instances with different types of handycaps. The most classical environment consisted of a finite, discrete, grid world where 4 predators tried to capture 1 prey and agents were only allowed to move to orthogonally adjacent cells (i.e. north, south, east or west). In this environment, agents moved sequentially and two agents were not allowed to be on the same cell.

As Stone&Veloso stated [9], that classical environment could be varied by changing the size and shape of the world, the legal moves, the concurrency on agent movements, the size of agent's field of vision (FOV) in cells, the presence of objects, the definition of capture, the behaviour of the prey/s and the way predators communicate or not. Among this characteristics, we find three of them to be key for the environment to be challenging enough: using a toroidal world, restricting perception of agents to their FOV and making predators move concurrently.

Proposed characteristics could be simulated inside Kok&Vlassis' Pursuit Domain Package (PDP)[6]. PDP is a software package that simulates a pursuit domain environment. It lets modifying the parameters previously mentioned to instantiate different experimental scenarios. Concretelly, PDP was tuned for the purposes of our research to reflect some exact characteristics that are described as follows: (1) Toroidal world with a discrete, orthogonal grid of squared cells, (2) Availability for the agents to move to every adjacent cell each turn (9 possible options), (3) Concurrency in the execution and movement of predators, (4) Limited FOV for agents in the world affecting all agent sensors, (5) Agent's capability to communicate with other agents inside FOV, (6) Programability of prey behaviour, (7) Selection of the capture method; in our case, 4 predators occuping the 4 orthogonally adjacent cells (i.e. north, sourth, east and west).

Defined this way, PDP has some challenges to face. As we stated before, the three most remarkables ones are: (1) Concurrency lets predator move to the same cell in the same timestep (i.e. they collide). If this occurs, colliding predators are penalized by replacing them randomly. (2) FOV makes exploration necessary, and (3) the toroidal world removes the possibility of cornering the prey.

3   Methodology

Initially, Korf [7] considered a solution quite simple yet effective. The approach was to consider an "attractive" force which pushed predators towards the prey. The method was to calculate this force as fitness function for each of the possible cells to go next, and finally select the most attractive one. This solution had the problem that predators piled up and disturbed themselves; then, it turned difficult to achieve the final surrounding capture position. Korf overcomed this problem considering a "repulsive" force which pushed each predator away from the nearest other predator. With this new force, predators attacked the prey more jointly, not piling themselves up.

The reduced number of cycles that predators took to capture the prey with Korf's method seemed good enough not to consider the necessity of improving it. However, the differences between the environment used by Korf and new environments like PDP [6] lead to reconsider it. For instance, Korf reported that his algorithm captured the prey in 119 cycles in average. The experiments we have run in the most similar conditions possible to Korf's inside PDP take 366 cycles in average. In this case, which is the best one for Korf, the toroidal world and the collisions between agents multiply time to capture the prey by 3.

When conditions get worse, namely when the FOV of predators is reduced, the performance of Korf's approach deteriorates exponentially, as it is shown in the left graph of figure 2.

This means that it is necessary to extend Korf's algorithm to deal with the new issues of the environment. One possible way to extend it is to reconsider the way Korf treated atractive and repulsive forces between agents. In his proposal, predators were atracted by the prey and repelled by the nearest other predator. This leads to situations where one predator may be repelled directly against other predator, resulting in a collision. Then, the first approach to take is to make predators repel from all other predators. Equation 1 shows the fitness function used to do this. This function depends on the (x, y) coordinates of the cell and calculates distances from that cell to prey location (X_p, Y_p) and to other n predators locations (X_i, Y_i) using Manhattan Distance $d(x, y, x', y')$. To balance the relative amount of repulsive forces against the atractive one, a scale constant k is added. We will call Extended Korf, or ExtKorf for short, to the algorithm which works like Korf's but with the fitness function shown by equation 1.

$$f(x, y) = d(x, y, X_p, Y_p) - k \sum_{i=1}^{n} d(x, y, X_i, Y_i) \qquad (1)$$

The Extended Korf algorithm dramatically outperforms results of the Korf algorithm. The main reason for this is that it reduces collisions between predators by an order of magnitude, thus avoiding penalties. Results supporting this are shown and explained in section 4 (see figure 2).

3.1   Cascading Sight Notice (CSN)

In the environment where Korf did his experiments, communication between agents were not necessary, as he demonstrated. The main reason was that his agents were able to see the whole world at once. But, the more we limit the FOV of the predators the more they need to get more information to efficiently capture the prey. When predators have a reduced FOV, most of the times happens that when some predators have found the prey, others are still wandering around. This delay in founding the prey could be avoided if the predators were able to effectively tell where the prey is to others when they had found it.

Consider that an agent located at x, y and having a FOV of n cells means that the agent is only able to perceive what happens in the cells $\{(x', y')/x - n <= x' <= x + n, y - n <= y' <= y + n\}$. Take into account that this refers to sensing in general, and not seeing in particular. Therefore, an agent is only able to communicate with other agents being inside its FOV. Moreover, agents never know their global location, nor global coordinates of other agents. They are only aware of the relative location other agents are with respect to them.

In strict sense, the probability of a predator indefinitely not finding the prey in this conditions is not 0, and that is definitely a problem to overcome. But communication is not as simple as telling others directly where the prey is; there is no way to do that. In order to communicate where the prey is, we

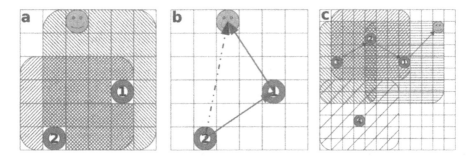

Fig. 1. a) Two predators with FOV 3 seeing each other, predator 1 seeing the prey. b) Predator 2 can figure out prey location from message of predator 1. c) Predators 1, 2 and 3 can figure out prey location, predator 4 cannot.

propose a simple protocol called Cascading Sight Notice (CSN). The idea is that a predator P seeing the prey Y has to communicate the relative location of Y that P is perceiving to each other predator P^i that P can see (i.e. P^i is inside the FOV of P). Then, each P^i not seeing Y could locate it by listening to P. P^i will then be aware of the relative location of P with respect to P^i and also aware of the relative location of Y with respect to P. So, P^i is able to calculate the relative location of Y with respect to P^i by adding the vectors of the two relative locations it knows. Then, when P^i has located the prey, P^i resends this new relative location to other predators in its FOV. The cycle continues until no predator is hearing or hearing predators already know where prey is (see figure 1).

This simple protocol lets predators with reduced FOV find the prey earlier than predators without communication do, and this turns into an improvement in the average number of cycles needed to capture the prey. The results supporting this are shown and explained in section 4 (see figure 3).

3.2 NEAT Coordination Protocol (NECool)

Inside PDP, collisions occur when two or more predators move to the same cell on the same timestep. As long as predators decide where to move in a concurrent fashion, they have no opportunity of avoiding collisions unless they establish an appropiate coordination protocol. One possibility to look for an optimal coordination protocol is to evolve a neural network that decides the next movement to do, taking into account the fitness values of the 9 possible cells to go next. If the neural network of predator P receives as input the location of all the other predators P^i that are inside the FOV of P, then the neural network will be able to output the next move that P should do to optimize the capture of the prey without colliding with any P^i.

Following this idea, algorithm 1 lets predators learn how to optimally coordinate and improve their performance in capturing the prey. To make algorithm 1 understandable, it is necessary to clarify some insiders. First of all, the function *compressAllFitnesses*(D) takes as argument a matrix with the 9 fitnesses associated to each one of the 9 adjacent cells where P^0 could move next. This is a biyective function that transforms the matrix D into a real value in $[-1, 1]$. This value is sent to other predators which use it as input to their neural networks. The neural networks, having locations and compressed fitnesses of predators as inputs, output a real value in $[-1, 1]$. This value is passed to the inverse function of *compressAllFitnesses*, that is *getNextCellToMove*(c). This last function treats the output from the neural network as a new compressed fitness: it "decompresses" the value, reconstructing a 3x3 matrix of fitnesses, and then it returns the number of the cell with best fitness value.

It is important to point some details. The functions *compressAllFitnesses* and *getNextCellToMove* do not directly compress the 9 fitness values into 1: there is no biyective function to do that. But that is not a problem, because the most relevant information for predators in order to coordinate their actions is not exactly the fitness itself, but the priority to choose each cell as next movement. Therefore, *compressAllFitnesses* forms a unique number λ by concatenating the numbers of the 9 cells ordered by their fitness. For example,

---

Algorithm 1. Coordinate decisions of predator P^0 with each P^i decision

---

Require: P^0 = predator with a 3-to-1 recurrent neural network
1: Let P be a vector of predators
2: Let D be a 3x3 real matrix
3: Let F be a vector of real numbers
4: Let f, d be real numbers
5: **if** *seesPrey*(P^0) **then**
6:    $(X_p, Y_p) \Leftarrow getPreyRelativeLocationTo(P^0)$
7: **else**
8:    $(X_p, Y_p) \Leftarrow (0, 0)$
9: **end if**
10: $P \Leftarrow getAllPredatorsInsideFOVOf(P^0)$
11: **for all** $((x, y) \mid 1 \le x \le 3, 1 \le y \le 3)$ **do**
12:    $D_x y \Leftarrow calculateExtendedKorfFitness(x, y)$
13: **end for**
14: $f \Leftarrow compressAllFitnesses(D)$
15: $sendCompressedFitnessToOtherPredators(f, P)$
16: $F \Leftarrow receiveCompressedFitnessesOfPredators(P)$
17: **for all** $(P^i \in P)$ **do**
18:    $f \Leftarrow getCompressedFitnessOf(P^i, F)$
19:    $(x, y) \Leftarrow getLocationOfPredator(P^i)$
20:    $activateNeuralNetworkWithValues(x, y, f)$
21: **end for**
22: $f \Leftarrow getCompressedFitnessOf(P^0, F)$
23: $(x, y) \Leftarrow getLocationOfPredator(P^0)$
24: $d \Leftarrow flushNeuralNetworkWithValues(x, y, f)$
25: $c \Leftarrow getNextCellToMoveTo(d)$
26: $movePredatorTo(P^0, c)$

---

compressAllFitnesses could form the number $\lambda = 854713269$ meaning that the cell number 8 is the best fitted one, while the cell number 9 is the poorly fitted one. Then, as long as λ is a discrete integer value, it is now possible to associate an $\alpha \in [-1, 1]$ though a biyective function. *compressAllFitnesses* finally returns α, while *getNextCellToMove* reconstructs λ from an α and returns the first digit (8 in our previous example).

Regarding the neural networks, they are trained using Neuroevolution of Augmenting Topologies (NEAT [8]). Populations of predators are created each epoch, and each predator has its own neural network. Each neural network has 3 inputs and 1 output. The 3 inputs are designed to receive the (x, y) location of a predator P^i, scaled to $[-1, 1]$ depending on the FOV, and the compressed fitness value P^i. The neural network is expected to sequentially receive these 3 inputs from each of the predators inside the FOV of P^0, and to activate all its neurons once for each triplet of inputs. Finally, the neural network receives the 3 inputs of P^0, activating and flushing the net to get its final output value.

4   Results

To validate our approach we compared the results of the 3 methods (ExtKorf, ExtKorf+CSN and ExtKorf+CSN+NECool) with the original of Korf in the same environment conditions, but variating the FOV. We have measured predators against two different preys: a random moving prey, and an evading prey. The second prey moves to the adjacent cell that is more distant from the closest predator. These tests let us show the magnitude of the improvements and their relative relevance. For running the simulations we used Kok&Vlassis' Pursuit Domain Package (PDP). Concretely, we used a 30x30 cells field, allowing agents to move diagonal, with the prey starting on the center and predators starting randomly placed. We lauched 4 predators to capture 1 prey, following capture method 2 (4 predators orthogonally surrounding the prey, without touching it). Finally, in case of collision, only predators colliding were penalized. Simulation was always ran for 500 consecutive episodes, and we got the average results.

Our first comparative experiment was to measure the improvement in cycles and collisions of the Extended Korf algorithm against original Korf's. For this experiment the results show an improvement of an order of magnitude in most cases. In figure 2 we see that the improvement is much greater when the FOV is more limited (3 is the minimum FOV considered). It is normal, though, that the minimum improvement in cycles and collisions happens when agents have 15 cells of FOV (i.e. they can sense the whole world at once). In this case, agents do not lose cycles in trying to find the prey, and they go straight to capture it.

As we stated in previous section, figure 2 clearly shows that there are two major ways of improvement: more efficiently finding the prey and avoiding collisions. We have made two proposals, each one to cover each of these two ways. Our first proposal was about the CSN protocol, enabling predators to locate the prey by using the indications got from other predators. In order to check the relative improvement of using this protocol, we have compared Extended Korf's model

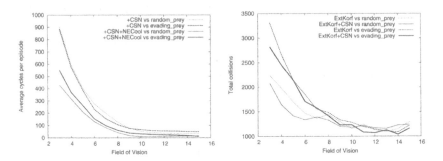

Fig. 2. Comparison between original and Extended Korf's model with respect to average cycles per episode and total collisions in 500 episodes

against itself with and without CSN. Figure 3 shows the results of this comparison. As expected, results suggest that there are plenty of situations in which CSN saves cycles of exploration to the predators. So, CSN represents an improvement which leads predators to earlier find the prey on average, and CSN is more significant when FOV is minimal.

However, CSN is not a definitive solution. CSN turns less effective when dimensions of the world increase due to the necessity of predators to be inside FOV of others to hear them. This limits the relative improvement that could be achieved with CSN to a factor depending on the relation of FOV with the size of the world. The less proportion of cells a predator is able to perceive, the more difficult to find the prey and the more difficult to communicate with others.

Although these results suggest that CSN could be improved, it is not an easy task because FOV restricts communication between agents. Therefore, other way to globally improve performance is to reduce collissions between predators. NECool addressed this issue. To test NECool we set up a training session of 250 generations, with a population of 100 predators. Each predator was tested by 50 episodes against each type of prey, with 6000 cycles as maximum episode time to capture it. The fitness function used to train predator was $f = \frac{6001}{n+10c+1}$,

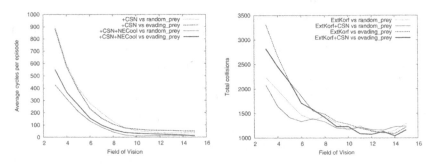

Fig. 3. Comparison between Extended Korf's model and Extended Korf's model with CSN with respect to average cycles per episode and total collisions in 500 episodes

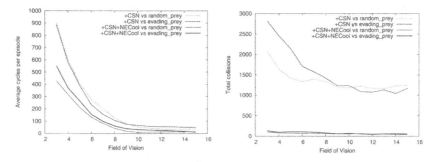

Fig. 4. Comparison between Extended Korf's model with CSN and with CSN+NECool with respect to average cycles per episode and total collisions in 500 episodes

which depends on the average number of cycles to capture the prey (n) and the average number of collisions (c). All agents had 6 cells as FOV.

Once we had trained NECool predators, we run for them the same 500 episodes test we run earlier, but this time against ExtKorf+CSN predators. The result (see figure 4) was a dramatic reduction in the number of total collisions, and this reflected directly in an improvement in the average number of cycles to capture the prey, by around $25 - 35\%$. It is interesting to notice that predators were trained with a FOV of 6 cells but tested with different FOVs.

5   Conclusions and Further Work

This paper describes a new proposal for improving cooperation between predators in domains. This new proposal mixes the efficiency of greedy approaches with Machine Learning techniques to get the best of both. The proposal suggests to extend Korf's approach (ExtKorf) and to add two cooperatives strategies: Cascading Sight Notice (CSN) and NEAT Coordination Protocol (NECool).

To validate this approach we compared the results of ExtKorf, ExtKorf+CSN and ExtKorf+CSN+NECool between them pairwise and with Korf's using Pursuit Domain Package (PDP) in more challenging environment conditions. Our first experiment measured performance in cycles and collisions of Extended Korf's algorithm against Korf's. Results shown an improvement of an order of magnitude in most cases. Our second experiment demonstrated that CSN improves the average cycles to capture the prey, but only significantly in few cases. This was mainly due to the necessity of predators to be inside FOV of others to communicate with them. Our third experiment added NECool and compared it with ExtKorf+CSN. Results shown a dramatic reduction of total collisions between predators, which maps directly to a significant improvement (25 to 35%) in average number of cycles to capture the prey.

Therefore, we conclude that mixing greedy and evolutive approaches is a promising path to explore, as our experiments have shown. Our final algorithm, ExtKorf+CSN+NECool achieved great results mainly due to its ability to make predators collaborate in an efficient way to lower down collisions with minimum impact in the greedy way to chase the prey. However, there remains room for improvements. For instance, it is still needed a way to early find the prey, what could be achieved if predators coordinate to explore the world, rather than exploring it randomly. Our future work will address this issue and it will also focus on lowering down collisions to 0, with the minimum impact on chasing efficiency.

References

1. Benda, M., Jagannathan, V., Dodhiawalla, R.: On optimal cooperation of knowledge sources. Technical Report Tech. Rep. BCS-G2010-28, Boeing AI Center, Boeing Computer Services, Bellevue, WA (1986)
2. Chainbi, W., Hanachi, C., Sibertin-Blanc, C.: The Multi-agent Prey-Predator problem: A Petri net solution. In: Proceedings of the IMACS-IEEE-SMC conference on Computational Engineering in Systems Application (CESA 1996), Lille, France, pp. 692–697 (1996)
3. Haynes, T., Sen, S.: Evolving behavioral strategies in predators and prey. In: Sen, S. (ed.) IJCAI 1995 Workshop on Adaptation and Learning in Multiagent Systems, Montreal, Quebec, Canada, pp. 32–37. Morgan Kaufmann, San Francisco (1995)
4. Jim, K.-C., Giles, C.L.: Talking helps: Evolving communicating agents for the predator-prey pursuit problem. Artificial Life 6(3), 237–254 (2000)
5. Katayama, K., Koshiishi, T., Narihisa, H.: Reinforcement learning agents with primary knowledge designed by analytic hierarchy process. In: SAC 2005: Proceedings of the 2005 ACM symposium on Applied computing, pp. 14–21. ACM, New York (2005)
6. Kok, J.R., Vlassis, N.: The pursuit domain package. Technical Report Technical Report IAS-UVA-03-03, Informatics Institute, University of Amsterdam, The Netherlands (August 2003)
7. Korf, R.E.: A simple solution to pursuit games. In: Proceedings of the 11th International Workshop on Distributed Artificial Intelligence, Glen Arbor, MI, pp. 183–194 (February 1992)
8. Stanley, K.O., Miikkulainen, R.: Evolving neural networks through augmenting topologies. Evolutionary Computation 10(2), 99–127 (2002)
9. Stone, P., Veloso, M.M.: Multiagent systems: A survey from a machine learning perspective. Autonomous Robots 8(3), 345–383 (2000)
10. Tan, M.: Multi-agent reinforcement learning: Independent vs. cooperative learning. In: Huhns, M.N., Singh, M.P. (eds.) Readings in Agents, pp. 487–494. Morgan Kaufmann, San Francisco (1997)

The Evolution of Negotiation and Impasse in Two-Party Multi-issue Bargaining

Fernando Lopes[1], A.Q. Novais[1], and Helder Coelho[2]

[1] INETI, Dep. de Modelação e Simulação, Est. Paço Lumiar, 1649-038 Lisboa, Portugal
{fernando.lopes,augusto.novais}@ineti.pt
[2] Universidade de Lisboa, Dep. de Informática, Campo Grande, 1749-016 Lisboa, Portugal
hcoelho@di.fc.ul.pt

Abstract. Automated negotiation systems are becoming increasingly important and pervasive. Most previous research on automated negotiation has focused on understanding and formalizing "successful" negotiations, *i.e.*, negotiations that do not become contentious to the point of impasse. This paper shifts the emphasis to negotiations that are "difficult" to resolve and can hit an impasse. It analyses a situation where two agents bargain over the division of the surplus of several distinct issues to demonstrate how a procedure to avoid impasses can be utilized in a specific negotiation setting. The procedure is based on the addition of new issues to the agenda during the course of negotiation and the exploration of the differences in the valuation of these issues to capitalize on Pareto optimal agreements. This paper also lays the foundation for performing an experiment to investigate how the evolution of negotiation contributes to the avoidance of impasses, paying particular attention to the expansion of the number of issues to be deliberated and its impact on the frequency of impasses.

1 Introduction

Negotiation is an important and pervasive form of social interaction — it may involve two parties (bilateral negotiation) or more than two parties (multilateral negotiation), and one issue (single-issue negotiation) or many issues (multi-issue negotiation). This paper concentrates on two-party and multi-issue negotiation. We are interested in Pareto optimal outcomes (because Pareto optimality ensures that resources are not wasted), the uniqueness of these outcomes (because this allows agents to know their actual shares of the issues under dispute), and the computational complexity of different negotiation procedures and strategies (because agents should be able to negotiate in a reasonable amount of time).

Negotiation is usually understood as proceeding through three distinct phases [6]: a beginning or initiation phase, a middle or problem-solving phase, and an ending or resolution phase. The initiation phase focuses on preparation and planning for negotiation (usually referred to as pre-negotiation), and is marked by each party's efforts to posture for positions. The problem-solving phase focuses on movement toward a final agreement (usually referred to as actual negotiation), and is characterized by strategic maneuvers and jockeying for positions. The resolution phase focuses on elaborating details and implementing the final agreement.

H. Geffner et al. (Eds.): IBERAMIA 2008, LNAI 5290, pp. 213–222, 2008.

Negotiation may end in an agreement, wherein the parties mutually agree to a proposal, or in an impasse, wherein the parties do not reach a settlement. An impasse (a stalemate or a deadlock) is a condition or state of negotiation in which there is no apparent quick or easy resolution — the parties are unable to create mutually advantageous deals that satisfy their aspirations [6]. Productive communication stops. The issues are viewed is such a way that the parties do not believe that there is any possible compatibility between them, or they cannot find a middle ground where agreement is possible. The cost of a failed or faulty negotiation can be high in many different ways (e.g., in the quantity of physical resources). Thus, effective negotiators need to understand why negotiation breaks down and be familiar with specific techniques to avoid or resolve impasses.

Artificial intelligence (AI) researchers have traditionally focused on understanding and formalizing "successful" negotiations — most researchers have assumed that negotiations result in agreement (see, e.g., [3,4,5]). Few researchers have attempted to formalize "difficult" negotiations, i.e., negotiations that can become contentious to the point of impasse (see, e.g., [2,7,12]). At present, despite these and other relevant pieces of work, there is still a lack of theoretical and practical understanding and important questions are still waiting to be addressed more thoroughly. We highlight the following:

- Why and how negotiations become "difficult" to resolve and reach impasse? What are the causes of impasse?
- How to manage "difficult" negotiations? Which are the actions that autonomous agents can take jointly to return negotiations to a productive phase?
- Which individual approaches to impasse avoidance or resolution are effective?

This paper addresses some of these questions in a domain-independent way.

Recently, we have proposed a model that accounts for systematic preparation and planning for negotiation, describes equilibrium strategies for the bargaining game of alternating offers, and formalizes a procedure for assisting agents to avoid impasses [9]. The procedure involves the following main actions:

- re-definition of the agenda, i.e., addition of new issues to the agenda during the course of negotiation;
- exploration of the differences in the valuation of the new issues to capitalize on Pareto optimal agreements.

Taken together, these actions add an evolutionary dimension to negotiation — some elements of the situation are not fixed, but evolve over time. Abandoning a static view simply unveils new opportunities for mutually acceptable agreements.

In this paper, we analyse a situation where two agents bargain over the division of the surplus of several distinct issues to demonstrate how the impasse avoidance procedure can be utilized in a specific negotiation setting. We also lay the foundation for performing an experiment to investigate how the evolution of negotiation contributes to the avoidance of impasses, paying particular attention to the expansion of the number of issues to be deliberated and its impact on the frequency of impasses.

2 Pre-negotiation

Successful negotiators agree on one thing [6,13]: the keys to success in negotiation are preparation and planning (pre-negotiation). Let $Ag = \{ag_1, ag_2\}$ be the set of autonomous negotiating agents. Let $I_i = \{is_{i1}, \ldots, is_{iz}\}$ be the set of independent issues of an agent $ag_i \in Ag$. The issues are quantitative variables, defined over continuous intervals. Negotiation usually involves a number of major or primary issues (e.g., price) and several minor or secondary issues (e.g., maintenance policies). Let $MI_i = \{is_{i1}, \ldots, is_{in}\}$ and $SI_i = \{is_{in+1}, \ldots, is_{iz}\}$ be the sets of major and minor issues of ag_i, respectively. A brief description of various activities that negotiators make efforts to perform in order to carefully prepare and plan for negotiation follows (see our earlier work for an in-depth discussion [7,9]).

Effective pre-negotiation requires that negotiators prioritize the issues, define the limits, and establish the agenda. Priorities are set by rank-ordering the issues, *i.e.*, by defining the most important, the second most important, and so on. The priority pr_{il} of ag_i for each issue $is_{il} \in I_i$ is a number that represents its order of preference. The weight w_{il} of is_{il} is a number that represents its relative importance. The limit lim_{il} is the point where ag_i decides that it should stop to negotiate, because any settlement beyond this point is not minimally acceptable. The negotiating agenda is represented by $Agenda$ and specifies the final set of issues to be deliberated. Its definition involves interaction with the opponent. Specifically, negotiators disclose and combine their individual sets of major issues. For the sake of simplicity, we consider that the sets MI_i and $Agenda$ contain the same issues.

Additionally, effective pre-negotiation requires that negotiators agree on an appropriate protocol that defines the rules governing the interaction. The protocol can be simple, allowing agents to exchange only proposals. Alternatively, the protocol can be complex, allowing agents to provide arguments to support their negotiation stance. However, most sophisticated protocols make considerable demands on any implementation, mainly because they appeal to very rich representations of the agents and their environments (see, e.g., [4]). Therefore, we consider an alternating offers protocol [10]. Two agents or players bargain over the division of the surplus of $n \geq 2$ issues (goods or pies) by alternately proposing offers at times in $T = \{1, 2, \ldots\}$. The negotiation procedure, labelled the "joint-offer procedure", involves bargaining over the allocation of the entire endowment stream at once. An offer is a vector $(x_1, \ldots, x_n)$ specifying a division of the n goods. Once an agreement is reached, the agreed-upon allocations of the goods are implemented. This procedure permits agents to exploit the benefits of trading concessions on different issues.

The players' preferences are modelled by assuming that each player ag_i discounts future payoffs at some given rate δ_i^t, $0 < \delta_i^t < 1$, (δ_i^t is referred to as the discount factor). The cost of bargaining derives from the delay in consumption implied by a rejection of an offer. Practically speaking, the justification for this form of preferences takes into account the fact that money today can be used to make money tomorrow. Let U_i be the payoff function of ag_i. For simplicity and tractability, we assume that U_i is separable in all their arguments and that the per-period delay costs are the same for all issues:

$$U_i(x_1, \ldots, x_n, t) = \delta_i^{(t-1)} \textstyle\sum_{l=1}^n w_{il} \, u_{il}(x_l)$$

where w_{il} is the weight of is_{il} and x_l denotes the share of ag_i for is_{il}. The component payoff function u_{il} for is_{il} is a continuous, strictly monotonic, and linear function. The distinguish feature of time preferences with a constant discount rate is the linearity of the function u_{il} [10]. The payoff of disagreement is normalized at 0 for both players.

Finally, effective pre-negotiation requires that negotiators be able to select an appropriate strategy. Traditionally, AI researchers have paid little attention to this pre-negotiation step. In the last several years, however, a number of researchers have developed models that include libraries of negotiation strategies (see, e.g., [3,4,5]). Some strategies are in equilibrium, meaning that no designer will benefit by building agents that use any other strategies when it is known that some agents are using equilibrium strategies (see, e.g., [10] for an in-depth description of the standard game-theoretic concept of equilibrium). Thus, for some situations, the agents can be designed to adopt equilibrium strategies and to negotiate according to these strategies. This paper follows this line of work.

3   Actual Negotiation

The negotiation process is modelled as an extensive game. For convenience, we consider the standard game-theoretic situation of two players completely informed about the various aspects of the game. The players are assumed to be rational, and each player knows that the other acts rationally. Also, we consider a particular setting in which the players have different evaluations of the issues, as described below.

Two players are jointly endowed with a single unit of each of four goods, $\{X_1, \ldots, X_4\}$, and alternate proposals until they find an agreement. Each good is modelled as an interval $[0, 1]$ (or as a divisible pie of size 1). The players' preferences are as follows:

$$U_i = \delta_i^{(t-1)} \left(a\,x_1 + b\,x_2 + x_3 + x_4 \right)$$

$$U_j = \delta_j^{(t-1)} \left[(1 - x_1) + (1 - x_2) + c\,(1 - x_3) + d\,(1 - x_4) \right]$$

where x_l and $(1 - x_l)$, $l = 1, \ldots, 4$, denote the shares of ag_i and ag_j for each pie, respectively. The parameters a, b, c, and d allow the marginal utilities of the players to differ across issues and players. We consider $a > b > 1$ and $d > c > 1$, i.e., ag_i places greater emphasis on goods X_1 and X_2 while ag_j values goods X_3 and X_4 more. Also, we consider that δ_i and δ_j are close to 1 and the parameters a, b, c, and d are close to one another. Let $p_{j \rightarrow i}^{t-1}$ and $p_{i \rightarrow j}^{t}$ denote the offers that ag_j proposes to ag_i in period $t-1$ and ag_i proposes to ag_j in period t, respectively. Consider the following strategies:

$$str_i^* = \begin{cases} \text{offer } (1,\, 1,\, x_{i3}^*,\, 0) & \text{if } ag_i\text{'s turn} \\ \text{if } U_i(p_{j \rightarrow i}^{t-1}) \geq U_i^* \quad \text{accept else reject} & \text{if } ag_j\text{'s turn} \end{cases}$$

$$str_j^* = \begin{cases} \text{offer } (1,\, x_{j2}^*,\, 0,\, 0) & \text{if } ag_j\text{'s turn} \\ \text{if } U_j(p_{i \rightarrow j}^{t}) \geq U_j^* \quad \text{accept else reject} & \text{if } ag_i\text{'s turn} \end{cases}$$

where $U_i^* = U_i(1, x_{j2}^*, 0, 0)$, $U_j^* = U_j(1, 1, x_{i3}^*, 0)$, and the shares are the following: $x_{i3}^* = \frac{\delta_i \delta_j (a+b) - \delta_j (a+b+bc+bd) + bc + bd}{bc - \delta_i \delta_j}$ and $x_{j2}^* = \frac{\delta_i (\delta_i \delta_j (a+b) - \delta_j (a+b+bc+bd) + bc + bd) + (bc - \delta_i \delta_j)(a\delta_i + b\delta_i - a)}{b(bc - \delta_i \delta_j)}$.

Remark 1. For the two-sided four-issue bargaining game of alternating offers with an infinite horizon, in which the players' preferences are as described above, the pair of strategies (str_i^*, str_j^*) form an equilibrium. The outcome is the following:

$$x_1^* = 1, \quad x_2^* = 1, \quad x_3^* = \frac{\delta_i \delta_j (a+b) - \delta_j (a+b+bc+bd) + bc + bd}{bc - \delta_i \delta_j}, \quad x_4^* = 0$$

Agreement is immediately reached with no delay. The outcome is Pareto optimal. Letting $\delta_i \to 1$ and $\delta_j \to 1$, the equilibrium division is $(1, 1, 0, 0)$.

The formal proof is based on the familiar necessary conditions for equilibrium: ag_i is indifferent between waiting one period to have its offer accepted and accepting ag_j's offer immediately, and ag_j is indifferent between waiting one period to have its offer accepted and accepting ag_i's offer immediately. Let $\mathbf{x}_i^* = (x_{i1}^*, \dots, x_{i4}^*)$ and $\mathbf{x}_j^* = (x_{j1}^*, \dots, x_{j4}^*)$ be the equilibrium proposals of ag_i and ag_j, respectively. The problem for ag_i is to find an offer that maximizes its payoff (because it is a payoff maximizer) subject to being acceptable to its opponent, *i.e.*,

maximize:
$$U_i(x_1, \dots, x_4, t) = \delta_i^{(t-1)} (ax_1 + bx_2 + x_3 + x_4)$$

subject to:
$$(1 - x_{i1}^*) + (1 - x_{i2}^*) + c(1 - x_{i3}^*) + d(1 - x_{i4}^*) =$$
$$\delta_j [(1 - x_{j1}^*) + (1 - x_{j2}^*) + c(1 - x_{j3}^*) + d(1 - x_{j4}^*)]$$
$$0 \le x_{il}^* \le 1, \quad 0 \le x_{jl}^* \le 1, \quad \text{for } l = 1, \dots, 4$$

The problem for ag_j is stated in a similar way and is omitted. Solving both maximization problems yields the outcome specified in the statement of the Remark. In the limit, letting $\delta_i \to 1$ and $\delta_j \to 1$, the outcome of the equilibrium is $(1, 1, 0, 0)$. This outcome is on the Pareto frontier and corresponds to the utility pair $(a+b, c+d)$.

4 Bargaining Impasse

Negotiators can adopt different orientations (and strategies) to accomplish their goals. Two bargaining orientations are commonly discussed in the literature [11]: individualistic or competitive and cooperative or problem solving. Individualistic negotiators show a strong interest in achieving only their own outcomes — getting this deal, winning this negotiation — and tend to pursue competitive strategies (e.g., appearing firm and imposing time pressure). Cooperative negotiators are concerned with both their own and the other's outcomes — building, preserving, or enhancing a good relationship with the other party — and tend to pursue problem solving strategies (e.g., logrolling and compensation).

The last section has considered a typical bargaining situation of two cooperative agents and a "win-win" philosophy (formalized, at least in part, by the strategic choices of the players). The agents were assumed to be sufficiently creative to devise the Pareto frontier and able to settle for the outcome that maximizes their benefit (resources were not wasted and money was not squandered).

This section addresses a different bargaining situation — it considers a cooperative agent, say ag_i, and a competitive agent, ag_j, who wants to "win" the negotiation. Now, ag_j pursues a strategy compatible with its negotiating style (e.g., starting with high demands and making a few small concessions throughout negotiation [7,8]). In period 1, ag_i proposes the offer $\mathbf{x}_i^*$ specified in Remark 1, and ag_j either accepts this offer or rejects it. We restrict attention to the case in which ag_j rejects the offer $\mathbf{x}_i^*$. The play passes to period 2 and ag_j proposes an offer $\mathbf{y}_j$, which ag_i rejects (considering that $U_i(\mathbf{y}_j, 2) < U_i(\mathbf{x}_i^*, 3)$). The agents continue to negotiate in this manner and, therefore, negotiation can become "difficult" to the point of impasse.

In this situation, ag_i can try to draw ag_j into a more constructive process. Specifically, ag_i can manage the sets of major and minor issues constructively by performing the following actions:

- analysis of the set SI_i of minor issues; selection of issues that are believed to cost less than they are worth to ag_j;
- addition of new issues to the set MI_i of major issues (and subsequent re-definition of the agenda);
- exploration of the differences in the valuation of the new issues.

The basic idea is to allow ag_i to prepare a new proposal that maximizes its benefit and simultaneously is more favourable to ag_j (than any previous proposal). Taken together, the suggested actions add an evolutionary dimension to the analysis. They can enable the enlargement of the space of feasible settlements, thus facilitating movement towards an optimal agreement.

Consider a new two-sided five-issue bargaining situation obtained from the two-sided four-issue situation introduced in the previous section by changing the agenda, $i.e.$, by adding a new good X_5. For the new bargaining game of alternating offers, time starts at period 1. However, the players' preferences take into account the costs of bargaining derived from the delays in consumption implied by the rejection of offers in the "initial" situation, $i.e.$,

$$U_i = \delta_i^{(t-1)+\tau}(a\,x_1 + b\,x_2 + x_3 + x_4) + \delta_i^{(t-1)}x_5$$

$$U_j = \delta_j^{(t-1)+\tau}[(1-x_1)+(1-x_2)+c\,(1-x_3)+d\,(1-x_4)] + \delta_j^{(t-1)}e\,(1-x_5)$$

where τ is a time period, $a > b > 1$ and $d > c > e > 1$. Consider the following strategies:

$$str_i^{**} = \begin{cases} \text{offer } (1,\,1,\,0,\,0,\,x_{i5}^{**}) & \text{if } ag_i\text{'s turn} \\ \text{if } U_i(p_{j\rightarrow i}^{t-1}) \geq U_i^{**} \quad \text{accept else reject} & \text{if } ag_j\text{'s turn} \end{cases}$$

$$str_j^{**} = \begin{cases} \text{offer } (1,\,x_{j2}^{**},\,0,\,0,\,0) & \text{if } ag_j\text{'s turn} \\ \text{if } U_j(p_{i\rightarrow j}^{t}) \geq U_j^{**} \quad \text{accept else reject} & \text{if } ag_i\text{'s turn} \end{cases}$$

where $\qquad U_i^{**} = U_i(1, x_{j2}^{**}, 0, 0, 0), \qquad\qquad U_j^{**} = U_j(1, 1, 0, 0, x_{i5}^{**}),$

$$x_{i5}^{**} = \frac{(a+b)\delta_i^\tau \delta_j^{\tau+1} - (a+b+bc+bd)\delta_i^{\tau-1}\delta_j^{\tau+1} + (bc+bd)\delta_i^{\tau-1}\delta_j^\tau - be\delta_i^{\tau-1}(\delta_j-1)}{be\delta_i^{\tau-1} - \delta_j^{\tau+1}}, \qquad \text{and}$$

$$x_{j2}^{**} = \frac{(abe+b^2 e)\delta_i^\tau - abe\delta_i^{\tau-1} - (b+bc+bd)\delta_j^{\tau+1} + (bc+bd)\delta_j^\tau - be(\delta_j-1)}{b(be\delta_i^{\tau-1} - \delta_j^{\tau+1})}.$$

Remark 2. For the new bilateral five-issue bargaining game of alternating offers with an infinite horizon, in which the players' preferences are as described above, the pair of strategies (str_i^{**}, str_j^{**}) form an equilibrium. The outcome is Pareto optimal:

$$x_1^{**} = 1, \qquad x_2^{**} = 1, \qquad x_3^{**} = 0, \qquad x_4^{**} = 0,$$

$$x_5^{**} = \frac{(a+b)\delta_i^\tau \delta_j^{\tau+1} - (a+b+bc+bd)\delta_i^{\tau-1}\delta_j^{\tau+1} + (bc+bd)\delta_i^{\tau-1}\delta_j^\tau - be\delta_i^{\tau-1}(\delta_j-1)}{be\delta_i^{\tau-1} - \delta_j^{\tau+1}}$$

Agreement is immediately reached with no delay. Letting $\delta_i \to 1$ and $\delta_j \to 1$, the equilibrium division is $(1, 1, 0, 0, 0)$.

The formal proof is similar to the proof of Remark 1. At this stage, it is worth noting that the offer specified in Remark 2 is more favourable to ag_j than the offer specified in Remark 1. Thus, this new offer can be accepted, $i.e.$, the negotiation process may end successfully and the Pareto optimal agreement may be implemented.

Example 1. Consider a sales agent and a logistics agent operating in a multi-agent supply chain system. The sales agent is responsible for acquiring orders from customers, negotiating with customers, and handling customer requests for modifying or canceling orders. The logistics agent is responsible for coordinating the plants and distribution centers of a manufacturing enterprise − it manages the movement of materials and products across the supply chain, from the suppliers of raw materials to the customers of finished goods. In particular, consider the following situation:

"David, the director of Sales, is trying to arrange for production of its two new orders, one for 10000 and the other for 5000 men's suits. Martin, the director of Logistics, is stating that the job will take four months. Together, they will gross over 25000 Euros, with a fine profit for the company. The problem is that Martin insists that the job will take four months and David's customer wants a two-month turnaround. Also, David claims that it can't afford to lose the customer".

There are four major issues of concern in negotiation, namely quantity_1 and date_1 (for the 10000 suit order), and quantity_2 and date_2 (for the 5000 suit order). The sales agent places greater emphasis on quantity_1 and date_1 (due to the inherent customer demands). On the other hand, the logistics agent values quantity_2 and date_2 more. Figure 1 shows the joint utility space for the agents (the small squares represent a few possible agreements). The Pareto frontier is represented by the dotted line OAO' and the optimal outcome referred to in Remark 1 by the point A. This outcome provides a (normalized) benefit of 0.65 to each party (letting $\delta_i \to 1$ and $\delta_j \to 1$).

Additionally, there is one minor issue for the sales agent: meeting_attendance, $i.e.$, the right to attend a number of Sales Division meetings that are of interest to the Logistics Division. The inclusion of this issue unveils new opportunities for mutually acceptable agreements, thus changing the location of the Pareto frontier. Figure 1 shows the new location of the frontier (line OBO'). The optimal outcome referred to in Remark 2 is represented by the point B and provides a (normalized) benefit of 0.725 to Martin and 0.55 to David (again, letting $\delta_i \to 1$ and $\delta_j \to 1$). Thus, Martin may re-analyze the negotiation situation, adopt a different negotiating style, and respond favourably to this new solution.

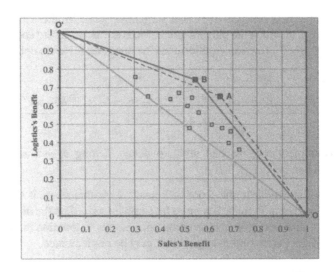

Fig. 1. Joint utility space for the sales and logistics agents

5   Experimental Analysis: Preliminary Report

The analytic results just given ensure the benefits of adding new issues to the agenda for the negotiation setting discussed here. However, the theory does not articulate how fast the convergence of negotiation is. Specifically, negotiation may become contentious to the point of impasse, even if the agents are sufficiently creative to re-define the agenda and exploit the differences in the valuation of the new issues to capitalize on Pareto optimal agreements. We intend to address this issue by empirically investigating how the evolution of negotiation contributes to the avoidance of impasses, paying particular attention to the expansion of the number of issues to be deliberated and its impact on the frequency of impasses. Accordingly, we describe below the experimental method, discuss the independent and dependent variables, and introduce the preliminary hypotheses. In so doing, we lay the foundation for the experimental work.

The experimental method is controlled experimentation [1]. The experiment involves three types of agents: (i) competitive agents, (ii) creative agents, and (iii) impasse avoidance agents. Competitive agents are individualistically oriented and pursue a strategy str. This strategy models an optimistic opening attitude and successive small concessions [7,8]. Creative agents are cooperatively oriented and pursue a strategy str^* (see Remark 1). Impasse avoidance agents are also cooperatively oriented and pursue a strategy str^* at the beginning of negotiation and a strategy str^{**} after the rejection of the first offer (see Remark 2).

Research on human negotiation has shown that motivational orientation (and strategy) affects both process and outcome in bilateral interaction (see, e.g., [11,13]). A cooperative orientation has increased the joint benefit of negotiators. Also, when aspirations were high and inflexible, negotiations were more likely to be broken off under an individualistic as opposed to a cooperative orientation. Accordingly, the hypotheses are as follows (a dyad is composed by a sales agent and a logistics agent):

Hypothesis 1. Dyads whose sales agent is cooperatively oriented (cooperatively oriented dyads) will reach higher quality outcomes (higher joint benefits) than dyads whose sales agent is individualistic oriented (individualistic oriented dyads).

Hypothesis 2. The impasse rate will be lower in cooperatively oriented dyads than in individualistic oriented dyads. The impasse rate will be lowest in cooperatively oriented dyads composed by an impasse avoidance sales agent.

Hypothesis 3. The cost of bargaining (the time spent in negotiation) will be lower in cooperatively oriented dyads composed by an impasse avoidance sales agents than in cooperatively oriented dyads composed by a creative sales agent.

The independent variable is the bargaining orientation of the sales agent (manipulated by assigning a specific strategy to this agent). This variable has three levels, namely the three strategies mentioned earlier. The dependent variables are the impasse rate, the time spent in negotiation, the Pareto efficiency, and the joint benefit provided by the final agreement. The first dependent variable is the impasse rate, *i.e.*, the frequency of impasses. The second variable is the time spent in negotiation (measured in terms of the total number of offers exchanged by the agents). The next variable is the Pareto efficiency, *i.e.*, the extent to which an agreement approaches the frontier (a fully Pareto efficient agreement is Pareto optimal). The last dependent variable is the joint benefit provided by the final agreement, *i.e.*, the sum of the two agents' benefits in the final agreement.

The experiment involves three groups of trials. Each group corresponds to a level of the independent variable. A trial is a single run of the experimental system and involves a bargaining session. Trials of the same group will, in general, differ from one another. The detailed experimental procedure is a follows:

- for each group of trials, the experimenter manipulates the independent variable, *i.e.*, assigns a strategy to the sales agent;
- for each trial in each group, the experimenter randomly determines the agent that starts the bidding process and the orientation of the logistics agent, *i.e.*, its strategy (from a library containing competitive and problem solving strategies [7,8]);
- for all trials of each group, the experimenter measures the dependent variables and computes averages on the measures taken.

6 Related Work

Traditionally, AI researchers have focused on modelling "successful" negotiations, *i.e.*, negotiations that result in agreement (see, e.g., [3,4,5]). There are, however, some researchers that have studied various techniques that autonomous agents can use to resolve impasses on their own (see, e.g., [2,7,12]). Faratin [2], for example, presented a model that incorporates a mechanism to assist agents in dynamically including or retracting issues from the set of negotiation issues. The author acknowledged the usefulness of the mechanism to escape negotiation deadlocks. However, he pointed out that the mechanism is complex and deferred to future work both its specification and its empirical analysis. Lopes et al. [7] developed a model that formalizes a structure for the problem under negotiation and supports the dynamic change of that structure to achieve movement towards agreement (problem restructuring). The authors pointed out that problem restructuring facilitates the resolution of impasses. However, they observed that problem restructuring is a highly creative and challenging task and postponed its formal treatment to future work. Sycara [12] developed the Persuader system for resolving conflicts in the domain of labor relations. Problem restructuring may take place during the modification of a proposal.

At present, despite these and other relevant pieces of work, the study of negotiations that are "difficult" to resolve, the formalization of approaches to impasse avoidance, and the empirical evaluation of agents capable of managing "difficult" negotiations are still in its infancy. This paper has addressed these issues in a specific negotiation setting.

7   Conclusion

This paper has shifted the emphasis to negotiations that are "difficult" to resolve and can hit an impasse. It has analysed a particular situation where two agents bargain over the division of the surplus of several distinct issues and has demonstrated the benefits of an impasse avoidance procedure involving the re-definition of the agenda during the course of negotiation. It has also laid the foundation for performing an experiment to investigate how the evolution of negotiation contributes to the avoidance of impasses.

Autonomous agents able to negotiate and avoid impasses under complete information are currently being developed using the Jade framework. Our aim for the future is to perform a set of experiments to validate the key components of the agents. In addition, we intend to develop more sophisticated agents that are able to negotiate and avoid impasses under incomplete information.

References

1. Cohen, P.: Empirical Methods for Artificial Intelligence. MIT Press, Cambridge (2001)
2. Faratin, P.: Automated Service Negotiation Between Autonomous Computational Agents. Ph.D. Thesis, Queen Mary & Westfield College, UK (2000)
3. Ito, T., Hattori, H., Zhang, M., Matsuo, T.: Rational, Robust, and Secure Negotiations in Multi-Agent Systems. Springer, Heidelberg (2008)
4. Jennings, N., Faratin, P., Lomuscio, A., Parsons, S., Wooldridge, M., Sierra, C.: Automated Negotiation: Prospects, Methods and Challenges. Group Dec. and Neg. 10, 199–215 (2001)
5. Kraus, S.: Strategic Negotiation in Multi-Agent Environments. MIT Press, Cambridge (2001)
6. Lewicki, R., Barry, B., Saunders, D., Minton, J.: Negotiation. McGraw Hill, New York (2003)
7. Lopes, F., Mamede, N., Novais, A.Q., Coelho, H.: A Negotiation Model for Autonomous Computational Agents: Formal Description and Empirical Evaluation. Journal of Intelligent & Fuzzy Systems 12, 195–212 (2002)
8. Lopes, F., Mamede, N., Novais, A.Q., Coelho, H.: Negotiation Strategies for Autonomous Computational Agents. In: ECAI 2004, pp. 38–42. IOS Press, Amsterdam (2004)
9. Lopes, F., Fatima, S., Wooldridge, M.: Pre-Negotiation and Impasse in Automated Negotiation. Group Dec. and Neg. (submitted, 2007)
10. Osborne, M., Rubinstein, A.: Bargaining and Markets. Academic Press, London (1990)
11. Pruitt, D., Kim, S.: Social Conflict: Escalation, Stalemate, and Settlement. McGraw Hill, New York (2004)
12. Sycara, K.: Problem Restructuring in Negotiation. Management Sci. 37, 1248–1268 (1991)
13. Thompson, L.: The Mind and Heart of Negotiator. Prentice-Hall, Englewood Cliffs (2005)

Characters with Character

Isabel Machado Alexandre

ISCTE/ADETTI
Ed. II - Av. Forças Armadas
1646-026 Lisboa, Portugal
isabel.alexandre@iscte.pt

Abstract. How good is a story without a good protagonist, or even a good plot? One of the flaws that are pointed to edutainment and entertainment applications is that they do not have an underlying story, and their characters end up without character. With this we mean that each character do not exhibit any qualities or features that distinguishes one person, group or thing from another. If the characters that populate a game, an educational or an edutainment application do not have specific goals, behaviours or more generally a role, the aim of such application can be seen as shallow and might contribute to poor interactions. This paper explores novel and alternative ways to enrich such characters with more social capabilities, promoting a more engaging experience for the users.

Keywords: narrative intelligence, interactive storytelling, believable characters.

1 Introduction

How good is a story without a good protagonist, or even a good plot? One of the flaws that are pointed to edutainment and entertainment applications is that they do not have an underlying story, and their characters are characterless. With this we mean that each character do not exhibit *any qualities or features that distinguishes one person, group or thing from another.* If the characters that populate a game, an educational or an edutainment application do not have specific goals, behaviours or more generally a role, the aim of such application can be seen as shallow and might contribute to poor interactions. One can argue against this claim by saying that players of first-person shooter (FPS) games do really enjoy game interactions, and do not need any narrative to guide or shape the interactions. Some researchers have argued that in these situations users are bound to violent interactions and miss social interactions [Magerko 2004]. The drive is what if an interactive drama approach is applied to commercial games, would it improve the interactions, would it be an added value for the users and their interaction's experiences.

In *interactive drama* the user has an important and active role in the interaction since he intervenes in the play by acting with the story characters and by participating within the achievement of the story. Therefore, the audience leaves its traditional role of spectator to incarnate the role of someone that can influence the story progression by acting in it. Several Artificial Intelligence (AI) researchers have developed several approaches to the development of interactive drama systems. For example, Mimesis,

H. Geffner et al. (Eds.): IBERAMIA 2008, LNAI 5290, pp. 223–232, 2008.

architecture for integrating intelligent control in games [Young 2005]; Virtual Sitcom, which developed a character-based approach, and represents the story as the set of HTN plans for the characters [Cavazza 2001]; Façade, a virtual sitcom which represents the story as annotated story beats [Mateas 2002]. This paper presents another approach for interactive drama which mixes a character-based approach with a centralised story control, provided by a Director agent (similar to [Magerko 2005]). The novelty of this approach is that it is grounded on *narratology* theories and educational drama [Bolton 1998], which empowers the user with the possibility to better understand the actions taken during the interactions, by providing them with an opportunity to reflect. The approach here presented was developed in the context of a Support and Guidance Architecture (SAGA) for story creation activities [Machado 2005].

The next sections present the definition of the characters that populate the interactive drama application, and how we envision achieving interactivity through this approach. To provide an informed interaction to the user a reflection engine is also presented and discussed.

2 Characters as Dramatis Personae

In this approach the concept of character is achieved as a ***dramatis personae***, adapted from Propp's work [Propp 1968] and it stands for the following definition:

Def.: A dramatis personae is defined as a virtual actor with an associated role to play within the story, i.e., the concept of dramatis personae is the conjunction of two different concepts: actor and role. The role played by a dramatis personae may vary along the story.

M. Bal's definition [Bal 1985] of an actor as: "the agents that perform actions" helped to reach the *actor* definition as the physical representation or appearance of a character in the story world.

Def.: An actor is defined as the physical representation or appearance of a dramatis personae (character) in the story world.

The *role* concept is based on B. Hayes-Roth's definition: "a set of behaviors that are known to both the characters and the audience (...)" [Hayes-Roth 1997]. This definition of role is also compliant with what M. Bal identifies as the set of distinct traits associated with each actor, which enrich the actor as an individual and convert him into a particular character – *dramatis personae*. This notion of ***dramatis personae*** is strongly related with the character concept defined by Aristotle [Aristotle 1996], since he states that a character (*ethos*) depends on what kind of assignments and interpretations are made by the audience – in our case the users. The assignment of a particular behaviour to a specific *role* is done by establishing a direct connection with the different *types of character* defined by Propp.

Def.: A role is defined as a class of individuals whose prototypical behaviours, relationships, and interactions are known both to the actors and to the audience.

Following Propp's morphology, there are five different role types, which can be assigned to the characters: *villain, donor, helper, others,* and *hero* – each of them being characterized by a set of *plot points[1]* (implicitly to the *functions* as defined by Propp). There is the need to generalize Propp's morphology in order to accommodate as large a number of situations as possible. For example, as an ending for a story or even a game, one does not want that the protagonist of the story always marries a beautiful prince(ss). At this stage, we go a step further in the specification of plot points and we establish that associated with each *plot point* is a set of *generic* goals. A **generic goal** is nothing more than a deeper elaboration of what the *plot point* stands for. For example, the plot point *villainy* has five associated different generic goals: theft, kidnapping someone, casting of a spell, imprisonment, and an order to kill/murder someone. Within each set, each *generic* goal is equally valid for reaching a particular *plot point*.

The definition of the set of generic goals associated with each plot point was based on the analysis of Propp's proposed morphology. Therefore, the *variable story schema*, which defines the structure of a story is:

$$(A \mid a)BC\uparrow DEFG \underline{HIK\downarrow Pr\text{-}RsL} \text{ } QEx \text{ } TUW$$
$$LMJNK\downarrow Pr\text{-}Rs$$

In this variable story schema, each of the letters stands for a *function*, which can be understood as both the actions of the characters and the consequences of these actions for the story. These *functions* can be seen as *plot points*, and can be decomposed into a set of *generic goals* for each *plot point* (see Table 1. – the plot points associated with the villain role).

Table 1. Roles, Plot Points, and Generic Goals (villain)

ROLE	PLOT POINT	GENERIC GOALS
VILLAIN	A - VILLAINY	THEFT KIDNAPPING SOMEONE CASTING OF A SPELL IMPRISONMENT ORDER TO KILL/MURDER SOMEONE
	H – STRUGGLE	HERO STRUGGLES WITH THE VILLAIN FIGHT CONTEST COMPETITION GAME
	PR – PURSUIT	ATTEMPT TO DESTROY THE SOUGHT PERSON OR ACQUIRE SOME SOUGHT OBJECT

Taking into account the specification of character's characteristics presented by L. Egri [Egri 1960], it is possible to define the following three dimensional characteristics for the *dramatis personae*: (**a**) **physiological** - this dimension characterizes the physical appearance of the character. The actor type is highly dependent on the story creation application but its definition can also influence the character's credibility in the story; (**b**) **emotional** - the emotional dimensions reflect the actual emotional state of the character. The model being developed only considers one bipolar emotional dimension: *sad – happy*, but more complex emotional models can be considered; and, (**c**) **social** - this dimension is determined by the role played by the character, since the role played, by a particular *dramatis personae*, has impact on some specific spheres of

---

[1] An important moment in the story [Mateas 1999].

action. These spheres of action define which characters, playing some specific roles, must interact in order to make the story go a step further.

As we saw, a *dramatis personae* is a virtual actor that performs a particular role in a story, so at this point there is the need to understand how a virtual actor is conceptualized and specified to take its part in an interactive story.

3 Achieving Interactivity

Within our view, interactivity is reached by providing the users with the possibility of deciding the flow of a specific story. To do this, each user should have the means to participate in the story and decide which action should be performed next by a specific character. This direct influence on the behaviour of the characters, and indirectly on the story, features the concept of *agency* defined by J. Murray [Murray 1997]. This interactivity is possible, because within our approach to support and guide a story creation activity, it is considered that each story is not pre-defined or written by an author before the story creation process starts. In that sense, each story starts with an initial story situation which only specifies the principal ingredients of a story and establishes a main purpose to be attained during the story creation activity. Therefore, if another story creation activity is begun from the same initial story situation, the result of such activity is certainly a different story with a different meaning to the users involved in its creation. This approach merges the actor, author and spectator roles, since users are invited *to act* in an interactive story along with the other characters (autonomous characters controlled by the architecture or by other users), to create/author such a story by acting in it and to understand the others characters' actions – being a spectator – in order to respond to their behaviours. This new concept aims at overcoming one of the typical problems of interactive narratives/stories – *the higher degree of freedom that is given to the user to intervene in the narrative flow, the weaker is the power given to the author to decide on the progress of the story* [Clarke & Mitchell 2001] – since the users and authors of the story are the same.

Since these different roles impose a set of new responsibilities to the users, there is the need to ease such burden and provide them with intuitive processes to carry on their task. Therefore, to act within the story we envision each user controlling a specific character and commanding it throughout the story creation activity. However, besides having user-controlled characters, there is the possibility to consider autonomous characters that play a pre-defined role within the story and interact with user-controlled characters. The question that rises at this point is how a character is – following the taxonomy a *dramatis personae* - specified and conceptualised within our approach. This issue is going to be discussed and presented in the following sub-section **Control of a Dramatis Person**.

To perform the role of the author and simultaneously being part of the audience of the story, we think that the best strategy is to provide the user with the possibility to be supported and guided throughout the story creation process. These support and guidance directives aim at providing the user with full understanding of what is happening within the story. Through these directives, users are provided with correct information for continuing the story *authoring,* and being an informed spectator during the process.

To do this, our approach considers a centralised control of the story, which tries to provide the users with support and guidance directives, sometimes achieved through the generation of some reflection threads. These support and guidance directives aim at clarifying the reasons behind the behaviours and actions taken by the characters. The goal is to promote the justification and context of the behaviours taken by the characters (autonomous or user-controlled) during the story progression. This justification aims at providing the users with some *meaning-making* and *meaning-finding* [Bolton 1998] about what happens inside the character's mind.

3.1 Control of a Dramatis Personae

Given the definition of what is a *dramatis personae*, it is time to understand how a *virtual actor* plays its role within the story. This *virtual actor* can perform its role in two different modes: user-controlled or autonomous mode. In both modes, *interactivity* represents an important factor to take into account when specifying a virtual actor. In particularly, in the autonomous mode, a virtual actor must not only perform accordingly to the role being played in the story, but must also take into account the actions taken by the other characters, specially because some characters' actions may not comply with the character model maintained by the autonomous character. This situation happens whenever a user-controlled character performs some actions that go against the role being played within the story. Of course, this means that the user controlling this character decided to direct his character differently; implicitly what he is indicating is that he is not happy with the role played by his character or is misunderstanding what is happening within the story.

Thus, a *dramatis personae*, that plays its role autonomously in the story, can be specified as an ***autonomous agent***. Along with this, if it is also implied that the agent must perform its story role in a credible manner, i.e., it must stay in character, a different concept is implicitly implied: the concept of ***believable character*** [Bates 1994]. In the user-controlled mode, the user has the possibility to control a *dramatis personae* during the story creation activity. In our view, this character can be seen as a semi-autonomous *avatar*. This concept was proposed by some researchers, who state that control can be seen as a combined task shared between the avatar/agent and the user. These avatars are somehow an extension of the user since they do not just behave, but sense the environment and provide the user with the character's perspective of what happened, which were defined by M. Mateas [Mateas 1997] as *subjective avatars*. J. Cassell and her colleagues [Cassell & Vilhjalmsson 1999] found evidence to show that users feel more in control when their avatars are able to exhibit a certain degree of autonomy and act by themselves when not controlled by the user.

Furthermore, the *dramatis personae* that are controlled by the users can also *become* autonomous *dramatis personae*. For instance, if a user controlling a character decides that she does not want to control it anymore, the system *takes care* of this character and it starts to act in the story according to its pre-defined role. Therefore, one could state that both approaches are to some extent two boundaries of a continuous spectrum, in the sense that any *dramatis personae* can go from being a ***semi-autonomous avatar*** – when controlled by a user – to an ***autonomous agent*** – when performing according to its pre-defined role, or vice versa.

3.2 Support and Guidance Directives

To provide the support and guidance directives, we considered the existence of a centralised narrative control module. This idea follows the work of P. Weyhrauch [Weyhrauch 1997] and M. Mateas [Mateas 2002], which defines this centralized narrative control module as a drama manager. In the work conducted by P. Weyhrauch, the drama manager has as a major goal subtly guiding the experience of the user, so that he would maintain his freedom, while attaining his destiny. This drama manager has an *aesthetic* evaluation function – which is able to evaluate the degree of quality the user experiences, and an adversary search mechanism that can effectively guide user experience based on the assessment provided by the evaluation function. In the work conducted by M. Mateas and A. Stern [Mateas 2002], the drama manager assures the dramatic consistency of the story state. To do this, the drama manager changes the story's dramatic values in response to the user's activity and guarantees that a good plot arc is achieved.

Within our theoretical framework, this centralised narrative control module is called the *Director Agent*. This *Director Agent* has the following capabilities: (1) to be able to inspect the changes occurring in the story world; (2) to be able to introduce new story elements whenever needed in order to achieve story progression;(3) to be able to ask for the generation of a reflection moment; (4) to be able to construct a story from the different *dramatis personae*'s perspectives, and; (5) to be able to accommodate the needs/opinions expressed by the users playing in the story world.

Capabilities three, four, and five are crucial to the enrichment of our theoretical framework with a user-centred approach. This user-centred approach is quite important since we aim to empower the user with the means to participate in an interactive story not only by influencing the flow of the story but also by understanding the meaning of the actions being taken in the story world by her or by the others *dramatis personae*. This full understanding of the reasons and motivations behind the behaviour of the *dramatis personae* is crucial for the user to act in the interactive story.

The generation of the appropriate reflection moments is of the responsibility of the *Reflection Engine*, which receives an information update from the *Director Agent* and triggers a reflection moment that tries to establish the right interaction with the user. This reflection moment aims at establishing the motivations of the user when directing a specific character and his opinion about the behaviour of the other characters in the story.

3.2.1 Director Agent

The *Director Agent* follows the specification of a narrative agent that K. Dautenhahn has established in a set of models for narrative agent. These different models are introduced along different levels of narrative complexity, by following a bottom-up strategy. It starts from the simplest case of a narrative agent and moves forward to the human narrative intelligence [Dautenhahn 2001]. Dautenhahn's definition of a type IV narrative agent represents an agent that possesses a form of narrative intelligence that is usually found in humans. This type of narrative agent makes use of its autobiographic memory to interact with others and respond with a new story. An agent that possesses an autobiographic memory can create and access information about sequence of actions, which it experienced during its lifetime. Following such definition, it is possible to catalogue the *Director Agent* as a Type IV narrative agent. Our agent fits this categorisation because it makes use of its memory to interact with the story characters and respond with support and guidance directives not only to those characters but also to the users. Nevertheless, we opted not to call our agent's memory autobiographic because it does not have the capability to learn from the facts collected from the stories. However, our agent does not limit itself to collect and store information from the stories, but organises such information in accordance with the different perspectives of the different *dramatis personae*.

3.2.2 Narrative Memory
This memory is created from the sequences of actions, which the Director Agent experiences while performing its guiding and supporting task during each story creation process. Furthermore, we assume that the *Director Agent's* lifetime is determined by the time of a particular story, i.e., the *Director Agent* only knows what happened within each story. Following Dautenhahn's classification, the *Director Agent* can be considered an agent of type IV, since it is embodied and situated in the story world, and because it dynamically reconstructs its individual *history* based on the story action/events experienced.

The memory of the Director Agent was named within this theoretical framework as a *narrative memory*. This *narrative memory* is organised in the form of episodes and contains information about the story progression from each story *dramatis personae*'s point of view. Each episode is constituted by three important events: crisis, climax and resolution [Freytag 1900] and are organized in a temporal sequence and with cause-effect links.

Def.: An episode – e – can be defined as a sequence of three events. Each of these events is of a specific type: crisis, climax, and resolution. The events are organized in a temporal sequence and with cause-effect links.

Def.: An event – ev - is characterized as a sequence of situations – one or more situations - and the type of the event, which can assume the following values crisis, climax and resolution.

From the approach presented in Computer as Theatre [Laurel 1993], these events have the following specification: - a **crisis event** can be characterised as a sequence of actions that comprise the revelation of the context (the possibilities, the characters and situations) and the initiation of an action that will become the central one; - a **climax event** is characterised as a sequence of actions that makes it evident that some possibilities are eliminated and others are emerging; a **resolution event** is characterised as the sequence of actions that exposes the consequences of the actions that happened within the climax event. Each situation can be of two categories: sensorial or behavioural, i.e., the former can be characterised as a *dramatis persona* internal state and the latter by a behaviour performed by such a *dramatis personae*.

Def.: A situation, st, is characterized by the identification of the dramatis personae that is experiencing such situation and the type of situation being experienced – sensorial or behavioural – and the situation itself.

Def.: A sensorial situation, $st_{sensorial}$, is characterized by a dramatis personae internal state.

Def.: A behavioural situation, $st_{behavioural}$, is characterized by a behaviour performed by a dramatis personae.

Thus, the *Director Agent*'s narrative memory can be specified as:

Def.: The narrative memory – M – can be defined as a vector of memory objects, where each of the entries of such vector is characterized by the identification of the dramatis personae to whom such entry is relevant.

3.2.3 Reflection Engine

The *Reflection Engine* aims at generating the reflection moments that are presented to the users during the story creation activity. The theory behind the design of this agent was based on the research of Dorothy Heathcote on acting in classroom drama [Bolton 1998]. The idea is that a user is asked to freeze her character's actions and explain the meaning of her character's current behaviour. By assuming that the plot associated with each story remains unsettled until users start the story creation process, we give them the opportunity of feeling the tension in the form of a problem, which they have to discover by their own means how to solve. From this tension, they move to the recognition of the problem and its implications, which would lead to a cognitive and affective response. In Heathcote's opinion *emotion is at the heart of the drama experience*, but each user should be kept in a safe position, like the self-spectator which remains safely protected because it is a drama experience but at the same time both *engaged* and *detached*. The *Reflection Engine* must provide the same guarantees in the sense that we do not want to betray any user's confidence by disrespecting his opinion about a character's behaviour or character's emotional state and simultaneously we want to provide her/him with any clarification or support that he may need to progress in the story creation activity. By experiencing the emotions conveyed in the drama experience, users can experience an empathic relation with the story and with its characters, and they can go through the three different levels of accomplishment identified by Stein [Thompson 2001], which means that: (1) they can watch the experience of others in the drama activity, even if he is the one playing one role, what is happening within the drama is not happening with her/him but with his character; (2) each user can then transpose himself to the place of the character in order to understand the character's experience, and; (3) finally, to react in accordance to his interpretation of the experience. The ability to transpose oneself into the place of the character is realised in our *user-supported interactive story creation* approach through the triggering of a reflection moment. The *Reflection Engine* is responsible for generating and sequencing the reflection moments to be presented to a particular user – meaning that in each reflection thread several reflection moments can be presented. Each reflection moment is composed by a statement about what a specific *dramatis personae* has done, which tries to make the users think and justify their agreement or disagreement with such a statement. The reflection moments are triggered whenever the *Director Agent* detects a conflict between a situation – before inserting such situation in the *dramatis personae*'s memory – and the *dramatis personae*'s expected behaviour. The *dramatis personae*'s expected behaviour is determined by its current goals, which should comply with the role performed by such *dramatis personae* in the story. As we have seen previously, a situation can be of two types: sensorial and behavioural, which implies that the statements portrayed within each reflection moment should be of similar nature. Thus, we decided to categorise such statements along three different categories: behaviour, personality, and emotional. The *behaviour statements* should refer to a particular action or a pattern of behaviour that should be performed by a specific character. The *emotional category* usually takes the form of a statement that establishes the emotional state of a specific character. The *personality category* is somehow similar to the emotional one but instead of trying to establish the current emotional state of a specific character, it tries to inquire about a specific character personality trait.

4   Conclusions

In this paper we present a novel approach to enrich game, educational and edutainment applications in order to provide a more wide variety of experiences. To do this, we devised an architecture based on character approach and centralized control achieved by the introduction of a *Director Agent*. Additionally, we enriched the approach with a reflection engine, which provides the user with an informed perspective of the actions taken within the application. This additional information helps the user to understand the motivations of the other characters within the application and adapt his strategy. This approach was already used in an educational application, Teatrix, a collaborative virtual environment for story creation. In this context, and from the evaluation experiences conducted in a real setting, it was possible to realize that the introduction of this approach improved the children experiences and the stories created. The next step would be to apply the same approach to a commercial application and assess its impact in the users' interaction experiences.

References

1. Aristotle 330 B.C. Poetics. Translated with an introduction and notes by Malcolm Heath, Penguin Classics (1996)
2. Bal, M.: Narratology: Introduction to the theory of narrative. University of Toronto Press, Toronto (1985)
3. Bates, J.: The Role of Emotion in Believable Agents, Technical Report CMU-CS-94-136, Carnegie Mellon University (1994)
4. Bolton, G.: Acting in classroom drama: a critical analysis. Trentham, Stoke-on-Trent (1998)
5. Cassell, J., Vilhjalmsson, H.: Fully embodied conversational avatars: Making communicative behaviours autonomous. Autonomous agents and Multi-Agent Systems 2(1) (1999)
6. Cavazza, M., Charles, F., Mead, S.J.: Agent's Interaction in Virtual Storytelling. In: de Antonio, A., Aylett, R.S., Ballin, D. (eds.) IVA 2001. LNCS (LNAI), vol. 2190. Springer, Heidelberg (2001)
7. Clarke, A., Mitchell, G.: Film and Development of Interactive Narrative. In: Balet, O., Subsol, G., Torguet, P. (eds.) ICVS 2001. LNCS, vol. 2197. Springer, Heidelberg (2001)
8. Dautenhahn, K., Coles, S.: Narrative Intelligence from the Bottom Up: A Computational Framework for the Study of Story-Telling in Autonomous Agents. The Journal of Artificial Societies and Social Simulation, Special Issue on Starting from Society - the application of social analogies to computational systems (2001)

9. Egri, L.: The art of dramatic writing - its basis in the creative interpretation of human motives. Touchstone Book - Simon and Schuster (1960)
10. Freytag, G.: Freytag's technique of the drama: an exposition of dramatic composition and art. Scott. Foresman, Chicago (1900)
11. Laurel, B.: Computers as Theatre. Addison-Wesley, Reading (1993)
12. Machado, I., Brna, P., Paiva, A.: Tell Me a Story. Journal of Virtual Reality (2005)
13. Magerko, B.: Story Representation and Interactive Drama. In: 1st Artificial Intelligence and Interactive Digital Entertainment Conference. Marina Del Rey, CA (2005)
14. Magerko, B., Laird, J.E., Assanie, M., Kerfoot, A., Stokes, D.: AI Characters and Directors for Interactive Computer Games. In: Proceedings of the 2004 Innovative Applications of Artificial Intelligence Conference, San Jose, CA. AAAI Press, Menlo Park (2004)
15. Mateas, M.: An oz-centric review of interactive drama and believable agents. In: Veloso, M.M., Wooldridge, M.J. (eds.) Artificial Intelligence Today. LNCS (LNAI), vol. 1600, pp. 297–328. Springer, Heidelberg (1999)
16. Mateas, M., Stern, A.: Towards Integrating Plot and Character for Interactive Drama. In: Dautenhahn, K., Bond, A., Cañamero, D., Edmonds, B. (eds.) Socially Intelligent Agents - creating relationships with computers and robots of the Multiagent Systems. Artificial Societies, and Simulated Organizations Series. Kluwer, Dordrecht (2002)
17. Murray, J.H.: Hamlet on the Holodeck - The future of the narrative cyberspace. MIT Press, Cambridge (1997)
18. Propp, V.: Morphology of the folktale. University of Texas Press, Austin (1968)
19. Weyhrauch, P.: Guiding interactive drama, Ph.D. thesis, School of Computer Science, Carnegie Mellon University (1997)
20. Young, R.M.: Cognitive and Computational Models in Interactive Narratives. In: Forsythe, C., Bernard, M.L., Goldsmith, T.E. (eds.) Cognitive Systems: Human Cognitive Models in Systems Design. Lawrence Erlbaum, Mahwah (2005)
21. Thompson, E.: Empathy and Consciousness. Journal of Consciousness Studies 8(5–7), 1–32 (2001)

Automatic Generalization of a QA Answer Extraction Module Based on Semantic Roles[*]

P. Moreda, H. Llorens, E. Saquete, and M. Palomar

Natural Language Processing Research Group
University of Alicante
Alicante, Spain
{paloma,hllorens,stela,mpalomar}@dlsi.ua.es

Abstract. In recent years, improvements on automatic semantic role labeling have grown the interest of researchers in its application to different NLP fields, specially to QA systems. We present a proposal of automatic generalization of the use of SR in QA systems to extract answers for different types of questions. Firstly, we have implemented two different versions of an answer extraction module using SR: a) rules-based, and b) patterns-based. These modules work as part of a QA system to extract answers for location questions. Secondly, these approaches have been automatically generalized to any type of factoid questions using generalization rules. The whole system has been evaluated using both location and temporal questions from TREC datasets. Results indicate that an automatic generalization is feasible, obtaining same quality results for both original type of questions and new auto-generalized one (Precision: 88.20% LOC and 95.08% TMP). Furthermore, results show that patterns-based approach works better in both types of questions (F1 improvement $+40.88\% LOC$ and $+15.41\% TMP$).

Keywords: Semantic Roles, Question Answering, Semantic Rules, Semantic Patterns, Internet Search Engines.

1 Introduction

Recently, automatic semantic role labeling (SRL) has experimented much progress. There is a growing interest in the study of the influence of using semantic roles (SR) on different natural languages processing (NLP) areas in which its contribution is believed to be beneficial, such as information extraction, summarization or textual entailment. However, several studies about automatic assignment of roles [6] indicated that one of the most outstanding contributions of SR will be in their application to QA systems.

Simplifying, the goal of a QA system is the answering by computers to precise or arbitrary questions formulated by users in natural language (NL). In this

---

[*] This paper has been partially supported by the Spanish government, project TIN-2006-15265-C06-01 and project GV06/028, and by the framework of the project QALL-ME, contract number: FP6-IST-033860.

H. Geffner et al. (Eds.): IBERAMIA 2008, LNAI 5290, pp. 233–242, 2008.

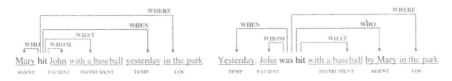

Fig. 1. Application of semantic roles in QA

manner, using a natural language input, the objective of a QA system is determining "WHO did WHAT to WHOM, WHERE, WHEN, HOW and WHY?" [7].

For each predicate in a sentence, SR identify all constituents, determining
their roles (agent, patient, instrument, etc.) and also their adjuncts (locative,
temporal, manner, etc.). In this way, SR represent 'WHO did WHAT to WHOM,
WHERE, WHEN, HOW and WHY?" in a sentence (see figure 1), which indicates
that its use in answer extraction could be very useful.

Therefore, the first objective of this paper is to analyze the influence of SR
on QA systems by evaluating two different methods of answer extraction based
on SR for location type questions. The second one is proposing an automatic
generalization process to other types of questions defining a set of generalization
rules, and testing it with temporal type questions.

The paper is structured as follows: Section 2 exposes the background of SR
field applied to QA systems, Section 3 provides detailed information of implemented proposals, and its generalization to temporal type. After that, Section
4 includes the evaluation and results discussion. Finally, some conclusions and
orientations for future work are presented.

2 Semantic Roles Applied to QA: Background

In general, QA systems architecture is composed of four main modules: question
analysis, document retrieval, passage retrieval and answer extraction [2]. QA
systems using SR are characterized by: (1) the set of SR applied and (2) how
SR are used.

Regarding the semantic role sets, most systems have used: the set used in the
corpus developed in PropBank (PB), the Proposition Bank project [18], such
as [21,22,10,14]; the set developed in the FrameNet (FN) project [3], such as
[17,20,5]; or a combination of both [15,8]. Other systems have selected a subset
of the role sets given by these corpora, as [9], which is only using PropBank roles
A0, A1 and A2.

Regarding how SR are used, two main categories of systems using SR can
be differentiated. On one hand, systems using SR to obtain extra information
and complement other methods, normally based on named entity recognition
[22,9,20,10], which are only giving information about how SR complements other
solutions. On the other hand, systems using SR as a core method of a module
in the QA architecture, being the type we are interested into. A brief summary
of the main systems is presented in Table 1.

Table 1. Summary of the use of SR in QA systems (QC: Question Classification, AE: Answer Extraction, AC: Answer Classification, AR: Answer Reranking)

SYSTEM	ROLES	USE	METHOD
Narayanan	FN	QC	Mapping Q. Pattern − Answer Pattern
Stenchikova	PB	AE	Rules type Q. − Answer role
Ofoghi	FN	AE	Mapping Q. Pattern − Answer Pattern
Kaisser	FN,PB	AE	Mapping Q. Pattern − Answer Pattern
Moschitti	PB	QC, AC, AR	Supervised Machine Learning
Fliedner	FN	AE	Mapping Q. *Frame* − Ans. *Frame*

As shown in the table, most of the systems are using a mapping between the semantic information of the question and the semantic information of candidate answers. Narayanan and Harabagiu's [15] applied SR to determine the type of the answer of complex questions. Their evaluation results over an ad-hoc set of 400 questions indicated a precision of 73.5% in which the type of the answer was properly detected. Ofoghi et al. [16] implemented a manual proof over a set of 15 questions in order to extract candidate answers to a question using SR. This system looks for the absent role of the question in the roles of the candidate answers. The evaluation of this approach using TREC2004 question corpus showed an MRR of 38.89 %. Kaisser's system [8] is a very similar proposal to the one explained before. It was evaluated with a subset of TREC2002 question corpus and obtained a precision of 36.70%. Fliedner [4] proposes a representation of both question and passages containing a possible answer as FrameNet style structures. The answer is obtained by a mapping process between both structures. Results for open domain questions achieved a precision of 66% and a 33% in recall.

Besides, another system like Stenchikova [21] establishes a set of rules that relate some types of questions (who,when,where or what) with the role type for the expected answer. In this case, the evaluation of the system obtains an MRR of 30%.

Otherwise, Moschitti [14] proposes a supervised learning algorithm using information of semantic analysis tree composed of the sentence predicate and its arguments tagged with SR. Results obtained prove the usefulness of this information for classification (MRR 56.21%) and re-classification (MRR 81,12%) of answers, but not for the question classification.

One of the most important problems of all these systems is the extraction of the SR of the question due to the fact that the SRL tools have serious problems to annotate questions.

Once the different proposals have been analyzed, it seems obvious that the main contribution of SR to QA systems is in the answer extraction module. However, previous works are not comparable between them due to the fact that these systems are using different set of measures, questions, documents and roles to achieve different objectives[1].

---

[1] For this reason it will not be possible to compare our proposal that uses SR in QA systems with the proposals presented to date.

Our work analyzes the contribution of SR to QA, using them in the answer extraction module in order to avoid the problem of annotating questions with SR, and presents an stable environment to measure, under the same conditions, the influence of two different SR-based answer extraction approaches.

3   Implementation

In order to analyze the influence of using SR on QA systems, specifically in the answer extraction module, and study if an automatic generalization to different types of questions is possible, two main steps have been taken in the implementation. Firstly, a base QA system including a SR-based answer extraction module for location questions has been implemented. Secondly, the answer extraction module has been automatically extended to temporal questions by using the proposed generalization rules.

3.1   Base System

A QA system has been developed following the steps indicated in Pizzato et al. [19] where all parts of it are detailed. In our system (see figure 2), the information retrieval module uses snippets obtained from several Internet search engines. Moreover, the answer extraction module has been modified in order to apply SR approaches. SemRol tool [13] has been used in order to determine the role of the arguments. This SRL tool uses PB role set, avoiding in this way the problem of adjuncts coverage of FN. In the next two subsections the implemented answer extraction methods will be described.

Answer extraction based on rules. Depending on the question type, and therefore on the expected answer type, a different set of SR could be considered as a possible answer. In that manner, it is possible to define a set of semantic rules that establishes relationships between the type of the question and SR. For instance, location questions such as "Where", "In what + location expression" or "What + location expression" must be answered with the location SR (AM-LOC). Making use of this rule, the answer extraction module will select the arguments of the snippets returned by the information retrieval module, that play the location role.

Answer extraction based on patterns. The PB role set prevents making consistent generalizations about adjunct or numbered arguments [18]; for instance, as [12] showed, in PB, the location can be represented by the roles: A2, A3, A4 or AM-LOC depending on the verb.

Therefore, the answer extraction module based on rules is not able to detect all the possibilities. To solve this problem, and considering the work presented in [23] about an answer extraction module based on patterns using named entities, the automatic construction of a set of semantic patterns based on SR is proposed. This set of semantic patterns will allow to detect which arguments represent

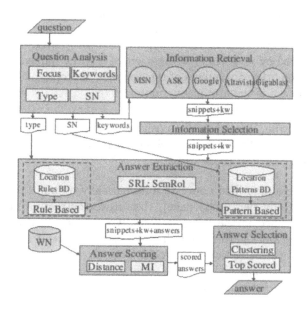

Fig. 2. Architecture of the QA system using SR in answer extraction

location in combination with which verbs covering a wide range of possibilities. Following the work of [23] and using pairs of question-answer, the automatic construction of a set of semantic patterns based on SR is proposed. This process consist of four stages:

1. *Snippet retrieval.* For each question-answer pair, the set of terms that a relevant document should contain is defined. Then, a query using these terms is submitted to different search engines[2] and the snippets retrieved that contain some of the terms are selected. The set of relevant terms is composed of 1) the noun phrases of the question, and 2) all the possible combinations of sub-phrases of the answer. The first 100 snippets retrieved for each search engine that contains in the same sentence the terms of the question and at least, one of the terms of the answer, are selected.

2. *Semantic Filtering of snippets.* Selected snippets are validated according to the semantic relation that they contain. Since the semantic relation generally appears as the main verb of the question, all verbs in the selected snippets are examined. Sentences of snippets containing synonyms, hyperonyms or hyponyms of the question verb, are selected. This semantic information is obtained from WordNet [11].

3. *Generating the answer pattern.* Finally, the selected sentences are generalized in semantic patterns using information about SR.

   (a) Each sentence is annotated with SR, using SemRol tool, in order to identify location arguments (AM-LOC, A2, A3 or A4).

---

[2] MSN, AskJeeves, Google, Altavista and Gigablast.

(b) Then, the arguments corresponding to some of the sub-phrases of the answer are replaced by its SR tag.

(c) Next, the arguments corresponding to the noun phrases of the question are replaced by $< QARG_n >$ tags, where n is the phrase counter.

(d) Finally, the other arguments of the sentence are replaced by $< ARG_n >$ tags, where n is the argument counter.

(e) All other words are removed.

4. *Pattern clustering.* Regardless the position of the tags, if two patterns have the same tags but different verbs, a single pattern is obtained containing the set of tags and a list of those verbs.

After the process described above to automatically obtain a database of semantic patterns (only performed once), the answer extraction module of the QA system is modified in the following way: when a new location question is formulated, one or more patterns for the returned snippets of this question are obtained (one for each location role: AM-LOC, A2, A3, A4 in the sentence). Then the patterns are matched with the set of patterns in our database. If there is a coincidence, the text corresponding to the SR tag in the pattern is retrieved as an answer.

3.2   Generalization Proposal

In order to generalize to other types of questions, we have defined an automatic generalization process that uses a set of rules [12] establishing relationships between the type of the question and SR (see table 2). Using these rules, the system knows which roles are used to answer which types of questions.

Otherwise, as explained in 3.1, we can not use rules to directly extract answers in all cases because, for instance, although AM-LOC always represent a location, locations can be also represented by the roles: A2, A3 or A4, depending on the verb. Therefore, we need patterns to decide when to take them into account.

3.3   Generalization Example to Temporal Type Questions

In order to demonstrate the validity of these generalization rules, we have automatically generalized the system described in section 3.1, that was originally implemented for location type questions. Once generalized, the system has been evaluated using both location and temporal type questions.

4   Evaluation

4.1   Evaluation Benchmark

A set of 100 questions has been used for each question type, meaning 100 location and 100 temporal questions. These sets have been built using TREC1999 and TREC2000 factoid questions and answers. Before carrying out the test, a

Table 2. Question-SR semantic relation set (R: Semantic Rules and P: Semantic Patterns)

Q. TYPE	ROLE	PB ROLE	ROLE NO	METHOD
LOCATION	Location	AM-LOC	ProtoAgent	R,P
		A2	Mode	P
		A3	Temporal	P
		A4	Cause	P
			ProtoPatient	
TEMPORAL	Temporal	AM-TMP	ProtoAgent	R,P
			Mode	
			Location	
			Cause	
			ProtoPatient	
MANNER	Mode	AM-MNR	ProtoAgent	R,P
	Theme (if it is a diction verb)	A1	Location	P
			Temporal	
			Cause	
			Patient	
			Beneficiary	
HUMAN (Who)	Agent − ProtoAgent	A0	Mode	P
	Patient − ProtoPatient	A1	Temporal	P
			Location	
			Theme	
			Beneficiary	
HUMAN (Whose)	Receiver	A2	Agent	P
	Beneficiary	A3	Location	P
	Patient		Mode	
	ProtoPatient		Temporal	
			Theme	
			Cause	
REASON	Cause	AM-CAU		R,P
	Theme	A1		P

patterns database for the patterns-based answer extraction module has to be built, as explained in section 3. It has been built using a set of 300 factoid location and temporal questions and answers, composed of a subset of TREC2003, TREC2006 and OpenTrivia.com data.

As explained in section 3.1, our system uses Internet search engines results as corpus to answer the questions. We judged answers to be correct if they represent or contain the correct answer. The measures used to evaluate the system are precision (*questions answered correctly/total questions answered*), recall (*questions answered correctly/total questions*), F1 (*(2*Precision*Recall)/(Precision+Recall)*) and MRR (*Mean Reciprocal Rank measure used in TREC*).

4.2   Results Analysis

The QA system has been executed for both implemented answer extraction modules and for both location and temporal question types (results in table 3). Neither manual review of sub-processes outputs nor post-execution adjustments have been made to automatic processes of the presented system.

On one hand, comparing the two different approaches of the answer extraction module based on SR, we can conclude that patterns-based approach is better than the rules-based one (F1 improvement: +40.88% *LOC*, +15.41% *TMP* and F1 error reduction: +19.06% *LOC*, +25.59% *TMP*) for two main reasons:

- Patterns-based approach improves rules-based in recall because of the inclusion of A2, A3 and A4 roles as possible answers for some patterns. Moreover, considering synonym, hyperonym or hyponym verbs in patterns database building process widens the approach coverage by including more than only questions verbs.
- Patterns improve rules in precision because while rules-based module extracts all location roles as possible answers, patterns-based only considers location roles whose pattern represent one of the contained in Patterns DB. That way, patterns-based approach does a kind of semantic filtering of sentences that results in a more precise extraction of answers.

Table 3. Implemented approaches results for location and temporal questions

		Answer type	
Approach	%	LOC	TMP
SR Rules	Pre	65.60	73.97
	Rec	21.00	54.00
	F1	31.80	62.42
	MRR	22.50	60.33
SR Patt.	Pre	88.20	95.08
	Rec	30.00	58.00
	F1	44.80	72.04
	MRR	31.50	62.83

On the other hand, results prove that an automatic generalization is possible. In this case the original system was implemented to solve location questions and it has been automatically extended to temporal questions with equal quality results, what proves that the proposed generalization process is valid. With this simple generalization process, results achieved for temporal questions are even higher than the ones for location questions. This is due to the fact that the SRL system used (SemRol tool) obtains better results for temporal roles than for locations ones (F1: 70.26% LOC - 83.21% TMP).

5   Conclusions and Further Work

The aim of this paper is to analyze the influence of using SR on question answering systems, as well as proving that an automatic extension of this systems from one type of question to others is feasible. To reach this goal a simple QA system has been developed and two proposals of a QA answer extraction module based on SR have been implemented for location questions. In the first proposal, a set of semantic rules that establishes relationships between the type of the question and a SR for the answer is defined. In the second one, the automatic construction of a set of semantic patterns of possible answers based on SR is proposed. Once this system has been implemented, we successfully extended it automatically to temporal questions by using generalized rules.

The whole system has been evaluated for both location and temporal questions. On one hand, results corroborate that patterns-based approach is better than rules-based one (F1 improvement $+40.88\%LOC$ and $+15.41\%TMP$). On the other hand, results prove that the proposed generalization is valid, obtaining equal quality results for the new auto-generalized type (Precision: 88.20% LOC and 95.08% TMP).

As further work, it could be interesting an study of the application of a specific SR set made for QA (see [12]) in our system comparing its results to the ones we have obtained with the generic SR set. Otherwise, improvements on base QA system could be oriented to adjusting answer scoring and ranking, as well as implementing an Answer Clustering module, to better select the final answer.

References

1. Deep Linguistic Processing Workshop in 45th Annual Meeting of the Association for Computational Linguistics (ACL), Prague, Czech Republic (June 2007)
2. Ferrández, A.: Sistemas de pregunta y respuesta. Technical report, Universidad de Alicante (2003)
3. Fillmore, C.J.: Framenet and the linking between semantic and syntactic relations. In: Proceedings of the 19th International Conference on Computational Linguistics (COLING), Taiwan, pp. xxviii–xxxvi (2002)
4. Fliedner, G.: Linguistically Informed Question Answering. Saarbrücken Dissertations in Computational Linguistic and Language Technology, vol. XXIII. Universität des Saarlandes und DFKI GmbH, Saarbrücken (2007)
5. Frank, A., Krieger, H., Xu, F., Uszkoreit, H., Crysmann, B., Jorg, B., Schafer, U.: Question answering from structured knowledge sources. Journal of Applied Logic. Special issue on Questions and Answers: Theoretical and Applied Perspectives 5(1), 20–48 (2007)
6. Gildea, D., Jurafsky, D.: Automatic labeling of semantic roles. Computational Linguistics 28(3), 245–288 (2002)
7. Hacioglu, K., Ward, W.: Target Word Detection and Semantic Role Chunking Using Support Vector Machines. In: Proceedings of the Human Language Technology Conference (HLT-NAACL), Edmonton, Canada (June 2003)
8. Kaisser, M.: Question Answering based on Semantic Roles. In: Proceedings of the Deep Linguistic Processing Workshop in 45th Annual Meeting of the Association for Computational Linguistics (ACL 2007) (2007) [1]
9. Lo, K.K., Lam, W.: Using semantic relations with world knowledge for question answering. In: Proceedings of The Fifteenth Text Retrieval Conference (TREC 2006) (2006)
10. Melli, G., Wang, Y., Liu, Y., Kashani, M.M., Shi, Z., Gu, B., Sarkar, A., Popowich, F.: Description of SQUASH, the SFU Question Answering Summary Handler for the DUC-2005 Summarization Task. In: Proceedings of the Document Understanding Conference 2006 (DUC 2006), New York City (June 2006)
11. Miller, G., Beckwith, R., Fellbaum, C., Gross, D., Miller, K.: Five Papers on WordNet. CSL Report 43. Technical report, Cognitive Science Laboratory, Princeton University (1990)
12. Moreda, P., Navarro, B., Palomar, M.: Corpus-based semantic role approach in information retrieval. Data and Knowledge Engineering 61(3), 467–483 (2007)

13. Moreda, P., Palomar, M.: The Role of Verb Sense Disambiguation in Semantic Role Labeling. In: Salakoski, T., Ginter, F., Pyysalo, S., Pahikkala, T. (eds.) FinTAL 2006. LNCS (LNAI), vol. 4139, pp. 684–695. Springer, Heidelberg (2006)
14. Moschitti, A., Quarteroni, S., Basili, R., Manandhar, S.: Exploiting Syntactic and Shallow Semantic Kernels for Question Answer Classification. In: Proceedings of the Deep Linguistic Processing Workshop in 45th Annual Meeting of the Association for Computational Linguistics (ACL 2007), pp. 776–783 (2007) [1]
15. Narayanan, S., Harabagiu, S.: Question answering based on semantic structures. In: Proceedings of the 20th International Conference on Computational Linguistics (COLING), Switzerland (August 2004)
16. Ofoghi, B., Yearwood, J., Ghosh, R.: A hybrid question answering schema using encapsulated semantics in lexical resources. In: Advances in Artificial Intelligence, 19th Australian Joint Conference on Artificial Intelligence, Hobart, Australia, pp. 1276–1280 (December 2006)
17. Ofoghi, B., Yearwood, J., Ghosh, R.: A semantic approach to boost passage retrieval effectiveness for question answering. In: Computer Science 2006, Twenty-Nineth Australian Computer Science Conference, Hobart, Australia, Enero, pp. 95–101 (2006)
18. Palmer, M., Gildea, D., Kingsbury, P.: The Proposition Bank: An Annotated Corpus of Semantic Roles. Computational Linguistics 31(1), 71–106 (2005)
19. Sangoi Pizzato, L.A., Mollá-Aliod, D.: Extracting Exact Answers using a Meta Question answering System. In: Proceedings of the Australasian Language Technology Workshop 2005 (ALTW 2005), Sidney, Australia (December 2001)
20. Shen, D., Wiegand, M., Merkel, A., Kazalski, S., Hunsicker, S., Leidner, J.L., Klakow, D.: The Alyssa System at TREC QA 2007: Do We Need Blog06? In: Proceedings of The Sixteenth Text Retrieval Conference (TREC 2007), Gaithersburg, MD, USA (2007)
21. Stenchikova, S., Hakkani-Tur, D., Tur, G.: Qasr: Question answering using semantic role for speech interface. In: Proceedings of the International Conference on Spoken Language Processing (Interspeech 2006 - ICSLP), Pittsburg, PA (September 2006)
22. Sun, R., Jiang, J., Tan, Y.F., Cui, H., Chua, T., Kan, M.: Using Syntactic and Semantic Relation Analysis in Question Answering. In: Proceedings of The Fourteenth Text Retrieval Conference (TREC 2005) (2005)
23. Yousefi, J., Kosseim, L.: Using semantic constraints to improve question answering. In: Kop, C., Fliedl, G., Mayr, H.C., Métais, E. (eds.) NLDB 2006. LNCS, vol. 3999, pp. 118–128. Springer, Heidelberg (2006)

A Multilingual Application for Automated Essay Scoring

Daniel Castro-Castro[1], Rocío Lannes-Losada[1], Montse Maritxalar[2], Ianire Niebla[2],
Celia Pérez-Marqués[3], Nancy C. Álamo-Suárez[3], and Aurora Pons-Porrata[4]

[1] Development Center of Applications, Technologies and Systems, Cuba
{daniel.castro,rocio.lannes}@sc.datys.co.cu
[2] Department of Languages and Information Systems,
University of the Basque Country
{montse.maritxalar,ianire.niebla}@ehu.es
[3] Center for Applied Linguistics, Ministerio de Ciencia, Tecnología y Medio Ambiente, Cuba
{celiap,alamo}@cla.ciges.inf.cu
[4] Center for Pattern Recognition and Data Mining, Universidad de Oriente, Cuba
aurora@cerpamid.co.cu

Abstract. In this paper, we present a text evaluation system for students to improve Basque or Spanish writing skills. The system uses Natural Language Processing techniques to evaluate essays by detecting specific measures. The application uses a client-server architecture and both the interface and the application itself are multilingual. The article also explains how the system can be adapted to evaluate Spanish essays written in Cuban schools.

Keywords: Assessment, Writing, Natural Language Processing in ICALL.

1 Introduction

In recent years, research has been carried out on computer-based Automated Essay Scoring (AES) systems for English ([4, 8, 9, 10, 11, 12]). The AES systems provide students with feedback to improve their writing abilities. Nevertheless, the results so far have been disappointing due to the difficult nature of defining objective criteria for evaluation. Indeed, the evaluation of essays is controversial. In fact, many factors influence the scoring of essays: the topic, time limits, handwriting skills and even the human raters themselves. Most AES systems are based on expert rater evaluations, although some authors [7] use expert writings to develop the evaluation models of such systems.

One of the advantages of AES systems is that they measure all essays using the same scoring model. Moreover, they provide empirical information about the evaluation process itself. In the case of AES systems which use evaluation models based on the criteria of expert raters, the empirical information of the evaluation process provides experts with feedback related to their evaluation criteria. This way, AES systems offer "objective" data to improve on the controversial task of essay evaluation by hand. In this article we address the results obtained from an evaluation of 30 essays and the way these results have influenced the criteria of human raters. Moreover, we explain the steps followed to define evaluation criteria and how it works in our AES system.

H. Geffner et al. (Eds.): IBERAMIA 2008, LNAI 5290, pp. 243–251, 2008.

The proposed system uses Natural Language Processing (NLP) techniques to detect specific evaluation measures in the analyzed essays. The application uses a client-server architecture and both the interface as well as the application itself are multilingual. Nowadays, there are few multilingual systems in this field [6]. In this paper, we present a multilingual system, describing the way in which different NLP tools have been integrated for two different languages: Spanish and Basque. Throughout the evaluation, the user gets feedback regarding erroneous linguistic structures, lexical variability and discourse information in both languages as well as information about the grammatical richness of Basque.

In the next section, we will explain the functionality and the architecture of the developed AES system. In section three we define the features detected by the system as well as the NLP tools used. Section four explains the building process of the system's criteria and the evaluation of the system for Spanish essays. Finally, conclusions are outlined in the last section.

2 Functionality and Architecture

We present a bilingual AES system for Spanish and Basque. The system features a Client-Server architecture (see Figure 1).

The server includes a request manager which calls the language modules of the server depending on the language requested by the client. Those language modules are composed of two different types of modules related, respectively, to the linguistic process and to criteria specification. The linguistic process module for text analysis and error management detects those linguistic features that the client will use to calculate each evaluation measure. This module extracts spelling errors and lexical and discourse information for both languages, as well as syntactic data in the case of Basque essays. The criteria specification module includes information about the detection of linguistic features (maximum length of a short sentence, word repetition, number of repeated word endings, number of words and different lemmas, specific features of the language such as the written accent in the case of Spanish, etc.). The modules are communicated to the corresponding NLP tools in order to detect the necessary features for each evaluation measure.

We defined three evaluation measures: spelling correction, lexical variability and discourse richness. The linguistic features provided by each evaluation measure are as follows: spelling errors and accentuation (spelling correction), redundancy or word repetition, monotony or repeated word endings, adjective usage (lexical variability), conjugated verbs, sentence length and pronoun usage (discourse richness).

The language modules compute the linguistic features at four different levels: word, sentence, paragraph and text. The result is calculated at one of those levels depending on the linguistic features of the application. For example, word repetition is computed at paragraph level because the client uses the redundancy of the texts at that level. Monotony is also calculated at paragraph level. Pronoun, adjective and conjugated verb usages are considered to be at text level.

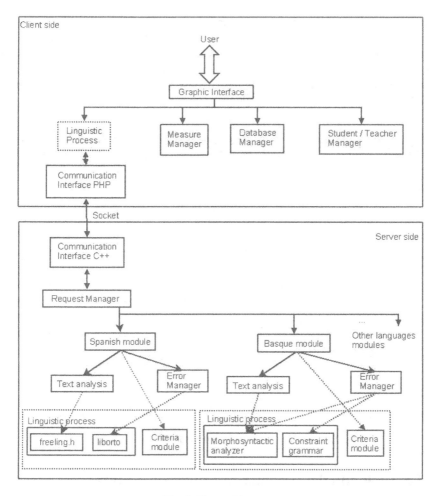

Fig. 1. The architecture

The client interprets the linguistic features calculated by the server in order to compute the evaluation measures that the application will give the user via the results of the evaluation. The application (graphic interface) adapts the interface depending on the language of the essay. The functionalities of the interface are: a text editor to write essays, consultation of previous evaluations and a source of quantitative and qualitative results. Although a score is provided for each evaluation measure, the user can consult the specific linguistic features related to each one. For example (see Figure 2), redundancy (word repetition) in the text is a linguistic feature which influences lexical variability. When the user clicks the button named *Redundancia en el texto* (*Redundancy in the text*), the application marks all the repeated words (one color for each different word)[1] in each paragraph. The user employs this kind of feedback to decide which words are justifiably repeated and which ones must be changed.

---

[1] In figure 2 we use geometric figures to represent different colors.

There are two types of users: students and teachers. The main difference between them is that teachers can consult the raw formulae used to calculate each evaluation measure. The formulae give information about the linguistic features used when calculating each evaluation measure and the weight given to each feature in the formulae.

The proposed system can be used in both, Windows and Linux operating systems. The client is programmed with *php* while the server modules are written in *C++*.

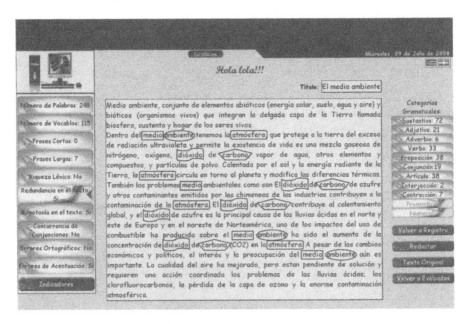

Fig. 2. Screenshot of the results provided by the evaluator

3 NLP Tools and the Detection of Linguistic Features

As seen in figure 1, the system makes use of the open source morphological analyzer, named *freeling* (version 1.5) ([3, 5]), in the Spanish module and our *liborto* library as a basis for the detection of spelling errors in Spanish. In the case of Basque, the morphological analyzer, [1] apart from dividing the words into corresponding lemma and morphemes, provides the morphosyntactic information necessary for the evaluation of the essays. This analyzer is also able to analyze erroneous words. Moreover, the Constraint Grammar formalism [2] includes linguistic rules for the detection of errors at sentence level.

We think that it is worthwhile to provide users with feedback, despite the limitations of NLP tools. For example, in the case of *freeling*, the information related to the part-of-speech is helpful in deciding whether a word must be taken into account when detecting redundancy or monotony. Likewise, the number of adjectives in an essay is another important aspect when evaluating its lexical variability. Hence, the number of adjectives, redundancy and monotony are the three linguistic features used to calculate the lexical variability of the Spanish essays. Discourse richness is based on the number of conjugated verbs and of pronouns, as well as sentence length. We are aware of the limits of this approach since some features, such as the use of conjunctions and coordination or subordination phrases, should also be considered when measuring the discourse level of an essay. However, the *freeling* open source software does not provide this kind of information. As explained in the next section, the raters did not take the mentioned features into account when evaluating the essays. Therefore, they were aware of the limits of the NLP tools before giving a strict evaluation.

4 Evaluation of Spanish Essays

In this section we explain the process followed to develop the system's criteria to evaluate essays written in Spanish in Cuban schools. During the identification of the criteria, the raters changed the formulae used in the evaluation in order to adapt automatic results to their evaluation done by hand. These changes were made in the criteria module. That means that in the future, when we have a wide-coverage analyzer for Spanish, raters will be able to change their formulae in order to take aspects such as subordination and coordination into consideration. The empirical information of the evaluation process provided the raters with specific evaluation criteria feedback and, based on the feedback, the experts changed the weighting assigned to the linguistic features in the formulae.

4.1 The Process

In order to define the criteria module for Spanish, we collected a sample consisting of 30 Spanish essays written by 9th grade students in Cuban schools. In general, the average text length was 237 words.

At the beginning, two experts evaluated a sampling of the compositions in order to define a formula for each evaluation measure. For example, in the case of lexical variability, the experts provided special weights for redundancy and monotony of the text. The lack of adjectives was weighted lower than the previous ones. Indeed, during different interviews with the raters, we realized that we had to give a specific weight to each linguistic feature. That task proved to be difficult as we strived to be as objective as possible.

The raters used a hundred-point scale to evaluate the compositions and a number of points were subtracted each time a linguistic feature was used erroneously. It was not obvious whether the score was the same in the case of each rater, which is related to subjectivity bias. However, by common consent, they defined the number of points to subtract for each linguistic feature. Once they agreed on all linguistic features, we defined the weight that would be given to each. We went on to make up the formulae to be applied in the automatic process. When it came to developing the system, we compared the automatic results and the hand-made evaluations of those 30 essays. We conducted the experiment with three different evaluation measures: spelling correction, lexical variability and discourse richness. In the case of all measures, the totals are counted without considering prepositions, conjunctions or articles.

4.2 The Experiment

For this experiment, spelling correction, lexical variability and discourse richness measures were analyzed. In this case, scores ranged between 1 (the lowest) and 10 (the highest), following the criterion currently used at Cuban schools. The scores provided by our system were compared to scores recorded by hand. The scores reflected precision, recall and F_1.

In this context, we defined these measures as follows:

$$Precision = \frac{Number\ of\ correct\ system\ evaluated\ essays}{Number\ of\ system\ evaluated\ essays}$$

$$Recall = \frac{Number\ of\ correct\ system\ evaluated\ essays}{Number\ of\ manually\ evaluated\ essays}$$

$$F1 = \frac{2 * Precision * Recall}{Precision + Recall}$$

Table 1 shows the results obtained by the evaluator while factoring in spelling correction. In the table, the first column shows possible test scores. The second column represents the number of texts that raters manually assigned to each score. The third column represents the number of texts for which the evaluator assigned the correct score. The fourth column represents the number of texts to which raters (and not the system) assigned each score. The fifth shows the number of texts to which the system (and not raters) assigned each score. Finally, the last three columns show precision, recall and F_1 values. Likewise, Table 2 shows the results obtained for lexical variability, Table 3 describes the results related to discourse richness and Table 4 shows the results yielded for a global evaluation, where the three mentioned evaluation measures were considered together. The structure of these tables is the same as that of Table 1.

Several observations can be made by analyzing the results in Tables 1, 2, 3 and 4. First, despite the difficulty of this task, the system achieves encouraging values of recall, precision and F1 for all evaluation measures. Second, the quality results with respect to spelling correction measure decrease in essays with scores of 9. This is due to the fact that the evaluator recognizes fewer spelling errors than do the raters because it does not identify context errors. In future research, we will improve the *liborto* library to help identify these types of errors.

Table 1. Results obtained by the automatic evaluator for spelling correction

Scores	According to raters	Correctly scored	Missed	Spurious	Precision	Recall	F1
10	26	25	1	2	92.59	96.15	94.33
9	4	2	2	1	75	50	60
Total	30	27	3	3	90	90	90

Table 2. Results obtained by the automatic evaluator for lexical variability

Scores	According to raters	Correctly scored	Missed	Spurious	Precision	Recall	F1
10	24	22	2	0	100	91.67	95.65
9	6	3	3	2	60	50	54.55
8	0	0	0	2	0	-	-
7	0	0	0	1	0	-	-
Total	30	25	5	5	83	83	83

Table 3. Results obtained by the automatic evaluator for discourse richness

Scores	According to raters	Correctly scored	Missed	Spurious	Precision	Recall	F1
10	30	30	0	0	100	100	100

Table 4. Results obtained by the automatic evaluator for the global evaluation of the texts

Scores	According to raters	Correctly scored	Missed	Spurious	Precision	Recall	F1
10	13	9	4	1	90	69.23	78.26
9	14	10	4	4	71.43	71.43	71.43
8	2	2	0	3	40	100	57.14
7	1	0	1	0	-	0	-
6	0	0	0	1	0	-	-
Total	30	21	9	9	70	70	70

When it comes to lexical variability, the obtained results are highly dependent on the morphological analyzer. Unfortunately, errors in part-of-speech tagging and unknown words influence these results. Another factor that affects the precision and recall of the evaluator is related to the manual calculation of monotony and redundancy. This is a challenging task for raters, who often detect only minimal repetition.

Another fact that also clearly emerges from the tables is that all essays have high scores, due to the advanced writing ability of the students. We will plan further experiments including a greater number of essays.

5 Conclusions

An essay evaluation system has been presented to help students improve their Basque or Spanish writing skills. This system is the core of the first bilingual web application developed to handle the two aforementioned languages. In addition, it may be easily adapted to other languages thanks to the modularity of the architecture. Moreover, the formulae used for the evaluation can be updated depending on the needs of the human raters. In the near future, we plan on conducting experiments using machine learning techniques to update the formulae.

Analyses of the essays of Spanish students show encouraging results. For evaluation purposes, we have taken three measures into account: spelling correction, lexical variability and discourse richness. Each measure is meant to provide information which must be considered in order to emulate real life scoring as accurately as possible, as a human rater would do. We must recognize that the evaluator is unable to grade in a manner as detailed and elaborated as a teacher would. However, it does provide students with an opportunity to practice their writing skills and it is a way to improve their knowledge of languages, in this case Spanish and Basque.

For future research, we will analyze comparisons with other similar systems, measure the level of rater agreement when evaluating essays and try to include experiments with participants with a wide range of abilities. Coherence and discourse analysis of texts will also be an important line of research in the near future.

Acknowledgments. This research is supported by the Basque Ministry of Education (FOCAD-PRO-2005K2/0001 project).

References

1. Alegria, I., Artola, X., Sarasola, G.K.: Automatic morphological analysis of Basque. In: Literary & Linguistic Computing, vol. 11(4), pp. 193–203. Oxford University Press, Oxford (1996)
2. Aduriz, I., Arriola, J., Artola, X., Díaz de Ilarraza, A., Gojenola, K., Maritxalar, M.: Morphosyntactic disambiguation for Basque based on the Constraint Grammar Formalism. In: Proceedings of Recent Advances in NLP, pp. 282–287. Tzigov Chark, Bulgary (1997)
3. Atserias, J., Casas, B., Comelles, E., González, M., Padró, L., Padró, M.: FreeLing 1.3: Syntactic and semantic services in an open-source NLP library. In: Proceedings of the 5th international conference on Language Resources and Evaluation, Genoa, Italy (2006)
4. Burstein, J., Kukich, K., Wolf, S., Lu, C., Chodorow, M., Braden-Harder, L., Harris, M.D.: Automated Scoring Using A Hybrid Feature Identification Technique. In: Proceedings of the 36th Annual Meeting of the Association of Computational Linguistics, Montreal, Quebec, Canada, pp. 206–210 (1998)
5. Carreras, X., Chao, I., Padró, L., Padró, M.: FreeLing: An Open-Source Suite of Language Analyzers. In: Proceedings of the 4th International Conference on Language Resources and Evaluation, Lisbon, Portugal, vol. 1, pp. 239–242 (2004)
6. Elliot, S.: IntelliMetric: from here to validity. In: Shermis, M.D., Burstein, J.C. (eds.) Automated Essay Scoring: A Cross Disciplinary Perspective, pp. 71–86. Lawrence Erlbaum Associates, Mahwah (2003)

7. Ishioka, T., Masayuki, K.: Automated Japanese Essay Scoring System based on Articles Written by Experts. In: Proceedings of the 21st International Conference on Computational Linguistics and the 44th Annual Meeting of the Association of Computational Linguistics, Sidney, Australia, pp. 233–240 (2006)
8. Kelly, A.P.: General Models for automated essay scoring: Exploring an alternative to the status quo. Journal of Educational Computing Research 33(1), 101–113 (2005)
9. Landauer, T.K., Laham, D., Foltz, P.W.: Automated Essay Scoring and Annotation of Essays with the Intelligent Essay Assessor. In: Shermis, M.D., Burstein, J.C. (eds.) Automated Essay Scoring: A Cross Disciplinary Perspective, pp. 87–112. Lawrence Erlbaum Associates, Mahwah (2003)
10. Larkey, L.: Automatic Essay Grading Using Text Categorization Techniques. In: Proceedings of the 21st ACM-SIGIR Conference on Research and Development in Information Retrieval, Melbourne, Australia, pp. 90–95 (1998)
11. Page, E.B., Poggio, J.P., Keith, T.Z.: Computer analysis of student essays: Finding trait differences in the student profile. In: AERA/NCME Symposium on Grading Essays by Computer (1997)
12. Vantage Learning (n.d.). My Access, http://www.vantagelearning.com

Combining Frequent and Discriminating Attributes in the Generation of Definite Descriptions

Diego Jesus de Lucena and Ivandré Paraboni

Escola de Artes, Ciências e Humanidades – Universidade de São Paulo (EACH / USP)
Av.Arlindo Bettio, 1000 - 03828-000, São Paulo, Brazil
{diego.si,ivandre}@usp.br

Abstract. The semantic content determination or attribute selection of definite descriptions is one of the most traditional tasks in natural language generation. Algorithms of this kind are required to produce descriptions that are brief (or even minimal) and, at the same time, as close as possible to the choices made by human speakers. In this work we attempt to achieve a balance between brevity and humanlikeness by implementing a number of algorithms for the task. The algorithms are tested against descriptions produced by humans in two different domains, suggesting a strategy that is both computationally simple and comparable to the state of the art in the field.

1 Introduction

When producing documents in natural language, we need to use appropriate linguistic forms to describe the entities that we talk about, e.g., "John", "he", "the man with a yellow umbrella" and so on. In computer-based natural language generation (NLG) this is known as the task of referring expressions generation (REG) In this work we focus on the task of determining the semantic content of these expressions, i.e., the task of deciding *what* to say, and we largely ignore linguistic realisation issues (i.e., *how* to say it.) Moreover, we shall limit the discussion to the selection of attributes to be realised as *definite descriptions* (e.g., "the old table bought in London"), assuming that the choice for this particular linguistic form has already been made.

The computational task of attribute selection (AS) has received a great deal of attention in the NLG field for at least two decades now [1,3,4,7,8,9, 10,11], and has been the subject of two recent REG competitions [e.g., 12]. At the most basic level, the challenge consists of designing algorithms that guarantee *uniqueness*, i.e., producing uniquely identifying descriptions denoting the intended referent and no other object in the context. In addition to that, AS algorithms are often required to take *humanlikeness* into account (i.e., selecting sets of attributes as close as possible to what a human speaker would have selected in the same context) whilst paying regard to *brevity* to avoid the generation of overly long or otherwise clumsy descriptions. Our own work attempts to achieve a balance between brevity and humanlikeness in REG by presenting several variations of a general strategy that combines a greedy and a frequency-based approach to AS. In doing so, we arrive at an attribute selection strategy that is both simple (from the computational point of view) and comparable to the state of the art in the field.

H. Geffner et al. (Eds.): IBERAMIA 2008, LNAI 5290, pp. 252–261, 2008.

2 Background

The work in [1] captures the essence of the problem of producing definite descriptions with the purpose of identification, proposing an approach that later became influential in the field, called the *Incremental algorithm*. The algorithm aims at generating descriptions that can be successfully identified by the hearer whilst avoiding false conversational implicatures in the sense defined by H. P. Grice [2]. In this approach, domain objects are characterised as sets of attributes and their corresponding values. Attribute-value pairs are called properties, as in (*colour*, black). All objects have an attribute *type*, corresponding to the properties typically realised as head nouns, e.g., (*type*, dog), which could be realised as "the dog" .

The input of the algorithm is a target object r (i.e., the entity that we want to identify), a context set C containing the distractors of r (i.e., the set of domain objects to which the reader or hearer is currently attending, and from which r has to be distinguished) and the attribute sets associated with each object. The algorithm also makes use of a list of preferred attributes P which specifies, in order of preference, which attributes should be considered for inclusion in the description under generation. For example, in a particular domain the list P may determine that descriptions should make use of the attributes P = <*type*, *size*, *colour*>, in that order.

Generating a description of a target object r consists of producing a set of properties L of r, such that L distinguishes r from all its distractors in C. The resulting set of attributes corresponds to the semantic content of a description of the target, and it can be realised as, e.g., a noun phrase. The set L is built by selecting attributes that are true of r but which do not apply to at least one of its distractors, in which case these properties are said to rule out the distractors. A set of attributes that rules out all the distractors in C comprises a uniquely distinguishing description of r. Consider the following example of three domain entities and their properties from [1]:

Example 1. A simple context of reference [1].

```
Entity1: (type, dog), (size, small), (colour, black)
Entity2: (type, dog), (size, large), (colour, white)
Entity3: (type, cat), (size, small), (colour, black)
```

Assuming the order of preference P = <*type*, *size*, *colour*>, a description of *Entity1* can be represented by the set of properties L = {(*type*, dog), (*size*, small)}, which could be realised as "the small dog". The use of the first property (i.e., the property of 'being a dog') rules out *Entity3* (which is a cat), and the use of the second property (i.e., the property of 'being small') rules out *Entity2* (which, despite being a dog, is not small but large). Similarly, *Entity2* can be described as "the large dog" and *Entity3* can be described simply as "the cat".

The Incremental algorithm attempts to avoid the inclusion of properties that do not help ruling out distractors by selecting those attributes which have discriminatory power and by terminating as soon as a uniquely distinguishing set of properties is obtained. The approach is generally considered to perform well, and remains the basis of many (if not most) REG algorithms to date.

3 Algorithms

At the heart of the Incremental algorithm - and many of its successors - is the list P which determines in which order the available attributes are to be selected. Clearly, by changing the contents or the order of attributes in P, it is possible to obtain a wide range of REG algorithms with different effects on e.g., brevity or humanlikeness. For instance, had we defined the list as P = <colour, size, *type*> in the previous example 1, *Entity3* would have been described as "the small black cat" and not simply as "the cat" as P = <*type*, *size*, *colour*> would have permitted.

The work in [1] does not elaborate on how exactly the ordering of attributes in P should be defined to meet these criteria, but it is made sufficiently clear that P should be worked out from the domain. One possible way of ordering the list is according to the *discriminatory power* of the existing attributes, i.e., by selecting first the attribute capable of ruling out the largest number of distractors. To this end, a number of so-called *Greedy* or *Minimal* approaches to REG have been proposed [3,8]. For instance, a minimal description of *Entity2* in previous example 1 would be simply "the white (one)". Descriptions produced in this way tend to be as brief as possible, which may be desirable in some applications, but they may simply look unnatural in others.

By contrast, instead of favouring highly discriminating attributes, another way or ordering P is to favour a perhaps more 'human-like' strategy and select, for instance, the attributes most commonly used in the domain. Descriptions produced in this way may seem closer to real language use, but for paying little or no attention to brevity they may become overly long or clumsy.

Which strategy might a human speaker favour? In this work we are interested in a family of algorithm that favour humanlikeness, that is, algorithms that select sets of 'typical' attributes as close as possible to what human speakers would produce, whilst taking brevity into account[1]. To this end, we take a simplified view of humanlikeness and regard 'typical' attributes as those found most frequently in the domain, and then we derive a general (and arguably 'human-like') AS strategy in which the attributes in P are selected in descending order of *relative frequency*[2] as seen in a corpus of definite descriptions. Besides implementing the policy of selecting typical attributes first, this allows the desirable inclusion of attributes such as *type* (usually required to form a head noun) to be modelled in a more convenient, domain-independent way.

The implementation of a frequency-based approach of this kind - and its possible combination with a greedy AS strategy - gives rise to a number of research questions to be investigated. In what follows, rather than attempting to answer these questions directly, we will simply model each of them as a parameter in a general REG algorithm (in fact, a modified version of the Incremental approach) to be tested with all its possible input combinations.

A first question that we intend to investigate is what precise content the list P should convey. One possible approach is to follow the Incremental algorithm and

---

[1] As greedy algorithms and indeed human speakers may attempt to achieve as well.

[2] In [4], the order of attributes in P is determined by their *absolute* frequency in the data. However, we assume that *relative* frequencies (e.g., the number of counts of each attribute divided by the total number of attributes) is more appropriate for unbalanced data.

others and define a list P of preferred *attributes*, e.g., P = <*type, size, colour*>. On the other hand, this may be further refined to build an ordered list P of individual *properties* (i.e., attribute-value pairs), e.g., <*type*-dog, *type*-cat, *size*-small, *colour*-black, *colour*-white, *size*-large> also ordered by relative frequency. We will therefore model the choice as a binary parameter *useProperties* such that, if *useProperties* is true, it will force the use of a list of properties instead of the standard list of attributes.

Secondly, we would like to investigate whether highly frequent attributes or properties *above a certain threshold frequency value* v should be included in any description regardless of discriminatory power. Thus, assuming that such value can be determined empirically as we discuss later, we will define a binary parameter *useThreshold* to determine (when *useThreshold* is true) the compulsory inclusion of 'typical' (i.e., highly frequent) information. When *useThreshold* is false, no compulsory inclusion is performed.

Finally, we intend to test whether our frequency-based strategy should pay any regard to brevity. To this end, we will focus on a particular kind of combined frequency-based greedy strategy based on two simple assumptions:

(a) When facing a complex context with a large number of objects, an attempt to compute the precise attribute capable of ruling out the largest possible number of distractors may not only hard (from the computational point of view), but also less natural than simply using 'typical' attributes.

(b) On the other hand, as the number of distractors decreases, it may become gradually clearer for the speaker which attributes are most helpful to achieve uniqueness, up to the point in which she may naturally switch to a 'greedy' strategy and finalize the description at once.

In order to test (a-b) above, a binary parameter *isGreedy* will determine whether to switch from frequency-based attribute selection to a greedy strategy at all. If *isGreedy* is true, before every inclusion the algorithm will first search the entire list P for an attribute / property capable of ruling out all distractors at once. If successful, such attribute or property is selected and the algorithm finalizes. If *isGreedy* is false, no greedy search will take place, i.e., the algorithm behaviour remains entirely frequency-based.

The three parameters - *useProperties*, *useThreshold* and *isGreedy* - and their possible (binary) values give rise to $2^3 = 8$ input combinations, each of them corresponding to a distinct AS strategy as follows.

Table 1. Proposed attribute selection strategies

Strategy #	1	2	3	4	5	6	7	8
useProperties	n	y	n	y	n	y	n	y
useThreshold	y	y	y	y	n	n	n	n
isGreedy	y	y	n	n	y	y	n	n

We implemented a modified version of the Incremental algorithm [1] in which the parameters *useProperties*, *useThreshold* and *isGreedy* are additionally taken as an input. Among these strategies, Algorithm 7, in which all parameters are set to 'no', corresponds to the original Dale & Reiter Incremental algorithm, and will be used as a baseline for the others[3].

By varying the values of these parameters, we were able to generate descriptions according to each of the eight proposed strategies. The general algorithm is illustrated below, in which the function *RulesOut* is intended to return the set of objects in the context C whose value for the attribute A_i is different from (and hence ruled out by) the selected value V_i.

Example 2. A frequency-based greedy attribute selection strategy[4].

```
L ← ∅                                  while (C ≠ ∅) and (P ≠ ∅)
if(useProperties)                          if(isGreedy)
    P ← preferred properties                   // greedy attempt
else                                           for each Aᵢ ∈ P do
    P ← preferred attributes                       if(RulesOut(Aᵢ,Vᵢ)=C)
                                                       L ← L ∪ {<Aᵢ,Vᵢ>}
// compulsory inclusion above threshold v           return(L)
if(useThreshold)
    for each Aᵢ ∈ P do                         // frequency-based selection
        if (frequency(Aᵢ) > v)                 P ← P - Aᵢ
            P ← P - Aᵢ                          if(RulesOut(Aᵢ,Vᵢ) ≠ ∅)
            L ← L ∪ {<Aᵢ,Vᵢ>}                      L ← L ∪ {<Aᵢ,Vᵢ>}
            C ← C -RulesOut(<Aᵢ,Vᵢ>)               C ← C - RulesOut(<Aᵢ,Vᵢ>)
    repeat                                 repeat
                                           return(L)
```

4 Evaluation

In order to evaluate the algorithms proposed in the previous section, we used a subset of trials taken from the TUNA corpus [6], a database of situations of reference collected primarily for the study of reference phenomena and referring expressions generation algorithms. The TUNA data are available in two domains (Furniture and People, comprising references to pieces of furniture and people's photographs), and each trial conveys two kinds of information:

(a) a context representation containing a target object (i.e., the intended referent) and several distractors, with their corresponding semantic properties represented as sets of attribute-value pairs. For example, a set of chairs of various sizes and colours, one of which is the target object.

(b) a description (also represented as a set of attributes) of the target as uttered by a native or fluent speakers of English, participant in a controlled experiment.

The following is a fragment of one such trial in the Furniture domain, showing the referring expression (b) only. The context information (a), not shown, would be represented in a similar fashion, as a collection of (possibly larger) attribute sets for each domain object in the same XML format. For details we report to [5,6].

---

[3] Also, Algorithm 3 will be used in the same way for reasons discussed in the next section.
[4] For simplicity, we used a slightly imprecise notation in which we remove *attributes* from the list P, although depending on the value of *useProperties,* P may actually contain properties.

Example 3. A description (e.g., "the large red chair") in TUNA [5,6].

```
<ATTRIBUTE-SET>
  <ATTRIBUTE ID="a295" NAME="size" VALUE="large" />
  <ATTRIBUTE ID="a296" NAME="colour" VALUE="red" />
  <ATTRIBUTE ID="a297" NAME="type" VALUE="chair" />
</ATTRIBUTE-SET>
```

We used a subset of 741 TUNA trials (399 references in the Furniture domain and 342 in the People domain) originally distributed as training and development data for the REG-2008 Challenge[5]. Given that our eight possible strategies take either the relative frequency of properties or attributes into account, we started by computing these frequency lists in both domains[6]. In all four lists, we observe a sudden drop in frequency after the first few instances, which allowed us to establish a clear divide between highly frequent attributes/properties and the others. More specifically, we chose a threshold value v = 0.80 to determine – in the AS strategies in which v should play a role – the compulsory inclusion of attributes / properties. In practise, this grants special treatment to the attributes *type* and *colour* in the Furniture domain, and to the attribute *type* in the People domain. The same principle is applied to the most frequent properties in each case.

To illustrate the divide between the highest frequencies and the others, the following Tables 2 displays the most frequent attributes in each domain.

Table 2. Most frequent Furniture and People attributes, showing a significant frequency drop after the (Furniture) *colour* attribute, and also after the (People) *type* attribute

Furniture domain		People domain	
Attribute	Freq.	Attribute	Freq.
type	97.18%	type	92.70%
colour	86.52%	hasBeard	44.89%
Size	36.99%	hasGlasses	42.70%
orientation	33.23%	y-dimension	31.02%

The resulting lists and the context information (a) above provided by the TUNA data were used as input to our eight possible strategies, producing eight output sets (hereby called *System* output sets) in each domain. In total, (8 * 399) + (8 * 342) = 5928 referring expressions were generated.

Given the descriptions produced by humans in each TUNA trial provided in (b) above (hereby called *Reference* set), evaluation proper was carried out by comparing each of our 5928 *System* descriptions with their *Reference* counterparts using the tool provided by the REG-2008 team to compute Dice, MASI and Accuracy scores[7]. Briefly, Dice and its variation MASI measure the degree of similarity between two sets, and Accuracy counts the number of exact matches between them.

---

[5] http://www.itri.brighton.ac.uk/research/reg08/

[6] Interestingly, in the list of properties in the Furniture domain we observe that certain *colour* properties are more frequent than some of the existing *types*.

[7] The tool also computes minimality and uniqueness scores, but these are not relevant to our discussion as all the proposed algorithms uniquely identify the target object, and none of them are expected to generate (unless by chance) minimal descriptions.

The tests revealed that – at least for our data - there are only 6 distinct outputs, that is, algorithms 3 and 7 and algorithms 4 and 8 turned out to produce the same results. These correspond to the four strategies in which *isGreedy* is false, in which case the threshold v had no effect. The coincidence can be explained by the fact that the threshold is used precisely to improve greedy strategies by forcing the inclusion of highly frequent attributes, and thus its effect in non-greedy strategies is minimal[8]. These results are shown in Tables 3-5 below with best performances underlined.

Finally, although our work concerns content determination only, we have also generated output strings using the English surface realisation module developed by Irene Langkilde-Geary for the REG-2008 Challenge, and computed String-edit Distance

Table 3. Dice scores (similarity)

	Overall		Furniture		People	
Strategy	mean	sd	mean	sd	mean	sd
1	0.717	0.253	0.779	0.230	0.646	0.260
2	0.716	0.247	0.773	0.218	0.651	0.262
3	0.706	0.249	0.768	0.240	0.634	0.241
4	0.733	0.231	0.761	0.224	0.699	0.235
5	0.373	0.292	0.389	0.300	0.354	0.281
6	0.378	0.293	0.392	0.302	0.360	0.282

Table 4. MASI scores (similarity)

	Overall		Furniture		People	
Strategy	mean	sd	mean	sd	mean	sd
1	0.481	0.378	0.549	0.392	0.401	0.346
2	0.468	0.373	0.518	0.385	0.409	0.350
3	0.437	0.343	0.536	0.367	0.322	0.271
4	0.468	0.355	0.505	0.363	0.424	0.341
5	0.183	0.210	0.190	0.236	0.175	0.176
6	0.184	0.211	0.190	0.237	0.178	0.176

Table 5. Accuracy scores (exact match)

	Overall		Furniture		People	
Strategy	mean	sd	mean	sd	mean	sd
1	0.323	0.468	0.406	0.492	0.225	0.418
2	0.305	0.461	0.366	0.482	0.234	0.424
3	0.233	0.423	0.348	0.477	0.099	0.300
4	0.275	0.447	0.316	0.465	0.228	0.420
5	0.039	0.194	0.055	0.229	0.020	0.142
6	0.040	0.197	0.058	0.233	0.020	0.142

---

[8] The only effect of using of a threshold value in a purely frequency-based strategy (and never observed in our data) is that all compulsory attributes are added *before* the first test for uniqueness, which in some cases may produce non-minimal descriptions where the Incremental algorithm would obtain one.

(i.e., the number of tasks required to make a *System* description identical to the corresponding *Reference*) and String Accuracy scores (the number of exact matches) for each *System-Reference* pair[9]. The following Table 6 and Table 7 present these results, which are not to be interpreted as an evaluation of the work done by Lang-kilde-Geary in any way, but simply as further evidence for a comparison among the alternatives. Notice that none of the strategies produced exact string matches for People descriptions, which can be explained by the complexity of the domain, subject to a much greater variety in surface realisation alternatives.

Table 6. String-edit distance

Strategy	Overall		Furniture		People	
	mean	sd	mean	sd	mean	sd
1	6.235	3.293	5.193	3.213	7.450	2.956
2	6.406	3.282	5.476	3.223	7.491	3.008
3	6.947	3.856	5.170	3.062	9.020	3.650
4	6.914	3.621	5.647	3.166	8.392	3.561
5	7.260	2.943	7.108	2.956	7.439	2.921
6	7.308	2.987	7.160	2.993	7.480	2.975

Table 7. String accuracy (exact match)

Strategy	Overall		Furniture		People	
	mean	sd	mean	sd	mean	sd
1	0.031	0.174	0.058	0.233	-	-
2	0.027	0.162	0.050	0.218	-	-
3	0.024	0.154	0.045	0.208	-	-
4	0.024	0.154	0.045	0.208	-	-
5	0.003	0.052	0.005	0.071	-	-
6	0.003	0.052	0.005	0.071	-	-

5 Discussion

The following Table 8 summarises the three best-performing strategies according to each evaluating criteria and domain as described in the previous section.

Table 8. Winning strategies

Criteria	Overall	Furniture	People
Dice	4,1,2	1,2,3	4,2,1
MASI	1,2,4	1,3,2	4,2,1
Accuracy	1,2,4	1,2,3	2,4,1
String-edit distance	1,2,4	3,1,2	5,1,2
String-accuracy	1,2,4	1,2,4	-

---

[9] In doing so we take advantage of the word string information provided by the TUNA corpus, representing the actual descriptions uttered by each participant in the experiments.

The overall winning strategy in all criteria but Dice is Algorithm 1 (greedy strategy using a list of preferred attributes and threshold value), which fares best in 8 out of 15 criteria / domain combinations. This was closely followed by its property-selecting variation Algorithm 2, and then Algorithm 4 (non-greedy strategy, using a list of preferred properties and threshold value.) The baseline Algorithm 3 (the implementation of the Dale & Reiter Incremental algorithm) appears only three times among the best results, and comes first in only one test (String-edit distance in the Furniture domain.) In the light of these results our original research questions - modelled by the parameters *useProperties*, *useThreshold* and *isGreedy* - can be interpreted as follows:

(1) the use of a list of attributes (Algorithms 1,3,5 and 7) is preferred in the Furniture domain, but the use of properties produced consistently superior results for People. This may suggest that simply iterating over a list of preferred attributes (as in the Incremental algorithm) may be unsuitable to all but extremely simple domains.

(2) the use of a threshold value (Algorithms 1,2,3 and 4) has greatly improved results in all scenarios, and none of the strategies whose *useThreshold* was set to 'no' appeared among the three best-performing alternatives, except for Algorithm 5 in one single occasion. This is consistent with our general frequency-based strategy used as the basis to the eight proposed algorithms.

(3) the decision to finalize the description as soon as a 'final' attribute (i.e., capable of ruling out all distractors at once) becomes available (Algorithms 1,2,5 and 6) has also improved results, although the gain in this case was slightly larger in Furniture than People. This partially supports our assumptions (a-b) in Section 3 regarding the change from frequency-based to a greedy strategy.

At the time of writing Algorithm 1 was to take part in the REG-2008 Challenge[10] using previously unseen data, and it was to be evaluated against competitors according to the criteria used in this paper and others (in particular, involving human judgements as well.) Although the results of the competition are yet to be known, it is interesting to notice that despite its simplicity, this algorithm is a close match to the participants of the previous challenge (called GRE-2007) - see for example [7] for the overall best–performing algorithm in that competition.

6 Final Remarks

In this paper we have proposed a number of competing algorithms for the task of semantic content determination of definite descriptions. The algorithms were implemented and tested against a corpus of descriptions produced by humans in two different domains, evidencing a selection strategy that is both simple (from the computational point of view) and comparable to the state of the art in the field. As future work we intend to expand our current evaluation work to different domains and use one of the present algorithms as part of an NLG system under development.

---

[10] http://www.itri.brighton.ac.uk/research/reg08/

Acknowledgments

The first author is supported by CNPQ-Brazil. The second author acknowledges support from FAPESP (2006/03941-7) and CNPq (484015/2007 9.)

References

1. Dale, R., Reiter, E.: Computational interpretations of the Gricean maxims in the generation of referring expressions. Cognitive Science (19) (1995)
2. Grice, H.P.: Logic and Conversation. In: Cole, P., Morgan, J.L. (eds.) Syntax and Semantics. Speech Acts, vol. iii, pp. 41–58. Academic Press, New York (1975)
3. Dale, R.: Cooking up referring expressions. In: Proceedings of the 27th Annual Meeting of the Association for Computational Linguistics (1989)
4. Kelleher, J.D.: DIT - Frequency Based Incremental Attribute Selection for GRE. UCNLG+MT, pp. 90–91 (2007)
5. Gatt, A., van der Sluis, I., van Deemter, K.: Evaluating algorithms for the generation of referring expressions using a balanced corpus. In: Proceedings of the 11th European Workshop on Natural Language Generation, pp. 49–56 (2007)
6. van Deemter, K., van der Sluis, I., Gatt, A.: Building a semantically transparent corpus for the generation of referring expressions. In: INLG 2006 (2006)
7. Bohnet, B.: IS-FBN, IS-FBS, IS-IAC: The Adaptation of Two Classic Algorithms for the Generation of Referring Expressions in order to Produce Expressions like Humans Do. UCNLG+MT, pp. 84–86 (2007)
8. Gardent, C.: Generating minimal definite descriptions. In: Proceedings of the 40th Annual Meeting of the Association for Computational Linguistics (2002)
9. Krahmer, E., Theune, M.: Efficient Context-Sensitive Generation of Referring Expressions. In: van Deemter, K., Kibble, R. (eds.) Information Sharing Reference and Presupposition in Language Generation and Interpretation, pp. 223–264. CSLI Publications, Stanford (2002)
10. Horacek, H.: Generating referential descriptions under conditions of uncertainty. In: 10th European workshop on Natural Language Generation, Aberdeen, pp. 58–67 (2005)
11. Siddharthan, A., Copestake, A.: Generating referring expressions in open domains. In: Proceeding of ACL 2004 (2004)
12. Beltz, A., Gatt, A.: The Attribute Selection for GRE Challenge: Overview and Evaluation Results. UCNLG+MT, pp. 75–83 (2007)

A Machine Learning Approach to
Portuguese Pronoun Resolution

Ramon Ré Moya Cuevas and Ivandré Paraboni

Escola de Artes, Ciências e Humanidades – Universidade de São Paulo (EACH / USP)
Av.Arlindo Bettio, 1000 - 03828-000, São Paulo, Brazil
{fusion,ivandre}@usp.br

Abstract. Anaphora resolution is an essential component of most NLP applications, from text understanding to Machine Translation. In this work we discuss a supervised machine learning approach to the problem, focusing on instances of anaphora ubiquitously found in a corpus of Brazilian Portuguese texts, namely, third-person pronominal references. Although still limited to a subset of the more general co-reference resolution problem, our present results are comparable to existing work in the field in both English and Portuguese languages, representing the highest accuracy rates that we are aware of in (Brazilian) Portuguese pronoun resolution.

1 Introduction

Anaphora resolution - the computational task of identifying linguistic antecedents of referring expressions in discourse (e.g., identifying the relation between "the man" and "he") such as pronouns, definite descriptions etc - lies at the heart of a variety of NLP applications, including text understanding, machine translation (MT), summarization and many others. Accordingly, the problem has received a great deal of attention in the field for many years now [e.g., 1,3,4,5,6,7]. Speaking of the Brazilian Portuguese language, research on anaphora resolution is not novel either [e.g., 13], and it has indeed experienced a new surge of investigation in recent years [e.g., 8,9,10,14], a change that might be explained by the now more wide-spread availability of basic NLP tools such as parsers, taggers and large corpora.

Existing approaches to anaphora resolution range from purely algorithmic or rule-based solutions to, more recently, unsupervised and supervised machine learning techniques. Our own work is related to the latter, addressing a supervised method used in [5,14] and others, and making use of some of the learning features proposed in [4] for general co-reference resolution. In addition to that, we favour the use of so-called 'low-cost' features readily obtainable from basic (Portuguese) NLP tools such as PoS taggers, largely by-passing the need for in-depth analysis. In this sense, our work is also related to [3], a knowledge-poor re-interpretation of the 'classic' algorithm proposed by Lappin and Leass [12] that has influenced the definition of some of our present 'low-cost' learning features.

Our investigation is presently limited to a particular instance of anaphora, namely, the Portuguese third person plural pronouns ("Eles/Elas") as required by a MT project under development. The choice - mainly based on the assumption that these (as well

H. Geffner et al. (Eds.): IBERAMIA 2008, LNAI 5290, pp. 262–271, 2008.

as their Spanish counterparts) are less prone to ambiguity and arguably easier to resolve than the English equivalent ("They") - may suggest an interesting multilingual
approach to anaphora resolution not unlike, e.g., [7], which we intend to investigate as
future work. In addition to that, by focusing on a single case of anaphora, we expect
to achieve higher accuracy rates than what would be possible, e.g., by training an all-
purpose pronoun resolution model, even though a direct comparison between the two
models is not appropriate as we shall argue.

2 Background

Likewise [4,5,6] and others, we regard the task as a classification problem. More
specifically, a pronoun j and a potential antecedent term i (i.e., a candidate to co-
reference) may be classified as co-referent or not, that is, for each pair (i, j) in a given
text, we intend to 'learn' a binary class *coref* whose possible values (or labels) are
true (co-referent) and false (non co-referent.)

Positive instances of co-reference will consist of pairs (i, j) explicitly defined as
co-referential in the training data by human annotators, i.e., in which i is the actual
antecedent term of j. Negative instances will consist of all pairs (i, j) in which i is an
intermediate NP between j and its actual antecedent in the left-to-right word order of
the text. For example, the pronoun j in the following text gives rise to one positive ($i1$,
j) and three negative ($(i2, j)$, $(i3, j)$ and $(i4, j)$) instances of co-reference[1]:

Example 1. A pronoun (j) with its actual antecedent ($i1$) and three intermediate NPs
($i2$-$i4$).

A researcher from Embrapa Genetic Resources and Biotechnology in Brasilia, Ales-
sandra Pereira Fávero, has managed to select [wild species]$_{i1}$ that carry [genes]$_{i2}$ that
provide [resistance]$_{i3}$ to [these diseases]$_{i4}$. But [they]$_j$ cannot be crossed with the cul-
tivated ones on account of the different number of chromosomes.

Candidates outside the range between j and the actual antecedent i as annotated in
training data are never consider in the resolution model, and in the unlikely occurrence
of one such long-distance reference in real language use our approach will simply fail
to find the actual antecedent. Notice that the present definition of training instances is
different from the one adopted in co-reference resolution machine learning approaches
[e.g., 4,14], in which entire co-reference chains have to be taken into account.

In this work we take advantage of the training data used in [15] comprising instances of third person plural pronouns (male) "Eles" and (female) "Elas" identified
by two independent annotators in the Portuguese portion of an English-Portuguese-
Spanish parallel corpus tagged using the PALAVRAS tool [2]. The corpus proper
consisted of 646 articles (440,690 words in total) from the Environment, Science,
Humanities, Politics and Technology supplements of the on-line edition of the *Revista
Pesquisa FAPESP*, a Brazilian journal on scientific news.

Given that many documents in this domain conveyed highly ambiguous or even ill-
formed instances of co-reference, all noise that could compromise the quality of the

---

[1] Example taken from *Revista FAPESP*.

training data was eliminated[2], thus limiting the annotation task to the cases which the annotators could immediately agree upon. As a result, [15] arrived at a set of 2603 instances of co-reference, being 484 positive and 2119 negative, with an average of 4.4 intermediate antecedents between each pronoun and the actual antecedent. About 10% of the positive instances were set aside with their negative counterparts for testing purposes, and the reminder 2393 instances (being 436 positive or co-referential, and 1957 negative or non co-referential) became our main training data.

It was shown in [15] that a simple set of syntactically-motivated features (based on distance, gender and number agreement, among others) extracted from tagged Portuguese text may achieve overall positive results in pronoun resolution (70.30% success rate in F-measure over the positive instances, using ten-fold cross-validation decision-tree induction) and that comparable results can be obtained using unsupervised statistical methods as well. However, this simple approach still suffered from low precision for the co-referential cases, making the resulting algorithm only partially useful for practical purposes.

3 Current Work

In this work we extend the set of the features originally proposed in [15] to include several features intended to capture syntactic constraints that are central to pronoun resolution, besides additional semantic information required to disambiguate cases of co-reference in which there is no number agreement between pronoun and antecedent (e.g., "The company" and "They".) At the same time, we shall keep the same general principle of limiting the feature set to the kind of knowledge available from the PALAVRAS tag set.

By contrast, the work in [6], for instance, not only makes use of features extracted from resources such as Wordnet (which may be considered to be less developed for the Brazilian Portuguese language), but also relies on features such as *binding*, which is intended to determine whether an NP violates certain conditions of the binding theory. Whilst we do not dispute the usefulness of these features to pronoun resolution, our set of features will be defined so as to avoid such 'costly' knowledge sources, a decision that is to a certain extent due to the lack of suitable resources for the Portuguese language.

Apart from the extended set of features, we will also present a more comprehensive evaluation work in a second linguistic domain, and an initial attempt to cover singular instances of pronouns, which were not originally included in the training data. In addition to that, as the current approach reaches (in our view) satisfactory success rates, we will presently use for the first time the original test data left aside in our previous work. To this end, we will consider the following 13 learning features (plus the *coref* class to be learned.) Given a pair comprising an antecedent *i* and a pronoun *j*, our present set of features can be summarized as follows.

---

[2] However, the selective nature of this task does not apply to our test data set, as we discuss in the next section.

Table 1. Set of learning features extracted from the tagged text

Feature name	Description
distance	sentences between i and j.
words_between	number of words between i and j.
pronoun_type	1=personal (eles/as); 2=possessive (deles/as); 3=location (neles/as.)
number_agreement	true if i and j agree in number.
gender_agreement	true if i and j agree in gender.
same_sentence	true if i and j occur in the same sentence.
i_defined	true if i is a definite description.
i_subject	true if i is the sentence subject.
i_direct	true if i is a direct object.
j_subject	true if j is the sentence subject.
is_hh	true if i is a group of humans.
is_inst	true if i is an institution.
is_civ	true if i is a city, country, province etc.

The features *distance* and *words_between* are intended to capture – perhaps rather redundantly – distance constraints that usually play a role in co-reference resolution. However, this overlap should be of no concern in our approach as we intend to leave to a machine learning algorithm the task of selecting the useful features and discarding those that do not play a role in the solution.

The *pronoun_type* feature is intended to verify whether the pronoun follows a preposition denoting possession ("deles", or "theirs"), place ("neles", or "in them") or no preposition at all, and how this might impact resolution. The features *gender_agreement* and *number_agreement* are self-explanatory, corresponding to features that clearly perform a major role in the resolution of personal pronouns.

The features *same_sentence*, *i_defined*, *i_subject*, *i_direct* and *j_subject* represent a low-cost – albeit certainly less than ideal –alternative to in-depth syntactic parsing, capturing some of the constraints associated to a pronoun and its antecedent.

Finally, the last three features (*is_hh*, *is_inst* and *is_civ*) take advantage of the semantic tags *<hh>*, *<inst>* and *<civ>* provided by the PALAVRAS tagger, and are intended to help the resolution of those less typical (but nevertheless genuine) cases of co-reference in which there is no number agreement between antecedent and pronoun, as in, e.g., "The company" referred to as "They".

The distributions of each individual feature-value in the training data are illustrated as follows. For the two numeric features (*distance* and *words_between*), Table 2 presents the corresponding distribution of values. For the nominal features *pronoun_type* Table 3 presents the number of instances covered by each possible label (1-3.) The binary features (i.e., all the others) are shown in Table 4.

Table 2. Numeric features distribution

Feature name	Range	Mean	SD
Distance	0-15	1.397	2.59
words_between	0-301	28.173	51.263

Table 3. Nominal features distribution

Feature name	Coverage
pronoun_type	1=1743; 2=627; 3=23.

Table 4. Binary features distribution

Feature name	True	False	Feature name	True	False
same_sentence	947	1446	i_direct	344	2049
number_agreement	1010	1383	j_subject	1342	1051
gender_agreement	1494	899	is_hh	78	2315
i_defined	963	1430	is_inst	60	2333
i_subject	335	2058	is_civ	80	2313

4 Evaluation

We carried out a number of supervised experiments using the data described in the previous section and additional, previously unseen material. Our main test (hereby called test 1) consisted of a standard C 4.5. decision-tree induction approach [16] using the training and test sets as above. The following Table 5 summarizes our findings, and Table 6 shows the corresponding confusion matrix.

Table 5. Test 1: Pronoun resolution in science magazine articles (Revista Fapesp.)

Class	Precision	Recall	F-measure
Co-referential	0.857	0.875	0.866
Non Co-referential	0.963	0.957	0.960

Table 6. Confusion matrix for Test 1

	True	False
True	42	6
False	7	155

The results show an average 93.81% correctly classified instances, but since our data is heavily imbalanced due to the much greater number of negative instances, we take a conservative view and regard the F-measure for co-referential cases (86.6%) to be a more accurate evaluation measure. Even so, and despite some limitations that we shall discuss in the next section, these scores are the highest that we are aware of among existing pronoun resolution algorithms for the Brazilian Portuguese language.

Given that our test data are somewhat biased as they excluded ill-formed and ambiguous instances of co-reference, we decided to evaluate the model performance in a second linguistic genre, namely, articles taken from the 1994 politics supplements of the *Folha de São Paulo* newspaper. However, as we are presently unable to build the required (and necessarily large) training data in the new domain, we decided to verify how much loss in accuracy the existing model (trained on science magazines) would experience if applied to the resolution of pronouns found in newspapers.

To this end, we built a second test data set by randomly selecting 81 instances of co-reference (each of them taken from a different newspaper issue) and all their 396 negative counterparts. Differently from our training data, though, the new test data did not exclude any ill-formed cases of co-reference[3], and contained even a number of pronouns denoting compound antecedents (e.g., "John and Mary") that our model is currently unable to handle, and which will inevitably result in error. Using the original (science magazines) training data we obtained the following results.

Table 7. Test 2: Pronoun resolution in newspapers using training data from science magazines

Class	Precision	Recall	F-measure
Co-referential	0.683	0.691	0.687
Non Co-referential	0.937	0.934	0.936

Table 8. Confusion matrix for Test 2

	True	False
True	56	25
False	26	370

As expected, the results (with an average 89.31% correctly classified instances, or 68.7% F-measure for co-referential cases) are significantly lower than in Test 1, but still comparable to existing work in the field as we will discuss later. Moreover, we believe that the present results would most likely improve had we used proper (i.e., newspapers articles) training data. Although we presently do not seek to prove this claim, the general idea is hinted at by our third test, now using the entire (and hence mixed) data set (2603 instances in the science magazines domain and 477 instances in the newspapers domain), and performing 10-fold cross validation. The results are shown in the following Tables 9 and 10.

Despite the still insufficient amount of training instances in the newspapers domain (recall that the amount of instances from the science domain is over six times larger)

Table 9. Test 3: Pronoun resolution in both domains using 10-fold cross validation

Class	Precision	Recall	F-measure
Co-referential	0.724	0.703	0.713
Non Co-referential	0.934	0.940	0.937

Table 10. Confusion matrix for Test 3

	True	False
True	397	168
False	151	2363

---

[3] This task was considerably simpler than in the science magazines domain as the newspapers presented far less ambiguity – see for example the work in [8], whose overall best results in pronoun resolution were obtained precisely in the same domain.

the results show considerable improvement, with an average 89.64% correctly classified instances (71.3% F-measure in co-referential cases.) Again, notice that this data set included a number of references to compound antecedents, in which our approach simply fails.

Finally, although the present set of features was not originally designed to model singular instances of reference[4], it is tempting to verify to which extent it may be still applicable to those cases. As our training and test data sets did not convey any singular pronouns, we randomly selected 50 instances of co-referent personal pronoun "ele / ela" (he / she) and their 164 non co-referent counterparts (making 214 training instances in total) from the newspapers domain. The following Tables 11 and 12 summarize our findings using 10-fold cross validation decision-tree induction.

Table 11. Test 4: Singular Pronoun resolution in newspapers using 10-fold cross validation

Class	Precision	Recall	F-measure
Co-referential	0.571	0.480	0.522
Non Co-referential	0.849	0.890	0.869

Table 12. Confusion matrix for Test 4

	True	False
True	24	26
False	18	146

Despite an overall success rate of 79.44%, these results are obviously low if we consider F-measure for positive instances (52.2%). Although perhaps this was only to be expected from such small training data set (50 pronouns), we notice that even these tentative results - presented here for illustration purposes only - are still comparable to some of the approaches to Portuguese pronoun resolution as we discuss in the next section. and we believe that they would match the results for plural pronouns had we used a similarly-sized training data set (which in that case was over ten times larger than the one currently employed.)

5 Discussion

The results of our present investigation show major improvement over our previous work [15]. They are in principle comparable to existing work in the field in both English and Brazilian Portuguese languages and, at least with respect to the latter, may be indeed superior to results obtained by traditional (i.e., non-learning) pronoun resolution algorithms. However, differences in the choice of language and in the instances of the co-reference phenomena addressed may limit the possible comparisons in a number of ways.

Firstly, it should be pointed out that our results are not directly comparable to similar work using pruned trees for unrestricted co-reference resolution. For example, the

---

[4] Recall that in Portuguese-English MT we are mainly interested in resolving (English) plural pronouns (e.g., they), which unlike singular pronouns (e.g., he / she) are not gender-specific.

work in [5] obtained F-measure of 86.0% using a much larger set of features, but since we are addressing only a subset of the more general co-reference problem, perhaps our results can only be expected to be similar to those in [5]. On the other hand, it should be pointed out that pronouns – which convey little or no information about the identity of the antecedent term – might be arguably more difficult to resolve than, e.g., definite descriptions, which may greatly benefit from features based on substring matching (e.g., "the man who bought the flat" may co-refer with "the man", but probably not with "the girl".)

Secondly, as pointed out earlier, a major limitation of our current work is the fact that we do not address instances of reference to compound antecedents (e.g., "John and Mary".) We are aware that in doing so we may have simplified the task considerably, as some of the most difficult cases to be resolved may have simply been left out. However, given our present results we believe that references to compound antecedents could be handled by a simple heuristics to detect when two candidates are linked by a conjunction. This possible extension of our current work is currently underway and will be described elsewhere.

Given the wide scope of the pronoun resolution problem, a more direct comparison with existing work focused on the Portuguese language is not straightforward either. For example, the work in [14], focused on the general co-reference resolution task, achieved 56.0% F-measure for co-referential instances. However, it does not seem possible to compare these results to ours since we are not concerned with the task of clustering co-referent terms together, but simply finding an antecedent for each pronoun. Moreover, pronouns in the work in [14] correspond to only 4.82% of all referring expressions that the system attempts to resolve, and they most likely include reflexive and demonstrative cases as well, which does not allow us to draw a fair comparison with our (much more limited) investigation.

One of the few studies that are more directly relevant to ours is [9], describing an implementation of the Lappin & Leass algorithm [12] for Portuguese third person pronoun resolution. The proposed algorithm was tested against 297 pronouns, achieving 35.15% success rate. According to [9], this relatively low performance was mainly due to the use of a rather complex linguistic domain of texts on legislation, with long sentences and structural ambiguity.

A more recent approach, focusing on an implementation of the Hobbs' algorithm [11] for Portuguese pronoun resolution is described in [10]. In this case, the test involved a set of 916 instances of non-reflexive pronouns in three linguistic genres, with accuracy rates ranging from 40.40% (texts on legislation) to 50.96% (magazine articles.) Interestingly, the work in [10] achieves much higher success rates for reflexive pronouns (not covered in our work), which may suggest that having individual resolution algorithms tailored for each kind of reference phenomena may be more successful than an all-purpose anaphora resolution approach. We believe that more research on this issue is still required.

Finally, Portuguese third person pronouns are also investigated as an implementation of the algorithm of R. Mitkov [1] presented in [8]. The success rates in this case are the highest that we have found in the surveyed work for the Portuguese language, ranging from 38.00% (novels domain) to 67.01% (newspapers articles) depending on the linguistic genre under consideration.

A comparison between the best results achieved by these rule-based approaches to pronoun resolution and ours suggests that they are at least comparable to each other. Moreover, being trainable from corpora, our work is in principle domain-independent, and much less prone to the wide fluctuations in results experienced by the above-mentioned studies. Bearing in mind these differences, the following summary in Table 13 is presented for illustration purposes only.

Table 13. A comparison with previous work for the Brazilian Portuguese language

Algorithm	Success rate[5]
[9] Coelho & Carvalho (2005)	35.15%
[10] Santos & Carvalho (2007)	50.96%
[8] Chaves (2007)	67.01%
[15] Cuevas & Paraboni (2008)	70.30%
present work	86.60%

6 Conclusions

In this paper we have described a machine learning approach to Portuguese personal pronoun resolution. Using a small set of so-called 'low-cost' learning features (i.e., easily obtainable from the output of a PoS tagger) and previously unseen test data in two different linguistic domains, the present approach shows major improvement in resolution accuracy over our previous work, besides a partially successful attempt to cover additional (namely, singular) instances of pronouns as well. The results obtained so far, although still limited to a subset of the more general co-reference resolution problem, are comparable to existing work in the field in both English and (Brazilian) Portuguese languages.

Acknowledgements

This work has been supported by CNPq-Brazil (484015/2007-9) and FAPESP (2006/03941-7 and 2007/07356-4).

References

1. Mitkov, R.: Anaphora Resolution. Longman, New York (2002)
2. Bick, E.: The parsing system PALAVRAS: automatic grammatical analysis of Portuguese in a constraint grammar framework. PhD Thesis, Aarhus University (2000)
3. Kennedy, C., Boguraev, B.: Anaphora for Everyone: Pronominal Anaphora Resolution without a Parser. In: 16th International Conference on Computational Linguistics (COLING-1996) Copenhagen, pp. 113–118 (1996)

---

[5] With respect to the surveyed work, we show the maximum accuracy reported in [8,9,10]. Regarding our own work, we show F-measure for co-referential cases only (and not the overall success rates, which range from 85.81% to 93.81%.)

4. Soon, W.M., et al.: A Machine Learning Approach to Coreference Resolution of Noun Phrases. Computational Linguistics 27(4) (2001)
5. McCarthy, J.F., Lehnert, W.G.: Using Decision Trees for Coreference Resolution. In: 14th International Conference on Artificial Intelligence IJCAI 1995 (1995)
6. Ng, V., Cardie, C.: Improving Machine Learning Approaches to Coreference Resolution. In: 40th Annual Meeting of the Association for Computational Linguistics (ACL), Philadelphia, pp. 104–111 (2002)
7. Mitkov, R.: Multilingual Anaphora Resolution. Machine Translation 14(3-4), 281–299 (1999)
8. Chaves, A.: A resolução de anáforas pronominais da língua portuguesa com base no algoritmo de Mitkov. M.Sc. dissertation, University of São Carlos, Brazil (2007)
9. Coelho, T.T., Carvalho, A.M.B.R.: Uma adaptação de Lappin e Leass para resolução de anáforas em português. In: Anais do XXV Congresso da Sociedade Brasileira de Computação (III Workshop em Tecnologia a Informação e da Linguagem Humana – TIL 2005), São Leopoldo, Brazil, pp. 2069–2078 (2005)
10. Santos, D.N.A., Ariadne, M.B.R.: Carvalho Hobbs' algorithm for pronoun resolution in Portuguese. In: Gelbukh, A., Kuri Morales, Á.F. (eds.) MICAI 2007. LNCS (LNAI), vol. 4827, pp. 966–974. Springer, Heidelberg (2007)
11. Hobbs, J.: Resolving pronoun references. Lingua 44, 311–338 (1978)
12. Lappin, S., Leass, H.J.: An algorithm for pronominal anaphora resolution. Computational Linguistics 20(4), 535–561 (1994)
13. Paraboni, I., de Lima, V.L.S.: Possessive Pronominal Anaphor Resolution in Portuguese Written Texts. In: 17th International Conference on Computational Linguistics (COLING 1998), pp. 1010–1014. Morgan Kaufmann, Montreal (1998)
14. Souza, J., Gonçalves, P., Vieira, R.: Learning Coreference Resolution for Portuguese Texts. In: International Conference on Computational processing of the Portuguese Language (Propor 2008), Aveiro, Portugal (September 2008)
15. Ramon Ré Moya, C., Honda, W.Y., de Lucena, D.J., Paraboni, I., Oliveira, P.R.: Portuguese Pronoun Resolution: Resources and Evaluation. In: Gelbukh, A. (ed.) CICLing 2008. LNCS, vol. 4919, pp. 344–350. Springer, Heidelberg (2008)
16. Quinlan, J.R.: C4.5: programs for machine learning. Morgan Kaufmann Publishers Inc., San Francisco (1993)

Text Classification on Embedded Manifolds

Catarina Silva[1,2] and Bernardete Ribeiro[2]

[1] School of Technology and Management, Polytechnic Institute of Leiria, Portugal
[2] Dep. Informatics Eng., Center Informatics and Systems, Univ. of Coimbra, Portugal
catarina@dei.uc.pt, bribeiro@dei.uc.pt

Abstract. The problem of overfitting arises frequently in text mining due to high dimensional feature spaces, making the task of the learning algorithms difficult. Moreover, in such spaces visualization is not feasible. We focus on supervised text classification by presenting an approach that uses prior information about training labels, manifold learning and Support Vector Machines (SVM). Manifold learning is herein used as a pre-processing step, which performs nonlinear dimension reduction in order to tackle the curse of dimensionality that occurs. We use Isomap (Isometric Mapping) which allows text to be embedded in a low dimensional space, while enhancing the geometric characteristics of data by preserving the geodesic distance within the manifold. Finally, kernel-based machines can be used with benefits for final text classification in this reduced space. Results on a real-world benchmark corpus from Reuters demonstrate the visualization capabilities of the method in the severely reduced space. Furthermore we show the method yields performances comparable to those obtained with single kernel-based machines.

1 Introduction

Text classification is becoming a crucial task to analysts in different areas. In the last two decades the production of textual documents in digital form has increased exponentially [1], consequently there is an ever-increasing need for automated solutions for organizing the huge amount of digital texts produced. Documents are represented by vectors of numeric values, with one value for each word that appears in any training document, making it a large scale problem. High dimensionality increases both processing time and the risk of overfitting. In this case, the learning algorithm will induce a classifier that reflects accidental properties of the particular training examples rather than the systematic relationships between the words and the categories [2]. To deal with this dimensionality problem, feature selection and dimensionality reduction methods are applied, such as, stopword removal, stemming and removing less frequent words. However, these standard methods are usually very mild and do not avoid the curse of dimensionality. Current research is probing into more aggressive dimensionality reduction methods, namely manifold learning, e.g. Isomap [3] and discriminative Gaussian process using latent variable models [4].

Manifold learning is an effective methodology for extracting nonlinear structures from high-dimensional data in many applications [5]. Finding the structure

H. Geffner et al. (Eds.): IBERAMIA 2008, LNAI 5290, pp. 272–281, 2008.
© Springer-Verlag Berlin Heidelberg 2008

behind the data may be important for a number of reasons. One possible application is data visualization. Graphical depiction of the document set has the potential to be a powerful tool, since it makes possible to quickly give large amounts of information to a human operator [6]. To this purpose it is appropriately assumed that the data lies on a statistical manifold, or a manifold of probabilistic generative models [7].

When applied to classification problems, like text mining, manifold learning was originally considered as simply a pre-processing technique to reduce the feature space dimensionality. However, it can also be regarded as a supervised learning method, where the training labels play a central role. In such a scenario, manifold learning can be used not only with the traditionally associated algorithms, such as K-Nearest Neighbors (K-NN), but also with state-of-the-art kernel-based machines like support and relevance vector machines (SVM and RVM). SVM are a learning method introduced by Vapnik [8] based on the Statistical Learning Theory and Structural Minimization Principle. When using SVM for classification, the basic idea is to find the optimal separating hyperplane between the positive and negative examples. The optimal hyperplane is defined as the one giving the maximum margin between the training examples that are closest to it. Support vectors are the examples that lie closest to the separating hyperplane. Once this hyperplane is found, new examples can be classified simply by determining on which side of the hyperplane they are. RVM were proposed by Tipping [9], as a Bayesian treatment of the sparse learning problem. RVM preserve the generalization and sparsity of the SVM, yet also yielding a probabilistic output, as well as circumventing other limitations of SVM, such as the need for Mercer kernels and the definition of the error/margin trade-off parameter.

We propose the use of manifold learning, with an Isomap (Isometric Mapping) based nonlinear algorithm that uses training label information in the dimensionality reduction step, combined with kernel-based machines in the classification step. We show that kernel-based machines can be used with benefit albeit severe dimensionality reduction techniques are employed.

The rest of the paper is organized as follows. In the next section, we introduce supervised dimensionality reduction methods that are the base of the proposed approach. In Section 3, we establish a text mining background, including representation methods, and the benchmark corpus used. In Section 4, we introduce our approach for the use of manifold learning in text mining, with an Isomap-based nonlinear dimensionality reduction algorithm combined with kernel-based machines in the classification step. Experiments and results are described and analyzed in Section 5. Finally, Section 6 addresses conclusions and future work.

2   Supervised Dimensionality Reduction

Dimensionality reduction methods aim at choosing, from the available set of features, a smaller set that more efficiently represents the data. Such reduction is not needed for all classification algorithms as some classifiers are capable of feature selection themselves. However for some other classifiers feature selection is mandatory, since a large number of irrelevant features can significantly weaken the classifier accuracy. Dimensionality reduction techniques can be divided into supervised and unsupervised. The latter are more common and simply use the representation of inputs and some fitness function to determine a reduced representation, with existing or synthesized features. We focus on supervised dimensionality reduction techniques that are usually more computationally demanding, but also more effective in performance results.

Many approaches have been proposed for dimensionality reduction, such as the well-known methods of principal component analysis (PCA) [10], independent component analysis (ICA) [11] and multidimensional scaling (MDS) [12]. All these methods are well understood and efficient and have thus been widely used in visualization and classification. Unfortunately, they share a common inherent limitation: they are all linear methods while the distributions of most real-world data are nonlinear.

An emerging nonlinear dimensionality reduction technique is manifold learning, which is the process of estimating a low-dimensional structure which underlies a collection of high-dimensional data. Manifold learning can be viewed as implicitly inverting a generative model for a given set of observations [13]. Let Y be a d dimensional domain contained in a Euclidean space $\mathbb{R}^d$. Let $f : Y \rightarrow \mathbb{R}^D$ be a smooth embedding for some $D > d$. The goal of manifold learning is to recover Y and f given N points in $\mathbb{R}^D$. Isomap [3] provides an implicit description of the mapping f. Given $X = \{\mathbf{x}_i \in \mathbb{R}^D | i = 1 \ldots N\}$ find $Y = \{\mathbf{y}_i \in \mathbb{R}^d | i = 1 \ldots N\}$ such that $\{\mathbf{x}_i = f(\mathbf{y}_i) | i = 1 \ldots N\}$. However, learning such mapping between high dimensional spaces from examples is fundamentally an ill-posed problem [14]. Therefore certain constraints have to be exploited, for instance using nonlinear manifold learning where the sequences are mapped to paths of the learned manifold. The simplest case is a linear isometry, i.e. f is a linear mapping from $\mathbb{R}^d \rightarrow \mathbb{R}^D$, where $D > d$. In this case PCA recovers the d significant dimensions of the observed data. Classical Multidimensional Scaling (MDS) produces the same results but uses the pairwise distance matrix instead of the actual coordinates.

2.1   Isomap

Recently, a novel manifold learning method has been proposed, namely Isomap [3], that tries to preserve as well as possible the local neighborhood of each example, while trying to obtain highly nonlinear embeddings.

For data lying on a nonlinear manifold, the *true distance* between two data points is the geodesic distance on the manifold, i.e. the distance along the surface of the manifold, rather than the straight-line Euclidean distance. The main purpose of Isomap is to find the intrinsic geometry of the data, as captured in the geodesic manifold distances between all pairs of data points. The approximation of geodesic distance is divided into two cases. In case of neighboring points, Euclidean distance in the input space provides a good approximation to geodesic distance. In case of faraway points, geodesic distance can be approximated by adding up a sequence of *short hops* between neighboring points. Isomap shares some advantages with PCA and MDS, such as computational efficiency and asymptotic convergence guarantees, but with more flexibility to learn a broad class of nonlinear manifolds. The Isomap algorithm takes as input the distances $d(\mathbf{x}_i, \mathbf{x}_j)$ between all pairs $\mathbf{x}_i$ and $\mathbf{x}_j$ from N data points in the high-dimensional input space. The algorithm outputs coordinate vectors $\mathbf{y}_i$ in a d-dimensional Euclidean space that best represent the intrinsic geometry of the data. Isomap is accomplished following these steps:

Step 1. Construct neighborhood graph: Define the graph G over all data points by connecting points $\mathbf{x}_i$ and $\mathbf{x}_j$ if they are closer than a certain distance ε, or if $\mathbf{x}_i$ is one of the K nearest neighbors of $\mathbf{x}_j$. Set edge lengths equal to $d(\mathbf{x}_i, \mathbf{x}_j)$.

Step 2. Compute shortest paths: Initialize $d_G(\mathbf{x}_i, \mathbf{x}_j) = d(\mathbf{x}_i, \mathbf{x}_j)$ if $\mathbf{x}_i$ and $\mathbf{x}_j$ are linked by an edge; $d_G(\mathbf{x}_i, \mathbf{x}_j) = +\infty$ otherwise. Then for each value of $k = 1, 2, \ldots, N$ in turn, replace all entries $d_G(\mathbf{x}_i, \mathbf{x}_j)$ by $min\,\{d_G(\mathbf{x}_i, \mathbf{x}_j), d_G(\mathbf{x}_i, \mathbf{x}_k) + d_G(\mathbf{x}_k, \mathbf{x}_j)\}$. The matrix of final values $\mathbf{D}_G = \{d_G(\mathbf{x}_i, \mathbf{x}_j)\}$ will contain the shortest path distances between all pairs of points in G.

Step 3. Apply MDS to the resulting geodesic distance matrix to find a d-dimensional embedding.

The mapping function given by Isomap is only implicitly defined. Therefore, it should be learned by nonlinear interpolation techniques, such as generalized regression neural networks, which can then transform the new test data into the reduced feature space before prediction.

2.2   Supervised Isomap

In the supervised version of Isomap [15], the information provided by the training class labels is used to guide the procedure of dimensionality reduction. The training labels are used to refine the distances between inputs. The rationale is that both classification and visualization can benefit when the inter-class dissimilarity is larger than the intra-class dissimilarity. However, this can also make the algorithm overfit the training set and can often make the neighborhood graph of the input data disconnected. To achieve this purpose, the Euclidean distance $d(\mathbf{x}_i, \mathbf{x}_j)$ between two given observations $\mathbf{x}_i$ and $\mathbf{x}_j$, labeled y_i and y_j respectively, is replaced by a dissimilarity measure [15]:

$$D(\mathbf{x}_i, \mathbf{x}_j) = \begin{cases} \sqrt{1 - e^{\frac{-d^2(\mathbf{x}_i, \mathbf{x}_j)}{\beta}}} & y_i = y_j, \\ \sqrt{e^{\frac{-d^2(\mathbf{x}_i, \mathbf{x}_j)}{\beta}}} - \alpha & y_i \neq y_j. \end{cases} \tag{1}$$

Note that the Euclidean distance $d(\mathbf{x}_i, \mathbf{x}_j)$ is in the exponent and the parameter β is used to avoid that $D(\mathbf{x}_i, \mathbf{x}_j)$ increases too rapidly when $d(\mathbf{x}_i, \mathbf{x}_j)$ is relatively large. Hence, β depends on the *density* of the data set and is usually set to the average Euclidean distance between all pairs of data points. On the other hand, α gives a certain possibility to points in different classes to be *closer*, i.e.

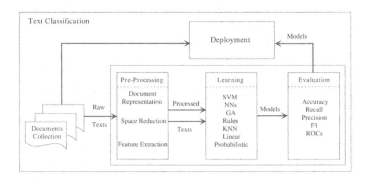

Fig. 1. Text classification overview

to be more similar, than those in the same class. This procedure allows a better determination of the relevant features and will definitely improve visualization.

3 Text Classification

The text classification task consists of setting learning models for a given set of classes and applying these models to new unseen documents for class assignment. It is mainly a supervised classification task, where a training set consisting of documents, with previously assigned classes, is provided, and a test set is used to evaluate the models. Text classification is illustrated in Figure 1, including the pre-processing steps (document representation and space reduction/feature extraction) and the learning/evaluation procedure (support vector machines, neural nets, genetic algorithms, etc.). Great relevance has been rightfully given to learning procedures in text classification. However, a pre-processing stage must be done before the learning process, usually representing up to 80% of both time and computational efforts [1]. Typically, text documents are unstructured data. Before learning, we must transform them into a representation that is suitable for computing. We employ the vector space model, also known as the bag-of-words, widely used in information retrieval, to represent the text documents. This representation method is equivalent to an attribute value representation used in machine learning. Each separate word is a feature (or index term), and its value is the number of times the word occurs in the document (term frequency). Pre-processing alters the input space used to represent the documents that are ultimately included in the training and test sets, used by machine learning algorithms to learn classifiers that are then evaluated. After the representation of documents common text-specific dimensionality reduction techniques are employed, viz., stopword removal, stemming and low frequent word removal.

3.1 Benchmark Text Corpus - Reuters-21578

Reuters-21578 was used in the experiments. It is a financial corpus with news articles documents averaging 200 words each. Reuters-21578 is publicly available at http://kdd.ics.uci.edu/databases/reuters21578/reuters21578.html. In this corpus 21,578 documents are classified in 118 categories. Reuters-21578 is a very heterogeneous corpus, since the number of documents assigned to each category is very variable. There are documents not assigned to any of the categories and documents assigned to more than 10 categories. Furthermore, the number of documents assigned to each category is also not constant. There are categories with only one assigned document and others with thousands of assigned documents. The ModApte split was employed, using 75% of the articles (9603 items) for training and 25% (3299 items) for testing. Moreover only the 10 most frequent categories widely accepted as a benchmark were used, since 75% of the documents belong to at least one of them.

4   Proposed Approach

Our approach is a manifold learning strategy, underpinned by supervised Isomap [15]. Thus, we use the training labels in the corpus to provide a better construction of features. We further apply the dissimilarity measure (1) to enhance the baseline Isomap Euclidean distance using label information, with α taking the value of 0.65 and β the average Euclidean distance between all pairs of text data points.

When a reduced space is reached, our aim is to learn a kernel-based model that can be applied in unseen documents. We use a support vector machine (SVM) with a linear kernel. For testing, however, Isomap does not provide an explicit mapping of documents. Therefore we can not generate the test set directly, since we would need to use the labels. Hence, we use a generalized regression neural network (GRNN) [16] to learn the mapping and apply it to each test document, before the SVM prediction phase, as can be gleaned from Figure 2 that summarizes the proposed approach. In the training phase the supervised Isomap procedure, that runs on features and label training instances, is captured by the GRNN using only the features. Furthermore, the reduced featured space ($\mathbb{R}^d$) is the place for the SVM modeling. When a new testing instance is to be classified, the GRNN maps it from $\mathbb{R}^D$ to $\mathbb{R}^d$ and the SVM model predicts the class.

5   Experiments and Results

This section presents the conducted experiments and obtained results. First the performance criteria are defined and then experiments and results are presented and analyzed.

5.1   Performance Criteria

In order to evaluate a binary decision task we first define a contingency matrix representing the possible outcomes of the classification, as shown in Table 1. Several measures have been defined based on this contingency table, such as, error rate ($\frac{b+c}{a+b+c+d}$), recall ($\frac{a}{a+b}$), and precision ($\frac{a}{a+c}$), as well as combined

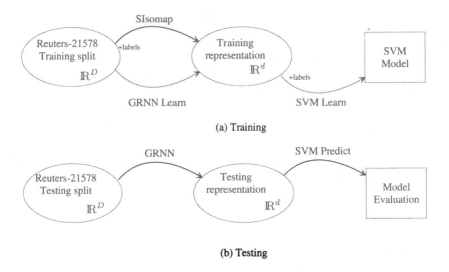

(a) Training

(b) Testing

Fig. 2. Proposed approach: SIsomap+SVM

Table 1. Contingency table for binary classification

	Class Positive	Class Negative
Assigned Positive	a	b
	(True Positives)	(False Positives)
Assigned Negative	c	d
	(False Negatives)	(True Negatives)

measures, such as, the van Rijsbergen F_β measure [17], which combines recall and precision in a single score, $F_\beta = \frac{(\beta^2+1)P \times R}{\beta^2 P + R}$. The latter is one of the measures best-suited to text classification used with $\beta = 1$, i.e. F_1, and thus the results reported in this paper are macro-averaged F_1 values.

5.2 Results and Analysis

Experiments were carried out on the Reuters-21578 corpus on both the baseline Isomap and the proposed approach, hereafter denominated SIsomap+SVM. Table 2 presents the F_1 performances for both settings.

The supervised Isomap combined with the SVM presents a global performance improvement of around 9%, showing that the training label information should be considered in the dimensionality reduction step. While some categories are only slightly better or poorer, there are several for which the improvement is considerable, viz., Grain improves around 17% and Ship improves around 20%. Even in the hardest categories, like Wheat with less than 5% of positive examples, the proposed approach can obtain significant improvement in performance.

Table 2. Comparison of performances of baseline and proposed approaches

Category	Baseline Isomap	SIsomap+SVM
Earn	92.02%	94.48%
Acquisitions	73.45%	86.25%
Money-fx	71.79%	70.77 %
Grain	60.71%	77.55%
Crude	60.87%	69.57%
Trade	57.78%	66.67%
Interest	70.83%	81.82 %
Ship	26.67%	46.15%
Wheat	52.63%	71.43%
Corn	47.06%	42.86%
Average	61.38%	70.76%

Table 3. Comparison of the proposed approach with Isomap, RVM and SVM

	Baseline Isomap	SIsomap+SVM	RVM	SVM
Features	150	150	498	7568
F_1	61.38%	70.76%	70.95%	79.68%

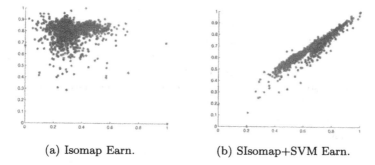

(a) Isomap Earn.   (b) SIsomap+SVM Earn.

Fig. 3. Separation of classes in the reduced dimensionality space for Earn category

Therefore, severe supervised dimensionality reduction should be considered as a pre-processing step in text mining applications. Comparing classification performance with baseline kernel-based machines, the proposed approach presents in this phase comparable results with RVM, using far less features, as can be seen in Table 3. Moreover, the proposed SIsomap+SVM is competitive with RVM where training times are concerned, since RVM have scalability problems and time and resource-consuming training. The huge difference in the number of features makes it possible to use and develop more advanced learning mechanisms, such as boosting and ensembles, to improve classification.

Figures 3 and 4 demonstrate the visualization capabilities of the proposed method using the first two dimensions given by the supervised Isomap algorithm for Earn and Money-fx categories, when compared with the baseline Isomap.

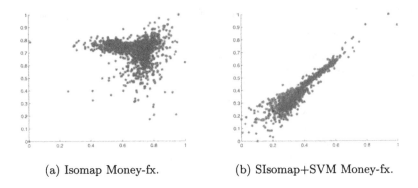

(a) Isomap Money-fx.   (b) SIsomap+SVM Money-fx.

Fig. 4. Separation of classes in the reduced dimensionality space for Money-fx category

One can see that, as expected, the supervised version permits a much better distinction between categories. Note that for SVM and RVM, the visualization is only possible for a two-dimensional problem and infeasible for the 7568 or 498 features respectively (see Table 3).

6   Conclusions and Future Work

In this work we have shown how severe dimensionality reduction techniques can be successfully applied to text classification problems. Moreover we concluded that manifold learning can be used not only with the traditionally associated algorithms, such as K-NN, but also with state-of-the-art kernel-based machines.

The proposed approach, an Isomap-based nonlinear algorithm using training label information in the dimensionality reduction step, combined with kernel-based machines in the classification step, proved to have similar performance to the baseline RVM and be competitive with the SVM. Furthermore, unlike kernel-based machines, it allows for graphical visualization of the datasets, which can be extremely important in real-world applications. Moreover, in real situations, the reduced dimensionality and resulting time reduction can become crucial.

Future work will aim at expanding the learning abilities making use of the reduced dimensionality.

References

1. Sebastiani, F.: Classification of Text, Automatic. In: Brown, K. (ed.) The Encyclopedia of Language and Linguistics, 2nd edn., vol. 14. Elsevier, Amsterdam (2006)
2. Eyheramendy, S., Genkin, A., Ju, W., Lewis, D., Madigan, D.: Sparse Bayesian Classifiers for Text Classification. Journal of Intelligence Community R&D (2003)
3. Tenenbaum, J., Silva, V., Langford, J.: A global geometric framework for nonlinear dimensionality reduction. Science 290(5500), 2319–2323 (2000)
4. Urtasun, R., Darrell, T.: Discriminative Gaussian Process Latent Variable Models for Classification. In: International Conference on Machine Learning (2007)

5. Kim, H., Park, H., Zha, H.: Distance Preserving Dimension Reduction for Manifold Learning. In: International Conference on Data Mining, pp. 1147–1151 (2007)
6. Navarro, D.J., Lee, M.D.: Spatial Visualization of Document Similarity. In: Defence Human Factors. Special Interest Group Meeting (2001)
7. Zhang, D., Chen, X., Lee, W.S.: Text Classification with Kernels on the Multinomial Manifold. In: SIGIR 2005, pp. 266–273 (2005)
8. Vapnik, V.: The Nature of Statistical Learning Theory, 2nd edn. Springer, Heidelberg (1999)
9. Tipping, M.: Sparse Bayesian Learning and the Relevance Vector Machine. Journal of Machine Learning Research I, 211–214 (2001)
10. Jolliffe, I.T.: Principal Component Analysis. Springer, New York (1986)
11. Comon, P.: Independent Component Analysis: a New Concept? Signal Processing 36(3), 287–314 (1994)
12. Cox, T., Cox, M.: Multidimensional Scaling. Chapman & Hall, London (1994)
13. Duraiswami, R., Raykar, V.: The Manifolds of Spatial Hearing. In: International Conference on Acoustics, Speech and Signal Processing, pp. 285–288 (2005)
14. Elgammal, A., Lee, C.: Inferring 3D body pose from silhouettes using activity manifold learning. IEEE Computer Vision and Pattern Recognition 2(27), 681–688 (2004)
15. Geng, X., Zhan, D.-C., Zhou, Z.-H.: Supervised Nonlinear Dimensionality Reduction for Visualization and Classification. IEEE Transactions on Systems, Man, and Cybernetics 35(6), 1098–1107 (2005)
16. Specht, D.: A General Regression Neural Network. IEEE Transactions on Neural Networks 2(6), 568–576 (1991)
17. van Rijsbergen, C.: Information Retrieval, 2nd edn. Butterworths, London (1979)

An Improved Connectionist Translator between Natural Languages*

Gustavo A. Casañ[1] and Maria Asunción Castaño[2]

[1] Dept. Lenguajes y Sistemas Informáticos, Jaume I University, Av. Sos Baynat s/n, 12071,
Castellón, Spain
ncasan@lsi.uji.es
[2] Dept. Ingeniería y Ciencias de los Computadores, Jaume I University, Av. Sos Baynat s/n,
12071, Castellón, Spain
castano@icc.uji.es

Abstract. The RECONTRA translator, a simple connectionist translator between natural languages, has been able to approach several simple MT tasks. In this paper we create a variant of the RECONTRA topology which takes into account what seems to be the natural work of the human brain in the translation process: complete paragraphs or sentences are translated, not individual words. Thus, the RECONTRA translator is modified to present as output several words at the same time. Experimentally, this simple modification has shown an improvement in the translation results.

Keywords: Machine Translation, Neural Network, Improved RECONTRA.

1 Introduction

Neural Networks can be considered an encouraging approach to Machine Translation (MT), as the translation schemes presented in [1] and [2] have empirically shown. Encouraging results have been obtained for text-to-text limited domain applications using a simple Example-Based recurrent connectionist translator called RECONTRA (Recurrent Connectionist Translator) [3]. It directly carries out the translation between the input and the output languages and, at the same time, automatically learns the semantic and syntax implicit in both languages.

In this approach the vocabularies involved in the translations can be represented according to local codifications. However, in order to deal with large vocabularies, they would lead to networks with an excessive number of connections to be trained., which has discouraged most research. One solution is to use distributed representations of both source and target vocabularies [4]. In [5] an automatic encoder which used a simple neural model to create this type of codifications was designed and further experimentation with this encoder was presented in [6] and showed how medium size tasks could be approached with good results.

In this paper we aim to directly improve the RECONTRA translator including an output window which has two advantages: 1) it forces the translator to remember its previous outputs; 2) it's more similar to the work of a human translator.

---

* Partially supported by the Generalitat Valenciana Project number GV/2007/105.

H. Geffner et al. (Eds.): IBERAMIA 2008, LNAI 5290, pp. 282–291, 2008.

The paper is divided in several parts. First, we explain the RECONTRA translator and it's modification; next, the codifications used and the translation task approached in this paper are explained and finally the experimental results obtained and the conclusions.

2 The RECONTRA Translator

The basic neural topology of the RECONTRA translator is an Elman network [7], a Simple Recurrent Neural Network in which the activations of the preceding step in the hidden units of the networks are feedback as inputs in the hidden layer. The architecture of RECONTRA includes time delays in the input layer of an Elman network, in order to reinforce the information about past and future events (Fig. 1).

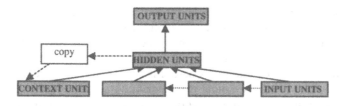

Fig. 1. RECONTRA translator

The words of the sentence to be translated are sequentially presented to the input of the network, and the net has to provide the successive words of the corresponding translated sentence. The time delays of the input layer allow the net to simultaneously see the successive $m+1+n$ words of the input sentence; for instance, the words $i\text{-}m$ ... $i\text{-}1$ i $i+1$ ... $i+n$. In the next step, the *words $i\text{-}m+1$ ... i $i+1$ $i+2$ ... $i+n+1$* are presented and so on.

The modification we propose in this paper is very simple: the output of the network is changed to be several words output, producing a moving window similar to the input window (in Figure 2). Including an output window has two advantages: 1) it forces the translator to remember its previous outputs and to take into account all the words in the input; 2) it's more similar to the work of a human translator, which doesn't translate one word but one paragraph or sentence at the same time, or at least take into account this information. Also, the use of several output words instead of only one, is related to the phrase-based approach to machine translation which has provided good results in the last years (see [8], [9] and a mixed approach in [10]). An example of the translation process can be seen in Table 1.

As extended RECONTRA produces several output words we need to decide which of them is the best; or how to combine the words. Although there are a lot of possible methods (as we can approach the problem as if we have an ensemble of RECONTRA models, see [11] for a complete vision of the field), experimentally we would see how in most cases the same word position (First) always obtains better results than the others.

Table 1. Example for the pair of sentences: Voy a marcharme hoy por la tarde . # I am leaving today in the afternoon . with input window format 2+1+2 and output window format 1+1.

Input window format 2+1+2					Output 1+1	
@	@	Voy	a	marcharme	@	I
@	voy	A	marcharme	hoy	I	am
Voy	a	marcharme	hoy	por	am	leaving
A	narcharme	hoy	por	la	leaving	today
marcharme	hoy	Por	la	tarde	today	in

Both the extended and basic (non-extended) RECONTRA translator are trained by using an "on-line" version of the Backward-Error Propagation (BEP) algorithm [12]; that is, the weights of the net are modified after each input is processed. The standard algorithm is modified to ignore the recurrent connections of the net in the process of adjusting the weights; these connections are considered additional external inputs to the architecture. Later, the hidden unit activations are copied onto the corresponding context units. This time cycle is continuously repeated until the target values mark the end of the translated sentence. The gradient of the error is truncated in the estimation of the weights; that is, it is not exactly computed. However, this learning method runs well in practice as it is shown in [3]) where it is compared to (more computationally costly) methods which exactly follow the gradient. A sigmoid function (0,1) is as-sumed as the non-linear activation function and context activations are initialized to 0.5 at the beginning of every input-output pair.

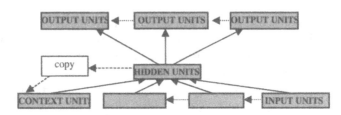

Fig. 2. Extended RECONTRA: RECONTRA with output window

The updating of the weights requires estimating appropriate values for the learning rate term and momentum term. The learning rate concerns the convergence speed to-wards a minimum in the error surface; and the momentum term is related to how the old weights change for the computation of the new change (it avoids some oscillation problems common with the BEP algorithm when the error surface has a very narrow minimum area). The choice of learning rate and momentum for the BEP algorithm is carried out inside the unitary bidimensional space which they define (using values 0.1, 0.3, 0.5, 0.7 and 0.9), by analyzing the residual mean squared error (MSE) of a network trained for 10 random presentations of the learning corpus. In same cases smaller parameters were used (0.01, 0.03, ... 0.09) trying to reduce the instability. Training continues for the learning rate and momentum which led to the lowest MSE and stops after 150 training epochs.

The activations provided by the network are interpreted as the word associated to the nearest pre-established codification of the target vocabulary. Word accuracy is computed by comparing the obtained and expected translations corresponding to every source sentence in the test sample using a conventional Edit-Distance procedure [13]. In the extended RECONTRA, the different word outputs are computed separately, like if they were from different translator. Integrating the multiple output is still a pending work, but it's partially explored in point 5.5.

3 Codification of Vocabularies

There are two distinct types of representation used for symbolizing short-term data at the input/output of connectionist models: local and distributed representations.

In a local representation each concept (each word) is represented by a particular unit. This means that each input or output unit of the network represents one word of the vocabulary. To this end, one unit is on (his value is, for instance, 1) and the other units are off (value 0). The main problems with local representations concern inefficiency, as the networks grow enormously for large sets of objects.

A distributed representation is defined [14] as one in which each concept is represented over several units, and in which each unit participates in the representation of several concepts.

Main advantages of distributed codifications are the efficient use of representational resources and the ability to have an explicit representation of relevant aspects of objects, analogical representations (similar representation for similar objects) and continuity (representation in a continuous vector space). Disadvantages of distributed codifications are the problem of creating adequate ones for each problem and how to represent arbitrary associations (for instance, several words with the same meaning) and variable bindings (a word with several meanings). Also, translators in which distributed codifications are adopted usually require more training time.

3.1 MLP with Output Window

A Multi-Layer Perceptron (MLP) with output window was presented in [5] as an encoder which automatically generates the codifications required for RECONTRA. It's based on the known capabilities of a network to develop its own internal representations of the input. The MLP has three layers of units and is trained to produce the same output as the input (a word of the vocabulary). When the MLP has been sufficiently trained, the activations of the hidden units have developed its own representations of the input/output words and can be extracted and used for the translation task. Consequently, the size of the (unique) hidden layer of the MLP determines the size of the distributed codifications obtained. After training, a word is presented to the MLP and the activations of the hidden units are extracted and assumed to be the internal representation developed by the MLP for this input word.

In order to take into account the context in which a word appears, the previous and following words in a sentence are also shown at the output of the MLP. The resulting topology for the MLP encoder is shown in Figure 3. In addition, the importance of the input word over its context can be made equal, decreased or increased in the encoder. If the input word had less importance at the output than its context, the codifications of words with the same syntactic function were too similar to be adequate for translation purposes, as the translator could not differentiate between the different nouns or verbs. This was achieved by repeating the input words several times at the output window of the MLP encoder. According to this, a possible output window of size 8 for the *x-th* input word w_x could be w_{x-2} w_{x-1} w_x w_x w_x w_x w_{x+1} w_{x+2}, where w_{x-2}, w_{x-1} are the two previous words in its context and w_{x+1}, w_{x+2}, the two following words. To simplify the nomenclature, from now on, we will refer to such example of format for the output window as *x-2 x-1 x x x+1 x+2*.

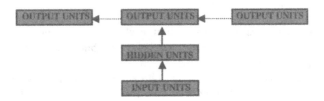

Fig. 3. MLP encoder with output window

The size of the codifications extracted from the MLPs has been automatically determined using a simple pruning method [15]. Moreover, the codifications extracted from these MLPs can be used to train other MLPs which lead to new codifications, in a sort of feedback. Finally, to mention that BEP has been used to train the encoders, but also a combination of BEP and a Scaled Conjugate Gradient method [16]. More details about the encoder, the types of output windows, and the pruning and the training methods used can be found in [5], [6] and [7].

4 The Traveler Task

The task chosen in this paper to test the RECONTRA translator and the encoders was the Spanish-to-English text-to-text Traveler MT task, which was designed within the first phase of the EuTrans project [17]. This task is restricted to a limited domain and approaches typical situations of a Traveler at the reception of a hotel in a country whose language he/she does not speak. The scenario has been limited to some human-to-human communication situations in the reception of a hotel: asking for rooms, wake-up calls, keys, and moving the luggage; asking for information about and changing them; notifying a previous reservation; signing the registration form; asking and complaining about the bill; notifying the departure; and other common expressions. The task has 683 Spanish words and 513 English words.

The corpora adopted in the translation task were sets of text-to-text pairs: a sentence in the Spanish language and the corresponding sentence in the English one. 10,000 pairs were used for training and 3,000 for test. The test-set perplexity of the Spanish sentences is 13.8 and 7.0 for the English ones. The medium size of the sentences in Spanish is 9.5 and 9.8 in the English ones. These are several examples of this task:

¿ Reservé una habitación tranquila para hoy a nombre de la señorita Soler . # I booked a quiet room for today for Miss Soler .

¿ les importaría bajar el equipaje a recepción ? # would you mind sending the luggage down to reception ? EndOfSentence

The corpora used for the training of the MLP encoders were sets of text-to-text pairs, each of them consisting of an input word and the same input word together with its context as output. All pairs were extracted from sentences which appeared in the training corpus of the translation task, but repetitions were not allowed. There were no test corpora for the codification process; it was indirectly evaluated later in the translation process.

As reported in [18] the best translation results previously obtained with the task using other inductive algorithms (based on finite-state transducers) and the same corpora sets had a best results of 3.9% Word Error Rate (WER). There are newer results, as this task has become lately a sort of first step with new translation techniques before approaching more complex natural task, like Hansards. The best results reported in [19] with mixtures of IBM2 models, with phrase based hidden markov models (PHMM) [10] and with different translation rules for IBM2 models [20] are also shown in Table 2, but they don't improve the previous results. The best results using basic RECONTRA were 16.3% WER with a pair of distributed codifications (explained in Table 3 where they are called $I\ mlp^2\ P$) previously presented in [6]).

Table 2. Best results obtained with other methods [18], [19], [10] and [20]

Method	WER
OMEGA	3.9%
MGTI	8.0%
OSTIA	8.3%
PHMM	7.8%
Rules+IBM2	10.0%
IBM2 Mixtures	12.6%

5 Experimental Results

The Traveler task was approached using RDCs and later using codifications obtained from encoders which used initial local codifications at their input/output and others from encoders trained using initial RDCs. Previous experimentation with the task [6] suggested adopting a RECONTRA model with an input window of 9 words and 450 hidden units, and this was the base topology used in the paper. We present experiments with different number of output words in RECONTRA (2, 3 and 4 words) and the same pairs of codifications. A sigmoid function (0,1) was assumed as the non-linear function. The experiments were done using the Stuttgart Neural Network Simulator [21].

5.1 Codifications Employed

In order to compare the benefits of the extended RECONTRA with the benefits of the basic (non-extended) RECONTRA, in the experimentation of this paper we adopted codifications previously presented in different works by Casañ and Castaño ([5], [6] and [7]). In Table 3 we can see some of the characteristics of these codifications: size of the codifications for the Spanish and English vocabularies (which are denoted by |Spanish|/|English|, respectively) and when codifications were extracted from MLPs, some of the characteristics of the networks: the use or not of pruning, the use of feed-back and the output window format of the network. More details can be found in the original papers [5], [6] and [7]. The nomenclature adopted for the names of the codi-fications is as follows: a roman number for binary RDCs (the same as in [7]); in codi-fications extracted from MLPs trained with initial RDCs, mlp was added to the name of the original codification (for instance $V\ mlp$); if it was a codification extracted from a MLP in which the initial codifications were extracted from other trained MLP, we add mlp^2 to the name of the codification ($I\ mlp^2$); and when the MLPs have been pruned, a P is added ($IV\ mlp\ P$).

Table 3. Characteristics of the codifications employed in the paper and translation results pre-viously obtained

Codifications	MLP				WER
Name	Feedback	Pruning	|Spanish| / |English|	Output Format	
IV mlp P	No	Yes	49/46	x-1 x x x+1	20.3%
V	No	-	30/30	-	36.6%
V mlp	No	No	30/30	x-1 x x x+1	23.5%
V mlp P	No	Yes	17/14	x-1 x x x+1	47.5%
I mlp P	No	Yes	121/94	x-1 x x x x x+1	21.9%
I mlp² P	Yes	Yes	121/94	x-1 x x x x x+1	16.3%

5.2   Two Output Words

RECONTRA was modified to have two output words instead of one. When we com-pare the translation results with those obtained using basic RECONTRA and the same codifications (in Table 4 and Table 3) we can see a clear improvement. It's also im-portant to note that one of the output words consistently provides better results than the other. The following experiments will show how this is a consistent occurrence.

Table 4. Translation results with extended RECONTRA with two output words

Name	|Spanish| / |English|	Learning Rate	Momentum	Second	First
V	30/30	0.1	0.3	29.5%	24.2%
V mlp	30/30	0.1	0.1	20.3%	18.9%
V mlp P	17/14	0.1	0.3	37.5%	32.5%
IV mlp P	49/46	0.1	0.1	18.7%	16.6%
Imlp P	121/94	0.1	0.1	28.7%	19.2%
		0.09	0.01	27.1%	16.9%
Imlp² P	121/94	0.09	0.03	15.9%	14.2%

5.3   Three Output Words

Adding two new words to the output of RECONTRA was the logical next step and the results provided by the resulting networks for the same codifications as in previ-ous experiments were better (compare Tables 5 and 4). But the increase was not as significant as expected for all the pairs of codifications. Part of the problem seems to come from the increasing size of the networks and the instability that it tends to pro-duce. In some cases using smaller training parameters helped to reduce the instability and increase the translation results (see results for $I\ mlp\ P$ and $I\ mlp^2\ P$).

Table 5. Translation results with extended RECONTRA with three output words

Name	|Spanish| / |English|	L. R.	Mom.	Third	Second	First
V	30/30	0.1	0.1	30.1%	24.5%	22.4%
V mlp	30/30	0.1	0.1	19.7%	17.5%	17.2%
V mlp P	17/14	0.1	0.1	35.9%	29.9%	27.0%
IV mlp P	49/46	0.1	0.1	19.4%	16.4%	15.7%
Imlp P	121/94	0.1	0.1	38.8%	27.5%	17.2%
Imlp^2 P	121/94	0.1	0.3	20.0%	16.5%	15.4%
		0.09	0.03	18.2%	15.3%	14.3%

5.4 Four Output Words

We finally tested an extended RECONTRA with four words output (translation results in Table 6) and in some cases the translation results still improved. But at this point stability problems become common during training (in Table 6 we can see how smaller parameters for *I mlp P* provided better results) and its size (specially for *I mlp P* and *I mlp^2 P*, as the codifications are bigger) made their training time very long.

Table 6. Translation results with extended RECONTRA with four output words

Name	|Spanish| / |English|	L. R.	Mom.	Fourth	Third	Second	First
V	30/30	0.1	0.1	30.7%	23.8%	21.9%	20.7%
V mlp	30/30	0.1	0.1	20.4%	17.8%	17.2%	17.4%
V mlp P	17/14	0.1	0.1	35.7%	29.4%	27.3%	25.9%
IV mlp P	49/46	0.1	0.3	19.6%	15.9%	15.6%	15.2%
		0.07	0.09	20.0%	16.8%	16.0%	15.3%
I mlp P	121/94	0.1	0.1	43.7%	30.7%	27.5%	25.3%
		0.05	0.01	39.9%	23.1%	19.6%	18.0%
I mlp^2 P	121/94	0.1	0.1	23.5%	18.7%	16.6%	15.7%

5.5 How to Integrate the Outputs

In this section we present several experiments to integrate the output. We used codification *I mlp^2 P*, and two output words in all cases, as the best results had been obtained with this experiment. Two different basic techniques were employed, with and without weights: *average*, in which the average of the two outputs was calculated; and *distance*, in which the distance from each output to the nearest codification was used as a decision term (the codification which was nearest its corresponding word was selected). The results can be seen in Table 7 and are disappointing: the best results are

Table 7. Translation results with weighted media and distance

Method	Second Weight	First Weight	WER
	0.1	0.9	14.1%
	0.3	0.7	16.1%
Average	0.5	0.5	45.3%
	0.7	0.3	25.4%
	0.9	0.1	23.0%
	0.1	0.9	14.8%
	0.3	0.7	14.8%
Distance	0.5	0.5	15.1%
	0.7	0.3	16.2%
	0.9	0.1	16.5%

obtained when more importance is given to the output word which will, anyway, provide better translation results (not an unexpected result). Better methods are needed to integrate or interpret the extended RECONTRA outputs.

6 Conclusions and Future Work

The results improve consistently when using an output window in the RECONTRA translator, but the network can grow so much that it can become instable and slow to train, specially when working with "big" codifications. On the other hand, small size codifications (like V mlp P) which tend to provide worse results have a huge improvement with multiple output words, maintaining a reasonable network size. This combination of techniques seems to be a promising approach to the translation problem, although the translation results are still not as good as the best ones obtained with other methods [10].

The big question right now is how to interpret the outputs. It's true that one of the output words (First) tends to provide the best results, but examining the results word by word when First fails, in some cases other output words (Second, Third...) will provide the correct one. Thus, if we had a perfect selection or combination method, the translation results obtained could be better. There are lots of possibilities to explore, as this problem is similar to that presented when using ensembles of neural networks and a lot of work has been done in this field of research (see [11]).

References

1. Koncar, N., Guthrie, G.: A Natural Language Translation Neural Network. In: Procs. of the Int. Conf. on New Methods in Language Processing, Manchester, pp. 71–77 (1994)
2. Waibel, A., Jain, A.N., McNair, A.E., Saito, H., Hauptmann, A.G., Tebelskis, J.: JANUS: A Speech-to-Speech Translation System using Connectionist and Symbolic Processing Strategies. In: Procs. of the International Conference on Acustic, Speech and Signal Processing, pp. 793–796 (1991)
3. Castaño, M.A.: Redes Neuronales Recurrentes para Inferencia Gramatical y Traducción Automática. Ph.D. dissertation, Universidad Politécnica de Valencia (1998)
4. Casañ, G.A., Castaño, M.A.: Distributed Representation of Vocabularies in the RECONTRA Neural Translator. In: Procs. of the 6th European Conference on Speech Communication and Technology, Budapest, vol. 6, pp. 2423–2426 (1999)
5. Casañ, G.A., Castaño, M.A.: Automatic Word Codification for the RECONTRA Connectionist Translator. In: Perales, F.J., Campilho, A.C., Pérez, N., Sanfeliu, A. (eds.) IbPRIA 2003. LNCS, vol. 2652, pp. 168–175. Springer, Heidelberg (2003)
6. Casañ, G.A., Castaño, M.A.: A New Approach to Codification for the RECONTRA Neural Translator. In: Procs. Ninth IASTED International Conference on Artifical Intelligence and Soft Computing, pp. 147–152 (2005)
7. Elman, J.L.: Finding Structure in Time. Cognitive Science 4(2), 279–311 (1990)
8. Wang, Y., Waibel, A.: Modeling with structures in statistical machine translation. In: Procs. of the 36th annual meeting on Association for Computational Linguistics, Canada, vol. 2, pp. 1357–1363 (1998)
9. Zens, R., Och, F.J., Ney, H.: Phrase-based statistical machine translation. In: Jarke, M., Koehler, J., Lakemeyer, G. (eds.) KI 2002. LNCS (LNAI), vol. 2479, pp. 18–32. Springer, Heidelberg (2002)

10. Andrés-Ferrer, J., Juan-Císcar, A.: A phrase-based hidden markov model approach to machine translation. In: Procs. New Approaches to Machine Translation, pp. 57–62 (2007)
11. Kuncheva, L.I.: Combining Pattern Classifiers. John Wiley & Sons, Chichester (2004)
12. Rumelhart, D.E., Hinton, G., Williams, R.: Learning Sequential Structure in Simple Recurrent Networks. In: Rumelhart, D.E., McClelland, J.L., PDP Research Group (eds.) Parallel distributed processing: Experiments in the microstructure of cognition, vol. 1. MIT Press, Cambridge (1981)
13. Marzal, A., Vidal, E.: Computation of Normalized Edit Distance and Applications. IEEE Transactions on Pattern Analysis and Machine Intelligence 9(15) (1993)
14. Hinton, G.E., McClelland, J.L., Rumelhart, D.E.: Distributed representations. In: Rumelhart, D.E., McClelland, J.L. (eds.) Parallel Distributed Processing: Explorations in the Microstructure of Cognition. Foundations, vol. 1. MIT Press, Cambridge (1986)
15. Mozer, M.C., Smolensky, P.: Skeletonization: a Technique for Trimming the Fat from a Network via Relevance Assessment. In: Touretzky, D.S. (ed.) Advances in Neural Information Processing, vol. 1, pp. 177–185. Morgan Kaufmann, San Francisco (1990)
16. Möller, M.F.: A Scaled Conjugate Gradient Algorithm for Fast Supervised Learning. Neural Networks 6, 525–533 (1993)
17. Amengual, J.C., Castaño, M.A., Castellanos, A., Llorens, D., Marzal, A., Prat, A., Vilar, J.M., Benedí, J.M., Casacuberta, F., Pastor, M., Vidal, E.: The Eutrans-I Spoken Language System. Machine Translation, vol. 15, pp. 75–102. Kluwer Academic Publishers, Dordrecht (2000)
18. Prat, F., Casacuberta, F., Castro, M.J.: Machine Translation with Grammar Association: Combining Neural Networks and Finite-State Models. In: Procs. The Second Workshop on Natural Language Processing and Neural Networks, Tokio, pp. 53–61 (2001)
19. Civera, J., Juan, A.: Mixtures of IBM Model 2. In: Proc. of EAMT 2006, pp. 159–167 (2006)
20. Andrés-Ferrer, J., García-Varea, I., Casacuberta, F.: Combining translation models in statistical machine translation. In: Procs. of The 11th Int. Conference on Theoretical and Methodological Issues in Machine Translation (TMI 2007), pp. 11–20 (2007)
21. Zell, A., et al.: SNNS: Stuttgart Neural Network Simulator. User manual, Version 4.1. Technical Report no. 6195, Institute for Parallel and Distributed High Performance Systems, Stuttgart: University of Stuttgart (1995)

A Framework for Information Retrieval Based on Fuzzy Relations and Multiple Ontologies

Maria Angelica A. Leite[1,2] and Ivan L.M. Ricarte[2]

[1] Embrapa Agriculture Informatics
PO Box: 6041 - ZIP: 13083-970 - Campinas - SP - Brazil
angelica@cnptia.embrapa.br
http://www.cnptia.embrapa.br
[2] School of Electrical and Computer Engineering, University of Campinas
PO Box 6101, Postal Code: 13083-970 - Campinas, SP, Brazil
{leite,ricarte}@dca.fee.unicamp.br
http://www.fee.unicamp.br/

Abstract. The use of knowledge in the information retrieval process allows the return of documents semantically related to the initial user's query. This knowledge can be encoded in a knowledge base to be used in information retrieval systems. The framework for information retrieval based on fuzzy relations and multiple ontologies is a proposal to retrieve information using a knowledge base composed of multiple related ontologies whose relationships are expressed as fuzzy relations. Using this knowledge organization a new method to expand the user query is proposed. The framework provides a way that each ontology can be represented independently as well as their relationships. The proposed framework performance is compared with another fuzzy-based approach for information retrieval. Also the query expansion method is tested with the Apache Lucene search engine. In both cases the proposed framework improves the obtained results.

Keywords: Fuzzy information retrieval, ontology, knowledge representation.

1 Introduction

An information retrieval system stores and index documents such that when users express their information need in a query the system retrieves the related documents associating a score to each one. The higher the score the greater is the importance of the document [1]. Usually an information retrieval system returns large result sets and the users must spend considerable time until find items that are really relevant. Moreover, documents are retrieved when they contain the index terms specified in the queries. However, this approach will neglect other relevant documents that do not contain the index terms specified in the user's queries. When working with specific domain knowledge this problem can be overcome by incorporating a knowledge base which depicts the relationships between index terms into the existing information retrieval systems. Knowledge bases can

H. Geffner et al. (Eds.): IBERAMIA 2008, LNAI 5290, pp. 292–301, 2008.

be manually developed by domain experts or automatically constructed from the knowledge in the document collection [2,3]. To deal with the vagueness typical of human knowledge, the fuzzy set theory can be used to manipulate the knowledge in the bases. It deals with the uncertainty that may be present in document and query representations as well in their relationships.

Knowledge bases in information retrieval cover a wide range of topics of which query expansion is one. A recent approach is to use ontologies to infer new terms to be added to the queries [4]. Particularly, fuzzy ontologies are being constructed [5,6,7] to model the uncertainty in the domain knowledge. Usually information retrieval systems use just one conceptual structure to model the knowledge and compose the knowledge base. But the knowledge indexing a document collection can be expressed in multiple distinct domains each one consisting of a different conceptual structure represented by a lightweight ontology. Lightweight ontologies include concepts, concepts taxonomies, relationships between concepts and properties that describes concepts [8].

In this paper we focus on the fuzzy encoding of an information retrieval framework which is supported by fuzzy related lightweight ontologies each one representing a distinct area of the knowledge domain. The framework provides means to represent each ontology independently as well as their relationships. Based on the knowledge from the ontologies the system carries an automatic fuzzy query expansion. The documents are indexed by the concepts in the knowledge base allowing the retrieval by their meaning. The results obtained with the proposed framework are compared with the results obtained using just the user's entered keywords and with the results obtained by another fuzzy information retrieval system [9,10]. The proposed expansion method is also employed in expanding queries for the Apache Lucene [11] search engine. The results show an enhance in precision for the same recall measures.

2   Related Work

This section presents some information retrieval models that encode the relationship among terms as a way to improve the retrieval performance. By combining lexico-syntactic and statistical learning approaches a fuzzy domain ontology mining algorithm is proposed for supporting ontology engineering [6]. The work uses one ontology as knowledge base and presents empirical studies confirming that the use of a fuzzy domain ontology leads to significant improvement in information retrieval performance. A fuzzy query expansion and a fuzzy thesaurus are used to solve the Medical Computational Problem (MCP) [12]. In the experiments the system was capable of retrieving the same MCP for distinct descriptions of the same problem. The system uses a unique fuzzy thesaurus for query expansion. In the keyword connection matrix model [2] the knowledge about the relevant keywords or terms is encoded as a single fuzzy relation that expresses the degree of similarity between the terms. The information retrieval process uses the fuzzy keyword connection matrix to find similarities between the query terms as a way to improve query results. The multi-relationship fuzzy concept network information retrieval model [9,10] considers the knowledge encoded as a fuzzy conceptual network. In the network each node can be related to another one by three relation types: fuzzy positive association, fuzzy generalization association and fuzzy specialization association. These relations are constructed automatically based on word co-occurrence at syntactic level in the documents. The documents are associated to the concepts by a fuzzy relation. Using the relationships in the concept network the system infers new concepts to be associated to the documents. The query is composed with concepts from the concept network. When a query is executed the system calculates the documents similarity based on the weight of the concept in the document. The fuzzy ontological relational model [13] considers a knowledge base as a fuzzy ontology with concepts representing the categories and the keywords of a domain. When the user enters a query, composed of concepts, the system performs its expansion and may add new concepts based on the ontology knowledge. After expansion the similarity between the query and the documents is calculated by fuzzy operations.

The presented works use just one conceptual structure to encode the knowledge. The proposed framework considers the knowledge being expressed in multiple lightweight ontologies allowing representing each ontology independently as well as their relationships.

3   Information Retrieval Framework

3.1   Knowledge Representation

The knowledge is represented in multiple lightweight ontologies each one corresponding to a distinct domain. Each ontology representing a knowledge domain is a concept set $D_k = \{c_{k1}, c_{k2}, \cdots c_{ky}\}$ where $1 \leq k \leq K$, K is the domains number and $y = \|D_k\|$ is the concepts number in each domain. These ontologies are related composing the framework knowledge base. The concepts inside the ontology are organized as a taxonomy and are related by fuzzy specialization association (S) and fuzzy generalization association (G). Concepts pertaining to distinct ontologies are related by fuzzy positive association (P).

Definition 1. *Consider two distinct concept domains sets D_i and D_j.*

1. *Fuzzy positive association is a fuzzy relation: $(R^P_{ij} : D_i \times D_j \to [0,1])$ not symmetric, not reflexive and not transitive.*
2. *Fuzzy generalization association is a fuzzy relation: $(R^G_i : D_i \times D_i \to [0,1])$ not symmetric, not reflexive and transitive.*
3. *Fuzzy specialization association is a fuzzy relation: $(R^S_i : D_i \times D_i \to [0,1])$ not symmetric, not reflexive and transitive.*

The fuzzy generalization association is the inverse of the fuzzy specialization association. The implicit relationships between concepts from the same domain are given by the transitive closure of the fuzzy generalization and fuzzy specialization associations. The transitive closure of the associations R^G_i and R^S_i where $1 \leq i \leq K$, results the relations R^*_{Gi} and R^*_{Si} respectively.

Definition 2. *The transitive closure* R^* *of a fuzzy relation* R *can be determined by an iterative algorithm that consists of the following steps:*

1. *Compute* $R' = R \cup [we_t \times (R \circ R)]$ *where* $we_t \in [0, 1]$, $t = \{G, S\}$;
2. *If* $R' \neq R$, *rename* $R = R'$ *and go to step 1; otherwise* $R^* = R'$ *and the algorithm terminates.*

The $(R \circ R)$ means the composition between two fuzzy relations. The composition between two fuzzy relations [14] $P : X \times Y$ and $Q : Y \times Z$ is the fuzzy relation $R : X \times Z$ as in (1).

$$R(x, z) = (P \circ Q)(x, z) = \max_{y \in Y} \min [P(x, y), Q(y, z)] . \tag{1}$$

The weight we_t, with values $0 < we_t < 1$, penalizes the association strength between distant concepts in the ontology. As the distance between concepts increase their association values decrease. Concepts with higher strength value are considered to have stronger meaning association. In order to discard concepts associations with lower strength value a boundary b establishes the minimum value such that the corresponding association is to be considered.

3.2 Document and Query Representation

The documents d_l are represented by the DOC set where $1 \leq l \leq \|DOC\|$. A fuzzy relation $U_j (d_l, c_{jy}) = u_{ly} \in [0, 1]$, where $1 \leq l \leq \|DOC\|$, $1 \leq j \leq K$ and $1 \leq y \leq \|D_j\|$ indicates the association degree between the concept $c_{jy} \in D_j$ and the document $d_l \in DOC$. The relations U_j, $1 \leq j \leq K$ are represented as matrices $p \times m$ where $p = \|DOC\|$ and $m = \|D_j\|$. The U_j fuzzy relation indicates the relevance of the concept to represent the document content. Its value is calculated following a *tf-idf* schema [1].

The query is expressed with the concepts from the distinct domains connected by logical operators. The query is transformed into the conjunctive normal form and is represented by sub-queries connected by the AND logical operator. Each sub-query is composed by a set of concepts connected by the OR logical operator. Given the domains $D_1 = \{c_{11}, c_{12}, c_{13}\}$ and $D_2 = \{c_{21}, c_{22}, c_{23}, c_{24}\}$ a valid query in this format would be $q = (c_{11} \vee c_{22}) \wedge (c_{13} \vee c_{24})$. Once the query is in the conjunctive normal form each sub-query is performed independently and retrieves a document set. The intersection of the document sets is the final result of the query. Therefore, in the sequence, only aspects related to the sub-query are presented. The documents are associated to the domain concepts using distinct relations. To consider this the sub-queries are partitioned to take the concepts from each domain separately. Each partition is a vector with dimension equal to the associated domain concepts number and is composed by values that indicates the presence (1) or absence (0) of the concept in the query. A sub-query q is partitioned in q_i vectors where $1 \leq i \leq K$ and K is the domains number. In the previous example the sub-query $q = (c_{11} \vee c_{22})$ is partitioned as $q_1 = [1\,0\,0]$ and $q_2 = [0\,1\,0\,0]$.

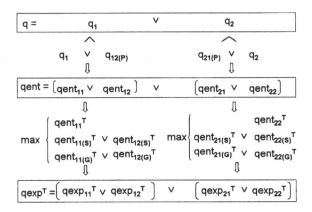

Fig. 1. Query expansion process result

3.3   Query Expansion

The query expansion is performed in two phases. In the first one each partition q_i, from the initial sub-query q, is expanded to consider the relations between the domain D_i associated to the partition and the other domains from the knowledge base. For each partition q_i new $K-1$ vectors are generated each one containing concepts from the others domains D_j, $j \neq i$, $1 \leq i,j \leq K$ associated to concepts present in q_i. This process generates a new expanded query denoted $qent$. The first expansion is translated in (2). The variable i refers to the domain of the partition q_i and the variable j refers to the remaining domains from the knowledge base.

$$qent = \bigcup_{i=1}^{K} \bigcup_{j=1}^{K} \begin{cases} q_i & j = i \\ w_P \left(q_i \circ R_{ij}^P \right) & j \neq i \end{cases}. \tag{2}$$

To expand the query to consider other domains the fuzzy positive association R_{ij}^P between concepts from the domains D_i and D_j is used. The framework allows to associate a weight $w_P \in [0,1]$, that defines the influence the fuzzy positive association will have in the expansion. Each expansion generates a new vector with domain D_j concepts. The values in the vectors denote the degree the concepts from the domain D_j are related to the concepts from the partition q_i. Consider two domains D_1 and D_2 and a sub-query $q = q_1 \vee q_2$ partitioned in both domains. Figure 1 shows the result of the expansion process. Each partition q_i, $1 \leq i \leq 2$ is expanded in the other domains generating the $qent_{ij}$ partitions, $1 \leq j \leq 2$ that compose the expanded sub-query $qent$.

After expansion among the domains the second phase is performed. This phase expands the sub-query $qent$ considering the knowledge inside the ontologies. This expansion generates the final transposed expanded query $qexp^T$. Equation (3) presents the expansion. The association type is given by $r = \{S, G\}$.

$$qexp^T = \bigcup_{i=1}^{K} \bigcup_{j=1}^{K} \max \begin{cases} \begin{cases} qent_{ij}^T & j = i \\ w_r \left(R_{rj}^* \circ qent_{ij}^T \right) & \end{cases} \\ w_r \left(R_{rj}^* \circ qent_{ij}^T \right) & j \neq i \end{cases}. \tag{3}$$

Considering the knowledge inside the domains each transposed partition $qent_{ij}^{\mathrm{T}}$, $1 \leq i, j \leq K$ is expanded to take into account the fuzzy generalization and fuzzy specialization associations between the concepts from their domain D_j. The framework allows to associate a value $w_r \in [0, 1]$, $r = \{S, G\}$ that defines a weight to the association type. This way the expansion can be adjusted to consider more one association type than the other. Figure 1 shows the expansion inside domains for the sub-query $qent$. For example, the transposed partition $qent_{12}^{\mathrm{T}}$ is expanded considering the fuzzy specialization association, $qent_{12(S)}^{\mathrm{T}}$, and the fuzzy generalization association, $qent_{12(G)}^{\mathrm{T}}$, among concepts from the D_2 domain. The final expanded partition given by $qexp_{12}^{\mathrm{T}} = \max\left(qent_{12(S)}^{\mathrm{T}}, qent_{12(G)}^{\mathrm{T}}\right)$ is the maximum value between the fuzzy associations types $r = \{S, G\}$ for the D_2 domain.

3.4   Similarity Function

The documents relevance is given by the similarity function between the documents representation and the expanded fuzzy sub-query $qexp^{\mathrm{T}}$. The similarity is calculated by the product between the relations U_j with each partition $qexp_{ij}^{\mathrm{T}}$, as in (4), resulting the retrieved documents set V:

$$V = \bigcup_{i=1}^{K} \bigcup_{j=1}^{K} \left(U_j \times qexp_{ij}^{\mathrm{T}}\right) . \tag{4}$$

Each relation U_j associates the collection documents to the D_j domain concepts, where $1 \leq j \leq K$. The vector $qexp_{ij}^{\mathrm{T}}$ represents the expansion of the concepts from the partition q_i to the D_j domain where $1 \leq i, j \leq K$. It is constituted from the D_j domain concepts and its values indicates the degree the concepts from domain D_j are associated to the concepts in partition q_i. The arithmetic product $U_j \times qexp_{ij}^{\mathrm{T}}$ indicates the documents associated to the D_j domain that are related to the q_i partition. The $\bigcup$ symbol designates union and denotes the max operator. The arithmetic product adjusts the associations of the documents to the concepts (expressed in the relations U_j) by the strength of the relationships between concepts present in $qexp_{ij}^{\mathrm{T}}$. If a concept c_{1i} is associated to the concept c_{2j}, from domain D_2, by a value degree $\in [0, 1]$ then a document related to the concept c_{2j} is associated to the concept c_{1i} adjusted by the same degree. The $V(v_l)$ set represents all the documents in the collection and its value $v_l \in [0, 1]$ indicates the degree a document d_l, $1 \leq l \leq \|\mathrm{DOC}\|$ is similar to the initial user query. Documents with $v_l > 0$ are presented to the user in decreasing order.

4   Experimental Results

The experimental evaluation is carried out using a document collection sample referring to the agrometeorology domain in Brazil, a query set, a lightweight ontology referring to the geographical brazilian territory and a lightweight ontology referring to the climate distribution over the brazilian territory.

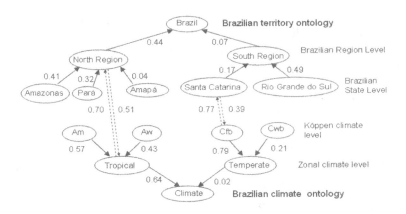

Fig. 2. Brazilian territorial and brazilian climate lightweight ontologies and their fuzzy associations

The ontologies are manually constructed considering a brazilian map [15] that contains the Köppen climate [16] distribution over the country. The first ontology refers to the brazilian territory, say domain D_1, with three levels. The root node is labeled 'Brazil', the descendant nodes are labeled with brazilian regions and each region node has the respective brazilian state nodes as descendants. Figure 2 shows a sample of the brazilian territory ontology. For the brazilian territory ontology the fuzzy generalization association and the fuzzy specialization association relates the spacial relationship between the territory entities they refer to. The second ontology refers to the climate distribution over the brazilian territory, say domain D_2. The root node is labeled 'Climate', the root descendant nodes are labeled with brazilian zonal climates and each zonal climate has the respective associated Köppen climate nodes as descendants. Figure 2 shows a sample of the brazilian climate ontology. For the brazilian climate ontology the fuzzy generalization association and the fuzzy specialization association relates the spacial relationship between the climate entities they refer to. The fuzzy positive association between the ontologies is established by the distribution of the climate over the brazilian territory. The association is settled in two levels. The first one is between the brazilian regions and the zonal climates and the second one is between the brazilian states and the Köppen climates. The dashed lines in Fig. 2 illustrate both associations levels.

The document collection is composed of a sample of 128 documents selected from a base of 17,780 documents from the agrometeorology domain. This sample considers documents containing just one of the concepts from the ontologies as well as a combination of concepts from both ontologies. The queries set contains 35 queries considering just one concept from each ontology or two concepts from both ontologies connected with AND or OR boolean operators. For each query the relevant documents from the sample document collection are selected by a domain expert.

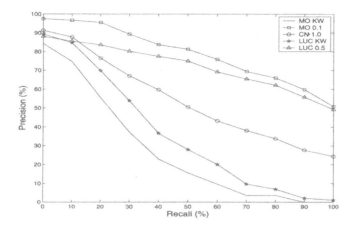

Fig. 3. Recall and precision measures for the models

4.1 Experimental Analysis

The experiment is ran to test the proposed framework performance and to compare its performance with a similar approach, that is, the multi-relationship fuzzy concept network information retrieval model presented in Sect. 2. The experiment also tests the use of the query expansion method in the Apache Lucene text search engine. The Apache Lucene allows boosting a search concept increasing the relevance of documents indexed by the concept.

Several experiments were ran considering many combinations of the weights we_t, $t = \{S, G\}$ and w_r, $r = \{S, G, P\}$. After many tests all the models showed a behavior tendency concerning the precision and recall measures. Given a query, recall is the ratio between the number of documents retrieved and considered relevant, and the total number of documents considered relevant in the collection and precision is the ratio between the number of documents retrieved and considered relevant, and the total number of retrieved documents [1]. As the addition of general concepts tends to add more noise in the search results then a lower weight value is assigned to the fuzzy generalization association like $w_G = 0.3$. A higher value is assigned to the fuzzy specialization association like $w_S = 0.7$. For transitive closure calculation the assigned weights are $we_G = 0.2$ and $we_S = 0.8$. The fuzzy positive association is tested with four different weights like $w_P = 0.0$, $w_P = 0.1$, $w_P = 0.5$, and $w_P = 1.0$.

Figure 3 presents the performance results for the models. For each model its best result represents its behavior tendency considering the tested w_P variations. So the best result for each one is recorded to keep the graphic understandable. The proposed framework is represented by MO curves, the multi-relationship fuzzy concept network model by the CN curve and the Apache Lucene by LUC curves. In the curves legend, the KW means the use of just the entered keywords (without performing query expansion) and the numbers refer to the corresponding w_P value when query expansion is considered. As the proposed framework and the Apache Lucene use the same query expansion method their performances have the same tendency. When considering just the user entered keywords the precision for lower recall values is high but it decreases fast as the recall values increase. When query expansion is performed the precision is high for low recall values and maintains around 50% for high recall values. The fuzzy concept network model presents high precision values for low recall values but as the recall values are higher it maintains the precision values around 25%. Comparing the three models results, the proposed framework exhibits better performance (MO 0.1 curve) when knowledge is considered in the query expansion process.

5 Conclusions

The use of knowledge in the information retrieval process can enhance the quality of the results by returning documents semantically related to the initial user's query. To deal with the uncertainty and vagueness present in the knowledge the fuzzy set theory has been used. When working with specific document collections one way to accomplish that is to represent the knowledge in distinct domains each one being represented as an independent lightweight ontology. These domains knowledge can be related to each other composing a knowledge base. To explore these issues this work presents an approach for improving the document retrieval process. Contrary to other approaches that consider the knowledge base composed of just one ontology, the proposed framework explores knowledge expressed in multiple ontologies whose relationships are expressed as fuzzy relations. This knowledge organization is used in a novel method to expand the user query and to index the documents in the collection.

Experimental results show that the proposed framework achieves better performance when compared with other fuzzy information retrieval approach. The manually constructed knowledge base offers a semantic knowledge that leads to good retrieval performance when compared with a model that uses a knowledge base constructed considering just the syntactic word co-occurrence. There is an effort to develop an iterative strategy, using machine learning techniques, to relate concepts extracted from a corpora of documents in some discourse area. Initial tests show that this strategy is a promising one in developing the fuzzy positive associations between ontologies concepts. The possibility of using some semi-automatic strategy to construct the semantic positive relationships between distinct related ontologies will allow to consider larger ontologies. This will enable the information retrieval framework to achieve scalability. Associations based on semantic meaning are more stable and less sensible than those based on word co-occurrence. Thus this framework can also achieve good results in other knowledge areas. For example, in a document collection about plant pathology an ontology about plants can be related to an ontology about plant diseases to improve document retrieval.

References

1. Baeza-Yates, R.A., Ribeiro-Neto, B.A.: Modern Information Retrieval. ACM Press / Addison-Wesley, New York (1999)
2. Ogawa, Y., Morita, T., Kobayashi, K.: A fuzzy document retrieval system using the keyword connection matrix and a learning method. In: Fuzzy Sets and Systems, vol. 39, pp. 163–179. Elsevier B. V, Amsterdam (1991)
3. Widyantoro, D.H., Yen, J.: A fuzzy ontology-based abstract search engine and its user studies. In: 10th IEEE International Conference on Fuzzy Systems, pp. 1291–1294. IEEE Computer Society, Washington (2001)
4. Bhogal, J., Macfarlane, A., Smith, P.: A review of ontology based query expansion. In: Information Processing and Management, vol. 43, pp. 866–886. Elsevier B. V, Amsterdam (2007)
5. Abulaish, M., Dey, L.: A fuzzy ontology generation framework for handling uncertainties and nonuniformity in domain knowledge description. In: International Conference on Computing: Theory and Applications, pp. 287–293. IEEE Computer Society, Washington (2007)
6. Lau, R.Y.K., Li, Y., Xu, Y.: Mining fuzzy domain ontology from textual databases. In: IEEE/WIC/ACM International Conference on Web Intelligence, pp. 156–162. IEEE Computer Society, Washington (2007)
7. Parry, D.: A fuzzy ontology for medical document retrieval. In: Second Workshop on Australasian Information Security, Data Mining and Web Intelligence, and Software Internationalisation, pp. 121–126. Australian Computer Society Inc., Darlinghurst (2004)
8. Gomez-Pérez, A., Fernández-Lopez, M., Corcho, O.: Ontological Engineering. Springer, London (2003)
9. Chen, S.M., Horng, Y.J., Lee, C.H.: Fuzzy information retrieval based on multirelationship fuzzy concept networks. In: Fuzzy Sets and Systems, vol. 140, pp. 183–205. Elsevier B. V, Amsterdam (2003)
10. Horng, Y.J., Chen, S.M., Lee, C.H.: Automatically constructing multi-relationship fuzzy concept networks for document retrieval. In: Applied Artificial Intelligence, vol. 17, pp. 303–328. Taylor & Francis, Philadelphia (2003)
11. Apache lucene overview, http://lucene.apache.org/java/docs/index.html
12. Bratsas, C., Koutkias, V., Kaimakamis, E., Bamidis, P., Maglaveras, N.: Ontology-based vector space model and fuzzy query expansion to retrieve knowledge on medical computational problem solutions. In: 29th IEEE Annual International Conference on Engineering in Medicine and Biology Society, pp. 3794–3797. IEEE Computer Society, Washington (2007)
13. Pereira, R., Ricarte, I., Gomide, F.: Fuzzy relational ontological model in information search systems. In: Sanchez, E. (ed.) Fuzzy Logic and The Semantic Web, pp. 395–412. Elsevier B. V, Amsterdam (2006)
14. Pedrycz, W., Gomide, F.: An introduction to fuzzy sets: Analysis and Design. MIT Press, Cambridge (1998)
15. Sisga - Ensino Mapa do Clima no Brasil, http://campeche.inf.furb.br/sisga/educacao/ensino/mapaClima.php
16. Köppen, http://en.wikipedia.org/wiki/Koppen_climate_classification

Recommendation System for Automatic Recovery of Broken Web Links*

Juan Martinez-Romo and Lourdes Araujo

Dpto. Lenguajes y Sistemas Informáticos. UNED, Madrid 28040, Spain
juaner@lsi.uned.es, lurdes@lsi.uned.es

Abstract. In the web pages accessed when navigating throughout Internet, or even in our own web pages, we sometimes find links which are not valid any more. The search of the right web pages which correspond to those links is often hard. In this work we have analyzed different sources of information to automatically recover broken web links so that the user can be offered a list of possible pages to substitute that link. Specifically, we have used either the anchor text or the web page containing the link, or a combination of both. We report the analysis of a number of issues arising when trying to recover a set of links randomly chosen. This analysis has allowed us to decide the cases in which the system can perform the retrieval of some pages to substitute the broken link. Results have shown that the system is able to do reliable recommendations in many cases, specially under certain conditions on the anchor text and the parent page.

Keywords: information retrieval, World Wide Web, broken links.

1 Introduction

The web is a highly dynamic system with a continuous creation, deletion and movement of web pages. This often causes page links to become broken some time after the page creation. We now and then find this situation in Internet. This problem also forces us to verify frequently our own pages to check if their links are still valid. The search of the new location of a page that has been moved, or of a new page whose contain is similar to a disappeared page, is sometimes a difficult task. In the case of our own pages, the task can be easier, but still tedious.

There have been some attempts to recover broken links. Most of them are based on information annotated in advance with the link. Davis [1] has studied the causes that provoke the existence of broken links and has proposed solutions focussed on collecting information on the links in its creation or modification. The Webvise system [2], integrated with Microsoft software, stores annotations in hypermedia databases external to the web pages. This allows the system to provide a certain degree of capacity to recover integrated broken links. The information is stored when the links are created or modified. Shimada and Futakata

* Supported by project TIN2007-67581-C02-01.

H. Geffner et al. (Eds.): IBERAMIA 2008, LNAI 5290, pp. 302–311, 2008.

[3] designed the Self-Evolving Database (SEDB), which stores only links in a centralized fashion while documents are left in their native formats at their original locations. When a document is missing, the SEDB reorganizes all links formerly connected to the missing document in order to preserve the topology of links.

Nakamizo et al. [4] have developed a software tool that finds new URLs of web pages after pages are moved. The tool outputs a list of web pages sorted by their plausibility of being link authorities. Links contained in the link authority pages are expected to be well-maintained and updated after the linked pages are moved. In this work, a page v is called a link authority of another web page u if (1) v includes the link to u, and (2) if u is moved to u_{new}, the link to u in v is always changed to the link to u_{new}. This system uses a link authority server which collects links to u and then sorts them by plausibility. This plausibility is based on a set of attributes concerning the relations among links and directories.

Thought with a purpose different to repairing broken links, other works have investigate mechanisms to extract information from the links and the context they appear in. Some of these mechanisms have been tested in our system for recovering broken links. McBryan [5] proposed to use the anchor text as a help to the search of web resources. This work describes the tool WWWW intended to locate resources on the Internet. The WWWW program surfs the Internet locating web resources and builds a database of these. Each HTML file found is indexed with the title string used in there. Each URL referenced in an HTML file is also indexed. The system allows searching on document titles, reference hypertext, or within the components of the URL name strings. Chakrabarti et al. [6] have developed an automatic resource compiler which, given a topic that is broad and well-represented on the web, seeks out and returns a list of web resources that it considers the most authoritative for that topic. The system is built on an algorithm that performs a local analysis of both text and links to arrive at a "global consensus" of the best resources for the topic.

Our work differs from previous proposal since it does not rely on any information about the links annotated in advance, and it can be applied to any web page.

Sometimes we can recover a broken link by entering the anchor text as a user query in a search engine. However, there are many cases in which the anchor text does not contain enough information to do that. In these cases, we can compose queries adding terms extracted from other sources of information — the text of the web page that contains the link, the page stored in the cache of the search engine, if it exists, the Url, etc.— to the anchor text of the broken link.

In this work we have developed a system to perform this process automatically. Our system checks the links of the page given as input. For those which are broken, the system proposes to the user a set of candidate pages to substitute the broken link. The candidate pages are obtained by submitting to a search engine queries composed of terms extracted from different sources. In order to tune the results, the pages recovered in this way are ranked according to relevance measures obtained by applying information retrieval techniques. The resulting list of pages is presented to the user. Figure 1 presents a scheme of the proposed system.

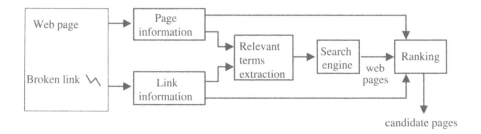

Fig. 1. Scheme of the system for automatic recovering of broken links

This work has begun by analyzing a large number of web pages and their links in order to determine which ones are the most useful sources of information and which of them are the most appropriate in each case. This study has allowed us to extract criteria to determine, for a particular broken link, whether it makes sense to look for candidate pages to recommend to the user, or whether the available information is not enough to attempt the recovering.

The remaining of the paper proceeds as follows: section 2 describes the methodology we have followed to evaluate the suitability of the sources of information considered; section 3 presents the analysis of those sources of information; section 4 is devoted to describe the process to rank the candidate documents; section 5 describes the scheme resulting of the previous analysis, as well as the results of applying it to a set of broken web links. Finally, section 6 draws the main conclusions of this work.

2   Methodology

If we analyze the usefulness of the different sources of information directly employed on broken links, it is very difficult to evaluate the quality of the candidate pages to replace the link. Therefore, at this phase of analysis, we employ random web links, which are not really broken, and we called *pseudobroken* links. Thus we have the page at which they point and we are able to evaluate our recommendation.

2.1   Selection of Links to Recover

To carry out the analysis, we take links from pages selected randomly by means of successive requests to *www.randomwebsite.com*, a site that provides random web pages. Certain requisites are imposed to our test pages. We tried to restrict the language to English, considering the following domains: ".com ", ".org ", ".net ", ".gov " and ".edu". Pages with at least 250 words are required for using its text to characterize this page. Moreover, the text will have to contain at least ten terms that are not stop words, that is, words that are so common that they are ignored in information retrieval (e.g. articles, pronouns, etc.) We also demand that the page have at least five potentially *analyzable links*, which means:

- The system analyzes external links, therefore links that point to the same site are discarded.
- The anchor text must neither be empty nor be a number or an URL.
- If the anchor text is only formed of one character and it also coincides with a punctuation mark, this link is discarded.

Pages not fulfilling these requirements are discarded, and the selection process does not finish until one hundred pages are collected, what amounts to having at least 500 links to study. Some preliminary experiments indicated us that it is frequent to find pages in which most of the links are online and others in which most of them are broken. When these pages have many links, they bias the results in some way or another. Because of this we have decided to limit the number of links taken per page to ten. This subset of links is randomly chosen among the analyzable links in the page.

3   Sources of Information

In this section we analyze each source of information considered, extracting statistics of its usefulness for the recovery of links when they are applied separately or combined.

3.1   Anchor Text in a Hyperlink

In many cases the words which compose the anchor text of a hyperlink are the main source of information to identify the pointed page. To verify this theory we have performed a study which can be observed in the Table 1. This table shows the number of cases in which the broken links have been recovered, searching in Google the anchor text in inverted commas.

A combination of different tests to consider that a link has been recovered has been used. First of all it is verified if the Url from the page candidate to replace the link matches the analyzed link (remember that in this analysis the link is not really broken). Nevertheless, we have found some cases in which the recovered page has the same content as that of the pseudobroken link, but different Url. Therefore if the Urls do not match, we verify whether the web page content is the same. We have also found several cases in which the page content is not identical, but they were very similar: there are some small changes like advertisements, dates, etc. For this reason, if the contents are not exactly the same, we apply the vector space model [7], i.e we represent each page by a term vector and calculate the cosine distance between them (similarity). If this value is higher than 0.9, we consider that the page has been recovered. For lower values than this threshold (e.g. 0.8), we sometimes recover different pages. We have measured the number of recovered links according to this threshold. Table 1 shows these results. We can observe that using a similarity threshold of 0.9, 41% of the links are recovered in the top ten results (*Google*). In addition, 66% of the recovered links appear in the first position. These results prove that the anchor text is a good source of information to recover a broken link. Lowering the similarity threshold adds very

Table 1. Results of searching the anchor text in Google in terms on the similarity degree used. First column indicates the similarity degree used. *1st pos.* represents the number of pseudobroken links recovered in the first position from the results of the search engine, and *1-10 pos.* the number of those recovered among the first 10 positions. *N.R.L.* represents the links have not been recovered.

Sim. Degree	1st pos.	1-10 pos.	N.R.L.
0.9	253	380	536
0.8	256	384	529
0.7	258	390	521
0.6	262	403	504
0.5	266	425	478

few additional links to the list of recovered ones. Besides, doing this increases the number of wrong results. For these reasons, we have chosen for the degree of similarity a threshold value of 0.9.

Sometimes the anchor terms are little or no descriptive at all. Let us imagine a link whose anchor text is "click here". In this case, finding the broken link might be impossible. For this reason it is very important to analyze these terms so as to be able to decide which tasks should be performed depending on their quantity and quality.

In this work we have chosen to carry out a recognition of named entities (persons, organizations or places) on the anchor text in order to extract certain terms whose importance is higher than the remaining ones. There exist several software solutions for this task, such as *LingPipe, Gate, FreeLing*, etc. There also exist multiple resources, like *gazetteers*. But none of these solutions have provide precise results working with the anchors, perhaps because we are working in a wide domain. In addition, the size of the anchor texts is too small for the kind of analysis usually performed by these systems.

Accordingly, we have decided to use the opposite strategy. Instead of finding named entities, we have chosen to compile a set of dictionaries to discard the common words and numbers, assuming that the rest of words are named entities. Although we have found some false negatives, as for example the company "Apple", we have obtained better results using this technique.

Table 2 shows the number of pseudobroken links recovered depending on the presence of named entities in the anchors, and on the number of anchor terms. We can see that when the anchor does not contain any named entity, the number of links that are not recovered is much higher than the number of the recovered ones, whereas both quantities are similar when there exist named entities. This proves that the presence of any named entity in the anchor favors the recovery of the link. Another result is the very small number of cases in which the correct document is recovered when the anchor consists of just a term and it is not a named entity[1]. When the anchor contains named entities, even if there is only one, the number

---

[1] These few cases are usually Url domains with a common name, e.g. the anchor "Flock" has allowed recovering www.flock.com, the anchor "moo" the Url www.moo.com/flicker, etc.

Table 2. Analysis of not recovered (*N.R.L.*) and recovered links (*R.L.*) according to the type of anchor — with (*Named E.*) and without (*No Named E.*) named entities— and to the number of anchor terms. *4+* refers to anchors with four or more terms.

	Type of anchor			
	Named E.		No Named E.	
Terms	N. R. L.	R. L.	N. R. L.	R. L.
1	102	67	145	7
2	52	75	91	49
3	29	29	27	45
4+	57	61	33	47
total	240	232	296	148

of retrieved cases is significant. Another fact that we can observe is that from two terms on, the number of anchor terms does not represent a big change in the results.

3.2 The Page Text

The most frequent terms of a web page are a way to characterize the main topic of the cited page. This technique requires the page text to be long enough. A clear example of utility of this information are the links to personal pages. The anchor of a link to a personal page is frequently formed by the name of the person to whom the page corresponds. However, in many cases, the forename and surname do not identify a person in a unique way. For example, if we search in Google "Juan Martínez", we obtain a huge amount of results (99.900 aprox. at the time that this paper was wrote). The first result of the search engine which corresponds to Juan Martínez Romo appears in the tenth position. However, if we expand the query using some term present at his web page, such as "web search", then his personal web page goes up to the first position. This example shows how useful is using a suitable choice of terms.

We have applied classical information retrieval techniques to extract the most representative terms from a page. After eliminating the stop words, we generate a term list ranked by frequencies. The first ten terms of this list are used to expand the query formed by the anchor text, i.e. the query is expanded with each of those terms, and the first ten documents retrieved in each case are taken.

In Table 3 we can observe that the expansion considerably increases the number of links recovered in the first ten positions. In spite of this, the number of recovered links in the first position is reduced.

Table 4 shows the number of cases in which the expansion has improved or worsened the results. We can see that, although the number of cases in which the expansion improves the results is quite higher (almost twice: 90 against 52), the number of cases in which it get worse is not negligible. Accordingly, we think that the most suitable mechanism is to apply both recovery ways, later ranking the whole set of results to present the user the most important ones in the first places.

Analyzing the cases in which it becomes possible to recover the correct page with and without named entities and according to the number of terms of the

Table 3. Analysis of the number of retrieved documents in the first position (*1st pos.*), those retrieved among the first 10 positions (*1-10 pos.*) and the links that have not been recovered (*N.R.L.*), according to whether we use query expansion (*EXP*) or not (*No EXP*).

Analysis	1st pos.	1-10 pos.	N.R.L.
No EXP	253	380	536
EXP	213	418	498

Table 4. Number of cases in which the query expansion improves and worsens the results

Expansion	N of Cases
Improvements	90
Worsenings	52

Table 5. Number of not recovered (*N.R.L.*) and recovered links (*R.L.*) according to the type of anchor, with (*Named E.*) and without (*No Named E.*) named entities, and to the number of anchor terms, when the query expansion method is applied. *4+ term.* refers to anchors with four or more terms.

	Type of anchor			
	Named E.		No Named E.	
Terms	N. R. L.	R. L.	N. R. L.	R. L.
1	104	65	127	25
2	55	72	70	70
3	30	28	22	50
4+	59	59	31	49
total	248	224	250	194

anchor (Table 5) we observe that the results are better than without expansion. However, they present the same trends as in the case without expansion: the worst result corresponds to the case with an only term and without named entities, and, in general results are better if there are named entities. Nevertheless, with the current method (query expansion) the number of recovered links, when the anchor consists of just a term and it is not a named entity, is 25. This last value can be considered as a significant quantity. This suggests trying to recover using query expansion in this case too, as long as it is possible to validate the obtained results. This validation is explained in section 4.

4   Ranking the Recommended Links

At this point we have retrieved a set of candidate pages to replace the broken link. These pages are the results of searching in the web with the anchor and with

Table 6. Occurrences of the best candidate page in the elaborated ranking, selecting the N best candidates according to the similarity with the reference page: cache or parent page

Occurrences of the Best Candidate							
First N selected docs	10	20	30	50	80	100	110
Cache page	301	305	306	307	310	312	313
Parent page	47	105	132	191	263	305	313

the anchor plus terms from the parent page. Now we want to present the results to the user in decreasing order of relevance. To calculate this relevance we have considered two sources of information. First, if it exists, we use the page pointed to by the broken link saved in the search engine cache, in this case *Google*. If this information does not exist, then we use the parent page which contains the broken link. The idea is that the pointed page's topic will be related to one of the parent page.

Once again we have applied the vector space model [7] to study the similarity between the analyzed page and its broken links. With this technique, we calculate the similarity either with the cache page or with the parent page. Table 6 shows the obtained results ranked by similarity with the cache and the parent page. In the first case, most of the correct retrieved documents appear between the first ten documents, therefore if we can retrieve the cache page, we will be able to do very trustworthy recommendations. In the second case, using the similarity with the parent page, the order of the results is worse. Thus, we will resort to this information only if we can not get the cache page.

5   Strategy for Automatic Recovery of Links

The results of the analysis described in the previous sections suggest several criteria to decide for which cases there is enough information to try the retrieval of the link and which sources of information to use. According to them, we propose the following recovery process. First of all, it is checked whether the anchor number of terms is just one and whether it does not contain named entities. If both features are found, the retrieval is only attempted provided the link of the missing page appears in the cache, and therefore we have reliable information to verify that the proposal presented to the user can be useful. Otherwise, the user is informed that the recommendation is not possible. If the page is in the cache, then the recovery is performed, expanding the query (anchor terms) with extracted terms from the parent page. Then the results are ranked and only if any of them is sufficiently similar to the cache content, the user is recommended this list of candidate documents. In the remaining cases, that is, when the anchor has more than one term or when it contains some named entity, the recovery is performed using the anchor terms and the terms from

Table 7. Number of recovered links (best candidate which content is very similar to the missing page) according to his cache similarity, between N first documents ranked by similarity with the parent page. The total number of broken links investigated were twenty five.

First N docs.	R.L.
1-10	12
10-20	7
20-50	6

the parent page. After that, all documents are grouped and ranked according to the cache page if it is available in Google, or according to the parent page otherwise.

We have applied this strategy to links that are really broken, but we have only used those that were present in the Google cache. The reason is that only in this case we can evaluate the results. Table 7 shows the quantity of recovered links (best candidate whose content is very similar to the missing page) ranking the results by means of the similarity with the parent page (the page cache is only used to measure relevance). We have verified that in some cases the original page is found (it has been moved to other Url). In some other cases, we have retrieved pages with very similar content. We can observe that, even if we are not using the cache similarity and we rank with the similarity with the parent page, the system is able to provide useful replacements documents between the first 10 positions in 48% of the cases, and between the 20 first ones in 76% of the cases.

6   Conclusions and Future Work

In this work we have analyzed different sources of information that we can use to carry out an automatic recovery of web links that are not valid anymore. Results indicate that the anchor terms can be very useful, especially if there are more than one and if they contain some named entity. We have also studied the effect of using terms from the page that contains the link for expanding the queries. In this way, we reduce the ambiguity that would entail the limited quantity of anchor terms. This study has showed that the results are better when the query is expanded than when using only the anchor terms. However, since there are cases in which the expansion worsens the recovery results, we have decided to combine both methods, later sorting the documents obtained by relevance, to present to the user the best candidate pages at the beginning. The result of this analysis has allowed us to design a strategy that has been able to recover a page very similar to the missing one in the top ten of the results in 48% cases, and between the top 20 in 76%. At this moment we work in analyzing other sources of information that can be useful for the retrieval, as the Urls or the pages that point to the page which contains the broken link.

References

1. Davis, H.: Hypertext link integrity. In: ACM Computing Surveys Electronic Symposium on Hypertext and Hypermedia, vol. 31(4) (2000)
2. Grønbæk, K., Sloth, L., Ørbæk, P.: Webvise: Browser and proxy support for open hypermedia structuring mechanisms on the world wide web. Computer Networks 31(11-16), 1331–1345 (1999)
3. Shimada, T., Futakata, A.: Automatic link generation and repair mechanism for document management. In: HICSS 1998: Proceedings of the Thirty-First Annual Hawaii International Conference on System Sciences, Washington, DC, USA, vol. 2, p. 226. IEEE Computer Society, Los Alamitos (1998)
4. Nakamizo, A., Iida, T., Morishima, A., Sugimoto, S., Kitagawa, H.: A tool to compute reliable web links and its applications. In: SWOD 2005: Proc. International Special Workshop on Databases for Next Generation Researchers, pp. 146–149. IEEE Computer Society, Los Alamitos (2005)
5. McBryan, O.A.: GENVL and WWWW: Tools for Taming the Web. In: Nierstarsz, O. (ed.) Proceedings of the first International World Wide Web Conference, CERN, Geneva, p. 15 (1994)
6. Chakrabarti, S., Dom, B., Gibson, D., Kleinberg, J., Raghavan, P., Rajagopalan, S.: Automatic resource list compilation by analyzing hyperlink structure and associated text. In: Proceedings of the 7th International World Wide Web Conference (1998)
7. Manning, C.D., Raghavan, P., Schütze, H.: Introduction to Information Retrieval. Cambridge University Press, Cambridge (2008)

Conceptual Subtopic Identification in the Medical Domain

Rafael Berlanga-Llavori[1], Henry Anaya-Sánchez[2], Aurora Pons-Porrata[2], and Ernesto Jiménez-Ruiz[1]

[1] Department of Languages and Computer Systems
Universitat Jaume I, Castelló, Spain
{berlanga,ejimenez}@lsi.uji.es
[2] Center for Pattern Recognition and Data Mining
Universidad de Oriente, Santiago de Cuba, Cuba
{henry,aurora}@cerpamid.co.cu

Abstract. In this paper we present a novel approach for identifying and describing the possible subtopics that can be derived from the result set of a topic-based query. Subtopic descriptions rely on the conceptual indexing of the retrieved documents, which consists of mapping the document terms into concepts of an existing thesaurus (i.e. UMLS meta-thesaurus). Subtopic identification is performed by selecting highly probable concept bigrams whose support sets are homogeneous enough. The evaluation of the method has been carried out on a real biomedical example, which demonstrates both the effectiveness and usefulness of the proposed method.

Keywords: conceptual indexing, text mining, biomedical applications.

1 Introduction

One of the more challenging issues of forthcoming decision support systems will be to integrate the potential knowledge of document sources to the decision-making processes. Unfortunately, nowadays the only way analysts have to discover such a knowledge consists of manually exploring a ranked list of documents retrieved with a keyword-based query. There exist some preliminary approaches that aim to build a conceptual space from a document collection (e.g. [1]) by associating frequent word co-occurrences to concepts of an external knowledge source. In the medical domain, novel tools also aim at capturing interesting co-occurrences from tagged text collections to show users the implicit knowledge behind them. EbiMed[1] and MedStory[2] are two good examples. However, these approaches have the disadvantage of relying on a very limited subset of co-occurrences, which may not be representative of the relevant topics behind the collection. Indeed, some strong co-occurrences are common phrases that do

---

[1] http://www.ebi.ac.uk/Rebholz-srv/ebimed/
[2] http://www.medstory.com/

H. Geffner et al. (Eds.): IBERAMIA 2008, LNAI 5290, pp. 312–321, 2008.

not imply any topic. Unfortunately, statistical interest measures as those used in these works are not able to capture the topic aboutness of the co-occurrences.

More recently, there has been a great interest within the Information Retrieval community about the Subtopic Retrieval task [4,7]. This basically consists of re-arranging the query result so that documents implying different subtopics of the query can be accessed from the top of the rank. Notice that this task can be very interesting in a medical scenario, where clinicians can fetch broad queries about a disease or treatment and then explore the different methods or viewpoints associated to them. However, notice also that they are not able to identify all the relevant documents that would be associated to a concrete subtopic as they only get a representative part of the subtopic.

In this paper we propose a new method for the conceptual identification of subtopics. As in the Subtopic Retrieval task, we identify the subtopics by pro-cessing the result set of a document search query. However, we aim at retrieving all the relevant documents to each identified subtopic rather than re-ranking the result set. Similarly to the approaches based on word co-occurrences, our method uses highly probable concept bigrams to guide the identification of subtopics. But contrary to them, the quality of each concept bigram is measured with the coherence of its document support set. The resulting method has two main ad-vantages: we can ensure the aboutness of the identified subtopic and, we can describe the subtopic with the concept bigram that originates it.

The proposed method has been developed in the context of the Health-e-Child european project[3], which aims at developing an integrated platform for biomedical information and decision-support tools to assess the decision-making processes in the Paediatrics domain. Thus, this work can be seen as part of the process of linking patients data to external document sources such as MEDLINE[4] and OMIM[5].

The paper is organized as follows. Section 2 is mainly dedicated to describe the process of conceptual indexing of a document collection. Section 3 concerns with the identification of subtopics from the result of a topic-based query. Section 4 shows the experiments carried out over a real example in Biomedicine. Finally, we give some conclusions and future works.

2   Conceptual Indexing

In Figure 1, we depict the overall process of the conceptual subtopic identifica-tion. Broadly speaking, it can be divided into two main phases: the conceptual indexing of the results obtained via a topic-based query (e.g. a specific dis-ease) and, the identification of the document groups that can be associated to subtopics of the user query. This section is devoted to the former phase.

Conceptual indexing of a collection consists of finding a set of concepts to describe its contents. Usually concepts are taken from well-established external

---

[3] http://www.health-e-child.org
[4] http://www.ncbi.nlm.nih.gov/pubmed/
[5] OnlineMendelianInheritanceinMan:http://www.ncbi.nlm.nih.gov/omim/

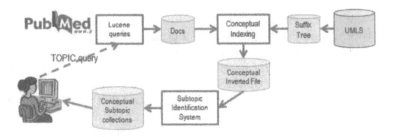

Fig. 1. General architecture of our proposal

knowledge sources such as WordNet or specific-purpose thesauri. External knowledge sources usually consist of two parts, namely: a very large lexicon with the different lexical variants of the concepts and, a set of semantic relationships between concepts (e.g. "is a", "part of", etc.). In the context of this paper, conceptual indexing allows us to homogenize the terminology used in the medical documents and, additionally to organize the detected subtopics according to the concept hierarchies provided by the external knowledge sources.

2.1   Medical External Knowledge Sources

In the medical domain, conceptual indexing is critical for managing the huge volumes of scientific documents stored in publicly available repositories. For example, MEDLINE, the world's largest repository of medical publications, is indexed through the Medical Subject Heading (MeSH), which allows users to search and browse the publications more effectively. However, MeSH concepts are too much broad to be useful for other purposes like document analysis. Moreover, as MeSH concepts are assigned by authors, the resulting annotations may not cover properly the interesting details contained in the documents. For this reason, it is preferable to automate as much as possible the conceptual indexing of the document contents.

In this work, we use the Unified Medical Language System (UMLS) [3] as the external knowledge source. The UMLS Metathesaurus is one of the three components of the UMLS Project and comprises many different controlled and well-known vocabularies[6] such as MeSH, SNOMED CT or ICD. Each UMLS concept is linked to a set of synonyms available in the associated vocabularies. In addition, UMLS provides relations between concepts such as taxonomic relations and relations provided by the UMLS Semantic Network. The UMLS Semantic Network is an additional component in the UMLS Project and aims to be the Upper Level Ontology for the Biomedicine domain, defining around 135 semantic types (e.g. 'Disease or Syndrome', 'Gene Function', etc.) for term categorization.

Unfortunately, there are few approaches for automatically identifying concepts from medical documents. MetaMap [2] is the more referenced and widely accepted tool for such a purpose. The main limitation of MetaMap is that of

---

[6] UMLS Source Vocabularies: http://www.nlm.nih.gov/research/umls/metaa1.html

efficiency, which makes it non escalable for large document collections. An alternative method recently proposed in [6], called MWT (MultiWord Tagger), consists of applying pure dictionary look-up techniques based on finite state automata. This approach is very efficient, more precise than MetaMap but with lower recall values [5]. However, its main limitation is the enormous space required to allocate large lexicons. In fact, experiments carried out over a lexicon of 1,500,000 strings required of several piped MWTs, each one for a different subset of the UMLS [5].

2.2 Building the Conceptual Index

In this work we have avoided the problem of tagging a large collection by taking a global strategy. That is, instead of tagging one by one the documents of a collection, we aim to index with concepts the whole collection by merging both the vocabulary of the collection and the external lexicon.

We start with the inverted representation of the document collection. Thus, now each collection item is a single term (e.g. lemmatized word present in the collection) which has associated the set of its document hits. Obtaining the inverted representation of a document collection is straightforward.

On the other hand, the UMLS lexicon is organized into a suffix tree as follows. First, each lexicon string is processed to identify its head noun. This is done with a few simple rules that detect prepositions. Meaningless words are removed from the lexicon strings. Then, the string tokens are ordered so that the head appears first and its modifiers appear at the back. The resulting list is inserted into the suffix tree, where each token is associated to a tree node. Finally, concepts associated to each string are attached to the node of its last token. Figure 2 presents a fragment of the resulting suffix tree. In this case, concepts are expressed as CUIs (Concept Unique Identifiers) of UMLS. Notice that some paths of the tree lead to ambiguous conceptual representations.

The process of merging both the inverted file and the suffix tree is described in Algorithm 1. This basically follows a greedy strategy so that paths of the suffix tree are transformed into queries for the inverted file. As a result, each concept

```
joint|C0444497,C0555829,C0022417,C1706309,C1269611,C0558540
        spherical|C0224504
        pastern|C1279617
        Jaw|C0039493
        zygapophyseal|C0224521
                entire|C1267117
                thoracic|C0504605
        tibiofemoral|C1269072,C0447795
                right|C0834358
                left|C0834359
        xiphisternal|C0447790,C1280647
```

Fig. 2. Fragment of the suffix tree of the UMLS lexicon

Algorithm 1. Algorithm for merging lexicons and inverted files

---

Input: Suffix Tree FP; Inverted File FI.
Output: Conceptual Inverted File $FCUI$.
  1. **for all** maximal path p in FP (ordered by length) **do**
       Normalize p according to the rules applied to the inverted file FI
       Revise.append($p[0]$)
       while $|p| > 1$ **do**
           if p has concepts in FP **then**
               $R=FI.query(p)$
               if $|R| > 0$ **then**
                   update $FCUI$ with $FCUI[FP.concepts(p)]=R$
                   update FI removing the elements of R associated to p
               end if
               p.removeLastToken()
           end if
       end while
    end for
  2. **for all** p in *Revise* **do**
       $R=FI.query(p)$
       if $|R| > 0$ **then**
           update $FCUI$ with $FCUI[FP.concepts(p)]=R$
       end if
    end for

---

accessed through a path is associated to the documents retrieved with its query. More specifically, the algorithm takes each maximal path of the suffix tree and produces a query for each of its subpaths with length greater than one. If such a query successes, the retrieved documents are associated to the concepts reached with the corresponding path. Consequently, the references of the retrieved documents are removed from the inverted file entries associated to the query. In this way, these references are not regarded again when checking other subpaths. It is worth mentioning that inverted file queries are evaluated as boolean expressions, which takes into account plural/singular forms and proximity contraints between query terms.

3   Subtopic Identification

As previously mentioned, our aim is to discover the subtopics comprised in the set of documents retrieved for a query, and simultaneously provide a short descriptive label for each one. We assume that no prior knowledge about the subtopic distribution exists, and therefore our subtopic identification strategy is completely automatic.

Starting from the set of documents $D = \{d_1, \ldots, d_n\}$ retrieved for a topic-based query (documents are represented as bag of words build from the conceptual index), our method involves two main processes: *subquery generation* and *subtopic identification*. The subqueries are generated from concept bigrams likely to occur in the document set, which guide the search for a "good" subtopic structure in the discovery process. We define the probability of generating a concept bigram $\{c_i, c_j\}$ from D as:

$$P(\{c_i, c_j\}|D) = \sum_{d \in D} P(c_i|d)P(c_j|d)P(d|D)$$

where $P(d|D)$ is the probability of selecting document d from among all documents in D, and $P(c_i|d)$ and $P(c_j|d)$ represent the probability of generating concepts c_i and c_j from d respectively.

As the elements of a bigram could represent the same concept because of the conceptual indexing method, we filter out those concept bigrams that identify a collocation in D using the log-likelihood ratio test. We have restricted ourselves to concept bigrams in order to simplify the discovery of subtopics. In the future work, we will extend this framework to consider unigrams and n-grams.

Thus, starting from the most probable concept bigram, its support set (i.e., the set of documents in D that contain both concepts c_i and c_j) is built. If this set is *homogeneous in contents*, a subtopic consisting of the *set of relevant documents for the contents labeled by the bigram* is identified. The concept bigram becomes the subtopic's descriptive label. In case that the support set is not homogeneous in contents, the bigram is discarded.

We define a support set $D|_{\{c_i, c_j\}}$ to be homogeneous in contents if the "pure" entropy of the partition induced by the connected components of the β-similarity graph of $D|_{\{c_i, c_j\}}$ is less than 1. Given a similarity function s, the β-similarity graph is an undirected graph whose vertices are the documents in $D|_{\{c_i, c_j\}}$, and there is an edge between documents d_i and d_j if they are β-similar (i.e., $s(d_i, d_j) \geq \beta$). We estimate β from the average similarity of each document and its $\sqrt{n}$-most similar documents.

The pure entropy of a partition $\Theta = \{\Theta_1, \ldots, \Theta_k\}$ is calculated as follows:

$$H(\Theta) = -\sum_{i=1}^{k} P(\Theta_i|\Theta) \log_2 P(\Theta_i|\Theta)$$

where $P(\Theta_i|\Theta)$ can be estimated as $\dfrac{|\Theta_i|}{\sum_{j=1}^{k} |\Theta_j|}$.

As entropy expresses the average number of bits required to encode some information, this definition stems from the following fact: if less than one bit is needed to encode a partition, then it includes a predominant component representing the contents of the support set. We will call *core*, denoted as $core(D|_{\{c_i, c_j\}})$, to this predominant component.

We define the set of relevant documents for the contents labeled by $\{c_i, c_j\}$, $Rel(D|_{\{c_i, c_j\}})$, as:

$$core(D|_{\{c_i, c_j\}}) \cup \{d \in D \,|\, \exists d' \in core(D|_{\{c_i, c_j\}})[s(d, d') = \max_{d'' \in D} s(d, d'') \geq \beta]\}$$

that is, the core of its support set together with those documents in D whose most β-similar document belongs to the core.

Algorithm 2. Subtopic Identification Method.

Input: A set of documents $D = \{d_1, \ldots, d_n\}$ retrieved for a query.
Output: The identified subtopics, each one labeled with a concept bigram.

1. Subquery generation:
    (a) Find all concept bigrams $\{c_i, c_j\}$ such that:
        i. it maximizes the probability $P(\{c_i, c_j\}|D)$, and
        ii. it is not identified as a collocation in D by the log-likelihood ratio test.
    (b) If there are no concept bigrams satisfying the previous conditions then
          Return the identified subtopics.
2. Subtopic identification:
    (a) For each subquery $\{c_i, c_j\}$:
        i. If $D|_{\{c_i, c_j\}}$ is homogeneous in contents then
             Identify $Rel(D|_{\{c_i, c_j\}})$ as a subtopic labeled by $\{c_i, c_j\}$.
    (b) Remove all documents belonging to the identified subtopics from D.
    (c) Go to Step 1.

Once a subtopic has been identified, its documents are removed from D. Then, a new subquery is generated from the remaining document set, and the subtopic identification process is carried out again. These processes are repeated until no more concept bigrams can be found. The general steps of our proposal are shown in Algorithm 2.

4   Evaluation

In order to evaluate our proposal, we have conducted several experiments over a collection of 7654 documents related to the *Juvenile Idiopathic Arthritis* (JIA), which have been retrieved from MEDLINE (a collection with 17M biomedical abstracts). The topic-based query has been built with a boolean query expanded with all the lexical variants of the concept JIA found in UMLS.

For evaluating the precision of the conceptual indexing process, we compare the conceptual inverted file obtained with Algorithm 1 with one representing the same collection but tagged with MWT [6]. As earlier mentioned, the latter approach can be only applied on separate subsets of UMLS. For this evaluation we have included the subsets that correspond to the semantic types: *disease, tissue, protein, organ* and *treatment*. The MWT approach identifies 6810 concepts in the JIA collection, against 11274 identified in our approach. The overall agreement between the hit lists of the common concepts identified by both approaches is around 0.89. However, there are 11% of concepts detected by MWT that are not detected by our approach. Some of these missing concepts are associated to lexicon forms that cannot be properly detected with inverted file queries as they contain tokens that are not indexed (e.g. numbers). Other missing concepts correspond to wrong annotations produced by MWT taggers, mainly those involving acronyms. In any case, a deeper study should be done in the future to determine the real precision and recall of our approach. Despite the potential loss of coverage of our approach, we consider the estimated precision good enough to perform with some certainty the subtopic identification.

Algorithm 2 divides the JIA collection into 424 non-single groups. Table 1 describes the top-15 subtopics ranked according to their size. Comments associated to each subtopic have been contrasted with knowledge provided by experts of the HeC project and the Wikipedia entry for this disease. In general, the identified subtopics correspond to real subtopics of JIA, although there are some subtopics that are rather related to Rheumatoid Arthritis (RA). This is because JIA can be seen as a negation of other arthritis with known causes, so it is frequent to find comparisons between them along the document collection. Moreover, JIA and RA shares some drug therapies to treat their common symptoms. Notice that thanks to the subtopic descriptions, users can detect easily the false subtopics, enabling them to focus on those more related to their needs. Thus, subtopics 6, 8, 10 and 15 of Table 1 can be considered out of focus for the JIA topic.

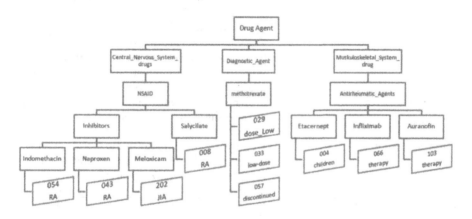

Fig. 3. Subtopics related to drugs according to UMLS hierarchy

Finally, in order to show the usefulness of the concept indexing, we have arranged the subtopics according to the concept hierarchies provided by UMLS. Figure 3 shows a fragment of the obtained hierarchy associated to drugs (not all subtopics have been included). It is worth mentioning that this hierarchy has been automatically generated from the subtopic descriptions (i.e. concept bigrams) and the "is-a" relationships of UMLS. In the figure, the subtopics are represented as instances of the concepts in the subtopic description (leaves in the hierarchy). The name of each instance includes the rank number of the subtopic and the other concept of the bigram. Notice that the concepts "therapy" and "RA" are the most frequent.

Table 1. Top-15 identified JIA subtopics

ID	Concept Bigram	Size	Explanation
1	Still's disease & adult	147	The still's disease (systemic JIA) has as main feature its persistance into adulthood and it can have an adult onset (AOSD).
2	Uveitis & childhood	72	Two main extra-articular manifestations characterize JIA diseases, namely: uveitis (eye inflammation) and growth disturbance. Both of them only affect to children.
3	Levels & Soluble	70	Many proteomics experiments involving JIA diseases measure the levels of soluble proteins associated to antigens and receptors.
4	Etacernept & children	65	Etarcernept is a TNF inhibitor recently applied to treat severe JIA (see also subtopic 12).
5	Gene allele & susceptibility	63	This subtopic covers the main research publications concerning the possible genetic origins of JIA diseases.
6	Treatment & gold	61	Gold salts have been applied to reduce inflammation in Rheumatoid Arthritis (RA) and more infrequently in JIA.
7	version & JIA	58	The Childhood Health Assesment Questionaire (CHAQ) is widely use for JIA patients. This subtopic covers different versions of CHAQ adapted to different cultures.
8	salycilate & RA	51	Non-steroid Antiinflammatory drugs (NSAID) are frequently used in RA and JIA. Salycilates are the main representatives of this drug group.
9	IgA & juvenile	49	Due to its autoimmune nature, JIA research concerns with the immunologic factors (e.g. IgA, IgM, etc) which are used in patient diagnosis and follow-up (see also subtopic 14).
10	patient & density bone	49	Bone erosion is one of the main side-effects of RA and JIA. Bone mineral density is a relevant indicator of disease progress.
11	transplatation & autologous	47	Autologous transplantation has been experimented on severe autoimmune diseases such as JIA but it has a high risk of fatal complications.
12	Etacernept & treatment	46	(see subtopic 4)
13	parents & questionaire	46	Parents play a relevant role in the follow-up of JIA patients. This is done through a series of questionaires.
14	IgM & hidden	45	(see subtopic 9)
15	total & replacement hip	45	Severe cases of JIA requires surgery. Hip replacement is one of the techniques.

5   Conclusions

In this paper a new approach for the identification of the subtopics comprised in the set of documents retrieved from a topic-based query has been presented. The major novelty of the proposal consists of the combination of both the use of a conceptual representation of documents and the generation of conceptual subqueries for guiding the identification of subtopics. The experiments carried out over a collection of documents relevant to the JIA disease retrieved from MEDLINE show the usefulness of the proposed method. Future work includes both improving the subtopic labeling and obtaining an ontological visualization of the identified subtopics.

Acknowledgements. This work has been partially supported by the Spanish National Research Project ICARO with contract number TIN2005-09098-C05-04.

References

1. Anaya-Sánchez, H., Berlanga-Llavori, R., Pons-Porrata, A.: Retrieval of Relevant Concepts from a Text Collection. In: Borrajo, D., Castillo, L., Corchado, J.M. (eds.) CAEPIA 2007. LNCS (LNAI), vol. 4788, pp. 21–30. Springer, Heidelberg (2007)
2. Aronson, A.R.: Effective mapping of biomedical text to the UMLS Metathesaurus: the MetaMap program. In: Proceeding of the AMIA Symposium 2001, pp. 17–21 (2001)
3. Bodenreider, O.: Lexical, Terminological, and Ontological Resources for Biological Text Mining. Text Mining for Biology and Biomedicine. Artech House (2006)
4. Dai, W., Srihari, R.: Minimal Document Set Retrieval. In: Herzog, O., Schek, H.-J., Fuhr, N., Chowdhury, A., Teiken, W. (eds.) Proceedings of the 14th ACM International Conference on Information and Knowledge Management, pp. 752–759. ACM, New York (2005)
5. Jimeno-Yepes, A., Jimenez-Ruiz, E., et al.: Assessment of diseases named entity recognition on a corpus of annotated sentences. BMC Bioinformatics 2008 9(suppl. 3), S3 (2008)
6. Rebholz-Schuhmann, D., et al.: Text processing through Web services: Calling Whatizit. Bioinformatics 24(2), 296–298 (2008)
7. Zhai, C., Cohen, W.W., Lafferty, J.D.: Beyond Independence Relevance: Methods and Evaluation Metrics for Subtopic Retrieval. In: Proceedings of the 26th Annual International ACM SIGIR Conference on Research and Development in Information Retrieval, pp. 10–17. ACM, New York (2003)

Real-Time Open-Domain QA
on the Portuguese Web

António Branco, Lino Rodrigues, João Silva, and Sara Silveira

University of Lisbon, Portugal
{antonio.branco,lino.rodrigues,jsilva,sara.silveira}@di.fc.ul.pt

Abstract. This paper presents a system for real-time, open-domain question answering on the Web of documents written in Portuguese, prepared to handle factual questions and available as a freely accessible online service. In order to deliver candidate answers to input questions phrased in Portuguese, this system resorts to a number of shallow processing tools and question answering techniques that are specifically geared to cope with the Portuguese language.

Keywords: natural language processing, question answering, QA, real-time QA, open-domain QA, web-based QA, factoids, QA online service.

1 Introduction

The Web allows the access to unparalleled amounts of publicly available online information. A credible estimate from the year 2005 places the indexable Web at 11.5 billion pages [1] and, since then, it has certainly kept growing.[1] Though expectedly smaller, the size of the Portuguese Web, consisting of documents written in Portuguese, should not be underestimated since Portuguese is likely to be one of the most used languages on the Internet—viz. the fourth most used according to an estimate published in the year 2002 [2].

Such a volume of data implies a considerable degree of redundancy as a given piece of information often happens to be phrased in many different ways and published in different sites. All this makes the Web a very attractive source of information when looking for answers to a large range of questions. Current Information Retrieval technology and popular search engines, however, do not deliver actual answers, even when simple factual questions are entered. Instead, for a list of input keywords, they return a list of documents and it is up to the user to seek a possible answer for his question within those documents.

Question Answering (QA) technology aims to go beyond the mere retrieval of relevant documents by returning possible answers to questions worded in plain natural language. This requires additional and more complex procedures which—this being the crucial point—are dependent on the specific idiom at stake.

In this paper we present XisQuê, a system for real-time, open-domain QA over the Portuguese Web. In order to deliver candidate answers to input questions

---

[1] http://www.worldwidewebsize.com, for instance, estimates 47 billion pages.

H. Geffner et al. (Eds.): IBERAMIA 2008, LNAI 5290, pp. 322–331, 2008.

phrased in Portuguese, this system resorts to a number of QA techniques and shallow processing tools, e.g. for part-of-speech annotation, morphological analysis, lemmatization or named entity recognition, that are specifically designed to cope with the Portuguese language.

This system supports a freely accessible online QA service, which can be found at `http://xisque.di.fc.ul.pt`.

Paper structure. Section 2 presents the architecture adopted for the QA system, and describes its major modules. Section 3 addresses other QA systems for Portuguese. In Section 4, the performance of XisQuê is evaluated and compared with that of other systems. Finally, in Section 5 we discuss ongoing work and paths for future development, and present concluding remarks.

2   The QA System

XisQuê is a QA system that has been developed to comply with the following major design features:

Portuguese input: the admissible input are reasonably well formed, fully-fledged questions from Portuguese (e.g. *Quem assassinou John Kennedy?*).

Real-time: upon receiving a question, the service provides output to human users in real-time, i.e. without any QA-specific pre-processing indexing procedure of documents that are the source of information for getting answers.

Web-based: the possible answers to the input question are searched in and extracted from documents retrieved on the fly from the Web.

Extraction-based: the returned answers are excerpts extracted verbatim from the retrieved documents, and displayed with no further processing.

Portuguese Web: the possible answers are those that can be found and extracted from the Portuguese Web, that is the collection of documents written in Portuguese and publicly available online.

Open-domain: the input questions may address issues from any subject domain (e.g. Sports, History, etc.)

At the heart of the system heart lies the QA infrastructure described in [3], which is responsible for handling the basic non-linguistic functionality. This includes the managing of requests to the QA service, the submitting of the queries to search engines, and the downloading of selected documents.

On top of this infrastructure, the natural language driven modules were implemented by using existing, state-of-the-art shallow processing tools, developed by our group [4,5,6].

The underlying architecture for this set of modules follows what has become a quite standard configuration, that has been explored and perfected in similar QA systems for other natural languages: The first phase deals with question processing; This is followed by a stage of document retrieval; Finally, the answers are extracted from the retrieved documents. The modules responsible for these functionalities are addressed in the following Sections.

2.1 Question Processing

In our system, the stage of question processing is concerned with three tasks: (i) Extraction of the main verb and major supporting noun phrase (NP) of the question; (ii) Detection of the expected semantic type of the answer; and (iii) Extraction of relevant keywords. Tasks (i) and (ii) deliver elements that will play a key role in a subsequent phase of processing, viz. the answer extraction stage. Task (iii), in turn, helps to create the query to be used in the document retrieval step.

Phrase extraction. The main verb and the major supporting NP of the question (e.g. *John Kennedy* in *Quem assassinou John Kennedy?*) are extremely useful for helping to pinpoint the candidate answer in the answer extraction stage. For example, in many cases, the simple inversion between that NP and the main verb will help match declarative sentences that may contain an answer:

> Q: Quando [nasceu]$_V$ [Nelson Mandela]$_{NP}$?
> *When was Nelson Mandela born?*
> A: [Nelson Mandela]$_{NP}$ [nasceu]$_V$ em...
> *Nelson Mandela was born in...*

In order to detect its phrases, and in particular its supporting NP, the question is firstly annotated with part-of-speech (POS) by a state-of-the-art tagger for Portuguese [4]. The phrases are then extracted with the help of patterns defined by regular expressions.

With respect to the patterns for capturing the main verb, they permit to grab simple verbs (e.g. assassinou), verbs with proclisis (e.g. se casaram), and verbs with other auxiliary verbs (e.g. foi assassinado).

As for the NPs, we adapted the pattern coming out of the detailed study of their structure in [7, p. 69]. This pattern builds upon a number of syntactic slots reflecting precedence constraints in terms of word order:

1. predeterminers (e.g. todos);
2. determiners (e.g. aquela);
3. prenominal possessives (e.g. suas);
4. cardinals, ordinals, vague quantifiers (e.g. três, terceira, muitos);
5. prenominal adjective phrases (e.g. grande);
6. *head* (e.g. bicicleta);
7. adjectival arguments (e.g. americana);
8. adjective phrase adjuncts, prepositional phrase arguments, prepositional phrase adjuncts, adverbial phrase adjuncts, postnominal possessives, postnominal demonstratives (e.g. intensa, com pedais, do Iraque, ali, teus, esse).

These slots can be mapped into the POS categories assigned by the tagger.[2] Naturally, this kind of "shallow" chunking is limited by the expressive power of regular expressions, but tends to produce satisfactory results given the purpose and the application at stake, and has the upside of being quick and efficient.

---

[2] The correspondence is specific to the tagset used. Readers interested in these details are referred to [4,7].

Answer type detection. Detecting the expected semantic type of the answer allows the system to narrow down the search space in the answer extraction stage. In that subsequent stage, we resort to a named entity recognizer (NER), which is able to identify expressions that behave like proper names for entities, and semantically classify them with one of a small set of pre-defined types, viz. PERSON, ORGANIZATION, LOCATION, NUMBER, MEASURE or TIME [6].

Accordingly, the answer that can be expected on the basis of the analysis of the input question is thus classified as being of one of these semantic types.

In many cases, the interrogative pronoun found in the question is a major clue and may be enough to anticipate the semantic type of the answer. For instance, the answer to a "Quando... ?" *(When... ?)* question will likely take the form of a time expression.[3]

In questions with the format "Que X... ?" *(Which X... ?)*, the interrogative pronoun does not provide enough information about the answer type. In these cases, the system uses a WordNet-like ontology which, though small, is yet large enough for the application at stake as it includes all the relevant sub-ontologies under the concepts that can be identified by the NER (PERSON, ORGANIZATION, etc.). For a given "Que X... ?" question, this ontology is instrumental in finding the hypernym of "X" that is the semantic type of the expected answer. For instance, in the following question

> Q: **Que pintor criou a Mona Lisa?**
> *Which painter created the Mona Lisa?*

the hypernyms of **pintor** will be recursively retrieved until one that corresponds to an answer type (viz. PERSON in this case) is found, as illustrated below.

$$\begin{array}{ccccc} \text{pintor} & \rightarrow \cdots \rightarrow & \text{artista} & \rightarrow \cdots \rightarrow & \text{pessoa} \\ \textit{painter} & & \textit{artist} & & \textit{person} \end{array}$$

Keyword extraction. For a given input question, the retrieval of documents where to look for its possible answers is done on the basis of a query. These queries are just a set of keywords. In order to obtain these keywords the system simply removes, from the input question, words belonging to the so-called closed, functional morphosyntactic categories. This implies that the keywords to be used for document retrieval are the words in the question pertaining to open classes.

For instance, for the question in the previous example, **Que pintor criou a Mona Lisa?**, the keywords would be **pintor**, **criou**, **Mona** and **Lisa**.

2.2 Document Retrieval

In order to perform the document retrieval task, the QA system acts as a client of several established high-quality search engines (viz. Ask, Google, MSN Live and

---

[3] This generalization has to be used with care. Exceptions to it can be found in cases like: Q: *When was Sting in Portugal?* A: *In Rock in Rio–Lisboa.* Though the question is introduced by *when,* the expected answer is not an expression denoting time but denoting an event. Exceptions with respect to the typical expected semantic type can also be found for other pronouns like *where* or *who.*

Yahoo!). The system thus needs only to submit the list of keywords extracted from the question to each search engine, taking care also to select the option that, for that engine, limits the search to online pages that are written in Portuguese.

However, after the search engines return their list of result links, there are still many tasks that are performed to prepare the documents for the next stage:

- The links to the resulting documents are extracted from the HTML page with the results provided by the search engine. The top 10 results of each search engine are retrieved, avoiding repeated URLs, for a total of 40 links;
- The extracted URLs are used to download the documents in case there is an HTML version of them available. To ensure that the system provides a quick answer, the size of the download is capped at 512 Kb, and a timeout mechanism is used to safeguard against site accessibility problems;
- The character encoding of the downloaded documents is made uniform by converting them to Windows-1252 (roughly, a superset of ISO-8859-1);
- For documents that happen to be downloaded more than once (i.e. from more than one site), duplicates are discarded to avoid irrelevant processing;[4]
- Documents are stripped from HTML markup (formatting, tables, frames, menus, etc.), leaving only plain text.

2.3   Answer Extraction

The answer extraction stage is divided into two tasks: (i) candidate selection, where the best sentences, i.e. those most likely to contain an answer, are selected using an heuristic; and (ii) answer extraction itself, where candidate answers are extracted from the selected sentences.

Candidate selection. The documents that were gathered are split into sentences, which are then ranked. The top ranking sentence are selected as possibly containing answers to the input question. These sentence are the ones that proceed to the answer extraction task, thus reducing the number of sentences that must be processed in that (more computationally expensive) step.

The criterion to select the sentences that should be retained is based on the number of keywords that are in the query that came out of the input question and occur in those sentences. The threshold function is $q \geq \lfloor \sqrt{Q-1} \rfloor + 1$ where q is the number of keywords found in the sentence and Q is the number of keywords in the query, following the heuristic adopted in [8].

If they happen to pass this threshold, the retained sentences are ranked, receiving a higher rank if they contain a higher number of keywords and these keywords occur adjacent to each other.

Answer extraction. The candidate sentences that remain in the final set are then annotated with a variety of linguistic information obtained with shallow

---

[4] Currently, a simple heuristic is used to determine if two documents are duplicates: If the snippet of a document, that is returned by the search engine, is contained in the other document, one of them is discarded.

processing tools, including POS, inflection features and lemmas.[5] The NER is then run over this annotated material. This is an hybrid tool, using regular expressions to detect entities with well-defined formats, mostly based on numbers (e.g. dates, measures, etc.) but relying on statistical methods for entities with a larger variation in format, mostly based on names (e.g. persons, organizations, etc). In addition, this tool also classifies entities according to their semantic type: PERSON, ORGANIZATION, LOCATION, NUMBER, MEASURE or TIME [6].

After the candidate sentences have been annotated, a set of patterns—defined by regular expressions—is applied to them to pinpoint and extract the desired answer. These patterns are specific to the semantic type of the question, hence the importance of detecting that type during the question processing stage.

Extraction patterns. As a way of illustration, here we will discuss only those patterns that are being used for "Quem...?" *(Who...?)* questions since space restrictions prevent us from presenting an exhaustive coverage. The description of the full set of patterns—16 in total—will be postponed for future publications.

Take, for instance, the following question, shown here after the question processing stage, with the main verb and supporting NP already identified:

Quem [escreveu]$_V$ [Hamlet]$_{NP}$?
Who wrote Hamlet?

For such questions, the system applies the patterns described below to detect and extract the answer, viz. a named entity of type PERSON (marked by angle brackets in this example):

1. A pattern that matches the phrases in the question, but with the answer in the place of the interrogative pronoun, i.e. $\langle \cdots \rangle$ $[\cdots]_V$ $[\cdots]_{NP}$

   ⟨William Shakespeare⟩ [escreveu]$_V$ [Hamlet]$_{NP}$
   William Shakespeare wrote Hamlet

   Relative clauses are accounted for by extending this pattern to allow an optional **que** pronoun after the named entity

   ⟨Shakespeare⟩ , que [escreveu]$_V$ [Hamlet]$_{NP}$
   Shakespeare, who wrote Hamlet

2. A pattern that matches the passive form of the first case: $[\cdots]_{NP}$ $[\cdots]_V$ ⤳ $\langle \cdots \rangle$

   [Hamlet]$_{NP}$ [foi escrito]$_V$ ⤳ ⟨Shakespeare⟩
   Hamlet was written ⤳ *Shakespeare*

   To match the passive voice, the pattern uses the lemma and inflection information that has been added to the sentence by the shallow processing annotation tools. The ⤳ is used here to indicate that the pattern allows anything after the verb up to the first named entity with the PERSON type, for instance: **pelo dramaturgo inglês** *(by the English playwright)*

---

[5] For a detailed account of these tools, see [4,5].

3. A pattern that matches the common writing convention where the name of a work (book, painting, play, sculpture, etc.) is followed by the name of its author: [⋯]ₙₚ , de ⟨⋯⟩

> [Hamlet]ₙₚ , de ⟨William Shakespeare⟩
> *Hamlet, by William Shakespeare*

2.4 Web Service

The XisQuê system supports a freely available Web service, which can be found at the following address: http://xisque.di.fc.ul.pt

The user introduces a question phrased in Portuguese and the system returns a list of 5 answers. Each answer (termed as short-answer from this point onwards) is accompanied by the sentence from where it was extracted (termed as long-answer), as a way of providing some extra context, together with a link to the original, full document. In case no short-answer is extracted from a top-5 scoring sentence, this sentence is still provided as a long-answer to the input question.

3 Related Work

There are some QA systems for Portuguese reported in the literature[6] though, for most of them, their performance is not comparable to that of XisQuê. On the one hand, these systems have no interface for searching the Web that could be used to collect comparable results, by running the test-set used here. On the other hand, running the CLEF test-set of questions [14] with XisQuê leads also to non comparable results since there is no guarantee that the answers in the CLEF corpus for these questions are available in the Web.

Moreover, while the preliminary application of indexing techniques to the closed corpus containing the answers is an option for QA systems evaluated over that corpus, as in CLEF, that is not an option for QA systems evaluated over the Web, as applying such techniques on such an amount of data is out of reach for any academic research team.

Esfinge [9] is the only of these QA systems that currently provides an interface for searching the Web.[7]

4 Evaluation and Comparison

Evaluating a QA system running over the Web raises non negligible issues as the Web's content is constantly changing. The results for a certain question

---

[6] Esfinge [9], L2F's [10], Priberam's [11], Raposa [12], Senso [13].

[7] Vd. http://www.linguateca.pt/Esfinge. We should note however that it is unclear to which extent this Web service is supported by the system reported in [9] since the system reported therein pre-processes and indexes the documents where the answer is to be searched, which does not happen in the Web-based version.

in different runs may thus vary due to external factors, such as document or website availability, etc. [15]. Hence, there is no gold standard against which the system can be compared. However, it is possible and useful to obtain system performance indicators through sampling, by manual evaluation of a test set.

The test-set was built by randomly picking questions from Trivial Pursuit® cards, 15 for each of the interrogative pronouns that XisQuê handles (viz. **Quem**, **Quando**, **Onde** and **Que**), for a total of 60 questions,[8] which were submitted to each Web service. The following metrics are used:

Short answers is the proportion of questions for which the system provided at least a short answer—regardless its rank in the five answer list or its being correct. It serves as an indication of how good a system is at extracting short answers from candidate sentences.

Accuracy is the proportion of questions for which a correct answer was provided. In "all", a long-answer is counted in the lot of the correct ones in case it is correct and no short-answer (correct or not) was extracted from it. This is further divided into accuracy concerning only the top result and accuracy regardless of rank. It indicates the quality of the candidate sentences.

MRR stands for mean reciprocal rank. It is a measure commonly adopted in QA evaluation of how highly, on average, the first correct answer is ranked in the answer list [16].[9] For instance, if all questions have a correct answer and these all appear in position 1, the MRR scores 1; in case they would all appear in position 2, the MRR would score 0.5. It serves as an indication of the quality of the sentence ranking procedure.

XisQuê is compared with Esfinge and with Google, the latter serving as a baseline non-QA system on which QA systems should be able to improve since Google does not return short answers and thus only the result page is considered when checking for answers, i.e. we do not search within the returned documents and take the snippets provided in the results page as long-answers.

The results are summarized in Table 1.

4.1   Result Analysis

XisQuê provides short-answers to 56.67% of the test set questions, which is slightly better than Esfinge. Google, naturally, does not provide short answers.

Since XisQuê returns a correct short-answer to 55.00% of the test set questions, a short-answer, when returned, is almost always correct. In this regard, Esfinge is similar, albeit with fewer short answers being returned.

For XisQuê, the long-answer acts as an effective fallback for those cases where a short answer was not provided, since a correct answer (short- or long-) is returned to 98.33% of the test set questions. In this respect, it is better than the Google baseline and it vastly improves on Esfinge's score since this system, when unable to provide a short-answer, does not return a long-answer. If we only look

---

[8] The full test-set may be found at http://xisque.di.fc.ul.pt.

[9] If no correct answer is given, a rank of 0 is used.

Table 1. System comparison

	XisQuê		Esfinge		Google	
short answers	56.67%		53.33%		n/a	
rank	1st	1–5	1st	1–5	1st	1–5
accuracy (short)	45.00%	55.00%	36.67%	51.67%	n/a	n/a
accuracy (all)	73.33%	98.33%	38.33%	53.33%	40.00%	91.67%
MRR (short)	0.4819		0.4500		n/a	
MRR (all)	0.7372		0.4667		0.5956	

at the top ranked answer, these values are naturally lower, with XisQuê scoring 45.00% accuracy for short answers and 73.33% for short- or long- answers.

The overall MRR value obtained for XisQuê is 0.7372 when short- and long-answers are considered, and is 0.4819 when only short-answers are taken into account (i.e. when a rank of 0 is used for questions without any short-answer).

The difference between the "short" and "all" accuracies for XisQuê is a strong indication that the system still has room for improvement in the answer extraction stage: It is good at choosing candidate sentences (long-answers), but it is not always able to extract short-answers from them. However, those that it does extract tend to be correct.

4.2   A Short Note on QA Timeliness

To assess the performance of a QA system, specially one with real-time as a design feature, one has to measure how fast the system is in the delivering of answers to end-users. In this regard, what matters to the end-user, and his perception of the usability of the service, is how long it takes for an answer to be returned since a question is asked to the system. From a system development point of view, however, it is instructive to also determine how much of that time is spent searching for and downloading documents, since those tasks are contingent on search engines that lie outside the QA core system proper.

On average, XisQuê takes 22 sec. to display the results, with 14 sec. (ca. 64% of total time) being spent in tasks performed "outside" the QA core system. This compares favorably with Esfinge, which takes 91 sec. on average to answer (from 21, for questions with no answers, to 342, for questions with answers).

5   Future Work and Conclusions

XisQuê has room for improvement and extension with new functionality. One of the first efforts will be towards broadening the system to support other question formats, e.g. requests for lists, definitions, question sets, etc.

Together with this extension in width, the system will also be extended in depth in an attempt to retrieve more and better answers. In this regard, there are several research avenues that are being pursued. Of particular interest are query expansion techniques, such as searching for synonyms, morphological expansion, detecting paraphrases (e.g. changing between active and passive voices), etc. Ultimately, we will move away from the shallow processing methods we currently use and apply deep linguistic processing [7].

In this paper we presented XisQuê, a real-time, open-domain, freely accessible online factoid QA service for the Portuguese Web with encouraging performance scores. Run over the 60 question test set, it returns a correct short answer for 55% of them, raising to 98% if long-answers are also taken into account. As for the salience of the correct answers, it got a 0.48 MRR score, raising to 0.75 if long-answers are also considered.

References

1. Gulli, A., Signorini, A.: The indexable web is more than 11.5 billion pages. In: Proceedings of the 14th International Conference on WWW, pp. 902–903. ACM, New York (2005)
2. Aires, R., Santos, D.: Measuring the Web in Portuguese. In: Proceedings of the Euroweb Conference (2002)
3. Rodrigues, L.: Infra-estrutura de um serviço online de resposta a perguntas com base na web portuguesa. Master's thesis, Universidade de Lisboa, Portugal (2007)
4. Silva, J.R.: Shallow processing of Portuguese: From sentence chunking to nominal lemmatization. Master's thesis, Universidade de Lisboa, Portugal (2007)
5. Nunes, F.: Verbal lemmatization and featurization of Portuguese with ambiguity resolution in context. Master's thesis, Universidade de Lisboa, Portugal (2007)
6. Ferreira, E., Balsa, J., Branco, A.: Combining rule-based and statistical methods for named entity recognition in Portuguese. In: Actas da 5ª Workshop em Tecnologias da Informação e da Linguagem Humana (2007)
7. Costa, F.: Deep linguistic processing of Portuguese noun phrases. Master's thesis, Universidade de Lisboa, Portugal (2007)
8. Zheng, Z.: AnswerBus question answering system. In: Proceedings of the 2nd Human Language Technology (HLT), pp. 399–404 (2002)
9. Cabral, L., Costa, L., Santos, D.: Esfinge at CLEF 2007: First steps in a multiple question and multiple answer approach. In: [14] (2007)
10. Mendes, A., Coheur, L., Mamede, N., Romão, L., Loureiro, J., Ribeiro, R., Batista, F., Matos, D.: QA@L2F@QA@CLEF. In: [14]
11. Amaral, C., Cassan, A., Figueira, H., Martins, A., Mendes, A., Mendes, P., Pinto, C., Vidal, D.: Priberam's question answering system in QA@CLEF 2007. In: [14] (2007)
12. Sarmento, L., Oliveira, E.: Making RAPOSA (FOX) smarter. In: [14]
13. Saias, J., Quaresma, P.: The Senso question answering approach to Portuguese QA@CLEF-2007. In: [14] (2007)
14. Nardi, A., Peters, C. (eds.): Working Notes for the CLEF 2007 Workshop (2007)
15. Breck, E., Burger, J., Ferro, L., Hirschman, L., House, D., Light, M., Mani, I.: How to evaluate your question answering system every day and still get real work done. In: Proceedings of the 2nd LREC, pp. 1495–1500 (2000)
16. Voorhees, E.: The TREC8 question answering track report. In: Proceedings of the 8th Text REtrieval Conference (TREC) (1999)

Hyponymy Extraction and Web Search Behavior Analysis Based on Query Reformulation

Rui P. Costa and Nuno Seco

Cognitive and Media Systems Group, CISUC
University of Coimbra, Portugal
racosta@student.dei.uc.pt, nseco@dei.uc.pt

Abstract. A web search engine log is a very rich source of semantic knowledge. In this paper we focus on the extraction of hyponymy relations from individual user sessions by examining, search behavior. The results obtained allow us to identify specific reformulation models as ones that more frequently represent hyponymy relations. The extracted relations reflect the knowledge that the user is employing while searching the web. Simultaneously, this study leads to a better understanding of web user search behavior.

Keywords: Semantic Web Usage Mining, Query Reformulation, Hyponymy Extraction, Web User Search Behavior.

1   Introduction

Web Usage Mining applies concepts from the field of data mining to the information banked on the Web (e.g. to the logs of a web search engine). In this study we consider a log to be "an electronic record of interactions that have occurred during a searching episode between a web search engine and users searching for information on that web search engine" [1]. Web Usage Mining is a new field fueled by a huge amount of data, an amount that grows every second, for example, the data that Google stores in its logs every second. Taking into account the fact that it is mainly humans that conduct the search requests contained in these logs, this work attempts to extract a representation of the knowledge being used by looking into search behaviors. Log analysis fits well in this type of research because it provides the "most naturally-occurring and large-scale data set of query modifications" [2].

The driving assumption in this paper is that there are semantic relations between the terms contained in a session. The semantic relation studied is the hyponymy.

Many statistical studies have been conducted (as can be found in [1,3]), but very few have used logs from a generic web search engine. In our study the logs are from a generic search engine, thus providing an interesting longitudinal study [3].

A previous study has looked at ways of building taxonomies given an initial set of 14 main categories [4]. For every query issued they analyzed the category of pages returned and added the query terms to that category. Another study related to user

H. Geffner et al. (Eds.): IBERAMIA 2008, LNAI 5290, pp. 332–341, 2008.

behavior and semantics concluded that by using a specific extraction methodology an ontology may be extracted [5].

Several studies have been concerned with hyponymy extraction [6,7] and ontology learning [8]. These studies usually apply lexico-semantic patterns (e.g. *is a* and *such as*) in order to extract hyponymy relations and build ontologies.

Regarding query reformulation, one study examined multiple query reformulations on the Web in the context of interactive information retrieval [2]. The results indicate that query reformulation is the product of user interaction with the information retrieval system. They used a log that corresponded to a particular day, cleaned it manually and obtained 313 search sessions. However, results regarding semantics were not presented. This study is further explained in section 2.

Two studies focused on the Portuguese language and web search logs. In the work of [9], 440 people were emailed from a Computer Science Department in a Brazilian University, and asked to keep track of their queries during a one month period. The purpose was to study the application of natural language in formulating queries. The second work studied the identification of user sessions in a generic log with the intent of conducting future work enabling the extraction of semantic relations [10]. Regarding the Portuguese language we did not found any study dealing with the semantic aspects.

This paper proposes a new approach for hyponymy extraction and gives some clues towards the understanding of typical web user search behaviors, both based on query reformulation within individual user sessions. The relations extracted can enrich well-known ontologies like Wordnet[1] with new hyponymy relations. Considering that knowledge is growing every day this may provide an interesting way of updating ontologies, as we believe that this new knowledge will be reflected in the logs.

This paper is organized in the following manner: Section 2 describes a theoretical framework for web user search behavior, in Section 3 the hyponymy extraction method is explained, in Section 4 preliminary experiments are presented, and finally in Section 5 we conclude the paper.

2   Web User Search Behavior

The theoretical framework of interactive information retrieval that was applied was the one from Rieh [2] that derives from Saracevic [13]. Saracevic defines interaction as the "sequence of processes occurring in several connected levels of strata" ([13] p. 316). As can be deducted from the Figure 1, the interaction between the user and the system is complex. On the users side, there are three levels: cognitive (interaction with texts and their representations), affective (interaction with intentions) and situational (interaction with given or problems-at-hand). On the other side, we have the computer, where there are the engineering, processing and content levels. Both sides meet at the surface level where adaptation through feedback occurs.

A unique, non-intrusive way to understand the user (cognitive, affective and situational facets) is by web log mining, but the current search engines do not seem to

---

[1] http://wordnet.princeton.edu

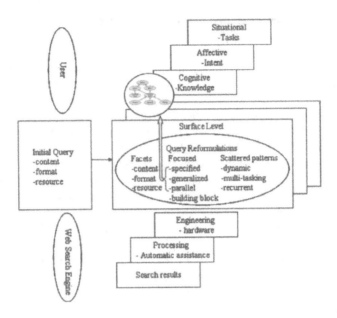

Fig. 1. Model of web query reformulation [2] (with user knowledge extraction link)

use this to their advantage. Rieh [2] reveals three main categories of reformulation within user sessions:

- *content* - 80.3% (changes to the meaning of a query);
- *format* - 14.4% (changes without altering the meaning of the query);
- *resource* - 2.8% (changes in types of information resources (e.g. news and images)).

The category studied in this paper is content since, it is the most frequent category and the most related to our study. The sub-facets studied are: specialization, generalization and parallelization. Specialization corresponds to the addition model, generalization to the deletion model and finally parallelization to the substitution model (see section 3). Figure 1 was updated from [2] with a link between query reformulation and user knowledge.

Our conclusions are in contrast to [14,15] who comment that transaction logs can only deal with the actions of the user, not their perceptions, emotions or background. Our study proposes a new method that can be used to extract a portion of the user knowledge (hyponymy relations).

Table 1. Three queries that exemplify a session

IP	Search URL	Date/Time
127.0.0.1	GET /pesquisa?lang=pt&index=sidra&terms=**virtual&books**	01/Oct/2003:00:00:07
127.0.0.1	GET /pesquisa?lang=pt&index=sidra&terms=**free&virtual&books**	01/Oct/2003:00:01:07
127.0.0.1	GET /pesquisa?lang=pt&index=sidra&terms=**virtual&libraries**	01/Oct/2003:00:10:47

Table 2. User reformulation model of addition (specialization)

Term(s) addition beginning/middle/end	This behavior happens when the user wants to specify the search.
Patterns	1. The new expression is a hyponym of the old one. 2. The old expression is a hyponym of the terms entered. 3. The new expression is a hyponym of the terms entered. 4. The new expression is a hyponym of the terms before the new term (just for middle case). 5. The old expression is a hyponym of the terms before the new term (just for middle case).
Examples	1. seguro (insurance), seguro escolar (scholar insurance). *Conclusion*: Insurance scholar is a hyponym of insurance. 2. pinheiro (pine), pinheiro árvore (pine tree). *Conclusion*: Pine is a hyponym of tree. 3. nações unidas (united nations), organização das nações unidas (united nations organization). *Conclusion*: United nations organization is a hyponym of organization. 4. dia sem carros (day without cars), dia europeu sem carros (european day without cars). *Conclusion*: European day without cars is a hyponym of day. 5. região oeste (west region), região turismo oeste (west region tourism). *Conclusion*: West region tourism is a hyponym of region.

3   Hyponymy Extraction Using User Reformulation Models

In the present study we consider a session as a sequence of queries that the user issues to satisfy his information needs [10]. An example of a session is shown in Table 1.

The algorithm used to detect sessions is presented in [10]. Our session detection algorithm used a 15 minute time limit as the maximum duration of a session. This threshold is based on the work of [11] where it was concluded that the optimal session interval is somewhere within the range of 10 to 15 minutes.

Hyponymy is the semantic relation of being subordinate or belonging to a lower rank or class; for instance apple is a fruit.

The new method that we propose for hyponymy extraction must be applied on a per session basis and on each two sequential queries. The user reformulation models proposed are based on the work of [12], where three different patterns of query reformulation were identified: substitution, addition and deletion.

Tables 2, 3, 4 and 5 explain the three user reformulation models studied (addition, deletion and substitution). Different positions of query reformulation (at the

Table 3. User reformulation model of deletion (generalization)

Term(s) deletion beginning/middle/end	This behavior happens when the user wants to generalize the search.
Patterns	1. The old expression is a hyponym of the new one. 2. The new expression is a hyponym of the deletion term. 3. The old expression is a hyponym of the deletion term. 4. The old expression is a hyponym of the expression before the deletion terms (just for middle case). 5. The new expression is a hyponym of the expression before the deletion terms (just for middle case).
Examples	1. planeta terra (planet earth), planeta (planet). *Conclusion*: Planet earth is a hyponym of planet. 2. orientação desporto (orientation sport), orientação (orientation). *Conclusion*: Orientation is a hyponym of sport. 3. parque de campismo (camping park), campismo (camping). *Conclusion*: Camping park is a hyponym of park. 4. tribunal penal internacional (international criminal court), tribunal internacional (international court). *Conclusion*: International criminal court is a hyponym of court. 5. desenvolvimento ambiental sustentável (sustainable ambiental development), desenvolvimento sustentável (sustainable development). *Conclusion*: Sustainable development is a hyponym of development.

beginning, in the middle and at the end) were studied. Each table contains several hyponymy extraction patterns and the respective examples. These patterns were identified during manual log analysis. The examples given are extracted from the logs of the Tumba[1], a search engine focused on Portuguese language. Therefore the reformulation patterns are only applicable to Portuguese (the English translation is given to assist the reader).

4   Experiments

The data used corresponds to 1,7 million cleaned query entries from 2003 from the Tumba. The log was cleaned by removing all entries that did not correspond to true search queries (e.g. bots and watchdog server queries). We found 75320 distinct sessions after applying the method presented in Section 3.

The following two topics present different evaluation strategies. The first does not need human intervention while the second is completely manual.

---

[1] http://www.tumba.pt

Table 4. User reformulation model of substitution (parallelization)

Term(s) substitution beginning/middle/end	This behavior happens when the user wants to do a parallel move (co-hyponymy).
Patterns	1. The new expression is a hyponym of the constant terms. 2. The old expression is a hyponym of the constant terms.
Examples	1. agência de actores (actors agency), agência de publicidade (advertising agency). *Conclusion*: Advertising agency is a hyponym of agency. 2. agência de actores (actors agency), agência de publicidade (advertising agency). *Conclusion*: Actors agency is a hyponym of agency.

Table 5. User reformulation model of total substitution (generalization | specialization)

Total substitution	This behavior happens when the user wants to specify or generalize.
Patterns	1. The old expression is a hyponym of the new one (generalization). 2. The new expression is a hyponym of the old one (specification).
Examples	1. mba (mba), pós graduação (pos graduation). *Conclusion*: Mba is a hyponym of pos graduation. 2. anti virus (anti virus), norton (norton). *Conclusion*: Norton is a hyponym of anti virus.

Using an approach similar to [16] we used Google in order to evaluate the extracted hyponymy relations. The idea is simple, using the extraction method presented and a pattern between the terms extracted it is possible to validate semantic relations. The pattern is linked by the semantic relation. For instance, if we have the terms *mouse* and *animal,* and the pattern "is an" (for hyponymy) between them, Google returns 900 results. Therefore, we can say that *mouse* is an hyponym of *animal* with a frequency of 900. However, there are sometimes false positives, mainly because of the missing words. For instance, *education is a ministry* has a frequency of 7240, but the correct form would be *ministry of education is a ministry.* This problem can be smoothed by adding articles before the terms (e.g. *an education is a ministry,* returns 0 results).

To reinforce the results evaluated from the Google search, a sub-set of 30 hyponym relations were randomly chosen. For each sub-set we selected a number of

Table 6. General model results for hyponymy extraction

Model	Model amount	Google	Correct	Some sense	Wrong
Addition end	17073	231	55,33%	21,67%	23%
Addition beginning	5665	163	58%	20,67%	21,33%
Addition middle	3421	52	89,33%	7,33%	3,33%
Deletion end	7281	107	53,66%	19,67%	26,67%
Deletion beginning	7170	49	64,67%	25,34%	10%
Deletion middle	3333	49	89,66%	8,34%	2%
Substitution end	27755	553	88%	12%	0%
Substitution beginning	15767	21	32,5%	21,66%	45,83%
Substitution middle	2286	27	64%	14%	22%
Total substitution	70382	41	38,34%	30,67%	31%
Total	160133	1295	61,92%	19,58%	18,5%

pattern examples proportional to the total amount of each pattern. When the patterns did not have at least 30 relations, we used logs from others years. However, for the substitution at the beginning, the maximum number of possible relations was 25. The evaluation was done by 10 people. For each relation the evaluator had to choose one of the following options: wrong, some sense or correct. The "some sense" option allows the evaluator to state that s/he is not sure about the relation, making the study more realistic.

We used Google to evaluate our method, and manual verification to evaluate Google in order to ensure a threshold of confidence regarding the results given by Google. Table 6 shows the results from the experiments using the Tumba logs from 2003. The third column holds the number of unique relations that Google evaluated and the subsequent columns hold the manual evaluation results. Table 7 shows the quantity and evaluation of each pattern within each model. For instance, in the

Table 7. Model patterns results. Each cell contains the total number of hyponymy relations validated by Google search and within parenthesis the manual validation results (both for a specific pattern).

Model	1st (C;SS;W)	2nd (C;SS;W)	3rd (C;SS;W)	4th (C;SS;W)	5th (C;SS;W)
Addition end	76 (82;15;3)	152 (35;23;42)	3 (53;40;7)		
Addition beginning	0	138 (38;30;32)	25 (99;1;0)		
Addition middle	0	2 (45;15;40)	1 (50;40;10)	30 (96;4;0)	19 (92;7;1)
Deletion end	48 (84;13;3)	48 (32;24;44)	1 (70;30;0)		
Deletion beginning	0	28 (53;35;12)	21 (78;14;8)		
Deletion middle	0	0	0	39 (90;8;2)	10 (90;10;0)
Substitution end	279	274			
Substitution beginning	11	10			
Substitution middle	18	9			
Total substitution	20	21			

C - Correct (%)   **SS** - Some Sense (%)   **W** - Wrong (%)

second row, second column are the results of validation to the addition end model (1st pattern). The manual evaluation of the substitution model was not divided into patterns since, substitution patterns were equal between them. Some instances of the relations extracted are presented in tables 2, 3, 4 and 5.

The most interesting patterns are (ordered first by quantity and then by correctness):

1. Term(s) substitution at the end (1st and 2nd): 553 - 88%;
2. Term(s) addition at the end (1st): 76 - 82%;
3. Term(s) addition in the middle (4th and 5th): 30 - 96% 19 - 92%;
4. Term(s) deletion in the middle (4th and 5th): 39 - 90% 10 - 90%;
5. Term(s) deletion at the end (1st): 48 - 84%;
6. Term(s) addition at the beginning (3rd): 25 - 99%;
7. Term(s) deletion at the beginning (3rd): 21 - 78%;

Joining these seven patterns results in a total of 821 hyponymy relations.

It is possible to get better results by changing the search engine requirement. This can be done by restricting the relations added to those that obtained more than x hits. For instance, empirically we chose that addition end(2nd, 3rd), deletion beginning(2nd, 3rd) and total substitution(1st, 2nd), needed more than one entry to be assumed as a relation. But this value could be larger and thus the semantic relation would become stronger.

After discovering the most promising method (substitution end) using the search engine evaluation method, a sub-set of 1000 unique relations of this pattern was selected. From these 1000 relations we studied only 749 since the remaining relations contained orthographic errors. We then decided which were hyponyms and which were not. In the end about 40% were correct, 20% had some sense and 40% were wrong. We therefore estimate that among all the 27000 relations in the substitution end model, it is possible to extract about 12150 hyponymy relations.

Patterns with less than 20 relations have a very low frequency, thus do not represent the typical user search behavior and should not be used in hyponymy extraction.

5   Conclusions

Hyponymy extraction from logs reinforces the idea that human knowledge is organized like an ontology where parent-child relations exist [17]. Interestingly, users prefer to make a horizontal move in the ontology, as the frequency in the substitution model demonstrates. This movement allows us to extract co-hyponymy relations by connecting two hyponyms extracted in each of two queries.

The proposed user reformulation models can be used to extract hyponymy relations that can be added to ontologies. Taking into account the results obtained, we recommend the use of the 1st/2nd Substitution End and the 1st Addition End patterns in order to extract hyponymy relations. This method can improve ontologies by adding recent relations. The relations extracted tend to represent the knowledge of the community that more frequently uses the search engine.

Using Google alone and the best behavior patterns it was possible to extract 821 hyponymy relations. With the manual method it was estimated to be possible to extract about 12150 hyponymy relations with a single model.

In this paper we present a method to capture part of the web user knowledge, leading to an important update in the model of web query reformulation (Figure 1). With the capture of user knowledge it will be possible to develop web search engines that perform searches more efficiently.

In the future the study of other semantic relations (e.g. meronymy and holonymy), other logs[1] and other query reformulation patterns/models (e.g. analyzing the entire session or combining different sessions) should be performed.

Acknowledgments

We thank Paulo Gomes for his important support. A special thanks to everyone who participated in the experiments, without whom the study would not have been so complete. Part of this work was performed under a research grant given by CISUC/FCT.

References

1. Jansen, B.J.: Search log analysis: What it is, what's been done, how to do it. Library and Information Science Research 28, 407–432 (2006)
2. Rieh, S.Y., Xie, H.I.: Analysis of multiple query reformulations on the web: The interactive information retrieval context. Information Processing & Management 42, 751–768 (2006)
3. Wang, P., Berry, M.W., Yang, Y.: Mining longitudinal web queries: Trends and patterns. J. Am. Soc. Inf. Sci. Technol. 54, 743–758 (2003)
4. Chuang, S.L., Chien, L.F.: Enriching web taxonomies through subject categorization of query terms from search engine logs. Decision Support System 30 (2003)
5. Noriaki, K., Takeya, M., Miyoshi, H.: Semantic log analysis based on a user query behavior model. In: ICDM 2003: Proceedings of the Third IEEE International Conference on Data Mining, Washington, DC, USA, p. 107. IEEE Computer Society, Los Alamitos (2003)
6. Hearst, M.A.: Automatic acquisition of hyponyms from large text corpora. In: Proceedings of the 14th International Conference on Computational Linguistics, Nantes, S2K-92-09 (1992)
7. de Freitas, M.C.: Elaboração automática de ontologias de domínio: discussão e resultados. PhD thesis, Universidade Católica do Rio de Janeiro (2007)
8. Buitelaar, P., Cimiano, P.: Ontology Learning and Population: Bridging the Gap between Text and Knowledge. Frontiers in Artificial Intelligence and Applications, vol. 167. IOS Press, Amsterdam (March 2008)
9. Aires, R., Aluisio, S.: Como incrementar a qualidade dos resultados das maquinas de busca: da analise de logs a interaccao em portugues. Ciencia de Informacao 3, 5–16 (2003)
10. Seco, N., Cardoso, N.: Detecting user sessions in the tumba! query log (unpublished) (March 2006)

---

[1] http://ist.psu.edu/faculty_pages/jjansen/academic/transaction_logs.html

11. He, D., Göker, A.: Detecting session boundaries from web user logs. In: 22nd Annual Colloquium on Information Retrieval Research (2000)
12. Bruza, P., Dennis, S.: Query reformulation on the internet: Empirical data and the hyperindex search engine. In: RIA 1997 Conference Computer-Assisted Information Searching on Internet, pp. 488–499 (1997)
13. Saracevic, T.: The stratified model of information retrieval interaction: Extension and applications. In: 60th annual meeting of the American Society for Information Science, vol. 34, pp. 313–327 (1997)
14. Hancock-Beaulieu, M., Robertson, S., Nielsen, C.: Evaluation of online catalogues: An assessment of methods (bl research paper 78). The British Library Research and Development Department, London (1990)
15. Phippen, A., Sheppard, L., Furnell, S.: A practical evaluation of web analytics. Internet Research: Electronic Networking Applications and Policy 14, 284–293 (2004)
16. Cimiano, P., Staab, S.: Learning by googling. SIGKDD Explor. Newsl. 6(2), 24–33 (2004)
17. Collins, A.M., Quillian, M.R.: Retrieval time from semantic memory. Journal of Verbal Learning and Verbal Behavior 8, 240–247 (1969)

Semantics of Place: Ontology Enrichment

Bruno Antunes[1], Ana Alves[1,2], and Francisco C. Pereira[1]

[1] CISUC, Department of Informatics Engineering
University of Coimbra, Portugal
{bema,ana,camara}@dei.uc.pt
[2] ISEC, Coimbra Institute of Engineering, Portugal
aalves@isec.pt

Abstract. In this paper, we present an approach to a challenge well known from the area of Ubiquitous Computing: extracting meaning out of geo-referenced information. The importance of this "semantics of place" problem is proportional to the number of available services and data that are common nowadays. Having rich knowledge about a place, we open up a new realm of "Location Based Services" that can behave more intelligently. Our approach builds on Ontology Engineering techniques in order to build a network of semantic associations between a place and related concepts. We briefly describe the KUSCO system and present some preliminary results.

Keywords: Point of Interest, Place, Semantic of Place, Ontologies, Ontology Enrichment, Ontology Evaluation.

1 Introduction

The current ubiquitous availability of localization technologies (particularly GPS) has driven to the emergence of many new applications (the "Location Based Services" or LBS) and enormous amounts of geo-referenced data. However, although we have already available rich and sophisticated knowledge representation and techniques (e.g. Semantic Web and Ontology Engineering) that allows for elaborate uses, information on location or *place* tends to be poor, with little or no directly associated semantics (e.g. the typical Point Of Interest or POI simply has a description and a generic type; in other cases we only have the latitude/longitude pair; and sometimes an LBS has its own purpose driven semantics, unusable to others). The association of a set of semantic concepts to a place should allow the application of those sophisticated techniques and foster the quality of current and future LBS (e.g. with better indexing). For example, knowing simply that "Goldener Adler" is placed at "47.268430 N 11.392230 E" and that it is a restaurant misses much of its essential meaning: what kind of food do they make? how expensive is it? where exactly is it? is it open now?

KUSCO is a system that intends to find and associate a set of semantic tags to Points Of Interest (or POI's). A POI is a geo-referenced tag that contains a latitude/longitude pair, a name and a type (e.g. restaurant, museum, gas station).

H. Geffner et al. (Eds.): IBERAMIA 2008, LNAI 5290, pp. 342–351, 2008.

Such information is used by KUSCO, which applies a number of techniques to automatically extract information from the Web about that POI. The system starts by doing a web search (e.g. using Yahoo), then it extracts and calculates statistics about the main words used. Afterwards, it associates these words to concepts (of WordNet [1]), and finally it determines the relationships of these concepts with the POI by using Place Ontologies.

In this paper, we describe the Ontology Enrichment process of the KUSCO system. This process is necessary to establish the association between the Generic Place Ontologies and specific POI instances, which is also normally called Ontology Instantiation. Given a POI and an Ontology, KUSCO seeks for the associations between the Ontology *Terms* and the more relevant words found in the Web pages most related to the POI. In the next section, we present "Semantics of Place" problem, well known in the area of Ubiquitous Computing. Then, we present some Ontology Engineering concepts that are essential to this work: Learning and Evaluation. In section 4, we present KUSCO and show some preliminary results. We end the paper by discussing next steps (section 5) and final remarks (section 6).

2   Semantics of Place

First introduced in [2], Jeffrey Hightower argues that location must have more associated information than simply the absolute position in a global coordinate system. Location representation needs more human-readable information including geographic, demographic, environmental, historical and, perhaps, commercial attributes. The meaning of place derives from social conventions, their private or public nature, possibilities for communication, etc. [3,4]. As argued by [5] on distinguishing the concept of place from space, a place is generally a space with something added - social meaning, conventions, cultural understandings about role, function and nature - having also temporal properties, once the same space can be different places at different times. Thus, a place only exists if it has some meaning for someone and the construction of this meaning is the main objective of our research.

As a formal definition, location models can be classified into four main types [6]: Geometric, Symbolic, Hybrid or Semantic. While the first three models (the third considers both geometric and symbolic) are mainly devoted to spatial relationship between locations, the last one, the Semantic Location Model, is orthogonal to symbolic and geometric representations. The semantic representation provides other information around its place, such as a bus route or a snapshot of interest. For instance, a hybrid location model was proposed by Jiang and Steenkiste [7] where they decompose the physical environment in different levels of precision and feature a self-descriptive location representation to each level. At a lower level of decomposition, they use a local and 3D coordinate system (Latitude, Longitude, Altitude) to define points or areas for which there is no name in the hierarchical tree. As an example, they can identify a specific printer in the Carnegie Mellon University campus by the identifier *cmu/wean-hall/floor3/3100-corridor#(10,10,0)*. In a different perspective, the HP Cooltown [8] introduces a semantic representation of locations. Its main goal is to support web presence for people, places and things. They use Universal Resource Indentifies (URIs) for addressing, physical URI beaconing and sensing of URIs for discovery, and localized web servers for directories in order to create a location-aware ubiquitous system to support nomadic users. In the same line, Ubiquitous Web [9] was envisioned as a pervasive web infrastructure in which all physical objects are socially tagged and accessible by URIs, providing information and services that enrich users experiences in their physical context as the web does in the cyberspace.

While the focus of our work is the Semantic aspect of Location Representation, we also take advantage of information available on the Web about public places. With the growth of the World Wide Web, we think that almost every commercial and non-commercial entities of public interest are or tend to become present on-line by proper web sites or referred by other related institutions. This should become even more relevant for places considered interesting for a group of people (i.e. they are in a sense *Points Of Interest*). But differently from the two previous semantic models, we don't assume that the Semantic Web is already a reality, with all information semantically structured and tagged. Actually, it is widely accepted that the majority of on-line information is composed of unrestricted user-written texts, so we get mainly dependent on the Information Extraction (IE) capabilities. IE is a research subtopic within Information Retrieval (IR) devoted to extract useful information from a body of text, including techniques like Term Extraction and Named Entity Recognition. In the Natural Language Processing field, there are other techniques which will be further used in our work, including part-of-speech tagging and word sense disambiguation to discover meaningful key concepts from the Web and contextualize it within a Common Sense Ontology (see the following sections).

3   Ontology Engineering

The growing amount of information available on the web demands for the development of efficient and practical information extraction approaches, in order to avoid the actual user's overloading of information. This need for new ways of extracting information from the web stimulated a new vision, the Semantic Web [10], where resources available have associated machine-readable semantic information. For this to come true, a knowledge representation structure for representing the semantics associated to resources would be necessary, and that was where ontologies [11] assumed a central role in the movement of the Semantic Web. Because it is nearly impossible to design an ontology of the world, research focused on the development of domain-specific ontologies, in which construction and maintenance are time-consuming and error-prone when manually done. In order to automate this process, research on ontology learning has emerged, combining information extraction and learning methods to automatically, or semi-automatically, build ontologies.

3.1 Ontology Learning

According to [12], ontology learning can be described as *"the process of automatic or semi-automatic construction, enrichment and adaptation of ontologies"*. It relies on a set of algorithms, methods, techniques and tools to automatically, or semi-automatically, extract information about a specific domain to construct or adapt ontologies. The process of ontology learning comprises four different tasks: ontology population, ontology enrichment, inconsistency resolution and ontology evaluation. Ontology population is the task that deals with the instantiation of concepts and relations in an ontology, without changing its structure. On the other hand, ontology enrichment is the task of extending an ontology by adding new concepts, relations and rules, which results in changes on its structure. Because errors and inconsistencies can be introduced during ontology population and enrichment, inconsistency resolution aims to detect these inconsistencies and generate appropriate resolutions. Finally, the ontology evaluation task assesses the ontology by measuring its quality with respect to some particular criteria (see section 3.2).

The ontology learning process can be performed through three different major approaches [12]: the integration of ontologies by capturing the features that are shared between them; the construction of a new ontology from scratch, based on the information extracted from data about a specific domain; and the specialization of a generic ontology by adapting it to a specific domain.

Following the work of Buitlaar et al. [13], the ontology learning process deals with six different aspects related with the structure of an ontology: *Term Identification*, which is in the basis of every ontology learning process; *Synonym Identification*, for identifying sets of terms that refer to the same concept or relation; *Concept Identification*, which is done through the realizations of the concept (i.e. terms); *Taxonomy Construction*, using inclusion relations (usually known as "is-a" relations); *Semantic Relations Extraction*, for identifying non-taxonomic relations that connect semantically related concepts; and *Rule Acquisition*, the least explored aspect of ontology learning.

3.2 Ontology Evaluation

The need for well defined techniques of ontology evaluation arise from the fact that different ontology conceptualizations can be constructed from the same body of knowledge. Much of the work developed in this field came from the context of ontology learning and enrichment, where different evaluation approaches were explored to evaluate the resulting ontologies. Also, the increasing development of semantic-aware applications, that make use of ontologies, uncovered the need to evaluate the available ontologies and choose the one that best fits the specific needs of the application.

According to [14], there are four different categories of techniques used for ontology evaluation: those based on a "golden standard", those based on the results of an application that makes use of the ontology, those based on the use of a corpus about the domain to be covered by the ontology, and those where evaluation is done by humans.

When the semantic characterization of place involves the construction and enrichment of place ontologies, it becomes necessary to apply some of the techniques developed for ontology evaluation, in order to assess the quality of the ontology produced and validate the proposed ontology enrichment approach.

4   KUSCO

The problem of "position to place" is a well known challenge within the area of Ubiquitous Computing and relates deeply with the connection humans have with places, their functionality and meaning. Attached to a tag name, even when a category is included, a place needs a richer semantic representation in our perspective in order to be understood. This knowledge can be used for whatever processes that demand semantics of place (e.g. understanding POI's while in navigation; searching for a place that has specific characteristics; route planning using locations with specific functionalities; inferring user's activity, etc.). We formally name this process as Semantic Enrichment of Place and it consists of using available Common Sense Ontologies and Web information to build a collection of generic and instance facts about these places. Figure 1 shows the internal architecture of KUSCO System. The following sections will explain in detail each component of this system.

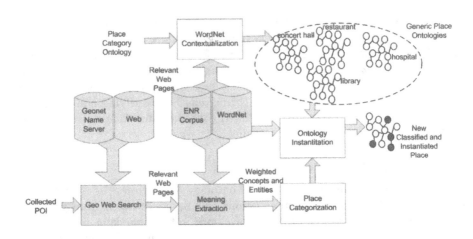

Fig. 1. The architecture of KUSCO

4.1   Generic Place Ontologies

The module of Generic Place Ontologies represents a collection of commonsense and generic information about well-known place categories, like restaurants, cinemas, museums, hotels, hospitals, etc. At a first stage, this information is manually collected from well-known and shared Ontologies (retrieving and selecting the most popular using ontology search engines like [15]). But as the system is used, it is dynamically fed by new examples, and thus instantiated and populated by specific facts about these instances that represent real-world places (see fig. 1). At a first stage, only concepts are extracted from Web describing places. Furthermore we also want to instantiate relations between these concepts using the original context where they appear. In order to infer place meaning, ontologies are contextualized on WordNet. For each term in an ontology, a WordNet's definition will be looked for (see section 4.4 for an example of this process).

4.2   Geo Web Search

This module is responsible for finding Web pages using only POI data as keywords: place name and geographical address. This last element is composed of the City name (where POI is located) and is obtained from Gazetteers [1] available on Web). This search is presently made by the freely available Yahoo API. For the moment, we are applying a simple heuristic that use the geographical reference as another keyword in the search. Thus, assuming a POI is a quadruple (Latitude, Longitude, [Category,] Name)[2], the final query to search will be: "City Name" + ["Category" +] "Name". In the near future, however, we think that works like Geotumba[17] and Wikipedia[18], with their geo-reference annotated information, will contribute to get better precision of this process, once the search on the Web can be localized only in a given geographical region. At this moment our system is very sensitive to geographical location of Place Name. For example, after looking for specific Web information for a given POI named "Carnegie Hall" in New York, we find many relevant results all referring to the same place: a concert venue. In another example, given a POI in the same city about "Mount Sinai" (a hospital), a geographical search gives us definitions such as a hospital and a metropolitan neighborhood. This shows us that this approach can become very dependent of search algorithms and of the Web's representativeness of places. At the end of this process, the N more relevant pages are selected (as suggested by the search engine).

4.3   Meaning Extraction

Having the set of Web pages found earlier, keyword extraction and contextualization on WordNet is made at this point. This processing includes POS tagging, Named Entity Recognition and Word Sense Disambiguation using available NLP tools [?,19,20]. On completion of these sub tasks for each web page, we are able to extract the most relevant terms (only common or proper nouns) that will be used in the categorization task (next module). The common nouns are contextualized on WordNet and thus can be thought not only as a word but more

---

[1] A geographical dictionary (as at the back of an atlas) generally including position and geographical names like Geonet Names Server and Geographic Names Information System [16].

[2] This category refers to the type of POI in question, a museum, a restaurant, a pub, etc. This information is optional, once sometimes it may not be present in the POI.

cognitively as a concept (specifically a synset - family of words having the same meaning, i.e., synonyms [?]). Each concept importance is computed by TF/IDF weighting [21] considering the most relevant WebPages for all POI's on that category.

4.4   Place Categorization

In order to evaluate the capacity of categorizing POI's (i.e. if they represent restaurants, museums, bars, etc.) we selected a set of ontologies using a popularity based criteria [22]. The result of this ontology selection process was a set of four ontologies about different domains: restaurants[3], museums[4], travel[5] and shows[6].

In an initial phase, already described, POI's were associated to a set of WordNet concepts. To facilitate the categorization of the POI's against this set of ontologies, we also map the concepts of the selected ontologies in WordNet. The mapping comprises three phases:

1. *Term Extraction.* The terms are extracted from the name of the concepts contained in the ontology. Because these names are usually comprised of one or more terms, they are split by upper case letters and special characters such as '-' and '_'.
2. *Term Composition.* In a preliminary analysis of the results obtained in the previous phase, we found that some of the terms, extracted of the split concept names, represented composed entities such as 'fast food' or 'self-service'. To avoid loosing these composed entities, the different terms extracted from each concept are combined and the resulting combinations are included as terms associated to the concept.
3. *Concept Identification.* The terms and combinations of terms, extracted in the previous phases, are then searched in WordNet. When more that one sense is found for each term, these are disambiguated by selecting the sense with the greatest tag count value. The tag count is a value given by WordNet for each word sense and represents the frequency of that word sense in a textual corpus.

The result of the mapping process is that all the concepts of each ontology became associated to one or more concepts of WordNet. With the ontologies already mapped in WordNet, the categorization process proceeds with three different approaches:

- *Simple Approach.* The simple approach, as its name tells, is the most simple approach and represents the direct mapping between the concepts associated to POI's and the concepts associated to the ontologies. The mappings between concepts of the two structures are counted and the POI is categorized in the ontology with the greatest number of mappings.

---

[3] http://gaia.fdi.ucm.es/ontologies/restaurant.owl
[4] http://cidoc.ics.forth.gr/rdfs/cidoc_v4.2.rdfs
[5] http://protege.cim3.net/file/pub/ontologies/travel/travel.owl
[6] http://www-agentcities.doc.ic.ac.uk/ontology/shows.daml

Table 1. Percentages of correctly categorized POI's

	Simple	Weighted	Expanded
Restaurants (I)	71%	29%	59%
Restaurants (II)	70%	41%	69%
Museums (I)	0%	15%	15%
Museums (II)	14%	14%	14%

- *Weighted Approach.* The weighted approach takes advantage of the TF/IDF [21] value of each one of the concepts that are associated to POI's. The TF/IDF value represents the weight of the concept in relation to the POI it is associated to. This way, each mapping has a weight equal to the weight of the concept that originated the mapping. The POI is then categorized in the ontology with the greatest sum of mapping weights.
- *Expanded Approach.* The expanded approach is based on the idea that the expansion of the concepts to their hyponyms make the mapping more tolerant and extensive. One may argue that when searching for *restaurants*, we are implicitly searching for every kind of restaurant, such as an *italian restaurant* or a *self-service restaurant*. Following this idea, the concepts associated to POI's are expanded to their hyponyms and the concepts that result from this expansion are associated to the POI. Then, the mapping between POI's and ontolgies is performed as in the simple approach.

4.5   Preliminary Results

In order to evaluate the three categorization approaches described before, we conducted some preliminary experiments with four sets of POI's, manually categorized as restaurants and museums. We then used the three categorization approaches to categorize the POI's according to the four ontologies previously selected and mapped in WordNet. The percentages of correctly categorized POI's for each set are presented in Table 1.

Although this is a preliminary experimentation, using a total of 116 POI's, the results obtained reveal interesting hints. As expected, the quality of the ontologies is crucial to the results of the categorization process. In our experimentation scenario, the ontology representing the restaurants domain was clearly more detailed than that representing the museums domain. Furthermore, the museums ontology was very abstract, which decreases the probability of matching with the specific concepts associated to POI's. In part, this explains the bad results of the POI's representing museums. Another interesting result is that the simple approach performs better than the weighted approach in most cases. This reveals that somehow the TF/IDF value used for weighting the concepts associated to the POI's is not reflecting the real weight of the concept, which should be improved in a near future. Also, we can conclude that the expanded approach stays very close to the simple approach. In this situation, there is not an evident gain on expanding the concepts to their hyponyms. Again, the quality and detail of the ontologies used may have a strong impact in the results obtained with this approach in the way that when ontologies are not specific enough there is no point on specializing the concepts associated to the POI's.

5   Future Work

This is an ongoing work and a lot of ideas are planned to be tested in the near future, some of them were extracted from the results obtained so far. One of the things we plan to improve is the way the TF/IDF of each concept associated to the POI's is calculated. Actually, it is calculated only taking into account the set of six web pages that were selected for each POI. Clearly, this set of documents is too small for obtaining relevant TF/IDF values. We believe that calculating the TF/IDF value taking into account all the web pages selected to the whole set of POI's will improve its relevance. Another fact already referred is that the quality of the ontologies used in the process is crucial to the results obtained, which demands for a more carefully selection and evaluation of such ontologies. Some of the approaches developed in areas such as ontology evaluation (see section 3.2) may be applied, in order to guarantee the quality of the ontologies used in the system. The next step is the ontology instatiation process, which will make use of the information generated in the previous steps to create instances of concrete POI's in the Generic Place Ontologies.

6   Conclusions

It is clear that, in order to improve current and future location based services, more information must be associated to common POI's. Location representation needs more human-readable information including geographic, demographic, environmental, historical and, perhaps, commercial attributes. KUSCO, the system we are developing, implements a process that we call as Semantic Enrichment of Place, which consists of using available Common Sense Ontologies and Web information to build a collection of generic and instance facts about these places. We have described the system architecture and foccused in the process of association between the Generic Place Ontologies and specific POI instances. Interesting results were obtained in a preliminary experimentation, which revealed important hints that will be used for future improvements.

References

1. Fellbaum, C. (ed.): Wordnet, an Electronic Lexical Database. MIT Press, Cambridge (1998)
2. Hightower, J.: From position to place. In: Proc. of the Workshop on Location-Aware Computing. Part of the Ubiquitous Computing Conference, pp. 10–12 (2003)
3. Genereux, R., Ward, L., Russell, J.: The behavioral component in the meaning of places. Journal of Environmental Psychology 3, 43–55 (1983)

4. Kramer, B.: Classification of generic places: Explorations with implications for evaluation. Journal of Environmental Psychology 15, 3–22 (1995)
5. Harrison, S., Dourish, P.: Re-place-ing space: the roles of place and space in collaborative systems. In: CSCW 1996: Proceedings of the 1996 ACM conference on Computer supported cooperative work, pp. 67–76. ACM Press, New York (1996)
6. Ye, J., Coyle, L., Dobson, S., Nixon, P.: A unified semantics space model. In: Hightower, J., Schiele, B., Strang, T. (eds.) LoCA 2007. LNCS, vol. 4718, pp. 103–120. Springer, Heidelberg (2007)
7. Jiang, C., Steenkiste, P.: A hybrid location model with a computable location identifier for ubiquitous computing (2002)
8. Kindberg, T., Barton, J., Morgan, J., et al.: People, places, things: Web presence for the real world. In: Proc. of WMCSA 2000 (2000)
9. Vazquez, J.I., Abaitua, J., Ipiia, D.L.: The ubiquitous web as a model to lead our environments to their full potential. In: W3C Workshop on the Ubiquitous Web (2006) (position paper)
10. Berners-Lee, T., Hendler, J., Lassila, O.: The semantic web. Scientific American 284, 34–43 (2001)
11. Zuniga, G.L.: Ontology: Its transformation from philosophy to information systems. In: Proceedings of the International Conference on Formal Ontology in Information Systems, pp. 187–197. ACM Press, New York (2001)
12. Petasis, G., Karkaletsis, V., Paliouras, G.: Ontology population and enrichment: State of the art. Public deliverable d4.3, BOEMIE Project (2007)
13. Buitelaar, P., Cimiano, P., Magnini, B.: Ontology Learning from Text: Methods, Evaluation and Applications. IOS Press, Amsterdam (2005)
14. Brank, J., Grobelnik, M., Mladenic, D.: A survey of ontology evaluation techniques. Technical report, Josef Stefan Institute (2005)
15. Swoogle: Semantic web search engine (2008)
16. Geonet names server (gns). National imagery and mapping agency (2008)
17. Cardoso, N., Martins, B., Andrade, L., Silva, M.J.: The xldb group at geoclef 2005. Technical report (2005)
18. Wikipedia (2008)
19. Patwardhan, S., Banerjee, S., Pedersen, T.: Senserelate: Targetword-a generalized framework for word sense disambiguation. In: AAAI, pp. 1692–1693 (2005)
20. Krishnan, V., Manning, C.D.: An effective two-stage model for exploiting non-local dependencies in named entity recognition. In: ACL 2006: Proceedings of the 21st International Conference on Computational Linguistics and the 44th annual meeting of the ACL, Morristown, NJ, USA, pp. 1121–1128. Association for Computational Linguistics (2006)
21. Salton, G., Wong, A., Yang, A.C.S.: A vector space model for automatic indexing. Communications of the ACM 18, 229–237 (1975)
22. Sabou, M., Lopez, V., Motta, E., Uren, V.: Ontology selection: Ontology evaluation on the real semantic web. In: Proceedings of the Evaluation of Ontologies on the Web Workshop, held in conjunction with WWW (2006)

Explicit Dynamic User Profiles for a Collaborative Filtering Recommender System*

M. Ilic, J. Leite, and M. Slota

CENTRIA, Universidade Nova de Lisboa, Portugal

Abstract. User modelling and personalisation are the key aspects of recommender systems in terms of recommendation quality. While being very efficient and designed to work with huge amounts of data, present recommender systems often lack the facility of user integration when it comes to feedback and direct user modelling. In this paper we describe ERASP, an add-on to existing recommender systems which uses dynamic logic programming – an extension of answer set programming – as a means for users to specify and update their models, with the purpose of enhancing recommendations. We present promising experimental results.

1 Introduction

Nowadays, almost every e-commerce application provides a recommender system to suggest products or information that the user might want or need [19].

Common techniques for selecting the right item for recommendation are: collaborative filtering (e.g. [15]) where user ratings for objects are used to perform an inter-user comparison and then propose the best rated items; content-based recommendation (e.g.[8]) where descriptions of the content of items are matched against user profiles, employing techniques from the information retrieval field; knowledge-based recommendation (e.g. [9]) where knowledge about the user, the objects, and some distance measures between them are used to infer the right selections; and hybrid versions of these where two or more techniques (collaborative filtering being usually one of them) are used to overcome their individual limitations. For further details on this subject the reader is referred to [10].

The extent to which users find the recommendations satisfactory is the key feature of a recommendation system, and the accuracy of the user models that are employed is of significant importance to this goal. Such user models represent the user's taste and can be implicit (e.g. constructed from information about the user behavior), or explicit (e.g. constructed from direct feedback or input by the user, like ratings). The accuracy of a user model greatly depends on how well short-term and long-term interests are represented [7], making it a challenging task to include both sensibility to changes of taste and maintenance of permanent preferences. While implicit user modelling disburdens the user of providing direct feedback, explicit user modelling may be more confidence inspiring to the user since recommendations are based on a conscious assignment of preferences.

---

* Partially supported by FCT Scholarship SFRH/BD/38214/2007.

H. Geffner et al. (Eds.): IBERAMIA 2008, LNAI 5290, pp. 352–361, 2008.

Though most recommender systems are very efficient from a large-scale perspective, the effort in user involvement and interaction is calling for more attention. Moreover, problems concerning trust and security could be approached with a better integration of the user and more control over the user model [16].

This calls for more expressive ways for users to express their wishes. The natural way to approach this is through the use of symbolic knowledge representation languages. They provide the necessary tools for representing and reasoning about users, while providing formal semantics that make it possible to reason about the system, thus facilitating trust and security management.

However, we want to keep the advantages of the more automated recommendation techniques such as collaborative filtering and statistical analysis, and benefit from using large amounts of data collected over the years by existing systems that use these techniques. Unfortunately, the use of these methods makes it impossible to have the explicit user models we seek. A tight combination between expressive (logic based) knowledge representation languages and sub-symbolic/statistical approaches is still the Holy Grail of Artificial Intelligence.

One solution to tackle this problem is through the use of a layered architecture, as suggested in [17], where expressive knowledge based user models, specified in *Dynamic Logic Programming* (DLP) [2,18,3], are used to enhance the recommendations provided by existing recommender systems.

In a nutshell, DLP is an extension of Answer-set Programming (ASP) [14] introduced to deal with knowledge updates. ASP is a form of declarative programming that is similar in syntax to traditional logic programming and close in semantics to non-monotonic logic, that is particularly suited for knowledge representation. Enormous progress concerning the theoretical foundations of ASP (c.f. [6] for more) have been made in recent years, and the existence of very efficient ASP solvers (e.g. DLV and SMODELS) make it possible to investigate some serious applications. Whereas in ASP knowledge is specified in a single theory, in DLP knowledge is given by a sequence of theories, each representing an update to the previous ones. The declarative semantics of DLP ensures that any contradictions that arise due to the updates are properly handled. Intuitively, one can add newer rules to the end of the sequence and DLP automatically ensures that these rules are in force and that the older rules are kept for as long as they are not in conflict with the newly added ones (c.f. [18] for more).

In this paper we describe the architecture, implementation and preliminary performance results of ERASP (Enhancing Recommendations with Answer-Set Programming), the system that resulted from following this path. Specifically, ERASP takes the output of an existing recommender algorithm (in this paper we used collaborative filtering, but it could be another) and enhances it taking into account explicit models and preferences specified both by the user and the owner of the system, represented in DLP. The main features of ERASP include:

– Providing the owner and user with a simple but expressive and extensible language to specify their models and preferences, by means of rules and employing existing (e.g. product characteristics) as well as user defined (e.g. own qualitative classifications based on product characteristics) concepts.

– Facilitating the update of user models by automatically detecting and solving contradictions that arise due to the evolution of the user's tastes and needs, which otherwise would discourage system usage.

– Taking advantage of existing recommender systems which may encode large amounts of data that should not be disregarded, particularly useful in the absence of user specified knowledge, while giving precedence to user specifications which, if violated, would turn the user away from the recommendation system.

– Enjoying a well defined semantics which allows the formal study of properties and provides support for explanations, improving interaction with the user.

– Having a connection with relational databases (ASP can be seen as a query language, more expressive than SQL), easing integration with existing systems.

– Allowing the use of both strong and default negation to reason with closed and open world assumptions, thus allowing to reason with incomplete information, and to encode non-deterministic choice, thus generating more than one set of recommendations, facilitating diversity each time the system is invoked;

The remainder of this paper is organised as follows: In Sect. 2, for self containment, we recap the notion of Dynamic Logic Programming, establishing the language used throughout. In Sect. 3 we present ERASP architecture, semantics and implementation. In Sect. 4 we present a short illustrative example and some experimental results. In Sect. 5 we discuss the results and conclude.

2   Dynamic Logic Programming

Let $\mathcal{A}$ be a set of propositional atoms. An **objective literal** is either an atom A or a strongly negated atom $\neg A$. A **default literal** is an objective literal preceded by not. A **literal** is either an objective literal or a default literal. A **rule** r is an ordered pair $H(r) \leftarrow B(r)$ where $H(r)$ (dubbed the head of the rule) is a literal and $B(r)$ (dubbed the body of the rule) is a finite set of literals. A rule with $H(r) = L_0$ and $B(r) = \{L_1, \ldots, L_n\}$ will simply be written as $L_0 \leftarrow L_1, \ldots, L_n$. A **generalised logic program** (GLP) P, in $\mathcal{A}$, is a finite or infinite set of rules. If $H(r) = \neg A$ (resp. $H(r) = not\, A$), then $\neg H(r) = A$ (resp. $not\, H(r) = A$). By the **expanded generalised logic program** corresponding to the GLP P, denoted by $\mathbf{P}$, we mean the GLP obtained by augmenting P with a rule of the form $not\, \neg H(r) \leftarrow B(r)$ for every rule, in P, of the form $H(r) \leftarrow B(r)$, where $H(r)$ is an objective literal. An **interpretation** M of $\mathcal{A}$ is a set of objective literals that is consistent, i.e. M does not contain both A and $\neg A$. An objective literal L is true in M, denoted by $M \models L$, iff $L \in M$, and false otherwise. A default literal $not\, L$ is true in M, denoted by $M \models not\, L$, iff $L \notin M$, and false otherwise. A set of literals B is true in M, denoted by $M \models B$, iff each literal in B is true in M. An interpretation M of $\mathcal{A}$ is an **answer set** of a GLP P iff $M' = least(\mathbf{P} \cup \{not\, A \mid A \notin M\})$, where $M' = M \cup \{not\_A \mid A \notin M\}$, A is an objective literal, and $least(.)$ denotes the least model of the program obtained from the argument program by replacing every $not\, A$ by not_A.

A **dynamic logic program** (DLP) is a sequence of generalised logic programs. Let $\mathcal{P} = (P_1, \ldots, P_n)$ be a DLP and P, P' be GLPs. We use $\rho(\mathcal{P})$ to

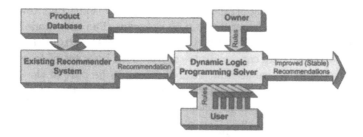

Fig. 1. ERASP System Architecture

denote the multiset of all rules appearing in the programs $\mathbf{P}_1, \ldots, \mathbf{P}_n$ and $(P, P', \mathcal{P})$ to denote the DLP $(P, P', P_1, \ldots, P_n)$. We can now set forth the definition of a semantics, *based on causal rejection of rules*, for DLPs. We start by defining the notion of conflicting rules as follows: two rules r and r' are **conflicting**, denoted by $r \bowtie r'$, iff $H(r) = not\, H(r')$. Let $\mathcal{P} = (P_1, \ldots, P_n)$ be a DLP and M and interpretation. M is a **(refined) dynamic stable model** of $\mathcal{P}$ iff

$$M' = least([\rho(\mathcal{P}) \setminus Rej(\mathcal{P}, M)] \cup Def(\mathcal{P}, M)) \text{ where:}$$
$$Rej(\mathcal{P}, M) = \{r \mid r \in \mathbf{P}_i, \exists r' \in \mathbf{P}_j, i \le j, r \bowtie r', M \models B(r')\}$$
$$Def(\mathcal{P}, M) = \{not\, A \mid \nexists r \in \rho(\mathcal{P}), H(r) = A, M \models B(r)\}$$

3 Framework and Its Implementation

In this Section, we introduce the architecture, its semantics and describe the implementation. ERASP's goal is to take the strengths of DLP as a framework for the representation of evolving knowledge, and put it at the service of both the user and owner of a recommender system, while at the same time ensuring some degree of integration with other recommendation modules, possibly based on distinct paradigms (e.g. statistical).

Fig. 1 depicts the system architecture, representing the information flow. To facilitate presentation, we assume a layered system where the output of an existing recommendation module is simply used as input to our system. We are aware that allowing for feedback from our system to the existing module could benefit its output, but such process would greatly depend on the particular module and we want to keep our proposal as general as possible, and concentrate on other aspects of the framework. The output of the initial module is assumed to be an interpretation, i.e. a consistent set of atoms representing the recommendations. We assume that our language contains a reserved predicate of the form $rec/1$ where the items are the terms of the predicate[1]. The owner policy, possibly used

---

[1] It would be straightforward to also have some value associated with each recommendation, e.g. by using a predicate of the form $rec(item, value)$. However, to get our point across, we will keep to the simplified version.

to encode desired marketing strategies (e.g. introduce some bias towards some products), is encoded as a generalised logic program. The user model (including its updates) is encoded as a dynamic logic program. The Product Database is a relational database that can easily be represented by a set of facts in a logic program. For simplicity, we assume such database to be part of the generalised logic program representing the owner's policy. A formalization of the system is given by the concept of Dynamic Recommender Frame:

Definition 1 (Dynamic Recommender Frame). *Let $\mathcal{A}$ be a set of propositional atoms. A Dynamic Recommender Frame (DRF), over $\mathcal{A}$, is a triple $\langle M, P_0, \mathcal{P} \rangle$ where M is an interpretation of $\mathcal{A}$, P_0 a generalised logic program over $\mathcal{A}$, and $\mathcal{P}$ a DLP over $\mathcal{A}$.*

The semantics of a Dynamic Recommender Frame is given by the set of dynamic stable models of its transformation into a DLP. This transformation is based on two natural principles: – the user's specification should prevail over both the initial recommendations and the owner's rules, since users would not accept a recommendation system that explicitly violates their rules; – the owner should be able to override the recommendations in the initial interpretation, e.g. to specify preference among products according to the profit. Intuitively, we construct a DLP with the initial program obtained from the initial recommendations, which is then updated with the owner's policy specification (P_0) and the user's specification ($\mathcal{P}$). A formal definition follows:

Definition 2 (Stable Recommendation Semantics). *Let $\mathcal{R} = \langle M, P_0, \mathcal{P} \rangle$ be a DRF and M_R an interpretation. M_R is a stable recommendation iff M_R is a dynamic stable model of $(P_M, P_0, \mathcal{P})$ where $P_M = \{A \leftarrow | A \in M\}$.*

According to this semantics, a Dynamic Recommender Frame can have more than one Stable Recommendation, each corresponding to one particular set of products that could be recommended to the user. This immediately represents a nice feature since it allows for the system to present the user with a different set of recommendations each time the user invokes the system adding diversity.

ERASP is implemented as an online application[2] using a PHP-based initial collaborative filtering recommender system. The product database consists of the complete MovieLens (http://www.grouplens.org/) dataset (3883 movies with title, genre and year). After rating some movies and receiving some initial recommendations (using the collaborative filtering algorithm), the user can edit his preferences encoded as a dynamic logic program using an interface which provides some help in rule creation. This program $\mathcal{P}$, the initial recommendations M, the product database and the owner specifications P_0 are given to a *SMODELS*-based solver. The solver computes the corresponding DLP $\mathcal{Q} = (P_M, P_0, \mathcal{P})$ and, using *Lparse*, produces an equivalent DLP $\mathcal{Q}_G$ without variables.

After the grounded dynamic logic program $\mathcal{Q}_G$ is parsed, it gets transformed into an equivalent normal logic program $\mathcal{Q}_G^R$. This transformation is described in detail in [5]. The stable models of $\mathcal{Q}_G^R$ directly correspond to the dynamic

---

[2] Available at http://centria.di.fct.unl.pt/erasp/

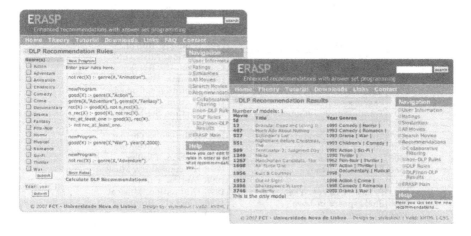

Fig. 2. ERASP Screenshots: a) User Model Interface b) Recommendations

stable models of Q. The transformed program is then passed to *Lparse* and *Smodels* in order to compute its stable models. Our program then writes the recommendations into an SQL database and presents them to the user. Fig. 2 presents two screen-shots of ERASP.

4 Illustrative Example and Experimental Results

In this Section, we show an example that illustrates some features of our proposal, and present the results of benchmark tests based on the example.

Let's consider a typical on-line movie recommender. Its product database contains information about a number of movies and its recommendations are based on some kind of statistical analysis performed over the years. The owner of the recommender system may want to explicitly influence the recommendations of the system in a certain way. She may also want to give the users the ability to specify some explicit information about their tastes in order to correct or refine the recommendations of the existing system. Below we will illustrate how our framework can help achieve both these goals in a simple way. A list of the movies involved in the example together with their relevant properties can be found in Table 1. We will also consider the initial interpretation M obtained from the statistical system to be constant throughout the example:

$$M = \{rec(497), rec(527), rec(551), rec(589), rec(1249),$$
$$rec(1267), rec(1580), rec(1608), rec(1912), rec(2396)\}$$

Let's consider the following owner specification:

$$P_0 : rec(12) \leftarrow not\, rec(15). \tag{1}$$
$$rec(15) \leftarrow not\, rec(12). \tag{2}$$
$$rec(X) \leftarrow rec(Y), year(Y, 1998), genre(Y, \text{``}Romance\text{''}),$$
$$genre(X, \text{``}Musical\text{''}), year(X, 1998). \tag{3}$$

Table 1. Movies used in the example with some of their properties

ID	Title	Year	Genres
12	Dracula: Dead and Loving It	1995	Comedy, Horror
15	Cutthroat Island	1995	Action, Adventure
497	Much Ado About Nothing	1993	Comedy, Romance
527	Schindler's List	1993	Drama, War
551	Nightmare Before Christmas, The	1993	Children's, Comedy
558	Pagemaster, The	1994	Action, Adventure, Fantasy
589	Terminator 2: Judgment Day	1991	Action, Sci-Fi
1249	Nikita	1990	Thriller
1267	Manchurian Candidate, The	1962	Film-Noir, Thriller
1580	Men in Black	1997	Action, Adventure
1608	Air Force One	1997	Action, Thriller
1856	Kurt & Courtney	1998	Documentary, Musical
1912	Out of Sight	1998	Action, Crime
2394	Prince of Egypt, The	1998	Animation, Musical
2396	Shakespeare in Love	1998	Comedy, Romance
3746	Butterfly	2000	Drama, War

Rules (1) and (2) specify that the system should non-deterministically recommend either movie 12 or 15[3]. Rule (3) encodes that the system should recommend all movies with the genre *Musical* from 1998 if any movie with the genre *Romance* from the same year is recommended. Adding an empty set of user specifications $\mathcal{P}_0 = ()$, the recommender frame $\langle M, P_0, \mathcal{P}_0 \rangle$ has two stable recommendations: $M_{R1} = M \cup \{rec(12), rec(1856), rec(2394)\}$ and $M_{R2} = M \cup \{rec(15), rec(1856), rec(2394)\}$. The reader can easily check that each of these two stable recommendations extend the results from the initial recommendation to reflect the wishes of the owner. We now turn to the user specifications:

$$P_1 : not\,rec(X) \leftarrow genre(X, \text{``Animation''}). \tag{4}$$
$$P_2 : good(X) \leftarrow genre(X, \text{``Action''}), genre(X, \text{``Adventure''}),$$
$$genre(X, \text{``Fantasy''}). \tag{5}$$
$$rec(X) \leftarrow good(X), not\,n\_rec(X). \tag{6}$$
$$n\_rec(X) \leftarrow good(X), not\,rec(X). \tag{7}$$
$$rec\_at\_least\_one \leftarrow good(X), rec(X). \tag{8}$$
$$\leftarrow not\,rec\_at\_least\_one. \tag{9}$$
$$P_3 : good(X) \leftarrow genre(X, \text{``War''}), year(X, 2000). \tag{10}$$
$$P_4 : not\,rec(X) \leftarrow genre(X, \text{``Adventure''}). \tag{11}$$

In the single rule (4) of program P_1, the user simply overrides any previous rule that would recommend an *Animation* movie. In program P_2, she introduces the notion of a good movie in rule (5) and rules (6) – (9) make sure there is always at least one good movie recommended[4]. Program P_3 extends the definition of a good movie and program P_4 avoids recommendations of *Adventure* movies.

With $\mathcal{P}_1 = (P_1)$, $\mathcal{P}_2 = (P_1, P_2)$, $\mathcal{P}_3 = (P_1, P_2, P_3)$, $\mathcal{P}_4 = (P_1, P_2, P_3, P_4)$, the recommender frames $\langle M, P_0, \mathcal{P}_1 \rangle$, $\langle M, P_0, \mathcal{P}_2 \rangle$, $\langle M, P_0, \mathcal{P}_3 \rangle$ and $\langle M, P_0, \mathcal{P}_4 \rangle$ have

---

[3] The even loop through default negation is used in ASP to generate two models.

[4] These rules are a classic construct of ASP. The actual recommendation system would, like most answer-set solvers, have special syntactical shortcuts for this kind of specifications, since we cannot expect the user to write them from scratch.

Table 2. All test results ordered by input and program (time in milliseconds)

Input	All				No title				1000				1000 no title			
User DLP	$\mathcal{P}_1$	$\mathcal{P}_2$	$\mathcal{P}_3$	$\mathcal{P}_4$	$\mathcal{P}_1$	$\mathcal{P}_2$	$\mathcal{P}_3$	$\mathcal{P}_4$	$\mathcal{P}_1$	$\mathcal{P}_2$	$\mathcal{P}_3$	$\mathcal{P}_4$	$\mathcal{P}_1$	$\mathcal{P}_2$	$\mathcal{P}_3$	$\mathcal{P}_4$
Parsing	195	196	199	197	151	150	149	150	95	96	96	96	81	84	83	85
Grounding	1596	1591	1598	1639	1156	1159	1154	1181	468	470	475	476	329	330	332	339
Transformation	496	503	502	504	305	310	320	407	131	133	133	135	134	137	136	138
Stable models	1289	1294	1312	1320	919	922	963	859	308	310	326	310	218	220	235	223
Total	3576	3584	3611	3660	2531	2541	2586	2597	1002	1009	1030	1017	762	771	786	785

2, 2, 6 and 1 stable recommendations, respectively, which, for lack of space we cannot list here. Instead, we list only the final one and invite the reader to see how it complies with the user rules, how contradictory user rules are solved (e.g. adventure movies that are good, such as movie 558), as well as those between user and owner rules (e.g. movie 15 is no longer recommended).

$$M = \{rec(12), rec(497), rec(527), rec(551), rec(589), rec(1249), rec(1267),$$
$$rec(1608), rec(1856), rec(1912), rec(2396), rec(3746)\}$$

We now turn our attention to time performance. To investigate the importance of the size of the input, we tested using the programs specified above but with the following four databases with varying number of movies and concepts:

- **All:** 3883 movies, all concepts (17406 atoms)
- **No title:** 3883 movies, all concepts except $title(ID, Title)$ (9640 atoms)
- **1000:** 1000 movies, all concepts (4428 atoms)
- **1000 no title:** 1000 movies, all concepts except $title(ID, Title)$ (3440 atoms)

For each database and each recommender frame we computed all the stable recommendations 100 times using an Intel Pentium D 3.4 GHz processor with 2 MB cache and 1 GB of RAM. The average times for each step of the implementation are shown in Table 2. As can be seen from the table, the time it takes to compute the recommendations varies with the size of the database. As expected, the parsing time grows linearly. The size of the database directly determines the number of terms substituted for the variables in the grounding phase hence the number of generated rules. The transformation is then linear and the worst case upper bound is $2m + l$ rules after the transformation, where m is the number of rules in the grounded DLP and l is the number of atoms in the grounded DLP. The last phase, computation of stable models, is known to be NP-hard although, as usual, SMODELS performs quite well in keeping the computation time low, making ERASP look quite promising. Apart from that, it can be run on computers much faster than the one we had at our disposal. It is also worth noting that the addition of common user rules has little effect on performance.

5   Concluding Remarks

In this paper we proposed ERASP, a system that can work as an add-on for existing recommender systems. Owners of such systems should be able to plug in the application as a recommendation enhancer, for offering users the possibility of explicit preference creation, for defining specific system rules, or both. A rule-based language like DLP can empower owners of recommender systems with the necessary tools to employ marketing strategies with precision, while keeping the diversity of recommendations and following user's preferences. Moreover, it can be used as a query tool to extract information from the database using a more sophisticated language than for example SQL, allowing the system to be used on its own without the need of a previously existing recommender systems. Users of ERASP can find a rich language to interact with the recommender system, gaining control, if they so desire, over the recommendations provided.

ERASP has a formal declarative semantics based on ASP and DLP, thus inheriting many of their theoretical properties and efficient implementations.

ERASP also enjoys other formally provable properties, e.g. the property of both positive and negative supportiveness which insures there always exists an explanation for each recommended item. The provided semantics makes multiple recommendation sets possible, facilitating diversity and non-determinism in recommendations.

ERASP has been implemented and preliminary tests are very encouraging. For databases of some reasonable size (few thousand products) often found in specialised e-commerce applications, the system is readily applicable. For larger databases, not only there is still room for implementation optimizations, but we can drastically improve its performance with an iteration mechanism which would first try to compute the stable models only with a part of the database, of fixed size, chosen according to some criteria of the initial recommender system, e.g. according to the rating of the nearest neighbors in a collaborative filtering recommender system. If recommendations are found, they are presented to the user. If there are no recommendations, then they are recomputed with a bigger (or different) part of the database. The number of items chosen in each step and control over whether and how the iterative approach is being used could depend on the demands of the domain, it could even be controlled directly by the owner and/or user or change dynamically according to some immediate external changes, like the load of the server or similar.

Another way to improve the system in terms of speed would be to restrict the database used to concepts explicitly appearing in the rules, as shown in our tests when we used an input database without the concept $title(ID, Title)$. Furthermore, the grounding and transformation phase of the implementation still have room for optimizations.

One issue that needs to be tackled is that of the user interface, namely the task of writing rules, burdening for the user [12]. Without addressing this issue, ERASP can still provide added value for experts of specific domains that are willing to learn how o write such rules to satisfy their demand of higher accuracy and, more important, reliability of recommendations. Even for less demanding users, there are still some easy to write rules that provide some basic interaction with the recommender system that is of great help. Dealing with this issue includes transforming natural language sentences into logic programs [13], creating natural language interfaces for databases [4], creating rules by tagging and suggestion and learning rules by induction [1].

As for related work, in [11] Defeasible Logic Programming is employed in the ArgueNet website recommender system. Lack of space prevents us from comparing both architectures. To the best of our knowledge, ArgueNet has not been implemented yet.

References

1. Aitken, J.S.: Learning information extraction rules: An inductive logic programming approach. In: Procs. of ECAI 2002. IOS Press, Amsterdam (2002)
2. Alferes, J., Leite, J., Pereira, L., Przymusinska, H., Przymusinski, T.: Dynamic updates of non-monotonic knowledge bases. J. Logic Programming 45(1-3) (2000)
3. Alferes, J.J., Banti, F., Brogi, A., Leite, J.A.: The refined extension principle for semantics of dynamic logic programming. Studia Logica 79(1) (2005)
4. Androutsopoulos, I., Ritchie, G.D., Thanisch, P.: Natural language interfaces to databases–an introduction. Journal of Language Engineering 1(1), 29–81 (1995)
5. Banti, F., Alferes, J.J., Brogi, A.: Operational semantics for DyLPs. In: Bento, C., Cardoso, A., Dias, G. (eds.) EPIA 2005. LNCS (LNAI), vol. 3808, pp. 43–54. Springer, Heidelberg (2005)
6. Baral, C.: Knowledge Representation, Reasoning and Declarative Problem Solving. Cambridge University Press, Cambridge (2003)
7. Billsus, D., Pazzani, M.J.: User modeling for adaptive news access. User Model. User-Adapt. Interact 10(2-3), 147–180 (2000)
8. Billsus, D., Pazzani, M.J.: Content-based recommendation systems. In: Brusilovsky, P., Kobsa, A., Nejdl, W. (eds.) Adaptive Web 2007. LNCS, vol. 4321, pp. 325–341. Springer, Heidelberg (2007)
9. Burke, R.: Knowledge-based recommender systems. In: Encyclopedia of Library and Information Systems, vol. 69, M. Dekker, New York (2000)
10. Burke, R.D.: Hybrid recommender systems: Survey and experiments. User Model. User-Adapt. Interact 12(4), 331–370 (2002)
11. Chesñevar, C., Maguitman, A.: ArgueNet: An argument-based recommender system for solving web search queries. In: Procs. of the 2nd. International IEEE Conference on Intelligent Systems, pp. 282–287. IEEE Press, Los Alamitos (June 2004)
12. Claypool, M., Le, P., Wased, M., Brown, D.: Implicit interest indicators. In: Intelligent User Interfaces, pp. 33–40 (2001)
13. Fuchs, N.E., Schwitter, R.: Specifying logic programs in controlled natural language. Technical Report ifi-95.17,1 (1995)
14. Gelfond, M., Lifschitz, V.: Logic programs with classical negation. In: Procs. of ICLP 1990. MIT Press, Cambridge (1990)
15. Goldberg, D., Nichols, D., Oki, B.M., Terry, D.: Using collaborative filtering to weave an information tapestry. Communications of the ACM 35(12), 61–70 (1992)
16. Lam, S.K., Frankowski, D., Riedl, J.: Do you trust your recommendations? An exploration of security and privacy issues in recommender systems. In: Müller, G. (ed.) ETRICS 2006. LNCS, vol. 3995, pp. 14–29. Springer, Heidelberg (2006)
17. Leite, J., Ilic, M.: Answer-set programming based dynamic user modeling for recommender systems. In: Neves, J., Santos, M.F., Machado, J.M. (eds.) EPIA 2007. LNCS (LNAI), vol. 4874, pp. 29–42. Springer, Heidelberg (2007)
18. Leite, J.A.: Evolving Knowledge Bases. IOS Press, Amsterdam (2003)
19. Ben Schafer, J., Konstan, J.A., Riedl, J.: E-commerce recommendation applications. Data Min. Knowl. Discov. 5(1/2), 115–153 (2001)

Text Retrieval through Corrupted Queries*

Juan Otero[1], Jesús Vilares[2], and Manuel Vilares[1]

[1] Department of Computer Science, University of Vigo
Campus As Lagoas s/n, 32004 – Ourense, Spain
{jop,vilares}@uvigo.es
[2] Department of Computer Science, University of A Coruña
Campus Elviña s/n, 15071 – A Coruña, Spain
jvilares@udc.es

Abstract. Our work relies on the design and evaluation of experimental information retrieval systems able to cope with textual misspellings in queries. In contrast to previous proposals, commonly based on the consideration of spelling correction strategies and a word language model, we also report on the use of character n-grams as indexing support.

Keywords: Degraded text, information retrieval.

1 Introduction

The content of printed documents is hard to process because of the lack of automatic tools for dealing with it. In this sense, in order to make the available information accessible, the first step consists of converting it into an electronic format. Whichever the approach chosen, an expensive manual transcription or an *optical character recognition* (OCR) technique, the process will irremediably introduce misspellings and the final version could only be considered as a degraded version of the original text, which makes the subsequent processing difficult. Similarly, once the document collection is effectively integrated in an *information retrieval* (IR) tool, user-queries often continue to introduce not only new misspelled strings, but possibly also out-of-vocabulary words. Both document and query misspellings are undesirable but their impact on IR systems is different: a misspelled word in a document causes this document to be non-relevant for a query containing the intended word; however, a misspelled word in a query causes all the documents containing the intended word to be non-relevant for that query. In this context, spelling errors are a major challenge for most IR applications [16]. In effect, although formal models are designed for well-spelled corpora and queries, applying them in the real world implies having to deal with such errors, which can substantially hinder performance.

* Research partially supported by the Spanish Government under project HUM2007-66607-C04-02 and HUM2007-66607-C04-03; and the Autonomous Government of Galicia under projects PGIDIT07SIN005206PR, PGIDIT05PXIC30501PN, the Network for Language Processing and Information Retrieval and "Axuda para a consolidación e estruturación de unidades de investigación".

H. Geffner et al. (Eds.): IBERAMIA 2008, LNAI 5290, pp. 362–371, 2008.

With regard to the state-of-the-art in this domain, most authors study the problem exclusively from the point of view of text collection degradation, evaluating the improvement brought about by merging the IR system with a spelling corrector, usually based on a string-to-string edit distance [17]. In contrast to other applications in natural language processing, the correction task is here performed automatically without any interaction with the user, which supposes a serious inconvenience that some authors attempt to compensate for with extra resources. In this sense, a first attempt [18] consists of introducing term weighting functions to assign importance to the individual words of a document representation, in such a manner that it can be more or less dependent on the collection. In particular, if we want to be able to cope even with the degree of corruption of a large number of errors, it is important that the documents are not too short and that recognition errors are distributed appropriately among words and documents [10]. A complementary technique is the incorporation of contextual information, which adds linguistically-motivated features to the string distance module and suggests [16] that average precision in degraded texts can be reduced to a few percent. More recent works [19] propose that string similarity be measured by a statistical model that enables similarities to be defined at the character level as well as the edit operation level.

However, experimental trials suggest [3] that while baseline IR can remain relatively unaffected by character recognition errors due to OCR, relevance feedback via query expansion becomes highly unstable under misspelling, which constitutes a major drawback and justifies our interest in dealing with degraded queries in IR. With regard to this, some authors [6] also introduce modifications to relevance feedback methods combining similar recognized character strings based on both term collection frequency and a string edit-distance measure. At this point, a common objection to these IR architectures concerns [9] the difficulty of interpreting practical results. Indeed, whatever the misspelling located, retrieval effectiveness can be affected by many factors, such as detection rates of indexing features, systematic errors of scanners or OCR devices. It can be also affected by the simulation process, by the behavior of the concrete retrieval function, or by collection characteristics such as length of documents and queries.

In this paper, we propose and evaluate two different alternatives to deal with degraded queries on IR applications. The first one is an n-gram-based strategy which has no dependence on the degree of available linguistic knowledge. On the other hand, we propose a contextual spelling correction algorithm which has a strong dependence on a stochastic model that must be previously built from a POS-tagged corpus. In order to study their validity, a testing framework has been formally designed an applied on both approaches.

2 Text Retrieval through Character N-Grams

Formally, an n-gram is a sub-sequence of n items from a given sequence. So, for example, we can split the word "potato" into four overlapping character 3-grams: -pot-, -ota-, -tat- and -ato-. This simple concept has recently been

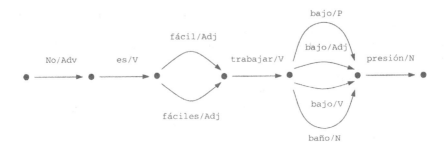

Fig. 1. Spelling correction alternatives represented on a lattice

rediscovered for indexing documents by the *Johns Hopkins University Applied Physics Lab* (JHU/APL) [7], and we recover it now for our proposal.

In dealing with monolingual IR, adaptation is simple since both queries and documents are simply tokenized into overlapping n-grams instead of words. The resulting n-grams are then processed as usual by the retrieval engine. Their interest springs from the possibilities they may offer, particularly in the case of non-English languages, for providing a surrogate means to normalize word forms and allowing languages of very different natures to be managed without further or language-specific processing, since the only processing involved consists of splitting the text into character n-grams. For the same reason, it can even be used when linguistic information and resources are scarce or unavailable.

This seems to be a promising starting point to introduce an effective indexing/recovering strategy to deal with degraded queries. Indeed, the use of indexes based on n-grams nips in the bud the main factor justifying the integration of spelling correction methods in robust IR applications, namely that classic text recovery strategies assume exact matching on entire and correct word indexes, which are usually normalized. So, by using n-grams instead of entire words, matching should only be applied on substrings of these. In practice, this eliminates both the impact of misspelling, to which no specific attention should be paid, and the need to apply normalization. More generally, it should also greatly reduce the inability to handle out-of-vocabulary words.

3   Contextual Spelling Correction

In order to justify the practical interest of our robust IR proposal based on n-grams, we also introduce a classic approach associated to a contextual spelling corrector [14], which will enable us to define a comparing testing frame. The idea now is to take advantage of the contextual linguistic information embedded in a tagging process to rank the alternatives supplied by the correction phase.

More formally, we apply a global finite-state error repair strategy [17], which searches for all possible corrections of a misspelled word that fall within a given edit distance threshold. When an error is detected in a word, elementary edit operations[1] are applied along all the positions in the string, which allows the algorithm to guarantee that all the closest words for a given misspelling will be provided. The algorithm reduces the search space dynamically, retaining only the minimal corrections and attempting to reach the first correction as soon as possible.

Once the repair candidates have been computed from the spelling corrector, additional linguistic information is integrated with the aim of ranking them. This role is played by a stochastic part-of-speech tagger based on a dynamic lattice-based extension of the Viterbi's algorithm [22] over second order *Hidden Markov Models* (HMMs) [5], which allows us to take advantage of syntactic and lexical information embedded in probabilities of transition between tags and emission probabilities of words.

To illustrate the process with an example, let us consider the sentence *"No es fácile trabajar baio presión"*, which is intended to be a corrupted interpretation of the phrase *"No es fácil trabajar bajo presión"* ("It is not easy to work under pressure"), where the words *"fácile"* and *"baio"* are misspellings.

Let us now assume that our spelling corrector provides *"fácil"*/Adj-singular ("easy") and *"fáciles"*/Adj-plural ("easy") as possible corrections for *"fácile"*. Let us also assume that *"bajo"*/Adj ("short"), *"bajo"*/Preposition ("under"), *"bajo"*/Verb ("I bring down") and *"baño"*/Noun ("bath") are possible corrections for *"baio"*. We can then consider the lattice in Fig. 1 as a pseudo-parse representation including all these alternatives for correction. The execution of the dynamic Viterbi's algorithm over it provides us both with the tags of the words and the most probable spelling corrections in the context of this concrete sentence. This allows us to propose a ranked list of correction candidates on the basis of the computed probability for each path in the lattice.

4   Evaluating Our Proposal

Our approach has been initially tested for Spanish. This language can be considered a representative example since it shows a great variety of morphological processes, making it a hard language for spelling correction [21]. The most outstanding features are to be found in verbs, with a highly complex conjugation paradigm, including nine simple tenses and nine compound tenses, all of which have six different persons. If we add the present imperative with two forms, the infinitive, the compound infinitive, the gerund, the compound gerund, and the participle with four forms, then 118 inflected forms are possible for each verb. In addition, irregularities are present in both stems and endings. So, very common verbs such as *"hacer"* ("to do") have up to seven different stems: *"hac-er"*, *"hag-o"*, *"hic-e"*, *"har-é"*, *"hiz-o"*, *"haz"*, *"hech-o"*. Approximately 30% of Spanish verbs are irregular, and can be grouped around 38 different models. Verbs also include enclitic pronouns producing changes in the stem due to the presence of accents: *"da"* ("give"), *"dame"* ("give me"), *dámelo*

---

[1] Insertion, deletion or replacement of a character, or transposition of two contiguous characters.

("**give it to me**"). There are some highly irregular verbs that cannot be classified in any irregular model, such as *"ir"* ("**to go**") or *"ser"* ("**to be**"); and others include gaps in which some forms are missing or simply not used. For instance, meteorological verbs such as *"nevar"* ("**to snow**") are conjugated only in third person singular. Finally, verbs can present duplicate past participles, like *"impreso"* and *"imprimido"* ("**printed**").

This complexity extends to gender inflection, with words considering only one gender, such as *"hombre"* ("**man**") and *"mujer"* ("**woman**"), and words with the same form for both genders, such as *"azul"* ("**blue**"). In relation to words with separate forms for masculine and feminine, we have a lot of models: *"autor/autora"* ("**author/authoress**"); *"jefe/jefa"* ("**boss**"); *"poeta/poetisa"* ("**poet/poetess**"); *"rey/reina"* ("**king/queen**") or *"actor/actriz"* ("**actor/actress**"). We have considered 20 variation groups for gender. We can also refer to number inflection, with words presenting only the singular form, as *"estrés"* ("**stress**"), and others where only the plural form is correct, as *"matemáticas"* ("**mathematics**"). The construction of different forms does not involve as many variants as in the case of gender, but we can also consider a certain number of models: *"rojo/rojos"* ("**red**"); *"luz/luces"* ("**light(s)**"); *"lord/lores"* ("**lord(s)**") or *"frac/fraques"* ("**dress coat(s)**"). We have considered 10 variation groups for number.

4.1   Error Processing

The first phase of the evaluation process consists of introducing spelling errors in the test topic set. These errors were randomly introduced by an automatic error-generator according to a given error rate. Firstly, a *master error topic file* is generated as explained below. For each topic word with a length of more than 3 characters, one of the following four edit errors described by Damerau [4] is introduced in a random position of the word: insert a random character, delete a character, replace a character by one chosen randomly or transpose two adjacent characters. At the same time, a random value between 0 and 100 is generated. Such a value represents the probability of not containing a spelling error. This way we obtain a master error topic file containing, for each word of the topic, its corresponding misspelled form, and a probability value.

All these data make it possible to easily generate different test sets for different error rates, allowing us to evaluate the impact of this variable on the output results. Such a procedure consists of reading the master error topic file and selecting, for each word, the original form in the event of its probability being higher than the fixed error rate, or than the misspelled form in the other case. So, given an error rate T, only $T\%$ of the words of the topics should contain an error. An interesting feature of this solution is that the errors are incremental, since the misspelled forms which are present for a given error rate continue to be present for a higher error rate, thereby avoiding any distortion in the results.

The next step consists of processing these misspelled topics and submitting them to the IR system. In the case of our n-gram-based approach no extra resources are needed, since the only processing consists of splitting them into *n*-grams. However, for our correction-based approach, a lexicon and a manually disambiguated training corpus are needed for training the tagger. We have chosen to work with the MULTEX-JOC Spanish corpus and its associated lexicon. The MULTEX-JOC corpus [23] is a part of the corpus developed within the MULTEXT project[2] financed by the *European Commission*. This part contains raw, tagged and aligned data from the *Written Questions and Answers* of the *Official Journal of the European Community*. The corpus contains approximately 1 million words per language: English, French, German, Italian and Spanish. About 200,000 words per language were grammatically tagged and manually checked for English, French, Italian and Spanish. Regarding the lexicon of the Spanish corpus, it contains 15,548 words that, once compiled, build an automaton of 55,579 states connected by 70,002 transitions.

4.2   The Evaluation Framework

The open-source TERRIER platform [20] has been employed as the retrieval engine of our system, using an InL2[3] ranking model [1]. With regard to the document collection used in the evaluation process, we have chosen to work with the Spanish corpus of the CLEF 2006 robust task [13],[4] which is formed by 454,045 news reports (1.06 GB). More in detail, the test set consists of the 60 training topics[5] established for that task. Topics are formed by three fields: a brief *title* statement, a one-sentence *description*, and a more complex *narrative* specifying the relevance assessment criteria. Nevertheless, only *title* and *description* fields have been used, as stated for CLEF competitions [13]. Taking this document collection as input, two different indexes are then generated.

For testing the correction-based proposal, a classical stemming-based approach is used for both indexing and retrieval. We have chosen to work with SNOWBALL,[6] from the Porter's algorithm [15], while the stop-word list used was that provided by the University of Neuchatel.[7] Both approaches are commonly used in IR research. Following Mittendorfer *et al.* [11,12], a second list of so-named meta-stop-words has also been used for queries. Such stop-words correspond to meta-level content, i.e. those expressions corresponding to query formulation without giving any useful information for the search, as is the case of the query *"encuentre aquellos documentos que describan ..."* ("**find those documents describing ...**").

On the other hand, for testing our *n*-gram-based approach, documents are lowercased, and punctuation marks, but not diacritics, are removed. The resulting text is split and indexed using 4-grams, as a compromise on the *n*-gram

---

[2] http://www.lpl.univ-aix.fr/projects/multext
[3] Inverse Document Frequency model with Laplace after-effect and normalization 2.
[4] These experiments must be considered as unofficial experiments, since the results obtained have not been checked by the CLEF organization.
[5] C050–C059, C070–C079, C100–C109, C120–C129, C150–159, C180–189.
[6] http://snowball.tartarus.org
[7] http://www.unine.ch/info/clef/

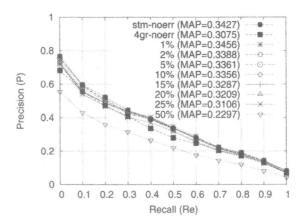

Fig. 2. Results for misspelled (non-corrected) topics using stemming-based retrieval

size after studying the previous results of the JHU/APL group [8]. No stop-word removal is applied in this case.

4.3 Experimental Results

Our proposal has been tested for a wide range of error rates, T, in order to study the behavior of the system not only for low error densities, but also for high error rates existing in noisy environments:

$$T \in \{0\%, 1\%, 2\%, 5\%, 10\%, 15\%, 20\%, 25\%, 50\%\}$$

The first set of experiments performed were those using the misspelled (non-corrected) topics in the case of a classical stemming-based approach. The results obtained for each error rate T are shown in the Precision vs. Recall graph of Fig. 2 taking as baselines both the results for the original topics (*stm-noerr*), and those obtained for such original topics but when using our n-gram based approach (*4gr-noerr*). Notice that *mean average precision* (MAP) values are also given in the same figure. As can be seen, stemming is able to manage the progressive introduction of misspellings until the error rate is increased to T=25%, when the loss of performance —MAP decreases by 9%— becomes statistically significant.[8]

Our second round of experiments tested the first of our proposals. Thus, Fig. 3 shows the results obtained when submitting the misspelled topics once they have been processed using our spelling corrector integrating PoS contextual information. On analysis, these results have shown that correction has, in general, a significant positive effect on performance. Moreover, the application of our corrector allows the system to outperform the original run —even for T=20%, with one in five query words incorrectly typed. This is due, probably, to misspellings existing in the original topics.

---

[8] Two-tailed T-tests over MAPs with α=0.05 have been used throughout this work.

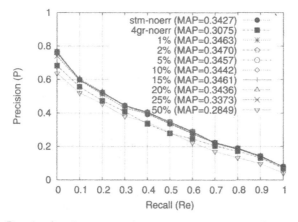

Fig. 3. Results for the corrected topics using stemming-based retrieval

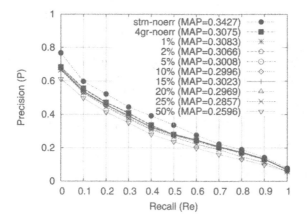

Fig. 4. Results for the misspelled (non-corrected) topics using 4-gram-based retrieval

Finally, we have tested our n-gram-based proposal. So, Fig. 4 shows the results when the misspelled (non-corrected) topics are submitted to our n-gram-based IR system. As can be seen, this approach is also very robust. No significant difference is found until the error rate is increased to T=20%, with only a MAP loss of 3% at that rate. Taking into account the relative loss of performance in relation to the original topics, n-grams behave in a similar way to stemming for low error rates — when no correction is applied—, but better for high ones. For example, in the case of stemming, MAP losses are 6% for T=20%, 9% for T=25% and 33% for T=50%; however, for n-grams, the equivalent losses are 3%, 7% and 16%, respectively.

5 Conclusions and Future Work

This paper studies the effect of misspelled queries in IR systems, also introducing two approaches for dealing with them. The first consists of applying a spelling correction algorithm to the input queries. This algorithm is a development of a previous global correction technique but extended to include contextual information obtained through part-of-speech tagging. Our second proposal consists of working directly with the misspelled topics, but using a character n-gram-based IR system instead of a classical stemming-based one. This solution avoids the need for word normalization during indexing and can also deal with out-of-vocabulary words, such as misspellings. Moreover, since it does not rely on language-specific processing, it can be used with languages of very different natures even when linguistic information and resources are scarce or unavailable.

After proposing an error generation methodology for testing, our approaches have been evaluated. Experiments have shown that both in the case of stemming and n-gram-based processing, they are able to manage error rates up to 20–25% with no significant impact on performance. Moreover, the application of our correction-based approach has a positive impact, since it is able not only to eliminate the loss of performance for stemming due to the misspellings introduced, but also to consistently outperform the results for original topics.

However, both stemming and our correction-based approach need language-specific resources in order to function: stemmers, stop-word lists, lexicons, tagged corpora, etc. On the contrary, the use of an n-gram-based proposal is a knowledge-light language-independent approach with no need for such resources, also having the same robust behavior in relation to misspellings.

With regard to our future work, it would be interesting to test the impact of the length of the query on the results. We would also like to make further experiments with our correction-based approach. One possibility is to study the behavior of the system when no contextual information is taken into account, i.e. when only the original global correction algorithm is applied [17]. Finally, new tests with other languages are being prepared.

References

1. Amati, G., van Rijsbergen, C.-J.: Probabilistic models of Information Retrieval based on measuring divergence from randomness. ACM Transactions on Information Systems 20(4), 357–389 (2002)
2. Cross-Language Evaluation Forum (visited, July 2008), http://www.clef-campaign.org
3. Collins-Thompson, K., Schweizer, C., Dumais, S.: Improved string matching under noisy channel conditions. In: Proc. of the 10th Int. Conf. on Information and Knowledge Management, pp. 357–364 (2001)
4. Damerau, F.: A technique for computer detection and correction of spelling errors. Communications of the ACM 7(3) (March 1964)
5. Graña, J., Alonso, M.A., Vilares, M.: A common solution for tokenization and part-of-speech tagging: One-pass Viterbi algorithm vs. iterative approaches. In: Sojka, P., Kopeček, I., Pala, K. (eds.) TSD 2002. LNCS (LNAI), vol. 2448, pp. 3–10. Springer, Heidelberg (2002)
6. Lam-Adesina, A.M., Jones, G.J.F.: Examining and improving the effectiveness of relevance feedback for retrieval of scanned text documents. Information Processing Management 42(3), 633–649 (2006)

7. McNamee, P., Mayfield, J.: Character N-gram Tokenization for European Language Text Retrieval. Information Retrieval 7(1-2), 73–97 (2004)
8. McNamee, P., Mayfield, J.: JHU/APL experiments in tokenization and non-word translation. In: Peters, C., Gonzalo, J., Braschler, M., Kluck, M. (eds.) CLEF 2003. LNCS, vol. 3237, pp. 85–97. Springer, Heidelberg (2004)
9. Mittendorf, E., Schauble, P.: Measuring the effects of data corruption on information retrieval. In: Symposium on Document Analysis and Information Retrieval, p. XX (1996)
10. Mittendorf, E., Schäuble, P.: Information retrieval can cope with many errors. Information Retrieval 3(3), 189–216 (2000)
11. Mittendorfer, M., Winiwarter, W.: A simple way of improving traditional IR methods by structuring queries. In: Proc. of the 2001 IEEE Int. Workshop on Natural Language Processing and Knowledge Engineering (NLPKE 2001) (2001)
12. Mittendorfer, M., Winiwarter, W.: Exploiting syntactic analysis of queries for information retrieval. Data & Knowledge Engineering 42(3), 315–325 (2002)
13. Nardi, A., Peters, C., Vicedo, J.L.: Results of the CLEF 2006 Cross-Language System Evaluation Campaign, Working Notes of the CLEF 2006 Workshop, Alicante, Spain, September 20-22 (2006) [2]
14. Otero, J., Graña, J., Vilares, M.: Contextual Spelling Correction. In: Moreno Díaz, R., Pichler, F., Quesada Arencibia, A. (eds.) EUROCAST 2007. LNCS, vol. 4739, pp. 290–296. Springer, Heidelberg (2007)
15. Porter, M.F.: An algorithm for suffix stripping. Program 14(3), 130–137 (1980)
16. Ruch, P.: Using contextual spelling correction to improve retrieval effectiveness in degraded text collections. In: Proc. of the 19th Int. Conf. on Computational Linguistics, pp. 1–7 (2002)
17. Savary, A.: Typographical nearest-neighbor search in a finite-state lexicon and its application to spelling correction. In: Watson, B.W., Wood, D. (eds.) CIAA 2001. LNCS, vol. 2494, pp. 251–260. Springer, Heidelberg (2003)
18. Taghva, K., Borsack, J., Condit, A.: Results of applying probabilistic IR to OCR text. In: Proc. of the 17th Int. ACM SIGIR Conf. on Research and Development in Information Retrieval. Performance Evaluation, pp. 202–211 (1994)
19. Takasu, A.: An approximate multi-word matching algorithm for robust document retrieval. In: CIKM 2006: Proc. of the 15th ACM Int. Conf. on Information and Knowledge Management, pp. 34–42 (2006)
20. http://ir.dcs.gla.ac.uk/terrier/ (visited, July 2008)
21. Vilares, M., Otero, J., Graña, J.: On asymptotic finite-state error repair. In: Apostolico, A., Melucci, M. (eds.) SPIRE 2004. LNCS, vol. 3246, pp. 271–272. Springer, Heidelberg (2004)
22. Viterbi, A.: Error bounds for convolutional codes and an asymptotically optimal decoding algorithm. IEEE Trans. Information Theory IT-13, 260–269 (1967)
23. Véronis, J.: MULTEXT-corpora: An annotated corpus for five European languages. CD-ROM, Distributed by ELRA/ELDA (1999)

Dynamic Velocity Field Angle Generation for Obstacle Avoidance in Mobile Robots Using Hydrodynamics

Claudia Pérez-D'Arpino, Wilfredis Medina-Meléndez, Leonardo Fermín, José Guzmán, Gerardo Fernández-López, and Juan Carlos Grieco

Simon Bolivar University, Mechatronics Group, ELE-302
Sartenejas 1080-A Miranda, Venezuela
{cdarpino,wmedina,lfermin,joseguzman,gfernandez,jcgrieco}@usb.ve

Abstract. In this work, a strategy for the generation of the angle reference for a Velocity Field Controller is presented. For an arbitrary trajectory given in its parametric form, it is possible to create a desired velocity field, that could be modified if obstacles were detected by an artificial vision system. Velocity fields are composed by vectors that can be expressed in polar form, i.e. $V_x = |\vec{V}| \cdot \cos(\alpha)$ and $V_y = |\vec{V}| \cdot \sin(\alpha)$. In the velocity field generation technique proposed, the problem is divided into two separate problems: the calculation of the orientation angle α and the calculation of the linear velocity $|\vec{V}|$. This paper addresses the calculation of α, using the hydrodynamics theory of an incompressible non-viscous fluid, plus the use of conformal mapping, thus generating a trajectory vector field that can evade obstacles. Results obtained show that a smooth and continuous field for both open and closed trajectories is achieved.

Keywords: Motion and Path Planning, Velocity Field Generation, Hydrodynamics, Conformal Mapping, Autonomous Navigation.

1 Introduction

Velocity fields consist in specifying a velocity vector to each point of the workspace of a robot, coding a specified task in terms of velocity. They were introduced in [1], and extended in [2] and [3], where authors proposed and tested a Passive Velocity Field Controller for a manipulator. There have been many other velocity field controllers developed for wheeled robots and manipulators [4], that focus on the study of the controller itself using time invariant velocity field theoretically obtained. However, the problem of generating those references in a dynamic fashion has not been addressed in depth. The work of Li et. al. [5], Yamakita et. al. [6] [7], Dixon et. al. [8] and Medina-Meléndez et. al. [9], are important contributions to the velocity field generation area, which is still an open problem in robotics, due to its high tasked dependency and the fact that it is not a trivial matter to solve [2]. This work is focused in the development of an algorithm able to generate velocity fields for coding desired tasks in environments with uncertain conditions.

H. Geffner et al. (Eds.): IBERAMIA 2008, LNAI 5290, pp. 372–381, 2008.
© Springer-Verlag Berlin Heidelberg 2008

The proposed algorithm changes the angle of each vector of a desired velocity field pattern in order to achieve obstacle avoidance. This is based on the theory of hydrodynamics and conformal mapping, so evasion is performed in the same way fluids surround obstacles in their paths. Previous works have been made using hydrodynamical potentials in obstacle's avoidance [10] [11] [12], exploiting its local-minima free characteristic and showing an exact solution for particular cases, in general very difficult to extend to an arbitrary situation in an automatic system. The technique based on hydrodynamics exhibits advantages over the well known Potential Fields Approach (PFA) [13], which uses electrostatic potentials, because it allows to establish a desired trajectory and does not present neither oscillations around the obstacles, nor local minima problems.

This paper is organized as follows: Section 2 presents an overview of the proposed algorithm; Section 3 describes the generation algorithm for the desired trajectory vector field, while the generation of the evader field based on hydrodynamics is explained in Section 4. The deformation of the desired field due to obstacles is shown in Section 5. Two examples are used along the paper to illustrate the process, while results for different trajectories are shown in Section 6. Finally, conclusions are presented in Section 7.

2 Overview of the Proposed Algorithm

The velocity field is given in its 2D components in polar form: $V_x = |\vec{V}| \cdot \cos(\alpha)$ and $V_y = |\vec{V}| \cdot \sin(\alpha)$. It is proposed that α and $|\vec{V}|$ can be generated by different methodologies. This paper is focused in the generation of the Angle Reference α, which is calculated using simple differential calculus, while the obstacles avoidance is reached using the equation of an incompressible non-viscous fluid, that presents a convenient evasive behavior.

The algorithm is divided into two parts: one responsible of the generation of the desired field, which is aware only of the desired trajectory, and the second part that deforms the desired field, as a consequence of the presence of obstacles in the workspace, using an approach based on the theory of hydrodynamics. The process in which fields are generated is illustrated in Fig. 1.

The Trajectory Planning Module processes the algorithm required to generate the values of the angle α reference for each point of the workspace captured by the artificial vision system, thus the robot's environment is discretized over the image using a 640×480 grid, i.e. a 2D equispaced grid, in which one vector

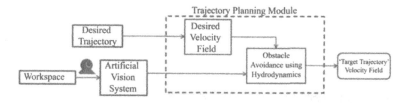

Fig. 1. Block Diagram of the target velocity field generation system

is calculated for each grid point (i, j). Depending of the particular application, vectors can be calculated only for the point where the robot is located.

3   Generation of the Desired Trajectory Vector Field

The desired trajectory is specified by the user in its parametric form, specifying $x = f(\theta)$ and $y = g(\theta)$, being able to define both open and closed trajectories, and to indicate an orientation, i.e. to specify a direction of travel, through the velocity vectors associated to the desired path, which are defined by (1).

$$V_x = direction \cdot \frac{\partial x}{\partial \theta}, \quad V_y = direction \cdot \frac{\partial y}{\partial \theta} \tag{1}$$

where *direction* is a binary variable having a value of 1 or -1, depending of the direction of travel. Also, starting and ending points can be specified, using the range of the parameter θ.

For example, a circle contour following task is defined by (2), and an open trajectory by (3).

$$x = 300 + 100 \, \cos(\theta), \quad y = 300 + 100 \, \sin(\theta), \quad \theta \in [0, 2\pi] \tag{2}$$

$$x = 300 + 100 \cos(\theta + 2) + 300 \cos(\frac{1}{2}\theta), \quad y = 200 + 100(\sin(\frac{1}{2}\theta))^3, \quad \theta \in [0, 1.7\pi] \tag{3}$$

These trajectories are illustrated in Fig. 2 together with their velocity vectors.

In order to obtain the desired field that encodes the desired trajectory, it is necessary to generate first two vector fields, which are the approaching and the tangential vector fields, and perform a weighted superposition of them that produces a field that converges smoothly to the desired trajectory, as it was proposed in [9].

3.1   Approaching and Tangential Vector Field

The Approaching Field is defined by the vectors that aim directly to the closest point of the desired trajectory, in which each vector $\vec{V}_{approach(i,j)}$ is obtained as the normalized substraction of the closest trajectory's point and the grid's point (i, j) being analyzed. The algorithm finds the closest trajectory's point

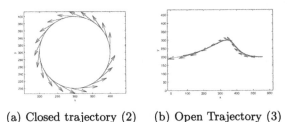

(a) Closed trajectory (2)   (b) Open Trajectory (3)

Fig. 2. Parameterized Trajectories

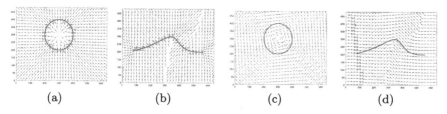

Fig. 3. Approaching Fields: (a) Closed Trajectory, (b) Open Trajectory. Tangential Fields: (c) Closed Trajectory. (d) Open Trajectory.

$(X_{closest(i,j)}, Y_{closest(i,j)})$ for all pairs (i, j), as the coordinate pair (X_{traj}, Y_{traj}) that satisfies (4),

$$MIN \left[\sqrt{(X_{(i,j)} - X_{traj_k})^2 + (Y_{(i,j)} - Y_{traj_k})^2} \right] \tag{4}$$

where k is the index of all points conforming the desired trajectory. The approaching field is defined by (5).

$$\vec{V}_{ap(i,j)} = \frac{(X_{closest(i,j)} - X_{(i,j)})\,\hat{x} + (Y_{closest(i,j)} - Y_{(i,j)})\,\hat{y}}{\|(X_{closest(i,j)} - X_{(i,j)})\,\hat{x} + (Y_{closest(i,j)} - Y_{(i,j)})\,\hat{y}\|} \tag{5}$$

The approaching fields generated for trajectories defined in (2) and (3) are shown in Fig. 3(a) and Fig. 3(b), respectively. This algorithm works in both open and closed trajectories.

In the generation of the Tangential Field, the directional derivative expressed in (1) is considered. This vector field is based on the previously calculated data $(X_{closest(i,j)}, Y_{closest(i,j)})$, and its generated using (6).

$$\vec{V}_{tg(i,j)} = \frac{(V_x(X_{closest(i,j)}))\,\hat{x} + (V_y(Y_{closest(i,j)}))\,\hat{y}}{\|(V_x(X_{closest(i,j)}))\,\hat{x} + (V_y(Y_{closest(i,j)}))\,\hat{y}\|} \tag{6}$$

The result for a closed trajectory is shown in Fig. 3(c). When the algorithm deals with an open trajectory, in the cases that $(X_{closest(i,j)}, Y_{closest(i,j)})$ coincides with the starting or ending points of the desired trajectory, it is necessary for the algorithm to evaluate the possibility of turn around the direction of the vector, in order to obtain vectors that aim tangentially to the trajectory. This case can be observed in Fig. 3(d), at the left side of the field, in which the vector's orientation differs from the other vector in the field. The algorithm is limited to trajectories with unique tangent at all points.

3.2 Desired Field

The desired field is generated performing the weighted sum specified in (7),

$$\vec{V}_{des(i,j)} = \frac{F1_{d_{(i,j)}} \vec{V}_{ap(i,j)} + F2_{d_{(i,j)}} \vec{V}_{tg(i,j)}}{\|F1_{d_{(i,j)}} \vec{V}_{ap(i,j)} + F2_{d_{(i,j)}} \vec{V}_{tg(i,j)}\|} \tag{7}$$

where $F_{1_{d_{(i,j)}}}$ and $F_{2_{d_{(i,j)}}}$ are functions of the shortest Euclidean distance $d_{(i,j)}$ between the grid's point (i,j) and the desired trajectory. The weight functions used are sigmoidal type [9], expressed in (8).

$$F_{1_{d_{(i,j)}}} = \frac{2}{1 + e^{-\gamma d_{(i,j)}}} - 1, \qquad F_{2_{d_{(i,j)}}} = 1 - F_{1_{d_{(i,j)}}} \qquad (8)$$

The behavior of these weight functions (in Fig. 7(a)) allows to obtain a field in which the direction of the tangential vectors prevail over the direction of the approaching vectors in the trajectory's vicinity, while the opposite effect occurs far from the path.

The results of performing this weighted sum over the fields presented in Fig. 3 are shown in Fig. 4, for both the closed and open trajectories. As can be noticed, the field is such as its flow, which is determined by tracing the arrows, converges to the desired trajectory in a smooth and continuous form. The rate of convergence can be modified varying the parameter γ of the Sigmoidal functions (8).

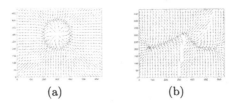

(a)   (b)

Fig. 4. (a) Closed Trajectory Desired Field. (b) Open Trajectory Desired Field.

4   Obstacles Avoidance Based on Hydrodynamics

Once the desired field has been established, the system takes the information provided by an artificial vision system which is able to determine the position and dimensions of the obstacles, from a top view image of the workspace [14]. Each obstacle is encircled, limiting the space that must be evaded by the mobile robot while executing the desired task.

The behavior of a laminar fluid flow can be applied in the obstacle-avoidance path planning problem due to the smoothness and continuity of the evader fluid motion through an obstacle. Considering a steady-state incompressible and non-viscous fluid, its velocity field $\overrightarrow{V}_{F_m}$ is calculated for each obstacle represented by the index m, thus the desired trajectory field can be deformed using a weighted sum of the desired trajectory field and the flow velocity fields.

An incompressible fluid satisfies $div\,\overrightarrow{V_F} = 0$, being divergence free [15], thus there is some velocity potential ϕ such as,

$$\overrightarrow{V_F} = grad\,\phi \qquad (9)$$

In view of these conditions, the velocity potential ϕ is a harmonic function because it satisfies the Laplace's Equation $\nabla^2\phi = 0$. Solving the equation for ϕ, the velocity field can be found using (9).

4.1   Conformal Mapping

The procedure used to find the stream lines around a disk (the obstacle) is to first solve the equation for a half complex plane, and then perform a conformal mapping to the disk. Conformal mapping is a mathematical technique used to convert a mathematical problem and its solution into another one using complex variables. The conformal mapping effect is illustrated in Fig.5 with a rotation angle ε, which is taken as the arrival angle of the desired trajectory field to the obstacle being analyzed.

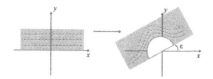

Fig. 5. Effect of the conformal mapping

The solution in the complex plane is based on two conditions over ϕ, expressed in (10) and (11),

$$\frac{\partial \phi}{\partial n} = 0 \tag{10}$$

$$\phi_{(x,y)} = \beta \cdot x \tag{11}$$

where (10) is a Neumann type boundary condition, that states that the velocity vectors $\overrightarrow{V}$ should be parallel to the disk's boundary, being n its normal vector; while (11) sets the flow's speed to a constant value β. This last condition implies that the fluid viscosity is equal to zero.

The solution of the fluid equation is given in the form of a complex potential $F_{(z)} = \phi + i\psi$, where ψ is the conjugate of ϕ, and Z is the complex variable, thus solving for ϕ in the plane and applying the conformal mapping to the disk, it is obtained (12).

$$F_{(z)} = \beta \left(e^{-i\varepsilon} Z + \frac{1}{e^{-i\varepsilon} Z} \right) \tag{12}$$

In polar coordinates, the real and complex components of $F(z)$ can be written as (13) specifies.

$$\phi_{(r,\theta)} = \beta \left[\left(r + \frac{1}{r} \right) \cos(\theta - \varepsilon) \right], \qquad \psi_{(r,\theta)} = \beta \left[\left(r - \frac{1}{r} \right) \sin(\theta - \varepsilon) \right] \tag{13}$$

The flow lines are the contours of the function ψ, which is plotted in Fig. 6(a), while the contour of the velocity potential is shown in Fig.6(b). The evader velocity field $\overrightarrow{V}_{flow_{k_{(i,j)}}}$ in which we are interested is shown in Fig. 6(c).

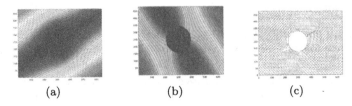

(a)   (b)   (c)

Fig. 6. Fluid Flow. (a) Contour of the Stream Function ψ. (b) Velocity Potential ϕ. (c) Evader Velocity Field $\mathbf{V}_{flow} = grad\phi$.

5   Field Overlapping

After the algorithm calculates an evader field $\vec{V}_{flow_{k(i,j)}}$ for each obstacle k detected, a weighted sum of these evader fields and the desired trajectory field (7) is performed, as it is specified in (14).

$$\vec{V}_{target_{(i,j)}} = Fg_{(i,j)} \vec{V}_{des(i,j)} + \sum_{k=1}^{obs} Fk_{d_{(i,j)}} \vec{V}_{flow_{k(i,j)}} \qquad (14)$$

F_k is the weight function for the evader fields that have the same behavior of F_2 (8), whereas $Fg_{(i,j)}$ is the weight function (15) for the desired field, constructed by centering a gaussian surface over each obstacle in order to obtain the opposite behavior of F_k. The $Fg_{(i,j)}$ calculated for the obstacles distribution used in the closed trajectory example is shown Fig. 7(b).

$$Fg_{(i,j)} = 1 - \sum_{k=1}^{obs} e^{-\left(\frac{X_{(i,j)}-Xobs_k}{Robs_k+\lambda}\right)^2 - \left(\frac{Y_{(i,j)}-Yobs_k}{Robs_k+\lambda}\right)^2} \qquad (15)$$

The overlapping equation (14) satisfies the superposition principle, because the solution vector field is obtained from the sum of several vector fields, allowing the system to be dynamic, because both the desired trajectory field and the evader fields represent a single term in the sum, which can be removed or added dynamically. When the number of obstacles is zero, $\vec{V}_{target_{(i,j)}}$ coincides with $\vec{V}_{des(i,j)}$.

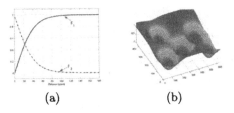

(a)   (b)

Fig. 7. Weight Functions. (a) Sigmoidal functions (8), with $\gamma = 0.05$. (b) Surface of the gaussian weigh function (15).

6   Results

The generation system was tested in several situations in both simulation and with a real robot, using different desired trajectories and distribution of obstacles, in order to verify that smooth obstacle avoidance is achieved, and to analyze the behavior of the fields in particular situations.

Overall results are presented in Fig. 8, in which the first row presents the velocity field generated for three different cases. It can be noticed in both open and closed trajectory cases that the original desired trajectory was smoothly deformed in order to avoid obstacles, producing a new visible main stream flow that will be followed by the robot once it has converged to the main trajectory. This fact is proved using a simulation, based on Runge-Kutta iterations, of the mobile robot trajectory. Results of these simulations are shown in the second row of Fig. 8, where Fig. 8(d) and Fig. 8(e) present the results for a desired trajectory without obstacles, and the behavior when obstacles are found, using several different starting points. Fig. 8(f) shows the result of the simulation in the case of an open trajectory.

The starting and ending points of open trajectories are of special interest due to the convergence of the fields to these points. When an obstacle is over the starting or ending point, the effect is to displace this checkpoint to another point outside the obstacle, as it is shown in Fig. 8(c).

Finally, the performance of the system was tested using a real differential drive robot under PID control, obtaining the results of Fig. 9. In real tests it is necessary to take into account the dimensions of the robot, by considering a security space around the obstacles, which is produced by the algorithm by simply increasing the radius of the obstacles. Smooth obstacle avoidance can be

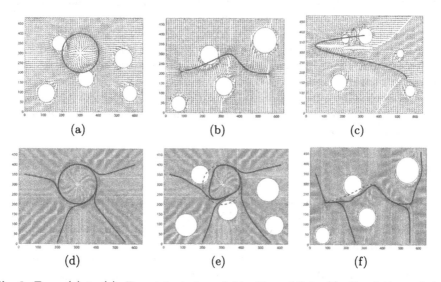

(a)   (b)   (c)

(d)   (e)   (f)

Fig. 8. From (a) to (c): Target trajectory fields. From (d) to (f): Simulations of the mobile robot trajectory.

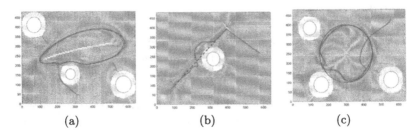

(a)   (b)   (c)

Fig. 9. Results of real tests using a differential drive robot

verified for all cases, as well as the convergence to the desired trajectory, even in those cases in which obstacles are in the main path of the desired trajectory, as it occurs in Fig. 9(b).

7 Conclusions

An algorithm for the generation of the angle component α of a velocity field was developed and tested. Using simple differential calculus, one can obtain a velocity field for an arbitrary desired trajectory, satisfying the condition of smoothness and convergence to the desired trajectory.

Obstacles avoidance is achieved using the theory of hydrodynamics, exploiting the natural evasive behavior of fluids. The method proposed for generating an evader velocity field using conformal mapping has the advantage of very low computational complexity. This fact, together with the condition that the equations satisfies superposition principle, allows the system to be used in dynamical and real time applications. Conformal mapping is a powerful technique that can be extended to avoid obstacles of different forms like an ellipse or a polygon, by changing the mapping function.

The system was evaluated through simulations and real tests with a differential drive mobile robot under a velocity field control, achieving reliable results in contour following tasks.

Future work will be focussed in the generation of the velocity component $|\vec{V}|$, as well as testing the performance of the mobile robot under control of both references: $|\vec{V}|$ and α.

References

1. Li, P.Y., Horowitz, R.: Passive Velocity Field Control of Mechanical Manipulators. IEEE Trans. on Robot. and Aut. 15, 751–763 (1999)
2. Li, P.Y., Horowitz, R.: Passive Velocity Field Control: Part I - Geometry and Robustness. IEEE Trans. on Robot. and Automat. 46, 1346–1359 (2001)
3. Li, P.Y., Horowitz, R.: Passive Velocity Field Control: Part II - Application to Contour Following. IEEE Trans. on Robot. and Aut. 46, 1360–1371 (2001)
4. Kelly, R., Sánchez, V., Bugarin, E.: A Fixed Camera Controller for Visual Guidance of Mobile Robots via Velocity Fields. In: Proc. IEEE Conf. on Rob. and Aut. (2005)

5. Li, P.Y.: Adaptive Passive Velocity Field Control. In: Proc. American Control Conf., San Diego, U.S.A, vol. 2, pp. 774–779 (June 1999)
6. Yamakita, M., Suh, J.H.: Adaptive Generation of Desired Velocity Field for Cooperative Mobile Robots with Decentralized PVFC. In: Proc. IEEE/RSJ Int. Conf. on Intell. Robot. and Syst. IROS 2000, Japan, pp. 1841–1846 (2000)
7. Yamakita, M., Suh, J.H.: Adaptive generation of Desired Velocity field for Leader-Follower Type Mobile Robots with Decentralized PVFC. In: Proc. IEEE Int. Conf. on Robot. and Automat., Seoul, Korea, pp. 3495–3501 (2001)
8. Dixon, W.E., Galluzo, T., Hu, G.: Adaptive Velocity Field Control of a Wheeled Mobile Robot. In: Proc. Int. Work. on Rob. Mot. and Cont., pp. 145–150 (2005)
9. Medina-Meléndez, W., Fermín, L., Cappelletto, J., Murrugarra, C., Fernández-López, G., Grieco, J.C.: Vision-Based Dynamic Velocity Field Generation for Mobile Robots. In: Robot Motion and Control. LNCIS, vol. 360, pp. 69–79 (2007)
10. Waydo, S., Murray, R.M.: Vehicle Motion Planning Using Stream Functions. In: Proc. IEEE Int. Conf. on Robot. and Automat., vol. 2, pp. 2484–2491 (2003)
11. Liu, C., Wei, Z., Liu, C.: A New Algorithm for Mobile Robot Obstacle Avoidance Based on Hydrodynamics. In: Proc. IEEE Int. Conf. on Aut. and Log. (2007)
12. Keymeulen, D., Decuyper, J.: The Fluid Dynamics Applied to Mobile Robot Motion: The Stream Field Method. In: Proc. IEEE Int. Conf. on Rob. and Aut. (1994)
13. Khatib, O.: Real-Time Obstacle Avoidance for Manipulators and Mobile Robots. Int. Journal of Robotics Research 5, 90–98 (1986)
14. Bolaños, J., Medina-Meléndez, W., Fermín, L., Cappelletto, J., Fernández-López, G., Grieco, J.C.: Object Recognition for Obstacle Avoidance in Mobile Robots. In: Rutkowski, L., Tadeusiewicz, R., Zadeh, L.A., Żurada, J.M. (eds.) ICAISC 2006. LNCS (LNAI), vol. 4029, pp. 722–731. Springer, Heidelberg (2006)
15. Marsden, E., Hoffman, J.: Basic Complex Analysis. W.H. Freeman, New York (1999)

Motion Planning for Cooperative Multi-robot Box-Pushing Problem*

Ezra Federico Parra-González, Gabriel Ramírez-Torres,
and Gregorio Toscano-Pulido

Centro de investigación y estudios avanzados del IPN
Laboratorio de tecnologías de la información
Carretera a Monterrey KM 6, Ciudad Victoria, Tamaulipas México
{eparra,grtorres,gtoscano}@tamps.cinvestav.mx

Abstract. The multi-robot box-pushing problem in cluttered environments has demonstrated to be a very complex problem with multiple practical applications. In this document we present a new strategy to solve it, inspired in the wavefront algorithm which it also includes some pertinent modifications to obtain trajectories that facilitate the box displacement for non-holonomic mobile robots. The proposed method obtains its benefits by the reduction of route distances, reducing the direction changes in the routes, and by searching the best pushing points for robots.

Keywords: Box-pushing, path planning, community of mobile robots.

1 Introduction

Researchers generally agree that multi-robot systems have several advantages over single-robot systems [1]. The most common motivations to develope multi robot system solutions are that: 1) the task complexity is too high for a single robot to accomplish; 2) the task is inherently distributed; 3) building several resource-bounded robots is easier than having a single powerful robot; 4) multiple robots can solve problems faster using parallelism; and 5) the introduction of multiple robots increases robustness through redundancy.

Box-pushing is related to the well-known "piano mover's problem" and is stated as follows: given an arbitrary rigid polyhedral environment, find a continuous collision-free path taking this object from a source configuration to a desired destination configuration. It was shown by Reif [2] that this problem is PSPACE-hard, which implies NP-hard.

The box-pushing task can be summarized as follows: We have N mobile robots that must drive a box B towards a target area T. The displacement of B requires at least the cooperation of a critical number Nc of mobile robots. Then the fundamental research challenge in these systems is to design the local control laws in order to generate the desired global team behavior (figure 1).

---

* This research was partialy funded by project number 51623 from "Fondo Mixto Conacyt-Gobierno del Estado de Tamaulipas".

H. Geffner et al. (Eds.): IBERAMIA 2008, LNAI 5290, pp. 382–391, 2008.
© Springer-Verlag Berlin Heidelberg 2008

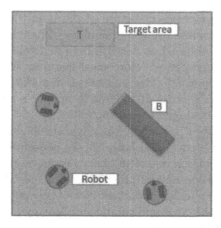

Fig. 1. Basic picture of a "box-pushing" systems

The rest of this paper is organized as follows. Section 2 presents a brief review of related published works. In section 3 we present the different strategies used to solve the path planning problem in the proposed method. The full description of the proposed method is presented in section 4 along with some numerical results. Finally, some concluding remarks and future works ideas are given in section 5 and 6.

2 Related Work

The box-pushing problem has a large number of practical applications that makes it particularly interesting to be studied. In this section we briefly report some of the most outstanding strategies proposed up to the moment.

Communication in multi-robot teams has been extensively studied since the inception of distributed robotics research. Yamada [3] reports that, independently of the configuration of the system (centralized or decentralized), the communication needs can be omitted and replaced by behavioral mechanisms based on local information. However these strategies do not vary dynamically and it is necessary to have a large amount of preprogrammed behaviors to solve new challenges. On the other hand, Muoz [4] reports how the communication can considerably improve the behavior of the multi-robot systems, increasing the coordination, the cooperation, the collisions handling and finally opening the possibility of implementing the client-server schemes to the involved robots.

Some studies address the problem by the well-known "Object closure" strategy. Wang [5] proposed the manipulation by surrounding the object with series of robots, then, the position of the object can be controlled by the position of each robot that enclose and push the object. Nevertheless, this theory bases its operations on an important number of holonomic robots.

One of the most studied strategies is the well-known "Pusher-Watcher" approach [6], [7]: A robot observes (watcher) the movement of the object and control the operations of the team (pushers) that manipulate the box.

Recent multi-robot strategies make use of the model known as "swarm intelligence". Li [8] experiments using communities of homogenous robots. These self-organized systems are based on decentralized and collective behaviors.

Another recent strategy is the reinforcement learning. Wang [9] implements a variant including a mechanism of decision based on a Markov process known as "Q-Learning". The main concern about this technique is related to the storage capacities and high demand of process capabilities.

Gene [10] and Lengegyel [11] model the environment by the construction of a configuration space (C-space) and both use the conventional wave front algorithm to compute the trajectories of the box. Lengegyel proposes a method to calculate collisions based on images processing with specialized hardware, nevertheless this method implies an important cost of processing. Gene works with cells maps to represent the environment and stores many parameters in each cell to calculate the trajectory.

3   Path Planning

The path planning problem can be defined as follows: given an initial and a final configurations, find a feasible continuous collision free trajectory between them. Path planning algorithms are responsible for maintaining many essential aspects of plausible agent behavior, including collision avoidance and goal satisfaction. Path planning also consumes a significant part of the computation time for many simulations, particularly in highly dynamic environments where most of the agents are moving at the same time.

In this paper we use the wavefront algorithm (figure 2A) to solve the path-planning problem. The wavefront algorithm uses a grid representation of the C-space, where all obstacles are marked on the grid as occupied cells. The wavefront algorithm places a value on every cell adjacent to the goal cell G and then a slightly higher value on all cells adjacent to the first ones, until all the squares have a value determined by their distance to the goal and any nearby occupied cells. The shortest path is given by any decreasing sequence of cells from the initial cell to the goal.

4   Proposed Method

The purpose of the this work is to obtain a new strategy to solve the box-pushing problem; the strategy is being developed to obtain compatible results with non-holonomic robots. The characteristics of the solution are listed below.

1. Find the shortest trajectories.
2. Look for trajectories with the smaller number of robot reconfigurations (from here we will define reconfigurations as the change of position of the robots around the object in order to obtain a valid position to push the object).
3. Preference to certain box rotations, in order to improve the pushing points.

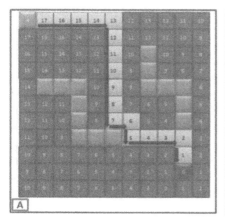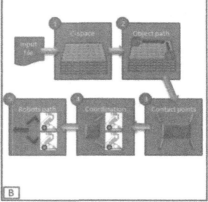

Fig. 2. A) Wavefront grid with lower numbers surrounding the goal, and higher numbers surrounding the robot. B) Big picture of the proposed method.

The proposed box-pushing method is realized in five stages: 1) From a predefined map construct the C-space representation; 2) Generate the object path trajectory using an alternative wavefront method which reduces the rotations of the object and not only look for the shortest path; 3) Determine the optimal pushing points that allow to execute the task precisely; 4) Determine the best coordination strategy for the N robots; 5) Calculate the individual robot trajectories including the non-holonomic characteristic of the robots.(figure 2B).

4.1   Space Representation

For this strategy it is necessary to obtain the configuration space representation (C-space). This representation is obtained from a convex polygonal description of the 2D environment, where each obstacle and the box are represented by a set of linear constraint as follows:

$$a_i x + b_i y \leq d_i, \ i = 1...P_k \ . \tag{1}$$

Where P_k is the number of faces of object k and for each $(a_i, b_i); a_i \neq 0$ or $b_i \neq 0$.

Finding intersections between polygons (collisions). We need a method to verify wether there is an intersection between 2 given polygons. This can be achieved if we find at least a segment of a line which satisfies both sets of constraints.

The general concept to make this evaluation is the following one: Given a line, defined by a point x_0 and a vector $\overrightarrow{m_0}$, we can find the intersection between this line and a set of linear constraints by finding the intersection of the line with each single constraint and use them to determine the limits of the segment (figure 3A).

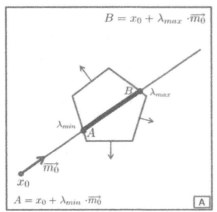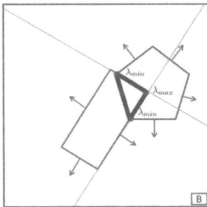

Fig. 3. A)Obtaining a segment of a line that satisfies the polygon's restrictions. B) Example of 3 segments that satisfy both sets of constraints of the polygons.

To verify the intersection between two polygons we use the previous method as follows. Given 2 polygons verify for each single constraint $n_i x \leq d_i$ if there is a segment on the line $n_i x = d_i$ which verifies both sets of constraints at the same time.

In figure 3B an example of an intersection between two polygons is shown, as we can see exist three line segments over the constraints that satisfies the restrictions of both polygons.

4.2   Building the C-Space

Assuming we have the mathematical representation of all the involved objects and the capacity to identify if an intersection exist between two polygons, the following step is the formal construction of the C-space. The C-space is a representation of all the configurations of the object (box) in the 2D space.

The configuration of the box is defined by its position (x,y) and orientation θ. Thus the C-space representation is a 3D matrix, where each cell defines if the configuration is collision-free or not. The computing of the C-space is made taking into consideration an increment of the box size (the increment would depend on the size of the robots), in order to guarantee that the box would never be against the wall and robots could move freely around the box.

The first step in the construction of the C-space, is to establish the resolution of the matrix that will represent it. In this implementation we use two different resolutions; one that defines the rotation step of the box, which is directly related with the number of layers in the three-dimensional matrix. The second resolution is the minimum step for horizontal and vertical motions.

In the example shown in figure 4A, we use resolution of 1 meter for horizontal and vertical movements and 5 degrees of rotation.

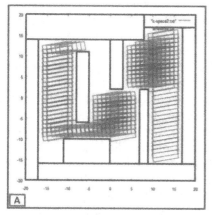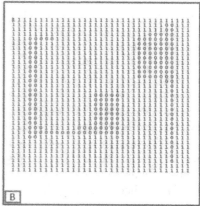

Fig. 4. A) Graphical representation of the C-space when the box is rotated 10 degrees; the positions where the box is not in collision are drawn. B) C-space binary layer that corresponds to figure A.

The final step is to verify for each cell if a collision exist between the object and, at least, one of the obstacles of the environment. This step is made by testing each cell $[x][y][c]$ of the matrix by moving the object to the (x,y) position and rotate (c * resolution of rotation) degrees. Finally we apply the function presented previously to detect collisions in order to verify if the configuration is collision-free ($[x][y][c] = 0$) or if a collision exists ($[x][y][c] = 1$) with any obstacle. In the figure 4B, the binary layer corresponding to figure 4A is presented.

4.3   Path Generation

In this section we are presenting the way we can obtain an optimal trajectory for the box. In the next subsection the proposed heuristic to find a semi-optimal box trajectory will be shown.

Wave front algorithm. As it was mentioned previously, the wave front algorithm allows calculating the shortest route between two points in a cluttered environment. The wave front algorithm is widely used for computing the trajectory of mobile robots and for this case, this algorithm is used to compute a base trajectory for the box since computing the trajectory is as simple as to start from a chosen point and follow the less value neighbor squares, up to the goal, as shown in fig 5A.

Trajectory computation with reduction of reconfigurations. It is obvious that working with non specialized mobile robots (in pushing task) it is necessary, along the path, to modify the position of those with respect to the box (reconfiguration) to be able to obtain a valid pushing position. In this work we use an heuristic of the neighbor selection which reduces the amount of robot reconfigurations throughout the trajectory.

The reduction of robots reconfigurations throughout the trajectory, allows in first instance to guarantee an important reduction of time, simply because the change of pushing points is a process that needs some time to be completed. Another aspect that can be improved when the robots reconfigurations are reduced is the increase of the precision of the movements. The continuous movements of the robots around the box can increase the possibilities of having collisions among them, and of course, the increase of the odometry errors by the constant movement of the robots can affect the precision of the pushes.

The proposed heuristic for reconfigurations reduction is based on the conventional wave front algorithm, with the inclusion of the following variations:

Once the wavefront matrix is computed, starts from a valid chosen point, validate all the neighbors (north, south, east, west, up and down). If at least 2 neighbors had an smaller value than the value of the starting point, the next step would be to measure the reach of all the possible routes again, following the direction of the less value neighbors. For instance, if we start from a defined point with a value of 99 and it has only two neighbors with smaller values, west with a value of 98 and up with a value also of 98, the following step is to evaluate and count the decreasing squares in the up and west directions. The counting will end when the decrement of the neighbors values finishes. Finally we have to compare the number of squares in both directions and follow the one that had the greatest value.

Figure 5B shows the obtained trajectory after implementing the proposed heuristic. If we compare it with the trajectory shown in figure 5A, we can verify that the changes of the box direction are reduced, therefore, the number of reconfigurations of robots is also reduced.

Trajectory computation including layer validation and reconfiguration reduction. Once we managed to obtain a route, the following aspect to improve

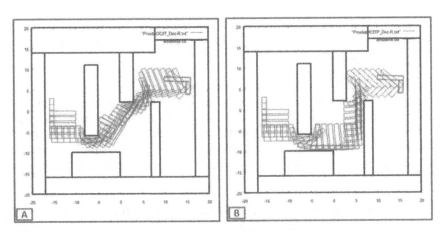

Fig. 5. A) Graphical representation of the box trajectory obtained without any heuristic to select the neighbors. B) Graphical representation of the box trajectory obtained with the proposed heuristic to reduce the reconfigurations.

is the robots pushing points. In this document we propose a method to privilege certain box rotations (0, 90, 180 and 270 degrees). With this method we try to improve the pushing points of the robots. This improvement will help to obtain a greater precision in the pushing task.

As we can see, it is possible to improve the pushing points if the movements north, south, east and west are made in certain box rotations, being thus, a method that privileges the use of certain box rotations to obtain routes with better pushing points.

In the previous section we suggested that the neighbors reach measure was made at the beginning of the process and whenever we arrive at the end of a route segment. In order to be able to privilege the use of certain layers of the C-space, we also consider we are evaluating belongs to one of those layers that are tried to be privileged. This action throws two results: one, in spite of following a specified direction, we must measure again searching new directions among some specified layers. Two, the fact of place new measurement points can clearly raise (sensibly) the quantity of robot reconfigurations.

For example: If we were paced in a square that has 3 possible directions to follow: north, west and up and after making the neighbor measurement we found that the reach of the routes is: north 21, west 19 and up 11. If we do not privilege any layers clearly the route to follow would be the one that has the north direction. The proposed change is to validate if the route that is going by the superior layer pass through some of the privileged layers, if it occurs, the value can be increased. In the present implementation the value of the route is duplicated ($11 * 2 = 22$), that is why the route with up direction will be followed to construct the final route.

In figure 6A we can see the heuristic to reduce reconfigurations and the layer validation applied. For this example, the heuristic helped to reduce the number of reconfigurations and it improves the pushing points in 2 of the four box movements.

4.4   Finding Pushing Points

Obtaining the pushing points for each sub route is a very important task since it will allow us to identify the points of the object that can be pushed in each sub trajectory and discard the drag points. For each sub route the manner to calculate them is the following one:

- Obtain the vector that defines the box movement dv, for example: for the North direction the vector is $(0,1,0)$, for the south direction the vector is $(0,-1,0)$. In the case of the rotations it is only necessary to define if it is clockwise or not, since the points for the rotations can be previously defined.
- For each point of the object, we have to obtain the projection of the vector dv on the two constraints that define the point.
- If at least one of the 2 projections is negative, the point is valid for pushing; however, if both are zero or positive, the point is not valid for pushing.

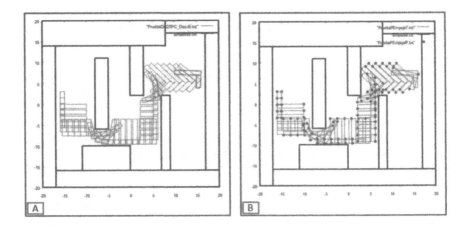

Fig. 6. A) Graphical representation of the box trajectory obtained with the proposed heuristic to reduce the reconfigurations and improve the pushed points by the layers validation. B) Valid pushing points for some steps of the route.

All the valid pushing points to move the box in the defined direction are marked with points in figure 6B.

5   Future Work

In future works the pushing points will be used to determine (by an optimization strategy) the best combination of robots and pushing points in each sub trajectory to diminish the amount of reconfigurations of the N robots. Also a module to find the advantageous robots locations is in development to place robots which are not participating in an interval of the movement in a favorable position for another sub trajectory. The main purpose is to continue reducing reconfiguration times.

Finally, all these locations will be used to compute the robots trajectories, considering their non-holonomic constraints.

6   Discussion and Conclusions

In this paper, we have developed a strategy to solve the Box-pushing problem that incorporates characteristics to improve the movement of objects in cluttered environments by a team of non-holonomics mobile robots. As it can be seen in the partial results, the proposed changes for the computation of the object trajectory improve the reduction of robots reconfigurations by the application of an alternative heuristic based on the wavefront algorithm. The reduction of reconfigurations is directly bound up with the reduction of necessary time to complete the task. Another point that throws good results was the improvement of pushing points by applying an heuristic to evaluate and privilege some layers of the C-space while the trajectory is being constructed; this action is directly related to the precision of the task.

References

1. Lynne, E.P., Tang, F.: Building multirobot coalitions through automated task solution synthesis. Proceedings of the IEEE 94(7), 1289–1305 (2006)
2. Reif, J.H.: Complexity of the mover's problem and generalizations. In: Annual IEEE Symposium on Foundations of Computer Science, pp. 421–427 (1979)
3. Yamada, S., Saito, J.: Adaptive action selection withouth explicit communication for multi-robot box-pushing. IEEE Transactions on Systems, Man and Cybernetics, Part C: Applications and Reviews 31(3), 398–404 (2001)
4. Muñoz Melendez, A., Drogoul, A.: Analyzing multi-robot box-pushing. Avances en la Ciencia de la Computacin. Memoria de los Talleres del Quinto Encuentro Internacional de Computacin. Universidad de Colima, pp. 530–539 (2004)
5. Wang, Z., Kumar, V.: Object closure and manipulation by multiple cooperating mobile robots. In: Proceedings of IEEE International Conference on Robotics and Automation, ICRA 2002, vol. 1, pp. 394–399 (2002)
6. Gerkey, B.P., Matari, M.J.: Pusher-watcher: An approach to fault-tolerant tightly-coupled robot coordination. In: Proceedings of IEEE International Conference on Robotics and Automation, ICRA 2002, vol. 1, pp. 464–469 (2002)
7. Kovac, K., Zivkovic, I., Dalbelo Basic, B.: Simulation of multi-robot reinforcement learning for box-pushing problem. In: Electrotechnical Conference, MELECON 2004. Proceedings of the 12th IEEE Mediterranean, vol. 2, pp. 603–606 (2004)
8. Li, Y., Chen, X.: Modeling and simulation of a swarm of robots for box-pushing task. In: 12th Mediterranean Conference on Control and Automation, Kusadasi, Aydin, Turkey (2004)
9. Wang, Y., de Silva, W.C.: Multi-robot box-pushing single-agent q-learning vs team q-learning. In: IEEE/RSJ International Conference on Intelligent Robots and Systems, 2006, pp. 3694–3699 (October 2006)
10. Gene, E.J., Tong-Ying, J., Jun-Da, H., Chien-Min, S., Chih-Yung, C.: A fast path planning algorithm for piano mover's problem on raster. Proceedings of the IEEE, 522–527 (2005)
11. Jed, L., Mark, R., Bruce, R.D., Donald, P.G.: Real-time robot motion planning using rasterizing computer graphics hardware. In: SIGGRAPH 1990: Proceedings of the 17th annual conference on Computer graphics and interactive techniques, pp. 327–335 (1990)

Multi-robot Exploration and Mapping
Using Self Biddings*

Juan C. Elizondo-Leal, Gabriel Ramírez-Torres, and Gregorio Toscano Pulido

Centro de Investigación y Estudios Avanzados del IPN
Laboratorio de Tecnologías de Información
Carretera a Monterrey KM 6, Ciudad Victoria, Tamaulipas México
{jelizondo,grtorres,gtoscano}@tamps.cinvestav.mx

Abstract. In this paper we propose a completely distributed multi-robot coordination algorithm to explore and map terrain. This algorithm is based on a market bidding process of unrevealed frontiers, where the bids are calculated by each robot. When it reaches the target the robot makes a decision by itself, which involves every one of the team members without lost of time in a distributed behavior and without the necessity of a central module. The result is an efficient and fault tolerant approach.

The bid function includes the distance of the actual robot towards the frontier, the distances to the others robots and theirs objectives. This function gives a tendency of robots separation in a minimum route towards the frontier.

1 Introduction

Exploration and mapping of the environment is a fundamental challenge in mobile robotics. There are several applications in the real world, such as search and rescue, hazardous material handling, planetary exploration, etc. The use of robot teams presents multiple advantages over single robot, such as concurrency, which can greatly reduce the time needed for the exploration and merging of overlapping maps so the error can be diminished. To achieve efficiency in exploration with a robotic team a good coordination is necessary. The coordination of the robots must be fault tolerant. This coordination might be achieved by a distributed coordination algorithm, since centralized coordination algorithms usually suffer from the single point of failure problem because if the leader breaks down, the exploration will fail.

The problem of multi-robot exploration can be defined as follows: *Given a set of n robots in an unknown area equipped with sensing, localization and communication capabilities. Design an efficient coordinated exploration algorithm to make a map of the unknown area.*

Recently, market economy approaches have arisen, which have demonstrated to reduce the time and traveling distance in previous works on multi-robot

---

* This research was partialy funded by project number 51623 from "Fondo Mixto Conacyt-Gobierno del Estado de Tamaulipas".

H. Geffner et al. (Eds.): IBERAMIA 2008, LNAI 5290, pp. 392–401, 2008.

exploration [1,2,3,4]. These approaches treat all robots as economic agents, which use a bidding mechanism in order to locally minimize the time and traveling distance.

In this paper, we present an approach based on market economy and the concept of frontiers [5], where the bid of each robot is calculated by the robot when it reaches the target, involving every member of the team without losing time, in a totally distributed scheme. The costs are computed in function of the traveling distances from the target of each robot towards the new frontier. We use evidence grids to represent the environment, so each cell of the grid is placed into one of three status by comparing its occupancy value to the initial value. The path planning is generated by a wavefront algorithm. The result is a reliable, efficient and totally distributed algorithm for mapping and exploration.

This paper is organized as follows: Section 2 expounds previous work in the area of multi-robot exploration. Section 3 outlines our approach to the problem and section 4 presents numerical results that show the performance of our method. In section 5, we present our conclusions and discuss future research.

2   Related Work

In mobile robotics the problem of exploring an unknown environment is very popular among the scientific community. Many approaches have been proposed to explore unknown environments with single robots [6,7,8]. In recent years the problem of exploring terrains with teams of mobile robots has received considerable attention, but relatively few approaches.

In 1997, Yamauchi [5] introduced an approach for exploration with a single robot based on the concept of frontiers, regions on the boundary between open space and unexplored space. The basic idea is to keep the robot moving to the closest frontier cell. In [9] Yamauchi applies the concept of frontiers to a distributed, asynchronous multirobot exploration algorithm, where robots exchange perceptual information continuously. This approach brings the fault tolerance capability, since if any robot breaks down, the exploration can be complete. However, there is no explicit coordination, so that multiple robots may end up covering the same area and may even physically interfere with each other.

Simmons et al. [2] developed a multi-robot approach which uses a concept of frontier and a simple bidding protocol. The team requires a central agent to evaluate bidding from all the other robots to obtain the most information gain while reducing the cost or the travelling distance.

Zlot et al. [1] presented a multi-robot exploration approach which exploited a market architecture. The team of robots continuously negotiate with each other, improving their current plans and sharing information about which regions have and have not already been covered. Their algorithm can improve the reliability, robustness and efficiency of the exploration. Nevertheless, the goal generation algorithm they used is not as efficient as the frontier based, and the negotiation process is complex.

Burgar et al. [3] developed a coordinated multi-robot exploration algorithm which simultaneously considers the utility of unexplored areas and the cost for reaching these areas, using evidence grids maps to represent the environment and the concept of frontiers. They investigate the impact of the limited-range communication. They use a central module dynamically selected which receives the local maps and combine them in a single global map which then is broadcasted to all robots. But using a central module suffers from a single point fault.

Sheng et al. [4] presented a coordinated multi-robot exploration algorithm based on a distributed bidding model. They address the problem caused by the limited-range communication. The authors introduce a nearness measure, and therefore the robots tend to stay close to each other. This approach does not guarantee that all the members of the team participate in the bidding.

Stachniss et al. [10] developed a multi-robot exploration strategy which considers the semantic place information, they apply a classifier learned with AdaBoost. This approach required learning and considering similar places.

Baglietto et al. [11] apply the concepts of entropy and frontier, where entropy quantifies the information gain associated with the frontier cell with the greatest information gains.

Poernomo and Shell Ying [12] proposed the separation of robots in the frontier selection, which reduces the chances of robots interfering with each other. However, they assumed that the size of robot is small enough, such that the collision is negligible.

In general, the proposals that are based on biddings require a central module that sometimes do not include all the team members. So we propose an algorithm where the team members are all included without the necessity of selecting a central module.

3   Approach

Our approach uses a bidding mechanism based on target assignment to coordinate the actions of the robots, which is totally distributed since each robot calculates the bid of the others and its own, and make its own decision. Thus adding efficiency and robustness, since it eliminates times of delay and single points of fault. We use evidence grids to represent the environment. Each cell of the grid is placed on one of three status by comparing its occupancy value to the initial value assigned to all cells:

occupied: occupancy value > initial value
free: occupancy value < initial value
unknown: occupancy value = initial value

The only time the occupancy value will be equal to the initial value is when it has never been sensed. During the exploration, the sensing and mapping is made continuously in each robot and the bidding is carried on when a frontier is reached. The frontier is considered reached when the robot is at a distance less than d and the frontier is detected explored.

3.1 Bid Compute

The bid is computed that each robot will be assigned to a near unexplored frontier, while keeping the robots far from each other. The bid of all robots (bid_k) includes the distance of robot towards its goal ρ_k plus the distance of this goal toward the frontier α_k, and the distances to the others robots toward their goals ρ_i plus the distance of these goals toward the frontier α_i. All bids are calculated by the current robot. Figure 1.

$$bid_k = \rho_k + \alpha_k - \sum_{i=0,i\neq k}^{n} (\rho_i + \alpha_i); \text{ for } k = 0,\ldots,n-1 \tag{1}$$

where i and k represent the index of each one of the robots and n is the quantity of robots.

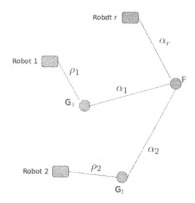

Fig. 1. Scheme of bid calculation. Where F is the current frontier, ρ distances to the frontier goals, α distance of the goals toward the frontier and G_x are the current goals.

In the bid every robot can only win one frontier in addition to their current goal. With the inclusion of the team data in the bid we manage to separate them from each other in a minimum route towards the frontier.

The current robot computes its bid and all the team's bids to reach each one of the frontiers. The complexity of the calculation of all the bids is $O((n^2-n)F)$, where n is the number of robots and F is the number of frontiers. Once all the bids have been computed, the frontiers are sorted (according to its bid value associated to the present robot) for the process of bidding.

3.2 The Distributed Bidding

This computation is used as follows: When a robot has reached its goal, it requests maps and targets of other robots and it waits for their answers. Then the robot merges the maps to its local map and compute the bids to the nearest frontier. If the robot provides the best bid, then this robot wins the bidding and

---

Algorithm 1. Robot exploration

```
start_MappingOnline()
My_target = My_pose
Send_MyTarget
while the Map is not Complete
   broadcast(Request MapTarget)
   update_MyMap
   update_OtherRobotTarget
   detectFrontier()
   bid_compute()
   iWin = 0
   for i=0 to number of frontiers
      if I win this frontier
         My_target=thisFrontier
         iWin=1
         break
   if does not win any frontier
      wait other new pose
      continue
   send my target
   travel to My_target
```

Fig. 2. Algorithm for robot exploration

Algorithm 2. Robot communication

```
while the Map is not Complete
   idRobot=receiveData()
   if request map and target
      sendTarget(idRobot, My_target)
      sendMap(idRobot, My_map)
   else if Receive target
      saveTarget(idRobot, target)
      if target is equal My_target
         stop travel and restart bidd
```

Fig. 3. Algorithm for robot communication

broadcast this frontier as its new goal. If this robot does not win, the process of bidding is repeated with the next nearness frontier until it wins, or no frontier is left. If the robot does not win any case then it stops until new data is received. Furthermore if the target frontier is selected by any robot, the travel is stopped and the process of bidding is restarted. The pseudocode of our approach is shown in Figure 2 and run in parallel with the communication protocol Figure 3. The complexity of this algorithm including calculation of bids is $O((n^2 - n)F^2)$, in the worst case where n is the number of robots and F is the number of frontiers.

3.3 Maps Updating

When a robot receives a map, it makes an average with its own map. The map computed by a robot can contain incorrect data, because of the own errors of the sensors. We exploit the advantage that multiple robots may produce more accurate maps by merging the overlapping information. When a robot receives a map (φ), each point (x, y) is overlapped with the local map (δ), but if the local point is marked as explored, the point is averaged with the new point, so the errors can be diminished.

$$\delta_{xy} = \begin{cases} \frac{\delta_{xy}+\varphi_{xy}}{2} & \text{if } \delta_{xy} \neq \text{initial value} \\ \varphi_{xy} & \text{if } \delta_{xy} = \text{initial value} \end{cases} \tag{2}$$

When the map is updated, the detection of frontiers is carry out by a clustering algorithm, so closer frontiers are considered as a single one. The clustering of frontiers is carried out by detection of neighboring frontiers. Once the cluster is generated, the geometrical center is located and it is taken like a single frontier. If the size of the cluster is less than the threshold, this cluster is does not considered frontier.

4 Numerical Results

We simulate our approach in the player/stage simulator [13] which models the interferences betwen robots. To carry out our experiments we used laser sensors with 360 degree of view in order to determine the occupied area and a ring of ultrasound sensor wich determines the free area, the sensors radius range is 4 meters, mounted on the robot Pioneer 2-DX.

An example environment is shown in figure 7. A number of robots are simulated by identical programs with each representing robot. We performed two experiments.

Firstly, we show the fault tolerant of approach, using the map shown in figure 4. We identify two cases: the robot fails while traveling to its goal, and the robot fails

Fig. 4. Map used for the demonstration of fault tolerant (15 × 15 meters)

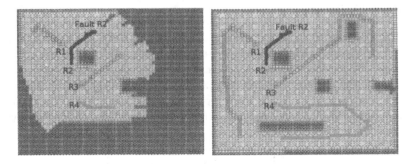

Fig. 5. The robot 2 has some failure during its travel

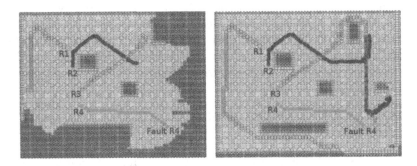

Fig. 6. The robot 4 has some failure during its bid process

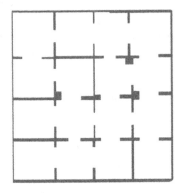

Fig. 7. Map used for the simulation (25 × 25 meters)

during its bidding process. In figure 5, robot 2 has some failures during its travel. When the others robots begin the bid process can not receive any new information from robot 2 and they do not include it in its bidding process and can complete the task. In figure 6, robot 4 has some failures during its bid process, but it does let affect the other robots since each robot makes a decision by itself.

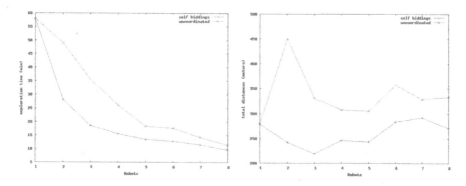

Fig. 8. Performances of the different coordination strategies for the environments shown in Figure 7

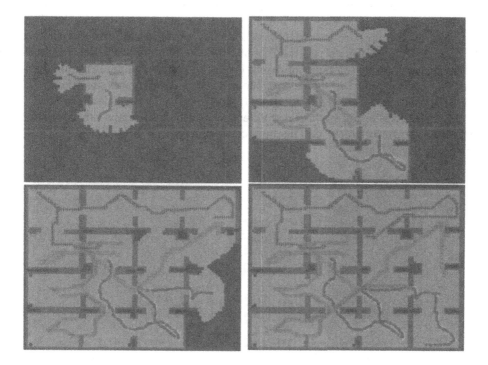

Fig. 9. Simulated exploration with four robots

The results of the previous cases prove that multi-robot exploration using self biddings is tolerant to faults. If any robot has a failure, the other robots can continue to explore the unknown environment.

Secondly, we compared our approach with the technique used by Yamauchi, in which each robot always approaches the closest unexplored area of a joint map.

From now on, this approach will be denoted as uncoordinated exploration since it lacks a component that arbitrates between the robots whenever they choose the same frontier cells. For each case and a fixed number of robots, ten test runs are conducted and the total exploration times are recorded. Figure 8 compares the total exploration time and distances needed for the one case with regard to the number of robots. For each comparison of the strategies, the robot team was started at the same randomly chosen location. The map used in our experiments is shown in figure 7. Screen shots of a simulation with five robots exploring the environment are shown in Figure 9. The robots started in the center of the map.

The results of the second experiment demonstrate a great efficiency in the selection of the frontier to explore by every robot.

5   Future Work and Conclusions

This work presents a novel completely distributed multi-robot coordination algorithm to explore and map terrain, based on a market bidding process. The key idea of this approach is take into account the cost of reaching an unexplored frontier and the distances to other robots and theirs objectives. The result is an efficient and fault tolerant approach. From the theoretical analysis and simulation experiments, it is shown that the method is feasible and can effectively distribute multiple frontiers to multiple robots in a totally uncentralized form.

Since the decisions are taken at different times, the local maps can be inconsistent as shown in figure 10. This may cause different robots select goals close to each other.

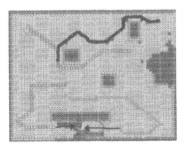

Fig. 10. Inconsistent map. Different robots select goals close each other.

References

1. Zlot, R., Stentz, A., Dias, M., Thayer, S.: Multi-robot exploration controlled by a market economy. In: Proceedings of the IEEE International Conference on Robotics and Automation, pp. 3016–3023 (2002)
2. Simmons, R.G., Apfelbaum, D., Burgard, W., Fox, D., Moors, M., Thrun, S., Younes, H.: Coordination for multi-robot exploration and mapping. In: AAAI/IAAI, pp. 852–858 (2000)

3. Burgard, W., Moors, M., Stachniss, C., Schneider, F.: Coordinated multi-robot exploration. IEEE Transactions on Robotics and Automation 21, 376–386 (2005)
4. Sheng, W., Yang, Q., Tan, J., Xi, N.: Distributed multi-robot coordination in area exploration. Robot. Auton. Syst. 54, 945–955 (2006)
5. Yamauchi, B.: A frontier-based approach for autonomous exploration. In: CIRA 1997: Proceedings of the 1997 IEEE International Symposium on Computational Intelligence in Robotics and Automation, Washington, DC, USA, p. 146. IEEE Computer Society, Los Alamitos (1997)
6. Albers, S., Kursawe, K., Schuierer, S.: Exploring unknown environments with obstacles. In: SODA 1999: Proceedings of the tenth annual ACM-SIAM symposium on Discrete algorithms, Philadelphia, PA, USA. Society for Industrial and Applied Mathematics, pp. 842–843 (1999)
7. Dudek, G., Jenkin, M., Milios, E., Wilkes, D.: Robotic exploration as graph construction. IEEE Transactions on Robotics and Automation, 859–865 (1991)
8. Thrun, S.: Learning metric-topological maps for indoor mobile robot navigation. Artificial Intelligence 99, 21–71 (1998)
9. Yamauchi, B.: Decentralized coordination for multirobot exploration. Robotics and Autonomous Systems 29, 111–118 (1999)
10. Stachniss, C., Martínez-Mozos, O., Burgard, W.: Speeding-up multi-robot exploration by considering semantic place information. In: Proceedings 2006 IEEE International Conference on Robotics and Automation, ICRA 2006, pp. 1692–1697 (2006)
11. Baglietto, M., Paolucci, M.S., Zoppoli, L.R.: Information-based multi-agent exploration. In: Proceedings of the Third International Workshop on Robot Motion and Control, RoMoCo 2002, November 9-11, pp. 173–179 (2002)
12. Poernomo, A., Ying, H.S.: New cost function for multi-robot exploration. In: 9th International Conference on Control, Automation, Robotics and Vision, ICARCV 2006, December 5-8, pp. 1–6 (2006)
13. Brian, P., Gerkey, R.T.V., Howard, A.: The player/stage project: Tools for multi-robot and distributed sensor systems. In: Proc. of the Intl. Conf. on Advanced Robotics (ICAR), pp. 317–323 (July 2003)

Coordinated Multi-robot Exploration with SRT-Radial

Alfredo Toriz P., Abraham Sánchez L., and Maria A. Osorio L.

Facultad de Ciencias de la Computación, BUAP
Laboratorio MOVIS
14 Sur esq. San Claudio, CP 72570 Puebla, Pue., México
alfredot@hotmail.com, asanchez@cs.buap.mx, aosorio@cs.buap.mx

Abstract. A multi robot system can be highly beneficial for exploration, a core robotic task. This work presents an approach to multi robot exploration based in a parallelization of the single-robot SRT method. Each robot in the team constructs a SRT, taking into account the presence of others robots by means of a suitable redefinition of its local frontier and planning its motion towards areas that have not been explored by itself, and by the rest of the team. The strategy is completely decentralized and can be implemented with a limited communication range. Simulation results in various environments are presented to show the performance of our proposed strategy.

1 Introduction

The problem of exploring an environment belongs to the fundamental problems in mobile robotics. The field of cooperative robotics is a relatively new research area, with origins in the 80s, when researchers began to investigate issues in multiple robot systems. A multi-robot system can be highly beneficial for exploration, which is a core robotics task. Application domains include for example surveillance, reconnaissance, planetary exploration or rescue missions. When using a team of robots, the overall performance can be much faster and more robust.

Multi-robot systems are emerging as a the new frontier in Robotics research, posing new challenges and offering new solutions to old problems. The research in multiple robots naturally extends research on single robot systems, but it also a topic in itself because of the complexity of dealing with multiple robots and new constraints. Multiple robot systems are more complex than other distributed systems because they have to deal with the environment (real world), which is more difficult to model since most of the time it is dynamic, noisy, etc. The use of multiple robots for exploration has several advantages over single robot systems [1]. In the following paragraph, we summarized the most important approaches in exploration with multiples robots.

Yamauchi implemented a technique for multi-robot exploration which is decentralized, cooperative and robust to individual failures. He demonstrated a

H. Geffner et al. (Eds.): IBERAMIA 2008, LNAI 5290, pp. 402–411, 2008.

frontier-based exploration which can be used to explore office buildings [2]. In a-
nother study, Simmons et al., emphasized the importance of coordination among
robots in order to explore and create a map. This approach is based on cost of
exploration and estimation of expected information gain [3]. Zlot el al., present
a new approach for coordination using a market-based approach. The market
architecture aims to maximize utility, this is achieved by minimizing the costs
and maximizing the benefits [4]. A decision-theoretic approach to coordinate
multiple robots was presented in [1], the aim is to maximize the overall utility
and minimize the potential overlap. In most exploration strategies, the boundary
between known and unknown territory (the frontier) is approached in order to
maximize the information gain.

This paper presents a strategy to explore an unknown environment by multiple robots. The strategy is a parallelization of the SRT method, which was
presented in [5]. The SRT method, is an exploration method based on the random generation of robot configurations within the local safe area detected by the
sensors. A data structure is created, which represents a roadmap of the explored
area with an associated safe region (SR). Each node of the SRT consists of a free
configuration with the associated local safe region (LSR) as reconstructed by the
perception system; the SR is the union of all the LSRs. The LSR is an estimate
of the free space surrounding the robot at a given configuration. In general, its
shape will depend on the sensor characteristics. To this simple extension, the
following functionalities were added to it: *cooperation* to increase the efficiency,
coordination to avoid conflicts and *communication* to cooperate and to coordinate. A decentralized cooperation mechanism and two coordination mechanisms
are introduced to improve the exploration efficiency and to avoid conflicts. The
basic steps of the exploration approach are presented in Section II. Simulation
results in different environments are discussed in Section III. Finally, conclusions
and future work are detailed in Section IV.

2   Cooperative SRT-Based Exploration

Espinoza et al., presented in [6] a method for sensor-based exploration of unknown environments by nonholonomic mobile robots, they proposed a strategy
called SRT-Radial [7]. The original SRT method [5] presents two techniques:
SRT-Ball and SRT-Star. The form of the safe local region (LSR) reflects the
sensors characteristics, and the perception technique adopted. Besides, the exploration strategy will be strongly affected by the form of the LSR. The SRT-
Radial strategy takes advantage of the information reported by the sensors in
all directions, to generate and validate configurations candidate through reduced
spaces.

The design of the cooperative exploration strategy proceeds from the parallelization of the basic SRT method, each robot builds one or more partial maps
of the environment, organized in a collection of SRTs. First, the procedure
BUILD_SRT is executed, i.e., each robot builds its own SRT, $\mathcal{T}$ is rooted at
its initial configuration q_{init}. This procedure comes to an end when the robot

---

BUILD Multi-SRT(q_{init})
1 $\mathcal{T}.init(q_{init})$
2 BUILD_SRT($q_{init}.\mathcal{T}$);
3 SUPPORT_OTHERS(q_{init});

Fig. 1. The Multi-SRT algorithm

can not further expand $\mathcal{T}$. Later, the robot executes the SUPPORT_OTHERS procedure, this action contributes to the expansion of the SRTs that have been built by others robots. When this procedure finishes, the robot returns to the root of its own tree and finishes its exploration. The exploration algorithm for each robot is shown in Figure 1.

The procedure BUILD_SRT is shown in Figure 2. In each iteration of the BUILD_SRT, the robot uses all available information (partially collected by itself and partially gained through the communication with other robots) to identify the group of engaged robots (GER), i.e. the other robots in the team with which cooperation and coordination are adequate. This is achieved by the construction of the first group of pre-engaged robots (GPR), or robots that are candidates to be members of the GER, and are synchronized with them (BUILD_AND_WAIT_GPR). Then, the robot collects data through its sensory systems, builds the current LSR (PERCEIVE) and updates their own tree $\mathcal{T}$. The current GER can now be built (BUILD_GER). At this point the robot processes its local frontier (the portion of its current LSR limit leads to areas that are still unexplored) on the basis of $\mathcal{T}$ as well as any other tree $\mathcal{T}_i$ gained through communication and stored in its memory (LOCAL_FRONTIER).

If the local frontier is not empty, the robot generates a random configuration contained in the current LSR and headed towards the local frontier, if not, the target configuration is fixed to the parent node with a backward movement (PLANNER). If the GER is composed only by the same robot, the robot moves directly to its target. Otherwise, the paths advanced by the robot in the GER are checked for mutual collisions, and classified in feasible and unfeasible paths (CHECK_FEASIBILITY). If the subset $\mathcal{G}_u$ of robots with unfeasible paths is vacuum, a coordination stage takes place, perhaps, confirming or modifying the current target of the robot (COORDINATE). In particular, the movement of the robot can be banned by simply readjusting the target to the current configuration. Then, the function MOVE_TO transfers the robot to the target (when this is different from q_{act}). The loop is repeated until the condition in the output line 15 is verified: the robot is unable to expand the tree $\mathcal{T}$ (no local frontiers remaining) and therefore it has to move back to the root of its SRT.

Two robots are GPR-coupled if the distance between their target configurations is less than $2R_p$, i.e. twice the range of perception of the sensorial system. The GPR of the robot is then built by grouping all robots and connecting a chain of coupled GPRs. To achieve synchronization, the GPR is calculated and updated until all its members are immobile (BUILD_AND_WAIT_GPR). The range of communication, R_c, clearly plays an important role in the construction

---

BUILD_SRT$(q_{init}, \mathcal{T})$
1 $q_{act} = q_{init}$;
2 **do**
3   BUILD_AND_WAIT_GPR();
4    $S(q_{act}) \leftarrow$ PERCEIVE(q_{act});
5   ADD$(\mathcal{T}, (q_{act}, S(q_{act})))$;
6    $\mathcal{G} \leftarrow$ BUILD_GER();
7    $\mathcal{F}(q_{act}) \leftarrow$ LOCAL_FRONTIER$(q_{act}, S(q_{act}), \mathcal{T}, \bigcup \mathcal{T}_i)$;
8    $q_{target} \leftarrow$ PLANNER$(q_{act}, \mathcal{F}(q_{act}), q_{init})$;
9   **if** $q_{target} \neq NULL$
10   **if** $|\mathcal{G}| > 1$
11     $(\mathcal{G}_f, \mathcal{G}_u) \leftarrow$ CHECK_FEASIBILITY$(\mathcal{G})$;
12   **if** $\mathcal{G}_u \neq \emptyset$
13       $q_{target} \leftarrow$ COORDINATE$(\mathcal{G}_f, \mathcal{G}_u)$;
14   $q_{act} \leftarrow$ MOVE_TO(q_{target});
15 **while** $q_{target} \neq NULL$

Fig. 2. The BUILD_SRT procedure

of the GPR; for this method two cases have been considered, according to the communication range:

Limited communication range. Since the maximum distance between the robot and any other robot GPR-coupled is $3R_p$ (the other robot can still be moving to its target, which however could not be further away than R_p of the current configuration) , it is sufficient to assume that $R_c \geq 3R_p$ to ensure that the GPR accounts for all the robots that are candidates to belong to the GER.

Unlimited communication range. Given the nature of this communication, the robot always knows the status of the other robots, and therefore will know which robots are candidates to be GPR-coupled; the distance to be GPR-coupled as in the above case will remain $3R_p$. In this way, as in the previous case, it is ensured that the GPR accounts for all the robots that are candidates to belong to the GER.

The SUPPORT_OTHERS procedure is detailed in Figure 3, it ca be divided in two main phases, which are repeated over and over. In the first phase, the robot picks another robot to support it in its exploration, or, more precisely, another tree that helps it to expand (there may be more than one robot acting on a single tree). In the second phase, the selected tree is reached and the robot tries to expand it, tying subtrees constructed by the procedure BUILD_SRT. The main cycle is repeated until the robot has received confirmation that all the other robots have completed their exploration.

In the first phase, the robot takes in a set $\mathcal{I}$, the trees belonging to $\bigcup \mathcal{T}_i$ that may require support for expansion. In particular, defining the open frontier of a tree (subtree) as the sum of the lengths of local frontiers associated with its nodes, a tree $\mathcal{T}_i$ is put in $\mathcal{I}$, if its open frontier is at least equal to a constant $\bar{F}$ multiplied by the number of robots that are active on $\mathcal{T}_i$, according to the most

---

SUPPORT_OTHERS(q_{act})
1 **do**
2   **for** $i = 1$ to n
3   **if** OPEN_FRONTIER($\mathcal{T}_i$) $\geq \bar{F} \cdot$ ACTIVE_ROBOTS($\mathcal{T}_i$)
4   ADD($\mathcal{T}, \mathcal{T}_i$);
5    $\mathcal{T}_s \leftarrow$ SELECT($\mathcal{T}$);
6   **if** $\mathcal{T}_s \neq$ NULL
7      $q_{act} \leftarrow$ TRANSFER_TO($\mathcal{T}_s.root$);
8   BUILD_SRT($q_{act}, \mathcal{T}_s$);
9      $q_{act} \leftarrow$ TRANSFER_TO($\mathcal{T}.root$);
10 **while** EXPLORATION_RUNNING()

Fig. 3. The SUPPORT_OTHERS procedure

recent information available. If $\mathcal{I}$ is not empty, the robot selects a particular tree $\mathcal{T}_s$ of $\mathcal{I}$, according to some criteria (for example, the tree with the closest root, or the most recent update), and move to its root. Once there, it makes the construction of GPR/GER perception and processing of the frontier. If the frontier of the local root is not empty, the robot begins an expansion of the subtree using the procedure BUILD_SRT. If not, it makes a random selection among the children of the node, using a probability, proportional to the open frontier of the corresponding subtree (the function returns NULL if the subtree does not have an open frontier), and establishes as the target, the selected children. The unfeasible path within the current GER is then verified and if needed, a coordination takes place, after which the robot is transferred to the target, and the internal loop is repeated. As soon as the robot reaches a node with a local frontier, it initiates a expansion subtree using the procedure BUILD_SRT. The robot is kept trying to add subtrees $\mathcal{T}_s$ until it has returned to the root of $\mathcal{T}_s$ and its open frontier is zero. At this point, the robot returns to the root of its own tree (i.e. its initial configuration) and becomes available to support the expansion of other trees. This phase is only used when an unlimited communication range is handled, because the robot who is providing assistance can count with updated information of the other robots and its last states at any time, in contrast with a limited communication range with probably partial and not updated information.

3   Simulations

In order to illustrate the behavior of the Multi-SRT exploration approach, we present two strategies, the Multi-SRT_Radial and the Multi-SRT_Star. The strategies were implemented in Visual C++ V. 6.0, taking advantage of the structure of the the MSL library[1] and its graphical interface that facilitates the visualization of the working environment, by the selection algorithms, and the

---

[1] http://msl.cs.uiuc.edu/msl/

animation of the obtained path. The library GPC developed by Alan Murta was used to simulate the sensor of the perception systems[2]. GPC is a C library implementation of a new polygon clipping algorithm. The techniques used are obtained from Vatti's polygon clipping method [8].

We use two different environments (see Figure 4). Both are square, the first contains a single obstacle that forms a narrow passage with the limits of the environment. The second contains many obstacles, where each area can be reached from different access points. One can consider two possible initial deployments of the robots. In the first, the robots are initially scattered in the environment; in the second, the exploration is started with the robots grouped in a cluster. Since the Multi-SRT approach is randomized, the results were averaged by 10 simulation runs. The performance of the method is evaluated in terms of the exploration time (in seconds), the environment coverage is not an important parameter because it was performed in all our simulations.

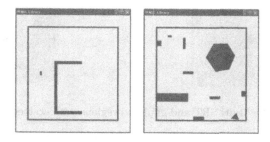

Fig. 4. Environments for the tests of the Multi-SRT approach

Figures 5 and 6 show the Multi-SRT and the explored region for the first environment with a team of 3 robots in the case of the unlimited communication range. We can see the difference between robots evenly distributed or clustered at the start. At the end, the environment has been completely explored and the SRTs have been built. In these figures, we can observe how each robot built its own SRT and when one of them finished, enters the support phase. The union of the trees, as in the center of Figures 5 and 6, indicates that the support phase took place.

The two strategies Multi-SRT Star and Multi-Srt Radial were compared through simulations. We used the same environment to prove the better efficiency of Multi-SRT Radial over Multi-SRT Star with the same free parameters. Figure 7, above, presents the explored and safe regions obtained with the Multi-SRT Star strategy for the second environment, for a team of 7 robots in the case of unlimited communication range. The bottom images of the Figure 7 illustrates the explored and the safe regions with Multi-SRT Radial. The final number of nodes in the tree and the exploration time are significantly smaller with Multi-SRT Radial than with Multi-SRT Star.

---

[2] http://www.cs.man.ac.uk/~toby/alan/software/

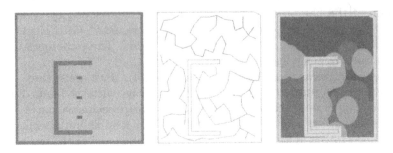

Fig. 5. The Multi-SRT and explored regions with cluttered start

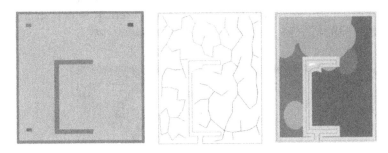

Fig. 6. The Multi-SRT and explored regions with scattered start

Table 1. Results of experiments performed for the first environment. Cardinality for limited communication range.

# of robots	Scattered Star	Scattered Radial	Clustered Star	Clustered Radial
2	340.253	68.891	216.791	64.492
3	183.362	45.021	236.891	40.424
4	254.530	35.290	147.278	32.935
5	130.654	9.980	218.031	56.836

Table 1 shows the simulation results for the first environment, the exploration time of teams of different cardinality for limited communication range can be observed. For the limited communication range case, the exploration time is greater with a scattered start, because the robots that are far apart at the start can exchange very little information during the exploration. As the number of robots increases, communication chains are more easily formed.

Table 2 shows the simulation results for the second environment, where teams of different cardinality versus exploration time for unlimited communication range can be observed.

Polygonal models have several interesting characteristics[3], they can compute geometric properties, such as areas and visibility regions. Representing a workspace as a polygonal region is not the same as saying that the workspace is polygonal.

---

[3] They can represent complex environments at any degree of precision.

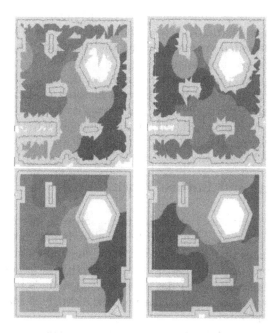

Fig. 7. Comparative map quality between Multi-SRT Star and Multi-SRT Radial for the second environment

Table 2. Results of experiments performed for the second environment. Cardinality for unlimited communication range.

# of robots	Scattered Star	Scattered Radial	Clustered Star	Clustered Radial
2	382.503	40.586	332.334	40.023
3	218.685	39.265	301.783	38.725
4	138.444	35.624	247.750	34.378
5	184.109	30.201	162.939	37.281
7	150.854	27.113	106.468	27.389
10	68.766	18.732	98.673	19.360

The local coordination procedure implemented in our work guarantees that the collective motion of the robots is feasible from the collision viewpoint. The approach does not need a central supervision. The selection of exploration actions by each robot is spontaneous and it is possible on the basis of the available information.

Architectures for multi-robot exploration are usually classified as centralized, and descentralized or distributed. In centralized architectures a central entity plans the actions of all the robot team, while in the descentralized approaches each robot makes use of local information to plan its exploration. Our approach is a decentralized cooperative exploration strategy for mobile robots, with coordination mechanisms that are used to guarantee exploration efficiency and avoid conflicts.

Single robots can not produce accurate maps like multi-robots. The only advantage of using a single robot is the minimization of the repeated coverage. However, even if repeated coverage among the robots decreases the mission's efficiency, some amount of repeated coverage is a desirable situation for a better efficiency. Additionally, this better efficiency can be achieved by coordination among robots. As a matter of fact, the goal in robot exploration must be to minimize the overall exploration time, and multiple robots produce more accurate maps by merging overlapping information that helps to stabilize the sensor uncertainty and to reach the goal.

4   Conclusions and Future Work

Mapping via exploration is a fundamental problem in mobile robotics. The different approaches to mapping could be roughly divided into two categories: theoretical approaches that assume idealized robots and environments without uncertainty, and practical approaches that contend with issues of a real environment. The theoretical approaches provide lower bounds for the exploration problem while the practical approaches produce algorithms that operate in environments under uncertainty.

We have presented a different approach for cooperative exploration based on the SRT-Radial. The Multi-SRT considers two decentralized mechanisms of cooperation at different levels. The first simply consists of making an appropriate definition of the local frontier that allows each robot to plan its motion towards the areas apparently unexplored for the rest of the team. The second allows a robot that has finished with its individual exploration phase, to support others robots in their exploration task. Additionally, we compared Multi-SRT Radial strategy with Multi-SRT Star strategy, the results obtained with our proposal are faster than other previous works.

Multi-robot systems are emerging as a the new frontier in Robotics research, posing new challenges and offering new solutions to old problems. Multi-robot systems are not a collection of robots performing a once-for-ever fixed task in a settled and static environment. They are collections of interacting, coopera-ting autonomous agents with physical embodiment that impose restrictions on what they can do, but also give themselves power to do some specific things. Thus, the paradigms of Multi-Agent and Multi-robot systems are somehow related and the recognition of this parallelism may foster new avenues for research and solutions. Autonomous Systems are endowed with some kind of intelligence. In the field of Computational Intelligence, the paradigm of Hybrid Intelligent Systems encompasses the most flexible definitions and constructions of systems fusing the most diverse approaches: evolutionary computation, neural networks and statistical classifiers, fuzzy systems and lattice computing, hidden Markov models, and formal concept analysis, ...

Exploration and localization are two of the capabilities necessary for mobile robots to navigate robustly in unknown environments. A robot needs to explore in order to learn the structure of the world, and a robot needs to know its own location in order to make use of its acquired spatial information. However, a problem arises with the integration of exploration and localization. A robot needs to know its own location in order to add new information to its map, but it may also need a map to determine its own location.

The integration of a localization module into the exploration process based on SLAM techniques will be an important topic for a future research. We can consider an extension of the Multi-SRT exploration method, where the robots constantly maintain a distributed network structure.

References

1. Burgard, W., Moors, M., Schneider, F.: Collaborative exploration of unknown environments with teams of mobile robots. In: Beetz, M., Hertzberg, J., Ghallab, M., Pollack, M.E. (eds.) Dagstuhl Seminar 2001. LNCS (LNAI), vol. 2466, pp. 52–70. Springer, Heidelberg (2002)
2. Yamauchi, B.: Decentralized coordination for multirobot exploration. Robotics and Autonomous Systems 29, 111–118 (1999)
3. Simmons, R., Apfelbaum, D., Burgard, W., Fox, D., Moors, M., Thrun, S., Younes, H.: Coordination for multi-robot exploration and mapping. In: 17th Conf. of the American Association for Artificial Intelligence, pp. 852–858 (2000)
4. Zlot, R.M., Stentz, A., Dias, M.B., Thayer, S.: Multi-robot exploration controlled by a market economy. In: IEEE Int. Conf. on Robotics and Automation, pp. 3016–3023 (2002)
5. Oriolo, G., Vendittelli, M., Freda, L., Troso, G.: The SRT method: Randomized strategies for exploration. In: IEEE Int. Conf. on Robotics and Automation, pp. 4688–4694 (2004)
6. Espinoza León, J.: Estrategias para la exploración de ambientes desconocidos en robótica móvil, Master Thesis, FCC-BUAP (2006) (in Spanish)
7. Espinoza, J.L., Sánchez, A.L., Osorio, M.L.: Exploring unknown environments with mobile robots using SRT-Radial. In: IEEE Int. Conf. on Intelligent Robots and Systems, pp. 2089–2094 (2007)
8. Vatti, B.R.: A generic solution to polygon clipping. Communications of the ACM 3(7), 56–63 (1992)

On the Selection of a Classification Technique for the Representation and Recognition of Dynamic Gestures

Héctor H. Avilés, Wendy Aguilar, and Luis A. Pineda

Department of Computer Science
Instituto de Investigaciones en Matemáticas Aplicadas y en Sistemas
Universidad Nacional Autónoma de México
Circuito Escolar, Ciudad Universitaria, D.F.
04510 México
{haviles,weam}@turing.iimas.unam.mx, luis@leibniz.iimas.unam.mx

Abstract. Previous evaluations of gesture recognition techniques have been focused on classification performance, while ignoring other relevant issues such as knowledge description, feature selection, error distribution and learning performance. In this paper, we present an empirical comparison of decision trees, neural networks and hidden Markov models for visual gesture recognition following these criteria. Our results show that none of these techniques is a definitive alternative for all these issues. While neural nets and hidden Markov models show the highest recognition rates, they sacrifice clarity of its knowledge; decision trees, on the other hand, are easy to create and analyze. Moreover, error dispersion is higher with neural nets. This information could be useful to develop a general computational theory of gestures. For the experiments, a database of 9 gestures with more than 7000 samples taken from 15 people was used.

Keywords: Gesture recognition, hidden Markov models, neural networks, decision trees, human-machine interaction.

1 Introduction

Visual recognition of dynamic gestures is important for machines to naturally interact with humans. Hidden Markov models (*HMMs*) and artificial neural networks (*ANNs*) have become standard classification techniques in this problem. However, previous efforts have focused on recognition performance [1], at the expense of feature selection, learning performance, error distribution and clarity and comprehension of knowledge representation. Notwithstanding, accurate recognition is not the only factor to take into account for developing computational models and for judging knowledge representation techniques.

In this paper we present a set of experiments to evaluate ANNs, HMMs and decision trees (*DTs*) to recognize gestures following the criteria mentioned above. Decision trees have become a cornerstone in many pattern classification problems; however, it is not a commonly used technique to represent dynamic gestures. Our experimental results show that ANNs and HMMs obtained high recognition results, but sacrifice clarity, while DTs are clearer, although have a marginal decrease in performance. We also

H. Geffner et al. (Eds.): IBERAMIA 2008, LNAI 5290, pp. 412–421, 2008.

present a gesture database with more than 7000 samples taken from 15 people and executed with the person's right-arm. These gestures are oriented to instruct a mobile robot. We propose this database as a testbed for comparison of different techniques in gesture recognition, as well as in machine learning and analysis of sequential data.

Section 2 discusses various techniques proposed for gesture recognition, and previous experimental comparisons of these techniques. Section 3 briefly describes DTs, ANNs and HMMs. Section 4 describes the gesture database used in our experiments. Section 5 presents our experiments, results and analysis. Finally, in section 6 we discuss our conclusions and future work.

2   Related Work

Recognition of dynamic gestures can be seen as a pattern classification problem; a wide range of techniques have been used for this purpose, like temporal templates [2], comparison of body posture streams using Viterbi-based alignment [3] and dynamic time warping. However, the most succesfull and widely used techniques for gesture recognition are HMMs [4] and ANNs [1]. On the one hand, HMMs effectively represent gestural phases *via* state transition probabilities, and noisy observations by means of observation conditional probability functions. On the other hand, ANNs are successful classifiers in many pattern recognition problems, due to their capability to model complex pattern functions [5].

Some of the previous work have evaluated recognition performance of these techniques. In [6] is presented a comparison between support vector machines and feed forward neural nets for 13 mouse cursor movements executed by three people. In those experiments, ANNs slightly outperformed support vector machines by 2% of recognition rate. Corradini and Gross [1] present a comparison of three architectures based on combinations of ANNs and HMMs, and dynamic time warping. Their database is composed by 1350 samples of 6 gesture classes executed by 5 people. They obtained better recognition results by combining HMMs and radial basis fuctions networks to compute state probabilities. These authors state that due to the small training set their results do not mean that one classifier always outperform the other. Surveys on gesture recognition with comprenhensive reviews on gesture classification have been presented as well [7,8]. Other comparison efforts have focused on extensive tests of different gesture attributes using HMMs [9].

Decision trees have been frequently used to classify static gestures –or postures [10,11]. However, its most important usage is in areas such as machine learning and data mining to discover useful information in large size datasets. Despite its usefulness, DTs is not commonly selected as a classifier to recognize dynamic gestures [12].

3   Classification Techniques

Decision trees are frequently used in classification problems where classes can be represented by a set of features. DTs are a tree-based representation of a collection of *if-then* rules. The antecedent part of a rule is composed by *and* operations between feature values. The consequent corresponds to the desired class or target. Following the tree representation, each node represents a unique feature. Each branch emerging from the node represents one possible value of the feature. Leaves correspond to the values of the class variable. Decision trees are constructed by iterative selection of the most discriminative features [13]. Some features may not appear in the tree since they do not provide with a large enough discriminative capability –*i.e., attribute selection*. This technique allows us to represent continuous and categorical data, and its knowledge and classification process is easy to interpret and understand.

Hidden Markov models are probabilistic models that represent statistical properties of dynamic processes [15]. Dynamics is described in terms of the system states and their transitions. States are not visible directly, they are estimated only through the observations generated by the process –states are "hidden". HMMs suppose independence of the future with respect to the past given the present, and that the probabilities do not change over time. In gesture recognition, HMMs-based classifiers are frequently constructed by training a single HMM for each gesture class. The parameters of a HMM are computed through well-known training procedures such as the *Baum-Welch* algorithm. For the recognition, the probability –or *likelihood*– of an observation sequence for each HMM is calculated using the *Forward* algorithm [15]. It can assumed that the HMM with the highest probability correspond to the desired gesture class.

Artificial neural networks [5] are composed by a set of interconnected elements called artificial neurons. Neurons are usually grouped into input, hidden and output layers. When used as classifiers, a learning step consists on training neurons to be activated or inhibited given an input pattern. The activation of a neuron is propragated as input to other neurons of the network. On testing, a given example is presented to the input nodes, and the learnt responses are propagated through the network to the output nodes. The activation states of the output neurons define the class of the original input pattern. Common learning strategies include 3-layer topologies, backpropagation learning to take into account error changes, sigmoidal activation functions for non-linear neural responses, and adaptive number of hidden neurons.

4   Gesture Database

In this work we used a gesture database with a set of 9 dynamic gestures performed by 10 men and 5 women. Gestures were executed with the user's right-arm –See Fig. 1. The complete set of examples is composed of 7308 gestures. Every person contributed a different number of samples; however, at least 50 samples of each gesture per person were recorded [1].

Each sample is composed by the length T of the gesture observation sequence –that ranges from 6 to 42 observations in the entire database– and the gesture data itself. Every observation of the sequence is composed of: i) (x, y)-coordinates of the upper and lower corners of the rectangle that segments the right-hand, ii) (x, y)-coordinates of the upper and lower corners of the rectangle that segments the user's torso, and iii) (x, y)-coordinates of the center of the user's face. These coarse posture data enable us to convert the information to different feature sets easily [9]. All coordinates are

---

[1] This database is available at:
http://sourceforge.net/projects/visualgestures/

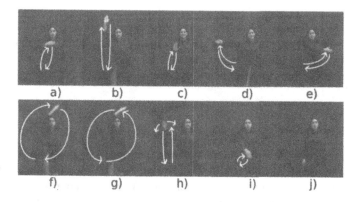

Fig. 1. Gesture set: a) come, b) attention, c) stop, d) right, e) left, f) turn-left, g) turn-right, h) waving-hand and i) pointing; j) initial and final position for each gesture

relative to the usual upper-left corner of the image and assuming a resolution of 640 × 480 pixels. Data were recorded on plain text files. Gestures were obtained using our monocular visual system[2] based on skin–color described in [16]. A spatial criterion about the position of the hand was used to start and end the capture of each gesture example. Every person executed his gestures in front of the camera at a distance of aproximately 3m. Observations were sampled every 4 images at a rate of 30 images per second.

5 Experiments and Results

5.1 Gesture Attributes

From the coarse posture information described in section 4 the following 7 gesture attributes were extracted: a) 3 features to describe motion, and b) 4 to describe posture. Motion features are $\Delta area$ –or changes in hand area–, Δx and Δy –or changes in hand position of the XY-axis of the image. The conjuction of these three attributes allows us to estimate hand motion in the Cartesian space XYZ. Each one of these features takes only one of three possible values: $\{+, -, 0\}$ that indicate increment, decrement or no change, depending on the area and position of the hand in a previous image of the sequence. For example, if the hand moves to the right, then $\Delta x = +$, if its motion is to the left, $\Delta x = -$ and if there is no motion in the X-axis, $\Delta x = 0$. Posture features named *form*, *above*, *right* and *torso* describe hand appearance and spatial relations between the hand and other body parts, such as the face and torso. Hand appearance is represented by *form*. This feature is discretized into one of three values: $(+)$ if the hand is vertical, $(-)$ if the hand is horizontal, or (0) if the hand is leant to the left or right over the XY plane. *right* indicates if the hand is to the right of the head, *above* if the hand is above the head, and *torso* if the hand is over the user's torso. These features take binary values, **true** or **false**, that represent if their corresponding condition is

---

[2] Available at the same location of the gesture database.

satisfied or not. The number of all possible combinations of these feature values is 648. In this work, every feature observation o_t is a vector of 7 features in the following order $(\Delta x, \Delta y, \Delta area, form, right, above, torso)$. In this setting motion attributes requires two consecutive observations to be calculated. This way, once features are extracted the first observation is eliminated and hence the new length of the feature observation sequences is $T - 1$.

5.2 Data Preparation

To obtain a more compact representation of the gestures and avoid missing data, gesture samples were normalized to 5 feature observations by subsampling the sequences at equal intervals. Five is the minimum sequence length found in our feature sequences. This preprocessing step is not unusual in gesture recognition [9,1]. We recorded our gesture data in the following order: $T, o_1, o_2, o_3, o_4, o_5$, where T is the original gesture length before feature extraction and normalization, and o_1, o_2, o_3, o_4, o_5 is the sequence of feature observations. T was included as a feature for DTs and ANNs.

5.3 Experimental Setup

We used the J4.8 tree learning algorithm, that is a Java implementation of C4.5 [13], and the 3-layer Perceptron implemented in the WEKA machine learning toolkit [17]. The learning strategy of Weka for multilayer Perceptron include adaptation of the number of hidden neurons and error backpropagation with gradient descendent. For HMMs, a modified version implemented in [18] to consider multiple observation sequences [15] was used. Training is performed using the Baum-Welch algorithm. Experiments were carried out using a PC with an Intel Core 2 Duo 2.33Ghz processor and 2Gb of RAM. These software suites were used to enable others to reproduce our experiments. We conducted experiments to evaluate recognition results, knowledge description, feature selection, error distribution and learning capabilities of ANNs, DTs and HMMs independently for each one of the participants. We did this for two reason: i) to compare the behaviour of these models for different people, and ii) because it has been suggested the need to construct personalized recognition systems for gesture recognition [16].

For DTs, WEKA's default parameters were used and no special setup was established –e.g., confidence threshold for pruning to 0.25, and 2 as the minimum number of instances per leaf. For ANNs we set learning rate parameter to 0.6 and the number of epochs to train through to 100. HMMs were set to discrete uniform distributions for observations and transition probabilities to follow a standard linear 5-state transition topology. The EM algorithm with *Forward* and *Backward* logarithmic probabilities was used to train HMMs. Convergence criteria are: 1) 10^{-26}, as the minimum difference between two consecutives estimations of a HMM and, 2) $10,000$ as the maximum number of iterations to train each model. However, the latter criterion was not observed to be triggered. For testing, the probability of each gesture sequence was computed using the scaled version of the *Forward* algorithm. Training parameters were selected arbitrarily; however, on various tests we observed that there is not a considerable impact of these values on the recognition performance of the classifiers. For

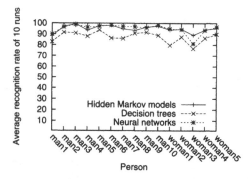

Fig. 2. Average recognition rates of 10 runs for each person using hidden Markov models, decision trees and neural networks

example, by modifying the minimum training threshold of HMMs to 10^{-6}, only the number of training iterations is decreased, without affecting recognition rates significantly.

Initially, for each person, we extracted 50 samples of each gesture to construct 15 personal databases. These examples are the base of all our experiments: from these 50 examples, we selected randomly 30 samples to construct the training data set, and the remaining 20 samples for testing. The three models were trained and tested using the same examples.

5.4 Results

We performed 10 repetitions of the previous experiment for each person. Following this configuration, 150 DTs, 150 ANNs and 1350 HMMs –9 HMMs per classifier– were constructed. Figure 2 shows the average recognition rates obtained with these classification techniques. Average recognition rates of all the participants are 95.07% for neural networks, 94.84% for HMMs and 87.3% for DTs. To analyze how classification erros are distributed among classes we computed cumulative confusion matries by adding the 150 individual confusion matrices of each model. Tables 1, 2, and 3 show these matrices. Rows are true classes and columns corresponds to classification results. Percentages on each row account for recognition results of 3000 classification tests. Table 4 presents the best and worst case of: i) computational time used for training and ii) the number of parameters required by the classifiers. For HMMs classifiers, the number of parameters is fixed and stands for discrete observation distributions –640 parameters– of each state, plus transition probabilities –25 parameters– and initial state distribution –5 parameters– for each one of the 9 hidden Markov models. Decision tree parameters correspond to the number of tree nodes. Parameters of neural networks are the number of connection weights between nodes required by networks with 122 and 155 hidden neurons in the best and worst cases, respectively. We conducted a visual inspection of these classifiers to give us an idea about the description capabilities of these models.

Table 1. Cumulative confusion matrix for recognition results of each person with HMMs. Gestures are: **C** = come, **A** = attention, **R** = right, **L** = left, **S** = stop, **T-L** = turn-left, **T-R** = turn-right, **P** = pointing, **W-H** = waving-hand. Percentage on each row corresponds to 3000 classification tests.

	C	A	R	L	S	T-L	T-R	P	W-H
C	**95.1**	0.7	0.57		1.33			1.43	0.87
A	0.87	**94.83**			0.47	0.7	0.13		3
R	0.13		**99.17**		0.17	0.03			0.5
L	0.17			**93.83**				6.0	
S	1.93	0.47	0.07		**90.63**			0.87	6.03
T-L	0.1	0.1	0.03		0.1	**99.47**		0.03	0.17
T-R		0.17	0.03	0.03			**99.67**	0.07	0.03
P	1.6		0.1	5.37	0.67	0.07		**91.87**	0.33
W-H	0.47	3.43	0.2		6.7	0.03	0.03	0.1	**89.03**

Table 2. Cumulative confusion matrix for classification results of each person using DTs

	C	A	R	L	S	T-L	T-R	P	W-H
C	**85.73**	0.87	2.97	0.13	4.1	0.5		2.87	2.83
A	2.13	**87.67**	0.23		0.97	6.4	0.77		1.83
R	0.47	0.17	**97.33**		0.6	1.43			
L	0.77			**96.73**			0.67	1.83	
S	4.13	1.67	0.57		**87.37**	0.70	0.10	1.47	4
T-L	4.37	8.5	4.23		0.73	**80.7**	1.13	0.13	0.2
T-R	6.73	0.83		4.33		1.23	**85.03**	1.60	0.23
P	6.70	0.03		4.77	0.47	0.23		**86.77**	1.03
W-H	5.27	5.03	1.07		7.20	1.07	0.2	0.03	**80.13**

5.5   Analysis

Recognition rates of the proposed techniques show that there are no considerable differences between recognition rates of ANNs and HMMs. This is somewhat coincident with previous comparisons of these classifiers, although we are using neither the same type of models, nor the same implementations. Recognition performance of DTs is below the other classifers in all cases. However, results of DTs are positive enough in accordance with their small number of parameters. Notwithstanding, more experimentation must be executed to test different criteria for tree learning, and evaluate its impact on the classification performance. An interesting case of low recognition rate is woman3. We analyzed her individual confusion matrices. Misclassifications are concentrated in attention and waving-hand gestures for the three models. By displaying these gestures we found there are fairly similar examples of these classes –*i.e.*, raising the hand around the heads top with a little hand waving.

In addition to recognition rates, we used three different measures to quantify error of these models. Results are presented on Table 5. The first one is *Shannon's entropy* [20] to evaluate error dispersion. This measure shows that dispersion for decision trees is higher in comparison to HMMs and ANNs. However, entropy is sensible to the error

Table 3. Cumulative confusion matrix for the recognition results of each person using ANNs

	C	A	R	L	S	T-L	T-R	P	W-H
C	95.77	0.83	0.23	0.03	1.83	0.1	0.07	1.03	0.1
A	1.1	91.6	0.83		0.67	2.17	1.23	0.27	2.13
R	0.03	0.03	99.3		0.2	0.1	0.07	0.13	0.13
L	0.17			96.13		0.03	0.1	3.57	
S	1.8	0.6	0.07	0.37	93	0.17	0.07	0.9	3.03
T-H	0.13	1.27	0.67	0.03	0.23	97.43	0.03	0.07	0.13
T-R	0.03	0.3	0.03	0.23	0.03	0.03	98.57	0.73	0.03
P	1.37		0.03	3.4	0.93	0.27	0.23	93.63	0.13
W-H	0.2	2.27	1.3	0.03	4.33	1.23	0.8	0.23	89.6

Table 4. Minimum and maximum number of parameters and training time (in seconds) for the three classifiers

	Number of parameters		Training time (*Sec*)	
	Best case	Worst case	Best case	Worst case
Hidden Markov models	29,070		1.03	849.83
Neural Networks	25,173	42,483	207.06	760.67
Decision trees	31	519	0.02	0.09

rate. To avoid this, we follow the method introduced by R. van Son to calculate error dispersion measures independent of the error rate, with information taken directly from the confusion matrix [19]. This method relies on entropy-based measure *perplexity* to calculate the "effective" mean number of error classes. Measures are d_s and d_r. d_s can be interpreted as the mean number of wrong responses per correct class; d_r is the mean number of samples incorrectly classified on each possible response. These measures account for dispersion through the horizontal and vertical dimensions of the confusion matrix, respectively. The higher the dispersion is, the higher the value of these measures should be. Error dispersion values show that NNs generated more error dispersion in comparison to HMMs and DTs. Error dispersion is important because confusion matrices could be used by machines to decide whether a gesture has been executed or not, and classifiers with low error distribution should be preferred. Finally, we propose *Confusion Ratio*. This measure is defined as the quotient of the total error over the total correct recognition rate; the lowest the confusion ratio, the lowest the value of this measure is. Here, again the results are similar for HMMs and NNs, and better than DTs.

Clarity in knowledge representation has not been correctly valued in the past on gesture recognition. While it has been shown that ANNs and HMMs provide good recognition engines, gestural information is better described by decision trees. In particular, HMMs represent internal information as numerical data, making it difficult to assign physical meanings and make judgments without the aid of adequate graphical tools. With ANNs the situation is even worse. Decision trees represent their information in a suitable form to be readable for everyone with a little understanding of them and using only a few parameters. For example, DTs enable us to visually analyze the structure

Table 5. Dispersion measures for cumulative confusion matrices of HMMs, DTs and NNs

	Shannon's entropy	d_s	d_r	Confusion Ratio
Hidden Markov models	3.51	1.88	1.88	0.054
Decision trees	3.94	3.36	3.46	0.142
Neural Networks	3.54	3.60	3.62	0.052

of gestures by identifying relevant observations for each gesture class –that it is a first step for feature selection. We have seen that gestures with similar evolutions are frequently grouped together into the structure of DTs. This help us to identify in advance which gestures are similar and could be potentially misclassified before making extensive testing. In addition to descriptiveness capabilities of DTs, the low training time of these models can be important for fast prototyping when designing gestural interfaces.

6   Conclusions and Future Work

In this paper, an empirical comparison of decision trees, neural networks and hidden Markov models in gesture recognition has been presented. Our analysis extends previous efforts to issues not considered before such as knowledge description, feature selection, error distribution and computational time for training. We have found that there is not a single best alternative to cope with all these questions. Neural nets and hidden Markov models obtained high recognition rates in comparison to decision trees. However, knowledge description of decision trees allows us to analyze interesting information such as the similarity of gestures or relevant observations. Moreover, due to the required computational time for training, decision trees could be adequate for fast prototyping in the design of gestural interfaces. We used a gesture database with more than 7000 samples performed by 15 people.

We believe decision trees can be applied to gestural analysis beyond gesture recognition. As a future work we plan to test different configurations for the current attributes and different sets of feature vectors to evaluate its impact on recognition performance and gesture description. In addition, we plan to develop a methodology for using decision trees as a preprocessing step to automatically analyze gestures, their relevant attributes, and to identify possible confusions before testing other more complex representations.

Acknowledgments. The authors would like to thank Dr. Rob van Son for his valuable comments and for proofreading the document, and anonymous reviewers for their constructive suggestions.

References

1. Corradini, A., Gross, H.M.: Implementation and Comparison of Three Achitectures for Gesture Recognition. In: IEEE International Conference on Acoustics, Speech, and Signal Processing, pp. 2361–2364 (2000)
2. Davis, J.W., Bobick, A.F.: The Representation and Recognition of Human Movement Using Temporal Templates. In: IEEE Computer Society Conference on Computer Vision and Pattern Recognition, p. 928 (1997)

3. Waldherr, S.: Gesture Recognition on a Mobile Robot, Diploma's thesis Carnegie Mellon University. School of Computer Science (1998)
4. Yang, J., Xu, Y.: Hidden Markov model for Gesture Recognition, Techincal report CMU-RI-TR-94-10, Carnegie Mellon University (1994)
5. Duda, R.O., Stork, D.G.: Pattern Classification, 2nd edn. Wiley-Interscience, Chichester (2001)
6. Dadgostar, F., Sarrafzadeh, A., Fan, C., De Silva, L., Messom, C.: Modeling and Recognition of Gesture Signals in 2D Space: A comparison of NN and SVM approaches. In: 18th IEEE International Conference on Tools with Artificial Intelligence, pp. 701–704 (2006)
7. Watson, R.: A Survey of Gesture Recognition Techniques, Technical Report TCD-CS-93-11, Trinity College (1993)
8. Pavlović, V., Sharma, R., Huang, T.S.: Visual Interpretation of Hand Gestures for Human-Computer Interaction: A Review. IEEE Trans. on Patt. Anal. and Mach. Intell. 19(7), 677–695 (1997)
9. Campbell, L.W., Becker, A.D., Azarbayejani, A., Bobick, A.F., Pentland, A.: Invariant features for 3-D Gesture Recognition, Techinical report 379, M.I.T. Media Laboratory Perceptual Computing Section (1996)
10. Spiegel, D.: A Gesture Recognition System (1997), http://alumni.media.mit.edu/~spiegel/papers/gesture.pdf
11. Hai, W., Sutherland, A.: Dynamic gesture recognition using PCA with multi-scale theory and HMM. In: Proc. SPIE, vol. 4550, pp. 132–139 (2001)
12. Mardia, K.V., Ghali, N.M., Hainsworth, T.J., Howes, M., Sheehy, N.: Techniques for online gesture recognition on workstations. Image Vision Comput. 11(5), 283–294 (1993)
13. Quinlan, J.R.: C4.5: Programs for Machine Learning. Morgan Kaufmann, San Francisco (1993)
14. McNeill, D.: Hand and Mind: What gestures reveal about thought. University of Chicago Press, Chicago (1992)
15. Rabiner, L.R.: Readings in Speech Recognition, A Tutorial on Hidden Markov Models and Selected Applications in Speech Recognition, pp. 257–286. Morgan Kaufmann Publishers, San Francisco (1990)
16. Avilés, H.H., Sucar, L.E., Mendoza, E.: Visual Recognition of Gestures. In: 18th International Conference on Pattern Recognition, pp. 1100–1103 (2006)
17. Witten, I.H., Frank, E.: Data Mining: Practical machine learning tools and techniques, 2nd edn. Morgan Kaufmann, San Francisco (2005)
18. Kanungo, T.: Hidden Markov Models Software (Last retrieved May 26, 2008), http://www.kanungo.com/
19. van son, R.J.J.H.: The Relation Between the Error Distribution and the Error Rate in Indentification Experiments. Proceedings 19, Institute of Phonetic Sciences, University of Amsterdam, pp. 71–82 (1995) (Last retrieved May 26, 2008), http://fonsg3.hum.uva.nl/Proceedings/Proceedings_19/ErrorDispersion_RvS/ErrorDispersion.html
20. Shannon, C.E.: A Mathematical Theory of Communication. Bell System Technical Journal 27, 379–423, 623–656 (1948)

A Fuzzy Hybrid Intelligent System for Human Semen Analysis

Esmeralda Ramos[1], Haydemar Núñez[1], and Roberto Casañas[2]

[1] Laboratorio de Inteligencia Artificial, Centro de Ingeniería de Software y Sistemas Escuela de Computación, Facultad de Ciencias, Universidad Central de Venezuela
esmeralda.ramos@ciens.ucv.ve, haydemar.nunez@ciens.ucv.ve
[2] Cátedra de Física y Análisis Instrumental, Escuela de Bioanálisis, Facultad de Medicina Universidad Central de Venezuela
robertoc@med.ucv.ve

Abstract. This paper describes a fuzzy hybrid system to support the human semen analysis, that integrates the case and rule based reasoning. The module of case based reasoning uses a recovery scheme in two phases: first, recovery rules are used to generate a spermatic classification; second, the k-nearest neighbor technique (KNN) with a fuzzy similarity measure, is used to determine the degrees of severity to each alteration. In order to complete the solution of the new case, a module of rule based reasoning gives suggestions and observations from variables that do no affect this classification. Experimental results obtained show that the system provides a good percentage of successes; therefore it could be used as an instrument to support the decision-making process that carries out the professionals of this domain.

Keywords: Case based reasoning, rule based reasoning, fuzzy similarity measure, human semen analysis, hybrid intelligent systems.

1 Introduction

The human semen analysis (HSA) or spermogram is a study applied in several processes such as the evaluation of the male fertility, the detection of infectious processes, the monitoring of vasectomy and control before and after surgical interventions [7]. In order to carry out this analysis in an effective way, professionals in this area apply not only empirical knowledge gained from their own experience (solved cases), but also declarative knowledge (which can be expressed in production rules). This knowledge could be available in a software application that supports the classification process. Thus, we can observe how the paradigms of case based reasoning (CBR) and rule based reasoning (RBR) can be adapted to this domain. The rules allow to represent the fundamental and general knowledge, and the cases represent the specific knowledge [10]. The integration of both schemes in a hybrid system could take the advantages that each offers. The integration of CBR with RBR has received special attention [5], as it is demonstrated in [3], [12], [13], where they have produced satisfactory results.

In this work a fuzzy hybrid system of RBC and RBR is proposed, which tries to emulate the decision-making process of experts from this domain. The module of case

H. Geffner et al. (Eds.): IBERAMIA 2008, LNAI 5290, pp. 422–431, 2008.

based reasoning uses a recovery scheme in two phases: first one, rules are used to retrieve cases whose spermatic classification matches the class of the new case. These cases will constitute a *reduced case base*. The second one, are recovered from the reduced case base using the k-nearest neighbor technique (KNN) and a fuzzy similarity measure, the cases whose sub-classifications (severity degrees) are more similar to the new case. This recuperation of two levels produces a part of the solution constituted by the spermatic classification and the degrees of severity to each alteration. In order to complete the solution of the new case, a module of rule based reasoning gives suggestions and observations from variables that do no affect this classification.

This document is structured as follows: Section 2 introduces the human semen analysis problem. In Section 3 the proposed hybrid system and the experimental results are presented. Section 4 shows how, when the case base is edited, a significant improvement of performance system is obtained. Finally, the conclusions and future works are presented.

2 Human Semen Analysis

Human semen analysis consists in two sets of evaluations [7]: the macroscopic tests, where characteristics like aspect, color, liquefaction, volume, viscosity and pH are evaluated, and the microscopic tests which allow to consider motility, vitality and spermatic morphology, agglutination and others.

Diagnosis of the human semen quality is a complex process. There are multiple options of classification, determined by the alterations of the variables measured in the HAS, and the different degrees of severity of each them (mild, moderate, severe) [6]. Because of the diversity of possible classifications, professionals use the nomenclature and criteria established in the laboratory manual of the World Health Organization (WHO) [8], and their own experience (see Table 1).

If the alterations of the variables which determine the spermatic classifications are conjugated, it is possible to obtain up to 51 possible classes. Moreover, those

Table 1. Nomenclature for classifying the ejaculate quality (* Classification with severity degree)

Classification	Description
Normozoospermia	Normal Ejaculated according to the Reference Values (RV).
Oligozoospermia *	Spermatic concentration fewer than RV
Asthenozoospermia *	Spermatic motility fewer than RV
Teratozoospermia	Amount of sperms with normal forms fewer than RV
Hipospermia *	Volume fewer than RV
Hiperespermia	Volume bigger than RV
Necrozoospermia *	Vitality fewer than RV
Azoospermia	No spermatozoa in the ejaculate

classifications whose alterations have a severity degree (indicated with "*"), can be sub-classified by 3 to 81 subclasses. In the other hand, the professionals can give recommendations and suggestions based on variables that don't determine the classification. This information completes the diagnosis.

For example, in a sample with the following results: Color =Yellow; Viscosity =Normal, Volume =2.5 ml, Concentration =16.5 millions/ml, Normal Forms =9.00%, Live immotile =45.99%, Rapidly progressive =16.79%, Slowly progressive =11.66% and Total progressive =28.45%; would be obtained as spermatic classification: *"Mild Oligozoospermia, Moderate Necrozoospermia, Astenozoospermia, Teratozoospermia"*. As the color of the sample reports yellow, the professional would make the following observation: *"It is possible that the sample is infected with urine. Also, it can indicate the existence of seminal infection"*.

In despite of the standardization of the procedures suggested in the WHO laboratory manual [8], there are difficulties to realize the classification. This is due to the diversity of terms and the subjectivity and complexity of the test. In addition, the lack of skills increases the difficulty of the examination.

3 Architecture of the Hybrid System

In order to support the decision-making process in the HSA a fuzzy hybrid system of RBC and RBR is proposed. Figure 1 shows the architecture of the system, which has the capacity to carry out the following tasks: a) To Analyze the variables reported in the spermograms and to determine the spermatic classification, b) To Determine the degrees of severity of each one of the alterations in the classification, c) To Analyze the variables of the spermogram that do not determine the classification of the ejaculation, and based on this information, give suggestions that complement the result. At next, the proposed system is described, following the stages of the cycle of life of the RBC [1].

3.1 The Case Base

The Case Base (CB) stores spermograms of patients, which were provided by a laboratory of fertilization. This data set was inspected with the purpose of identify absences, inconsistencies, outliers, among other aspects that could alter the results of the recuperation techniques [4]. Once finished the data cleaning under the supervision of experts, the CB was made up of 2663 spermograms, each one of them represented by a record of two components: the first one describes the problem (variables of spermogram) and the second one; the solution (spermatic classification, degree of severity, observations and suggestions). This structure is showed in Table 2.

In order to determine the recovery index, they were applied attribute selection techniques [9]. These methods can determine the features that are more important in predicting outcomes and improving retrieval. In particular, filter methods using different criteria of evaluation (information gain and chi square test) and wrapper methods (by training a support vector machine) were applied. Retrieval index obtained and verified by experts consists on variables such as: volume, concentration, PR + SM, % of Normal Forms and % of alive unmovable.

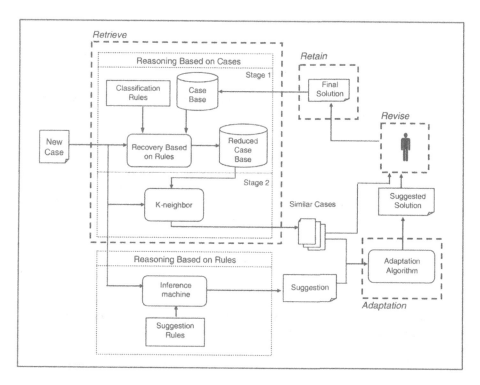

Fig. 1. Architecture of the fuzzy hybrid system

Table 2. Representation cases strutructure

Variables:

Identifier – Volume – Concentration – RP + SP - % Live immotile – Normal Forms Aspects – pH – Color – Viscosity – Agglutination – Rapidly Progressives (RP) – Slowly Progressives (SP) – Non Progressives – Live Immotile –Died Immotile– Abnormal Forms – Head Defects – Tail Defects – Peroxides' Cells

Solution: Spermatic Classification	Severity Degree	Observations
Suggestions		

3.2 Case Retrieval

Case retrieval is the process of finding, within a case base, those cases that are nearest to the current case. In the proposed system, this retrieval is applied in two phases: first, an inter-class classification is obtained (class shown in Section 2), second phase allows determining the severity degrees of the classification obtained in the previous step (intra-classes classification).

Phase 1: In this phase, the spermatic classification is obtained. Using a set of classification rules, which are generated from the retrieval index by applying the C4.5

algorithm [4], cases recovered where those whose spermatic classification matches the class of the new case. The recovered cases are stored in a *reduced case base* (Reduced BC in the Figure 1). This BC will be the input to the second phase of retrieval. Bellow we present an example of classification rule:

If   Volume < 2.0 ml AND % Live immotile < 50 AND (%PR + PM) < 50
Then   Classification = Hipospermia – Oligozoopemia – Asthenozoospermia.

Phase 2: In this phase, the severity degree of the spermatic classification is calculated. In order to realize this task we must consider the severity degree of each alteration in this classification given in Phase 1. Then, using the k-nearest neighbor technique (KNN), are retrieved from the *reduced case base* the cases whose sub-classifications (severity degrees) are more similar to the new case. To realize this task the following fuzzy similarity measure is used:

Let be X_{NEW} a new case and Y_{BC}, a case from de Reduced BC, where:

$$X_{NEW} = (x_1, x_2, x_3, x_4, x_5)$$

$$Y_{BC} = (y_1, y_2, y_3, y_4, y_5)$$

The $(x_1, x_2, x_3, x_4, x_5)$ and $(y_1, y_2, y_3, y_4, y_5)$, are the values for the variables of the retrieval index: volume, concentration, RP + SP, % Normal forms and % Immovable Alive, for each case.

The similarity between X_{NEW} and Y_{BC} is calculated as follows:

$$SIM(X_{NEW}, Y_{BC}) = \sum_i d_i \quad \text{where:}$$

$$d_i = \max\left[\min\left(\mu_{Severe}(x_i), \mu_{Severe}(y_i)\right), \min\left(\mu_{Moderate}(x_i), \mu_{Moderate}(y_i)\right), \min\left(\mu_{Mild}(x_i), \mu_{Mild}(y_i)\right)\right]$$

The fuzzy sets are determined from the data. For each variable of the index that has a severity degree, the minimum value and the maximum value, as well as the

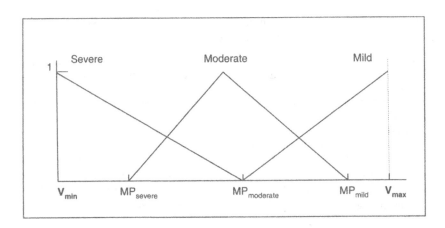

Fig. 2. Fuzzy sets determined from data

midpoint of the data associated to each of the linguistic labels (Severe, Moderate and Mild) are calculated. For example, for the volume variable, the minimum and maximum values are determined (V_{min}, V_{max}). Midpoints are also estimated from the data for mild Hipospermia (MP_{Mild}), Moderate Hipospermia ($MP_{Moderate}$) and Severe Hipospermia (MP_{Severe}). Such values are the basis for the construction of the fuzzy sets, as shown in Figure 2, with a triangular membership function.

Then, the 3 cases that are maximally similar to the new case are recovered, by computing the fuzzy similarity of this case to every case in the reduced BC. These cases have the smallest values for SIM. In order to determine the value of K, we practiced various experiments varying the vicinity (K=3, 5, 7, 9), applying 10-fold cross validation.

3.3 Cases Adaptation

Case adaptation is the process of transforming a solution retrieved into a solution appropriate for the new case. The adaptation proposal in this system is summarized in the following algorithm:

Step 1: The solution recovered is divided according to the variables of the index involved in the classification.
Step 2: To Determine, by simple majority, the severity of each variable.

For example (see Fig 3), a new case classified as: "Oligozoopermia – Hipospermia" (inferred in phase 1), applying the adaptation algorithm, the solution for the new case would be:

Mild Oligozoospermia – Moderate Hipospermia

Variables the index → involved in the classification	Concentration	Volume	
	Oligozoospermia	**Hipospermia**	← Classification of a new case (Stage 1)
Case recovered 1	Mild	Moderate	⎫
Case recovered 2	Moderate	Moderate	⎬ Severity degrees of the cases recovered
Case recovered 3	Mild	Mild	⎭
	Mild	Moderate	← The variables are analyzed separately and not the complete solution

Fig. 3. Example of applying adaptation algorithm

3.4 Suggestion Rules

Some variables measured in the ALS such as aspect, pH, viscosity, agglutination, do not have a effect on the spermatic classification of the sample that is evaluated. However, these values are reported by professionals, because they contribute to the diagnosis process and guide about the complementary tests or functional explorations. Therefore, a module of rule-based reasoning, able to analyze these variables and to emit suggestions, was incorporated to produce a complete solution. The rules were generated and validated by experts. An example of suggestion rule is as follows:

> **If** Agglutination > 10% **Then** "Immunological Disorders or Infections can exist, it is suggested to realize test of antisperm antibodies or *Martest*".

3.5   Case Revision and Case Retain

Solution provided by the system could be reviewed by professionals. If the solution is not satisfactory, they will be able to repair it and to give recommendations for the new case. This stage is done in a manual way through the interface of the system. In order to facilitate this process, the professional will be able to visualize the three cases more similar to the new case. This functionality is especially interesting since it allows supporting the professional to reach his conclusions. Moreover, it can be very useful for the inexperienced professionals who begin in the accomplishment of this type of examination.

New cases repaired or not by the expert, will be stored in a temporary table within the data base. This table will be examined periodically by the professionals to determine what cases would have to be inserted in the BC, in order to increase the knowledge of the system.

3.6   Experiments and Results

To evaluate the performance of the case based reasoning module during the classification process, we made experiments using the fuzzy similarity measure described in Section 2.2, with triangular and trapezoidal membership functions. The test case base was formed by 2073 spermograms. These spermograms represent the cases whose spermatic classification has severity degree (45 classes).

Table 3 shows the mean values on the percentage of accuracy using leave-one-one cross validation, using majority function to determine the degrees of severity from the 3 near neighbors. Also, a variation of KNN technique was used by applying average distance to determine these severity degrees. In order to determine the influence of the overlapping between adjacent fuzzy sets, this one was varied in a proportion of -10%, -5%, 5% and 10%. Table 4 shows the results using the same validation technique.

Table 3. Expermiental results on the case base

Membership function	Average percentage of successes	
	Majority	**Average distance**
Triangular	67.52	71.23
Trapezoidal	**72.23**	**75.68**

Table 4. Experimental results with varying degrees of overlap between adjacent fuzzy sets

Membership function	Average percentage of successes	
	Majority	**Average distance**
Triangular -5%	70.65	73.83
Triangular -10%	69.22	73.29
Triangular 5%	68.22	72.63
Triangular 10%	66.79	71.69
Trapezoidal -5%	74.41	**77.09**
Trapezoidal -10%	74.58	76.30
Trapezoidal 5%	**74.87**	76.44
Trapezoidal 10%	74.45	76.72

4 Case Base Edition and Results

To improve results reflected in Section 3, it would be advisable that the CB of the system presented characteristics such as: capacity (that the variety of classification problems could be successfully solved), effectiveness (low computer cost) and suitable size (a small CB could not have capacity to offer solutions to the great not representative for a class. We conducted a series of tests where two edition techniques were applied: Wilson [15] and Muliedit [2]. The obtained results on the amount of

Table 5. Experimental results on the edited CB

Membership function	Average percentage of successes	
	Majority	**Average distance**
Triangular	75.07	83.66
Trapezoidal	**77.79**	**90.17**

Table 6. Experimental results with varying degrees of overlap between adjacent fuzzy sets

Membership function	Average percentage of successes	
	Majority	**Average distance**
Triangular -5%	76.42	86.87
Triangular -10%	76.50	87.54
Triangular 5%	74.72	86.77
Triangular 10%	74.43	85.63
Trapezoidal -5%	77.75	90.57
Trapezoidal -10%	77.80	90.79
Trapezoidal 5%	77.83	91.26
Trapezoidal 10%	**78.03**	**91.33**

possible spermatic classifications and one great CB, although with more competition, it could be more susceptible to the utility problems). Thus, the CB was edited with the purpose of diminish the classification errors and those cases that are percentage of accuracy using leave-one-one cross validation are showed in Tables 5 and 6. It is important to stand out that the best results were obtained from an edited BC with Wilson technique, where the size of the BC was reduced approximately in a 22% and the percentage of accuracy increased in 14%.

5 Conclusions and Recommendations

Results obtained shown that the fuzzy hybrid system of case based and rule based reasoning provides a good performance given the percentage of accuracy achieved. Therefore, this system could be used as support in the decision-making process that carries out the professionals of this area.

Regarding the fuzzy sets used, it was observed a better performance for the trapezoidal case. Also, the results show that changing the degree of overlapping between the triangular and trapezoidal functions do not provide a significant improvement. In both cases the edition of the case base improved the results remarkably, as it is demonstrated in Tables 5 and 6. It is important to mention that also similar experiments with not fuzzy similarity measures (like Euclidean and city block) have been realized and so far, the best results have been achieved with the fuzzy measure.

Actually, we are working in the evaluation of techniques to be applied in a semiautomatic way by the maintenance of the case base in the Retention phase. In addition, this system constitutes the nucleus of a Classification Agent of an Agent-based System that is being developed for the support of the professionals of this domain. This application will also allow the analysis of the morphology sperm from scanned images of a semen sample, recovery of spermograms and medical records and the search of information of the HAS domain in an ontology that already has been implemented [11].

Acknowledgments

The authors thank Teresa Noriega and Víctor Fernándes, of the Medical Faculty, Central University of Venezuela (UCV), and Elizabeth Martínez, of the Leopoldo Aguerrevere Hospital, Venezuela. This research has been partially supported under grant PI-03.00.6653.2007 (Consejo de Desarrollo Científico y Humanístico, UCV).

References

1. Aamodt, A., Plaza, E.: Case-Based Reasoning: Foundational Issues, Methodological variations and System Approaches. AI Communications 7(1), 39–59 (1994)
2. Devijver, P.A., Kittler, J.: On the edited nearest neighbor rule. In: Proceedings of the Fifth International Conference on Pattern Recognition, Miami, Florida, pp. 72–80 (1980)
3. Huang, M., Chen, M., Lee, S.: Integrating data mining with case-based reasoning for chronic diseases prognosis and diagnosis. Expert Systems With Applications 32, 856–867 (2007)

4. Larose, D.: Discovering Knowledge in Data. An Introduction to Data Mining. Wiley Interscience, Chichester (2005)
5. Marling, C., Rissland, E., Aamodt, A.: Integrations with case-based reasoning. The knowledge Engineering Review 20(3), 241–245 (2005)
6. Mortimer, D.: Practical Laboratory Andrology. Oxford University Press, Oxford (1994)
7. Noriega, T., Orosa, J., Puerta, M., Goncalves, J.: Manual Práctico. I Curso de Actualización. Análisis del Líquido Seminal. Universidad Central de Venezuela. Facultad de Medicina. Escuela de Bioanálisis. Cátedra de Histología (2002)
8. de la Salud, O.M.: Manual de Laboratorio para el Examen del Semen Humano y de la Interacción entre el Semen y el Moco Cervical. Editorial Médica Panamericana. Madrid, España (2001)
9. Piramuthu, S.: Evaluating feature selection methods for learning in data mining applications. European Journal of Operational Research 156, 483–494 (2004)
10. Prentzas, J., Hatzilygeroudis, I.: Integrating Hybrid Rule-Based with Case-Based Reasoning. In: Craw, S., Preece, A.D. (eds.) ECCBR 2002. LNCS (LNAI), vol. 2416, pp. 336–349. Springer, Heidelberg (2002)
11. Ramos, E., Pereira, Y., Núñez, H., Castro, M., Casañas, R.: Aplicación de visualización de una ontología para el dominio del análisis del semen humano. Revista Ingeniería y Ciencia. Universidad EAFIT. Colombia 3(5), 43–66 (2007)
12. Rossille, D., Laurent, J., Burgun, A.: Modeling a decision-support system for oncology using rule-based and case-based reasoning methodologies. International Journal of Medical Informatics 74, 299–306 (2005)
13. Schmidt, R., Gierl, L.: Case-Based reasoning for antibiotics therapy advice: an investigation of retrieval algorithms and prototypes. Artificial Intelligence in Medicine 23, 171–186 (2001)
14. Sierra, B.: Aprendizaje Automático: conceptos básicos y avanzados. Pearson Education. Primera Edición (2006)
15. Wilson, D., Martinez, T.: Instance Pruning Techniques. In: Fisher, D. (ed.) Machine Learning: Proceedings of the Fourteenth International Conference, pp. 404–411. Morgan Kaufmann Publishers, San Francisco (1997)

Genetic Programming for Predicting Protein Networks

Beatriz Garcia, Ricardo Aler, Agapito Ledezma, and Araceli Sanchis

Universidad Carlos III de Madrid, Computer Science Department
Avda. de la Universidad 30, 28911, Leganes, Madrid, Spain
{beatrizg,aler,ledezma,masm}@inf.uc3m.es

Abstract. One of the definitely unsolved main problems in molecular biology is the protein-protein functional association prediction problem. Genetic Programming (GP) is applied to this domain. GP evolves an expression, equivalent to a binary classifier, which predicts if a given pair of proteins interacts. We take advantages of GP flexibility, particularly, the possibility of defining new operations. In this paper, the missing values problem benefits from the definition of *if-unknown*, a new operation which is more appropriate to the domain data semantics. Besides, in order to improve the solution size and the computational time, we use the Tarpeian method which controls the bloat effect of GP. According to the obtained results, we have verified the feasibility of using GP in this domain, and the enhancement in the search efficiency and interpretability of solutions due to the Tarpeian method.

Keywords: Protein interaction prediction, genetic programming, data integration, bioinformatics, evolutionary computation, machine learning, classification, control bloat.

1 Introduction

Nowadays, one of the challenges for molecular biology is to manage the huge amounts of genomic and proteomic data, which are increasing exponentially. The analysis of these data requires automatic methods in order to discover useful knowledge, which is infeasible with manual (i.e. visual inspections) techniques.

A significant part of the biological diversity and complexity is coded in the functional associations between molecules, such as the proteins [1]. Thus, understanding the protein interaction networks is essential to identify, explain and regulate the biological process dynamics in living systems. Therefore, if it is known how the cells in the organism work at molecular level, it will be possible to regulate certain processes, intervening in the appropriate interaction.

Traditionally, physical interactions or functional associations are detected by using experimental techniques [2] which are costly in resources and time. As a consequence, in recent years, an increasing interest in computational prediction methods which reduce these costs has arisen [3, 4, 5]. However no approach is the most suitable for each and every one of the protein pairs. Furthermore, the results about the analysis of proteins and their interactions (both at experimental and computational levels) are not unified; as well as, the information is distributed among multiple databases [6].

H. Geffner et al. (Eds.): IBERAMIA 2008, LNAI 5290, pp. 432–441, 2008.

In addition, comparing and combining data from different sources is very complicated, especially in protein-protein functional associations. This complexity is due to the respective biases of each source [7]. Moreover, most of the methods which determine functional associations lead to a significant number of false positives. Also, some methods have difficulties for retrieving particular types of interactions [7]. As a consequence of the previous aspects, the overlap among the outputs of the different methods is small. For this reason, the protein pairs predicted by these methods are complementary to each other. In other words, each method covers only a subset of the whole interaction network of the organism.

In this paper we intend to approach the problem of protein-protein functional association prediction, integrating the several available data sources, in order to centralize the current predictions, as a binary classification problem. This problem can be tackled by traditional Machine Learning methods and indeed, we will test them in this paper. But our long-term aim is to apply GP to this biological domain because of GP's potential flexibility.

Genetic Programming (GP) is a technique to automatically evolve computer programs [8]. In this paper, GP will be used to obtain an equation equivalent to a binary classifier. One of the reasons for choosing GP is that this technique allows the designer to define the primitives according to the requirements of the application domain. For example, we define the *if_unknown* (*if_?*) operator (explained below) in order to try to solve the missing values problem, which is a relevant question in this biological domain, because there is a great deal of them in the data sets.

A missing value is a feature without a known value in some of the instances. The most commonly used approaches to handle missing values in the Machine Learning literature are: (1) ignoring the complete instance or (2) filling in with the mean value for the feature. The first approach is appropriate when there are few missing values. However, in our domain almost all the instances have some missing values, and if these instances are ignored, the data is reduced considerably, down to less than 0.005%. The second approach gets a suitable approximation when there is noise while the data are collected, and consequently some values are missed or forgotten. But this is not our case, because it does not reflect the semantics of the actual data: most of our missing values represent non-existing data in a particular database (as opposed to unknown or forgotten). This is because the data sources (the output of several computational prediction methods) give an output only if all the method constraints are fulfilled. Therefore, you can not suppose any mean value as valid. Then the best solution is to manage missing values as special values.

Thus, in this paper we handle the non-existent values in a special way, with two new approaches: (1) replacing non-existent values with a specific numerical flag or (2) preserving the unknown in the data sets (represented by '?'). A drawback of the first approach is that numerical values now have two different semantic interpretations: actual values and flags. However, using the second approach a more meaningful representation is obtained in terms of biological interpretation. These new approaches for handling missing values are evaluated in the results section.

Furthermore, it is well known that GP suffers from the bloat problem [9]. That is, GP individuals tend to grow in size without apparent gain in fitness. Hence, to try to improve the accuracy and readability of equations evolved by GP, we use the Tarpeian bloat control mechanism, which biases evolution towards simple solutions [10]. We also expect that the Tarpeian method will speed-up the evolution of solutions.

This paper is organized as follows: Section 2 presents a brief introduction to the GP. In Section 3, the application domain, with the used information sources, is explained. Section 4 describes how to design the problem to apply GP. Results for the experimental phase are shown in Section 5. Finally, in Section 6, conclusions and future work are summarized.

2 Genetic Programming

Genetic programming (GP) is an evolutionary paradigm which applies genetic algorithms to breed computer programs automatically [8]. Each individual in the population is traditionally represented like a tree structure, with terminals in the leaves and operators or functions in the internal tree nodes. The fitness is determined by the individual performance in the specific task.

Excessive tree growth or bloat often happens in GP, greatly slowing down the evolution process [9]. Code bloat has three negative effects. First, individuals are difficult to understand by human users. This aspect may be important in protein interactions, if persons want to understand what GP learned after the evolution process. Second, it makes the evolution process very slow, because it takes longer to evaluate oversized individuals. And finally, and in the context of classification problems, oversized individuals may have a poor accuracy, because they tend to overfit the data.

The Tarpeian method [10], a well-founded bloat-control technique is applied in this research. Briefly, this method will stochastically abort some individuals in the evolution process, if its tree size is bigger than the average (in nodes or depth) in the population of the last generation. So, the solution size is limited in a flexible way and, decreasing the tree size, will improve its interpretation. It also reduces the execution time, since these individuals are not evaluated, and their fitness is the worst possible value. In addition, in learning tasks, reducing tree size is akin to Occam's Razor, and may improve prediction accuracy.

3 Protein-Protein Functional Association Prediction Problem

A pair or set of proteins interacts if they are associated by the function carried out. This is the definition of functional association used in this research. It means functional interaction, instead of physical one.

In this work, the application domain for the prediction task is the proteome of a specific procariota organism: *Escherichia Coli* (*E.coli*). It has 4,339 known proteins, whose functional interactions have to be determined.

The five computational methods used in this research are based on different evidences indicating if a pair of proteins physically or functionally interacts. The underlying fundamentals of every method are different [3].

The database sources where the 89,401 positive instances (without overlaps) are retrieved are BIND, DIP, IntAct, EcoCyc, KEGG, iHoP and Butland's set [11]. The number of pairs from each database is 58, 401, 2,684, 64,357, 20,860, 6,686, and 4,745, respectively. Each one contains information about evidence which indicates the possibility of an interaction between pairs of proteins. These databases can be grouped in several categories, according to the considered proof:

A) Pairs of proteins with a physical interaction, verified with experiments in a labo-ratory. Sources: BIND, DIP and the Butland's set.

B) Proteins belong to the same molecular complex. Sources: IntAct and EcoCyc complex.

C) Databases which take into account the co-regulation and regulation processes in the gene transcription. They include pairs of proteins (related with a specific gene) expressed at the same time, or when a protein catalyses a chemical reaction in order to the expression of the other gene to occur. Sources: EcoCyc regulated and EcoCyc coregulated.

D) Pairs of proteins which appear in the same metabolic pathway. Sources: EcoCyc functional associations and KEGG.

E) Databases with data retrieved from the scientific literature, using text mining tools. Source: iHoP.

Before beginning the description, it must be noted that there are several difficulties inherent to the nature of these biological data, which complicate solving successfully this task with a Genetic Programming or Machine Learning approach. The most important problems are: the intrinsic uncertainty in input data; the highly uneven distribution between the number of instances in the positive and negative classes (in general, the positive class means less than 1% instances); and the high percentage of missing values in several attributes (only 82 instances over 2,665,180 have a known value for the whole features).

4 Experimental Set Up

This section describes the necessary elements in order to apply GP to solve the pro-tein-protein functional association prediction problem. *lilgp 1.1* [12] is the GP tool used in the experimental phase. It is based on the first two Koza's books [8].

4.1 Data Set Representation

The data are represented in attribute-value pairs in order to be able to apply both GP and Machine Learning techniques. We define 9 features. On the one hand, 5 scores from five prediction computational methods [3] based on different evidences. On the other hand, 4 biological characteristics, the number of orthologous sequences and the length sequence, for every protein in the pair; both are ordered as minimum and maximum value for the pair.

The instances are divided in two classes: positive and negative class. The positive class includes pairs of proteins which appear in some of the databases previously mentioned.

The pairs of proteins in the negative class are extracted applying something similar to the "Closed-World assumption", which, in this domain, means that every pair of proteins whose functional associations has not been reported explicitly (i.e., that pair does not appear like a positive instance), is considered a pair which does not interact (i.e., a negative instance). Thus, the number of negative instances is very high (a total of 99% in all possible interactions set), due to the combinatorial explosion coming from the 4,339 proteins in *E.coli*, resulting in 9,411,291 possible interaction pairs.

Therefore, filters are applied to reduce this high quantity of negative instances. One filter only chooses the instances which have their two proteins belonging to pairs from the positive class. Another one removes homodimers pairs. Also, the instances without any known score are left out. To sum up briefly, the total number of available instances is reduced to 264,752 (16,566 positive and 248,186 negative ones).

For experimental reasons, train and test set have 10,000 instances each one, randomly chosen in each class among the available ones. The number of instances from the positive class and from the negative class is the same (5,000) in order to avoid the uneven distribution class problem (explained above).

4.2 Solution Coding

In GP, it is necessary to define the elements which are part of the trees that represent the different individuals in the population (i.e., the terminals and the operators).

There are 10 terminals: the 9 attributes explained above and 1 ERC (Ephemeral Random Constant) that represents any random numerical constant which can appear several times along the evolution process. Its value range is [0, 1].

Operational closure is a typical requirement in GP. So, all the terminals should have a value in any input instance. Therefore, the high quantity of missing values (or rather non-existing values in our domain) must be handled in a special way. In a first approach, we fill the non-existent values in with a specific flag: a numerical constant very different from the rest of the feature value (0 or -1, according to the minimum value reached in each terminal). Besides, all the terminals are normalized, in order to homogenize the results.

The operators used are the arithmetical ones (+, -, * and protected /), the conditional one *[if (a>=b) then x else y]*, and finally one new specific operator, tailored for this domain: if_? *[if (k is unknown) then x else y]*. This operator is defined as a second approach in order to manage the missing values, doing the non-existing values very different from the rest. So, when this operator is used, the missing values are preserved, without replacing them with any numerical constant (0 or -1). The rest of operations are operationally closed always returning the unknown value ('?') if any of their input values is '?'.

4.3 Evolutionary Process

Firstly, in order to predict functional association between two proteins *(p1, p2)*, the evolved individual f, is applied to them, and a threshold is used to give a positive or a negative class. Hence, *if (f >= threshold) then (p1, p2) functionally interact; else (p1, p2) do not interact*. In all the experiments presented in this work, the threshold is 0.5.

The fitness function in this work is the accuracy, it means, the percentage of correctly classified instances, in other words, *fitness=(TP+TN)/(TP+TN+FP+FN)*, according to the definition of True Positives (TP), True Negatives (TN), False Positives (FP) and False Negatives (FN) in [13].

In the evolutionary process, there are many parameters which must be set, resulting in different configurations for the experiments. A complete list, their meaning and a detailed description appears in the *lilgp* manual [12]. In addition, a new parameter is added to the *lilgp* tool: the Tarpeian factor. It is the probability of aborting an individual if its size is bigger than the average.

The main parameters have been tuned within the range of values shown in Table 1. An appropriate configuration for the parameters has been found from a few preliminary experiments (see Table 2).

The parameters in the base configuration were obtained from our preliminary tests, except for the *maximum depth* and *individual selection method*, which are the default values in the aforementioned Koza work [8].

Table 1. Range of values of the main parameters

Parameter	Range of values
Population size	1,000 - 25,000
No. generations	15 - 250
Maximum depth	17
Maximum no. nodes	25 - 300
Tree operators	+, -, *, /, >=, if_?
Genetic operators (probability)	crossover (0.3 - 0.9)
	reproduction (0.1 - 0.4)
	mutation (0.0 - 0.4)
Individuals selection method	tournament (size=7)
Tarpeian factor	0.0 - 0.9

Table 2. Values of the main parameters in the base configuration, without bloat control

Parameter	Value
Population size	1,000
No. generations	50
Maximum depth	17
Maximum no. nodes	200
Tree operators	+, -, *, /, >=
Genetic operators (probability)	crossover (0.5)
	reproduction (0.1)
	mutation (0.4)
Individuals selection method	tournament (size=7)
Tarpeian factor	0.0

5 Results

This section presents the results after applying GP to the protein-protein functional association prediction problem. All the configurations displayed come from averaging 30 GP runs.

In the base configuration a test accuracy of 60.83% on average and 61.44% for the best run are obtained, with a very low variance in both train and test.

5.1 Comparison with Other Machine Learning Techniques

Table 3 summarizes results from other Machine Learning techniques (from the *Weka* [14]) in order to make a comparison. All the parameters follow default *Weka* options.

Table 3. Genetic Programming and Machine Learning: accuracy comparison

Algorithm	% Train	% Test	% Test with unknown values	Test Sensitivity TP/TP+FN	Test Specificity TN/TN+FP
GP	62.34 / 62.92	60.83 / 61.44	60.67 / 61.22	58.87 / 63.54	62.62 / 59.34
ADTree	61.28	60.02	60.35	64.56	55.48
AODE	62.48	61.32	58.99	48.60	74.04
KStar	98.86	61.60	58.92	60.24	62.96
MLP	58.85	58.22	60.00	20.40	96.06
PART	64.06	61.96	58.33	60.84	63.08
Simple Logistic	60.29	60.70	57.61	56.34	65.06
SMO	59.17	59.96	57.62	56.98	62.94

Train and test results (first and second columns in table 3) are very close; accordingly we can assume that there is no overfitting. Table 3 shows that the accuracy in both train and test is nearly the same in all classifiers, with values around 60-61% in test (in GP, 60.83% on average and 61.44 for the best run). The single exception is Kstar in train which reaches an accuracy of almost 99%, because it stores the whole training set. In conclusion, GP gets accuracy about as high as most of traditional Machine Learning algorithms that we have tested.

Besides, the two last columns show sensitivity and specificity. Interpreting these measures as performance by class, the former for the positive class and the latter for the negative class, it can be noted that almost all algorithms get similar correct predictions in both classes. The exceptions are AODE and MLP, which are biased towards only the negative class, and the instances from the positive class are predicted worse than random.

The mix of the different data sources, the several transformations in attributes and the instances selection processes are very specific to this research. Therefore, it is very difficult to make a comparison with other protein-protein functional association prediction methods, which have their own biases.

5.2 Changing Significant Parameters: If_? Operator and the Tarpeian Method

This section describes what happens when a new operator is added to the existing arithmetical and conditional ones: it is *if_?*. It tries to manage the missing values problem which is very important in this domain due to its huge number in several features, as it was mentioned above. In the same way, the effects derived from the application of Tarpeian control bloat method are analyzed.

5.2.1 Missing Values Handling Comparison

Two different approaches for missing values handling are validated in this section. The former fills them in with a specific numerical flag (base configuration). The latter one preserves the missing values in the data, and each algorithm uses its own criteria for processing them. For example, GP adds the new operator (*if_?*), and *Weka* algorithms fill in with the mean or ignore the complete instance (see Introduction section for a more detailed explanation about missing values in this domain).

The second and third columns in table 3 show the test accuracy corresponding to the first and the second approach, respectively. Then, when the test accuracy column (the second one) is analyzed PART is slightly better than GP. However, looking at the third column, GP shows the highest value. It means, if unknown values are preserved in the data set, GP outperforms the other Machine Learning algorithms.

5.2.2 Different Configurations Comparison

Table 4 and Figure 1 show how several measures (such as train and test accuracy, tree size and execution time) change for six different experiment configurations. *Base* is the best configuration found, without bloat control, whose parameters were mentioned previously. *Base without limit* means the base configuration but without restricting the maximum tree size. *If_?* refers to base configuration including this new operator (see solution coding section for a description of *if_?* operator). Finally, *Tarpeian* configuration includes this control bloat method and the *without limit* characteristic. *if_? &*

without limit and *if_? & Tarpeian* are configurations which includes the elements of both of them.

In Figure 1, the Y-axis quantifies size (in number of nodes) and time (in seconds). The scale is the same for both measures.

Table 4. Influence of *if_?* and Tarpeian: train and test accuracy

Id	Configuration	% Train	% Test
a	base	62.34	60.83
b	base without limit	62.40	60.93
c	if_?	61.38	60.67
d	if_? & without limit	61.33	60.65
e	Tarpeian	60.89	60.43
f	if_? & Tarpeian	60.53	60.27

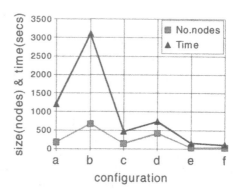

Fig. 1. Influence of *if_?* and Tarpeian: tree size and time average

Table 4 shows that the test accuracy is almost constant in all configurations, around 60.5%; while the train accuracy slightly goes down, when the *if_?* operator or/and the Tarpeian method are included. However, with reference to tree size (number of nodes) and time (see Figure 1), the values for the configurations with the *if_?* operator or the Tarpeian method are considerably lower than others. With the Tarpeian method the reduction is bigger than with the *if_?* operator, and even more when both are used together. From configuration 'b' to 'f', on average, the size decreases in more than 638 nodes and the time in almost 3000 seconds.

Moreover, when the *if_?* operator or the Tarpeian method is applied the solution size (i.e. number of nodes) is quite shorter than in PART algorithm, which is the best Machine Learning algorithm according to test accuracy (see previous section). In the decision list from PART there are 250 nodes (operands and operators) and in GP solution trees with 'f' configuration 38 nodes on average.

In conclusion, the *if_?* operator and the Tarpeian method reduce tree size and time, dropping scarcely test accuracy.

To sum up, as discussed previously, decreasing the tree size, only implies a scarcely lower accuracy than the base configuration. Nevertheless, the obtained trees have an easier interpretation and a very much faster evolution process. Therefore, it seems convenient to include in the solution both the *if_?* operator and the Tarpeian method.

6   Conclusions and Further Work

In this paper, we have applied Genetic Programming (GP) to the protein-protein functional association prediction problem. Our initial work shows that GP manages to obtain accuracy results similar to other Machine Learning methods (around 61%). The GP individual takes into account the intrinsic complexity which entails the biological nature of the data and its associated meaning. Besides, the predictor integrates information from different sources related with protein functional association, existing until now.

We have taken advantage of the flexibility offered by GP to define primitives in order to be closer to the real world problem conditions. We use a new operator (*if_?*) that takes into account the large number of unknown values in the data. GP gets to handle missing values slightly better than the rest of Machine Learning algorithms tested, in the sense that classification accuracy does not decrease significantly when missing values are used directly.

GP typically suffers from bloat, that is, the increase in size of the individuals with no apparent gain in fitness. In this paper, we have managed to reduce bloat by means of the *if_?* operator and the Tarpeian method. Some of the negative effects of bloat are controlled in this domain. First, the tree size has been reduced, even with respect to Machine Learning algorithms, therefore improving interpretation of the individuals. Second, the execution time goes down, due to do not wasting evaluating excessive big trees, improving the efficiency of the GP system. Both effects are achieved with almost no decrease in accuracy.

We believe that results could be improved further. The fitness function we have used is straightforward and perhaps more elaborate functions could achieve better results. In particular, our fitness functions measures only accuracy, but in this domain true positives is more important than true negatives, and this could be addressed very easily by GP. Extending the terminal and function set, and using ADFs [8] is also a plausible option, as well as using recent improvements over the Tarpeian method [9, 15]. Another interesting possibility would be to study if the output numerical value is suitable as functional association likelihood.

Acknowledgments

Data used in these experiments has been obtained in support of the Structural Computational Biology Group in Spanish National Cancer Research Centre (CNIO).This work has been supported by CICYT, TRA2007-67374-C02-02 project.

References

1. Rojas, A., Juan, D., Valencia, A.: Molecular interactions: Learning form protein complexes. In: Leon, D., Markel, S. (eds.) Silico Technologies in Drug Target Identification and Validation, vol. 6, pp. 225–244 (2006)
2. Causier, B.: Studying the Interactome with the Yeast Two-Hybrid System and Mass Spectrometry. Mass Spectrom. Rev. 23, 350–367 (2004)
3. Valencia, A., Pazos, F.: Computational Methods for the Prediction of Protein Interactions. Curr. Opin. Struct. Biol. 12, 368–373 (2002)
4. Fraser, H.B., Hirsh, A.E., Wall, D.P., et al.: Coevolution of Gene Expression among Interacting Proteins. Proc. Natl. Acad. Sci. U. S. A. 101, 9033–9038 (2004)

5. Yu, H., Luscombe, N.M., Lu, H.X., et al.: Annotation Transfer between Genomes: Protein-Protein Interologs and Protein-DNA Regulogs. Genome Res. 14, 1107–1118 (2004)
6. Gómez, M., Alonso-Allende, R., Pazos, F., et al.: Accessible Protein Interaction Data for Network Modeling. Structure of the Information and Available Repositories. Transactions on Computational Systems Biology I, 1–13 (2005)
7. Mering, C.v., Krause, R., Snel, B., et al.: Comparative Assessment of Large-Scale Data Sets of Protein-Protein Interactions. Nature 417, 399–403 (2002)
8. Koza, J.: Genetic programming II. MIT Press, Cambridge (1994)
9. Mahler, S., Robilliard, D., Fonlupt, C.: Tarpeian Bloat Control and Generalization Accuracy. In: Keijzer, M., Tettamanzi, A.G.B., Collet, P., van Hemert, J., Tomassini, M. (eds.) EuroGP 2005. LNCS, vol. 3447, pp. 203–214. Springer, Heidelberg (2005)
10. Poli, R.: A Simple but Theoretically-Motivated Method to Control Bloat in Genetic Programming. In: Ryan, C., Soule, T., Keijzer, M., Tsang, E.P.K., Poli, R., Costa, E. (eds.) EuroGP 2003. LNCS, vol. 2610, pp. 204–217. Springer, Heidelberg (2003)
11. Butland, G., Peregrin-Alvarez, J.M., Li, J., et al.: Interaction Network Containing Conserved and Essential Protein Complexes in Escherichia Coli. Nature 433, 531–537 (2005)
12. Zongker, D., Punch, B.: Lil-Gp Genetic Programming System (1998), http://garage.Cse.Msu.edu/software/lil-Gp/
13. Fawcett, T.: ROC Graphs: Notes and Practical Considerations for Data Mining Researchers (2003)
14. Witten, I.H., Frank, E.: Data mining: Practical machine learning tools and techniques, 2nd edn. Morgan Kaufmann, San Francisco (2005)
15. Poli, R., Langdon, W., Dignum, S.: On the Limiting Distribution of Program Sizes in Tree-Based Genetic Programming. In: Ebner, M., O'Neill, M., Ekárt, A., Vanneschi, L., Esparcia-Alcázar, A.I. (eds.) EuroGP 2007. LNCS, vol. 4445, pp. 193–204. Springer, Heidelberg (2007)

Fragmentation and Frontier Evolution for Genetic Algorithms Optimization in Music Transcription

Nuno Fonseca[1] and Ana Paula Rocha[2]

[1] ESTG – Polytechnic Institute of Leiria, Leiria, Portugal
[2] Faculdade de Engenharia da Universidade do Porto, Porto, Portugal
nfonseca@estg.ipleiria.pt, arocha@fe.up.pt

Abstract. Although traditional approaches in evolutionary computation encode each individual to represent the entire problem, the idea that an individual could be used to represent only part of it, is not new. Several different approaches exist that are based on decomposing the problem in smaller blocks/fragments, but the act of fragmentation can in some cases create unresolved issues, particularly on the fragments frontiers. This paper presents a method for optimizing some genetic algorithms applications, by fragment the problem in smaller ones, but keeping attention to frontier issues. While this paper focus on the application of the method to the music transcription problem, the proposed approach can be used on many other scenarios (signal processing, image analysis, etc.).

Keywords: genetic algorithms, local search, music transcription, fragmentation, divide-and-conquer.

1 Introduction

The goal of a music transcription system is to extract the musical notes from an audio stream. For instance, discovering all notes played during a piano recording. Although most systems use direct approaches based on signal processing [1][2][3], the problem can be resolved with a search space approach, i.e., looking for the right sequence of notes that better model the original audio stream. Although the search space is huge, Genetic Algorithms (GA) are known for their ability to work in big search spaces by using a very small subset of them [4]. Several authors, as Garcia[5], Lu[6] and Reis et al.[7], proposed possible ways to apply GA to the problem of music transcription by means of a GA evolution. Although the use of GA is a possible way to attack the problem, it suffers from a major handicap: the computational power/time required. So, the need for finding optimization processes is especially real.

Memetics approaches are known for getting very interesting results in some real applications or in special problems [8], by adding a local search operation inside the GA iterative process. Unfortunately, since most of the overhead of the music transcription system is placed on the evaluation of fitness, placing a local search operator (that evaluates several neighbors) inside the regular GA process would become prohibitive.

Traditional approaches in evolutionary computation encode each individual to represent the entire problem, but some methods work with slightly different concepts, by either dividing the problem in sub-problems and launching independent evolutionary

H. Geffner et al. (Eds.): IBERAMIA 2008, LNAI 5290, pp. 442–451, 2008.
© Springer-Verlag Berlin Heidelberg 2008

populations to solve each sub-problem; or by encoding only part of the problem on each individual, but with all individuals within the same population, interacting between them.

Probably the first use of one of these methods was on the "Michigan" approach [4], used for classifier systems and where each individual represents a single rule of the multi rule set that would represent the right answer to the problem. A similar concept is also used on the Parisian approach, with several applications in image analysis [9][10], by evolving individuals with partial representations of the solution, that are aggregated to form the global solution. Each individual is evaluated individually and also as a set. Instead of doing a global search as most traditional approaches, this permits a type of search with a scope somewhere between a global and a local search, which allows avoiding dominant solutions. In [11][12], the authors use GA to create halftoning images based on an original image. The image is fragmented in smaller blocks, and each fragment evolves in an independent GA population. Although [13] use individuals that represent the whole problem, it employs a recombination mechanism that present similar ideas. During recombination, the parent genes are fragmented, evaluated at fragment level, and their fragment fitness values are used in a fragment selection operator, that tries to get the best fragments to create new individuals. One interesting thing about this work is its application on the music transcription problem, offering some optimization (a computational cut around 50%), but doesn't take much in consideration issues present at the fragment neighborhoods.

This paper presents an optimization approach that tries to merge the advantages of fragmenting the problem in smaller ones, but minimizing the frontier issues common in these methods. In the section 2, the proposed approach is present. Section 3 explain how that approach can be applied to the music transcription problem, allowing a better understand of the method. Tests and results are presented on section 4. The last section (section 5) is used for conclusions and future work.

2 Proposed Method

Fragmentation can be a powerful tool for the optimization of GA, and the simple act of fragment the problem in smaller parts, creating independent populations to solve each sub-problem, can boost the performance of the GA, since the decrease of the search space is quite dramatic[1]. Nevertheless, it may not be so simple, since problems could arrive, especially on the fragment frontier zones. To handle that issues, a method was create that tries to get the benefits of fragmentation, but still resolving the frontier issues.

The proposed method has two important requirements that are quite common in similar approaches: the problem that we want to solve must allow its decomposition on smaller problems, and an independent evaluation of each sub-problem must be possible. The approach consists of several phases (see Fig. 1). On the first phase, the

---

[1] For instance, on a problem encoded as a 1024 bit sequence, the size of the search space is 2^{1024}, which is twice the size of a 1023 bit sequence (not of a 512 bit sequence). With the fragmentation of the 1024 bit sequence in 2 half's (with 512 bits), each fragment will have a search space reduction of 2^{512} times.

problem (that we want to resolve) is fragmented on smaller problems. For instance, if we are dealing with an audio file, the audio is split in small audio fragments; if it's an image, new smaller fragments of the image are created, etc. On the next phase, a population of genetic individuals will be created for each fragment and will try to resolve that fragment problem "at its own", evolving during a defined number of generations using a traditional GA approach: Individuals are evaluated, parents are selected, new individuals are created and mutated, etc. During this phase, there isn't any type of contact between different populations.

After the evolution of each fragment population (over a fixed number of generations), the phase of aggregation will occur: the best individual of each fragment population is chosen (that we will designate as the fragment champion) to represent that fragment on the candidate solution, i.e., all champions are merged to create our global candidate solution. After this aggregation, the method will analyze all genes present on the candidate solution, and mark the genes that might have been affected by standing on a fragment frontier. This decision will be based on the problem, and could be as simple as defining a fragment frontier neighborhood distance, or a much more complex task where several factors are evaluated for each gene.

On the final phase, a frontier evolution using a hill-climber approach, will perform a local search by applying special mutation operations only on the marked genes: during a defined number of iterations, a gene is randomly chosen between the genes that were mark on the previous phase (frontier genes), and a mutation is applied. If its overall fitness is better than the candidate solution, then it will become the new candidate solution. If the GA implementation supports several mutation operators, in this phase the system should only use mutation operators that might help to overcome problems created with the fragment cuts. This last phase, responsible for the frontier evolution, have a crucial impact, since there are situations that simply cannot be resolved (or evolved) during a fragment evolution.

By creating N fragments during Fragment Evolution, the number of evaluations increases N times (N fragments are evaluated instead of 1 global block). Nevertheless, since each fragment will have only 1/N of the original size, its evaluation tend to be N times faster, which will annul the impact of the increased number of evaluations.

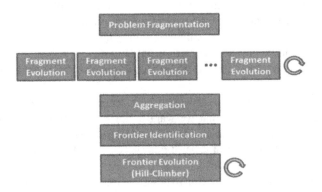

Fig. 1. Proposed method with 5 phases

Given that Fragment Evolution is the most demanding phase from the computational point of view, and since fragment populations evolve independently, the proposed method end up being highly parallelizable.

3 Music Transcription Application

Applying the proposed method to a music transcription system already based on GA it's more or less straightforward. For a better understand of the application, a little presentation of one of that systems are presented, based on [7].

3.1 Music Transcription Approach with GA

Each individual represents a solution to the problem, and is made of a sequence of notes. In this case, we can consider that each note is a gene, and that each individual may have a variable number of genes (notes) to represent the sequence of notes. Each note (gene) has 4 parameters: start time (onset), duration, pitch and dynamics (see Fig. 2).

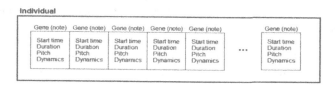

Fig. 2. Individual encoding for music transcription

To evaluate each individual, the note sequence is converted on audio (by the means of an internal synthesizer), that will be compared with the original audio stream.

The recombination is based on 1-point cut operator, but working on a time value: a time value is randomly chosen, and the notes (genes) of each individual are divided in two, based on their start time being before or after the random time value. If a note begins before that value and ends after, the note is split in two. The system also uses special mutation operators to do operations like: add random note, delete note, change pitch, change start time, change duration, change dynamics, split note in two with silence between, merge notes, etc.

3.2 Music Transcription and Proposed Method

During the phase 1 (fragmentation), the original audio is fragmented on smaller lengths. For instance, the user may specify that the original audio should be split on 3 seconds fragments.

During phase 2 (fragment evolution), each GA population will handle its fragment, trying to find the notes present on that fragment.

During phase 3 (aggregation), the best individual of each fragment population is chosen, and the candidate note sequence is created by merging the notes of all that individuals.

During phase 4 (frontier identification), the system will search for notes that are located near places where fragments were cut. For instance, the user could specify that the system should look from notes that start up to 250 ms after the fragmentation cut, or notes that end 250 ms or less before the fragment cut.

During phase 5 (frontier evolution/hill-climber), the system will enter an iterative cycle (e.g. 500 loops), where a special mutation is applied to one of the marked notes. At this phase, the focus is on resolving problems generated by the fragmentation cuts (e.g. notes were cut on 2; long notes that were detected in one fragment, but were missed, probably because of having lower energy, on the next fragment). As such, only some mutations make sense, like increasing notes durations on notes located before the cut, decreasing the start time of notes located after the cut, or merging notes. Apply mutations like adding new notes, or changing pitch does not resolve frontier issues.

4 Tests and Results

This section presents the tests made for analyzing the success of the proposed method on the music transcription problem. All tests try to transcribe a 30 second recording of a Mozart's Piano sonata using a GA music transcription method based on [7]. The fitness values are obtained by the sum of FFT (Fast Fourier Transform) differences over all frames (Eq. 1), where $O(t,f)$ and $X(t,f)$ represents the amplitude of frequency f at time t, in original and individual's synthesized audio stream. Since the fitness is based on the FFT differences, in this case lower values mean better fitted individuals, so fitness decrease over generations.

$$Fitness = \sum_{t=0}^{tmax} \sum_{f=27.5Hz}^{\frac{fs}{2}} \frac{||O(t,f)| - |X(t,f)||}{f} \tag{1}$$

Table 1 shows the main parameters of the GA system for the traditional approach (working on the entire 30s audio stream) and for the Fragment Evolution phase of the proposed method (working on fragments of the original audio). For each situation, 4 different runs of the GA were used, and the presented fitness values are average values within the different runs. Regarding the proposed method, during frontier identification, only notes ending near the fragment cuts (up to 250 ms) were considered. The hill-climber process will consider a 500 cycle, and only 2 mutation operators are used within this phase: increase duration (up to 1 second) and note merge (note is merged with the next occurrence of the same pitch).

Table 1. Main GA parameters

Population / Offspring	200 / 100
Elite size	200
Selection operator	Deterministic tournament (5 indiv.)
Recombination operator	1 point time cut
Recombination/Mutation prob.	75% / 10%

It can also be seen that the value used for fragment size have an important role. By decreasing the fragment size, each fragment population can evolve much more quickly since the search space is substantially reduced. But, by decreasing too much the fragment size, the impact of fragmentation on the genes will increase. The smaller the fragment size, the larger the number of genes directly affected (split, etc) or indirectly affected (genes near the fragmentation cut neighborhood). In this case, although the fragment size of 0.75 seconds presents the best evolution during the fragment evolution, as soon as the fitness is processed on a global base (instead of summing fragment fitness values), the impact of the frontiers shows up (due to note releases decay) and it ends on second place.

4.2 Impact of Mutation Probability

Traditional approach must handle bigger audio lengths, so its individuals will have a larger number of genes. As such, considering the same mutation probability (as the proposed method) could be wrong, since too much mutation may happen in each individual, which is bad from the performance point of view. To test if mutation probability values could be responsible for that performance gap, several tests were made with the traditional approach, considering mutation probabilities of 10%, 3.3%, 1%, 0.33% and 0.1%. Results are presented on Table 3.

Table 3. Test results with different mutation probabilities on the traditional approach

Mutation probability	Final Fitness
10 %	110.22
3.3 %	98.89
1 %	94.96
0.33 %	95.77
0.1%	103.26

As can be seen, although mutation probability could in fact affect the performance of the traditional approach, it still continues to have a performance evolution slower than the proposed method.

4.3 Frontier Evolution

Although the need of a frontier evolution could be validated from the theoretic point of view, since fragmentation might introduce issues that could not be resolved within the fragment evolution, it is important to analyze the importance of the frontier evolution from the practical point of view. Table 4 shows the fitness values before and after the hill-climber process. Based on these 2 values, Table 4 also presents the number of generations (prior to hill-climber) needed to achieve the same amount of fitness improve.

As can be seen, the smaller the fragment size, the greater the importance of the hill-climber process to resolve frontier issues. If we consider that during the hill-climber phase (500 cycles), 500 individuals are created; that each GA generation creates 100 new individuals (by fragment); and that the major task (from the computational point of view) is individual evaluation, results show us that hill-climber phase will also contribute for the performance gain of the proposed method.

Table 5 show us the same parameters but only for the 1,5 s fragment size, over 50 generations. In this case, with so little GA generations, the impact of the frontier evolution is very modest, since there is probably much more work to be done on the global scale, than on the local scale of the frontiers.

Table 4. Fitness values before and after the frontier evolution phase, after 400 GA generations. Generations (prior to hill-climber) needed to get the same amount of fitness improvement.

	Fitness before Hill-climber	Fitness after Hill-climber	Generations needed to get same fitness improve
Proposed method (6s)	85.00	84.26	27
Proposed method (3s)	77.26	76.80	32
Proposed method (1.5s)	73.87	73.24	52
Proposed method (0.75s)	76.13	74.99	125

Table 5. Fitness values before and after the hill-climber phase, but after 50 GA generations

	Fitness before Hill-climber	Fitness after Hill-climber	Generations needed to get same fitness improve
Proposed method (1.5s)	88.57	87.05	5

4.4 CPU Time

Although the first tests compare the same number of generations between traditional method and the proposed method, it is true that the fact that the proposed method has several genetic populations running, may add much more overhead. For instance, if the original problem is split in 10 fragments, there will be 10 times more recombination operations, 10 times more mutation operations, etc. So, it seems somehow unfair

Table 6. Fitness values and required CPU time required for each test to complete

	Fitness value (lower is better)	CPU time
Test A - Traditional approach - 400 generations - Mutation prob: 1%	94.96	27 645 secs (7:40:45)
Test B - Proposed method (1.5 s) - 30 generations - Mutation prob: 10%	93.37	1 518 secs (0:25:18)
Test C - Traditional approach - 1000 generations - Mutation prob: 1%	83.44	72 268 secs (20:04:28)
Test D - Proposed method (1.5 s) - 75 generations - Mutation prob: 10%	83.00	3 620 secs (1:00:20)

to take conclusions about its performance looking only to the same generation number. To analyze the real performance impact of the proposed method, an additional bank of tests was made, testing different situations and considering different number of generations. Table 6 shows the obtained fitness values and the required CPU time (considering a Core 2 Duo processor - 2.0 GHz) for each one of these tests.

By comparing tests A and B, we can notice that even using the traditional approach with the best mutation probability (1%) during 400 generations, it takes only 5.5 % of the CPU time for the proposed method, with only 30 generations, to achieve a better fitness result. But, if we continue to increase the number of generations of the traditional approach (test C with 1000 generations), the performance gain continue to increase, with the proposed method needing only 5.0 % of the CPU time (test D). The main reason is that the hill-climber phase requires the same amount of CPU time, independently of the number of generations. The greater the number of generations, the less impact will hill-climber has on the final CPU time, improving the performance gain of the proposed method.

5 Conclusion and Future Work

The results show us that the optimization is highly effective on the music transcription problem, requiring much less computational power. Some tests even suggest that performance benefits can achieve 20 times less CPU processing. Besides the performance boost, the method also takes special attention to internal damages created with its fragmentation. The advantages of the proposed method are maximized on the case of complex, high demanding, evaluation tasks, like this music transcription approach (using many FFT operations). If the evaluation is a simple process (from the processing point-of-view), although fragmentation could drastically reduce the search space, the overhead of creating additional population will have a bigger impact on the final performance.

Although the approach cannot be used in all kinds of problems, in the situations that have complex evaluation tasks and where fragmentation is possible, the method could present an interesting optimization approach.

In the future, besides deeper and longer tests, many variations could be used: different local search methods in the last phase of the method; instead of using only the best individual of each fragment, several individuals may be chosen to form a population, which could evolve by the means of a memetic algorithm; overlapping frontier regions as a way to decrease the impact of fragment cuts. The present approach should also be implemented in others problems (beside music transcription), as a mean to validate its generic advantages.

References

1. Moorer, J.A.: On the transcription of musical sound by computer. Computer Music Journal 1(4), 32–38 (1977)
2. Kashino, K., Nakadai, K., Kinoshita, T., Tanaka, H.: Organization of hierarchical perceptual sounds: Music scene analysis with autonomous processing modules and a quantitative information integration mechanism. In: IJCAI, pp. 158–164 (1995)

3. Klapuri, A.: Multiplitch analysis of polyphonic music and speech signals using an auditory model. IEEE Transactions on Audio and Language Processing 16(2), 255–264 (2008)
4. Holland, J.H.: Adaptation in Natural and Artificial Systems: An Introductory Analysis with Applications to Biology, Control, and Artificial Intelligence. MIT Press, Cambridge (April 1992)
5. Garcia, G.: A genetic search technique for polyphonic pitch detection. In: Proceedings of the International Computer Music Conference (ICMC), Havana, Cuba (September 2001)
6. Lu, D.: Automatic Music Transcription Using Genetic Algorithms and Electronic Synthesis. In: Computer Science Undergraduate Research, University of Rochester, USA (2006), http://www.csug.rochester.edu/ug.research/dlupaper.pdf
7. Reis, G., Fonseca, N., Ferndandez, F.: Genetic Algorithm Approach to Polyphonic Music Transcription. In: WISP 2007 - IEEE International Symposium on Intelligent Signal Processing (2007)
8. Hart, W., Krasnogor, N., Smith, J.: Memetic Evolutionary Algorithms. In: Recent Advances in Memetic Algorithms. Springer, Heidelberg (2004)
9. Collet, P., Lutton, E., Raynal, F., Schoenauer, M.: Polar {IFS}+Parisian Genetic Programming=Efficient {IFS} Inverse Problem Solving. Genetic Programming and Evolvable Machines 1(4), 339–361 (2000)
10. Dunn, E., Olague, G., Lutton, E.: Parisian camera placement for vision metrology. Pattern Recogn. Lett. 27(11), 1209–1219 (2006)
11. Aguirre, H.E., Tanaka, K., Sugimura, T.: Accelerated Halftoning Technique using Improved Genetic Algorithm with Tiny Populations. In: Proc. 1999 Conference on Systems, Man, and Cybernetics, vol. 4, pp. 905–910 (1999)
12. Aguirre, H., Tanaka, K., Sugimura, T.: Accelerated Image Halftoning Technique using Improved Genetic Algorithm. IEICE Trans. Fundamentals E83-A(8), 1566–1574 (2000)
13. Reis, G., Fonseca, N., Vega, F., Ferreira, A.: Hybrid Genetic Algorithm based on Gene Fragment Competition for Polyphonic Music Transcription. In: Giacobini, M., Brabazon, A., Cagnoni, S., Di Caro, G.A., Drechsler, R., Ekárt, A., Esparcia-Alcázar, A.I., Farooq, M., Fink, A., McCormack, J., O'Neill, M., Romero, J., Rothlauf, F., Squillero, G., Uyar, A.Ş., Yang, S. (eds.) EvoWorkshops 2008. LNCS, vol. 4974, pp. 305–314. Springer, Heidelberg (2008)

Applying Genetic Programming to Civil Engineering in the Improvement of Models, Codes and Norms

Juan L. Pérez[1], Mónica Miguélez[2], Juan R. Rabuñal[2], and Fernando Martínez-Abella[1]

[1] Departamento de Tecnología de la Construcción, University of A Coruña,
Campus de Elviña, A Coruña, Spain
[2] Departamento de Tecnologías de la Información y las Comunicaciones,
University of A Coruña, Campus de Elviña, A Coruña, Spain
{jlperez,mmiguelez,juanra,fmartinez}@udc.es

Abstract. This paper presents the use of Evolutionary Computation (EC) techniques, and more specifically the Genetic Programming (GP) technique, to Civil Engineering. This technique is applied here to a phenomenon that models the performance of structural concrete under controlled conditions throughout time. Several modifications were applied to the classic GP algorithm given the temporal nature of the case to be studied; one of these modifications was the incorporation of a new operator for providing the temporal ability for this specific case. The fitness function has been also modified by adding a security coefficient that adjusts the GP-obtained expressions and penalises the expressions that return unstable values.

Keywords: Information Extraction, Evolutionary Computation, Genetic Programming, Civil Engineering, Concrete Creep.

1 Introduction

The use of the Evolutionary Computation (EC) techniques in the field of Civil Engineering, more specifically Structural Engineering, dates from the end of 70s and beginning of 80s [1-3]. In such field the EC was mainly focused on structural optimisation problems, although some applications were related to the creative design of structures. These techniques were used due to the deficiencies and problems of formal calculation methods for the design in complex structural domains. This new way of tackling structural problems is currently known as Heuristic Methods, instead using the conventional ones, named as Formal Methods.

The present work shows the application of the GP techniques to a specific field such as the structural concrete. Due to the nature of the problem to be solved (modelling the creep phenomenon of the concrete under controlled lab conditions) several changes and adjustments to the GP algorithm were needed. After the changes, the GP was applied to creep data. Lastly, the obtained expressions were shown and compared with the current models.

H. Geffner et al. (Eds.): IBERAMIA 2008, LNAI 5290, pp. 452–460, 2008.

2 State of the Art

There are currently several approaches for the application of Artificial Intelligence (AI) techniques to the improvement of physics models related with Civil Engineering. Two specific studies related to this field are following presented.

Ashour et al. [4], by means of GP, obtained an expression that was able to predict the shear strength. The authors developed several expressions of variable complexity that achieve different precision levels from a data base related to 141 beam trials referenced in the scientific bibliography. This example cares for the simplicity of the expressions and only uses the addition, multiplication division and square operators.

Other example of the use of AI techniques in the development of new expressions and regulative codes is the contribution of Cladera and Marí [5], who studied, by means of Artificial Neural Networks (ANNs), the shear strength response of concrete beams without web reinforcement. These studies were based on experimental data gathered by Bentz and Kuchma, who identified 5 variables that had influence on the process and on the beam fracture values.

The authors have created with the ANN a virtual lab where they "test", within the variable range, new beams by exclusively varying only one of the parameters. In such way the individual dependence from every one of the variables can be studied and two new expressions, that outstandingly improve other already developed ones, can be formulated.

3 Problem Description

3.1 Creep Phenomenon in Structural Concrete

The creep phenomenon is the deformation that concrete endures under a constant load; it is observed by studying the deformation evolution experienced by cylindrical moulds under compression throughout time. In this type of trials the initial elastic deformation is followed by an increasing deformation that tends to an asymptotic value (this phenomenon is known as concrete creep). The creep deformation is a delayed deformation (DD) that includes delayed elastic deformation (DED) and delayed plastic deformation (DPD).

The creep depends on the age after the material is loaded and also on the type and amount of concrete used, which, together with the mixture water, determine the elastic deformability and the strength of the concrete. Linked with the migration of internal water particles, the concrete creep also will depend on the humidity of the material external environment and on the surface and volume affected by the external conditions.

3.2 Current Creep Models

There are different approaches for predicting creep deformations, generally expressed through codes or norms. The most extended ones are the ACI-209 regulation [6] developed by the 209 ACI Committee and the one proposed by the Béton European Committee, which is summarised in the CEB - MC90 Model [7] of the year 1990. This last model, showed in Equation 1 as example, has been adopted as a proposal for the Eurocode 2 [8]. For a better understanding Table 1 shows the description of the variables used.

$$J(t,t_0) = \frac{1}{E_{cmt_0}} + \frac{\phi}{E_{cm28}} \qquad \phi = \left(1 + \frac{t-h}{0.1(2V/S)^{1/3}}\right) \cdot \frac{16.8}{\sqrt{f_{cm28}}} \cdot \frac{1}{0.1+t_0^{0.2}} \cdot \left(\frac{t-t_0}{t-t_0+\beta_H}\right) \qquad (1)$$
$$\beta_H = 1.5\left[1 + (1.2h)^{18}\right](2V/S) + 250 \ < 1500 \ days$$

The J function represents the total deformation of concrete due to an unitary tension and includes an elastic component ($1/E_{cmt_0}$) and a delayed component or creep component, represented by the time-dependant creep coefficient (ϕ). The expression enables the observation of the fundamental parameters the deformation value depends on.

Table 1. Variables used in the CEB MC90 Model

Variables	Description
t	Concrete load age (days)
t_0	Concrete age when applying load (days)
f_{cm28}	Compressive strength after 28 days
E_{cmt28}	Concrete elasticity module after 28 days (MPa)
E_{cmt0}	Concrete elasticity module when applying load (MPa)
h	Relative humidity (decimal expressed)
(V/S)	Ratio (volume) vs. (lateral surface) (expressed in mm)

Another currently existing models are the B3 Model (Bazant and Baweja 1995)[9], the Atlanta 97 Model developed by Gardner in 1997 and, lastly, the GL2000 Model, developed by Gardner and Lockman[10].

3.3 Data Base

A set of experimental series internationally gathered in the data base of the Réunion Internationale des Laboratoires et Experts des Matériaux, systèmes de construction et ouvrages - RILEM (International union of laboratories and experts in construction materials, systems and structures) [11] was used. This data set, prepared by the TC 107 committee, includes comparable trials with different concretes where the same creep-related variables also appear: volume/area rate, relative humidity, curing time, age when load is applied, concrete type, water/concrete rate, deformation module in the initial load age and concrete compression strength after 28 days. The deformation data provided are obviously expressed in terms of classic J Function.

The whole of data refers to more than 2300 readings distributed among the 185 trials. Every trial has at least readings related to more than 500 days. The intervals for mould reading are irregular and, in some cases there are few records (5 or 6 experimental readings), or as much as 48 readings.

4 Development System

Most methods in Evolutionary Computation are inspired in the fundamental principles of neo-Darwinism or population genetics theory and the environment adaptation capability. Similarly to nature, several search techniques have arisen for solving problems in an automated and parallel way. The Evolutionary Algorithms (EA) are used for encoding such techniques.

The EA use individuals for produce solutions, and the data structure encoding the individual has different forms [12]: real valued vectors in Evolution Strategies [13], finite state machines in classical Evolutionary Programming [14], strings over a finite alphabet in Genetic Algorithms [15] and trees in Genetic Programming (GP) [16]; their differences rely on the options for individual representation and on the genetic operations. The GP, differently from other techniques, has the capability of generating solutions shaped as functions or formulations.

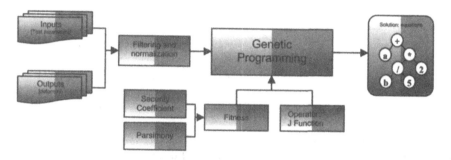

Fig. 1. Diagram of the developed system

The similarity with biological processes and its use for modelling complex adaptive problems have influence on the terminology used by EC researchers. The solution to a problem is named "individual", whereas a group of them is known as "population". The GP representation of every individual is performed by means of a "tree" where, for instance, a mathematic equation is encoded. This structure includes two types of nodes: terminal nodes, also named "tree leaves", where the constants and the variables are stored, and non terminal nodes, where the functions (arithmetic operations, trigonometric functions, etc.) applied to the terminal nodes are stored.

As in nature the "crossover operation" is needed for resulting in new "solutions" (descendants or children); if the solution has more fitness (it is better adapted/adjusted to the environment), the "selection" operation function will substitute, almost with no doubt, one of the individual of the current population, therefore leading to a new generation. Lastly, the "mutation" operation is used for exploring new search spaces.

The system performance is based on the iteration of successive generations from the previous ones. After the initial creation of random trees, successive generations are built from copies, crossovers and mutations of the individuals of the previous generation.

4.1 System Configuration Parameters

The classic GP was used in the first approaches with the data base of the trials for the symbolic regression. Several parameter configurations were obtained by changing, for instance, the selection algorithm (tournament, roulette, etc.), the crossover or mutation rates or the population size (100 – 1500). The Mean Square Error (MSE), obtained after the comparison of the real result with the one derived from applying the formulation to the input data, was used for fitness. The results achieved with this first set of trials were quite unsatisfactory, as they were similar but not better than the Mean Absolute Error

Table 2. Values of data normalized

Variable	Minimum	Maximum
V/S (mm)	0	220
h%[1]	0	110
t_c (days)	0	440
t_0 (days)	0	3600
t (days)	0	10000
c type	1	3
a (kg/m³)	1500	2200
w/c	0.2	0.8
$Ecmt_0$ (MPa)	10000	50000
fcm_{28} (MPa)	0	130
$J(t, t_0)$- $J(t_{inicial})$ x10^{-6} (1/MPa)	0	300

(MAE) obtained by the previously existing models. This fact was caused by the difficult adaptation of the classic GP to the temporal nature of this type of series. Several adjustments and changes were applied to the GP algorithm due to that reason. Fig. 1 shows the diagram of the system that was developed. In addition, and for achieving a higher fitness (despite being unnecessary for GP), a normalization process of all the variables was carried out. Table 2 shows the normalized values used for every variable.

Firstly, and after meticulously studying the performance of the used data set, a new operator linked to the temporal nature of the series (*j* factor expressed in the different regulations) was added. This operator is expressed mathematically as **Ln(t-t₀+1)** where **t** is the concrete load age in days and **t₀** is the concrete age when applying load in days. The operator *j* uses **Ln** because the series have exponential behavior. The individuals are considered as "valid" when they contain such operator (therefore

```
Function fitness(individual, patterns, rateParsimony, ratefSecurity)
{
  //Error of each individual.
  Set to Zero errorOfIndividual
  For each patter do {
   Calculate the errorOfIndividual
  }
  //Security term
  Set to Zero SecurityTerm
  For each patter do {
   If patter is unsafe
     SecurityTerm = SecurityTerm + (ratefSecurity * errorOfIndividual)
  }
  fitness = (errorOfIndividual + SecurityTerm / size(patterns)) +
   (rateParsimony * size(individual);
}
```

Fig. 2. Modified fitness function

---

[1] A normalization to a 0 -110 interval is performed in order to focus the real value from 20 to 100.

inducing its use) and the operator can be used only once. Another change performed was the modification of the fitness function in order to incorporate both, the parsimony value and the security coefficient. Fig. 2 shows the pseudo-code of the fitness-function.

A parsimony factor was included in the fitness in order to avoid, not only the redundancy in the expressions produced by the GP, but also their excessive growing[17]. This technique can be used for reducing the complexity of the tree that is being assessed; it works by means of the fitness penalty for the "i" individual. Equation 2 presents the function, where "α" represents the parsimony coefficient and "c_i" represents the individual complexity according to the number of nodes.

$$f(i) = P(i) + \alpha \cdot c_i \qquad (2)$$

4.2 Security Coefficients

As with the parsimony parameter, a penalisation process was applied to the GP algorithm in order to increase the security of the generated formulations. This process introduces a penalty for those individuals who predict unstable values; in this case values lower than the real ones. In this way, those individuals with good predictive capability returning unstable values will have less fitness than more conservative individuals who might have less accordance with the real values. This characteristic is extremely important in Civil Engineering, as the models should be conservative; the model is preferred to predict, not a lower but a higher level of deformation than the real one.

The fitness function used is shown in the Equation 3 (it already appears combined with Equation 2), where "x_i" represents the value predicted by the genetic formulation, "d_i" is the real value and "p" is the security penalty.

As the represented expression is considered as not good after obtaining unstable values, it will tend to disappear in future generations, though the evolutionary process. The obtaining of expressions with high security performance will be therefore boosted.

$$\frac{\sum |x_i - d_i| + s_i}{n} + \alpha \cdot c_i \qquad \text{where} \qquad \begin{array}{l} s_i = p \cdot \sum |x_i - d_i| \quad \text{if} \quad x_i > d_i \\ s_i = 0 \quad \text{if} \quad x_i \le d_i \end{array} \qquad (3)$$

5 Results

The following results were achieved after both, a normalization process of the information and the performance of trials with different configuration parameters. Table 3 presents the configuration that achieved the best result. For the verification process or test has been used 18 trials (10 % entire data set). The results presented are the union of training and test set.

The choice of operators or non terminal nodes was the following: addition, subtraction, product, protected division, square, cube root, square root ant the j temporal operator.

Table 3. Best parameters for GP configuration

Configuration parameters	Value
Selection algorithm	Tournament
Mutation rate	20
Crossover rate	95
Population size	400
Maximum tree height	9
Parsimony	0.00001
Security penalty	0.01

The previously explained normalized variables were used for the terminal nodes, together with constants varying from -1 to 1.

5.1 Obtained Formulations

The formulations commented here (Equations 4, 5, 6 and 7) were achieved after the optimal GP configuration was obtained. The F1 expression (Equation 4) (according to the current models) needed 450 generations, whereas the F4 (Equation 7, the best fitted one) needed 70000 generations.

$$F1 = 0.0685 \cdot \frac{W \cdot \ln(t - t_0 + 1)}{C} \tag{4}$$

$$F2 = \sqrt{-1.049 + t_0 - \frac{W}{C} + Ecmt_0 + h^2 \cdot \alpha} \tag{5}$$

$$\alpha = \left[\frac{1}{20} \ln(t - t_0 + 1) + \frac{1}{20} \sqrt[3]{t_c} - \frac{1}{10} \sqrt{t}_0 + \frac{1}{20} \sqrt[8]{t_c} - \frac{1}{10} VS \cdot Ctype - \frac{1}{5} Ecmt_0^{\ 2} \right]$$

$$F3 = \frac{-17}{125} \left[h\left(-\frac{72 \cdot W}{200 \cdot C} + 0.694 \right) + 0.583 t_0 - 0.835 \right] \ln(t - t_0 + 1)[-0.796 Ecmt_0 + 0.899] \tag{6}$$

$$F4 = -0.187 \cdot \alpha \ln(t - t_0 + 1)[-0.768 \cdot Ecmt_0 - 0.086 t_o + 0.927]$$

$$\alpha = h\left(1.268 \cdot \frac{W^2 (VS - 0.366)}{C^2} + 0.504 \right) - 0.1471 \cdot t_c + \frac{0.4172 \cdot t_0}{t_0 + VS} - 0.64 \tag{7}$$

5.2 Comparison of Results

Table 4, shows (from lower to high in the MAE row) the errors and the correlation coefficients related to the current models and to the obtained formulations.

As far as the results are concerned it can be stated that the expression F4 is the one that best models the creep performance by using 7 variables. Expression F2, although using more variables (9) achieves worse fitness. On the contrary, the use of 4 variables in expression F1 achieves a similar and even better mean error than the B3 model.

The correlation between the current models and the whole data set does not exceed 0.795, being the best model ever. Fig. 3 shows the correlation of experimental results with the model ones.

Table 4. Results of the different models (not normalized)

	F4	F3	F2	GL	CEB	ACI	ATL	S.B3	F1	B3
MAE	**10.491**	10.836	11.214	11.964	13.674	14.691	14.808	17.373	17.391	17.601
MSE	**276.3**	305.1	287.1	362.7	410.4	549.0	549.0	610.2	679.5	622.8
R^2	**0.8417**	0.8254	0.8384	0.7943	0.7820	0.7637	0.7324	0.6989	0.6143	0.7160

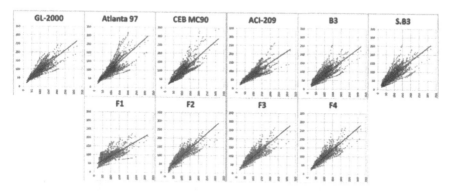

Fig. 3. Correlation current regulations – obtained equations

The use of GP has improved the correlation, which in expression 4 is close to 0.842.

6 Conclusion

One of the common procedures of the symbolic regression technique is the normalization data. Although normalization is not strictly necessary in GP, better results have been reached alter normalization the set of variables; this fact is mainly due to influence unification of the variables, no matter their range of variation.

The advantages of the evolutionary techniques enables it use in almost any science field. The present work shows that the use of GP techniques in Civil Engineering, more specifically regarding to structural concrete, has been quite satisfactory, since initially unknown information was extracted shaped as different equations. It has to be borne in mind that even with the low number of trials, (185) the results obtained had better fitness than the current models. The use of a refined and well chosen set of variables is a key factor for achieving the goal.

From the Civil Engineering viewpoint, the best result achieved might be used (according to experts of this area) as concrete creep model for the regulations of structural concrete.

Acknowledgements

This work was partially supported by the Spanish Ministry of Education and Science (Ministerio de Educación y Ciencia) (Ref BIA2005-09412-C03-01 and

BIA2007-60197), grants (Ref. 111/2006/2-3.2) funded by the Spanish Environmental Ministry (Ministerio de Medio Ambiente) and grants from the General Directorate of Research, Development and Innovation (Dirección Xeral de Investigación, Desenvolvemento e Innovación) of the Xunta de Galicia (Ref. PGIDT06PXIC118137PN and Ref. 07TMT011CT). The work of Juan L. Pérez is supported by an FPI grant (Ref. BES-2006-13535) from the Spanish Ministry of Education and Science (Ministerio de Educación y Ciencia).

References

1. Hoeffler, A., Leysner, U., Weidermann, J.: Optimization of the layout of trusses combining strategies based on Mitchel's theorem and on biological principles of evolution. In: 2nd Symposium on Structural Optimization, Milan (1973)
2. Lawo, M., Thierauf, G.: Optimal design for dynamic stochastic loading: a solution by random search. Optimization in structural design. University of Siegen: Bibl. Inst. Mannheim., 346–352 (1982)
3. Goldberg, D.E., Samtani, M.: Engineering optimization via genetic algorithm. In: Ninth Conference on Electronic Computation, pp. 471–482. University of Alabama, Birmingham (1986)
4. Ashour, A.F., Alvarez, L.F., Toropov, V.V.: Empirical modelling of shear strength of RC deep beams by genetic programming. Computers and Structures 81, 331–338 (2003)
5. Cladera, A., Marí, A.R.: Shear design procedure for reinforced normal and high-strength concrete beams using artificial neural networks. Part I: beams without stirrups. Eng. Struct. 26, 917–926 (2004)
6. ACI Committee 209: Prediction of Creep, Shrinkage and Temperature Effects in Concrete Structures. ACI 209-82. American Concrete Institute, Detroit (1982)
7. Müller, H.S., Hilsdorf, H.K.: Evaluation of the Time Dependent Behavior of Concrete. CEB Comite Euro-International du Beton. Bulletin d'Information No. 199, France (1990)
8. Eurocode 2 (European Committee for Standarization). Design of Concrete Structures, Revised final draft (2002)
9. Bazant, Z.P., Baweja, S.: Creep and Shrinkage Prediction Model for Analysis and Design of Concrete Structures - Model B3. Mater. Struct. 28, 357–365 (1995)
10. Lockman, M.J.: Compliance, relaxation and creep recovery of normal strength concrete. Thesis, Department of Civil Engineering, University of Ottawa, Ottawa (2000)
11. Réunion Internationale des Laboratoires et Experts des Matériaux, systèmes de constructionet ouvrages, http://www.rilem.net
12. Eiben, A.E., Smith, J.E.: Introduction to Evolutionary Computing. Natural Computing Series. Springer, Heidelberg (2003)
13. Rechenberg, I.: Cybernetic solution path of an experimental problem, vol. 1122. Royal Aircraft Establishment, Farnborough (1965)
14. Fogel, L.J., Owens, A.J., Walsh, M.J.: Artificial Intelligence through simulated evolution. John Wiley, Chichester (1966)
15. Holland, J.H.: Adaptation in natural and artificial systems. University of Michigan Press, Michigan, Ann Arbor (1975)
16. Koza, J.R.: Genetic Programming: On the Programming of Computers by Means of Natural Selection. MIT Press, Cambridge (1992)
17. Soule, T.: Code Growth in Genetic Programming. Thesis, University of Idaho, Idaho (1998)

Author Index